THE
SOCIALIST REGISTER 1985/86

SOCIALIST REGISTER
1985/86

EDITED BY

RALPH MILIBAND

JOHN SAVILLE

MARCEL LIEBMAN

and

LEO PANITCH

THE MERLIN PRESS
LONDON

First published in 1986
by the Merlin Press
3 Manchester Road
London E14 9BD

© The Merlin Press Ltd 1986

British Library Cataloguing in Publication Data

The Socialist register.——1985-86-
  1. Socialism——Periodicals
  335'.005   HX3

  ISBN 0-85036-339-X
  ISBN 0-85036-340-3 Pbk

Printed in Great Britain
by Whitstable Litho, Whitstable, Kent

Typesetting by Hems & Co
The Old Brewery, Tisbury, Wilts.

TABLE OF CONTENTS

PREFACE

This twenty second issue of the *Socialist Register* is a 'double' volume, spanning the years 1985/6. The reason for this is that we have long wanted the *Register* to appear at the beginning rather than at the end of the year; and the only way we could do this was by 'losing' a year. However, we hope that the volume makes up, both in interest and in bulk, for the loss.

Marcel Liebman became a third co-editor of the *Register* in 1984; and Leo Panitch has now become a fourth one. It is very unlikely that we shall go on adding co-editors at this rate. Leo Panitch has contributed to the *Register* in the past, is the author of *Industrial Militancy and Social Democracy* and other writings, and is Professor of Political Science at York University, Toronto.

Like its 1984 predecessor, this volume is mostly concerned with a single theme, namely 'Social Democracy and After'. What we present in this issue is a critical survey of social democracy in theory and practice, and an exploration of what, in socialist terms, lies beyond it. Social democracy has under various labels been the overwhelmingly predominant experience of Western labour movements, and retains that predominance today. The contributors to this volume are all highly critical of that experience but are well aware that the critique of social democracy, however necessary, is not enough, and that what is also badly needed is a careful exploration of what else is possible by way of socialist change in advanced capitalist countries with capitalist-democratic regimes. It is both to critique and exploration that the 1985/6 *Socialist Register* is intended to make a contribution.

In the opening essay, Marcel Liebman draws a sharp contrast between social democracy in its formative phase in the decades before 1914, and its subsequent evolution; and George Ross and Jane Jenson follow this up with a survey of the changes which have occurred since World War II in the nature of capitalism and the working class, and they discuss some of the crucial questions which these changes raise for the Left. As against those who would answer these questions in terms of the impasse of the socialist project that has allegedly been imposed by a declining working class and an orthodox Marxism, Leo Panitch presents a wide ranging critique, with particular reference to the Labour Party in Britain, which identifies social democracy's historical practice and continuing influence on working class politics as the critical obstacle on the Left to socialist advance.

The following seven articles are devoted to various aspects of working class and social democratic politics in a number of countries. William Graf contributes a detailed analysis of political trends within and beyond social democracy in the German Federal Republic; and Michal Bodemann analyses the experience and ambiguities of the Green Party. On the basis of a close reading of a rich documentation, Vicente Navarro provides an important corrective to the familiar view that the American working class has been won over to 'Reaganism'; and Peter Beilharz offers a searching analysis of present trends in the Australian Left. Mark Kesselman discusses the tensions in French social democracy under Mitterrand, and Michalis Spourdalakis analyses the record of the Papandreou Government in Greece. For his part, James Petras probes some of the major political problems which arise in regard to democratic forms in conditions of acute class struggle, such as these manifest themselves in Latin America in the transition from authoritarian capitalist to liberal democratic regimes, on the one hand, and to revolutionary regimes, on the other.

The following two articles discuss the year-long miners' strike in Britain in 1984–5 and its implications for socialists. John Saville provides a detailed account of how the Thatcher Government fought this battle, and considers the response of the National Union of Mineworkers and of the Labour Party; and Richard Hyman analyses the NUM's conduct of the strike and discusses some of the main questions which are suggested by the strike to the whole labour movement.

The last seven articles discuss critical issues facing socialism today. Andrew Gamble presents an analysis of the 'Austrian' critique of socialism and discusses how that critique may be answered; and Mario Nuti proposes some ways in which economic planning can be made to work in economies in which the market still plays an important role. Frank Webster examines the problems which the 'technological revolution' presents to socialists; and Roland Lew offers a critical review of a book which has had a considerable impact on the Left since its publication in 1983, namely Alec Nove's *The Economics of Feasible Socialism*. Ernest Mandel discusses the future of the working class in the context of capitalist crisis; and Mateo Alaluf discusses the ways in which views of the working class affect political strategies. Finally, a concluding essay by Ralph Miliband and Marcel Liebman considers the kind of socialist politics that could provide an alternative to present-day social democracy.

Among our contributors, George Ross is Professor of Sociology at Brandeis University, Massachusetts, and Jane Jenson teaches Political Science at Carleton University, Ontario; and Vicente Navarro is a Professor in the Department of Health Policy and Management at Johns Hopkins University, Maryland. Peter Beilharz teaches in the Sociology Department of the Phillip Institute of Technology, Bundoora, Australia;

and Mark Kesselman is a Professor in the Department of Political Science, Columbia University, New York. Michalis Spourdalakis is at Bishop's University, Quebec; and James Petras is a Professor of Sociology at the State University of New York, Binghamton. Richard Hyman is at the School of Industrial and Business Studies, University of Warwick, and Andrew Gamble teaches in the Department of Political Theory and Institutions, University of Sheffield. Roland Lew is a Research Fellow at the Institute of Sociology, Brussels. Ernest Mandel teaches political economy at Brussels University, and Mario Nuti is Professor of Economics at the European University, Florence. Frank Webster is at the Oxford Polytechnic and Mateo Alaluf at the Institute of Sociology, Nivelles, Belgium.

We are grateful to George Ross for his very helpful suggestions in the early stages of the planning of this issue of the *Socialist Register*; to Martin Eve and Sarah Tisdall for their help in the production of this volume; to David Macey for his translations; and to our contributors for their cooperation. Once again, we must stress that neither the editors nor the contributors necessarily agree with everything that appears in the following pages.

September 1985   R.M.   M.L.
                                                                            J.S.   L.P.

'REFORMISM YESTERDAY AND SOCIAL DEMOCRACY TODAY'

Marcel Liebman

It is now difficult to imagine that the term 'Social Democracy' once embodied socialism's greatest hopes. Shortly before the First World War, the German labour movement or German *Social Democracy*, which placed itself officially under the banner of Marxism, enjoyed a series of resounding successes that seemed to be full of promise. Within the space of a few years and despite the arsenal of laws and persecutory measures that were directed against it, it had become the major political force in the most powerful state in continental Europe. A membership of one million, the masses who voted for it and the group of deputies who represented it in the Reichstag, where they formed by far the most important group, all testified to its political strength. Its trade union strength could be measured in terms of millions of members. In organisational terms it seemed to embody both the genius of a nation and the irresistible emergence of a class. Its intellectual strength found expression in the voices of Karl Kautsky, Rosa Luxemburg, Edouard Bernstein and Rudolf Hilferding, who were rarely in agreement but who were all prestigious figures. In his memoirs Trotsky pays retrospective tribute to its strength: 'For us Russians, German Social Democracy was mother, teacher and living example.'[1]

The Russian Socialists were not alone in taking this view. Few people escaped the fascination of the example given by German Social Democracy. Even the term 'Social Democracy' was adopted in Russia, Holland, the Scandinavian countries and, in England, by the Social Democratic Federation.

The victories won by the German labour movement are not in themselves enough to explain the aura of prestige it enjoyed. Other considerations have to be taken into account, even though there is every reason to believe that they are bound up with the movement's victories. Social democracy was a persuasive option. It was both coherent and diverse, a shining example of the future that awaited organised workers in industrial countries. Under its leadership, the workers had been mobilised, educated and supplied with cadres; they seemed to be taking the path that would lead to the transformation of society. Many questions were still unresolved—notably the decisive question of 'reform or revolution'—but the social and political activity of the working class prefigured the develop-

1

ment of what, in terms of a different context and model, Gramsci was to describe as an irresistible hegemonic force within capitalist society. The anarchist vision of the 'great day' had been completely shattered. Much as its defenders might grumble, the bourgeois citadel was giving ground to its attackers. The only question was how long it would take them to undermine it. It might one day be necessary to make a frontal assault, but the progress of the socialist movement was such that many of its leaders and supporters were under the illusion that this was no more than an academic question. There was considerable tension between reformism, which was often vilified but still influential, and an orthodoxy which seemed radical but which offered only modest possibilities. Rosa Luxemburg eloquently and at times prophetically denounced all collusion with the 'right', as represented by Bernstein and others, and condemned an organisation which had already become trapped in the snares of a conservative bureaucratism. But this left-wing critique could itself be seen as further evidence of the theoretical and practical vitality of social democracy as a whole.

All the different currents and tendencies within social democracy agreed that bourgeois society should be undermined from within. The distinction between the reformist and revolutionary tendencies was less clear than it might now seem. It was not simply that the centrist nebula concealed differences by masking the divergences between them. Nor was it simply that the concrete gains the movement had made seemed to suggest that there was no urgent need for truly revolutionary action. What was more important was the general conviction that revolutionary action would take place over a relatively long period. Some argued that a radical break was therefore unlikely to occur, whilst others relegated it to the distant future. For many people the question of reform or revolution was not posed in clear terms, and the changes likely to result from the action of the socialist movement (and those which had already occurred) seemed to guarantee that the world would be completely transformed. Given that this seemed certain, the question of means (legal or otherwise, violent or non-violent) lost much of its relevance.

These developments lend a certain legitimacy to reformism, and particularly to forms of reformism which went by other names. By moderating its tone and avoiding the provocative formulations of men like Bernstein, these forms of reformism persuaded the entire movement to adopt a line which was reformist in everything but name. The term 'reformism' itself was still suspect, if not anathema. Reality was more accommodating.

The nature of the reformism which dominated the European labour movement at this time can be summed up as follows. There was a desire to bring about a profound social change and even to abolish capitalism itself by gradual, legal and peaceful means. It is true that many German social democrats—notably Kautsky and Bebel—did sometimes state that it might be necessary to resort to more radical means to overcome the resistance of the bourgeoisie, but they did so more and more infrequently. That eventuality seemed to them to be hypothetical, distant and above all abstract. It had no relevance when it came to determining practical policies and strategy. They expected a reactionary counter-offensive, which, in fact, was being prepared. But the social democrats were not even thinking about a real defence against it.

Until the First World War, this choice could be justified in terms of the growing strength of the working class. The working class appeared to be strong enough to use its organisations to take over the state. But even though it had made considerable gains, it seemed unlikely that it would do so in the near future. The exact form which the seizure of power would take was still uncertain. Negatively, Social democratic orthodoxy rejected ministerialism, i.e. the acceptance of governmental responsibilities within a bourgeois executive. Positively, hopes were all the greater for being so vague. There seemed to be little doubt as to which social agent would introduce socialism and Bernstein was one of the few theoreticians to argue that that social agent might be found elsewhere than in the only revolutionary class, namely the industrial proletariat. It was certainly assumed that the *party* would play a decisive role, particularly in terms of relations with trade union organisations. But no one had examined the role of the state, despite the disturbing questions that its repressive function could and should have raised. Nor did anyone have anything to say about the transitional period. Practically nothing had been done to elaborate the formula 'the dictatorship of the proletariat' since the days when Marx and Engels first referred to it.

1914 and then the final stages of the war changed everything. Patriotic collaboration led to two changes for Social Democracy, or rather for social democrats. Whilst Social Democracy had not lost its working-class base, it now seemed possible to extend that base to take in the middle classes and especially state employees. On the other hand, the presence of socialist ministers in bourgeois governments (or, as in the case of Germany after November 1918, in governments which respected and defended the capitalist system) finally helped to raise the problem of the state in new terms. The war economy had already led to increased administrative intervention into economic life. What was more important, the democratisation of electoral laws and the fact that socialist representatives were regularly present in the highest echelons of the executive inevitably overturned earlier conceptions of strategy. From now on, Social Democracy and, in more general terms, reformism, saw the state as one of the principal instruments of its policy. One of the major tendencies within the labour movement began to see its objectives as gaining more parliamentary power, extending state-run public services, appointing more socialist ministers, working to implement 'progressive' social legislation and bringing trade union organisations under the protection of the state. As a result, reformism came to be redefined. Its gradualism and peaceful legalism were now so blatant that they did not need to be spelled out. Its most obvious characteristic was the phenomenon of *integration into the state apparatus*. At the same time there was a complete break with the international Communist movement, which emerged at precisely the time when Social Democracy was becoming integrated into the state.

We will not analyse here either the significance of the Russian Revolution, its worldwide repercussions or its impact upon the world of labour. One point is, however, clear: it was at once a cause and an effect of the deep crisis into which the 1914–18 war had plunged Social Democracy both in Germany and in the rest of Europe. For a while Social Democracy was identified with a patriotism that bordered upon chauvinism and with a reformism that had become counter-revolutionary. Both took the form of class collaboration. As a result of the horrors of the interminable carnage and of the disappointments of an unsatisfactory peace, both revolutionaries and radical socialists regarded this collaboration as something shameful. And due to the fratricidal struggle, the communists obviously took the same view.

Political and above all moral condemnations of Social Democracy did not facilitate understanding of the phenomenon. That much is obvious from the label 'social traitors', which was applied to the social democrats at certain times and in certain milieux. The condemnation of Social Democracy was of course an expression of a polemic filled with hatred. Marxists and radical socialists judged it in terms which combined passion with ethics. Their attitude precluded any serious analysis of the logic and dynamics of reformism and particularly of the contradiction it had to deal with. Opting for legalism and gradualism looked like an easy choice. It seemed to promote prudence as opposed to heroism, a pusillanimous moderation as opposed to heroic energy. There were further differences at a level which is vitally important for socialism: Communism called for mass action whereas Social Democratic reformism at best turned its back on the masses or simply betrayed and crushed them.

This over-simplistic picture of Social Democracy was almost caricatural. It is not simply that it was an unfair picture. Matters were much more serious than that; it masked the true nature of Social Democracy by obscuring both its dynamics and its limitations. It failed to see the realities of a contradictory record, a combination of undeniable successes and of exhaustion and anaemia. There was no clear-cut distinction between the 'difficulties of the revolutionary path' and the 'easy option' of Social Democracy. The reformist path meant overcoming a whole series of pitfalls, obstacles and traps. They were very different from those obstructing the revolutionary path, but in their own way they were equally serious.

Overcoming them required more than tactical string-pulling on the part of mediocre politicians or drab bureaucrats; it required infinite resources of boldness and imagination. The issue becomes clearer if we examine the problems posed by relations between Social Democratic parties and the working masses, and clearer still if we look at the period in which reformist[2] organisations developed and enjoyed their greatest successes. To be more specific, matters become clearer if we grasp the fact that they owed their rise and their successes to the intervention of the proletarian masses. From that point of view, there is a great deal to be learned from the history of the Belgian socialist movement.

*   *   *   *   *

It might be argued that this is a somewhat minor example, but the 'Belgian case' was in fact of considerable importance at the turn of the century. It is no accident that both the major theoretical journals of German Social Democracy—Kautsky's *Neue Zeit* and the *Sozialistische Monatshefte*—were frequently involved in bitter controversies over the general strikes in Belgium. The explanation is that Rosa Luxemburg was at the time trying to justify a form of mass action that was distinct from both and not hostile to party action at a European level. In the East, the debate was fuelled by the first convulsions of the Russian Revolution; in the West it was fuelled by a repetition of the mass upheavals for which the Belgian working class had been famous for a decade. A small country and a relatively small party thus posed a serious problem and gave rise to a major debate.

When it was founded in 1885 the Parti Ouvrier Belge was little more than a set of political initials, a hypothetical organisation. The contrast between the future it saw for itself, its self-proclaimed vocation and its ambitions, and its real standing was considerable. In a country where industry was developing more rapidly than anywhere else in continental Europe, the proletariat was ill-informed, hyper-exploited and slow to mobilise. Enormous masses of workers were concentrated in the coal mines, the metal-working industries, the glass works and the textile mills. But these hundreds of thousands of illiterate workers could scarcely have been less politicised. In the great centres of economic development in the south of the country, this apoliticism had a very specific meaning. They rejected politics and refused to see that resorting to political means might provide a solution to their poverty, even though they regarded it as unjust and intolerable. This attitude, which was shared by many workers, was not unrelated to the influence of the most radical forms of Proudhonism. There was constant agitation in the industrial areas and in the coalfields, where the First International had enjoyed a certain success in about 1870. The agitation took the form of ill-planned strikes which were called without any regard for the conjuncture, which were poorly coordinated and badly led, if they were led at all, and which provoked severe repression. At times strikes broke out and spread without any demands ever being put forward. Was this in fact a *social movement*? It was more a matter of cries of protest, which became more violent and more strident than ever in 1886. Whole areas of the country were quite literally in flames. Tens of thousands of workers were involved in tumultuous demonstrations, in the destruction of property and in looting. All this was a prelude to a massacre in which the 'forces of law and order' displayed an unbridled savagery. It would have been difficult to imagine anything less political than these riots. The young Parti Ouvrier stood by passively, worried and unhappy. It took the view that any repetition of these events would be disastrous.

The young party, which was still little more than an embryo, saw its future in terms of the gradual and systematic organisation of a class which, under its leadership, would be able to win reforms that would improve or even transform workers' conditions. It believed that such transformations would not take place without social legislation which the state systematically refused to implement because of its rigid non-interventionism. How could the state be forced to shrug off a passivity which the bourgeoisie was doing its best to encourage? The only solution lay in political action. In other words, pressure had to be brought to bear upon governmental and parliamentary institutions. Obviously, the Parti Ouvrier did also encourage the workers to protect themselves by means of friendly societies, cooperatives and unions. But its strategy was primarily directed towards overcoming state resistance. *Universal suffrage* therefore became the emerging movement's primary objective. Unfortunately, conservative obstinacy was not the only obstacle it had to face. The workers themselves were not interested; their anarchistic tendencies made them sceptical about the virtues of political action, which they identified with institutional action.

The history of the first decades in the life of the Parti Ouvrier is the history of a double victory. It succeeded in awakening the political consciousness of the industrial proletariat and in channelling its militancy towards the conquest of universal suffrage. It also brought pressure to bear on successive governments and forced them to make major concessions both in the socio-economic domain and at the political level. The bourgeois state's unconditional *laissez-faire* attitude was overcome and the people were finally granted the right to take part in elections on a mass scale.

Both these developments—the politicisation of the working class, which went hand in hand with the establishment of an autonomous working-class organisation, and the reforms won from the government—resulted from a dynamic which was painful and frequently contradictory. It was, however, a real and very efficacious dynamic in that it allowed the relationship articulating party and masses to be outlined. As a result, a movement which, despite its occasional use of revolutionary rhetoric, made no secret of its basic reformism was able to force through major and promising reforms. They may well have been limited, but their importance could not be denied. Insofar as it was a 'classic' social democratic organisation, the Parti Ouvrier provides a very good illustration of the logic of reformism, of its workings, its development and of how it can become blocked.

The logic of the Parti Ouvrier was essentially *dialectical*. Its founders (a 'general staff without troops', as one of the leaders put it) feared, perhaps more than anything else, a repetition of the popular disturbances of 1886. Many of its leaders enjoyed privileged relationships, both personal and political, with the Liberals. They shared their anti-clericalism and often regarded them as intermediaries between themselves and the government, which was in the hands of the Catholics. Most of the party leadership wanted the state to adopt a more flexible attitude and to negotiate. But their opponents harsh moderates refused to do so. The 'agitators' and 'speech-makers' had no access to ministers and therefore looked ridiculous rather than dangerous. If it was to be taken seriously, the social democratic leadership had to make its presence felt, either directly or indirectly. Unless the leaders of the Parti Ouvrier could show that they had a winning card in their hand neither contacts with the government nor direct or indirect negotiations could produce even modest gains. The leaders soon realised that without the presence of the organised masses and without mass action they could do nothing and were nothing. They had no support from any influential group; the only secret weapon in their arsenal was a humanist rhetoric. They could conceive of no initiative that would sway or even impress the government. Reform was their very *raison d'être*, but they could not convince the government of the need for reform. They therefore had to rely upon threats, and their threats soon took a very concrete form: the threat of a *general strike*.

There is something of a paradox or rather a contradiction here. The only way in which a party of *moderates* could pursue its *moderate*, gradualist and basically *reformist* strategy was *to become radicalised* and to bare its teeth. The threat of a general strike, which was borrowed from the slogans and myths of the anarchists, frightened the social democrats as much as it frightened the bourgeoisie, if not more so. It suggested all the dangers or mirages of an anti-political strategy. It meant calling upon the proletariat to free itself by laying down its tools rather than by using the ballot box. It meant calling upon it to use its *economic* power (even if it was the power of inertia) rather than using or demanding the *political rights* which the Parti Ouvrier thought were essential.

There were also more serious problems. Assuming that it was possible to use this weapon, how could a general strike be controlled in such a way as to prevent 'extremists' taking over? The threat of a general strike was seen as a means of bringing pressure to bear in negotiations, but would the negotiators be able to control it? If they could not do so, the threat was useless and might backfire against the would-be negotiators. And although the Social Democratic leadership did state in 1889 that it was *in the last resort* ready to call a general strike in order to win universal suffrage, it qualified its ultimatum with reservations that expressed both its hopes and its fears. It was reluctant to take what looked like a leap into the unknown. It was afraid that it would lose the troops it had only just begun to recruit, that they would become discouraged and de-politicised. It hoped that its threats would be enough to make the government give way and that there would be no need to draw this double-edged weapon. But unless the militants were mobilised, the general strike organised and the demonstrations planned, such ultimatums would impress no one. And how could those preparations be made unless at least a verbal radicalism stirred up working-class anger?

For years, the social democratic leaders had no alternative but to oscillate between very moderate statements and increasingly rash calls for action. Elsewhere, I describe the life-giving but dangerous contradiction that social democratic reformism had to face, no matter how reluctantly, *if it was to become a true political force*: 'Between 1885 and the First World War, a whole generation of leaders and militants had to wrestle with contradictory demands. They had to maintain a demand and a virtual myth (universal suffrage). They had to inspire enthusiasm and at the same time keep it in check. They had to take one step at a time and to negotiate, sometimes displaying intransigence but usually recommending compromise. They had to build up hopes and at the same time call for realism. They had to whip up idealism and then temper it with reason. They had to rely upon both quasi-revolutionary energy and quasi-conservative common sense, to inspire passion and quell impatience. They had to vilify their adversaries without making enemies of them; they had to be considerate to their allies and had to chivvy them along at the same time. They had to recruit forces they hoped they would never have to use. They had to compromise and at the same time give the impression that they represented the inevitability of electoral reform, or even that of revolution. What a programme! And what skill, suppleness and intelligence were needed to implement a continuous programme of action that was continually threatened by the obstinacy of the bourgeoisie and continually placed in jeopardy by pressure from the proletariat![3]

Obviously, the social democratic option, as opposed to the revolutionary choice, was not an easy option! An examination of the general strikes organised by the Parti Ouvrier in 1893, 1902 and 1913 provides adequate proof of that. Let us look briefly at the events and at the lessons to be learned from them.

On all three occasions, the initiative behind the strike movement came from the anger and impatience of the masses. The Parti Ouvrier had succeeded only too well in convincing them of the importance of universal suffrage. The industrial proletariat mobilised and became politicised because it came to see electoral reform as more than a mere objective: it was a sacred cause which embodied its greatest hopes and for which no sacrifice was too great. The social democratic party and its leaders temporised for as long as possible and only called for a general strike when large sectors of the working class had already taken spontaneous strike action. In 1893 and 1902, the strikes were accompanied by serious disorders, which the party's cadres tried in vain to prevent. When the police savagely repressed the popular agitation, the social democratic leaders hastily called off the strikes before their objectives had been won. As Rosa Luxemburg pointed out at the time, on both occasions they entered into secret negotiations with the Liberal party, which acted as an intermediary with the government, and had become its hostages. Both strikes were called off without the appropriate party bodies being consulted. The more resolute workers bitterly protested that their leaders had betrayed them. When, in 1893, the conservatives agreed to a major concession and granted 'universal suffrage tempered by multiple votes'[4] the leadership described a partial victory as a complete triumph. The defeat of 1902 was put down to the influence of 'extremists' and the Parti Ouvrier began to concentrate on 'taming' the general strike by taking exclusive control. It succeeded in doing so in 1913, but it was less successful when it came to dealing with the government, which refused to grant universal suffrage pure and simple.

It is, however, true that, in these circumstances, the action of tens of thousands of workers did paralyse the industrial regions of the country on all three occasions. It is also true to say that the Belgian bourgeoisie found itself coming under almost constant pressure from a proletariat which had been both radicalised *and* held back by Social Democracy, which was both increasingly militant *and* increasingly contained. Social Democracy depended for its political credibility upon the power of a movement it distrusted and which it wanted to hold back; its ability to negotiate was determined by actions which both gave it its strength and threatened its reformist strategy.

The result of this kind of practice by European Social Democracy was very contradictory. Social Democracy had organised and radicalised workers. It had made a major contribution to the process whereby the working class became an agent of social change. It had forced the state to make major concessions which did improve the condition and status of the proletariat. But its accomplishments were also very limited; whatever anyone may have said, or sometimes feared, the social democrats had been reluctant to enter the struggle and had rapidly entered into negotiations, and the reforms secured by these methods did not constitute a step towards the abolition of capitalism. In this sense, while Social Democracy had been very successful when it came to organising the working class and strengthening it, it was a failure. It betrayed the aims of classic reformism in two ways: it owed its successes to methods which were much more brutal than those implied by its moderate philosophy and its legalism; and, valuable as they may have been, its successes did not open up the road to socialism. On the contrary, the fact that it had occupied a certain territory within the state apparatus meant that Social Democracy was rapidly integrated into that apparatus. As a result, it assumed that it no longer needed to rely upon the powerful but compromising weapon of mass action.

Until 1914, Social Democracy saw the assault upon the state as a necessary evil. After the First World War, a 'governmental' or 'responsible' social democracy developed, and assaults on the state were seen as an absolute evil. In the 1920s and 1930s no reformist party in Europe encouraged or even allowed the masses to take offensive action. In that sense, the Popular Front was never anything more than a defensive strategy designed to restrict the working class to a supporting role, to being an electoral auxiliary. It is not surprising that Social Democracy lost its oppositional strength. The resources of reformism, partly as a result of the effects of the economic crisis but also because the old strategy of *simultaneously encouraging and holding back* the most active workers, gave way to purely institutional action. Social Democracy had been discredited in 1914 and defeated in the 1930s and when, after the Second World War, a wind of reform began to sweep across Europe, it was only by deluding itself as to its strength and its future that it could hope for a renaissance. Obviously, it did derive some prestige from nationalisations and from the establishment of a social insurance system which was somewhat hastily baptised the 'welfare state'. Its representatives were often given important posts within the state, sometimes with temporary Communist support. But these successes were temporary, and Social Democracy was not being rewarded for its own merits. They represented the provisional defeat of a right wing which had been discredited by the fascist adventure and ·which had been forced on to the defensive by the joint victories of the Soviet Union and the Resistance.

*   *   *   *   *

A new era was opening up for Social Democracy. In its original or classic form, it was now a thing of the past. There was no longer any question of implementing a sequence of reforms so as to transform the state by legal means. Still less was there any question of abolishing capitalism. The reformism of the past, as incarnated by Kautsky, was dead. It was replaced by a strategy which owed its real inspiration to Keynes, who was no socialist, and which pursued objectives whose modesty would have astonished Bernstein himself. The foreign policy adopted by its various leaders is the best illustration of the profound change in social democratic ambitions. Prior to 1914, when it still represented a viable option, Social Democracy mobilised the working class to defend peace against imperialism, which Lenin was not alone in seeing as 'the highest stage of capitalism'. It inspired great hopes and when it failed to fulfil its promise, it attracted equally great opprobrium. Between the wars, it adopted more modest ambitions. It was merely an impotent, passive participant in the fight against fascism. The immediate post-war period was even more disastrous. Social Democratic foreign policy was increasingly effective, but it worked to the advantage of American capitalism, especially when men like Spaak, Blum and Bevin gave it the cachet of democracy. And whilst the aberrations of Soviet policy justified its harshest critics, no neo-reformist leader was every tempted by neutralism. In terms of the colonial question, the 'classic reformist' tendency within the Second International had never resolved the controversy between those who systematically opposed colonialism and those who wanted primarily to humanise it. Between the wars, Social Democracy paid little attention to a problem that had yet to come to the front of the political stage. During the Cold War period, its representatives enthusiastically took the side of the United States, and as the old reformism degenerated many social democratic parties lent their support to colonialism. Their supposed loathing for violence did not prevent them from taking part in the most bloody adventures, an area in which France's Guy Mollet particularly distinguished himself.

Foreign policy was merely one aspect of social democratic politics. Whereas the old socialist humanism had placed its hopes in international arbitration and the League of Nations, the neo-reformists invested NATO with a democratic mission, if not a civilising mission. In terms of domestic politics, neo-reformism collapsed into an unequivocal statism. Certain of its representatives had long been susceptible to the appeal of a 'strong state',[5] but the defeat of the authoritarian regimes in 1945 had put an end to those suicidal temptations. After the war, however, and lasting for a whole generation, statism took the form of the defence of a policy of collaboration between labour and capital, with the state intervening if the balance of power seemed to be shifting rather too blatantly towards the employers. Social democrats introduced protective social legislation which was, in theory, designed to protect the weak and a taxation policy which was designed to redistribute wealth. They argued that the state should have a major role in the task of economic modernisation. But when it came to putting their plans into practice, the social democrats showed no hesitation in introducing an incomes policy and in putting pressure on their 'social partners', and in that respect they showed no indulgence towards the trade unions.

There is no escaping the conclusion that the *new-style reformism* means *reformism without reforms.* Whilst reformism is only too ready to boast of its realism, as opposed to the 'dreams' of its detractors, it has for years been showing all the symptoms of chronic anaemia, particularly in terms of its stated aims of implementing far-reaching reforms leading to socialism and of making electoral gains.

There are many reasons why social democracy finds itself in this impasse and why it has betrayed itself. Only one such reason will be discussed here. It is important because it brings out the differences between the social democracy of the past and that of today. The social democrats of the past played a historical role whose inadequacy was revealed in 1914. Whilst that cannot be denied, this negative judgment is not in itself enough. Social democracy appeared at a time when the proletariat was just beginning to be concentrated and when its awakening class consciousness was still low. At a time when the great inadequacies of its emergent institutions made it a docile instrument of the bourgeoisie, social democracy (the reformist majority and the revolutionary minority alike) led the proletariat out of the political desert. It thus had the considerable merit of helping to constitute workers into a class. Although it was tangled up in thousands of contradictions, classic social democracy brought together the talents of journalists, agitators and administrators, united men of culture, militants and organisers and provided the proletariat with the many institutions without which it would have been impossible to develop the class independence essential to the development of any class consciousness. It provided the necessary but inadequate basis for the victory of socialism. This is why the working class identified so closely with social democracy, even though there was still considerable friction and tension.

The war was a moment of truth which left no room for hesitations or for confusion and it clearly revealed that the institutional base provided by these social, political, economic and cultural organisations did not provide a springboard for more decisive victories. On the contrary, whenever an increasingly organised working class became capable of making an assault on capitalist positions, they acted as so many brakes on the movement. The reformers' heirs had proved themselves efficient managers of socialist organisations and they now proved themselves to be aggressive managers of the bourgeois state. When the actions of the proletariat threatened the established order, they showed no compunction about resorting to violence. Noske, who had played the role of the 'bloody dog' in dealing with the Spartakists, almost met his match in the person of Salengro, the French social democrat who threatened to use force against striking workers in 1936. Almost ten years later, his compatriot and comrade Jules Moch matched action to words by using the police and gendarmerie against the miners of northern France.

Extra-parliamentary action was deemed not only dangerous but even sacrilegious. The most important effect of this development was to deprive Social Democracy of a weapon which was difficult to wield and which was rarely used, but which was at least theoretically available to it, namely mass action. Once that had been abandoned, the only weapon left in the arsenal of neo-reformism was the blunt sword of electoral pressure. A few exceptional periods aside, the desire for electoral success led to the dilution of the social democratic programme. Attempts to win over 'floating voters' inevitably led to a timid centrism. Statements of principle and party programmes of course sometimes used a rhetoric which evoked past epics, but that semblance of fidelity was itself a more or less centrist tactic designed to retain the loyalty of those workers and voters who were nostalgic for the real or imaginary audacity of the past.

If we compare the old social democracy with the modern version, we reach the following conclusions:

1. The reformists of the past, or at least such of them who preferred the discreet influence of Kautsky to the compromising patronage of Bernstein, still thought of themselves as radicals. They still thought that it might be possible to use the weapon of revolution, albeit in a hypothetical and distant future. In this context, it should be noted that revolution was seen as a possible response to initiatives from a reactionary bourgeoisie. Revolution was a possibility. But not in the foreseeable future.

2. With the exception of openly rightist elements, the reformists of the past realised that if they were to be able to exert pressure or even to become a serious political force, they had to rely upon working-class organisations or even upon the active and militant political intervention of the working class. The problem of how to use and control the masses was one of the main elements influencing the problematic and dynamics of social democracy. This was particularly important in terms of actions affecting the bourgeois state. Once it had forced its way into the state, social democracy increasingly acted *within* it and gradually abandoned any idea of transforming it, arguing that the state should in fact have a greater role, especially in the economic domain. Once it had abandoned the call to the masses and even the threat of making such a call, social democratic tactics were designed to make gains within a neo-capitalist society in which the mixed economy gave the administrators who had emerged from its ranks a relatively important role. This was the positional warfare described by Gramsci. . . without the fighting.

3. This development meant more than the end of any vision of socialism in the sense that the founders of socialism and the early reformists understood the term. Having lost its trump cards, this new version of social democracy has lost its ability to reform the capitalist

system in any real or lasting sense. At best, it hopes to hold parliamentary power for a period of office. This means that the right can
simply undo what the left has done if its initiatives go against the
interests of the ruling classes. Usually, the right leaves intact those
measures implemented by its timid adversary which appear to be in
its own long term interests. When the left is 'in power', its insistence
on moderation and its desire for appeasement normally lead it to
adopt policies which the more lucid or less demagogic elements on
the right would never seriously dream of rejecting.

*   *   *   *   *

The current Mitterrand experiment in France is a typical example. French
reformism, which has always rejected the pejorative label of 'social democracy' and which describes itself simply as 'socialism', is the heir to a
complex heritage, in which the spirit of the revolution is still present. It
has recently displayed evidence both of its remaining energy and of the
poor use it makes of it. The experiment which began when François
Mitterrand won the presidential election in May 1981 is still going on.
Without wishing to speculate as to its final outcome, it is possible to put
forward certain considerations and hypotheses as to its significance. All
these considerations relate to the problem which concerns us here: the
nature of modern social democracy and its historical links with classic
reformism.

If we wish to grasp the limitations of the 'Mitterrand experiment', 1936
is a more relevant point of comparison than the dynamic reformism of the
pre-1914 period. In 1936 a coalition similar to that led by the present
head of state came to power in Paris: a coalition of socialists, communists
and 'radical socialists', even if the latter were stronger than the modern
'left radicals'. There is one other point of comparison: in both 1936 and
1981 the programme which the left proposed to implement when it gained
power was modest. In both cases, it was designed to put an end to abuses,
and its reforms were a defensive reaction to the policies of the previous
government. In both cases, the left's electoral victory was a response to a
situation which the majority, albeit a slender majority, found intolerable.
Despite these similarities, there are many differences between the government of Léon Blum and that of François Mitterrand. The conjunctures
they were elected to change were also very different. In 1936, the political
climate was dominated by a serious European crisis, with deflation providing a dismal response to the poverty resulting from the crisis. The left felt
that it was faced with an active threat from the right and from the fascist
groups, and was convinced that the republic was in danger and that unity
was the way to defend it.

None of this applied in 1981. The victory of the left took place in a very different context. It was certainly a response to the right, but it had less to do with fear and anger than with exasperation and exhaustion. The right (and not merely the Giscardian right) was criticised because it had been in power for so long and because it was incapable of resolving the crisis. The President of the Republic had asked Raymond Barre, reputedly 'the best economist in France', to form a government. But the eminent professor was no more effective than the least distinguished of his students. Inflation was running at over 10%; there were over two million unemployed. Moreover, people were increasingly disenchanted with the authoritarianism of the right and increasingly outraged by the recurrent scandals.

There was one other crucial difference between 1936 and 1981. In 1936, the union of the left was the expression at the electoral level of a vast popular mobilisation which forced political leaders—and especially those of the Communist and Socialist parties—to put an end to their old quarrels. Hundreds of parliamentary candidates were backed up by millions of workers inspired by the call for unity. In 1981, the socialist-communist left, which had rallied together between 1974 and 1977, was more disunited than ever. The socialists did all they could to weaken the communists, who lapsed back into an extreme sectarianism which everyone thought had gone for ever. Thanks to their internal squabbles, both parties succeeded in demoralising their troops, who were in any case very passive.

The difference between 1936 and 1981 is astonishing. The left-wing government of 1936 came to power for two reasons: it won the elections, but there was also a gigantic offensive on the part of the masses. Not content with going on strike, two million workers occupied thousands of factories and other workplaces. Some of them believed that the revolution had begun. And the battle certainly unleashed the accumulated anger, joy and energy of the working class. The employers had to give way and the government had to radicalise a programme which had been designed to reassure.

Nothing of the kind happened on 10 May 1981, when 51.75% of the population of France dismissed Giscard from office. There were many elements involved in the spontaneous celebrations which lit up Paris that night. But they did not include social demands. This was a celebration, not a mobilisation. If we compare it with the unrest and tumult of 1936, Mitterrand's victory looks almost like an administrative measure or a phenomenon of electoral arithmetic. It was the culmination of a campaign which the future president had waged under the slogan *'la force tranquille'* with the accent falling on the adjective rather than the noun.

A month later the legislative elections resulted in a new victory. The Socialist Party (and its minority allies the Left Radicals) enjoyed a real triumph by winning 37.5% of the vote and a comfortable and unusual majority of 285 seats in the Assemblée Nationale. The stage was set for

Pierre Mauroy's government. The presence of four Communist ministers was some comfort to their party, and it also helped to stifle the debate that the Communist Party's defeat should have provoked. The stage was set for a second phase of 'socialist action' under the leadership of François Mitterrand, a past master of political tactics with an almost Florentine understanding of the arts of political manoeuvring. He had always courageously fought against De Gaulle's personal power and had worked skilfully for Socialist-Communist unity. Mitterrand is not even a social democrat. He is descended from the radical socialist line (defined in the broadest of terms), and simply claims to be a pragmatist with a wish for democracy. He joined the ranks of the Socialist Party without having any doctrinal convictions and without even trying to acquire any.

The government's first year has somewhat pompously been described as a 'state of grace'. This was a reforming government rather than what Kautsky or even Blum would have described as a reformist government. As soon as he took power, Mitterrand made it quite clear that his vocation was to unite the nation rather than to construct socialism, no matter how gradually. Even so, the balance sheet for the first year is far from negligible. A number of social measures helped to reduce the gap between rich and poor: the SMIG,[6] housing allowances and old age pensions were all increased, and a more rigorous wealth tax was introduced. Liberal policies did away with or restricted the effects of repressive measures taken by previous governments. It took a certain courage for the new government to abolish the death penalty and to regularise the situation of tens of thousands of foreign workers in the face of right-wing pressure and a strong current of reactionary populism. The government also introduced reforms prefiguring the 'Aurouix law' and designed to increase trade union power and to give workers the right to express their views inside the workplace. The working week was reduced to thirty-nine hours and holidays were extended to five weeks. This was not all. In accordance with the promises it had given, the Mauroy government introduced a plan for decentralisation which gave the regions considerably greater powers. Finally, it implemented a series of nationalisations which, at a cost of thirty-two billion francs compensation, brought twelve industrial giants—some of which, like Péchiney and Thomson, were on the verge of bankruptcy—and virtually all the banking system into the public sector. Whilst these measures were certainly impressive, they simply represented a further stage in a policy which had already been implemented by previous governments and they did not imply any major change in relations between the State and the private sector. It was no secret that the main aim of the reform was to make the public sector a major instrument, if not the principal locomotive, behind a policy of growth.

Even if we take into account the promises that were not kept (reducing the length of military service and more generally, commitments in matters of nuclear policy) and certain measures that were worthy of a conservative government (a temporary wage freeze in a period of inflation), the left and the working class had some reason to be pleased with the first year's record. There had been a real break with the attitudes of the right-wing government which the French electorate had voted out of office. This could have been the *beginning* of a policy of democratic or even socialist renewal.

Unfortunately, during the second half of 1982 it became obvious that what should have been a beginning had been a short-lived period of euphoria and that 'realism' had put an end to it. Most of the projected reforms were judged inopportune. Although the socialist leaders had said again and again that the fight against unemployment was their top priority, energetic measures soon gave way to resignation. The unemployment rate rose from two million to 2.2 million in 1983 and to 2.5 million in 1984. Reluctantly and not without some agonising hesitations, a government in which the Communists were still represented (though one wonders whether they were collaborators or hostages) put 'left-wing rigour' on the agenda. Amongst other things, this meant restrictions on social spending and the end of index-linked wages. The effects of the U-turn were soon reflected by public opinion. The Mitterrand–Mauroy tandem failed to win over the right, which effectively regarded the government as 'illegitimate', but it rapidly lost popularity with its own electorate. Neither the President's repeated calls for national unity, or 'harmony within the body social' as he put it, nor the attempts of the trade unions, including the pro-Communist CGT to spare the government from criticism did anything to prevent the Mauroy government and the President himself from making an increasingly bad showing in the opinion polls.

From 1983 onwards, it was no longer even a question of 'left-wing rigour'. In an attempt to respond to conservative pressure and to keep up with the new mood of liberal conservatism, Mitterrand forced his ministers to take an even more right-wing line. Taking their inspiration from fashionable ideologies and giving in to pressure from the employers and the middle classes, ministers unexpectedly made 'statism' the object of their attacks. In a remarkable speech made in September 1983, the President of the Republic adopted the language of the employers' federations and declared that France was suffering from 'excessive taxation which is suffocating the economy'. The government's objectives were redefined. The inflation rate had to fall. The franc was devalued to make industry more competitive. The austerity policy was tightened up: ordinary households were asked to make greater efforts, but at the same time taxation policy was overhauled to placate industry. Appalled at what was happening, the Force Ouvrière union federation, which can scarcely be accused of radicalism, claimed that the socialist government was looking to Mrs Thatcher for inspiration. Policy hardened still further when the 'liberal' Fabius took over from the 'doctrinaire' Mauroy in July 1984. With few exceptions, the general policy was now to cut state spending (especially social spending) in order to balance the budget and to restore financial orthodoxy (bringing the rate of inflation down to 8% by the end of 1984). One of the exceptions was spending on law and order, which was actually increased so as to avoid an open conflict with the ideology of 'security' stirred up by the right and the extreme right, which was not above pointing out that Robert Badinter, the over-liberal Minister for Justice, came from a Jewish background.

The days of 'everything for the State' were over, declared Laurent Fabius, as though France were emerging from an era in which the entire private sector of the economy had been sacrificed at the altar of a Leviathan-like state. By now the Communists had left the government which, according to one commentator, continued to make ordinary households swallow 'a bitter pill' and kept all the 'sweets' for the business world by cutting direct taxation and increasing indirect taxation. In 1984, net wages fell by an average of 2.5%, whilst those of civil servants fell even more. At the same time, the revenue of certain big companies was increasing by leaps and bounds. As a result, social spending fell even further.

Gratitude not being a political virtue, the right, the rich and the middle classes never dreamed of thanking François Mitterrand. On the contrary, student organisations, the medical and pharmaceutical professions, associations of managers and even police officers mobilised against the government and showed no hesitation about 'taking to the streets' in the immediate area of the Elysée itself. The demonstrations put constant pressure on the government and forced it on to the defensive. And when in 1983 the left tried to fulfil one of its election promises by turning the entire educational system (non-denominational and church schools alike) into a major public service, a groundswell of public opinion swept through *la France profonde* (in other words Catholic France) which united to defend its doctrine, its teachers, its financial privileges and its freedom, which were yet again being threatened by the 'statist left'. In June 1984 between a million and one and a half million gathered in the capital. Mitterrand gave in to their blackmail, converted to liberalism, abandoned his programme and turned his back on his electoral base.

His electorate returned the compliment. Since 1983, the left has met with one defeat after another at the polls. In the 1983 municipal elections it lost control of 31 towns with a population of over 30,000. Worse still, in the European elections of June 1984, the socialists and communists fell to only 21% and 11% of the vote respectively (Giscard and Chirac together polled 43%). The Communist Party won the same share of the vote as Jean-Marie Le Pen's 'National Front', the far right grouping which benefited more than any other party from the disillusionment provoked by Mitterrand's policies. The legislative elections of 1986 will probably produce another and more serious anti-socialist and anti-communist landslide. The only solution Mitterrand could think of was an electoral reform inspired by proportional representation and to force it upon all parties, his own included. The most likely outcome will be the emergence of a centre-left coalition which will put an end to France's 'socialist experiment'.

Even this schematic account would be incomplete without some discussion of foreign policy. Mitterrand's Atlanticism, combined with his liking for personal power, sowed even more confusion in the ranks of the left than his social and economic policies. His seven-year period of office had scarcely begun when Washington realised that the presence of Communist ministers in the government in no way altered France's diplomatic stance. In the State Department, there was even talk of a 'divine surprise'. Far from promoting a thaw in the Cold War, under Mitterrand's leadership Paris took a strong anti-Soviet position and the new President denounced his predecessor's servile attitude towards Moscow. In frequent and shamefully cordial meetings with Reagan, Mitterrand let it be known that he would not normalise relations with Moscow until Soviet troops were pulled out of Afghanistan. America was regarded as an ally, even though Mitterrand did have certain reservations about its attitude towards Latin America and, more generally, towards the Third World as a whole. The USSR, on the other hand, was more or less openly seen as a potential enemy. In terms of the arms race and particularly in terms of SS20, cruise and Pershing missiles, Mitterrand soon received the dubious accolade of being a 'model ally' of the Americans. The French head of state did all he could to influence the attitude of those European countries which had doubts about Reagan's policies. In 1983 he visited Bonn and then Brussels. On both occasions, he lent his support to the Atlanticist conformism of the right and criticised the socialist opposition for their slight leaning towards neutralism. 'Pacifism is in the West and missiles are in the East', he declared in Brussels, to the delight of the right and the consternation of the left.

It is true of course that Mitterrand's France also pleaded the case for the Third World and argued for concrete development aid. But such pious wishes did nothing to alter either American intransigence or France's pro-American position. Having savagely criticised Giscard for giving financial and military support to some of the most corrupt regimes in Africa, Mitterrand adopted a 'realistic' policy in that area too and soon became one of Mobutu's most reliable allies. J.P. Cot, his Minister for Cooperation, was so disillusioned that he resigned rather than support his policies.

In the last analysis, four years of 'socialist management' in France have resulted in two disasters. The right is stronger than ever, and the left has been demoralised. The case of the Communist Party needs little elaboration here: a combination of populist sectarianism, extreme opportunism and extreme bureaucratism have drained it of its life-blood. Whereas it once succeeded in maintaining close links with the organised working class and in inspiring its most active sectors, it is now little more than a secondary force. But how different the socialist movement's prospects had seemed! It has resurfaced in the early seventies, recruited members on a massive scale, strengthened its organisation, re-established its credibility and stood for government on the basis of policies which promised a break with capitalism. The accidents of the socio-economic conjuncture and the mysteries of electoral alchemy brought it a double triumph in 1981, when it occupied both the Elysée and the benches of the Palais-Bourbon. Changing politics was not enough. As its official anthem proclaimed the point was to 'change life'.

The 'state of grace' lasted for a year—and it was followed by three years of rapid decline, during which the heir to Jaurès and Léon Blum took Charles de Gaulle as his only model. Unfortunately, he did not adopt De Gaulle's anti-Americanism. But he did share his love of secrecy and rapidly conquered and consolidated a 'private domain' in which the personal authority of François Mitterrand was absolute. Dumbfounded and unhappy, the Socialist Party obeyed its leader, but wept over its past and present setbacks and foresaw the defeats of the future. It was incapable of reacting or even of formulating an autonomous policy.

The left wing provides a sadly eloquent example. The left wing was identified with CERES (Centre d'Etudes et de Recherches Socialistes) and was led by J.P. Chevènement; for a long time it sustained a current that was critical of François Mitterrand, accusing him of being reluctant to unite with the communists and of displaying an excessive opportunism and pragmatism that left little room for socialism. Chevènement and his friends did, however, go into battle to support the future president and the socialist majority. In the early Mauroy governments, Chevènement was given the Research and Technology portfolio. He supported a demand-led policy of economic recovery, even though his policies implied a measure of protectionism. He opposed the 'new line' (austerity, devaluation and left-wing rigour), left the government in 1983, but refrained from making any overt attack on its policies. A year later, he became a member of Laurent Fabius's cabinet, which was far to the right of the cabinet he had criticised for its excessive caution. When a minority current which claims to represent the oppositional forces within the party proves incapable of maintaining a coherent position; when its criticisms become muted and sybilline; when it wavers over its programme, becomes primarily concerned with unity and discipline and is prepared to endorse actions which take it further away from its objectives and closer to power; then its weaknesses affect the whole party and it reveals the sickness of the organisation as a whole. When it goes in for petty politicking and wheeling and dealing instead of uniting, educating and mobilising its leading militants, it leaves them directionless, sceptical and demoralised. And the Socialist Party does now look like a directionless, sceptical and demoralised party.

It retains the old reformist label. But its socialism had been diluted by a programme which is *in no sense* socialist and which is little more than a programme for *modernisation*. It retains the democratic pretentions of the old reformism. But whereas the internal party life of social democracy once thrived upon the open discussion of conflicting ideas, in Mitterrand's party obedience is regarded as the supreme virtue. It has been transformed into an apparatus in which unanimity is a pretence, in which dissidents keep quiet and which is almost totally obedient to orders from above. The one exception to the rule is Michel Rocard, who is more of a centrist than his comrades, more ambitious than his colleagues and who, it is said, has plans to use his talents outside the party organisation.

The Socialist Party was always an ambiguous quantity: it raised brief hopes but always refused to tap popular dynamism, to say nothing of calling for mass action. It has failed to deliver what might, in theory, have been expected of a party which claimed to be a reformist party, let alone a true reformist party with radical pretentions. It has now reached the point of exhaustion.

*   *   *   *   *

To conclude. The political skill which 'classic reformism' displayed when it articulated offensives on the part of social democratic parties, on the basis of the pressure exerted by a united and organised working class which it had to control if it was to have any autonomy in its negotiations with the bourgeoisie, has now degenerated into mere politicking. It is therefore impossible to elaborate any real programme or to raise any real hopes. The purpose of all the politicking is to strengthen centres of sectorial power within the state apparatus by maintaining the fiction that the party has broader ambitions and by appealing to the authority of a history which has lost all meaning.

Even the accomplishments of the old social democracy—the precious but limited reforms which did not even challenge the capitalist order—are beyond the grasp of contemporary reformism. Whilst tradition obliges us to use labels like 'reformism' and 'social democracy', only those who stand to gain from them are fooled by them. It should be quite clear to attentive readers, careful observers, informed critics and lucid participants in the political battle that the reformism of the past has fulfilled its historical mission, that it has lost its dynamism and that its narrow limitations are now obvious. It is no more than a shadow of its former self, a ghost, a form of nostalgia. A nostalgia, ridiculous and poignant, for something which once existed and will never exist again.

NOTES

1. Trotsky, *My Life* (New York: Grosset and Dunlap, 1960), p. 212.
2. Unless otherwise stated, the terms 'reformism' and 'social democracy' are used synonymously in the present article at least for a certain period.
3. Marcel Liebman, *Les Socialistes belges (1885–1914): La Révolte et l'organization* (Brussels, 1979), p. 76.
4. Under this system, the entire population had the right to vote, but multiple votes were also granted to property owners and heads of family.
5. Shortly before the Second World War this was true of both Henri de Man in Belgium and of François Déat in France. Significantly enough, both engaged in collaboration with the Nazis.
6. *Salaire Minimum Interprofessionel Garanti* (Guaranteed Minimum Wage).

Translated by David Macey

POST-WAR CLASS STRUGGLE AND THE CRISIS OF LEFT POLITICS

George Ross and Jane Jenson

The mass labour movement is in disarray throughout the advanced capitalist world. Its utopias, generations-old visions of a better social future, have ceased to mobilise. Its organisations—unions and parties—are in retreat. Its social base is more and more fragmented. Its erstwhile allies look in new directions. Its politics range from dogged defensiveness of past victories against powerful new capitalist opponents to 'reformulated' positions which, in fact, promise to do much of what these opponents desire. What has happened?

The argument presented in this essay is meant to provide a very general answer to this question based on an analysis of the development of class conflict in recent times. In the period immediately following World War II a new class compromise was reached in captalist societies, one which reconciled many of the pre-war goals of social democracy, broadly construed, with capital's determined pursuit of a new accumulation strategy. During the extraordinarily long period of post-war economic growth the dynamics of this compromise mutually modified the character and behaviour of capital, labour and the state. Part I shows how class structures and the cutting edge of class conflict were reshaped in important ways. When economic and social crisis finally broke the back of the post-war boom, it did its work not on any abstract situation of class division, but on these *specific* structures and relations of class conflict. What came apart in crisis for the labour movement were the very things which had been created in the post-war compromise, as Part II discusses. The results of this have been devastating. To the degree to which the post-war boom exhausted social democracy's stock of programmes the present crisis of the post-war compromise has left the mass labour movement bereft of creative perspectives. Part III reviews the political options which exist in this unprecedented situation.

I. CLASS CONFLICT REMODELLED: THE POST-WAR BOOM

Out of the turbulence of the Great Depression, World War II and the popular (and generally social democratic) political victories which immediately followed it, came a substantial reconstruction of capitalism. Along with this reconstruction came one of the longest continuous

23

moments of growth which capitalism has known. Fordist mass production by large corporations finally triumphed after its promising debut had been cut short by depression. Disposing of the product of such corporate jugger-nauts necessitated deepening domestic markets to make relatively expensive goods widely available to new sectors of the population. Working this new system also demanded new institutions, a new politics, and major changes in the role of the state. If class conflict was never abolished in all this, it was nonetheless substantially reshaped. Indeed, the post-war period in many advanced capitalist societies looked like the long-delayed denoue-ment of a script which the social democratic Second International had begun to write in the later 19th century. At the centre of this enactment was a complex new workplace compromise between big capital and much of organised labour, in which certain more vicious exploitative practices gave way to rising wages and greater work security, in exchange for labour cooperation to enhance productivity.

The focus of working-class concerns was altered by this new deal and by its consequences in the realm of consumption. In many ways the power of the organised working class—manifested in unions and political parties—was greatly strengthened. In turn, such strength was essential to promote the Keynesian and welfare state politics needed to provide the regulatory backbone to the post-war order. Workers' organisational and political strength was in itself not enough to make this politics happen, however. As always these organisations needed allies in their political quest. These allies were found, at least temporarily, in the new middle strata whose size and influence exploded in the post-war period in response to the need for new kinds of work in the circulation and administrative spheres of both the private and public sectors.

Post-war reconstruction was as much a new class compromise as any-thing else. Workers won substantial industrial and political power which affected the nature of working-class consciousness and capacities for mobilisation. At the same time, oligopolistic and monopolistic capital, with new space derived from post-war workplace and political deals, was able to pursue an immensely profitable Fordist-consumerist accumulation strategy. The state acquired new importance as the overseer of different aspects of this huge social deal. The entire compromise was remarkably successful while it lasted.

The complex system of class conflict and conciliation upon which the post-war compromise was built was not without its own specific contra-dictions, however. If the specific focus of workplace class conflict was altered in many ways, as we will see, such conflict never disappeared. The fragmentation of the working class which came out of the new compromise created new areas of unpredictability. The capacity of the state to perform necessary regulatory functions was premised on the maintenance of a class alliance between workers and middle strata which, in specific circumstances, might unravel or be politically defeated. The new deal depended upon containing such contradictions, yet generating such containment was never easy. What follows will explore the problems which did emerge.

Resettling the workers
Arguably the key element in the post-war remodelling of conflict between capital and labour was a new compromise in the workplace. The consolidation of new industrial relations systems almost everywhere—a major working-class, and particularly trade-union, victory—was the core of this new deal. Recognition of union legitimacy, the generalisation of seniority and work security rights for workers, the development of rules and procedures limiting certain of the prerogatives of capital on the shopfloor and the negotiation of fringe benefits were all goals for which workers and their unions had struggled for decades. The core of this compromise was, of course, a trade-off between capital and organised labour in which workers received predictably rising wages while allowing capital a relatively free hand to invest in increased productivity.

The coming of new industrial relations systems changed the shape of the workplace class struggle. The package of seniority, work security, and fringe benefits tended to tie workers to specific places of work. Where victories on such rights correlated with longevity in the firm they indirectly made the union more the 'property' of older workers. The collective bargaining of ever more complex contracts, the requirement of rank-and-file discipline to honour contracts once negotiated and for periodic 'punctual' strikes when needed, the place of expertise in interpreting and enforcing complex rules as well as to staff and administer protective institutions such as grievance procedures, taken together with the underlying effects of Fordism on the structure of work, crystallised unions as strongly formalised organisations. Over time grass-roots activism and spontaneous participation tended to lose their place and appeal. In all of this ordinary workers learned to perceive unions less as collectives for mutual struggle than as distinct and separate agencies which acted *for* them, to be sure, but more often than not *in their place*.

These workplace arrangements had important consequences for the creation of working-class consciousness and identity. By providing tickets of access to mass consumerism for many workers it altered their life situations dramatically. This, in turn, had important consequences for the balance between workers' private and point-of-production lives. One can easily discard facile 'embourgeoisement' theses, of course; essential class boundaries did persist. Nevertheless for major parts of the working class aspects of life did change and one result was a greater tendency for individual workers to 'instrumentalise' their work—to deemphasise its centrality and importance for their personal identity and instead to affirm themselves in private and family spheres. These were, of course, the chosen merchandising targets of the vanguard industries of the boom—housing, household appliances, the automobile, and, later, leisure. Although such changes could never abolish conflict in work, they did contribute to changing its cutting edge. Because higher incomes were the major avenue to the acquisition of the new goods which shaped private lives, the wage issue assumed a burning importance for workers. However wage demands might be separated from the daily social world of work, which could be 'instrumentalised' rather than collectivised.

Capital's post-war goal of 'deepening the domestic market'—plus, it must be added, demography—contributed to other changes in workers' lives and consciousness. Social geography itself changed with suburbanisation, resettlement following new growth centres and the like. Work culture and neighbourhood culture were therefore less and less likely to overlap. This, plus the effects of the electronic media and extended schooling clearly attenuated earlier practices of ghettoised working-class culture. In the household itself contradictions developed for some workers. Consumerism stimulated family-centredness and reinforced traditional definitions of the domestic division of labour. Yet, on the other hand, the boom rapidly drew more and more women into the wage labour force in ways which granted wives greater potential for economic independence.

The workers whose situation we have just described—male, unionised, deeply implicated in consumerism—were only *part* of the working class. As analyses of segmented labour markets have made abundantly clear, the post-war compromise decomposed and recomposed the working class into different major fractions, a process with its own significance for class identity and consciousness. Alongside the workers we have just discussed were others, a clustering of 'minorities'—women, recent immigrants, racially different groups, 'guestworkers' and the like. Often these 'minorities' were located in different labour markets and were much less protected in the workplace (low job security, rapid turnover, fewer rights), less well paid and more marginal to consumerism, less implicated in the trade off of rights and higher wages for productivity and less directly the target of capital's strategy to 'deepen the domestic market'. Although the size and conditions of this bloc of workers varied greatly from place to place here one found relative and absolute poverty and disproportionate resort to new 'safety net' social programmes.

Alongside such marginal workers were large numbers of service-sector operatives in new or greatly expanded sectors of clerical work, tourism (food, travel, lodging) and merchandising. Here one found numbers of feminised occupations in which, because of this fact and because unions found it persistently difficult to organise in such areas, working conditions, job security and wage levels were inferior to those in the blue-collar unionised sphere. The class conflict implications of such class fragmentation depended upon its specific national structures, of course. In general, however, one found working classes divided between those to whom socialists and unionists referred to rather hastily as 'the workers', full participants in the post-war compromise, and those who fell outside it in one or another way. In some places this latter group grew large enough to present a challenge to labour's right to speak on behalf of 'all the workers'.

For the 'fully included' segments of the working class the combined effects of the new workplace deal and changing relationships between workers' private and point-of-production lives were impressive while the boom lasted. Nevertheless, the package had its contradictions. One essential dimension of the industrial relations deal, for example, was the tradeoff by monopoly capital of collective bargaining, relative job security and predictably rising wages for a free hand in making productivity-enhancing investment. Yet the rush to increased productivity which ensued created one of the more important arenas of workplace class conflict in the post-war period. Fordism produced disagreeable work situations in the best of circumstances. Investment to enhance productivity tended over time to turn the merely disagreeable into the infernal. However conservatising the consequences of collective bargaining and higher wages, resistance to such 'infernalisation' occasionally broke through.

The 'high wage' part of the deal was contradictory in different ways. In the post-war order there was no natural equilibrium between rising wages and rising productivity. In contrast, there were limits to the amount of productivity increase possible in any period. Given inequality and the nature of consumer capitalism itself, the more money one could procure, the more access one could gain to what seemed, to most people, to be an infinitely expandable cornucopia of goods, services and lifestyle options. Thus workers were always likely to 'want more' than they could be 'reasonably' granted by capital. But rapidly rising wages would threaten profitability, other things being equal. Here, despite the fact that union organisations were often successfully enlisted as intermediaries to explain what was 'reasonable' to the rank and file, problematic outcomes were always possible. Sometimes unions and their members lined up against capital and there were strikes. When capital 'colluded' with unions and workers to pass on the cost of wage increases to consumers, inflationary trends already built into the system were enhanced. In either case some degree of instability followed.

Struggles around productivity questions and for higher wages were built into the post-war system. Nevertheless, even if these struggles were disruptive to capital in serious ways, they were usually cut off from any radical or system-transforming thrust. Work and private lives were more dissociated than they had been earlier and parts of personal identity *were* sought in consumerism. Changing workplace–private life boundaries combined with the reconstruction of industrial relations *within* the workplace meant that central working-class organisations such as unions, and parties in the electoral sphere, became less participatory and more distant, bodies which did things *for* workers rather more than being animated *by* workers. More generally, class identification became more abstract and less immediate.

Here there was huge irony. The contours of the post-war compromise represented precisely one kind of class compromise towards which Social Democracy had been pointing since the late 19th century. Yet one of its main effects was that workers became much less 'encapsulated' and 'encapsulatable' by the 'counter-society' of organisations which had been at the base of social democratic and other Left strategic assumptions. In general, then, workplace class conflict was contained both by tradeoffs made possible by growth and by the bureaucratisation, distanciation and de-radicalisation of the most salient working-class organisations. As against this, however, the conflict behaviour of groups only partially included in the post-war compromise was quite unpredictable.

Uncertain new actors: The new middle strata
The politics of the labour movement has almost always depended upon alliances with other classes and class fractions for success because workers and their organisations have never had enough weight alone to make deals in the workplace stick or to influence political regulation decisively. Post-war changes were also important for the possibility of alliance politics. Fordist-based accumulation developed in ways which presented workers with new potential allies. The basic facts are quite clear. The post-war boom brought a tremendous explosion of new intermediary social strata—salaried, educationally-credentialised non-manual workers. The bureaucratised large corporation advanced the decomposition-recomposition of capital's tasks into a multiplicity of hierarchically-organised managerial, administrative and technical occupations. In the circulation-finance (banking, insurance, advertising, marketing) areas, and in state bureaucracies there was much demand for the same kind of work. Finally the expanded provision of public and quasi-public goods and services—healthcare, education, social work and the like—created large numbers of analogous jobs.

What positions were new middle strata likely to take in the reformulated but still very real post-war class struggle between capital and labour, particularly in its political manifestations? To avoid the interminable disputes on this question, let us here be arbitrary. First of all one can draw a horizontal line across the internal stratification hierarchy of private and public-sector middle strata to exclude obviously bourgeois elements. Above this line there was clearly an expansion of non-propertied fractions of the ruling class, of considerable interest to sociologists but unlikely candidates for alliance with workers. Then one can draw a vertical line between private and public-sector groups. Those of the private sector were likely to side with capital against labour because, for the most part, they were involved in the managerial incentive structures which prevailed within large corporations, even if there were exceptions to this among certain technical and scientific workers. Those groups which remained after these lines were drawn, who were neither near-bourgeois nor, because of their private-sector situation, prone to seeing things in 'corporate' ways, were potential allies for the working class.

Potential did not mean certain, of course. Such middle strata had very different outlooks and goals from those of workers. Those in public-sector occupations were often educationally credentialised, hence placing their incumbents on the 'other side' of the massive cultural divide created by the enhanced social importance of post-secondary education in the post-war period. Moreover, work in such areas was more a 'career' than a 'job', a biographical assumption which tended to individualise social outlook and, moreover, one which was reinforced by specialised and pseudo-specialised professionalism. On the other hand, given certain post-war economic conditions, such groups had reasons to entertain at least electoral alliances with workers. They benefitted directly from the growing Keynesian welfare state which working-class struggle had largely created and whose expansion workers' votes fostered. Moreover, to the degree to which they unionised to ensure their own piece of the expanding state-provided pie, they moved closer, at least organisationally, to the unionised part of the working class. A 'progressive' sociopolitical coalition was there-fore conceivable between such groups and workers around the promotion of Keynesian methods to stimulate growth and full employment and on the desirability of redistribution of at least a part of the surplus generated by such growth into expanded social services.

Politics and the State

The state provided the economic and social glue which kept the post-war compromise on track. Keynesian macroeconomic manipulations (demand stimulation and contraction through fiscal and monetary policies) and the use of large state expenditures (which also provided leverage for sectorally directed industrial policies) tinkered with the general market framework within which the huge private 'locomotives' functioned. The new Keynesian state was thereby empowered to protect private capital from the more dangerous implications of its own activity. It also generated and re-distributed resources through taxation to provide a broad range of public services. Here there were not only 'welfare state' programmes strictly speaking, like healthcare, retirement pensions, disability payments, income supplements and 'safety net' provisions for those unable to work, all programmes in which the public sphere assumed responsibility for smooth-ing over the roughest edges of a capitalist market civilisation. There were also a range of 'reproductive' state activities which provided direct help for capitalist enterprises—education, research and development subsidies, information services and the like.

No divine ordination stood behind the post-war compromise creating symmetry between the needs of private capital and the new role of the state. In fact, the successful harmonisation of post-war capitalism through the state was the product of *politics,* or, to be more precise, of electoral class conflict which possessed its own stock of contradictions. For the post-war compromise to stick more or less intact there had to be a reasonably solid 'progressive' social and political alliance between labour and middle strata. To the degree to which an opposing 'conservative' alliance— capital, the traditional petite bourgeoisie and whatever middle strata and working-class recruits could be drawn into the electoral fold—was too strong, retreat from aspects of the post-war political deal was likely. There were problems as well should the 'progressive' alliance become *too* strong, relative to capital—an unlikely but conceivable situation, at least at some moments. Persistent Left political strength made full employment pledges operational, for example, and this, in turn, was likely to cut into profitability and enhance inflationary trends, 'taxing' different groups in ways which had domestic political and international economic consequences. In either case counter-cyclical state policies were indicated, but such policies, because they enjoined sacrifice rather than creating benefit, were difficult to achieve and politically costly. It was no accident, then, that in social democratic settings with very strong unions and sturdy 'progressive' political alliances between workers and middle strata 'neo-corporatist' arrangements were struck. Here tradeoffs between continuing union power and wage restraint—the conscious assumption by organised labour of the necessity for maintaining equilibria which would ensure capitalist profitability—were institutionalised. Needless to say, however, such arrangements were difficult to sustain over time.

There were other tendencies built into the post-war setting which also undercut the political strength of the 'progressive' political alliance upon which the Keynesian welfare state depended. The politics which emerged everywhere after 1945 was essentially a complex of large public bureaucratic organisations which, in day-to-day ways, dealt principally with similar large private bureaucratic organisations like corporations and unions. In all this the distance between individual citizens and public decisions expanded greatly. Politics became an arena in which public officials, politicians or non-public bureaucrats perhaps acted on one's behalf, but usually at several degrees removed from one's own involvement. 'Representation' tended to become a form of delegation to large bureaucratic organisations. In all this grass roots politics became simple electoralism with very little mobilisation, activism and participation.

Thus if the post-war compromise involved democratic advances against capital based on hard-fought and long working-class struggles, these advances remained profoundly contradictory. The representation of workers even by their own organisations easily became substitution for them. And social democratic 'substitutionism'—which, it must be said, had been immanent in social democratic politics for generations before 1945—had pitfalls. Passivity, quiescence and demobilisation of 'the base' were generally sought-after goals, allowing those who 'knew better' or were 'more responsible' to deal unhindered with one another. Yet the decline of mobilisation placed the labour movement at a distinct disadvantage in dealings with capital and the state. Capital, with the omnipresent 'mobilisational' logic of the accumulation process on its side, was bound to gain the upper hand.

The basic political equilibria of most post-war compromises were therefore much more precarious than many observers realised at the time. The balance between 'progressive' and 'conservative' political coalitions, as well as the actual substance of Keynesian welfare state policies, all revolved around continued stable growth. Growth transformed a potentially zero-sum class game into a situation in which class compromises could be mutually advantageous to most major actors. Growth could prod the kind of expanding productivity which would allow capital to pursue a high wage strategy in the workplace. Growth also allowed taxation policies which could facilitate some redistribution of surplus to public services in ways which ensured the positions of new middle strata. Without growth, however, the whole edifice might come crashing down.

II. CHANGING CLASS CONFLICT AND THE COMING OF CRISIS

All social things—good and bad—come to an end. The chronological beginning of the end of the post-war compromise is difficult to situate precisely, since much depends upon the theoretical eye of the beholder. At some point in recent years—the 1970s—the Fordist workplace-consumption deal began to unravel under pressure from capital's modified accumulation strategy. At about the same moment the Keynesian welfare state politics which had facilitated the post-war compromise ceased being effective. Contemporaneous was a progressive breakdown in the alliance between the working class and new middle strata which had been the prerequisite for such politics. Underlying all of this were processes of decomposition in the working class itself and altered perspectives among new middle strata. Not only did the long period of post-war economic growth conclude, then, but the complex and delicate social setting which had fostered it began to disappear.

Precocious signs of unravelling
Recent obsession with the 'economic crisis' as the root cause of all problems is misleading. In fact it was in the prosperous 1960s, a decade

during which Keynesianism swept away alternative perspectives and Professor Galbraith's pronouncement that 'the economic problem has been solved' became conventional wisdom, that the contradictions in the post-war class compromise first began to intensify. In an atmosphere of exceptionally high growth almost everywhere, to which American international economic and military actions added great strains, the 'high wage' concession of monopoly capital revealed its contradictory side. In heated-up, close-to-capacity economies the wage demands of unions, fuelled by strong rank-and-file militancy, were hard to resist. With other costs rising as well, capital began to price goods in anticipation of higher wage bills. Not surprisingly, unions and workers responded in kind. With everyone anticipating the behaviour of everyone else in this way, inflation rates began to climb. Simultaneously, the intensity of Fordist productivity-enhancing labour processes grew as well, reaching intolerable levels of psychic and physical tension for workers involved. Strikes and other forms of working-class militancy increased almost everywhere.

During roughly the same period, and sometimes (as in May–June 1968 in France) virtually simultaneously, parts of the new middle strata also exploded in protest. Here one saw a confusing mixture of phenomena, of which the so-called 'new social movements' were the most spectacular. 'New social movements', whose content and objects varied greatly were most often sparked by younger members of new middle strata. These strata were 'single issue' oriented (belligerently insouciant about alliances with others, in fact), and often highly moralistic in their appeals. Activists also seemed as much or more concerned with their personal identities as with collective goals, in particular with a strident cultural liberationism against restrictive social codes. Tactically and organisationally the new social movements behaved in unorthodox ways, gathering militants and masses together for punctual and often provocatively illegal actions, then demobilising without creating any significant membership organisation. These new movements defied the norms, procedures and goals of the mass organisational, representative politics pursued by all actors in the social democratic tradition.

At the time, the meaning of both sets of movements—working-class and middle strata—was unclear. Workers' militancy was often mistakenly interpreted as a return to a revolutionary tradition which had been momentarily undercut by the social democratic post-war compromise. Moreover, it was very often the case that new middle strata presented themselves as leftish—*gauchiste,* even—using old-fashioned revolutionary vocabularies that blurred distinctions between their cultural foci and more traditional working-class demands. It was easy to misperceive the moment, then. Renewed revolutionary radicalism was not on the horizon, however. Instead, the social democratic post-war compromise was beginning to break down.

Whatever their deeper meanings, these movements of class conflict and cultural protest were both economically and politically destabilising to the post-war compromise. Spiralling inflation taxed those who could not keep up and fed incipient international monetary and competitive problems. Increasing tax burdens pursuant to the expansion of the welfare state were unpopular. Strikes and protests, if they paid off in many ways, also provided political fuel to the Right against unions and for 'law and order'. More generally, the political life of many advanced capitalist systems had grown much more volatile by the early 1970s, reflecting such turbulence. Changes in government occurred more frequently while social and electoral alliances which had looked reasonably solid for many years began to be more shaky and less manageable. *The* crisis had, in fact, already begun.

The Crisis

As everyone knows, the post-war economic boom ended in the 1970s. Since the jury is still out on theoretical explanations for this major change, we will here simply list its symptoms. Inflation grew beyond tolerable levels in most advanced capitalist societies, both for domestic reasons and because of changes in the prices of critical raw materials, most notably oil. A moment of 'stagflation' (roughly from 1975–1980) followed, in which governments faced a policy choice between the equally unpalatable alternatives of pursuing relatively full employment at the cost of high inflation or lower levels of inflation with rising unemployment. Politics pushed towards the former, while the realities of international competition pushed to the latter. The ultimate result was simultaneous high inflation, low growth and rising joblessness. The gradual collapse of international monetary norms exaggerated the policy dilemma. Simultaneously the newly industrialising countries appeared on the scene—products of the internationalising thrust of capitalism—fully armed to compete effectively with advanced capitalism in product lines like steel, shipbuilding, auto-mobiles and textiles which had earlier been the exclusive preserve of Western economies.

Productivity growth in advanced capitalist economies dropped precipitously. Domestic economic policies and international trade levels began to fluctuate unpredictably, while unemployment rose steadily. Eventually, with exceptions in only the most die-hard social democratic states, failed Keynesianism gave way to neo-liberal deflationary and monetarist policies designed to restore price stability at whatever the cost in jobs. Beside the obvious fact that an era had come to an end, two things were clear in all this. First, capitalist accumulation had become a global process. National-centred accumulation perspectives for 'deepening the domestic market' gave way to capitalist visions of the entire planet as labour market, production locale and marketplace. This, plus the increased volatility of international trade and monetary uncertainty, made it more and more problematic for national governments to pursue Keynesian policies, since such policies demanded a margin of control over economic flows which could no longer be assumed. Secondly, the trans-nationalisation of capitalism either brought, or coincided with, an explosion of new technologies which had far reaching consequences for the balance of economic power between societies, for the nature of work and for the structure of the working class. Capitalism was not only 'in crisis', then, it was also 'turning a corner' both spatially and technologically.

Decomposing the working class

These changes in the character of accumulation called into question many of the most important components of the post-war compromise in very dangerous ways for trade unionism. Perhaps most dramatically, the combined effects of employer retrenchment, international competition and the coming of new technologies hit hardest in just those sectors—mass production, capital-intensive areas—where union victories and strength had been greatest in the boom years. With declining productivity growth, came reduced firm willingness to pay higher wages. Capital, often helped out by government policies, took the offensive. At first, in the 1970s, this involved simply closing down wage growth. As the crisis deepened, how-ever, 'slimming down' the labour force and 'making it more flexible'—i.e. firing and circumventing hard-won provisions for job security and control—rose to the top of capital's agenda. In certain privileged places where powerful social democratic parties and union movements sustained much of their strength (Sweden, Austria, to a degree West Germany), 'neo-corporatist' retrenchment was the major manifestation of such trends. In other places, changes were more brutal.

Premised on growing union weakness, sophisticated new tactics were developed to roll back the post-war compromise. Concession bargaining fostered hard-nosed union-busting (two-tier wage structures, abridgement of security rights, anti-union litigation, 'give backs' and the like). The increasing use of part-time, temporary, sub-contracted and even black-market labour had similar purposes. Other initiatives were undertaken to reassert control and revamp workplace social structures. The 'quality circles' which swept the advanced capitalist world like a prairie fire were only the most publicised of a number of class collaborative schemes designed to weaken unions and enhance productivity. Redesigning job and pay classification schemes to individualise employer-worker relation-ships (often in conjunction with lifetime 'career' lines modelled on Japanese arrangements), using supervisory personnel as communications conduits for grievances, suggestions and 'happy talk' (rather than discipline), profit-sharing and the like were all at least partly designed as union-busting tools.

The ways in which labour movements had adapted to the post-war years made response to this new situation quite difficult. The union bureaucratisation which had occurred limited mobilising for resistance. Moreover the structure of the workplace deal in most places intensified any natural tendencies the rank and file felt to respond 'particularistically' to crisis. Jobs were threatened, therefore what had to happen was that as many of them as possible had to be protected. In practice this came down to a notion that those who had work, and within this larger group those who had substantial seniority, should be protected in the first instance, almost whatever happened to anyone else.

This particularistic pressure, which union leaderships often encouraged and responded to, cut in a number of ways, many of which were negative. Depending upon political contexts, unions might thereby find themselves trapped in a spiral of 'concession bargaining' (the term is North American but the phenomenon is international) in which dwindling union resources were deployed against capital to consolidate some jobs in exchange for the loss of others, often with added concessions in areas of earlier-won seniority and fringe benefits. Inevitably such bargaining whet capital's appetite for greater concessions. It also undermined the morale of the union rank and file—especially younger union supporters with less seniority—and undercut their confidence in the effectiveness of unions and unionism. More generally, it played into the pro-capitalist portrayal of unions as 'special interests' and 'cartels' with little concern for anyone but their own members.

The situation was a trap for more militant unions as well. When they engaged in strikes and other forms of anti-crisis militancy, such struggles were often defeated. Even when they were not clearly defeated, they could still be used by capital and the state as weapons in a rapidly intensifying ideological struggle with union 'selfishness'. Public-sector unions, which were often very strong (largely because their post-war victories had statutory as well as contractual dimensions) were particular targets of this ideological campaign. To the degree to which public-sector unions were able to maintain employment and prevent retrenchment, governments and employers invariably broadcast messages to the public at large about the excesses of 'redundant' jobs and costly subsidies.

For unions, the new setting was perverse, then. Even short-run victories stood a good chance of becoming longer-run defeats. The post-war compromise had consolidated a form of unionism whose major purpose was to provide job security and produce higher wages. The changing conditions of accumulation made it more and more difficult for unions to produce what their bases expected. To the degree to which they nonetheless continued to try they did so at considerable damage to their public position. But when they did not try, they failed even more easily. The mildly positive-sum game established by the post-war class compromise between capital and labour had, in crisis, become a zero-sum one. That unions almost everywhere became weaker in the crisis was not surprising, even if they held out better in solid democratic settings like Sweden and Austria. Memberships declined from their 1960s heights (sometimes catastrophically, as in France and the USA), mobilising power waned and general union credibility was severely tarnished. And, of course, to the degree to which unions were weakened, the political power of the working class was indirectly undermined.

What was at issue was not simply a temporary retreat from the post-war order. Underlying changes in the structure of the working class itself meant that unravelling the post-war workplace deal would bring permanent change. The character of that class was first and foremost shattered by unemployment, of course, which everywhere shot to 10% and above, and in some places reached Great Depression levels. Workers with jobs were reluctant to be militant while the growing presence of 'reserve armies', both the unemployed at home and the employable abroad pressured wages and other bargaining items downwards. Rising unemployment also accentuated pre-existing tendencies to dualism. Whereas during the boom years such dualism had been visible mainly in the USA and other societies with domestic 'North–South' problems, it emerged virtually everywhere during the crisis. Thus many European societies discovered their own 'minorities' (often recent immigrants with accumulated citizenship rights) and their own endemic poverty. Ugly racist movements such as the British and French National Fronts sometimes came with this discovery. High levels of youth unemployment had their own sinister implications. With a disproportionate burden of unemployment on young people, whose bitterness and cynicism deepened commensurately, youthful workers gravitated less and less to the Left. In the medium run, organised workers in both political parties and unions, risked losing access to those very young people it needed to reproduce itself. When one put together the diverse components of this secondary segment of the labour force— minorities, youth, women, the 'new' poor—the potentialities for increased internal division in the working class were great. Racism, sexism and inter-generational hostility were but the most obvious forms.

One other decomposing tendency is worthy of mention, even if its implications are far from clear. The rapid introduction of high technology into industrial and circulation sectors, in addition to the expansion of industries producing 'high-tech' goods themselves promised changes in the structuring of the working class. At the high end of 'high-tech' employ- ment lay task recomposition and higher qualifications for certain workers, setting them off from more traditional Taylorised operatives as perhaps a new labour aristocratic stratum.

This partial decomposition of the post-war working class, with no recomposition in sight, occurred in the face of an international restructuring of capital itself. Organised labour's post-war acceptance of a 'hands off' attitude to productivity-enhancing investment by capital made less and less sense in this changing context because by leaving the investment planning to capital it permitted recourse to a range of new options such as moving to another country, restructuring to eliminate employment, national deindustrialisation and the like.

New middle strata in crisis: Striking out on their own?

Imperceptibly, beginning in the 1960s and extending into the years of economic crisis, the new middle strata seemed to move onto another political trajectory. As we earlier noted, social democrats and Marxists had always seen selected middle strata groups as essential allies for workers. While workers were the vanguard class of progressive change and middle strata would never completely share the progressivism of workers, at least some of them could be won over to a high common denominator of reformism with an anti-capitalist edge. Critical in all this was the position of intellectuals. Following *The Communist Manifesto* itself, it was expected that many intellectuals would recognise the vanguard status of labour and move directly to the side of workers' struggle. More often, intellectuals could help in accrediting the working-class cause ideologically among the middle strata themselves.

As the boom ended there were strong reasons to doubt these classic assumptions. Protest politics in the 1960s had a confusing face. While often making very strong pro-working class claims—as in Maoism, Third Worldism more generally and neo-Trotskyism—it was at the same time almost always stridently scornful of existing workers' organisations. Social Democrats and Communists, where they existed as plausible actors in mass politics, were routinely excoriated as 'revisionists' and 'stolid, unresponsive bureaucrats'. Moreover the social movement side of this protest, with its hit-and-run, disband and reassemble tactics, and its cutting edge of cultural liberationism was sometimes quite baffling to the traditional labour movement.

The 1970s brought rapid retreat from any veneer of ultra-Left workerism and the fragmentation of new social movements into single-issue crusades in which personal and cultural liberationism became the distinguishing characteristic. The list of such movements is very long, ecology, regionalism, communalism, consumerism, anti-nuclear energy, gay liberation, 'human potential'/quasi-psychotherapeutics, health foods, frenetic physical exercise, Oriental quietism, squatting, etc.

We here do not mean to pass judgment either on these movements or on the needs of the groups which they mobilised. What is essential to note, however, is that taken together they amounted to a distinctive form of *middle strata* politics. In the vast majority of cases, the notion that alliances with labour were necessary, or even particularly useful, disappeared, to be replaced, more often than not, with the proposition that labour, particularly in organised forms, was likely to be on the side of the enemy. In the case of several important social movements attempts were made to devise theories which discarded class analysis and posited new causal relation-ships as key historical variables. Intellectuals took up as well as contributed to this escape from class analysis. We think here, somewhat francophonical-ly, of Michel Foucault's analyses of power, Gorz's farewell to the working class, Touraine's welcome to post-industrial society and Laclau and Mouffe's dissolution of class into discourse.

The emergence of a quasi-theorised independent protest—and later electoral—politics located in new middle strata had a decisive effect on the political propensities of much of the radical intelligentsia. Tendencies to align oneself with the working class came to a rapid end. To the degree to which the emergence of an independent middle strata politics with radical pretensions could convince critical segments of the intelligentsia that the working class was *depassé* as an agent of change, then intellectuals ceased moving 'to the side of' workers. Not only did generations-honoured alliance notions become less plausible, then; equally traditional sources of intellectual and ideological support for working-class struggle tended to dry up as well.

What is different here from the post-war compromise period is not, to be sure, the fact of middle strata indignation, but rather the development of what seemed to be an *independent* form of *radical* new middle strata politics. If not denied altogether, the hegemony of labour and labour struggle was simply disregarded as archaic and irrelevant. Labour was not only not seen as the vanguard of progressive change, but in many, if not most cases, was regarded as an *arrière garde*, a 'special interest' standing obdurately in the way of needed social change. While independent and radical middle-class politics was not unprecedented in the history of capitalism—one thinks of North American populism and progressivism, for example, or various European small business movements—the coming of *this particular form* of independent middle class radicalism had the effect of undermining prospects for the political alliance which had under-pinned much of post-war politics.

Such a schematic analysis does not altogether explain either new middle strata radicalism or its particular concerns with personal identity and cultural liberation. Without venturing too far into detail, let us suggest that the personal self-affirmation inherent in such politics may be embedded in the force-feeding of individualism which occurs in middle strata socialisation. Extensive education, progressive specialisation and quasi-professionalism may promote a very strong sense of an individual's own centrality in the social world and a belief that the world *ought* to conform to preconceived visions of it. To the degree to which such groups had unequal access to income, they also gained privileged access to consumerism in ways which also accentuated individualism. Indeed, the 'grey flannel suit' era of conformity clearly gave way in the later 1960s to efforts at esoteric and individualised consumption as an avenue to unique self-definition (exotic food, furniture, clothes, travel and the like). Add to this the inevitable frustrations following from long-promised work autonomy turning out to be deeply limited by bureaucracy and the *salariat*. Self-affirmation in work turned out to be largely mythical. Careers turned out to be nowhere near as universalistically open as advertised—'merit' and 'science' may be less important in advancement than connections, social skills, sexual identity and the like. To the extent to which expectations and aspirations inculcated in schooling and socialisation turned out to be unrealistic, disillusionment followed.

Disillusionment, in turn, fed demands for *control* and participatory democracy as an avenue of self-realisation but with declining attention to the massive structural reforms proposed by the Left and social democratic tradition. Indeed, new middle strata perceptions of Left-promoted reforms often were that they pointed to a *uniformisation* of social situations, statisation in either its welfare state or 'existing socialist' forms. As a background for this analysis, the greyness, massification, social uniformity, bureaucratisation and lack of democracy under existing socialism became common new middle strata wisdom in the 1960s and 1970s as a decades-long intellectual flirtation with the Soviet Union finally came to an end. The renewal of Cold-War anti-Sovietism in the late 1970s hastened this. In a profound sense, new middle strata indignation grew completely out of phase with the utopias, both social democratic and communist, which had been the stock in political trade of the labour movement for a century. All the more reason for an independent new middle strata politics, then, which stressed diversity, difference, self-expression and pluralism.

There is another important dimension to this. The century-old tradition of the labour movement was one of mass collective organisations and politics based on unions and parties. In this tradition one sought broad unity around the primordial importance of a number of essential demands for political democracy, workplace rights, social services, and decent living standards. In this unity *point-of-production* concerns and their political ramifications were presumed to be paramount, the vanguard concerns of the vanguard class. In all this demands which were based on *differences*—i.e. which were not unifying—and demands which aimed to redress specific non-workplace grievances were toned down and subordinated to such vanguard concerns. Women's issues were a classic case in point. As a rule, the labour movement had been historically progressive on such issues. But when it had raised and struggled around such issues, which few other political traditions had deigned to do, it had consistently reshaped them to be part of the broader package of workers' demands. By so doing it had tended *a priori* to define women's issues as those of women workers or of women in working-class families, thereby subordinating any other concerns. Thus when middle strata radicalism turned to just such issues of *difference* it could anticipate and, more often than not was likely to find, misunderstanding from the labour movement. At best unions and parties would try to incorporate issues of difference into preexisting concerns, coalition building in ways which undercut the real purposes of those advancing such issues. At worst they would simply be hostile.

Crisis politics

Much of what we have already said points to the political changes brought by the crisis. Welfare state politics depended upon two things, the persistent power of a social democratic or 'progressive' political coalition composed of workers, their organisations and new middle strata, and the capacity of the national state to regulate essential economic flows. Both were undermined by the crisis. Working-class organisations were severely challenged as underlying structures of the working class itself were altered. The most essential component of any progressive social and political coalition thus lost resources needed to put forward its positions. Simultaneously its erstwhile allies began to do politics on their own. Even had the strength of progressive coalitions not been sapped in such major ways, however, the changing accumulation strategies of capitalism would have made the perpetuation of the post-war compromise extremely difficult. Simply put, even the largest national states proved no match for the internationalisation of economic processes. The leverage needed to regulate critical economic flows proved virtually impossible for single governments to generate.

The symptoms of all this are well known. Keynesian demand management techniques proved less and less effective as the 1970s went on. Under attack both politically and theoretically, they finally gave way to monetarism and neo-liberalism, both under social democratic and conservative regimes. Pledges to maintain close-to-full employment were abandoned willy-nilly in the process, again almost no matter what the political stripe of the government. Wage rises were deliberately and politically disengaged from rises in the cost of living. In many places there were direct and indirect attacks on key institutions of industrial relations and collective bargaining in the name of 'flexibility' and 'deregulation'. Likewise in many places there were attacks on welfare state services in the name of 'budgetary integrity'.

The specific forms of crisis politics varied. The worst onslaughts on the post-war compromise occurred in those societies—mainly Anglo-Saxon—where post-war reforms had been grafted or forced upon a capitalist class with virulent free market ideologies, societies in which social democratic notions had never been victorious. In such places when crisis emerged—bringing with it the weakening of progressive coalitions—older doctrines reemerged with a vengeance. Here one found the most dogmatic monetarism, state complicity in union-busting, frontal attacks on the welfare state and a renaissance in explicitly anti-egalitarian political thought. In contrast, there were other societies where social democratic coalitions maintained themselves and where 'neocorporatist' social alliances held firm. Here retrenchment occurred under social democratic auspices in ways which kept the most reactionary forms of *revanchard* politics at arm's length.

Perhaps the most puzzling form of 'new politics' to emerge in the crisis was the rise of a 'socialism without the workers' in Latin Europe (in France and Spain most notably). Here one found Left parties campaigning and being elected in mid-crisis on social democratic platforms—in the French case, at least, of quite a radical kind. Promises were made to stimulate domestic growth, work major reforms, reduce unemployment and expand the welfare state. Then, after but brief moments of hesitation, there were sharp shifts towards a very different programme which had very little to do with social democracy at all. The political core of this new programme was the use of state policy, often quite vigorously, to make the national economy more competitive in the changing international division of labour. Thus one found strong efforts to generate new labour market 'flexibility' by overturning earlier workplace victories now labelled 'rigidities'. And one also found a quite un-social democratic willingness to allow unemployment to rise rapidly. On the other hand, advocates of 'socialism without the workers' were more reluctant than the new Right to attack the welfare state, insisting only on better management.

Thus what many had argued to be a general convergence of capitalist politics around the forms of the social democratic post-war compromise rapidly gave way to a new pluralism of political strategies. On one extreme one found anti-egalitarian neo-liberalism à la Thatcher and Reagan, where emphases on 'freeing the capitalist market' coexisted with open repudiation of the compromise as a massive mistake. At another one found 'socialism without the workers', mainly in societies where economic *dirigisme* had deep roots. Here technocratic elites—often backed by new middle strata— seemed able to appropriate the political legacy of waning social demo- cracy, *via* attacks on a national bourgeoisie which was allegedly incapable of making the turn towards effective international competition, in order to use statist levers to begin the same turn themselves. In all this the 'traditional' politics of the post-war compromise were fast becoming a memory in most societies, an old tableau to be visited only in small, esoteric museums like Sweden and Austria.

III. LEFT POLITICS AND THE EROSION OF THE SOCIAL DEMOCRATIC COMPROMISE

This much seems clear. Except for a few small societies the post-war era of social democratic solutions—here meant in the broadest of ways—has come to an end. What was to become of Left politics in this unprecedented new and difficult situation? Politics, so far in the crisis, has been tremendously fragmented, constructed, as it has been, on top of a very fragmented class struggle. The notions of 'one working class' and 'one Left' have always been activists' myths because political pluralism has always existed on the Left, following the contours of a class struggle which has inevitably been complex. Yet for the better part of a century such myths could be sustained because it did seem as if historical tendencies to unification out of pluralism were stronger than those pushing towards fragmentation. Indeed, with all allowances duly made, the trajectory of social democracy, the dominant form of mass politics in capitalist societies in the 20th century, bore out such optimism. What ought to be sobering, indeed terrifying in some cases, about the current crisis in that it points to a *reversal* of such unifying tendencies. Moreover earlier crises of capitalism—that of the 1930s, for example—were, despite their horrible dimensions, moments when the labour movement kept faith with its own programme for the future. The current crisis is characterised not only by the collapse of political unification but also by the retreat of programmatic optimism about the future. The Left not only faces the material context of crisis, then. It does so with great new scepticism about its strategic and theoretical links with a better new society to come. This, plus the appearance of pro-capitalist strategies proposed in Left vocabularies, makes the situation difficult indeed.

The contradictions of defending social democracy

With social democracy and analogous movements under political siege in many places, a politics of 'defending social democracy' might seem, at first sight, to be justifiable. Experience demonstrates that such is not always the case, however. Where social democracy is under threat it has tended to react by giving up more and more of what counts—full employment, union rights, the welfare state, etc.—in order to 'protect the rest'. This has usually meant protecting the party itself. Put another way, the task of defending social democracy politically is often defined as moving rightwards in search of centrist voters in ways which tend to throw out both the post-war compromise baby and the bath water. No better example of this is to be found than the recent history of the British Labour Party which, led by its right wing, in its quest to stay in power in the later 1970s, held down living standards, attacked the welfare state, and discarded Keynesianism in the interests of monetarism. Meant to keep Mrs Thatcher out of power, this course paved the way for her and made it much easier for her to pursue her own nefarious projects after 1979. The strategy of 'doing what is unpleasantly necessary to save our party's chances' is destined to fail, ultimately undercutting such parties themselves. Similar arguments and strategies have been used to shore up President Mitterrand's political race towards the Centre and the analogous course followed by the American Democratic Party (a functional equivalent of social democracy), with similar long-term results. Confronting the problems raised by the evident halt in the 'forward march of labour' by eviscerating social democracy even of the political meaning of the post-war compromise, can only lead to a downward spiral. When one advocates the same policies as the Right, one helps the Right.

Another and quite different formula to 'save social democracy' is some-times advanced by left social democrats. It involves pasting together a patchwork alliance of workers and 'new social movements'. As we have noted, relatively autonomous new middle strata politics is a perplexing new reality in the crisis. The question is whether old working-class politics and such new middle strata politics can be patched together as is. To be sure, there are often parts of new social movements which persist valiantly in trying to connect the 'old' and 'new' Lefts, to use the condescending vocabulary of the 'new politics'. But such elements have been far from dominant. In fact, the 'new Left' is profoundly contradictory. The politics of peace, ecology and other movements, and their electoralist propensities, are often radical and progressive—in the sense of being change-oriented, while *simultaneously* harbouring deep anti-working-class feelings. At best such new middle strata politics seeks, in an interesting historical change of focus, to *subordinate* the workers' movement to its goals. At worst it simply disregards workers and their needs. Whereas denial of the progress-ive role of the working class and, even, denial that there *was* any such thing as the working class were favourite bourgeois arguments in the halcyon years of post-war compromise they have since been adopted by many 'new politics' advocates in the name of progress. It follows from all this that a political position which advocates that the labour movement strike deals with the 'new politics', as is, invites new problems. To the degree to which the labour movement is sufficiently strong to insist upon pro-working-class priorities in alliance, the alliance will be unstable. To the degree to which, out of organisational or ideological weakness it ends up 'tailing' such new middle strata movements simply because they seem 'radical' the result is likely to be very dangerous for workers.

Saving social democracy in more or less pure post-war compromise terms where there is some reasonable prospect that these different political downward spirals can be avoided is, of course, more plausible. In places like Sweden and Austria where strong labour movements tied to social democratic parties made unusually successful advances in taming local capital and in creating a general consensus around advanced welfare states, concessions such as consensual wage restraint may not lead to dramatic new weakness. But there are very few places where such strategies are feasible.

The new danger of 'socialism without the workers'
The technocratic politics which we have earlier labelled 'socialism without the workers' provide no solution at all. Here, in essence, everyone—workers and new social movement activists—are being told that 'nothing can be done until national capital accumulation is regenerated'. The supposed hard realities of new technology and the changed international division of labour are designated the primary obstacles to any progressive politics. What usually follows such assertions are propositions about 'industrial policy' and 'restructuring'. Such policies, which everyone acknowledges will harm workers' interests, are an inevitable bitter pill which must be swallowed. Somewhere further down the line, it is claimed, when national accumulation has been regenerated, the post-war compromise system of consumerism and the welfare state can be reinstated.

Here, of course, we must avoid know-nothingism. International capitalism is in a tumultuous period of change to which national economies and the labour movement, barring the discovery of any new strategy for transition to socialism in crisis, must pay serious and consciously adaptive attention. Technocratic 'socialism without the workers' à la François Mitterrand or Felipe Gonzalez is something different from this, however. It is rather a conscious abandonment of most principles of social democracy accomplished under the flag of 'socialism' itself and promoted by technocratic elites on the borderline between new middle strata and bourgeois class positions. Its purpose is not progressive social change but to supplant or complement the national bourgeoisie, portrayed as incompetent at working 'necessary adjustments', with new technocratic elites. It is far from clear, of course, whether it is even possible to regenerate national capitalism in such ways. The situation which would result if it were might be marginally more 'humane' than that proposed by Reagan and Thatcher but it would almost certainly also seal the doom of those limited principles of egalitarianism and redistribution which had characterised the post-war compromise.

The problematic optimism of the ultra-Left
It will take more than a huge crisis to destroy the faith of the ultra-Left. Imbued with a transhistorical vision of the revolutionary mission of the working class, this small, fiercely fissiparous cluster of intellectuals has historically always refused to give in to the prevalent gloom of crisis. Here uniquely one continues to find confidence that the future is bound to be better than the present, given the ineluctable contradictions and the likely eventual decline of capitalism. Moreover, for much of this ultra-Left the contemporary difficulties of both Social Democracy and Communism come as no surprise. The class collaborationism of the first and the revisionism, bureaucratism and Stalinism of the second have been roundly denounced for decades.

If long-term optimism and insistence upon socialist ideals, along with the courage to say *no* in the face of huge pressure to do otherwise, have been, and are, the virtues of this position, it has always had its concomitant faults. The greatest of these has consistently been analytical and practical distance from the day-to-day realities of the class struggle. The belligerent refusal to admit that the mass organisational labour politics of the post-war compromise were 'real', in the sense of being approximations of workers' goals, but were rather the concoctions of 'misleaders' in control of organisations which were the agents of capital and 'false consciousness', opened up space for consistent denunciation but provided little political effectiveness. If all mass working-class politics was a nearly closed circle of betrayal in which most workers themselves were dupes, those who perceive such processes were almost by definition excluded from them. It was no accident, then, that the ultra-Left was mainly composed of intellectuals.

Since ultra left politics is *residual*, it has an important historic role to play, that of the vociferous conscience. The present crisis, however, does pose serious problems for the ultra-Left because it has cast doubt on the credibility of its utopias. The Soviet model and derivations have lost their appeal, even in idealised Trotskyist forms. One-party dictatorships of the proletariat, vanguard parties, and centralised rule, even when debureau-cratised in theory, have little appeal to anyone, even intellectuals, any more. 'Council communist' utopias likewise sound ever more naive in an era where large organisations and complex social arrangements seem inevitable. In more immediate terms, it is evident that simply nationalising, or even abolishing, private property is likely to shift the locus of domina-tion to other agencies, the state in the first instance, rather than opening a path to socialism. 'Seizing state power', 'smashing the state' and other such slogans raise the same issues. It is not that these proposals—and others like them about abolishing the capitalist division of labour, for example—may not turn out to be steps toward a better society. It is rather that they presently exist outside of a genuinely convincing strategic trajectory which would persuade people that they were steps toward a better society. Thus many of the time-honoured positions which the ultra-Left had always condemned the rest of the Left for abandoning have lost their compelling edge. Because of this the effectiveness of its role as a conscience in the unfolding of a very uncertain future will be limited unless and until it can reflect anew and successfully on a meaningful socialism for the 21st century.

The limits of defensive workerism

'Workerism' involves the systematic defence in the face of crisis of what workers and their organisations, unions in particular, have achieved and desire to preserve. In practice this usually involves staunch support of the more militant struggles of unions and groups within unions. Lenin, of course, had some judicious remarks about the limits of simple, even militant, workerism which have lost little of their trenchancy. Unions, however militant, were unlikely to pursue radical change strategically and, because of this, would, sooner or later, create openings for capital to blunt or co-opt their struggles. Such thoughts remain pertinent in the crisis of the 1980s. Workers and their unions are particularly vulnerable in this crisis, given the declining power of unions, fragmentation of the working class and the decline of alliance support from middle strata.

Workerism is, therefore, a politics with little promise for positive change. Still, a huge amount is at stake in struggles to protect working-class victories in the workplace and in terms of broader political and social rights. Strong arguments can be made, therefore, in favour of workerist politics in a situation marked by the immediate absence of any broader strategic outlook. It is evident that the most determined 'roll-back' thrusts of the Right and capital are directed towards dismantling the workplace dimension of the post-war compromise and undercutting the legitimacy of unions and hard won workers' rights to a minimum of security in work. It is also clear that major, quite influential, segments of the new middle strata see workers and their organisations as mere 'special interests', and 'barriers to progress'. Whatever the limitations of worker-ism, then, in the absence of a general strategy for the Left which could build beyond existing conditions, workerism at least tries to defend what is most important. Without such a strategy, however, it will become more and more difficult to defend class positions through simple workerism. In short, unalloyed workerism is at best a politics of cutting losses in crisis in the hope that a recomposition of the working class and a regenerated Left strategy will ensue before the anti-labour politics of capital and the Right can achieve their goals. For the moment, however, it may be one of the few plausible Left positions we have.

Options for an agenda?
The present fragmented setting of mass Left politics is likely to be destructive of the solidarity needed to prevent the new politics of reaction from reversing some, if not a great deal, of what has been won by workers over the last century. Fragmentation facilitates capitalist strategies of dividing and ruling. The glaring new contradictions between workers and new middle strata provide new material for such strategies. The decline in social democratic alliance prospects for building opens the way to further fragmentation and separate new middle strata politics. This situation, in turn, gives a political hunting license to the Right. Better-off parts of the working class may be targets for 'populist' mobilisation by the Right, as the American and British examples show. Populist alliances including some workers, white-collar employees, capital, and cultural conservatives will be difficult to manage over time, however, given the complexities of conciliat-

ing anti-labour economic policies and the search for support, often on cultural grounds, from parts of the working class itself. Populist coalitions are therefore unlikely to be stable. They are, however, serious threats as agents for the further disaggregation of existing social democratic coalitions.

'Socialism without the workers', seen as one variant of capital's politics of crisis, may also spread because of Left fragmentation. Where techno-cratic elites are able to gain control over social democratic parties, they are then free, for a time, to manipulate an ambiguous stock of social demo-cratic symbols in the interests of 'industrial adaptation' and the like. Perhaps more important, because of their position at the head of nominal-ly Left political formations, they can also profit from long-standing electoral reflexes that 'socialists, no matter what their programme, will be better than the Right'. Here again, however, the problem of reconciling the maintenance of workers' electoral support with antiworking-class politics is likely to be difficult to resolve, as the contemporary French situation demonstrates best of all.

The path to such divide-and-rule strategies will remain open until the Left is able to devise, or reconstruct, a plausible mass political strategy which goes beyond appeals to restore the high points of the post-war compromise. Here the need for political creativity is immense. As a start-ing point one can construct an agenda of issues to be raised. Left utopias, plausible models for a substantially better society, desperately need rejuvenation. One can hardly mobilise large numbers of people for change unless one can inspire them with a vision of how such change will build new bridges to a more desirable world. The post-war compromise was, in many ways, the end of history for social democracy, a basis for a broad coalition of social groups to the degree to which it 'produced the goods' but which no longer pointed to a better future. When the 'goods' ceased to be forthcoming, therefore, social democracy lost much of its already limited capacity to inspire, especially because it then had little to offer except struggle to restore an unrestorable *status quo ante.* The main 'utopian' alternative to social democracy in the 20th century, Communism, has suffered a similar fate. 'Existing socialism', however one draws up its balance sheet, has clearly ceased to be a goal for anyone in advanced capitalist societies. Other minoritarian utopias on offer are, at best, the visions of sects. Why should workers and others take risks when the results are obscure. What might a socialism for our time look like? The problems which any open-minded progressive person would have in answering this indicates the huge need for new thought.

Needed as well is a Left strategy which would promote national economic integrity and social progress in an international context which has raised great barriers to both. Socialism in one country is, now even more than in the past, an illusory possibility. Complete affiliation with the bloc of 'existing Socialist' countries is also too costly. It is a dangerous form of know-nothingism to assert that political voluntarism will over-come the deep structures of the international market and division of labour. Movements for progressive change must therefore find space for manoeuvre in the interstices and contradictions of the new international setting. The neo-classical orthodoxy of the moment is that there is *no* margin for manoeuvre in this setting—one can only find ways to work astutely within a corset of near-complete international constraint. There is a great component of surrender to pro-capitalist ideology in this. Still, the Left needs policies, and not simply voluntaristic rhetoric, which will allow confrontation with the new international situation in ways which will open up, and not close down, progressive possibilities.

Alas, one finds only disconnected bits and pieces of plausible new strategies in the world today. Versions of the Meidner Plan—Employee Investment Funds—might be part of such a strategy of democratising capital *and* democratising economic and other decision-making, were it not for the facts that in Sweden such initiatives, in watered-down form, are being taken by labour bureaucracies in the place of workers for the purpose of restoring the basic conditions of the post-war compromise. Mobilisation from below to impose 'new criteria of management' in the economy and in political institutions, as proposed by the French Communists, is an intriguing prospect at present bogged down in France in workerist defensiveness and electoralism. Other formulations of essentially similar notions can be found which attempt to conciliate the need for genuine Left approaches with the control of economic and political decisions. They may point the way to alliances to move out of crisis towards better societies, with stress on the need for democracy in the ways such decisions are made. Proposals of this kind may be a way of addressing the problems of class fragmentation and mobilisation associated with the crisis. In these ways, a new basis for the construction of working-class identity may be found. There are some progressive flowers blooming. At present however they occupy only an alarmingly small corner of the garden.

The working class must be recomposed. What will help this along? Alliances between workers and ·middle strata must be reconstructed. How can this be begun? Beyond what we have already suggested, approaches which focus on democratic control over basic social decisions, beginning with those about work and the economy, seem the most promising path. Without major democratic advances in the shaping of fundamental economic decisions it seems clear that capital will attempt to regenerate accumulation on the backs of workers. Here, then, workers can be engaged beyond the boundaries between different fractions of the working class. Demands for democratic control are likewise the progressive side of the contradictory package of concerns which have come to motivate new middle strata politics. Demands for new democracy and personal freedom are thus shared across presently tenuous class boundaries, although recent developments in new middle strata politics have tended to move away from a focus on the workplace. The Left could bring to these movements both an analysis of and an insistence on the fundamental need to change working conditions in order to change any other life situations in a meaningful way. Stress on the democratic content of *struggle* for such goals of control may also begin to reverse the mobilisation problem created by the social democratic propensity to substitute organisational actions for those of people themselves. The involvement of workers and their organisations, in that order, in struggles for new beach-heads of control over central economic decisions about investment, national trade policies, industrial location and the structures of work and social programmes may be the beginning of the way. Adaptation to a changed international setting need not be the working of brutal social surgery by elites—whether technocrats or capitalists. It can also be social innovation promoted by workers and their allies in actions cemented by principled agreements. However, the Left's garden must be cultivated a great deal before such things grow.

THE IMPASSE OF SOCIAL DEMOCRATIC POLITICS

Leo Panitch

> There are three stages through which every new notion in England has to pass: 'It is impossible: It is against the Bible: We knew it before. Socialism is rapidly reaching the third of these stages. We are all socialists now,' said one of Her Majesty's late Ministers; and in sober truth, there is no anti-socialist political party. That which has long formed part of the unconscious basis of our practice is now formulated as a definite theory, and the tide of democratic collectivism is upon us.
>
> Sidney Webb, *English Progress Toward Social Democracy*, Fabian Tract, No. 15, December 1890.

I. INTRODUCTION

The notion of gradual but inevitable progress toward socialism through the vehicle of a paternalist parliamentary state has always entailed an historical determinism far more myopic than could ever be properly ascribed to Marxism. The rude shock administered by the establishment of the new right's 'market populism' as the governing ideology of the 1980s appears to have clearly and definitively shattered the complacency associated with the phrase, so oft repeated over the past century, 'we are all socialists now'.

At the same time it must also be recognised that the emergence of market populism amidst the current crisis of capitalism has simultaneously exposed in its wake the impasse of working class politics in the West. The long-standing assumption that a return to mass unemployment and an abandonment of bourgeois commitment to the Keynesian/welfare state would lead to political instability and a crisis of capitalist legitimacy, an assumption as common among liberals as among many Marxists, has been cast into doubt. For the moment at least, it is the weakness of the political forces associated with the working class—whether trade unions, or social democratic parties, or revolutionary socialist parties—that has come to the fore and brought home an old lesson: there is nothing automatic about the development of socialist consciousness when the capitalist economy is not generating material benefits or job security for the working class.

Indeed, the impasse that has been reached would appear to be the obverse of the one that many thought characterised the working classes in advanced capitalism since World War Two. Whereas it was earlier argued that that the ability of the system to generate immediate material rewards

50

foreclosed the possibility of developing sustained and broad interest in socialist ideas, it would today appear that the absence of widespread socialist conviction or understanding among the working classes in advance of the crisis has made many working people vulnerable to the new right's ideology and amenable to the 'common sense' remedies of restraint and sacrifice as a means of restoring capitalism's health. If the 'objective' economic conditions are present today, the no less 'objective' political and cultural conditions are not. In other words, the failure to generate socialist consciousness in the period of capitalist boom appears to have laid the grounds for a further failure in the period of bust.

The consequences of this has proved severe not only for socialist politics but for working class reformism. Reformism was able to retain popular support and programmatic direction when it appeared the system could support it, but it lost a good deal of both when economic conditions and the bourgeois onslaught against previous reformist gains in these new conditions combined to demonstrate how utterly dependent the system—and every individual within it—is on meeting the requirements set by capitalists for when and where they will invest. 'Common sense' has told all of us that reforms conceived and implemented within the logic of capitalism have to be re-examined once they really do begin to have the effect of scaring business away. At a minimum, a new defence of old reforms becomes necessary; inertia alone cannot be counted on. In the elaborate and complex poker game that is capitalist democracy, the new right used monetarism to call the old left's—including the unions'—bluff with regard to the hand it had been holding for some forty years. And it turned out that we had little strength in any suit.

It has been hardly surprising, therefore, that there has been a good deal of socialist 'rethinking' going on in recent years. Insofar as the primary form of working class politics in the West was that of reformist parties, this rethinking initially took the form (often drawing on the new intellectual revival of Western Marxism since the 1960s) of attempting to understand and transcend the limits and contradictions of social democracy both as state policy and as political and ideological practice. This inevitably involved an assault from the left on the 'we are all socialists now' ideology to match the one that had emerged from the right. This in turn produced considerable internal party strife as battles were fought out over the very meaning of socialism and democracy, amidst the heady revival within these parties of a form of radical discourse which the predominant leadership of these parties had long before stopped to take seriously. At the root of it all was the perception that if the history of the modern state was not one of inevitable gradual progress toward socialism this had much to do with the effective abandonment of the socialist project by working class parties. Tony Benn characteristically captured the spirit of this development in the British context at the beginning of the 1980s:

'We have persuaded the Labour movement that one of the reasons we have made so little progress over seventy years is the weakness of the Labour Party. That is the real issue that has been raised.'[1]

With rather astonishing haste, and long before the project of transforming these parties could be said to have been achieved, a remarkable shift of direction has taken place in the general orientation of leftist intellectuals towards understanding the roots of the impasse. Increasingly, this re-thinking has placed under scrutiny the very nature of the socialist project itself, above all as it has been classically conceived by Marxism. Brought into question has been the centrality, or at least the relative salience, of the working class as the agency of social change, whether because of the declining proportion of manual industrial workers in the labour force, or because of the inherent inability of workers to transcend militant trade union economism. At the same time, the vision projected by Marxism—and especially by 'actually existing' socialism's practice—of a centrally-planned non-market economy has come under increasing attack for associating the notion of socialism with authoritarian statism. While by no means unimportant issues have thus been raised, sometimes with considerable insight, the irony of this orientation to the problem is that it not only shifts attention away from the primary modern practice of the Western working class—reformist social democracy—but actually replicates, both in its critique of Marxism and in its strategic proposals, many of the essential tenets of that very practice.

The response of workers to the crisis must not be seen mechanistically or ahistorically as something inevitable, or as 'natural' or 'given'. It is rather a product of a range of previous practices which fostered certain structures and ideas that blocked the development of a viable socialist response to the crisis, and that excluded socialist options as 'unrealistic'. If we see the impasse in this way, as something constructed rather than given, we may also see that *the impasse pertains not only, indeed not so much, to the drag that the working class or Marxism imposes on the socialist project, as many would have it today, as to the drag that social democracy continues to exercise on the working class and the intellectual left.* For even though the Keynesianism and corporatism of social democracy have exhausted the limits of their reformist and electoral possibilities in the current crisis, they retain deep ideological and organisational supports which recent intellectual and party political experience indicates cannot be easily transcended.

To speak of the impasse of working class politics rather than the impasse of socialist politics involves a deliberate decision, therefore. It is designed to establish at the outset the problematic of the link between the achievement of socialism and the working class as its progenitor; and it is to emphasise that, contrary to much current misconception, *it is not only the viability of revolutionary socialism that is open to question as a result of the current crisis. The impasse we have been speaking of pertains far more to reformist gradualism precisely because this has been—and remains —the primary practice of Western working class parties.* This is not to deny the need for Marxian socialists to engage in a profound reexamination of a strategic kind with regard to their own forms of political practice, but this is hardly to be achieved through putting aside all of the difficult questions about how a transition to socialism in the face of bourgeois opposition is actually to be effected, which, as we shall see, the new revisionism is wont to do. Before turning to a critique of the latter however, it will be necessary to define in more concrete terms the exact nature of the impasse of working class politics.

II. THE CONTRADICTIONS OF SOCIAL DEMOCRATIC GOVERN-MENTS

To understand properly today's impasse, we must locate it in the historical context of the rise and fall of post-war social democracy. Until the post-war era, the socialist aspirations and rhetoric of social democratic parties had stood uncomfortably alongside their strategic commitments. How could public planning and control over the economy—which was the principal case offered not only for distributive reforms but for public ownership—be effected without offending the principle of inter-class compromise and cooperation upon which the gradualism, parliamentarism and tripartism practised by these parties ultimately rested? When a party like the British Labour Party finally committed itself to socialism in the sense of Clause Four—the taking into public ownership of the means of production, distribution and exchange—it never answered the question that arose over how this could be achieved while at the same time retaining its long-standing commitment to class cooperation as opposed to class struggle. As for the classic social democratic parties of the continent, their dilemma after World War One was no longer how their vulgar economic Marxism could be made consistent with their tepid political parliamentarism, but how their tripartite 'functional socialism' could retain its relevance when the bourgeoisie refused to cooperate in it (at least once the immediate revolutionary threat of at the end of the war had passed). This difficult question of how economic planning might be introduced without causing a massive political fissure was either avoided or it was answered in the face of capitalist opposition by the abandonment or marginalisation of such economic planning structures as had been initiated by social democratic governments at the end of the war.

After World War Two, on the other hand, in the context of the experience of the Depression, the defeat of fascism, and above all the onset of the greatest boom period the world economy has probably ever known, the conditions were established for social democracy's apparently successful resolution of the above dilemma. With Keynesianism and the welfare state coming to provide new substantive content to 'state intervention' and being accepted as such by significant sections of bourgeois opinion, it was no longer necessary for social democratic parties to emphasise public ownership as the centrepiece of planning or control over the economy. Indeed, to do so would involve throwing away the opportunity for class cooperation through tripartite indicative planning and, as was so often repeated at the time, confuse means with ends. Social democratic leaders discerned the emergence of an efficiency-oriented managerial class which had come to appreciate the limits of an unregulated capitalism and the virtues of macroeconomic planning, welfare reforms and stable industrial relations. In turn, capitalists and senior bureaucrats discerned a party leadership anxious to prove their 'soundness' and 'responsibility' by playing the key role of securing trade union cooperation in incomes policies so as to obviate the inflationary pressures of full employment capitalism. To one side this meant that we were all socialists now; to the other—and with rather more justice—that we were all capitalists now. But what did it matter? The terms were misleading in any case, were they not? This was after all the era of the end of ideology.

Or so it seemed. The so-called post-war settlement between labour and capital in the West may have concealed to some extent, but it hardly closed, the contradictions that give rise to class and ideological struggle and to economic instability under capitalism. In particular, the resurgence of industrial militancy in the late 1960s threw into sharp relief at one and the same time the economic strength of workers under the conditions of near full employment and the political weakness of labour *vis à vis* capital even under the tripartite economic planning arrangements of social democratic Governments. Moreover, the drawing to a close of the post-war boom in the 1970s underlined the instability of corporatism and revealed the fragility of the Keynesian/welfare state. A combination of special conditions had produced the high investment ratios of the 1950–73 period: the cleansing of unproductive and less dynamic capitals during the depression and the war; large post-war pools of skilled cheap labour; clusters of technological innovations favouring productivity growth and mass consumer demand; the weakening of trade union militancy during the Cold War; the abundance of cheap raw materials and the availability of new markets and relatively open trade under US economic leadership. Each of these ran out, however unevenly, by the early 1970s. This made particularly problematic for the economy and the state the consumerism and confidence of the workers which the boom had generated and which combined to sustain industrial militancy in the 1970s even as unemployment levels began their disastrous ascent. At the same time, the explosively expansive potential of public employment and state social expenditures became increasingly clear as the employment and growth performance of the private sector declined.

The collapse of the Keynesian era in the stagflation of the 1970s meant that the old 'settlement' had to be renegotiated—and not only between capital and labour, but also within labour, i.e. between social democratic leaderships and their trade union base. How to generate new capital investment while simultaneously extending the limits of reform so as to provide effective 'quid pro quos' for new rounds of wage restraint by the unions became the central question for social democratic governance in the 1970s. This did not in itself appear to entail an impasse for reformist working class politics. On the contrary, it seemed to provide the opportunity for a new testing of the limits of reform within capitalist democracies. And, indeed, a shift to the left, a resurgence of parliamentary *socialism*, was visible in one country after another. What was now taken up was what had been largely foregone in the post-war settlement in the way of industrial democracy and effective control over private investment decisions: the sphere of production rather than that of distribution became the primary focus of legislative reform. This was seen, for instance, in the turn by the DGB and SPD Government in West Germany towards 'Strukturpolitik' and investment planning as well as the attempted extension of codetermination beyond the iron and coal industry. It was seen in Sweden in the famous Meidner Plan and in the legislation in the mid-1970s which provided a legal framework for union challenges to managerial prerogatives on the shop floor and for worker participation schemes on works councils and company boards. It was seen in Britain in similar progressive labour legislation and the proposals of the Bullock Inquiry on industrial democracy as well as in the planning agreements and National Enterprise Board elements of Labour's 1973 programme. And it was seen, of course, in the emphasis on autogestion and nationalisation that characterised the phenomenal revival of the French Socialists under the umbrella of the Common Programme.

What has now become apparent after a decade is that in one country after another the much-vaunted social partnership, insofar as it ever existed beyond the most superficial and conditional levels, simply could not be reconstructed on a firm foundation. As social democratic parties took up demands for industrial democracy and investment planning, it now turned out that it was capital that balked at cooperation on such revised terms. In Germany and Britain this became clear very quickly in the mid-1970s, even though the SPD and Labour Governments adopted conventionally restrictive, virtually monetarist, macroeconomic policies. The German employers' constitutional challenge to the codetermination law and their 'taboo catalogue' on negotiations over work-time reduction led to the complete breakdown of Concerted Action in economic policy making in 1977 and to the six-week metal workers strike and lock-out in 1978 which presaged the even more protracted and bitter conflict of 1983 and shattered the myth of social consensus. In Britain, the radical thrust of the planning agreements and enterprise board proposals was quickly jettisoned in the face of business opposition, but neither this, nor the extensive wage restraint practised by the unions under the Social Contract until 1978, allayed capital's fears of 'union power'. Above all, as Colin Leys' interviews with CBI leaders have shown, the Bullock Report's majority recommendation for parity representation on company boards, although not taken up by the Labour Government, became the 'rallying point' for the conversion to Thatcherism by British industrialists regardless of its destructive implications for manufacturing industry. 'It was at this time that opinion among the CBI leadership shifted from a defence of collaborative relations with the state and the labour movement to one of more or less open rejection. . . In the mid-1970s a majority of manufacturing executives had come to feel that the survival of capitalism was at stake. They judged that unless trade union power was drastically reduced, control of capital would pass out of owners' hands and profits from manufacturing would progressively disappear. Consequently short-term business interests, and even the long-term interests of individuals or firms had to be sacrificed. Even those who were unconvinced by the Thatcherite project saw no realistic political alternative. . .'[2]

Just how widespread, and how fundamental, is the breakdown of the post-war consensus can be seen by looking at the Swedish case. Despite the defeat of the SAP in 1976, it seemed to many that the elaboration of the Meidner Plan laid the foundation for Swedish social democracy's inauguration of a new 'middle way' socialist society without having to disrupt economic growth and class harmony. These hopes have been disappointed not only by the severe watering down of the wage earners funds scheme after considerable strife in the social democratic party, but by the real and growing disenchantment shown by Swedish capital with the social consensus approach. This has been seen not only in the SAF's vociferous opposition to the wage earners funds even in their watered down versions as little more than forced savings schemes; it could also be seen in the Swedish employers' determination—and their recent success—to break the wage solidarity practice of the LO and the system of centralised bargaining upon which it was based. After the massive general strike of 1980, and the extensive strikes of the following year, protracted negotiations in 1982–3 were only concluded after the crucial metal sector settled separately without regard for the wage solidarity principle. Finally, in 1984 centralised bargaining was abandoned altogether in favour of sector by sector bargaining. This was a major victory for the employers and was achieved even in the face of the LO granting major concessions. This dramatic change in labour–capital relations has occurred in spite of the social democrats re-election in 1982. And it has occurred in spite of the introduction of a version of the wage earners funds that pose no challenge ·whatever to capital in terms of economic democracy and the socialisation of industry and in spite of the expressed hopes of the government that the funds will 'secure acceptance for a high level of profit in enterprise', 'reduce distributive conflict' and encourage restraint in collective bargaining'. Swedish capital's mobilisation against the funds and their dismantling of centralised bargaining shows that capital's own interest in social consensus is a highly conditional one: the attempt by working class institutions to pose fundamental challenges to managerial prerogatives or private ownership as a 'quid pro quo' for wage restraint finds capital withdrawing from the process.[3]

What this means is that the old dilemma has resserted itself: those social democratic parties which remain in office in the 1980s are primarily engaged in managing the crisis in a form increasingly reminiscent of the inter-war years. Where unemployment levels have been kept relatively low (as in Sweden and Austria compared with France) considerable credit is due to the cushioning effect of public sector institutions and practices forged during the era of consensus. But concern with reviving business profits and reducing the deficit have been the main themes of recent Budgets in Austria and Sweden; and this, along with the accelerating trend to decentralised bargaining in these countries as capital exploits and exacerbates labour's divisions and insecurity in this era of capitalist 're-structuring', clearly indicates that there is little prospect for a stable or unproblematic revival of the old consensus politics. And if this is the case for Sweden and Austria, it is most certainly the case for Britain where the crisis—economic, ideological and political—is incomparably more severe.

III. LABOURISM AND THE WORKING CLASS

To begin an examination of the impasse of working class politics by stressing the historical dilemmas of social democracy and the limits they impose on political practice, as we have done, stands in sharp contrast with current intellectual trends on the left.[4] From André Gorz's *Farewell to the Working Class* and Eric Hobsbawm's *The Forward March of Labour Halted?* the starting point for analysis of the impasse has been what it tells us about: a) the nature of the working class, and relatedly, b) the errors of 'orthodox' Marxist notions of class struggle as the focal point of socialist politics. Consequently, insofar as the practice of working class parties is criticised, it is for too close an attachment to traditional forms of class politics.

One must, of course, be careful to distinguish between a Gorz and a Hobsbawm, between a 'Green' and a 'Eurocommunist', analysis of the impasse. Gorz's polemic against 'Saint Marx' involves a fundamental displacement of the working class as a potentially revolutionary subject (by a vaguely-defined and rather amorphous 'non-class of non-workers'). Counterposing his position against a caricatured presentation of Marx as believing that the development of capitalist forces of production would directly give rise to a spontaneously unified, inherently 'universal', revolutionary class of industrial workers, Gorz presents an exactly opposite picture of an 'actual' working class which neither is, nor can be, anything more than a pale, and increasingly fading, reflection of capital itself, incapable of doing more than bargaining over the price of its labour. Gorz belittles in this fashion the enormous stress Marx put on the role of unions and parties in 'the formation of the proletariat into a class'[5] and he ignores the actual historical experience of the attachment of large sections of the working class to socialist parties. He shows little interest, therefore, in examining the practices of these parties to discern the extent to which they fostered or constrained its revolutionary potential. The matter is settled by his denial of this potential in face of the original Marxist sin of having based its political practice on chasing a false god. A rather more nuanced argument, but with a similarly one-sided reading of Marxism's alleged forces of production determinism, is offered by those 'discourse' theorists who grant the conjunctural preeminence of class conflict in certain historical periods but attack Marxism for its *a priori classism*, its tendency to privilege the working class among a plurality of possible hegemonic subjects 'whose forms of constitution and diversity it is only possible to think if we relinquish the category of "subject" as a unified and unifying essence'.[6]

The remit of these critiques of Marxism (apart from their misinterpretations, to which we shall return) obviously can have little salience in explaining the impasse in those countries where social democratic parties, which have long since rejected—or never adopted—Marxist analysis, have been the focal point of working class politics. Whatever their relevance to the Second International's pre-World War One practice or to the contemporary politics of the French Communist Party, they are largely beside the point if we are trying to understand the impasse today in Britain or West Germany or Sweden. Far more germane, therefore, is the interpretation of the impasse offered by Eric Hobsbawm in his attempt to confront the crisis of British Labourism. Hobsbawm has consistently identified a declining secular trend in Labour Party voting corresponding with the relative numerical decline of the manual working class and a growing sectionalism among trade unionists as the two fundamental problems which socialists had to analyse and overcome. Neither engaging in the caricature of Marxism so evident elsewhere, nor calling for the abandonment of the working class (his model is clearly the Italian Communist Party which 'is and wishes to remain a classical mass socialist labour party, attempting to rally the widest range of forces around its essential core of the working class'), Hobsbawm nevertheless insists that the old formula that governed socialist strategy in the first half of this century (i.e. 'class = support for the Workers' party = being against capitalism = for socialism') no longer automatically obtains. Even among the core of Labour's traditional manual working class support, as Hobsbawm increasingly has come to argue since the disastrous results of the 1983 election, and as Stuart Hall repeatedly warned before it, the long-standing pull of traditional loyalties have considerably frayed, especially under the impact of the dissolving effects of consumerism and mobility on working class communities.[7]

Although the tenor of the argument sometimes gave the impression of sociological reductionism regarding the declining working class, and of a remarkably uncharitable portrayal of trade union behaviour (which largely ignored the unrequited wage restraint practised under the Social Contract), it needs to be recalled that Hobsbawm insisted that what he was describing was an avoidable crisis:

> . . . Marxists are not economic and social determinists, and it simply will not do to say that the crisis of the working class and the socialist movement was 'inevitable', that nothing could have been done about it. . . If we are to explain the stagnation or crisis, we have to look at the Labour Party and the labour movement itself. The workers, and growing strata outside the manual workers, were looking to it for a lead and a policy. They did not get it. They got the Wilson years—and many of them lost faith and hope in the mass party of the working people.[8]

Because Hobsbawm was looking for, nay, insisting on, more than superficial analysis of the impasse and solutions to it, one might have expected that a serious and sustained analysis of the role of the Labour Party would have been undertaken, not as an academic exercise nor one directed at finding the appropriate culprits to blame, but in order to lay the basis for a truly innovative way forward. As sensitive and acute an historian as Eric Hobsbawm could hardly have imagined that the Wilson years or the Callaghan years which followed were accidents of Labour's history rather than products of it, nor that fundamental change in the leadership, and more importantly, the long-standing orientation of political parties is something that might be affected smoothly, without the pain and cost associated with rancour and division. Yet apart from the kind of passing comment offered above, this analysis of the party's historical contribution to the construction of the impasse has not been forthcoming. On the contrary, the brunt of Hobsbawm's attention (and ire) has been directed towards a polemic against those very forces in the Labour Party which have sought such changes in organisation, personnel, ideology and policy as would forestall a continuation of the practice of the Wilson/Callaghan years. The thrust of change is portrayed as irresponsibly divisive in the face of the need for a popular front against Thatcherite reaction. The attempt to require of the leadership a commitment to mobilisation and education towards a socialist transition is caricatured and derided as an ultra-leftist attempt to establish a 'correct position and wait for the British people to recognise how wrong they are in not agreeing with it', And, despite his insistence that the 'solution lies not in changing the workers, but the party' (as if the whole brunt of his analysis on economism and sectionalism does not belie such false polarities and does not implicitly require that the workers as well as the party be changed), it is he who insists that Labour return to the traditional presentation of itself as a 'broad people's party' as the fount of its politics. He demands that the party define its socialism in terms of 'a fair, free, socially just society', realistic policy, awareness of the conflicting sectional interests of workers, and, above all, in terms of Labour having an electoral chance to immediately form a government. This may indeed presage a different politics than practised during the Wilson/Callaghan years, but it is cast in such familiarly general terms as to invite the question of what is new?

Precisely because Hobsbawm no longer undertakes a serious examination of the Labour Party's role during what he takes to be a long period of decline rather than a sudden fall from grace, precisely because he levels his political critique against those who call for a more explicitly socialist orientation for the party, his intervention does indeed bring to mind the earlier revisionist debate at the end of the 1950s when it was argued that Labour had to abandon outmoded socialist nostrums to catch up with an embourgeoisified working class. The parallel has been repeatedly drawn in the debate that has raged around the new revisionism, but it is really only germane in one respect, and that is for a common crude determinism which moves directly from socio-economic changes to the orientations of the electorate, without a serious examination of the role of the party as an intervening variable. James Cronin has gone to the heart of the matter in contending that what is at issue is not the empirical validity of the new revisionism's descriptions of changes in social structure or voting behaviour, but rather that 'they remain embedded in a form of analysis which. . . is distinguished by the simplicity of its understanding of the link between politics and class structure'. In other words: 'The recourse to social structural explanation is had, therefore, even before the political dimensions of the problem are recognised and discussed, and certainly prior to the development and testing of any argument that assumes that the political crisis might in fact be rooted in factors that are in themselves primarily political in nature.'[9] This recalls Frank Parkin's riposte to the earlier revisionist contention that the deradicalisation of socialist parties was a necessary response to changing attitudes on the parts of its supporters. His point was that this approach ignored the extent to which parties are themselves critical to the formation of working class political perceptions: 'It seems plausible to suggest that if socialist parties ceased to present a radical, class-oriented meaning system to their supporters, then such an outlook would not persist of its own among the subordinate class. . . This is really to assert that the mass party has a potentially more formative influence on the political perceptions and understanding of the subordinate class than is generally acknowledged.'[10]

When cast in this light, it immediately becomes clear that Hobsbawm's equation regarding the period of 'forward march' (class = support for the workers' party = being against capitalism = for socialism), which captures so much of the new revisionism's assumptions regarding the historical trajectory of working class politics before the socio-economic changes that allegedly produced the impasse, actually represents a form of class reductionism which fails to acknowledge how indirect and tenuous the posited identities actually were. Hobsbawm acknowledges that even when a growing number of workers could have been relied on to accept the equation, that itself 'was not enough, as the history of the Labour Party shows'. But what he does not do is analyse to what extent the historical practice of the Party, during the period of 'forward march' no less than later, was not merely 'not enough' but actually served to render the equation invalid.

The first point that must be made in this respect is that the primary association between class identity and workers' party was always far more ambiguous in the case of the Labour Party than is currently admitted. It must be remembered that the attachment of the dense network of pre-existing working class institutions to the Labour Party in the first decades of this century took place in a manner, unlike the case in much of Western Europe, whereby the party was itself little involved as an agency in the formation of class identity and community. As Cronin puts it, the trade union leadership came to attach its organisations to Labour, thereby making it a mass workers party, by virtue of the political vacuum left by the Liberals resistance to growing union strength:

> Into this vacuum the Labour party stumbled. I mean stumbled in a very serious way, because it is impossible to detect any particularly keen political intelligence running through the party's organization or appeal in this period, nor can one find any particularly dramatic transformation of consciousness among working people. . . The Labour Party, in short, won the allegiance first of the leaders of the working class and its organizations and then of the workers as a whole, but less by its own organizational efforts than by default on the part of the other parties. This would mean, of course, that the fit between the outlook and policies of the party and the attitudes and beliefs of working people would be highly imperfect, and in general much less close than the organizational links between the party and the class. Only to the extent that the party's thinking was itself fuzzy and unclear and to the extent that its appeals were based upon class identity rather than program did it reflect what might be called the underlying consciousness of its supporters. This rather vacuous and negative compatibility would serve Labour well enough when the fortunes of the party and the class were for one or another reason on the rise, but it would do far less well in periods when the climate was unfavourable.[11]

It must immediately be added, moreover, that Labour's own ideological self-identification as a class party (and hence its very 'class appeal') was

always a particularly tortured and ambiguous one, despite its manifest
organisational, financial and electoral working class grounding. Hence the
extent to which it reinforced and extended class identity *vis à vis* its
supporters—actual and potential—is by no means something to be taken
for granted. Labour's predominant ideological orientation was consistently one of presenting itself as a national party, not in the Gramscian sense
of formulating and leading a hegemonic class project, but in the conventional idealist sense of defining a 'national interest' above classes. Fabianism and Macdonald's 'organic' conceptions of socialism (the watchword
of which was 'not class consciousness but community consciousness')
most clearly represented this 'national' as *opposed* to class ideological
orientation. This is not to say that the party did not represent and even
formulate working class demands, but it did so in a manner that *a priori*
conceived these demands as inherently partial and sectional. Labour
certainly lived off, electorally and organisationally speaking, the existing
consciousness of the class but far from carrying it to a hegemonic political
plane it attached itself to it through reinforcing and on many occasions
actively inducing those values of moderation, responsibility, and class
harmony that encapsulate class identity within a subordinate framework.
This orientation was never ubiquitous in the party and intra-party conflict
very often could be traced to implicit challenges to this predominant
thrust. But it gathered strength through the course of the century rather
than attenuated, particularly so long as social democracy was able to
conceal the fundamental contradiction contained in its planning plus class
harmony strategy by virtue of the conjunctural inter-class collaboration
that emerged around the mixed economy and the welfare state after 1945.

   The broad-based alliance that produced the 1945 Labour Government's
massive majority, did indeed contain within it considerable popular
radicalism. But, Gareth Stedman Jones is by no means wrong to point
out that 'the present appeal of 1945 is not primarily based upon an
assessment of its policies, but rather upon a nostalgia for the social and
political alliance upon which it was based'. From Morgan Phillips concern
as General Secretary of the party during the 1945 electoral campaign to
'remove at the outset any lingering impression that the Labour Party is
a class party'[12] to the predominance of Beveridge's liberalism and Durban's
Fabianism in the programmatic and ideological framework of the new
Government, the ideological orientation which promulgated planning
and class harmony as the embodiment of socialism remained dominant
and foreshadowed a series of reforms which, with great consequences for
future developments, foreclosed rather than opened up a 'forward march
for labour'. Stedman Jones, who shares a good many of the new revisionism's prescriptions for current strategy, is correct when he points out
regarding the 1945 Government that 'the assumption of social reform and
post-war reconstruction for the welfare of, rather than by the agency,

power and intelligence of, the working class remained deeply ingrained'.[13] Hobsbawm, of course, has contributed much himself to such an understanding of the historical limits of Labourism. Indeed, on the landslide of 1945, he once wrote: 'This does not mean that the reformist leadership of the labour movement has become any less wedded to the status quo; if anything the opposite has been the case. It is quite as easy to justify a moderate policy in socialist as it is in conservative phrases; the former may be even more effective.'[14]

What Hobsbawm did not recognise then and fails to acknowledge now is that Labourism is a practice that has had no little bearing not just on reproducing reformist attitudes among workers but on the actual withering away of the party's class base. And here we come to the nub of the matter. The discourse theorists are by no means wrong to place enormous stress on ideological and cultural factors in the formation of social and political subjects. Class identity, class consciousness, class politics, are indeed but one of a number of possible forms of collective expression even in a capitalist society, and it is by no means an automatic and inevitable outcome of economic locations in productive relations alone. Where the discourse theorists falter is in their utter relativism. They fail to recognise that the salience of relations of production provides great potential, by virtue of their central place in the constitution of social arrangements in general as well as their inherently exploitative and hence contradictory and conflictual character, for struggles about and around the formation of class subjects; and that in turn the possibility of realising a socialist project cannot conceivably do without working class identity, consciousness and politics forming its mass base and organisational core. This is not only because of the potential size of a collectivity which draws on those who occupy subordinate positions in production relations, but again because of the centrality of such a collectivity to the constitutive principle of the whole social order. If the issue is in fact social transformation, the supercession of capitalism as a system, then the mobilisation of the working class's potential range and power is the key organisational and ideological condition. It is hardly sufficient, but it *is* necessary.

But here is where Labour's 'discourse' precisely comes in. There was indeed no basis for an assumption that the class identities formed among manual workers in their trade unions and local communities through their experience of and struggles against an earlier industrial capitalism ('the making of the working class') would *automatically* persist, let alone extend to new occupational strata of workers or to new communities. Much less was there ground for thinking that left to itself, this old class culture would transcend occupational, industrial or local particularisms or the economism and sectionalism that so often are their trade union expression. And least of all should it have been thought that a hegemonic class self-identification and political orientation *vis à vis* other groups and classes, including that aspect of it that involves being 'against capitalism and for socialism', would directly flow from the numerical growth of workers (manual *or* other) or even their electoral 'support for a workers party'. The whole point of inserting the working class party into the equation as a mediating factor between class and socialism—and, putting it less abstractly and formally than equations allow, the historic importance of the formation of *mass* working class parties around the turn of the century— was precisely that they were potentially more than the electoral aggregators of individual expressions of pre-existing class identity, projecting them into the state arena as conduits for the attainment of governmental office by party leaders (socialist or otherwise). Mass working class parties were rather the essential condition in the twentieth century for the reinforcement, recomposition and extension of class identity and community itself in the face of a capitalism which continually deconstructed and reconstructed industry, occupation and locale. They were also the essential mechanism for the transcendance of sectionalism, particularism and economism not only through the national identity given to the class though its association with the party's project of winning state office, but through their potential role in socialist education and mobilisation. After all, if the notion of a hegemonic class project means anything, if the struggle for socialism *was* to be more than elitist, vanguardist, a war of manoeuvre (pick your anti-Leninist adjective), then it above all required class identity and community of a new kind. This had to include widespread understanding of how capitalism worked in general, of why supporting a workers party meant being against capitalism as a system, and of a socialist vision that meant more than 'more' in the particular and economistic sense, all leading to a self-confidence on the part of a very great number of working class activists to provide leadership in their wider communities in relation to multifarious forms of subordination, deprivation, and struggle.

That the Labour Party had not played this role has a great deal to do with the impasse of working class politics. In so far as non-manual workers in the service, commercial or retail sectors do not see themselves or politics in class terms, this has something to do, if we do not have an economic reductionist view of class formation (whether of a vulgar Marxist or modernisation school variety), with Labour's discourse. Labour tended, especially in the critical post-war period that witnessed the growth and even the unionisation of these new strata of workers, to define working class in terms of an old 'sectional' manual industrial stratum, to define white collar occupations as 'middle class' in the conventional bourgeois terms of income, education and status, and to take as evidence for the need to move even further away from the language of class politics the expansion of this grossly-conceived 'middle class'. As old manual working class communities declined and the locus of a new manual working class shifted to new industries and locales, a privatised 'instrumental collectivism' replaced old communal solidarities and became the fount of a largely apolitical trade union militancy. This cannot be separated however from the failure of the party even to try to refashion new class communities by engaging the 'affluent' worker in class terms—that is, other than trying to use the old class loyalties of the union leadership to prove that Labour could secure wage restraint from the unions where the Tories could not. It is all too often forgotten that Goldthorpe and Lockwood ended their famous study with this very observation, and one may perhaps be forgiven therefore for quoting them at length in this regard:

> It is. . . difficult to accept entirely at face value the argument typically advanced by those advocating a 'centrist' strategy that this is made *necessary* by the changing nature of economic and social conditions—that it represents the only realistic and responsible line of development of Labour politics within the affluent society. Rather, we would suggest, such advocacy must be understood as being itself a political initiative—an attempt at political leadership—intended to take the party away from radical politics of a class-oriented kind because a move in this direction is regarded as inherently desirable. . .
>
> However, the fact that the strategy in question is *not* empirically well-grounded has significant consequences. It means, for example, that Labour has in one sense underestimated the potential firmness of its support among the working class and thus the possibilities offered by retaining—and developing—its class base. On the other hand, though, it means that the effect that affluence and its concomitants most probably *have* had on the working-class Labour vote have been neglected. That is, the tendency for a purely affective or customary attachment to Labour to give way to one of a somewhat more calculative kind: an attachment likely to be more dependent on Labour clearly and consistently demonstrating it *is* the party of the working man. This neglect would appear to have become particularly far-reaching in its implications in the course of the second Wilson administration. Government economic policies—notably in regard to prices and incomes and industrial relations—have not been manifestly favourable to working class interests, and there have been few compensating measures of a radically redistributive or otherwise egalitarian kind. Under such circumstances, it is not hard to envisage the frustration of the affluent worker's private economic ambitions leading to still further attenuation of the links between localised trade union collectivism and electoral support for the Labour Party.[15]

The terrible irony of this prediction is that its coming to fruition, as manifest in the decline in the Labour vote in the 1970s and early 80s, is now taken as the basis for a renewed determinist reading of electoral trends (what might now be called the 'Crewe–Hobsbawm School of Psephology') which asserts the necessity again for a centrist strategy and an attack on radical politics of a class-oriented kind. If any critique of this new revisionism is to be more than facile, however, it must be recognised that the perverse electoral consequences of Labour's rejection of class politics are the remit, not merely of the policies of the previous Labour Government or the one before it, nor even of the revisionism of the 1950s, but of the much older and deeper practice whose effects in terms of the

withering away of working class political identities are by now very
difficult to reverse. The long term socio-economic changes, in other words,
have had many of the effects it was claimed they would precisely because
of *long-term* political and ideological practices, and immediate electoral
tactics are actually framed in terms of *their* all-to-real effects. The two
most systematic studies of working class attitudes which actually compare
British workers with Swedish and French (Scase and Gallie)[16] *do* find that
British workers are far less class conscious in any sense that is meaningful
for the prosecution of socialist politics and that the long-standing ideological and organisational practices of the working class parties in each
country are among the primary determinants of this difference. This
should hardly be surprising. Apart from the ambiguous and tenuous and
defensive nature of Labour's class appeal, the very fact that a mass party
of Labour's size and importance has not been able to sponsor or sustain
throughout the post-war years a mass readership socialist newspaper
speaks volumes to the failure of the party in defining the language and
terrain of politics in distinctive enough terms to make class politics viable.
This is not only a matter of failing to provide a class and socialist discourse
for new potential supporters, but of the consequences for traditional
supporters. Raymond Williams tells the story of his mother who took the
old Labour *Herald* because she was a trade unionist. When Hugh Cudlipp
took it over and changed its name and orientation in the 1950s with the
Labour Party's blessing to 'modernise' it, she continued taking it. And
when it was taken over by Rupert Murdoch and changed its name again in
1967, she also kept taking it. Whenever asked what happened to Labour
'opinion', Williams points to the history of this chauvinist newspaper,
The Sun.[17]

What all this means is that the roots of the impasse do indeed extend
very deep in British society. Those who would point to the growth of
trade union membership and the extensive militancy through the 1960s
and 1970s as evidence for the continued salience of class and class conflict
are by no means wrong to do so. But the fact is that the main expression of
class struggle took place on the limited terrain of the industrial sphere, and
was not attended by a politicisation which could overcome the sectionalism and economism of instrumental collectivism. This certainly belied
romantic assumptions regarding the direct revolutionary implications of this
militancy even as it increasingly confirmed the inherent instability and
contradictory character of the Keynesian/social democratic state. To be
sure, the constant tendency of the Labour leadership—in and out of office
and including the 1945 Government no less than subsequent ones—was to see
this militancy entirely as a 'problem' for the macroeconomic management of
the economy. It was something to be restrained and coopted *via* centralised
corporatist arrangements with the union leadership designed to insulate
them from membership pressures and instil capitalist growth criteria

within the formulation of union wage policy. This needs to be stressed as one of the major long-term practices which contributed to the construction of the impasse. Far from support for the workers party equating itself into being 'against capitalism', Labour Governments took any indications that trade union militancy involved such a dimension as the evil product of 'tightly knit groups of politically motivated men'.

The issue is not one of 'betrayals' by this or that Government. Of course, there were many betrayals, not least of the promise of full partnership for union leaders in the making of economic policy alongside capital and the state or of the promise that wage restraint would be compensated for by controls over investment and prices, and by income and wealth redistribution. But the union leadership's readiness to practise wage restraint short of these conditions being met, and the second-order prioritisation they gave to these aspects of the 'social contract' under each post-war Labour government as compared with industrial relations reforms which facilitated what Richard Hyman has recently pointed to as the *passive* growth of union membership ('boosting union numbers without winning workers' active commitment') must be counted in as part of the equation.[18] Yet, even given all this, it can hardly be said that the Labour leadership betrayed mass socialist aspirations, for these were far from the direct source either of the Labour vote or of union militancy. On the contrary, the very identification of socialism with the corporatist and bureaucratic practices of an increasingly cramped Keynesian/welfare state certainly did create considerable popular space for what finally became embodied in Thatcher's market populist appeal amidst a politically privatised and only instrumentally collectivist working class. The appeal of less taxation, law and order and chauvinism can be a strong one, even if only temporarily, when reformism has little else on offer.

IV. THE CHALLENGE FROM THE LEFT

If the foregoing argument would seem to indicate that the obvious strategic alternative to an increasingly cramped and beleaguered collaborationism lies in the attempt to turn social democratic parties towards a more explicitly socialist orientation, as was undertaken by the left in the Labour Party after 1979, it must at the same time be said that here is where the full awesome measure of the impasse becomes visible. For what the British experience indicates is that the very attempt to transform the party in such a way that it becomes a vehicle for socialist mobilisation is no easy task, however discredited pre-existing practices may have become. This is because the prerequisite working class identity and self-confidence, let alone the mass popular support for socialist ideas and alternatives, can hardly be said to be ready made after decades of social democratic practice but have in good part to be constructed anew. It is also because the very attempt to change the party in such a fundamental manner inevitably results in such severe internal party divisions as to undermine the immediate defensive role which such parties play against right wing forces, at least in immediate electoral terms. It is in no small part the recognition of this that has led many socialist intellectuals to turn against the Labour left with considerable vigour. Unfortunately, in their apportioning of blame for Labour's divisions they fall wide of the mark, as they do, moreover, in their facile promise of the viability of a return to reformist gradualism and consensus politics.

What took place in the Labour Party after 1979 was certainly the best organised, most inspired and most sustained attempt in the party's history at turning it from a party of defensive and tepid reform and integration into a party of socialist mobilisation and transformation. The profundity of this challenge has less to do with the specificities of the AES, the constitutional reforms, or the changes in defence policy, than with the strength of determination and the degree of talent and skill that was unleashed by a new understanding on the part of so many activists of the severe qualitative limitations of Labourism as ideology and practice. It was precisely Tony Benn's remarkable ability to articulate this understanding that allowed him to represent the disparate forces that composed the new Labour left. Whereas the old Tribune left tended to see its project as returning the party to its traditions, when the party was allegedly more socialist, the new Bennite left came far closer to defining its goals in terms of wrenching Labour out of its traditions, of breaking definitively with the class harmony orientation that from the inception of the party determined the integrative kind of parliamentarianism and the non-transformative kind of reformism that Labour practised.

It was the very novelty of this challenge, and the fact that it emanated from a far larger group of activists than could be directly associated with 'entryism', that ensured that far more was at stake than a slight alteration in the distribution of power in the party. The 'grand peur' induced by the British press with regard to what was happening in the Labour Party, fed and encouraged as it was by much of the old guard, may have been carica-ture but it was not mirage. The propaganda campaign against the Labour left—Tony Benn became for a period the most vilified man in the media next to the Ayatollah Khomeini—was not undertaken for nothing. Like all effective propaganda it had just enough of a rational kernel of truth to it to make plausible the dire warnings of the imminent victory of the socialist hordes over the old responsible and reasonable Labour leaders.

Perhaps the most superficial and damaging aspect of the new revision-ism has been its 'parti pris' attack on the Labour left as bearing primary responsibility for Thatcher's re-election in 1983. Whereas the 1979 defeat was portrayed in terms of the direct effect of long-term socio-economic changes on Labour's traditional vote, the 1983 defeat is attributed very largely to the immediate electoral effects of the Labour left's campaign to change the party. According to Hobsbawm, the left thought 'a Thatcher government was preferable to a reformist Labour government'.[19] According to many others the left sought a continuation of the old 'orthodox' social-ism which, with an astonishing gloss on Labour's actual history, they see as the root of Labour's long-term failure. The misrepresentation this involves, even if one agrees that Labour's divisions were a real factor in the defeat, is familiar enough for those acquainted with the heat generated in splits on the left, but this hardly makes it acceptable. This is not just a matter of insisting that the assault on the old leadership and ways of the party after 1979 were not just a product of the strategy of the Campaign for Labour Party Demo-cracy much less of Militant and even less of Tony Benn all by himself, but were a decade-long outgrowth of the severe crisis of Labourism and the spectacular disappointments which the Wilson and Callaghan Governments represented for so many Labour and trade union activists. Nor is it just a matter of insisting on the genuineness of the belief on the part of these activists that unity around a radical socialist programme (which obviously had to include, if unity was the condition for success, trying to ensure that the parliamentary leadership would subscribe to, campaign for and attempt to implement it) would alone create the popular understanding of the causes and dimensions of the economic crisis and hence renew Labour's credibility so that Thatcher could be defeated next time. Even if the immediate appeal of such a programme was over-optimistically presumed, any adequate reappraisal of the thrust for change and the direction it took after 1979 must surely put it in the context of the proximate failure of Callaghan's tired corporatist, 'give-the-social contract-another-chance' appeal in the 1979 election, the high number of working class abstentions in that election, the poor showing of Thatcher's Government in the opinion polls until the Falklands episode, and the fact that socialist parties won elections in Greece and France in 1981 on the basis of programmes more radical than the Alternative Economic Strategy.

Without denying the severity of reaction that the ideology that became known as Thatcherism represented, or even its ability to galvanise certain popular attitudes, it should at the same time be remembered that even those who first drew attention to the hegemonic potential of Thatcherism, most notably Stuart Hall in 'The Great Moving Right Show', insisted that 'the contradictions within social democracy are the key to the whole rightward shift in the political spectrum'. Hall identified Labour's corporatist practice, which 'requires that the indissoluble link between party and class be used not to advance but to *discipline* the class and the organisations it represents', as lying at the core of these contradictions: 'The rhetoric of "national interest" which is the principal ideological form in which a succession of defeats has been imposed on the working class by social democracy in power, are exactly the sites where this contradiction shows through and is being constantly reworked.'[20] To accuse the Labour left of bad political judgment for not taking Thatcherism seriously enough, as Hobsbawm did after the 1983 election, misses completely the understanding that was shown on the left of the basis for Thatcher's populist anti-corporatist appeal. It misses as well the importance of the Labour left having placed at the centre of its objective not more nationalisation (this was a minor strain after 1979, when most of the left was quite prepared to live with what had been articulated in the 1973 programme) but the democratisation of the party. The hardly ambiguous manner in which so many socialist intellectuals who have now taken their distance from Benn were earlier prepared to see Benn as their standard bearer had a great deal to do with Benn's own populist arguments for democratisation against a Labourism, which had not only become enmeshed in the state apparatus, but had used parliamentarism as a means of stifling the socialist aspirations that constantly resurfaced in the party.

But even if all this is granted, the truly astonishing aspect of the new revisionist quickie-history of the 1979–83 conflicts in the party is the extent to which it forgets that it takes two to tango. The resistance of the preponderant part of the parliamentary leadership to the constitutional reforms; the fuelling of the press hysteria on these reforms by labelling them as undemocratic on the basis of the most narrow parliamentarist nostrums; the readiness with which not only those MPs who left the party, but so many who stayed used adjectives like ultra, extremist and crazy with abandon—all this can hardly be ignored in assessing the 'suicidal civil war' in the party. Are socialist historians suddenly to cast themselves in the mould of those who understand political instability and conflict in terms of the responsibility that those who challenge the powers-that-be must bear for it?

A proper history of this period in the party obviously cannot be presented here, but perhaps the most critical illustration of the need for a more nuanced assessment of the causes and electoral consequences of the intra-party divisions may be signalled. What becomes especially clear as one reexamines the flow of events in this period is that the primary strategic consideration of the right wing of the Labour Party, the predominant part of which stayed in the party rather than joined tne SDP, was not unity but rather the belief that Labour could only win if it could be shown that the left were defeated inside the party before the election. This was particularly seen after Benn's narrow loss to Healey at the 1981 Conference. The 'peace agreement' insisted on and provisionally secured by the Trade Unions for Labour Victory at Bishop's Stortford in January 1982 was followed by a series of initiatives, most notably the drive to expel Militant, in which right wing union leaders like Sid Weighell, Terry Duffy and John Boyd took the lead, and whose inflammatory speeches against the left were echoed by Hattersley, Shore, and Healey in the context of trying to block reselections in the ensuing months. It was Benn who was led to warn in this context at a National Executive Committee meeting in March 1982:

'The Media will have a field day if we throw people one by one to the lions. I don't think we can gain by it.'[21] And so they did. For the last year and a half before the election, it was the left in the party that was on the defensive against a right that tenaciously clung to the view that the key to electoral success was to prove that the Bennite, Marxist, Marxist–Leninist, or Trotskyist left (the terms varied, but the scope assigned to them was commonly sweeping) had been marginalised in the party.

It is hardly anything new in the history of the Labour Party that on the basis of immediate electoral calculations it has been the left rather than the right which has tended to assume the burden of party unity. The tide in the party changed not after the disastrous defeat of the 1983 election, but a year and a half before, as not just the revolutionary entryist left but the Labour Co-ordinating Committee and the Campaign for Labour Party Democracy ran up against the most formidable barrier to change in the Labour Party: the need for party unity in order to maintain Labour's immediate electoral utility as a defensive agency for the working class. This is a real need always policed by the unions and one whose primacy was felt all the more urgently as the unions proved increasingly unable to provide, under conditions of mass unemployment, their own defence against Thatcherite reaction of the kind they had been able to mount against Heath's 'Selsdon man' a decade before. The case that unity around a radical socialist programme would alone renew Labour's credibility could not carry enough weight in the party particularly because the leading agents in the drive for defensive unity, that portion of the old Tribune left ranged around Foot, had a very strong base in the party. Their position rested, as always needs be in the case of the Labour Party, on a considerable part of the union leadership, but it also had a degree of appeal to consti-tuency activists of a kind that the right wing of the party could never muster on its own. This determined, moreover, that the shift in the balance of forces in the party after 1981 would outlast the run up to the 1982 election. Tariq Ali and Quintin Hoare's judgment in this respect that 'The Foot/ Kinnock recipe of fudging all issues in order to restore the old *status quo ante*' could not achieve longer-term success was severely mistaken: '[The] option, favoured by Foot and the bulk probably of the union leadership, is to strive to restore the Grand Old Party as before. . . It involves fudging over unwelcome conference policies and minimising the practical effect of recent constitutional changes, rather than defeating them as the right would like. . . At bottom, this option is a short term one, unlikely to survive either Foot himself or the next general election.'[22]

The strength of the Foot–Healey/Kinnock–Hattersley alliance, wherein the paramount concern for defensive unity is conjoined to the tenacious belief that the key to electoral success lies in marginalising the left, has very great implications, moreover, for the 'popular front' strategy advanced by the new revisionism. The impression is sometimes given that this strategy primarily entails the forging of alliances with the new social move-ments, articulating the demands of women, blacks and the peace move-ment to Labour's working class base in a hegemonic socialist project. Yet however attractive this may sound in abstract terms, this is not the sub-stantive element of the strategy actually being advanced, the key component of which entails ensuring that the old Gaitskellite right, with its enormous presence and respectability in the media, adheres to a broad anti-Thatcherite front centred around the Labour Party. This is not in the first instance a matter of entering into an electoral or parliamentary coalition with the Alliance (as, for instance, Hobsbawm's detractors have been too quick to insist) nearly as much as guaranteeing that the hazy compromises struck in the Foot-Healey era, which involved limiting the electoral damages done by the SDP split and preventing further defections by the Labour right, are fully stabilised in the Kinnock-Hattersley era. What the alliance with the parliamentary right means, however, is that the very attempt to restructure the party so that it might become a central site and vehicle for struggles by women and blacks as well as rank and file workers must be effectively constrained. The persistent refusal of the leadership and their trade union allies to proposals to give the Women's Conference effective powers in the party even if only to elect directly the women's representatives on the NEC (notably supported by the NUM alone at the 1984 Conference), their opposition to Black Sections, their inaction on the establishment of work-place branches (passed by the 1981 Conference)—all this tells us a great deal about the true nature of the alliances being (re)constructed in the Labour Party.

The critical factor that must be recognised is that the popular front strategy, as was so often the case with popular fronts in the past, has far less to do with the activation at the base than with alliances at the top among parliamentary and union elites, with the centre of gravity necessarily resting with those elites closest to the centre of the political spectrum whose adherence to an anti-Thatcher coalition is the central condition of success for the whole strategy. The main issue is not the question of the viability of popular fronts in the past, although it is tempting to point out as against the gloss that Hobsbawm puts on them that the parallel with the 1930s and the War is, to say the least, strained; that the fact that it was the Labour centre and right that rejected the popular front in the 1930s (to the point of expulsions of those on the left of the party who advanced it) goes strangely unmentioned; and that Hobsbawm astonish-ingly asserts that it was the popular front strategy that 'produced ten new states setting out to construct socialism' without mentioning the role of the Red Army in Eastern Europe or the readiness with which Communists were dropped from post-war governments in Western Europe when it suited their erstwhile partners. But the main issue is the here and now, and in this respect the real choices are not between an abstract 'broad alliance' line and an equally abstract 'class against class' line. What is on offer, what is available in the 'defensive unity' model Labour Party is a parliamentarist alliance under the hegemony of a party leadership whose centrist political strategy precisely embodies Bernard Crick's disarmingly honest prescription that 'however inadequate and over-empirical the old Butskellism was, we have to win the country back to that middle ground before we can move forward from it'.[23] Unfortunately, that very practice, as we have seen, precludes moving forward.

V. THEORISTS OF THE NEW SOCIAL CONTRACT

The widespread shift in opinion among socialist intellectuals towards a less 'orthodox' and more 'realistic' approach has been remarkable for its virtually exclusive concern with the tactical considerations involved in the formation of 'broad alliances' and for its relative silence and vagueness on programmatic questions. To Raymond Williams' charge that the anti-Thatcher 'coalitionists' appear basically content with reviving old Butskellite policies which are inadequate 'for any sustained recovery or advance', Hobsbawm has replied that the question of developing policies that go beyond 'trying to make the best of a bad job and give capitalism "a human face"' by trying to 'envisage a British socialism' is indeed a crucial one. But he consistently sets aside any further discussion of this for the prior tactical one of re-electing a Labour Government. However, a few others (all too few) who share the view that the failures of socialist politics have mainly to do with the narrow class-centredness of its practice in the face of a changing class structure, have attempted to address the difficult issues involved with the development of programmatic alternatives that would complement the 'realism' involved in the 'broad alliance' position. As Mike Prior and Dave Purdy argued in 1979: 'It cannot be too strongly emphasised that the politics of hegemony are not to be equated with the winning of allies, whether socially in terms of the broad demo-cratic alliance, or politically in terms of an alliance of political parties. What must underpin any such alliance and is the only safeguard against the degeneration of hegemonic politics into backroom deals and electoral manoeuvres, is a firm commitment to the *policies* of hegemony and the transformation of social practice.'[24]

Far less ink has been spilled on this since 1979 than on tactical questions, but as we shall see what has emerged in policy terms from this perspective evinces a clear tendency to return to slightly amended versions of those very reforms that were thrown up in the 1970s and failed to generate those crucial ingredients which would make them viable—the cooperation of the bourgeoisie and the commitment of the Labour leader-ship to them. Moreover, it is one of the paradoxical aspects of these pro-grammatic discussions that, although they insist that the working class can no longer occupy the exclusive or central place in socialist strategy, they nevertheless concentrate their attention very largely on developing policies for the participation of organised labour in national economic and enterprise-level decision making. A cynical explanation of this would be that, having abandoned the perspective that organised labour can be the fount of a socialist 'solution', they have come to the view that the trade unions are the central 'problem'. Yet it would appear that this is in fact a reflection of the fundamental ambiguity of the new revisionism in its attitude to the working class. Its hostility to trade union militancy and its insistence on the decline of the working class, is uncomfortably conjoined with an appreciation (even an exaggeration) of the salience of organised labour in the economy, and of its potential power as an agency for extending economic and industrial democracy.

This ambiguity is most clearly seen in the proposals that have re-emerged on the left for the development of a new social contract as the programmatic centrepiece of socialist strategy. In the view of Dave Purdy, Paul Hirst, Gavin Kitching, and Geoff Hodgson, among others, the traditional trade union obsession with economistic wage demands and their defence of unfettered collective bargaining has been reinforced by a romantic and pseudo-revolutionary perspective among socialists which condemns outright any involvement by the unions in the management of the capitalist economy, denies any responsibility for unions in causing—or solving—economic crises, and naively views the defeat of incomes policies by a militant wages struggle as a political as well as economic victory which presages a decisive confrontation. Although such a sweeping critique is a patent caricature both of past union behaviour and of the socialist opposition to incomes policies, it must nevertheless be said that many elements of their argument do contain important insights, even if these are not nearly as heretical nor as novel on the left as they insistently claim they are. Kitching, for instance, goes to the heart of the matter when he argues that: 'The tragedy of the British working class in fact is that it is neither radical enough nor self-confident enough to wish to change the system, yet it is too well-organised and economically militant to allow it to function "properly".'[25] The argument that he, like all the other advocates of incomes policy, makes to the effect that consistently high wage demands cannot be accommodated within an internationally competitive capitalist system without corresponding increases in productivity and profits is utterly conventional, but that in itself does not make it wrong, as Glyn and Sutcliffe among many others have insisted for a long time. Nor is Paul Hirst wrong, in making his case for 'national income planning', to insist on the importance in electoral as well as economic terms of overcoming the irrationalities of the wages structure: 'To see a minority enjoying a constant or increasing standard of living whilst one's own is declining or stagnant, and simply because of the accident of the trade, firm or place where they work will be generally unacceptable. . .

Pensioners, the unemployed, recipients of social security have votes too. Unless the Labour Party can provide a credible alternative to either a wage freeze or a "free-for-some", it could well find itself excluded from power.'[26] The well-worn insistence that collective bargaining is not in itself socialist, and that the planning of incomes has to be a feature of any socialist economic programme, may by now be tiresome, given how often it has been used by conventional Labour politicians to justify their equally conventional wage restraint policies, but again it is not wrong as cast in such general terms. All one can say is that it calls to mind once more the point made by Hobsbawm himself a long time ago, i.e. that 'it is quite easy to justify a moderate policy in socialist as it is in liberal or conservative phrases: the former may be even more effective'. Or, as he put it more recently, 'that what most Labour leaders have meant by "socialism" is rather different from what is in the minds of socialists'.[27]

Thus the fact that the advocacy of a social contract by socialist intellectuals provides a verbal meeting ground with those elements of the Labour leadership, such as Hattersley and Shore, for whom striking a wage restraint agreement with the union leadership along traditional Keynesian lines remained as much their central strategic concern through the early 1980s as it had been for Wilson, Brown, and Callaghan in the early 1960s and 1970s, does not invalidate such advocacy itself. The real question is whether this socialist advocacy provides different and better grounds for accepting the claim by both groups that the social contract they have in mind this time will indeed be different from what went before and was such an important element in producing the popular confusion, discord and disillusionment that led to Thatcherism.

The argument for why it is essential to premise a socialist strategy around a social contract rests on the view that it alone provides the opening within capitalism for a series of compromises between capital and labour that will both meet capital's needs for wage restraint and labour market flexibility and at the same time lay the grounds for a major extension of control by workers and their representatives over economic decision-making at the national and enterprise levels. Kitching has posed the issue most clearly and deserves to be quoted at length:

> . . . the central issue of economic policy in all advanced capitalist societies today is that of wage regulation—the need to keep wage rises broadly in line with productivity increases in order to ensure sustained growth without inflation. Monetarism is the capitalist class's response to the conviction that wage restraint cannot be attained 'voluntarily' under conditions of full employment. Yet it is also clear that wage restraint cannot be maintained with a highly unionized and compartmentalized labour market without a continuing level of mass unemployment that would threaten the very stability of capitalism, or at least would require the drastic abridgement or even the ending of democratic freedoms.
> It is quite likely therefore that after the monetarist experiment, advanced capitalist societies will return to Keynesian demand management and 'pump-

priming' for one more, and perhaps final experiment with more 'moderate' solutions. In doing so, they will once again confront the necessity of winning mass working-class compliance with wage restraint, and various forms of 'social contract' will be born again. . .

In short, capitalism in Britain may not need a 'responsible' and self-disciplined working class in order to survive. In the end, dictatorial solutions are always a possibility. But it is conceivable that capitalism in conjunction with parliamentary democracy needs such a class in order to survive. We may therefore see, in the not-too-distant-future, a crucial historical moment in which the British working class has an opportunity to extract major, indeed transforming, changes in the capitalist system in return for its cooperation.[28]

What Kitching proposes is that the unions seize this opportunity with both hands upon the ascension of a Labour or Labour/SDP government which he correctly discerns 'will want, sooner or later, to negotiate a "wages policy" (i.e. wage restraint) with the unions'. Instead of pushing for improved wages and conditions in the forlorn hope that capitalism's limitations in this respect will somehow radicalise workers, they should 'quite consciously offer whole-hearted cooperation to capitalism but demand in return for such cooperation concessions which aim quite consciously to change the fundamental nature of capitalism'. What he has in mind is that the unions go far beyond the usual price and dividend control and macro-economic policy demands on the social wage and unemployment, and undertake a radical 'pre-emptive unionism' by which long-term wage restraint bargains and redundancy agreements are exchanged for very precise demands, industry by industry, on 'investment policy, marketing, health and safety conditions, manning levels, retraining, an 'open books' policy'. This would entail developing within individual unions an extensive research and planning capacity (his model being the Lucas Aerospace Shop Stewards Combine and its alternative corporate plan in the 1970s), with union initiatives for joint management of enterprises being framed in overtly 'co-operative' and 'reasonable' terms 'for the good of the industry as a whole'. In this way management resistance can be portrayed as unreasonable and authoritarian and tactical ideological advantage can be gained by unions in management/labour relations. 'The essence of the matter is really very simple. If the British working class is to sell itself to capitalism, it must sell itself in a planned, thought-out and expensive fashion; in a fashion which, as its conditions are met, explores the limits of the concessions which capitalism can make without changing its fundamental nature.'[29]

A similar position is taken by Paul Hirst. Discerning that previous incomes policies have been rendered unstable by virtue of their effect on pay differentials that workers have struggled to maintain rather than their inequity in terms of the lack of equivalent controls on prices and high incomes, he argues that a 'socialist-egalitatarian' incomes policy should explicitly seek to close differentials among workers (by erasing them 'upwards') while offsetting workers discontent over their loss of relative status and benefits through 'a strategy of progressive increase in workers' control'. To this end he proposes linking incomes policy to the implementation of the Bullock Inquiry recommendations, so that unions can extend collective bargaining to include questions of enterprise policy and operation. Since management will not strike such bargains unless they limit the scope of trade union struggle, this will mean that the bargains will have to 'limit the right to strike, involve the reorganisation of jobs, etc. . . [and] commit the organised workers to the enterprise in a way that limited wage negotiations never did'. But extending the scope of bargaining would mean that 'the unions recognise that changed economic conditions and their own strength necessitate and make possible. . . new forms and methods of struggle' through Joint Representation Committees, company board representation and the development of management and economic policy knowledge and skills at the enterprise level among union personnel. Legislation by a Labour government along the lines of Bullock could serve as a catalyst for unions to enter this process as well as a means of compelling management to accept it. 'Bullock and incomes policy together represent a great lost opportunity for the trade unions and the Labour Party. It is a failure of political thinking which will have to be overcome if democratic socialism is to succeed in its objectives.'[30]

As Hirst acknowledges, this approach is very similar to that taken up by the Eurocommunist wing of the British Communist party in the late 1970s at the time when Hobsbawm first enunciated his analysis of the crisis of British working class politics. Although Hobsbawm was then—and has remained throughout the ensuing debate—remarkably vague with regard to programme or even policy, Mike Prior and Dave Purdy published at the same time a strong defence of the principle of the social contract ('as distinct from the Labour Government's current degenerated pay policy'). The novel element in the social contract they claimed, was that it embodied the notion that 'the trade unions should not accept or be expected to accept responsibility for the performance of the economy without a corresponding extension of power to influence national policy':

> This quid pro quo principle presents a major opportunity for subverting capitalism by linking the issues of pay and inflation with those structural issues—the volume, pace and composition of investment, the pattern of production and consumption, the scale, direction and composition of foreign trade, the character and consequences of technical innovation—which under capitalism are determined anarchically as the outcome of private action and decision beyond the scope of social control. Correctly used a social contract becomes an instrument for the assertion of a coherent working class strategy for the national economy. It offers a lever for shifting the terms of public debate and welding together a progressive social and political alliance.[31]

What are we to make of this programmatic alternative, which does indeed appear to be the one that will inform—at least in terms of the face it presents to the Labour Party—a Kinnock/Hattersley-led strategy for the next election? It must be said, first of all, that it is not quite as novel in many respects as its various authors claim. For the first two or three years of the 1945 Labour Government, it was the left in the Labour movement, and especially in the unions, which insisted on the importance of a wages policy, manpower planning and the democratisation of the administration of the newly nationalised industries as part of a strategy for transforming war-time planning into socialist planning. In the late 1950s and early 1960s a group of socialist intellectuals on the Labour left—Royden Harrison, Michael Barratt Brown, Ken Alexander and John Hughes—issued a series of pamphlets which presented a sustained argument for a wages policy as part of a socialist strategy for the Labour Party along very much the same lines as is being heard today. Nor is it the case that the unions did not try to make their support for the wage restraint they have undertaken for every Labour Government in the post-war era conditional upon 'a corresponding extension of power to influence national policy'. Even if all too few of them were as clear as Frank Cousins in insisting that fundamental change from what he called the 'trade union function' in the existing system was conditional on a Labour government actually trying to 'change the system', it should be recalled that the 1964 TUC's support for an incomes policy was not only made conditional on 'the planned growth of wages' as opposed to conventional wage restraint, but on 'the extension of public ownership based on popular control on a democratic basis at all levels'. It is certainly true that the unions' conditions for participation in the social contract a decade later were set out, under the influence of Jack Jones, much less vaguely and with less bombast and more detail than conference speeches and resolutions promote, particularly in terms of going beyond demands for Keynesian reflation and formal price and dividend controls to insist on the planning agreements, the closing of wage differentials and the industrial democracy proposals (that directly led to the Bullock Inquiry), all of which came to compose the social contract. The fact that the unions practised wage restraint under every Labour Government before these conditions were achieved and despite their not being achieved, may indeed say something about their priorities. But if so, it has as much, if not more, to do with the importance they have attached to the tactical considerations of getting and keeping a Labour government in office as with any unbending obsession with untrammelled wage bargaining.[32]

Just as those who are concerned primarily with such 'realistic' tactical considerations fail to grant sufficient weight to the historical role of the Labour Party in trying to understand and compensate for the decline of working class political identity, so those who concentrate on programmatic reform fail to appreciate the extent to which Labour's previous practice underlies, *especially among left-wing union leaders and activists*, the opposition to incomes policy today. The tendency to read this opposition off, in a quite reductionist and direct manner, from a natural or at any rate traditional trade union economism or a knee-jerk pseudo-revolutionary leftism, is all too easy, and belittles the actual political experience of participation of incomes policy at the national level (or Joint Representation Committees and their ilk at the industrial level). There can be no question that a socialist party that actually tries to undertake a radical programme involving a significant dimunition of the power and privileges of capital would have to depend on, and be either dishonest or naive if it did not demand and prepare for, some considerable material sacrifice and extensive change in the heretofore established adversarial industrial practices of its working class base. No serious socialist could argue against this, or fail to take this into her or his strategic concerns. There is far less originality about this insight, even on the British left, than our new socialist social contract theorists flatter themselves with. And there is at least some basis for thinking, especially regarding the 1945 period but also more recently, that had a Labour Government actually set out on this path, they could have counted on a considerable body of support in the trade unions. To put the onus on the unions for failing to realise what socialist potential existed in the social contract is perverse. As we have seen it was the danger that the unions in the mid-1970s were pushing Labour into too radical directions, *especially around Bullock* (and at a time when the wage restraint under the social contract had not yet broken down) that drove industrialists to identify their interests with Thatcherism.

What promise this gives for the future accommodation of British industrialists, even after the experience of Thatcherism, to a strategy which involves going beyond corporatist macroeconomic management to challenge their very control of their firms and the disposition of their capital by their own workers is unfortunately slight. It is not improbable that in the face of the experience of mass unemployment, the defeats that have been suffered, and the tenacity of the new right, that the unions might be prepared to yet again go quite far in practising wage restraint under a Labour government. Even if pre-election commitments remain characteristically vague, such cooperation would be enhanced especially if the government is in a minority situation, and the restraint may find no little compliance from an insecure and demoralised rank and file. In such a situation, it is even possible that capital will cooperate in a Keynesian reflationary policy again, although how far this can remedy the British economy's deep structural uncompetitiveness remains as dubious as ever. *If* the passivity of workers is great enough, something along the lines of the quality control circles and Quality of Working Life participatory schemes so widely being applied in American industry might find further acceptance and even encouragement in British industry. And if Labour's 'controls' over investment are vague and flexible enough, they too might find a cooperative response. But all this falls very far short of the kind of challenges to capital's managerial and investment prerogatives as our new realists propose. To imagine that wage restraint and plant level flexibility will forestall a major confrontation with capital in the face of *such* challenges, or that a Kinnock–Hattersley Labour government will risk them, is to stretch credulity to new limits.

The foreign examples which are so superficially adduced (Australia is a new vogue; Sweden and Austria remain mainstays, despite the latter's extremely centralist and top-down union structure) offer no evidence whatever for capital's preparedness to countenance co-operation in such a strategy. Indeed as we have seen it has been capital which has withdrawn its cooperation from long established corporatist wage bargaining in the face of such challenges. In so far as such countries have managed to maintain lower levels of unemployment their corporatist arrangements bear looking at seriously, although to what extent it is the strength of the labour movement in such arrangements as opposed to other factors that are at work here (Japan and the United States also have low levels of unemployment relative to Britain after all) needs to be examined seriously as well. In any case, one might wish for rather more of the kind of candour that one gets, for instance, from Goran Therborn when he recommends Swedish or Austrian policy to the British left. Therborn points out that not only the Eurocommunist and Latin socialist strategies for a move to the left did not bear fruit, but also that Scandinavian 'left-wing social democracy never materialised—a bitter lesson which Swedish social democrats. . . are learning now'.[33] He therefore admits that the policy pursued by the Swedish and Austrian governments 'is not a socialist one, and my socialist comrades may ask where socialism comes into all this if at all'.[34] His answer that socialism is not an overnight achievement but a long complex historical process and that full employment is necessary for further advances is a serious one if it can be shown that the conditions are now being put in place for the ascendancy of left-wing social democrats in the Swedish or Austrian labour movements rather than foreclosed as they were in the previous era of corporatist full employment. But in any case his tone is remarkably sanguine in comparison with the promise of the 'transformative' and 'subversive' phraseology of Britain's new social contract advocates (not least those British Eurocommunists who, having been inspired in the late 1970s by the Italian Communist Party's own version of the social contract at the time of its abortive alliance with the Christian Democratic Government, are strangely silent regarding its failure and the reasons for the subsequent abandonment of this approach by the PCI).

In fact, there is a marked ambiguity in the radical twist given to the social contract today. Hirst speaks in terms of a radical change in Britain's entire wage and salary structure yet he does not concern himself with whether and to what extent this is compatible with the continuing existence of a capitalist labour market. And is the closing of differentials 'upward' compatible with the increasing exposure of domestic labour markets to low foreign wage rates in an era of massive changes in the international division of labour brought about by competitive restructuring of industry in the crisis? Kitching, it may have been noted above, speaks on one page of aiming 'quite consciously to change the fundamental nature of capitalism' in exchange for the extensive cooperation he wants workers to give to capital, and on another page of 'exploring the limits of the concessions capitalism can make without changing its fundamental nature'. A similar ambiguity is seen in the 'realistic strategy' advanced by Geoff Hodgson, who does not explicitly advocate an incomes policy at the national level, but promotes extensive workers' participation within the capitalist enterprise as opposed to 'free collective bargaining' very much along the lines of Kitching and Hirst. Hodgson's case is based on the argument that workers' participation will raise productivity and thus be beneficial to both capital and labour, and that participation within the capitalist firm will presage and lay the ground for mobilisation around a 'wider and more egalitarian transformation of society as a whole' on the grounds that there always is 'room for manoeuvre under capitalism'. But Hodgson does not ask what the limits to this room for manoeuvre are today in Britain and what costs to the autonomy of working class organisation are entailed in the reforms he advances.[35]

The failure to ask these questions is the hallmark of social democratic discourse and it is no less present in the gradualist parliamentary democracy plus workers participation in the enterprise strategy than it is in the exclusively parliamentarist strategy itself. What if capitalists do not agree to more than minority representation in management or company boards, or to workers' representatives being solely accountable to those who elected them and subject to recall (which Hodgson suggests, almost in passing, are the conditions that will prevent loss of autonomy and co-optation)? Will participation still be promoted on a weaker basis and will such participation 'within the capitalism of the present' still prefigure 'the participatory socialist society of the future? Rosa Luxemburg's litmus test of dead-end parliamentarism, which is not to oppose participation but to ask whether it fosters illusions, is by no means inapposite here as well. The new realists have no more managed to square the circle of how to transform capitalism while cooperating fully with it than did traditional social democracy.

All this must reintroduce the old thorny question of for how long the issue of the socialisation of the means of production can really be put off in any serious socialist strategy. There are no easy answers, to be sure. Hodgson criticises 'orthodox socialist thinking' for insisting that an

extension of public ownership must be the first step before any extension
of participation in enterprise management and he quotes Wainwright and
Elliot's study of the Lucas plan to the effect that 'the extent to which
public ownership is an advance towards fuller socialism depends on the
extent to which workers create a changed relationship between themselves
and management in the course of achieving public ownership'. The point
is well taken although it would again appear to be a more relevant criticism
of the Morrisonian form of public ownership than of 'orthodox socialist
thinking'. It is indeed remarkable that Hodgson fails to point out that this
quotation from the Lucas study emerges in the explicit context of a
critique of the 'traditional Labourist formula' and of a discussion of what
a socialist government would have to do to make the implementation of
workers plans possible, the *first steps* in their view being 'the imposition of
exchange controls, the nationalisation of the banks and legislation for
trade union control over pension funds. In addition a socialist government
would back workers bargaining over proposals based on these plans, with
financial and other sanctions on the companies concerned. Where this met
determined resistance, a socialist government would need to be prepared
to socialise the company and/or industry under workers' control'.[36]

This inevitably brings us back to the nature of the Labour Party and the
meaning of the failure of the Bennite left to change it. Without this, the
reissued calls for incomes policy and workers participation must represent
nothing really new. In an important article in 1981, Dave Purdy soberly
examined the experience of Labour's 1974-8 Social Contract and argued
that, apart from the 'cloud of haziness' which hung over the Government's
economic policy targets and its vulnerability to external events and
pressures, its failure could be traced to the Government's dependence on
'the active collaboration, or at least the tacit consent of private industrial
and finance capital. The outcome of this dependent relationship is not
automatically predetermined in favour of private capital. Nevertheless,
it does set limits both to what any government can promise and on the
extent to which it can deliver on its promises. . . there is no way in which
private capitalist enterprises can be forced to invest against their better
judgment. Governments can persuade, cajole, create a favourable climate,
provide incentives and exert pressure. But they cannot compel unless
they acquire the legal rights of disposition over privately owned assets;
that is, requisition or nationalise them'.[37]

In light of this, Purdy endorsed the 'standard left response to these
difficulties. . . [which] envisages a radical and comparatively rapid shift
in the underlying balance between public and private economic power'
encompassing an extension of the powers and scope of the NEB, compulsory planning agreements, controls over private banking, extensive
restrictions on international flows of capital, while insisting that it is
inconsistent for the left to demand all this and defend free collective

bargaining. But the relevant point here is that the left that counted for something in the Labour Party and the unions *did* accept, for all practical purposes, wage restraint from 1975–1978 and even its obvious tacit inclusion in the framing of the social contract before the 1974 elections, while pushing for the very policies that Purdy agrees were essential to overcome the Labour Government's 'haziness' of purpose and capital's power. And what would have happened, we may ask, if the unions had acted upon Jack Jones' warning that Benn's dismissal from the Department of Industry (precisely for insisting on these policies) would be 'a grave affront to the union movement' rather than accepting wage restraint as they did on the traditional basis? Would not the unions have then been subject to the 'realistic left's' attack for endangering a Labour Government's survival, just as Benn was by his Cabinet 'colleagues' for insisting on policies that they, just as much as their Liberal parliamentary partners, saw as 'unrealistic' and 'dogmatic'?[38]

It was not Benn and the Labour left that were unrealistic, but those who clung to what Prior and Purdy themselves discerned in 1979 as the 'glaring and unresolved defect of the Labour Party. . . its inability to develop a strategy for socialism based on anything other than the equation between power and electoral success'. At this time they explicitly associated their strategy with 'the attempt, spearheaded by Benn, to develop a realistic alternative economic policy and to build popular involvement into the process of Government policy making around the themes of industrial democracy and planning agreements'.[39] The fact that so many socialist intellectuals have abandoned Benn today, indeed their denigration of him, appears to have much less to do with a change in Benn than in their own recognition of, and their accommodation to, the all too real logic of the equation between power and electoral success, even if it has little to do with socialism rather than minimal and temporary defence of the working class against the current reaction.

The truly innovative aspect about Tony Benn's personal development as a leading figure in the Labour Party lay in his realisation that a realistic long-term hegemonic strategy of the kind Purdy applauds can only be undertaken by a party that is unified around, and whose leadership is committed to, the social ownership of the means of production, distribution and exchange. This requires a party prepared to see through the confrontation with capital that this will inevitably involve when immediate reforms and the building of popular understanding of the value and necessity for socialism combine to make such a confrontation a viable possibility. If Benn and those who supported him as the representative of this strategy were wrong or naive or unrealistic, it was in their underestimation of two things. The first, which we have already discussed, was not only how deeply hostile but how deeply entrenched were those in the party who opposed such a hegemonic strategy in favour of the old equation between power and electoral success. Given this the constitutional reforms were not only bound to be inadequate but to be politically suicidal for Benn and the left as the immediate electoral costs of the conflict necessary to unify the party on a new basis became apparent. The second was the very deep incredulity among the British people that socialism could really be democratic and that those who proclaimed a determined belief in the need for socialism could really be democrats. This incredulity that was the fount of the success that those inside the party and out eventually achieved in defeating and marginalising the challenge and opportunity that 'Bennism' represented from its rise in 1971 to its eclipse in 1981. It is to this question of how to make a democratic socialist vision credible that we now need to turn.

VI. DOES MARKET SOCIALISM HELP?

To say that the new revisionists have failed to transcend the very limits of that social democratic practice which has in good part been constitutive of the impasse itself, does not at all mean that they have themselves abandoned a commitment to socialism. On the contrary, their concern with 'rethinking socialism' has at least as much to do with the need to reconceptualise and reformulate a vision of a future socialist society so as to rid it of the centralist and authoritarian connotations as it does with their immediate tactical or programmatic concern to reelect a Labour Government. To insist that this was also Benn's concern as well as that of many Marxists who are now relegated to the orthodox, 'class-reductionist' camp by the new revisionism, does not change the point except in so far as it should serve as a reminder that the debate over strategy should not be allowed to obscure what common ground continues to exist. Yet general agreement that socialism must involve some form of workers participation or control in the socialist enterprise or an even more vague consensus that any socialism worth its name must be democratic, has not carried socialists very far in overcoming the popular incredulity that socialism and democracy are really compatible.

In this regard, the really novel element that has been brought into the debate among socialists in the West in the 1980s has not been workers' participation but rather the idea of 'market socialism'. Although the question of market socialism has for some two decades been central to the intellectual agenda regarding actually-existing socialism, its extension to debates over socialist strategy in the West remained very much marginal. The impact of Nove's *The Economics of Feasible Socialism* has been such, however, as to have added an important dimension to the new revisionism. Although it is by no means yet clear to what extent its critique of Marxism and its perspective on the shape of a socialist economy is shared by all of those we have discussed above, Nove's concern to demonstrate that a socialist market is necessary for pluralism as well as efficiency is obviously intimately bound up with the common attempt to find a way out of the impasse of working class politics in the West. And other less celebrated interventions, such as Hodgson's *The Democratic Economy*, have certainly made the connection even more explicit than Nove himself.

This is hardly the place, towards the end of what is already a very long essay, to undertake a full discussion of the case for market socialism. I raise it at this point only to ask whether the projection of the retrieval of the market does indeed help to establish the conditions for a democratic socialism and enhance its desirability and credibility. There are some, of course, who insist that a market socialism is no socialism at all. I would prefer to remain, at least for the sake of this discussion, agnostic on this question. Nove's model, after all, does envision the social ownership of all the major means of production and designates as state corporations, subject to central planning and administration, not only banks and other credit institutions but also all those sectors which operate in large, inter-related units or have a monopoly position. Even with regard to the social-ised enterprises which would have 'full autonomy' as well as co-operatives and small-scale private enterprises (which would exist only 'subject to clearly defined limits'), central planning would have 'the vital task of setting the ground-rules for the autonomous and free sectors, with reserve powers of intervention when things got out of balance, or socially un-desirable developments were seen to occur'. Major investments and the share of GNP going to investment would be also centrally determined: this is no 'unplanned economy' obviously. Nove makes it clear that he expects that most final and intermediate goods and services will be bought and sold, but in so far as he explicitly designates that the management of the autonomous enterprises will be responsible to the workforce and establishes that a broader 'democratic vote could decide the boundary between the commercial or market sectors and those where goods and services could be provided free', this seems to put effective restrictions on the extent to which this 'market socialism' would be market *determined*, even if it could be said to be 'commodified'.[40]

It would therefore seem churlish to dismiss Nove's market socialism out of hand. The same applies to Hodgson who is less clear but also insists that 'the planning system dominates the system as a whole'. This must temper one's view, even if it does not Hodgson's own, when he claims that in his advocacy of market socialism he is 'uttering heresy'. Indeed, one might wish that Hodgson was himself rather less ready to smoke out heresies as he is when he astonishingly cites Tony Benn's occasional use of the term 'market economy' ('the incompatibility of a strong political democracy with a market economy'; 'the market economy upon which British capital-ism still relies for its motive force') as proof that Benn's *'bête noire* is markets *per se*, rather than capitalist hierarchy in industry, private owner-ship of the means of production, or the other integral features of a capital-istic economic system'.[41] Even the most determined exponents of democratic pluralism, it would appear, are not above a bit of witch hunting.

The question remains: to what extent does the market socialist model actually help resolve the socialism and democracy dilemma and aid us in the process of actually arriving at a democratic socialism? And here it must unfortunately be said that the answer is not very much. The transposition of the Eastern European advocacy of markets into a general model may be mystifying if the specific economic conditions and social forces involved are ignored. The interest of managers in securing discipline over a workforce whose only power in the system rests on their ability to resist managerial authority by virtue of their job security cannot be left out of consideration; nor can the interest of the ruling party in these systems in having freedom defined in terms of market freedom rather than actual political pluralism. Hodgson's own quotation from Brus regarding Eastern European reforms is relevant here: 'It is not "depoliticisation of the economy" but the "democratisation of politics" that is the correct direction for the process of socialisation of nationalised means of production. . . the problem of socialisation turns into the question of the democratic evolution of the state, of the political system'.[42] Unfortunately, Hodgson does not seem to grasp the extent to which this represents a criticism of the turn to markets in some actually-existing socialist states as a means of solving their problems as well as a statement on the necessity of not suppressing the question of the social ownership of the means of production in discussions of democracy as we have seen Hodgson is wont to do in his 'workers participation within capitalism' strategy.

Unfortunately, Nove offers even less in his own brief treatment of how a transition to his market socialism might be effected in the West. Apart from the obligatory sweeping denunciations of the 'extreme-left' and a critique of import and exchange controls and traditional nationalisation as a recipe for driving the centre into the arms of the right, which occupy most of his discussion, his own proposals are remarkably slight. 'The biggest obstacle of all' to 'a gradual shift in economic power away from big business' are 'trade unions pursuing the narrow sectional interests of their members'. But while he advocates limits on wage increases, he is at the same time opposed to price controls, import restrictions and material allocation. He advocates a new approach to nationalisation, whereby the nationalised firms would operate on 'normal commercial criteria' where competitive conditions exist, and where specific firms rather than whole industries are removed from the private sector. Industrial and service co-operatives would also be encouraged in so far as they also operated in a competitive environment. Both nationalised industries and private corporations would have to introduce 'elements of workers' participation into the management structures', a turn of phrase he apparently considers less vague than the 'totally undefined workers' control' he attacks the 'Marxist utopians' for advocating, since he provides absolutely no further elaboration of what this means except that to say there is much to be learned from West German *Mitbestimmung*.

In light of much careful argument and scholarship in the rest of the book, one cannot but be appalled at the slightness of Nove's chapter on the transition. West German capital's trenchant opposition to the exten- sion of *Mitbestimmung* receive no mention. The Scandinavian trade unions wages policies are adduced as proof that the regulation of incomes is a precondition for non-inflationary full employment without continuous conflict but no note is taken of the Swedish general strike of 1980, or the employers' dismantling of the centralised bargaining on which the system rested, not to mention the previous instability that led to the wage earners fund proposals as a gradual means of socialising capital and the capitalist opposition that determined their subsequent sorry fate. Whatever this Social Democratic-sounding bombast, which goes far beyond the social contract exponents we examined above in its acceptance of existing economic arrangements within capitalism, has to do with Nove's model of socialism is by no means clear—until, that is, he concludes his discussion of what he for some reason calls the 'Transition from Capitalism to Socialism' with the following: 'Of course, all this would imply a mixed economy, with the stresses and strains that inevitably accompany it. But stresses and strains we have already!'[43] *And so we do have a mixed economy!*

It would seem as though the existence of a market in the Western capitalist countries makes irrelevant for Nove the need for a serious discussion of how a social democratic reform programme would lead on to anything like Nove's model of socialism and of why the bourgeoisie would come to acquiesce in the social ownership and control of the means of production even if its political administration were conceived as demo- cratic and its economic dynamic as competitive. What is even worse, the connection posited between markets and pluralism seems to render irrelevant any discussion of the actual political institutions that would compose a democratic socialist state. The importance of the Brus quota- tion above and of Perry Anderson's comment on Nove's work, that 'only a *Politics of Feasible Socialism* could rescue it from the realm of utopian thought it seeks to escape', speaks precisely to this failure of the market socialists to cope with the socialism and democracy dilemma in a serious fashion.[44]

VII. TOWARDS SOCIALIST RECONSTRUCTION

We come, finally, to the real issue posed by how to make socialist advance possible in face of the impasse of working class politics today. If there is a really awesome gap in Marxism and a true need for revision, it is in its treatment of the state under socialism. Marx's three main concepts in this respect—the dictatorship of the proletariat, the smashing of the bourgeois state, the withering away of the state—all cover over the dilemmas involved in constructing a democratic socialist state rather than clarify them. The first conflates the notion of making the working class the dominant class (in the sense that the bourgeoisie is the dominant class in capitalist society) with the question of the limits that are imposed on democratic freedoms by a revolutionary confrontation and consolidation of power against the reactionary forces. The second has a destructive and negative connotation which conceals positive institution building of the kind envisaged by Marx on the basis of the experience of the Paris Commune, involving multi-tiered forms of representation, provision for the recall of representatives, elected officials, etc., and it discourages contemplation of the complex issues involved in the multiple sovereignties implied by this. The third seems to deny the very importance of the issue itself since the 'state' is apparently a passing socialist phenomenon anyway, even though in his dispute with Bakunin, Marx made it very clear that he saw some form of extensive public authority as necessary even in communist society (how could it be otherwise, even if this public authority is not conceived as imposed upon society, if people are to collectively determine their fate?).[45]

I have argued that a plan for achieving social control of the means of production and for building the mass popular support which will make such an achievement possible cannot be avoided if we are at all serious about a transition from capitalism to socialism. But such public support cannot be built if the limits of capitalist democracy cannot be demonstrated and if the difficult questions about the nature and form of democratic political institutions under socialism cannot be worked through. The terrible irony of the return in the 1980s to a widespread concern among 'realistic' socialists with the immediacy of the question of power is that it has embroiled itself in a beside-the-point attack on vulgar Marxism while ignoring and even caricaturing the enormous contributions that were set in motion in the 1970s by the developments in Marxist writings on the state which were just reaching towards breaking the theoretical logjam of Marxist politics when the tide among socialist intellectuals turned back towards reformism.

The initial purpose—and effect—of this work on the state was to provide a nuanced counterpoint to conventional liberal and social democratic understandings of capitalist democracy which claimed that the state had freed itself of the domination of capital and to demonstrate that far from becoming external to capital, the state had become an ever more integral element in its development and reproduction. It did not deny the state's autonomy from immediate pressures from capitalists, but on the contrary set out to demonstrate that such autonomy was an essential condition, given the competitive nature of the economy and the capitalist class itself, for the defence and reproduction of capitalism. Above all, its outstanding contribution was to provide strong invitation and useful tools for understanding both the variations and the *limits* of this general autonomy of the state. It provided a framework for understanding positive state responses in given conjunctures to working class (and other) demands while at the same time demonstrating the way these positive responses could be contained through the limits that the institutionalisation of political status tended to impose and through the state's own reading of the requirements of capital accumulation in given conjunctures. Thus to have developed the notion of relative autonomy was an accomplishment precisely because it focused attention on the balance of class forces (to see how relative this autonomy was in particular situations) and because it also drew attention to the limits beyond which reform and 'intervention' in the capitalist economy could not go without inducing a political fissure reflective of a crisis of hegemony and capital accumulation. It is extremely unfortunate that so much of the new revisionism has forgotten or ignored the essential lesson of this work.

This development, which marked an important departure from the Marxist classics even as it built on them, was certainly long overdue. Nor should the debates between the various tendencies that developed be overblown. What I have just described was common to Miliband, Poulantzas, Offe and others, with the debates among them pertaining more to language and particular focus than substantive incompatibilities: If the development of Marxist political theory had stopped here, however, it would indeed have had defeatist implications given the stress on reproduction and limits. But it did not, as toward the end of the 1970s both Miliband (in *Marxism and Politics*) and Poulantzas (in *State, Power, Socialism*) turned their attention to a revision of classical Marxism's fragile, contradictory and incomplete approach to a theory of the socialist state. To be sure, there were predecessors (not least Macpherson's attempt to point to the possibility of the retrieval of liberal democracy within socialism). But in Miliband's critique of Leninist Democratic Centralism and the Dictatorship of the Proletariat (very different from the opportunistic grounds on which Eurocommunists rejected it and the orthodox insurrectionary grounds with which their detractors defended it), as well as in his use of the notion of structural reformism to counterpose a strategy of administrative pluralism to social democratic reformism on the one hand and to 'smashing the state' on the other, a new start was made. So was it in Poulantzas' trenchant critique of the utopian notions of 'direct democracy' and in his insistence on thinking through the place and meaning of representative institutions in socialist democracy.[46]

It was only a start, to be sure. But that it was made at all and then ignored in a panic rush to traditional reformism and popular frontism and social contracts and workers participation in the capitalist firm has been a great diversion. Benn's attack on the undemocratic character of the Gentleman's club of Parliament and Whitehall in which the Labour Party had become structurally as well as ideologically enmeshed certainly needed more ballast than his populist appeals and the intra-party supports for constitutional change could provide. In 1981, as the struggle to change the Labour Party reached its climax, and while the TUC–Labour Party's Liaison Committee's subcommittee on industrial democracy and planning were examining five options for new planning structures, none of which involved any popular involvement in the process, Raymond Williams briefly set out some ideas on the radical reconstitution of the traditional forms of representation and administration of the kind that Marxist political theory was beginning to generate and was necessary if a socialist government in Britain were to have any chance of success.

> This is deliberately different from listing certain major political and economic policies. Of course these are crucial, but some of the best of them—the nuclear disarmament of Britain; the control of banks, insurance companies and pension funds for productive investment; exchange and import controls for the recovery of British industry—are typically presented as if they could be carried through on the basis of a parliamentary majority. This, even on the Left, is the Labourist perspective which is at the heart of the problem. For to carry through any of these policies. . . would require a degree of popular understanding and support which is of a quite different order from an inherited and in part negative electoral majority. . . The very powerful forces it is certain to encounter, in any of these initiatives—over a range from national and international institutions and companies, through widely distributed organizations for influencing public opinion, to the confusions among its potential supporters—are not of a kind to be defeated from the parliamentary centre alone. . . The 'alternative strategy', that is to say, is no more than an intellectual exercise unless it carries with it, and indeed as its priority, an alternative politics. . . The defining centre of any successful left politics is the radical extension of genuine popular controls. . . It is an attempted break beyond the most benevolent or determined representative administration.[47]

To this end Williams presented a series of particular proposals for a Labour Government's early priorities: to direct each nationalised industry to develop plans, based on the views of their workers, to democratise and socialise the 'nominally' publicly-owned institutions; the direct election of National Planning Councils and Consumers advisory bodies in industry and service with direct access to parliament as well as the relevant ministries; to break the 'system of monopolistic appointments to the control of public bodies which is in fact intended to ensure verticalism, concentration of power and dependence'; and to supplement the responsibility of elected government for public finance and investment 'with alternative and parallel forms of public responsibility'; public hearings conducted by qualified Planning Groups with access to all available public and industrial information in order to 'develop visible and publicly approved investment plans'; to make the planning process open and public so that it is not 'swamped, as always before, by capitalist power and its highly experienced market forces'; a Freedom of Information Act on which all of the above would depend; major public investment in new electronics communications and their use for public information, discussion and decision; professional companies in the older communications sectors being leased publicly-owned resources and made responsible to elected regional and local boards; the transfer of day-to-day administration of council housing to elected tenants' associations.

This much neglected article demonstrated precisely the enormous importance and immediate value of the kind of thinking that Marxist attention to the institutional forms of a democratic socialist state could provide—if there were a viable socialist party it could provide it to. To be sure, its immediate value seems now rather less clear given what has transpired in the Labour Party since 1981. A moderate Labour Government elected on a negative vote and committed to the idea that a return to Butskellism is the best way of moving forward is no less likely to fail and to set the stage for a return to Thatcherite reaction or worse than is one with radical policies but unable to transform political structures in a way that would alone make its policies popular and hence possible.

The real lesson of Thatcherism is this: Social democracy, over the course of the post-war period, took upon itself the responsibility—and the credit—for the expansion of the Keynesian/welfare capitalist state, and the solution it offered to the economic crisis that emerged in the 1970s was a defence of this state and a call for a further expansion of it. What came to be at issue ideologically and politically was not just the fact that the crisis itself had discredited this approach on its own prime criterion (the promise to end mass unemployment), nor the difficulty social democratic governments had in even maintaining previous reforms in this context. More important was the fact that this state had already become considerably unpopular in the eyes of most working people before the onset of the crisis. It *was* bureaucratic, inefficient and, above all, distant from popular control in any meaningful sense of the term. This was as true for those workers employed by the state as for the clients of its services. The word 'public'—whether attached to enterprise, employees or service—became in this context a dirty one in Western political culture after a decade of denigration by businessmen, politicians, and journalists of various political stripes. And although this denigration clearly represented an aspect of a bourgeois strategy in the crisis that involved turning the screws on workers, women, radical and ethnic minorities and the poor, it came to have a popular resonance even among some members of these groups because it threw up images that related to their own alienation from the capitalist state.

It is quite understandable that social democratic parties—especially those that had recently held government office—should have become most associated in the popular imagination with this alienation. They had always insisted it was their pressure in opposition and their policies in office that led to the expansion of the state's role. It was symptomatic of their ideology that what socialist rhetoric they retained or picked up again in the crisis took the form of an insistence that the Keynesian/ welfare state had been a 'teeny bit pregnant with socialism' and that what was now needed was a further gestation period. It had always been strategically mistaken to think that welfare state reforms, macroeconomic fiscal policy, and a few nationalised industries represented some way-station on a highway to socialism. It became for a period, and it is likely to become again at some point in the not too distant future, tactically disastrous even for reformist parties to seek to gain support by advocating the defence and expansion of such a state.

For socialists, the fact that a right-wing market populism representing the most blatantly reactionary elements of capitalist ideology rushed in to fill the vacuum left by the failures of social democracy and Keynesianism became, and must remain, a very great cause for concern. It underlines the urgency of our 'getting our act together', and it is the root of the new revisionism's tactics. But we must also learn from what the popular appeal of the radical right tells us. The strength of the monetarist assault should not have become the occasion for a knee-jerk defence of the Keynesian/ welfare state with all its ambiguous and constricted reforms, but rather treated as the occasion for proposing—for insisting on—the fundamental restructuring of the state and its relationship to society so that the communities it is supposed to serve and the people who labour for it together have great involvement in the public domain. Rather than leave the issue at 'less state' versus 'more state', socialists must recognise that popular antipathy to the state can also be addressed in terms of speaking of a *different kind of state*.

We are still left with the question of vehicle. The main theme of this essay has been that the impasse of the working class has much to do with the practice of social democratic parties: their acceptance of the structure of the state; their promulgation of class harmony; their concern with packaging policy programmes and mobilising activists around the next election; their excessive focus on parliamentary timetables and debates; their acceptance of a division of labour between industrial and political organisation with the necessary link between the two being cemented at the top of each structure—all this attests to their inadequacy. It must be said, however, that even if concentration on this kind of practice of working class politics is justified by its sheer predominance, one cannot pretend that parties to the left of social democracy have pointed a way forward.

Even if these parties were clearer in their socialist purpose, they tended far too often towards an easy use of the term 'nationalisation', leaving the impression that what was meant by this was merely state control of industry along the lines of what they themselves criticised as bureau-cratically-run public corporations in which the relationship between workers and managers did not change and in which popular control was offered only in terms of a highly tenuated form of ministerial responsibility. Although one cannot dismiss these parties' capacity to develop a limited number of very committed and skilled organisers who have often played important roles in popular organisations, their greatest problem has been the adoption of an internal political structure which put far too much—or at least far too permanent—an emphasis on discipline as opposed to participation and discouraged creative interaction, rather than instrumentalism, with popular organisations. Any political party which puts such a high priority on discipline that pursuing a common line becomes a form of keeping its members and supporters *in line*, is destined not to grow. This is entirely apart from problems associated with paying excessive attention to, let alone entering into a relationship of dependence on, foreign models of actually-existing socialism and defending too readily the tactical or even conjunctural positions taken by their governments. And not least problematic has been the tendency to search for immediate practical guidance and legitimation in the writings of Marx, Lenin, Stalin, Trotsky or Mao, which not only gave rise to a *practice* that was awkward in the Western context, but even a political *language* that had little apparent meaning to the uninitiated.

Fortunately, there is a notable awareness among a great many socialists today of the limitations of previous practice. At the same time, this has also induced a high degree of caution with regard to taking new socialist initiatives, of which the new revisionism is but one example. This caution is certainly understandable. It reflects the fact that the traditional Communist, Trotskyist, and Marxist–Leninist forms of political practice have largely played themselves out by this point in twentieth century history, at least in the English-speaking capitalist democracies and arguably in a good many other Western countries as well. It is not surprising that this should be so: they were the products of specific historical conditions and conjunctures, and it should hardly have been expected that they would crystallise revolutionary working class politics into a permanent mould. This is not to say that all the organisations they spawned will pass away, or that some of their ideas and practices will not continue to be relevant or in some situations actually operative. It does mean, however, that socialism as theory and movement will have to evolve new forms and new substance. We are at a new stage of socialist development and the confusion and hesitation that marks our time as socialist can only be seen in this light.

To this extent the new revisionists are right and although they are rather too ready to proclaim something new while clinging to the old, their caution does not necessarily reflect any lack of a sense of urgency or desire to move on. The promise of the attempt to change the Labour Party was that, especially through the voice of Tony Benn's insistent appeals for democratising the party and the state, it began addressing itself to the unity of socialism *and* democracy, democracy *and* socialism. The promise of Marxist theory was that, while not losing sight of the very difficult process of trying to convince people that social ownership of the means of production was necessary, it began a revision of traditional Marxist thought that enhanced understanding of the limits of the capitalist state and promoted thinking on the democratic structures appropriate to a socialist state.

That recapturing this promise and moving beyond it will be very largely, if by no means exclusively, dependent on the struggles of working people and mean the revitalisation and reconstitution of a political and cultural working class identity seems to be incontrovertible. I argued earlier that the withering away of old working class identities was indeed something real and would be difficult to reverse. To begin that process of reversal will mean, as this essay has tried to insist, not passively accommodating social-ist politics to a fatalistic 'realism', but setting out to connect with and helping to broaden and deepen the experience of collective labour out of which working class identity grows and can be nourished. The fact that older manual occupations have declined in relative numerical terms does not mean that exploitation has changed its character nor does it invalidate the classical Marxist project (based on its understanding of that exploita-tion) which, since the Communist Manifesto, has defined as the 'immediate aim' of working class parties 'the formation of the proletariat into a class'. Capitalism's insistent recomposition of occupations and communities must make this immediate aim an ever present one for socialist politics, and one that is particularly pressing today. But it is hardly an ephemeral goal, least of all today as capitalists, aided by the state, increase the level of exploita-tion and managerial domination and subject newer industries and occupa-tions, not least those in the service, commercial and public sectors, to the collectivising experiences—in terms of low status, limited mobility, low relative pay, and lack of autonomy—wherein labour's common predicament and potential can be recognised and acted upon. One of the main reasons why social democratic incomes policies and participation schemes have to be looked upon with suspicion is that they can so easily become the basis for undermining the utility and autonomy of unions as primary organisa-tional expressions of collective labour, devaluing the salience of class identity and struggle through their corporatist embrace.

Of course we must strive for a politics that seeks to transcend the sectionalism and particularism of trade union identity. But this is some-thing that is very different from a politics which pessimistically discerns the decline of the working class in the decline of the older industries and which promotes, on the basis of a presumed permanent minoritisation of the working class, alliances with vaguely defined 'new middle classes' and 'new social movements' with slender social bases. In the sense of those people who are unpropertied workers and who are not involved in the supervision of collective labour, there is indeed a working class majority in all advanced capitalist countries and the first task of a socialist party ought to be the nourishment of an understanding and consciousness of the existence and potential of this working class majority. The socialist potential of such identity, while by no means foreordained, lies in the sense of collective power as well as the sense of collective deprivation which an understanding of the centrality of class relations to the whole social order entails. To demand a politics that envisions creating a working class majority in terms of collective socio-political identity does not need to mean that other identities—of gender, or race, of ethnicity—have to be effaced. If anything, historical experience tells us that they cannot be effaced. And my own personal experience of working class community tells me that it is possible for working people to think of themselves as workers and to act politically in a way that allows for, in fact obtains strength from, a simultaneous expression of their other collective identities in so far as a popular socialist culture provides a common terrain of understanding, purpose and activity. It has fallen to socialists in the last decades of this century to undertake the daunting task of establishing new political directions and institutions, much as our forerunners had to do in the last decades of the last. As before, and despite the very different conditions, these will not come out of thin air but will involve the breaking up and the amalgamation and development of organisations that went before. That there will be enough immediate grievances and struggles, not least by workers, employed and unemployed, upon which to build in this terrible era of major capitalist crisis and restructuring, there can be no doubt. Even if it is by no means inevitable, least of all when the terror of nuclear holocaust gives a new and horrible visage to the meaning of barbarism, socialism remains the only human alternative.

NOTES

1. Speech to Campaign for Labour Party Democracy meeting, 1981 Labour Party Conference, Brighton, September 27, 1981.
2. Colin Leys, 'Thatcherism and British Manufacturing: a Question of Hegemony', *New Left Review* 151, May–June 1985, p. 17.
3. For a full discussion of these developments, see L. Panitch, *The Tripartite Experience*, Research study for the Royal Commission on the Economic Union and Development Prospects for Canada, Ottawa, 1985.
4. It should be noted that the term 'the new revisionism', although put to good use recently by Westergaard and Miliband, has in fact a much wider remit than the Eurocommunist-inspired analyses of British Labour's crisis in the 1980s, or even than the more general retreat from traditional positions among Marxists that has been evident in this decade. The very academic revival of Marxism since the late 1960s had already begun to produce in the 1970s a 'new revisionism' emanating from various political institutions and intellectual circles that were themselves traditionally anything but Marxist. Among academics whose values and assumpt-

ions rarely strayed from the tenets of Fabian, Keynesian, or Weberian analysis there was a tendency to recast their old conceptual gear in 'neo-Marxian' terminology, while continuing to explicitly reject the revolutionary implications of Marxism. And within social democratic parties, a good many of the new reformist strategies advanced in the 1970s were often formulated, even by elements of the old leadership and for the first time in decades, with the help of a vaguely Marxian vocabulary. What all this bespeaks, and has been far too little noted, is an important convergence of political and intellectual trends, coming so to speak from different directions, which has yielded a form of discourse and practice in our times that bears many of the earmarks of the revisionist and reformist Marxism of post-World War One social democracy. We are back at the original dilemma in more ways than one. For an earlier presentation of this 'new revisionism', see my review of C. Crouch (ed.), *State and economy in contemporary capitalism* (London, 1979) in the *International Journal of Urban and Regional Research*, 5:1, 1981, pp. 128–32. Cf. J. Westergaard, 'Class of '84', *New Socialist* , January–February 15, 1984; R. Miliband, 'The New Revisionism in Britain', *New Left Review*, 150, 1985; and B. Fine *et al.*, *Class Politics: An Answer to its Critics* (London, 1984), esp. pp. 9–11.

5. 'Manifesto of the Communist Party' in Karl Marx, *Political Writings Volume One: The Revolutions of 1948*, (ed. D. Fernbach), (London, 1974–80). It is worth noting that Marx speaks not only of the role of Communist parties in class formation here but of 'all proletarian parties' and of their expressing 'in general terms, actual relations springing from an existing class struggle, from an historical movement going on under our very eyes'. Gorz relies on a passage from *The Holy Family* ('It is not a question of what this or that proletarian, or even the whole proletariat, at the moment regards as its aim. It is a question of what the proletariat is, and what, in accordance with this being, it will historically be compelled to do.') It is therefore interesting to note that Gramsci saw *The Holy Family* as 'an occasional work. . . a vaguely intermediate state' in Marx, directly contrasting it with *The Poverty of Philosophy* which he saw as 'an essential moment in the formation of the philosophy of praxis', and that he makes this contrast directly in the context of citing the latter work as his 'point of reference for the study of economism and understanding relations between structure and superstructure. . . where it says that an important phase in the development of a social class is that in which the individual components of a trade union no longer struggle solely for their own economic interests, but for the defence and the development of the organisation itself.' *Selections from the Prison Notebooks of Antonio Gramsci*, (Q. Hoare and A.M. Smith eds.), London 1971, p. 162, cf. Gorz, *Farewell to the Working Class*, Boston, 1982, p. 16.
6. Ernesto Laclau and Chantal Mouffe, *Hegemony and Socialist Strategy*, London 1985, p. 181.
7. 'Labour's Lost Millions', *Marxism Today*, October 1983, p. 12; 'Labour: Rump or Rebirth?' *Marxism Today*, March 1984, p. 11.
8. *The Forward March of Labour Halted?* London 1981, p. 18.
9. 'The Labour Party and Class Formation in Twentieth Century Politics', paper presented at the Conference of Europeanists, Washington, D.C., October 1983, pp. 8, 10.
10. *Class Inequality and Political Order*, London 1971, pp. 98–9.
11. Cronin, pp. 23–4.
12. *The Labour Party: The Party with a Future*, May 1945, p. 1.
13. *Languages of Class: Studies in English Working Class History 1832–1982*, Cambridge, 1982, pp. 240, 246.
14. 'Trends in the British Labour Movement', in *Labouring Men: Studies in the*

History of Labour, London 1964, p. 330.

15. John H. Goldthorpe *et al.*, *The Affluent Worker in the Class Structure*, Cambridge 1969, p. 191.

16. Richard Scase, *Social Democracy in Capitalist Society: Working-class Politics in Britain and Sweden*, London 1977; Duncan Gallie, *Social Inequality and Class Radicalism in France and Britain*, Cambridge 1983.

17. Speech to Socialist Society meeting, 1983 Labour Party Conference, Brighton, October 3, 1983.

18. 'Class Struggle and the Union Movement', in D. Coates *et al.*, *A Socialist Anatomy of Britain*, Oxford 1985, p. 119.

19. 'Labour's Lost Millions', *Marxism Today*, October 1983, p. 8.

20. 'The Great Moving Right Show', in S. Hall and M. Jacques, *The Politics of Thatcherism*, London 1983, pp. 26-7.

21. Quoted in *The Guardian*, March 9, 1982.

22. Tariq Ali and Quintin Hoare, 'Socialists and the Crisis of Labourism', *New Left Review* 132, March-April 1982, pp. 74, 80.

23. 'The future of the left—but what then?', *New Socialist,* January 1985, p. 41. Hobsbawm's comments on the popular front experience are in 'The Retreat into Extremism', *Marxism Today*, April 1985, p. 10.

24. Raymond Williams, 'Splits, Pacts and Coalitions', *New Socialist*, March/April 1984, p. 33; Eric Hobsbawm, 'Labour: Rump or Rebirth?' *Marxism Today*, March 1984, p. 11; Mike Prior and Dave Purdy, *Out of the Ghetto*, Nottingham 1979, pp. 170-1.

25. Gavin Kitching, *Rethinking Socialism*, London 1983, p. 111.

26. Paul Hirst, 'The division of labour, incomes policy and industrial democracy', in A. Giddens and G. Mackenzie (eds.), *Social class and the division of labour*, Cambridge 1982, p. 256.

27. Hobsbawm, 'Labour: Rump or Rebirth?', *Marxism Today,* March 1984, p. 8.

28. Kitching, pp. 128-9.

29. Kitching, p. 125.

30. Hirst, pp. 263-4.

31. Prior and Purdy, pp. 129-30.

32. All this is discussed at length in my *Social Democracy and Industrial Militancy: The Labour Party, the Trade Unions and Incomes Policy 1945-1974*, Cambridge 1976.

33. 'Britain left out', in J. Curran (ed.), *The Future of the Left*, London 1984, p. 132.

34. 'West on the Dole', *Marxism Today*, June 1985, p. 10.

35. *The Democratic Economy*, London 1984, Ch. 5.

36. *The Lucas Plan*, London 1982, pp. 263-4.

37. 'The Social Contract and Socialist Policy', in M. Prior (ed.), *The Popular And The Political*, London 1981, pp. 108-9.

38. See my 'Socialists and the Labour Party: A Reappraisal', *The Socialist Register 1979*, p. 62.

39. *Out of the Ghetto*, pp. 183, 187.

40. *The Economics of Feasible Socialism*, London 1983, pp. 200-1, 207-8.

41. *The Democratic Economy*, pp. 181, 175.

42. Quoted in *The Democratic Economy*, p. 165.

43. *The Economics of Feasible Socialism*, pp. 160-175.

44. Perry Anderson, *In the Tracks of Historical Materialism*, Chicago 1984, p. 103.

45. I discuss this weakness of Marxism extensively in my 'The State and the Future of Socialism', *Capital and Class* 11, Summer 1980, pp. 51-66.

46. Ralph Miliband, *Marxism and Politics*, Oxford 1977, Chs. 5 and 6; Nicos Poulantzas, *State, Power, Socialism*, London 1978, Part Five.

47. 'An Alternative Politics', *The Socialist Register 1981*, pp. 1-10.

BEYOND SOCIAL DEMOCRACY IN WEST GERMANY?

William Graf

I

The theme of transcending, bypassing, revising, reinvigorating or otherwise raising German Social Democracy to a higher level recurs throughout the party's century-and-a-quarter history. Figures such as Luxemburg, Hilferding, Liebknecht—as well as Lassalle, Kautsky and Bernstein—recall prolonged, intensive intra-party debates about the desirable relationship between the party and the capitalist state, the sources of its mass support, and the strategy and tactics best suited to accomplishing socialism.

Although the post-1945 SPD has in many ways replicated these controversies surrounding the limits and prospects of Social Democracy, it has not reproduced the Left–Right dimension, the fundamental lines of political discourse that characterised the party before 1933 and indeed, in exile or underground during the Third Reich. The crucial difference between then and now is that during the Second Reich and Weimar Republic, any significant shift to the right on the part of the SPD leadership,[1] such as the parliamentary party's approval of war credits in 1914, its truck under Ebert with the reactionary forces, its periodic lapses into 'parliamentary opportunism' or the right rump's acceptance of Hitler's Enabling Law in 1933, would be countered and challenged at every step by the Left. The success of the USPD, the rise of the Spartacus movement, and the consistent increase in the KPD's mass following throughout the Weimar era were all concrete and determined reactions to deficiences or revisions in Social Democratic praxis.

Since 1945, however, the dynamics of Social Democracy have changed considerably. Each successive move by the SPD away from a socialist, anticapitalist course has at best invoked isolated, but never mass, sustained opposition on the Left. Until the emergence of the Greens in 1980, in fact, no alternative political organisation had been able to establish itself beyond Social Democracy. Allied occupation and intervention, the Cold War climate, and the spectre of the East German communist state have imposed narrow political parameters on the Federal Republic, placing the SPD in practically unchallenged occupation of the entire Left position and hence investing it with a quasi-automatic rightward tendency. It is symptomatic of this state of affairs that in the postwar period names like

Helmut Schmidt, Herbert Wehner, Heinrich Deist, Erich Ollenhauer, Carlo Schmid, Fritz Erler, Ernst Reuter and even Willy Brandt have come to symbolise the party's substance and direction, while leftists such as Viktor Agartz, Gerhard Gleissberg, Wolfgang Abendroth, Fritz Lamm and Arno Behrisch remain mere footnotes in the party's history.[2]

The absence of a political alternative to the left of the SPD has also meant that the West German political economy has not, on the strength of its inner constellations and alignments, been able even to pose the question: after Social Democracy, what? Apart from the situationally generated, spontaneously developing antifascist movement in the postwar period—which the respective Military Governments suppressed or administered away[3]—the West German Left since 1945 has been constrained, mediated, coopted and conditioned by the Social Democratic Party. In the Federal Republic, therefore, unlike elsewhere in Western Europe, the relevant question for the Left has been: what is and ought to be *the relationship between socialism and Social Democracy?* Even the posing of this question during the late forties and through the fifties was extremely problematic, since the conservative coalition headed by the Christian parties (CDU/CSU), supported by the restored and 'renazified' business and state elites, and propelled by the legitimacy conferred by the Economic Miracle, was able to consolidate its mass basis at successive elections and gain an absolute electoral majority in 1957. Integration of the West German partial state into a capitalist common market and an anti-Soviet military alliance combined with a 'total' ideology of 'clerical anticommunism'[4] to submerge real class conflict and social contradictions. This completed the formula for the all-embracing, anti-socialist CDU State.

In this context, the SPD was subject to powerful system-immanent pressures (1) to broaden its electoral appeal by expanding its social base beyond the working classes, (2) to defend itself against charges of communist tendencies or at least of being 'useful idiots' in the Soviet cause, and (3) to use every means to create intra-party solidarity to ensure that party members and followers would be prepared to adapt to the leadership's changing strategies. In particular, the post-Schumacher party leadership determined to 'modernise' Social Democracy, not by means of working through an anticapitalist, socialist programme corresponding to the specific development of the FRG, but by a strategy of initially *ad hoc,* and by 1959 conscious proximation of the CDU State. The party's platform thus increasingly amounted to a mere negation of the bourgeois coalition's tangible achievements and a vague assertion that, once in office, the SPD would expand and extend (or 'modernise') the existing state and economy. This policy of *Angleichung* involved abandoning or renouncing the party's traditional socialist 'ballast' and de-emphasising its essentially working-class base in an endeavour to adapt to perceived changing voter expectations and socio-economic conditions, a process which would transform the SPD into a 'pragmatic', 'moderate' and 'non-ideological' mass party employing the latest advertising and public relations techniques and basing its bid for power on image-making and the personalities of its leaders. This dual strategy of *moderation* (to attract voters from the 'progressive centre', especially the 'new' administrative and managerial classes) and *modernisation* (to stake a claim to be able to manage the CDU State more efficiently than the Christian Democrats and to win over the dynamic, export-oriented sectors of West German business) evolved, under the growing influence of the 'pragmatic' party grouping around Wehner, Erler and Brandt, into Western Europe's most comprehensive statement of *'Social Democratism'*[5] which may be summarised as a maximalist, system-immanent bid for political power within the logic and limits imposed by the capitalist state. The necessary corollary of Social Democratism is anticommunism—or in the West German case, the taking over and further 'modernisation' of clerical anticommunism—which both acts as a means of inner-party discipline to ensure acquiescence in pursuit of the new strategy of adaptation, and provides the necessary currency to purchase an image of responsibility and respectability.

The Bad Godesberg Programme of 1959, which formalised the SPD's renunciation of an alternative domestic policy (particularly 'socialist solutions'); Herbert Wehner's June 1960 Bundestag speech which proclaimed a 'mutuality' between the foreign policies of the SPD and CDU/CSU; Social Democratic support for pending emergency legislation in the mid-sixties; the party's failure to operate even as a *democratic* opposition in the face of such government violations of civil rights as the 1962 'Spiegel Affair'; and the formation of the Grand Coalition in December 1966; each of these developments was a further move toward what has been variously termed 'the party cartel', the 'amorphous middle-class society', and the apparent 'end of the opposition'.

The question of political alternatives also became more intense with every stage of the SPD's integration into the CDU State.[6] The already discredited and ineffectual KPD had been persecuted and banned in 1956. The sole attempt to create a political party to the left of the SPD, namely the Independent Labour Party (UAPD), was unable to attract mass support and simply disintegrated. The Trade Union Federation (DGB), like the SPD, had been deradicalised by the American Military Government and, by means of a 'Unified Trade Union' (*Einheitsgewerkschaft*) and the illusions of 'political party neutrality' and 'partial codetermination', integrated into a capital-dominated 'social partnership' sustained by rising economic prosperity. The intra-party Left, who in most cases merely persevered in advancing traditional socialist aspects of Social Democracy, were therefore constrained to choose between two equally bleak strategies: (1) 'hibernating' in the party or trade union while working and agitating from within, i.e. acting as a 'motor' to promote reforms and discussion on the one hand, and functioning as a 'brake' against even more substantial shifts to the right on the other; or (2) drawing the consequences of the anticommunist-motivated attacks and party discipline to which they were subjected and resigning or, in most cases, awaiting formal expulsion. In the first case, diminishing influence (Fritz Lamm and the *Funken*) or progressive cooptation (Peter von Oertzen and his *Sozialistische Politik* or *SoPo*) were the consequences. In the second case, isolation, defamation and alienation from the labour movement altogether were the results (Viktor Agartz and his *WISO-Korrespondenz*, Gerhard Gleissberg and Rudolf Gottschalk's *Die Andere Zeitung*). Even the fate of the socialist opposition to the Godesberg tendencies, embodied in Wolfgang Abendroth's 'Anti-Godesberg Programme',[7] was indicative of the 'misery of the German Left': the Programme was in fact passed by a hugh majority at the party conference.

During the period of official SPD opposition in the CDU State, then, prospects of the intra- and extra-party Left for gaining even a share in the formulation of Social Democratic programmes and policies were remote. The *'material' opposition*[8] lacked a coherent organisation, a minimal consensus-producing programme (as Abendroth's draft might have been), capable leaders, and—above all—a mass basis. 'Is it not deeply sad and perhaps also characteristic,' Viktor Agartz wrote in 1959, 'that today not the party, not the trade unions are in motion, not in action, but intellectuals, professors, free professionals and students?'[9]

In Agartz' rhetorical but nevertheless pointed question is contained an initial statement of the core of an emerging, specifically West German type of opposition: the issue-oriented, heterogeneous and rapidly mobilised (and demobilised) *Sammelbewegung*. Within the highly conformist, transnationalised and prosperous context of the postwar Federal Republic, the one issue still sufficiently sensitive to catalyse a popular *'post-material' oppositional movement* was that of rearmament and remilitarisation. This was so for a number of reasons. Popular opposition to rearmament rested, first, on immediate and direct historical experience of the war, the four-power occupation and the extensive anti-militarist propaganda disseminated as part of the Allied denazification programme. Secondly, it brought together oppositional forces from a variety of political or even 'pre-political' persuasions, such as pacifist and anti-conscription groups, neutralists from Left and Right, SPD members still supporting the Schumacherian primacy of reunification within bloc neutrality, religiously motivated anti-war groups, independent intellectuals, a critical minority within the media, and those who had suffered directly from the war and its effects. Third, rearmament was a relatively straightforward and comprehensible issue which could be defined in terms of a stark alternative: acceptance or rejection, and which affected the vital interests of most of the population. And fourth, no political party or labour organisation had made peace a central part of its programme, although public opinion polls consistently showed a large majority opposed to rearmament in any form. For these reasons, the peace movement became the central focus and rallying point for most of the oppositional forces, in particular the Left, in this period. As primarily a reaction to official government policy (and absence of alternatives on the part of the 'loyal opposition'), its development can be described in two important stages: *resistance to rearmament and conscription,* and *opposition to nuclear arms.*

Ironically, in view of its later adaptations, the SPD leadership itself had an important share in the formation of the peace movement in the Federal Republic. As the FRG under Konrad Adenauer moved towards making a German contribution to the 'defence of the West' in 1954 and 1955, a group of scholars, trade unionists, theologians and politicians, including SPD-leader Ollenhauer, convened a meeting in St. Paul's Church, Frankfurt which, in a mildly worded 'German Manifesto',[10] appealed to the government to avoid precipitate rearmament. The contemporary Left correctly argued that the 'movement' merely 'divert[ed] increasing radicalism among active party members and trade unionists into legitimate channels'[11] and that it in any event failed to prevent the Bundestag from ratifying the Treaty of Paris in February 1955. But this is to miss the importance of the incipient peace movement. For the first time it demonstrated that a variety of disparate groups, acting in concert on a single issue, could penetrate beyond the official consensus and influence the thinking of broad sectors of the population. The real significance of the St. Paul's Church movement was as a consciousness-provoking phenomenon.

Much the same can be concluded from the 'Göttingen Manifesto', a public appeal against the perceived intention of the government of the FRG to acquire nuclear weapons. On 12 April 1957, eighteen prominent scientists and scholars, with a 'non-political' self-image and careful to qualify their pronouncements with references to freedom 'as upheld by the Western world today against communism', appealed to the public to support the 'explicit' and 'voluntary' rejection of all forms of nuclear weapons by the Federal Republic. Within hours and days of its announcement, the appeal was joined by municipal councils, student bodies, women's leagues, church groups and prominent individuals such as Albert Schweitzer and his 'Appeal to Humanity' from Africa. The salient difference between the Göttingen appeal and the St. Paul's Church movement was that the former arose more or less spontaneously, unmediated by institutions or official organisations. Indeed, it proceeded mainly without them and even against their opposition. Resistance to atomic weapons went over to *ad hoc,* spontaneous and issue-focused organisations: the German Peace Society (DFG), the Union of Persons Persecuted by the Nazi Regime (VVN), the West German section of the War-Resisters International (IdK) and sectors of the Lutheran and Evangelical Churches.

This was followed by a further 'Appeal of the 44' professors and scholars calling for a nuclear arms-free zone in Middle Europe.

The SPD again sought to coopt the peace movement to overcome its own downward popularity trend. Together with the DGB and representatives from academia, the arts, and the churches, it instigated the Fight Atomic Death or KdA movement in Frankfurt in March 1958. Although the presence of the SPD and DGB provided some organisational coherence to the peace movement, it also affected the latter's strategy and tactics. Since the movement's goals contradicted government policy, they could only be realised by means of *consistent extra-parliamentary opposition*. Official protests, petitions and assemblies were no doubt effective ways of gaining popular support and producing mass awareness, but in themselves could not reverse a government decision, namely the Bundestag resolution of 25 March 1958 to equip the Bundeswehr with nuclear weapons. The realisation of the KdA's goals implied anti-parliamentary, anti-government and indeed anti-constitutional measures such as carrying out a national plebiscite, or instigating a political or general strike. As these extra-parliamentary implications became evident during the mass campaign and both SPD and DGB rank-and-file members became increasingly radicalised in favour of one or another form of direct, 'illegal' action, the leaderships of both organisations—for whom the KdA had in any case represented rather more an advertising campaign than a vital labour issue—withdrew from direct involvement, motivated not least of all by the anticommunist resentments invoked by the bourgeois coalition.

This discussion of the course of the peace movement in the CDU State is interesting not only in as much as it reveals obvious parallels with today's New Social Movements, but also because it suggests an abiding problem of what has been termed 'issue saliency' in contemporary politics. Popular support for Christian Democracy was scarcely affected by all this 'postmaterial' opposition. Its massive and historically unprecedented absolute majority of 1957 was registered while the Göttingen appeal was at the peak of its effectiveness. And during the Fight Atomic Death campaign the CDU gained a substantial victory in the North Rhine-Westphalia *Land* elections. How was the CDU/CSU, despite its pursual of unpopular policies, able to maintain its electoral hegemony? One useful explanation—though of somewhat less relevance in today's context, as will be explained below—is Hans-Karl Rupp's thesis of 'the secondary importance of non-economic and social motives' in voting behaviour.[12] So long as the Economic Miracle brought concrete and growing benefits to the great majority, issues of national survival and international peace, according to this theory, had to assume a secondary role in popular political action. In a word, therefore, *there was not yet a sufficient 'material' basis to sustain 'post-material' politics.*

Yet the Fight Atomic Death movement and its predecessors were not, for these reasons, insignificant. They demonstrated that ostensibly non-political groups could mobilise large numbers of people in support of vital, closely delimited issues. By their existence they showed the decline in the established labour organisations' theory and *praxis*. Further, they contributed to the development of a mass critical awareness. And finally, they may well have prevented the FRG from actually acquiring atomic weapons. After 1959, the peace movement appeared to have waned. but it re-emerged again in the sixties as part of the renewed campaign against nuclear weapons (Easter March Movement) and would figure in the growth of the Extra-Parliamentary Opposition (APO) of the late 1960s.

II

As the SPD's policy of *Angleichung* carried it toward a Grand Coalition, the 'material' and 'post-material' opposition it helped to generate increasingly coalesced into three interrelated but analytically separable currents, *viz.* a 'material', mainly traditional *democratic-socialist opposition,* a specifically *youth-oriented opposition,* and a greater *Sammelbewegung* concentrating on the issues of peace and evolving toward some form of party structure.

(1) The emergence of youth as a political factor imbued the opposition with new forces and new concerns. And here again, Social Democratic obsessions with probity and an image of respectability, rather than 'leftist factionalism', underlay this development. The SPD's Socialist Student League or SDS, long a reliable training school for higher party functionaries such as Helmut Schmidt and Erich Lohmar, contained a left wing which (implicitly) challenged the assumptions of party orthodoxy with its espousal of new currents in neo-Marxism (Frankfurt School, Third World liberation theory, etc.), its links with *konkret* magazine (edited by Klaus-Rainer Röhl and his then wife Ulrike Meinhof, a glossy periodical aimed at a young, anti-authoritarian and sexually liberated audience), its campaigns against former Nazis in high positions, its active involvement in the peace movement, its foreign policy that in every essential paralleled Willy Brandt's later *Ostpolitik,* and its willingness, under certain conditions, to undertake joint actions with communist organisations. For these reasons, the SPD leadership capitalised on an intra-SDS dispute in early 1960 to distance itself from the Left, support the Right's move to form a new, party-conforming group, and recognise and encourage the resulting Social Democratic University League or SHB. While the SDS then continued to operate outside the party (and to produce the theory and leadership of the West German 'New Left' as well as important elements in the Easter March Movement), the SHB in turn, pushed by the growing radicalisation of the student body and the popular awareness of the crisis

in higher education, adopted almost all the politics and concerns of the banished SDS. It was also eventually expelled from the SPD in the seventies.

(2) The socialist 'material' opposition, by contrast to the New Left, was unable to constitute itself into a mass movement. From the Society for the Promotion of the SDS (SFG)—a group of SPD members such as Abendroth, Flechtheim, Brakemeier, *et. al.* expelled from the SPD because of their continued support for the student movement—to its successor the Socialist League (SB) and the Union of Independent Socialists (VUS), these groups were unable to overcome the anti-communist propaganda, official sanctions and public indifference that prevailed in the Cold War-conditioned society of the FRG.

(3) The successes of the peace movement and growing popularity of the Easter Marchers led in 1960 to the formation of a single-issue party, the German Peace Union (DFU). Its minimal programme concentrated on foreign policy: military neutralisation of the FRG, peaceful reunification, disarmament, abolition of conscription, scrapping of the proposed emergency laws and removal of ex-Nazis from public office. Not unlike the Greens today, the DFU was thus essentially a protest movement and collection of various nationalist, neutralist, pacifist and some socialist oppositional groups, as well as most of the groups and individuals who had supported the St. Paul's Church and Göttingen movements. On this comparatively narrow basis, the party was able to register modest electoral successes of between one and two percent (1.9 per cent in the 1961 federal elections). As the DFU's strength subsequently ebbed both as a result of internal disagreements and official hostility, however, other forms of 'post-material' opposition emerged. The Easter March Movement went well beyond the KdA and, far from alienating the multifarious groups that supported it, increased its nationwide mobilisation from about 1,000 marchers in 1960 to 100,000 in 1964, to more than 150,000 in 1967.[13] At the same time, the anti-emergency laws movement, made up of diverse scholars, intellectuals, media employees, as well as the student movement and most of the Left, culminated in a popular anti-authoritarian campaign with a mass congress 'Democracy in Distress' in Bonn in May 1965.

Individually, the 'loss' of these oppositional groups was perceived as being of far less significance to the SPD leadership than the gain of supporters from the 'new' middle classes. Even collectively, the 'post-material' movements could be written off as a mere irritant—provided that the policy of adaptation could be vindicated by a share in state power. This the Grand Coalition of December 1966 furnished. But the agglutinating intra-party effect of shared opposition was also weakened by the SPD's new partnership with the CDU/CSU in a governing alliance. The coalition's programme of social peace and a 'tripartite alliance' of business, labour and the state so highly touted by SPD finance minister Karl Schiller, found bitter and protracted opposition in the party wards and within the DGB. In all the *Land* elections following the formation of the Grand Coalition, the SPD's share of the popular vote dropped considerably. And in the trade unions there was a renewed movement to dissociate the labour movement from the SPD. Following the expulsion of the SHB, even the Young Socialists or Jusos (the totality of all party members under 36) was rapidly politicised in opposition to the coalition.

The formation of the Grand Coalition may be seen as the culmination of a series of structural contradictions in the FRG which together generated several pressures pointing beyond Social Democratism. The most salient of these were probably (1) the slowing down of the expansionist phase of the Economic Miracle and its first structural crisis, with a corresponding loss of the political parties' main legitimating factor—prosperity—and sense of purpose; (2) connected to this, a series of pathologies in the social and economic spheres which revealed the need for long-overdue reforms and the class nature of society; (3) a substantial shift in the front lines of the Cold War; detente between the superpowers and erection of the 'Wall' reduced the credibility of the spectre of a one-dimensional, expansionist communist foe and hence called into question the ideological under-pinning of the CDU State; (4) increasing tendencies by the political elites in both parties to revert to authoritarian methods (emergency legislation, censorship, criminalisation of nonconformist groups) to enforce social discipline; and (5) a general sense of disillusion with politics and political parties regarded as monolithic, as parts of an all-embracing 'system' against which the individual was increasingly impotent and the object of powerful forces and interests.

From out of this multiplicity of structural contradictions emerged the Extra-Parliamentary Opposition. This qualitatively new oppositional form was based on a recognition that crucial vital interests, however defined, could not be realised within the existing political system and capitalist society which supported it. In particular, the SPD's entry into the Grand Coalition effectively ended any possibility of the parliamentary articula-tion and representation of the interests in preventing emergency legislation, in the anti-nuclear campaign, university reform, political justice, renazifica-tion, women's rights and an outmoded foreign policy regarded as a threat to peace. Spontanaeity was the really striking feature about the APO's development. As though on a signal—the formation of the Grand Coalition —hundreds of groups and movements came together in demonstrations, actions, mass petitions, etc. Among these groups, four main types can be distinguished, each of which in its own way represented a logical reaction to Social Democratism: (1) a pacifist-neutralist current consisting of people, many of them former DFU members, who had supported the Easter March and the various congresses and actions against rearmament and the Western military alliance; (2) a more or less traditional Marxist grouping, including members of the VUS, SB and supporters of *Die Andere Zeitung*, now generally referred to as the Old Left; (3) the New Left, which developed from the student movement and the SDS/SHB during the sixties; though divided into several factions, it constituted the real core of theorists, activists and mass basis of the APO.

This mass popular movement, as an anti-system opposition, mobilised hundreds of thousands of demonstrators and protestors for selected actions, triggered lasting reforms in the educational system, caused the established parties in some measure to rethink their tactics and, in the case of the SPD, their policies as well. Yet within three or four years it crumbled again, reverting to sectarian movements (R.A.F., Direct Action, Baader-Meinhof, etc.), dissolving into citizens' action groups, or re-entering mainstream political parties such as the re-legalised Communist Party, now called the DKP. In particular, many APO members found their way back to the SPD. (In fact, the speed with which the estranged Left returned to the SPD and the drastic rate of dissolution of anti-system opposition carry important lessons for the contemporary New Social Movements in the FRG and caution against a precipitate writing off of the staying power and mass basis of existing Social Democracy.)

Before this could happen, however, the SPD leadership, assailed by intra-party and extra-party, material and post-material opposition, deserted by traditional voters yet unable to balance these off with new supporters, was now forced to search for image-altering strategies to profile itself against its more successful coalition partner. These it found, having once achieved a share of national power, in the promise of Keynesian social reforms (education, pensions, limited co-determination, removal of 'morality laws', etc.) and above all in an alternative foreign policy—that is, precisely in those areas in which it had abandoned its independent stances with the Godesberg Programme and Wehner's speech!

With its participation in the Grand Coalition and its hard line against the socialist Left, the SPD could now use its image of respectability to address those social sectors who had hitherto remained immune to its 'modernising' appeal: the 'new' middle classes to whom it profferred a certain social orientation and the promise of a 'rationalisation' of the political economy, and the 'dynamic' export-oriented sectors of business who sought a more progressive *Ostpolitik* within the framework of which it could compensate for a lethargic world market by increasing trade with the East. A 'policy of domestic reforms' combined with a 'new *Ostpolitik*', made up the 'modern', technological image of a *Modell Deutschland* as one of the world's most successful capitalist economic and social systems.

In alliance with the also 'modernised' and 'rationalised' FDP under Walter Scheel, therefore, the SPD by 1969 was able to become the dominant partner in a Small Coalition based on an appeal to very diverse interests. As I wrote in last year's *Socialist Register*, *Ostpolitik* constituted the central element in this *Interessengemeinschaft:* 'To the Right it offered enhanced national power and prosperity, and to the Left it held out a more rational foreign policy, dialogue with the East, and a promise of ultimate detente and peace; for the Right Karl Schiller embodied techno-cratic efficiency, social partnership and state support of business interests, while for the Left Willy Brandt was the symbol of peace, liberalisation and compassion. In *Ostpolitik,* therefore, the "non-material" interests of politically separated families and friends combined with the "post-material" interests of the peace and anti-nuclear movements to constitute a mass basis for the very "materialist" interests of the more "dynamic" sectors of West German business'—to which I should have added the equally 'material' interests represented by the trade union movement and the recipients of social welfare benefits.

This 'reversion' to pre-Godesberg political and social policy alternatives, which undermined the apolitical consensus of the Grand Coalition era, very quickly 'repoliticised' the electorate around the central issues of foreign and domestic policy. Contrary even to the SPD's basic intent of merely establishing a distinctive profile in order to attract 'new' voters and 'progressive' business sectors, the policy shifts produced a rapid re-ideologisation and polarisation in West German politics. During the last months of the Grand Coalition and, especially, in the period before the 1972 elections, the Christian Democrats—initially scarcely able to cope with their unexpected role as official opposition—reached back to Cold War terminology and anticommunist defamation tactics:

> Whether in [CDU General Secretary] Biedenkopf's elegant High German or in the vapid, beery Bavarian dialect *[Bierdunstbayrisch]* of a Strauss, the basic tactical pattern is the same: they appeal to resentments and prejudices, speculate on stupidity and count on a lack of democratic sensitivity in a country where there has never been a successful bourgeois revolution and which, in contrast to other Western democracies, has not been able to develop a real, politically functioning democratic public.[14]

However, this strategy moved the CDU/CSU to the right, thus leaving important additional groups in the centre open to the Social Democrats. The illusion of a pending class struggle was reinforced by a corresponding 'information offensive' launched by the conservative sectors of business and their allied media, and supported by the 'old' middle classes. Mainly as a reaction to this conservative pressure, Social Democracy was com-pelled to assert its programme with a clarity and consistency dormant since the Schumacher era. For in addition to attracting mainstream managers, civil servants and technical intelligentsia, the SPD, in this polarising situation, had to retain its traditional 'material' support in the labour movement and attempt to win back its lost 'post-material' groups who had defected to the APO, DFU, or retreated into apathy. The relationship between these groups and Social Democracy was highly nuanced as a result of the SPD's participation in the Grand Coalition.

Within the DGB there had been a sharp rise in organised militancy—the 1969 Steelworkers strike, the 1971 Metal Workers strike in Baden-Württemberg, etc.—in response to low wage settlements, economic priority to business recovery (investment incentives) and the general climate of social discipline created by the recession of the late sixties. At the same time, the trade union leadership, as a (subordinate) partner in the corporatist tripartism of 'concerted action', was increasingly alienated from its mass basis, who responded to reductions in their entitlements with wildcat strikes, protests, and the like. Fearing a mass mobilisation outside their control, the DGB leadership reacted with militant pronouncements even as it cooperated in such tripartite arrangements as reducing labour's negotiating autonomy by means of linking wage settlements to ostensibly 'scientific', 'objective' economic indicators and subjecting settlements arrived at in the public service to ratification by parliament.[15]

Yet even as labour attempted to resist cooptation into SPD-induced corporatist arrangements, the party registered a substantial increase in members, sympathizers and voters among the working classes as well as wage earners in general. This phenomenon, which has rightly been used to adduce the thesis that the SPD had become a 'class party against its will', can only be stated here in its ambiguity, in terms of a double contradiction. To begin with, the adoption by the SPD of the class-collaborationist Keynesian model of 'modernisation' conflicted with its continued reliance on a working class core for its mass basis. And second, the structural affinity of the SPD and DGB leaderships was undermined from two sides: economic recession and integration via corporatism into the capitalist state clashed with class-motivated worker actions whose goals led beyond the structural coordination implied by 'concerted action'. Hence:

> The Social Democratic-leaning functionary apparatus, in this situation, was confronted by the contradictory task of having to defend the workers' social accomplishments, from which they lived and which the workers, in their own interests, sought to maintain, but without allowing scope for their mobilisation, which could have destroyed the existing level of institutionalisation.[16]

All these contradictions could be temporarily suspended, in a situation of economic growth and political polarisation, by a programme of domestic reforms. Prior to the 1972 elections, the unions engaged in a series of solidarity strikes, the so-called April Actions, to demonstrate labour support for the SPD/FDP coalition in the face of a non-confidence motion brought by the CDU/CSU. Not only did workers vote overwhelmingly for the SPD, therefore (one in two, cf. one in five or so among the 'new' middle classes), they also resorted to extraparliamentary action to advance their class interests.

Similarly complex developments characterised the post-material Left within, or at least at the margin of the party. Many of the socialist elements in the APO, it has just been suggested, 'relocated' or returned to the SPD and operated within its youth organisation, the Jusos. Although the Juso organisation as such scarcely constituted a 'post-material' opposition,[17] its university-based, APO-influenced vanguard did. On the one hand, the Jusos were constrained to practise solidarity with the SPD and to support and, if possible, expand the relatively progressive policies of reform and detente. But on the other hand the Jusos were concerned with pushing beyond Social Democratism toward a post-capitalist democratic socialism. The tension contained in these essentially contradictory goals was expressed in the concept—first developed within the SDS[18]—of a 'dual strategy' of socialist opposition. This meant first, defending and extending existing rights and opportunities within the advanced capitalist system: cooperation with citizens' action groups on specific, vital issues (which will be examined presently), asserting and testing the limits of crucial liberal rights such as freedom of speech and assembly, acting as a 'core' and 'motor' of the left wing within the SPD, and mobilising popular support for socialist strategies at the workplace, neighbourhood or university. And second, it meant extra-parliamentary action to place pressure on the party and government, as well as the formulation of anticapitalist theories and programmes. Jusos theory thus distinguished between 'system-immanent' reforms that merely shored up a declining capitalism, and 'system-overcoming' reforms whose cumulative effect would dismantle capitalist hegemony and in their ultimate effect 'transcend' that system. Like Harold Laski's 'revolution by consent' of the 1930s, the theory of system-overcoming reforms remained too subjective, too situation-dependent to be logically demonstrable; but it did suggest some of the central problems of evolving anticapitalist strategies from within Social Democracy. This theoretical ambiguity was also reflected in the factionalisation of the Jusos into a more or less Social Democratic wing, a socialist grouping, and a 'stamocap' (= state monopoly capitalism) faction, which during the seventies produced a lively discussion (and series of expulsions) within the Young Socialist organisation.

Paradoxically, however, the combination of *Ostpolitik* and domestic reforms—which pre-empted and/or reintegrated much of the 'material' and 'post-material' opposition, resulted in electoral victories for the Small Coalition in 1969 and 1972, and qualified Chancellor Brandt for a Nobel Peace Prize—at the same time clearly revealed the limits of Social Democracy in the advanced capitalist state, namely those 'given' by the Federal Republic's position in the capitalist world order and by the pattern of domestic socio-economic and political power distribution.

For *Ostpolitik* merely normalised and confirmed the *de facto* new international status quo which, objectively, ought to have been defined at the time of the formation of the two German states and, subjectively, had now penetrated into the consciousness of wide strata. Indeed, the SPD's own 1958 *Deutschlandplan,* renounced by Wehner's 1960 speech, had already contained all the essentials of Brandt's 1969 *Ostpolitik* (abolition of the Hallstein Doctrine, recognition of the Oder-Neisse Line, etc.). Besides, detente in Middle Europe was achieved entirely within, and as part of the respective bloc alliances. For the FRG, this meant in conformity with NATO and the Western Alliance as well as in the interests of the EEC and transnational business. Therefore, once these limits had been reached (and intersystem trade had been greatly enhanced), the progressive impulse *Ostpolitik* generated could not be developed into, for instance, the neutralisation and partial unification of all Europe or the demilitarisation of Middle Europe.

Similarly, the SPD's policy of domestic reforms, based on Keynesian 'modernising' and 'social engineering' premises, was unable to do more than respond to existing material needs and demands. To be sure, as a mere 'guest in power' in the peak institutions of the CDU State (i.e. legislature and chancellorship), the SPD was confined in its scope by the CDU-dominated Bundesrat, High Courts and most local governments as well as by the need to take account of the veto power of its coalition partner, the FDP. But such reforms were mainly constrained by the SPD's strategy of adaptation and voter-maximisation. Social Democratic reformism reveals that 'neither bureaucratic-technocratic visions, nor nationalisation visions uncoupled from reality can effect a transformation of structural social inequalities'.[19] In other words, social reforms implemented as part of an existing, capitalist-formed delivery structure are both inadequate and reversible. 'Structure-changing' measures, on the other hand, according to Axel Murswieck, would have had to entail decentralisation, popular participation, correction of the mechanisms of distribution and new forms of extra-state care such as the use of lay-persons in medicine or participatory types of non-state management. The specific example he cites is the health care system. Since social reformist policies left intact the private ownership principle as a foundation of health care—pharmaceutical industry, hospitals, doctors—and therefore the criterion of profitability, there has been no further scope for improvement beyond one-time legislated measures: 'Thus, e.g., the implementation of early-diagnosis examinations has become more a kind of financing for the middle class rather than an impetus toward the introduction of a broad system of preventive medicine extending into the workplace, which has everywhere been recognised as necessary.'[20]

From this perspective, Social Democratic reformism can be seen as finite and ultimately dysfunctional, if not framed in terms of a coherent set of goals, a vision. The point has been made that the SPD's *Kultur-politik* was incapable of dealing with the consequences of the 'modernisa-tion' process it set in motion. Reforms in education (greater accessibility, improved infrastructures, etc.) ought to have simultaneously concentrated on inculcating democratic and rational values as against traditional hierarchical thinking and authoritarian values. Social Democracy had therefore

> . . . not succeeded in destroying *the hard core of sovereign-statist and authoritarian*, pre-democratic traditions and attitudes characteristic of German political culture since even before fascism. Social Democratic modernization is an *external* process, not accompanied by a modernization of values, attitudes and forms of political association. Traces of an authoritarian, aggressive 'political naturalism' resting on categories of age, sex, nationality and race can be found as much today as in the Fifties.[21]

Since it did not or could not 'modernise' the political culture in this way, the SPD was a first victim when during the mid and late seventies the rightward *Tendenzwende* induced a rollback of 'welfarism'.

'Victim' here may be a less adequate term than 'architect'. The SPD's conscious policy of adaptation had led it to abandon the long-term goals for which it sought political power. From an opinion-making party it had transformed itself into an opinion-following organisation. In place of substantial social change, *Modell Deutschland* aspired merely to streamline and rationalise the CDU State.[22] Therefore, to argue that Social Demo-cracy had somehow failed to seize a historical opportunity to effect social progress is to impute to it a set of goals it no longer espoused. At the very peak of its 'progressive' period in 1972, for instance, it initiated the Anti-Radical Decree *(Berufsverbot)* which banned from public service employ-ment persons held to be 'extremists', 'radicals' or 'anti-democrats', and which has been used principally as a means of disciplining the Left.[23] The polarised election campaign of 1972, the temporary situation of being a 'class party against its will', a record turnout of issue-oriented voters (91.1 per cent), the mobilisation of mainly working-class voters despite the hesitant support of members of the 'new' middle classes, and the election itself which made the SPD the largest single party in the FRG—all these 'unforeseen' developments were not perceived as a mandate for social transformation but as an imperative to retrench, consolidate, 'depoliticise' and re-occupy the mainstream of the political system. In this context, not to deepen and link the reforms and to mobilise one's support-ers behind them is to go over to the political defensive. Adam Przeworski writes:

> The abandonment of reformism is a direct consequence of those reforms that have been accomplished. Since the state is engaged almost exclusively in those

activities which are unprofitable from the private point of view, it is deprived of financial resources needed to continue the process of nationalization. Having nationalized deficitary sectors, social democrats undermined their very capacity to gradually extend the public realm. At the same time, having strengthened the market, social democrats perpetuate the need to mitigate the distributional effect of its operation. Welfare reforms do not even have to be 'undone' by bourgeois governments. It is sufficient that the operation of the market is left to itself for any length of time and inequalities increase, unemployment fluctuates, shifts of demand for labour leave new groups exposed to impoverishment, etc.[24]

III

These considerations touch directly on what is surely the primary contradiction of contemporary social democracy. To satisfy the material needs and expectations of workers and consumers it must continuously extend the range and quality of state services, particularly welfare measures. The expending state structure, which social democracy consciously fosters and benefits from, must be financed by constant economic growth and productivity improvements in the private sector. Generally, therefore, social democracy has a *prior* interest in creating and maintaining conditions for the enhanced profitability of capitalist enterprise, especially its dynamic, monopoly sectors whose growth is as a rule more rapid and more responsive to state interests. The contradiction implied here, between furthering the interests of labour and capital simultaneously, is suspended, in a situation of constant economic growth, by the Keynesian welfare state.

The 'Keynesian equation' of economic prosperity, combined with public spending (emphasis on policy 'outputs' or demands to transfer purchasing power to the subordinate classes, so stimulating production) and social partnership (state as mediator between capital and labour) was and remains the foundation of social democratic politics in advanced capitalism. Although social democracy has been better situated (closer links with labour, 'modernising' ethos, social orientation), all mass political parties have, in varying degrees, taken the Keynesian welfare state as given; contemporary politics revolves mainly around the relative positions (or shares) of capital, labour and the state, but until the most recent sustained economic crisis, has not been concerned with the central role of the Keynesian equation itself.

For the welfare state, although able to incorporate almost all social groups into its nexus by offering something for everyone, arises in response to, and *primarily serves the interests of capital.* In Germany, its precedent was the complex of pre-emptive welfare benefits that legitimated the ruling authoritarian economic and political order of the Second Reich summed up in the concept of 'Bismarxianism'. In the FRG, as elsewhere in Western Europe, the rise of the welfare state can be regarded as a means of resolving the root contradictions of capitalism in the interests of what Marx called the collective capitalist. Offe, invoking Marx, explains the 'contradictions of the welfare state' in terms of a commodification/decommodification dichotomy,[25] which may be stated as follows. As capitalism moves from its *laissez-faire* and organised phases into advanced or monopoly capitalism, it tends increasingly to produce negative collective outcomes, such as environmental pollution, urban decay, intolerable income differentials and excessive unemployment. Particularised and segmented individual capitals are however unable to overcome these dysfunctional symptoms on their own strength. In other words, the continuous commodification of society, which capital needs, is undermined by the inherent development of capital itself. If these tendencies were left unchecked, they would produce decommodification in the sense of delegitimation, lack of a trained workforce, a society incapable of reproducing itself, counter-cultures and revolutionary movements.

The welfare state is implemented in order to resolve these contradictions: it selectively decommodifies, as it were, in order to maintain the commodified economy in new forms. As capitalism erodes the traditional social institutions that once ensured the reproduction of labour power—family, Church, charity organisations—the state increasingly assumes their functions, for instance by providing pensions, unemployment schemes, safety standards, housing construction, health care, and other 'catchment areas' for the old, infirm and unemployable. It introduces universal, compulsory education and underwrites a complex system of intermediate and higher education corresponding to the increasing division of labour in modern society. And it regulates and controls the interrelations among the various sectors of capital (anti-trust laws, fair competition) to ensure the coordination of the system as a whole. In each case, the primary objective, commodification, has long-term secondary effects: decommodification. Thus the measures intended to ensure reproduction of the labour force also create a certain autonomous sphere for individuals as citizens into which the capitalist mode of production cannot fully penetrate. Education and training do not only produce a skilled workforce, they also impart critical faculties and interests that remove individuals somewhat from the capital nexus (leisure time, private pursuits). The regulation of capital movements and powers creates certain legal safeguards for citizens.

The trade-off for this necessary decommodification is a far greater state involvement in the economy as a central actor. It not only subsidises the losses incurred by the capitalist economy (public services, infrastructures) and provides subventions, tax write-offs, etc. to facilitate private enterprise, it also moves into certain key sectors (defence, aircraft manufacture, telecommunications, nuclear energy) that drive the economy. The welfare state thus develops in several complementary directions: (1) It is a bigger state corresponding to the increased tasks it must perform in providing public services, propelling and coordinating the economy, and furthering the process of commodification. (2) It becomes a technocratic state with a 'modernising' mission. To cope with its growing 'load' it emphasises planning, regulation, rationality and efficiency, and extends its technocratic orientation into an 'administered society' and a process of 'social engineering'. (3) And in the narrower realm of politics it tends toward 'depoliticisation' and 'rationalisation' of contentious issues and conflicting interests. Politics is generally reduced to controlled competition among organised interests, and solutions are sought through expertise and/or compromise. 'The decline of legislatures', 'the end of ideology', 'the party cartel', 'bureaucratisation', 'the technocratic society', and 'pluralism' are all current expressions of the quality and direction of politics in the welfare state.

To sum up (and again following Offe), the Keynesian welfare state does several things simultaneously: (1) it maintains the domination of capital, even as (2) it erodes and challenges its power, and (3) it compensates for its disruptive, dysfunctional effects.

IV

The *conditio sine qua non* of the Keynesian model is therefore continuous growth and prosperity, which facilitate an intricate *ordering* of social relations, including potential class conflict, and *stabilisation* of economic development, which in turn legitimates and vindicates the capitalist socio-economic system over time. In this section I want to argue that when growth is interrupted, as it has been by the stagflation crisis since the early and mid-seventies, then the assumptions of order and stability are also called into question. The state's logical response, in the first case, is repression, including 'administrative repression', and in the second case, a kind of technologisation (or 'depoliticisation') of social life in the form of collective arrangements ('corporatism') and selective interest perception.

The post-OPEC economic crisis showed West German Social Democracy to be particularly vulnerable to the contradictions of the welfare state. The traumatisation of the population as a result of experiences of the inflation/depression cycle of the twenties and thirties, combined with a postwar 'regime legitimacy' that has rested more on economic prosperity and ability to deliver goods and services than on popular ideals or affective loyalties, rendered the FRG more susceptible than other advanced capitalist countries to the social-psychological effects of the crisis.

The crisis has also revealed that, in the words of Alan Wolfe, '. . . the particular class compositions that enabled social democratic experiments to take place are decomposing *faster* than other political coalitions, making social democratic parties as a rule the single most vulnerable to possible decomposition.[26] Wolfe's observation is borne out by the erosion in the SPD's mass basis after 1973/74. As the economic growth rate in

the seventies slowed to about one-third that of the 1950s[27] and became
virtually stagnant in the early eighties, the resulting scarcity undermined
the foundations of social partnership which quickly resorted to a Social
Darwinian contest of strength among organised groups.

On the *Right*, capital has become less willing to accept Social Democracy's mediating role in the social partnership and has come to see the
recession/depression as an opportunity to tighten social discipline.
Eschewing the once popular notion of a posited 'entrepreneurial social
conscience', it has reverted to a more expressly class-conscious, ideological
offensive aimed at a recommodification of social relationships: intensification of anticommunism, calls for the dismantling of the welfare state,
return to traditional values such as the work ethic, law and order, frugality
and self-reliance, coupled however with an advocacy of stronger national
defence, firmer control of dissent and nonconformity, and enhanced state
incentives to business as a motor of economic recovery.

At the *Centre*, the 'new' middle classes of experts and administrators
increasingly share with the 'old' middle classes of small businessmen,
artisans and farmers an unwillingness to continue to pay for the costs of
the welfare state and a desire to maintain status and income differentials
which they see it as corroding. Where the former classes were essentially
'on loan' to the SPD during the period of social modernisation and foreign
policy rationalisation, in times of economic reverse they tend to share with
capital and the old middle classes an apprehension of economic 'levelling'
and productivity decline, and therefore defect in increasing numbers from
Social Democracy.

On the 'material' *Left*—the 'post-material' Left will be discussed in the
next section—the labour movement becomes increasingly divided and
marginalised. While the weaker, less organised unions continue to advocate
labour solidarity and collective bargaining, the leaders of the stronger,
more central organisations tend to favour corporate arrangements in order
to maximise their particular interests:

> Even unions act as separate bureaucracies for managing interests. They are
> essentially busy defining and filtering out 'employee' interests so that they remain
> compatible with the capitalist modernization strategies and the structural changes
> determined by the world market—which means: representation of the wage
> interests of the (qualified, male, German) 'core employee groups' in the pro-
> duction and service sectors tied into the world market.[28]

The unions are further fragmented between a leadership that for its
own reasons is bent on continued collaboration, and a base directly
affected by the decline of the social partnership provisions and hence
increasingly militant. More and more divided between grass-roots pressures
for a larger share of 'outputs' and systemic adaptation at the top, between
the special interests of particular unions versus the need for labour

solidarity, and between organised and non-organised workers, many trade unionists have not been able to go beyond a strictly defensive strategy of attempting to uphold the status quo or—especially among the less skilled, less well paid—have retreated into apathy. Nevertheless, until the 1980s, workers have remained overwhelmingly loyal to the SPD in their voting behaviour, though increasingly critical and inclined toward industrial action and/or withholding their vote. Their general continued adherence to Social Democracy is explained by Andrei Markovits in this way: 'Faced with the choice of an SPD-led government that fulfilled fewer and fewer of their needs and the prospect of a CDU/CSU return to power, the unions chose to go with the lesser of two evils, thereby replicating the famous "hostage-to-a-friendly-government syndrome".'[29]

The crisis of the welfare state, in the FRG, is therefore at the same time a crisis of Social Democracy as the centre of a coalition of forces whose function is to commodify the capitalist state. Given the primacy of capital in the Keynesian equation and in the construct of *Modell Deutschland,* the SPD could hardly seek solutions that in any way countered the prevalent direction of the *Tendenzwende.* On the contrary, the party leadership, assumed in 1974 by Helmut Schmidt and a new 'management team', chose to abandon the party's reformist and foreign policies in favour of a strategy of 'crisis management' and 'pragmatic administration'. It moved from a demand-oriented economic polity to one of 'selected measures to restructure industrial production toward industries that are more competitive on the world market'.[30] In conformity with the dominant conservative theses of 'ungovernability' and 'system overload', it aimed at recommodifying the political economy by subjecting a greater part of it to market imperatives, e.g. by controlling unit wage costs, stimulating capital formation and encouraging productivity increases. In other words, the SPD turned to supply-side, monetarist economics as a way of breaking the impasse caused by stagflation. This policy was intended to

. . . structure problems so as to make them manageable. Quantity and skill level of the work force, energy and raw materials, the price level at which labor power and natural resources are available, and the level and rate of technical change are the foci of economic policies that no longer merely respond to problems but that try to change the nature of problems so as to make future responses possible.[31]

As analogous policy developments under Thatcher and Reagan have clearly indicated, monetarist economic policy is by no means merely a technical economic device; it is a conscious instrument to further the interests of capital. The stabilisation that it attempts to achieve is a stability of capital accumulation which, in a shrinking economy, necessarily takes place at the expense of the non-owners of capital. In fact, SPD monetarism

—or for that matter CDU/CSU–FDP monetarism; the policy effects are party-indifferent—has not only promoted an outflow of West German capital abroad (where wage demands are lower and labour discipline stronger), it has also led to capital intensification at home thus furthering structural unemployment[32] (or the 'natural rate of unemployment' as technocratic newspeak might put it).

In any case, crisis management and monetarism are comprehensible less in terms of their technical efficacy than as a means of 'depoliticising' a whole series of issues by placing them beyond the reach of liberal-democratic politics. Particularly, issues of redistribution and welfare entitlements, which are defined as the crux of the state overload problem, can be relegated to ostensibly technical problems to be dealt with by experts and therefore outside political debate. In this way economic policies directed toward business recovery can be passed off as in the interests of general economic progress. For instance, the 1973 system of price controls and wage freezes based on scarce money increased the relative strength of the financial sectors, did not harm big business, but had almost no redistributive effects at all. The 1974 programme of *'stabilitätsgerechter Aufschwung'* (recovery with stability) improved profits by means of tax and depreciation write-offs and government contracts (= subsidies) to business, but hardly reduced unemployment. And the 1975 public spending programme, which actually contained a reduced social welfare component, was spent mainly to aid business.[33] Austerity budgets, deflationary economic policies and an incapacity to generate jobs completed the economic policy package of the SPD.

The technocratic propensity of *Modell Deutschland* also extended to the institutionalisation and regulation of organised interests to engineer consent for what Hirsch has termed an 'authoritarian-democratic system based on bureaucratic mass organisations without mass participation.[34] One side of this institutionalised legitimation was the selective neo-corporatism described above. Concerted action, behind closed official doors, was able to induce tripartite consensus between the state, trade union and business elites and bypass the clogged channels of the 'overloaded' representative state institutions. As a consensus-producing mechanism that united the most powerful interests in the corporate and labour organisations. Social Democratic corporatism consciously excluded the weaker elements: foreigners, women, youth and older workers, thus converting class struggles to group struggles and doing nothing to reduce racism, sexism and anti-welfarism within the subordinate classes.

The other side of the 'authoritarian-democracy' formula is a vast, far-reaching bureaucratisation of political and social life, as summed up in the concept of a 'party-state' intertwined with the state bureaucracy, the broadcast media, judiciary and the powerful economic interests. These symptoms, Kenneth Dyson notes, correspond to a decline in intra-party democracy and increasing bureaucratisation of the parties themselves.[35] The political parties, in a word, can be seen as over-adapting, over-institutionalised, over-generalised and hence over-loaded.[36] Not without reason, therefore, the concept of *verdrossen*, in its dual sense of fed up and irritated, has become a popular catchword in the political lexicon of the FRG—*Staatsverdrossenheit*, *Parteiverdrossenheit*, indeed *Politik-verdrossenheit*.

One further and most telling aspect of this tendency toward de-politicisation should be considered, namely that *repression* necessarily inheres in it. In Offe's words, 'depoliticisation of conflict potentials and intensification of political repression. . . seem to be the two polar points of a spectrum of alternatives for describing the possible strategies of the capitalist state in advanced industrial societies.'[37] For where large numbers of people are alienated from political life, where stronger interests prevail over weaker ones, and where promised reforms founder on the superior 'veto power' of capital, the resultant conflicts stand to erupt even more sharply than would be the case under a system of more rationalised conflict resolution. Thus the 'progressive' *Ostpolitik*, as has been shown, coincided with the administrative terror of the *Berufsverbot*. During the last decade of SPD government, repression became an increasingly deploy-ed instrument to contain the conflicts generated by the decline in the Keynesian consensus. The anti-terrorist campaign of the mid-seventies, the law and order fetishism of the conservative parties which the SPD felt constrained to outdo, the expansion of the legal system (from the police force and special branch to the judiciary) and the criminalisation of political protest[38] were means of rationalising away the looming pathologies of Social Democratism.

So long as it remained the party of government, then, the SPD was locked into the contradictions of 'its' welfare state and hence the crisis of advanced capitalism. It was not that the SPD-led government posed a threat to *Modell Deutschland* or the class interests which underpinned it. On the contrary. Rather, the party could no longer mobilise mass support for government policy. Sectors within its core following among the work-ing class were lost to apathy or in some cases to other parties. 'Progressive' business groups had long since defected and the new middle classes were doing the same. The ecology and peace groups were also estranged and, following initial electoral successes in 1978 and 1979, constituted an alternative party by 1980. The SPD's coalition partner, the FDP, which was not committed to a working class mass basis, increasingly saw mone-tarism, a reduced state role and a more unmitigated reliance on market forces as the necessary solution to stagflation and economic immobilism. The Christian Democrats, though somewhat tardier in adapting to the *Tendenzwende* (e.g. in presenting Franz-Josef Strauss, an ultra-conservative identified with regional interests, as their chancellor candidate in the

1980 elections), were gradually able to appropriate the 'modernisation', 'in-tune-with-the-times' image of themselves once they had managed to divest themselves of their clerical Weltanschauung, their hidebound class image, their hardline anticommunism and other vestigial ideological elements. With a refurbished set of slogans related to performance, efficiency, rationality and flexibility, all adjusted to post-Keynesian exigencies, they emerged as the more pure 'protagonist for modern capitalism',[39] thus in a way emulating the SPD's breakthroughs of fifteen years earlier, though now advancing from the right.[40]

One is indeed tempted to advance the thesis that the SPD's 'objective function' in the West German capitalist state was to expand, humanise and rationalise the CDU State while the conservative forces were recovering and regrouping in the interval between Cold War clerical anticommunism and the new post-Keynesian recommodification. Electoral tendencies during the past decade seem to confirm this thesis. By 1976, the CDU at 48.6 per cent of the national vote recovered its lost voters, while the SPD at 42.6 per cent was reduced to its 1969 level. Even the 1980 candidature of Strauss did not aid the SPD, whose share remained at 42.9 per cent, but the FDP which went from 7.9 per cent in 1976 to 10.6 per cent in 1980. As the economic crisis heightened in 1980 and 1981 and the class bases of the parties became even clearer, the SPD–FDP coalitions in the various Länder came apart, so that by 1982 only Hesse was still governed by a Small Coalition. In 1981 the SPD also lost its majorities in all the big cities, notably Hamburg and West Berlin. The ten per cent gap between the CDU/CSU (48.8 per cent) and the SPD (38.2 per cent) in the 1983 elections—greater now than at any time since 1957—together with the decline of the Free Democrats (6.9 per cent) and the emergence of the Greens (5.6 per cent) sealed the Tendenzwende. Significantly, Social Democracy was said to have lost 750,000 voters to the Greens and 1.8 M to the Christian Democrats in that election.[41]

V

The disintegration of the Keynesian equation has not only caused a series of realignments in the existing party political system—particularly a dual 'material' and 'post-material' alienation from Social Democracy—it has also produced a mass basis for a 'New Politics' in part 'beyond' Social Democracy which however was already present in the 'post-material' opposition of the sixties.

Stagflation, relative scarcity and the shrinkage of the welfare state have coincided with a partial satiation of most material needs for at least the upper and middle classes in advanced capitalist society. Not only the assumption of the desirability of constant economic growth has been shaken, therefore, but even the belief that growth itself is possible and desirable. Without some vision of a 'post-material' 'no-growth' society, social relations are increasingly reduced to an already alluded to Social Darwinian zero-sum competition, replacing the cooperative, positive-sum ethos of the Keynesian welfare state. Moreover, as in 'post-industrial society' the numbers and importance of collective goods—defence, community well-being (including a clean environment), law and order—more and more occupy a central position in economic and social activity, politics tends to focus more on collective action either to demand such goods (roads, welfare benefits, security) or to avert the undesirable consequences of other goods (industrial pollution, urban decay). Such demands are necessarily addressed to the state, and the government in particular. Thus the class struggle is in part displaced from the axis of capital versus labour into the public sphere, in the form of conflicts for control over organisations that serve the commodity form (universities, public service, health system, etc.). The literature on 'post-material' social developments overwhelmingly demonstrates that strike actions, industrial disputes, collective bargaining, etc. are growing much more rapidly in the public, rather than the private sector. Within the public sector, however, the absence of adequate performance-measuring criteria *de facto* makes relative group strength, rather than one's own place in the process of production, the only consistent determinant of success in advancing one's group claims. To this complex of factors should be addressed the partially decommodified individual sphere, outlined earlier, of increased education, welfare, medical care and so on, which provides a relative degree of autonomy and the possibility of limited withdrawal from the commodity nexus for broad sectors of the population.

The picture that emerges is one of increasing politicisation of hitherto non-politicised areas of social life paradoxically espousing 'post-material' values on the strength of a range of material enablements; and this process is evolving within the context of official political forms anchored in the commodified form. The results, again as have been described, are apathy, cynicism, narrow interest-focused protest and an all-pervasive sense of *Verdrossenheit*. In a word, formal political institutions and concerns are less subject to political action even as the formerly 'private' or 'limited' aspects of everyday life are sharply 'politicised'. Where 'material' opposition once attempted to capture state power, 'post-material' opposition would dismantle it. And where the traditional Right sought to ward off modernisation and industrialisation as such, 'post-materialists' oppose the instrumentality of these processes. They argue, for instance, that the material benefits of the welfare state also entail bureaucratisation, étatism and social discipline (poverty traps, means tests, etc.); or that 'material' concern with national security has enhanced the risk of war; or that a growth-based economy is destructive of the environment.[42]

Hence 'post-material' politics today is measured against criteria for which no basis of legitimacy exists in either the economic or political orders. It is within this context that the broad movement of citizens' action groups (*Bürgerinitiativen* or BIs) in the FRG must be comprehended. It is important to recall that the BIs antedate the current economic crisis, but that that crisis has contributed to their development into a mass movement.

As the APO and its constituent groups receded in the late sixties and early seventies, the BIs increased proportionately, and the continuities between them in motives (overcoming state ossification and omissions), style (spontaneity, militancy) and tactics (protests, single-issue orientation, action in the extra-parliamentary sphere) are self-evident. The main difference is that the BIs generally are more locally concentrated (and therefore also fragmented) and espouse correspondingly more immediate causes. From the early-seventies actions on the issues of urban planning and highway construction to participation in the ecology and peace movements in the mid-seventies, the BI movement has grown to about 50,000 groups with a total membership of some 1.7 M—as many as are members of all the political parties.[43] Yet about two-thirds of these groups have a membership of less than 50, and may expect to survive from twelve months to a few years; only about 25 per cent 'present cultural, social and environmental issues in such a way as to achieve an impact on the whole of society'.[44] Dominated by civil servants (especially teachers), students, professionals and white-collar employees, their memberships contain only about ten per cent workers.[45]

Organised into small groups to place pressure on a local planning board or forming demonstrations of hundreds of thousands in favour of disarmament; operating in schools, at the workplace and in residential areas in cities and towns, the citizens' action groups generally practise unmediated, direct democracy; by their very existence they are a refutation of and challenge to established forms and methods of political interest representation and action.

For this reason, the various attempts to integrate and coordinate the BI movement by means of a peak association (or 'anti-party party' in Petra Kelly's coinage) have been problematic. Nevertheless, as the 'Alternatives' —the Green List in Bremen, the *Bunte Liste: Verteidigt Euch* in Hamburg, the Alternative List for Democracy and Environmental Protection in W. Berlin, the Free Greens in Constance, the Baden-Württemberg Green Action Future (GAZ), the Alternative/Green List in Leverkusen, etc.— began to reach the limits of isolated, 'hedonist' political action during the late seventies, they were more and more compelled to look beyond their 'grassroots fixations' and 'abstract anti-parliamentarism'[46] toward an organisational form combining their extra-parliamentary concerns with a collective political strategy in order to counter the organised hegemony of the established groups. Because the BIs are mainly single-issue oriented and locally operative, they tend not to compete with, but complement one another. Their common concern is group autonomy and individual liberation, and joint action is based on these common interests:

> They rally against the tendencies of mass democracy often perceived as willed by fate—the creeping levelling and replacement of the individual by anonymous mass social groups, the complete mediatization of the citizen under the aegis of the full-blown 'Party State'. Unlike the parties, they restore the ordinary citizen to the political stage as an acting subject. No longer is he merely the 'raw material' of rational administrative strategies, existing only to be 'consumed by the institutions'.[47]

Thus the alternative movement in many ways goes beyond the formal liberal definition of citizenship to emphasise full individual participation in a kind of neo-*Gemeinschaft*. Rejecting what Hirsch calls the 'Taylorisation of vital conditions'—the pervasive alienation and anomie of *Modell Deutschland*—it is antibureaucratic, decentralised and individualistic: a kind of 'do-it-yourself form of representation' (in Guggenberger's term) to compensate for deficiencies in the system of official political representation. This emphasis on methods relates to the important insight, first popularised by the Marcuse-influenced sectors among the New Left, that the means and ends of social action are closely interrelated and that therefore the quality and feasibility of social change are conditioned by the form and substance of the methods by which that change is sought. Thus the APO-pioneered means are still widely used by the New Social Movements: demonstrations, petitions, disruption of traffic, civil disobedience, etc. A characteristic and indeed brilliant strategy has been evolved by the squatters' movement, namely the practice of *Instandsbesetzung*, a practically untranslatable term that suggests not only occupation of housing units unutilised mostly as a consequence of property speculation, but also the restoration, beautification and 'human-friendly' renovation of such units—a most effective statement of what living conditions might be in a 'green' world.

Initial forays into the formal political sphere revealed the depth of support in West German society for the Alternatives: in 1978 the Green/Alternative Lists gained three per cent of the popular vote in the Hamburg elections and four per cent in Lower Saxony. These were followed by three per cent in the 1979 elections to the European Parliament and a first overcoming of the Five Per Cent Hurdle in the elections in Bremen in 1979 and Baden-Württemberg in 1980. On the strength of these gains, the G/AL was able to constitute itself as a party in 1980, and achieved a national share of 1.5 per cent of the total vote in that year's elections. By 1983, the 'Greens', as the party is popularly called, with 5.6 per cent of the federal vote, became the first new parliamentary party since the 1950s, and certainly the first since the mid-forties to suggest an actual, mass-based alternative politics beyond Social Democracy.

For reasons analogous to the diversity and heterogeneity of the BIs that make up their core, the Greens cannot be readily analysed in ('material') terms of Left and Right. The party's slogan, 'neither Right nor Left but out front' best captures its self-image. No doubt, the peace and ecology movements are the main pillars of the party—hence the popular designation 'ecopax'—but it is also strongly supported by the feminist, sexual-equality, alternative-lifestyle and other movements, as well as some sectors of the Left.

Not surprisingly, therefore, the Green programme[48] is designed as a minimal consensus-producing basis of action rather than a codified document like conventional party programmes. However:

> When one speaks of the Green/Alternative parties, it must first of all be remembered that they are based on trends, movements and cultures which must be understood specifically as the negation of prevailing socio-political conditions with all the consequent contradictions and ambivalences.[49]

The Green programme has been summarised as a general desire for decentralisation, democratisation and downsizing. Its primary concerns are the threats to peace and the environment which it sees as rooted in the growth-economy, the consumerism of capitalist society and the unequal distribution of resources among the members of society. It also eschews state ownership of the means of production with the argument that nationalisation produces bureaucratisation and domination, and advocates private property without exploitation. These are all formulated in terms of longer-term goals without, however, the specific means of realising them.

The means are rather implicit and must be inferred from the 'organisation' of the party itself as the instrument for the ultimate realisation of these goals. As already suggested, the BIs are the organisational basis of the Greens who merely guide and coordinate 'basis politics'. Still,

> these aggregation and articulation functions which the Greens undertake for both systemic and anti-system movements underline the equivocal role which the party plays in both rejecting the status quo of industrialized advanced monopoly capitalism through counter-hegemonic practice, and also in contributing to the legitimation of that system.[50]

This problem is replicated at the federal (as well as local and *Land*) level, where the Greens attempt to institutionalise principles of direct democracy by means of collective leadership, imperative mandates and two-year rotation of deputies. The further the Greens move from their initial role as forum and protest movement toward actual, sustained strategies and tactics for social change, the more *the organisational question divides the movement*. In particular, a pronounced division occurs between

(1) the elected deputies who, like Petra Kelly, see the need for 'competence' and 'continuity', for more 'efficient and reliable structures' (including parliamentary assistants) to carry out better research, and for a more adequate division of intra-party labour among the various local and regional levels,[51] or who, like federal deputy Dirk Schneider, see in the amateurism of party officials an accumulation by default of day-to-day leadership work on the part of the Greens' 27 Bundestag members[52] and (2) the party 'grassroots' such as Rudolf Bahro who see the parliamentary party as increasing its relative strength *vis-à-vis* the party basis and for whom intra-party democracy is thus jeopardised.[53]

These tensions are further complicated in as much as they are overlaid by contending basic currents within the party. (To speak of factions or organised groups would be to invoke a terminology not applicable to the Green situation; what is meant is the discussion about which means are appropriate to the realisation of joint long-term goals.) The multifarious intra-party currents may for analytical purposes be classified according to their class perspective. On one side is what might be termed an 'Ecopax-First' grouping, represented by figures such as Bahro and Kelly, who see the Green movement itself, with its primary and overriding aims of peace and a humanised environment, as transcending class politics. Bahro has expressed this position most coherently: 'We are the organ not of any particular interest but of the general interest. We are against the established interests, however, and most strongly against the interests of capital, the big corporations and the state.'[54] This group generally oppose any cooperation with Social Democracy, and, although critical of both superpowers, in part advocate unilateral disarmament of the FRG, if necessary, combined with citizen enlightenment and mobilisation as a deterrent against outside intervention. The antimilitarism of the *'Realpolitiker'*, on the other hand, is directed more or less equally against both superpowers. Prepared in some cases to undertake what Rudi Dutschke once termed 'the long march through the institutions', this group emphasises the need for Green organisational and technical 'counterstrength' to overcome the capitalist state, which may include temporary working arrangements with the SPD, or at least its progressive elements. These 'realists', represented by Joschka Fischer and Otto Schilly, are less ambiguous than the Ecology-Firsters about the constructive use of 'humanised' and 'controlled' modern technology.

Significantly, the socialist Left has been unable to find a consistent role within the Greens. Former members of various Marxist–Leninist associations, such as Rainer Trampert and Thomas Ebermann, have tended to agree with the Ecopax-First group in its differentiation of the perceived threat of Eastern and Western militarism respectively. But the independent socialists, such as Oskar Negt, Claus Offe and the late Rudi Dutschke—in so far as they do not remain at the fringe of the Greens—tend to ally with the *Realpolitiker* in as much as they are not prepared to abandon the possibility of collaboration with (sectors of) the SPD and trade unions. They are as a rule inclined to seek a fusion between 'material' and 'post-material' opposition groups and to regard the class struggle as the primary contradiction in capitalist society.

Both tendencies point beyond Social Democracy, however. For Bahro, the point is essentially a socio-cultural, rather than a class, struggle. The proletariat is for him no longer a revolutionary force since it has long since been integrated into the capitalist system, as demonstrated by its support for colonialism in the past and the trade unions' system-maintaining function in the present. Rather:

> It is the industrial system itself which is about to undo us—not the bourgeois class but the system as a whole in which the working class plays the role of house-wife. It would therefore be a most inappropriate strategy for survival to appeal to the working class. . . Today it is hard to say whether the small entrepreneur or the worker has the greatest interest in building something like the West Runway at Frankfurt Airport. In Berlin construction workers demonstrated against the squatters because they wanted jobs modernizing the squatted houses. The working class here is the richest lower class in the world. And if I look at the problem from the point of view of the whole of humanity, not just from that of Europe, then I must say that the metropolitan working class is the worst exploiting class in history.[55]

But the middle and upper classes, for their part, will recognise that the interests of survival precede those of class and thus bring about a supra-class 'movement of regeneration'. This is 'not a question of class collaboration but of a compromise in the face of crisis—atom bomb, nuclear power, ecological disaster—that threatens us all'.[56] Bahro proposes nothing less than a 'cultural revolution' to transform a capitalist society which, as it were, is simply withering away without conflict or class struggle. Like the Christian Church, which somehow 'took the place' of the Roman Empire, the ecopax movement will regenerate and transform capitalist society.[57]

For Offe, on the other hand, a successful transition to postcapitalist society must overcome the *veto power of capital* ('the foundation of capitalist power and domination is the institutionalised right of capital withdrawal of which economic crisis is nothing but the aggregate manifestation') while simultaneously avoiding *étatism* ('. . . whereas the capitalist nature of civil society constrains the capitalist state, the statist nature of any socialist society constitutes its major barrier'). He summarises the problem in terms of a 'contradiction': 'Socialism in industrially advanced societies cannot be built *without* state power and it cannot be built *on* state power'.[58]

The Bahro–Offe debate, at least as selectively recreated here, underlines both the strengths and weaknesses of the Green movement. As an essentially anti-political form of politics it is able to address the weaker, ignored groups in terms of their direct, immediate and personal interests and in this way marshal a very heterogeneous reservoir of support. But the moment the problem arises of how to realise their few, consensual ultimate goals in terms of specific measures and tactics, the movement tends to fragment. Moreover, these goals—no-growth society, disarmament, cleansing the environment—are in their implications revolutionary and challenge the interests of practically all organised groups, especially ruling groups, in the state and economy. The problem—and opportunity—for Green politics in the coming decade is therefore how to coordinate these disparate component groups, forge a minimal political programme and confront the problem of power and its use.

VI

The future of politics the other side of Social Democratism will thus depend to a substantial degree on the relative strengths of the SPD and the Greens, and upon their developing interrelationship. From all three of the perspectives implied here, too many qualifiers can be adduced to be able to construe more than a few sketchy projections and conjectures.

In this respect, one and only one tendency is unambiguous: when the SPD's electoral strength declines, the Greens' improves, and vice versa. All the Green 'victories' at the local, *Land* and federal levels from 1978–1984 have correlated with SPD losses. It is noteworthy that the SPD's recent turnaround elections in the Saarland in March 1985 (49.2 per cent of the popular vote) and North Rhine-Westphalia in May (52.1 per cent, combined with a CDU drop from 43.2 per cent to 36.5 per cent) were linked to Green reverses (2.5 per cent and 4.6 per cent respectively). Yet the correlation does not seem to be connected to the material or post-material policies of the Social Democrats. Where the Saarland SPD premier, Oskar Lafontaine, opened the party to the peace, ecology and democratisation concerns of the Greens, thus ostensibly in part coopting some of these issues, Johannes Rau, the North Rhine-Westphalian party leader, of whom *Der Spiegel* writes that he' is above all suspicion of being an ideologue, a left-winger',[59] clearly profiled the party *against* the Greens in pursuit of a 'moderate', anti-radical strategy aimed at re-occupying the centre of the political system.

Naturally, each of the currents among the Greens has interpreted these tendencies in different ways. For the Ecopax-Firsters, the party had co-operated and compromised with the SPD in too many other areas, thus blurring their distinct programme and image. But for the *Realpolitiker*, the failure to develop a coherent strategy based on a solid programme had lent the party an image of confusion, irresponsibility and unreliability. Although it is impossible to assign relative weights at this point, the *Realpolitiker* interpretation is enhanced by a recent poll showing that some 80 per cent of all Green members would prefer to see their party enter into a coalition or other working arrangement with the SPD.[60] These findings would also suggest an emerging tension between the party leadership, which in its majority support a distancing policy from the SPD, and the rank-and-file which want closer links.

There is actually much to be said for the Ecopax-First strategy, however. The West German Greens have grown into the world's largest and theoretically most sophisticated 'post-material' party formation mainly due to their ability to appeal to groups and interests neglected by Social Democracy. Without a clear delineation from it, the Greens stand to be eclipsed in the event that the SPD should find its way to relatively progressive positions on, e.g., disarmament and the environment. Besides, if one assumes, as Bahro does, that the Green movement represents 'the core of a new world order', and that perhaps half the SPD supporters belong to the 'conservative majority' in the FRG of about 75 per cent of the population.[61] then the need for a separate, uncompromising organisation beyond the existing parties, to which converts from the traditional Left (and Right) might be won, is self-evident. For him, this conversion process contains a certain inevitability:

> . . . those who voted Green have, in their thinking come more than fifty per cent of the way in our direction; while those who have now come only ten per cent towards us will in four years have come thirty per cent. The election results give absolutely no indication of this psychological shift.[62]

The problem here is that such assumptions do not allow for electoral reverses such as those experienced in the Saarland or North Rhine-Westphalia. What appears more probable and feasible, in the short-term, is a continuation of already developed locally (Darmstadt, Kassel) or *Land* (Hesse; but failure in Hamburg) based, *ad hoc* cooperative arrangements somewhere between mutual toleration and quasi-coalition. (Joschke Fischer speaks in this connection of a 'toalition'.[63])

For the SPD, still in some measure traumatised by its massive electoral defeat of 1983, yet in opposition freed now from the necessity to link programmatic decisions with concrete policies, the picture is even less coherent.

For one, the intra-party Left remains divided between its materially oriented groups, particularly in the trade union movement, and its post-material elements. Initially, the SPD in opposition appeared to be opening to its post-material side. Willy Brandt's early statement about 'a majority this side of the Union' alluded to a progressive centre-left coalition of all oppositional forces, including defecting FDP members (Günther Verheugen), when that party entered into the coalition with the CDU/CSU, and 'moderate' factions among the New Social Movements. Unlike

Helmut Schmidt, who tended to bypass the party to appeal directly to the electorate or, when required, to instrumentalise it, Hans-Jochen Vogel has been able to incorporate many of the goals of the more than 40 per cent of party delegates who supported a 1979 resolution calling for a halt to the government's nuclear energy programme, the more than 25 per cent of SPD voters opposed to stationing cruise missiles and Pershing IIs in the FRG, and the well over half of SPD voters against Schmidt's policy respecting the construction of nuclear power stations. A party resolution of 1983 reversed the 1979 missile decision that had created so much intra-party opposition and led to the first significant swing of SPD voters to the Greens; but until that decision, the Greens alone among all the parties reflected a majority of public opinion on the issue.

Otherwise, however, the 'post-material' party Left has seen its influence decline. Individual figures like Jochen Steffen have gone over to the Greens or retreated into private life, while Jusos membership has declined steadily despite attempts by their leaders (Johano Strasser) to develop links with the New Social Movements and to carry Social Democracy into state institutions, places of work, etc. Nevertheless, a desire for cooperation with the Green movement is strongest among the Jusos, and they have achieved some important successes at the local and factory levels.

Perhaps the most consistent proponent of 'post-material' concerns in the SPD is Lafontaine. He has strongly advocated reduced defence spending, the humanisation of the state, parties and enterprises, and the development of new, creative employment-generating forms of work, all within the framework of close 'Red-Green' collaboration. This alliance, he concedes, would be essential to rejuvenating the SPD which, due to tradition and inflexibility, would otherwise be unable to undergo a necessary 'learning process'. As a bridge between the two, he sees a common concern for the 'working people' and advocates 'an alternative progress':

> The alternative progress has a name: eco-socialism. It links the struggle against the exploitation of people with the struggle against the exploitation of nature... It is one and the same social structures that lead to the exploitation of man by man and to the exploitation of nature. This insight constitutes the basis of the necessary cooperation between the trade unions and the New Social Movements.[64]

This tactically essential sound assertion, however, is belied by the reservations of a 'material' trade union leadership (notably Hermann Raspe, head of the Chemical Workers Union) that nowadays must be mainly classified as on the party Right, a group motivated by its continuing fear of job losses in a no-growth economy and its suspicion of 'esoteric' Green policies. Yet the labour movement at the same time has not been able to develop an anti-conservative strategy in the absence of political leadership from the SPD. For instance, the unions have failed to organise the now around ten per cent of the population that are 'structurally unemployed', with the result that they are mainly lost to the labour movement.[65] To be sure, grassroots militancy does still recur, especially within the few more radical unions, such as the Metal Workers and Printers, but as a rule the industrial unions remain conservative forces within the party. (At the same time, the historically less radical white collar unions have very recently begun to adopt quality-of-life and environmental concerns into their programmes, thus bringing them into proximity with the party 'post-material' Left—a development which has interesting implications for future realignments.[66]) Also of interest here is the poor showing of the Greens in precisely those areas—the Saar, Ruhr—where industrial workers predominate in the population and make up a majority of SPD members.

The unpredictability of the SPD's future course is underscored by Willy Brandt's recent shift in the direction of a centrist strategy of vote-maximisation. In words reminiscent of Godesberg terminology, the party leader argues that, wherever the SPD operates, it must become as strong as possible in order to win elections or conclude favourable alliances. For him the slogan guiding party strategy is now 'consensus as far as possible, controversial arguments as far as necessary'.[67] Peter Glotz, the emerging spokesperson of the 'technocratic centre' within the party, has concretised the Brandt guideline with his proposed strategy of attracting or winning back the 'new' technical and economic intelligentsia of engineers, bank employees, high administrators, modern artisans, etc. by (re-)opening the party's post-material appeal with calculated references to environmental and peace issues.[68]

The renewed appeal—but by no means yet predominant—of the Brandt-Glotz line of a return to the *Volkspartei* strategy of the fifties and sixties is no doubt related to two important developments: the Rau victory just alluded to, and the mounting difficulties of the CDU/CSU–FDP ruling coalition.

For at least until the North Rhine-Westphalian elections, it had seemed that a combination of rising Green support and falling FDP votes—the latter perhaps to the point of extinction—meant that any successful 'majority this side of the Union' aimed at bridging the ten per cent voting spread between the Social Democrats and Christian Democrats would have to include the Greens and/or seek an SPD improvement at Green expense. Not only the Saar elections had appeared to confirm this, but the obverse case of massive SPD losses (down to 32.4 per cent of the popular vote) in West Berlin, also in March 1985, under the conservative, anti-Green strategy of Hans Apel. Rau's election appears to falsify that equation. If the SPD can now compete for votes at the centre and still pre-empt the Greens, the return to power could be not only quicker but ideologically less painful and entirely within the present leadership structure—perhaps with Rau himself as the party's new chancellor candidate.

At the same time, the governing bourgeois coalition, whose claim to power is rooted in policies that had proved successful in the fifties and sixties, has not managed to deliver on its promises of economic renewal based on further state incentives to business and welfare freezes (which, in periods of inflation, of course amount to rollbacks). Rather more a loose and somewhat contradictory coalition of capitalist and clerical interests, it has been more concerned with a restoration of conservative values and expedient intra-coalition politics than with coherent sets of policies. Therefore, 'serious economic strategy has fallen by default to those central bankers and business leaders who since at least 1980 have been calling for higher profits, tax relief, less welfare spending and a government willing to tough it out until the West German economy becomes competitive again'.[69] Beset by scandals (the 1984 Flick Affair), absolutely opposed by the peace and environmentally oriented New Social Movements, and unable to cope with the contradictions of the (shrinking) welfare state, the Christian Democrats are also very much on the political defensive.

It can be argued, therefore, that the logic of the peculiar situation of both SPD and CDU/CSU is moving toward a renewed Grand Coalition. For the former a big coalition would offer a share of power and hence respectability, a means of winning over (or back) sectors among the 'new' middle classes and 'dynamic' business groups, and an opportunity to over-whelm the post-material Left within the party. For the latter it would restore some of its lost social orientation, reduce the pressure of post-material demands, and assure labour peace.

That the SPD at present is at least interested in a renewed Grand Coalition seems to be indicated by a shift in policy emphasis from the peace and environmental concerns of the immediate post-1983 trauma to one of 'constructive opposition'. It has been prepared to 'bury' the Flick Affair and has shown a sense of 'national responsibility' in accepting the recent limited pension reforms. It has also taken a harder line toward the Greens, e.g. by positing an inseparability of material and post-material issues. Indeed, Rau has argued that the Greens, because they ignore or attack the labour movement, are really 'neo-conservatives'.[70]

If, as seems likely, a party cartel—whether or not in the form of a coalition—should re-emerge, and particularly if the FDP should go under as early as 1987, then the road beyond Social Democracy will almost certainly be a red-and-green one, though the appropriate mix of colours is impossible to foresee. If this 'scenario' should actually come about—or for that matter, even if a *'rechtsgeschrümpfte'* (as opposed to *'gesund-geschrümpfte'*) FDP should survive—this would make the Greens the sole party championing disarmament, democratisation, limited growth, environ-mental protection and other post-material concerns, just as it was until after the 1983 elections. In this case the Greens would almost certainly be able to detach large, progressive-minded sectors from the SPD and, along the lines foreseen by Bahro, establish an independent political party 'this side of Social Democracy'. If this were to happen, naturally, the relationship between socialist and ecopax concerns would become much more intense. But if, on the other hand, the Lafontaine-Strasser-Albrecht Müller tendency should prevail in opening the SPD to the central 'post-material' issues of West German society, the Greens will have to profile themselves very clearly and distance the party from Social Democratism. Most likely, as in the past, the SPD, *so long as it remains in opposition,* will again attempt to have it both ways, and if it does, the intra-party Left would again have to choose between a counter-hegemonic intra-party struggle against daunting odds, or extra-party, extra-parliamentary activity where, this time, a potential ally is already operating 'beyond' Social Democracy.

Either way, the Greens will surely have to develop a coherent 'post-material' programme rooted, however, in the 'material' realities of today. Above all other things, their relationship with actual and potential 'material' opposition must be redefined. For at this historical moment large sectors of the organised and unorganised working classes are alienated from and are indifferent toward Social Democracy. Objectively, it is argued here, 'material' and 'post-material' opposition are ultimately two sides of the same phenomenon: the contradictions and crises of advanced capitalism. The Greens' task, if they are to develop beyond a mere anti-party party, would be to link the theory and praxis of this latent anticapitalist coalition, perhaps in terms of common oppression or the need for democratisation and individual development, or even a common defence of the decommodified spheres of the welfare state. There is of course nothing inevitable about such a link, and only deliberate, determined and patient work in the spheres of economics, politics and culture stands to realise a convergence of interests and action of the two groups. However, the task is facilitated by the nature and composition of the New Social Movements. With their concern for people at their place of work, residence, and in other vital spheres, they are potentially able to mobilise the alienated, dispossessed, frustrated and disadvantaged sectors of the population who would otherwise remain excluded from the political process—this despite their present relatively privileged mass basis. And with their readiness to demonstrate, protest, and employ direct action, as well as to operate directly in neighbourhoods, inner cities, polluted areas, immigrant ghettos and the like, they have demonstrated an ability to enter into the extra-parliamentary realm which (apart from the APO) has hitherto been practically a monopoly of the Right with its presence in the churches, schools, clubs, mass media and other ostensibly 'non-political' areas of social life.

NOTES

1. On this see Ossip K. Flechtheim, 'Die Anpassung der SPD: 1914, 1933 und 1959', in *Kölner Zeitschrift für Soziologie und Sozialpsychologie*, Vol. 17 (1965), p. 584 *et seq*.

2. But do figure prominently in my *The German Left Since 1945: Socialism and Social Democracy in the German Federal Republic* (Cambridge U.K. and New York 1976), esp. Chs. IV–VIII.

3. For discussion and analysis, see *Ibid.*, Ch. II and the literature cited there.

4. For details see my 'Anticommunism in the Federal Republic of Germany', in *Socialist Register 1984*, pp. 164–213.

5. Entirely analogous to the notion of 'Labourism' in Britain, which John Saville has defined as 'the theory and practice of class collaboration'; see his 'The Ideology of Labourism', in R. Benwick, R.N. Berki and B. Parekh (eds.), *Knowledge and Belief in Politics: The Problem of Ideology* (London 1973), p. 215. Labourism, Ralph Miliband argues, is 'above all concerned with the advancement of concrete demands of immediate advantage to the working class and organised labour' which is '. . . not, like Marxism, an ideology of rupture but an ideology of adaptation'; 'Socialist Advance in Britain', in *Socialist Register 1983*, pp. 107 and 109.

6. All the developments described in the rest of this subsection are documented in Graf, *German Left. . .*, esp. Chs. VI and IX.

7. The complete version of Abendroth's counter programme is reproduced as 'Aufgaben und Ziele der deutschen Sozialdemokratie: Programm-Entwurf 1959', in *Der Sozialdemokrat*, Part I: No. 5/1959 and Part II: No. 6/1959.

8. Not without some reservations, I am here introducing the notion of 'material' (or 'acquisitive') versus 'post-material' ('post-acquisitive') opposition in order to develop the following analysis. The dichotomy starts from the assumption that needs and hence demands can be conceptually bifurcated between essentially material needs 'for physiological sustenance and safety' and non-material needs 'such as those for esteem, self-expression and aesthetic satisfaction'. (Ronald Inglehart, 'Post-Materialism in an Environment of Insecurity', in: *American Political Science Review*, LXXV, No. 4, December 1981, p. 881). Material values therefore include a strong economy with job security, an emphasis on tangible, immediate rewards, a predictable and ever improving material environment, and a concern for law and order as well as national defence. By contrast, post-material values are said to be of a different order: quality of life, regional or ethnic autonomy, greater involvement and participation in social matters, debureaucratisation and democratisation of social institutions, opportunities for self-realisation, 'humanisation' of interpersonal relationships, clean physical environment, disarmament, peace, and so on. These respective sets of values are then supposed to correspond to quite different social bases.

9. Viktor Agartz, 'Was haben wir Marxisten zum Entwurf des Grundsatz-Programms der SPD zu sagen?' speech delivered on 5 February 1959, issued as a brochure of the Karl-Marx-Gesellschaft (Munich 1959).

10. For text see *Jahrbuch der SPD 1954/55* (Bonn 1955), p. 354.

11. Theo Pirker, *Die SPD nach Hitler* (Munich 1965), p. 205.

12. Hans-Karl Rupp, *Ausserparliamentarische Opposition in der Ära Adenauer: Der Kampf gegen die Atombewaffnung in den fünfziger Jahren* (Cologne 1970), p. 264.

13. See 'Deutscher Ostermarsch', in *Studien von Zeitfragen*, No. 5/1967.

14. Johano Strasser, *Die Zukunft der Demokratie: Grenzen des Wachstums—*

Grenzen der Freiheit (Reinbek 1977), p. 39.

15. Here see Eberhard Schmidt, 'Gewerkschaften als Garant des sozialen Friedens', in F. Grube and G. Richter (eds.), *Der SPD-Staat* (Munich 1977), p. 87.

16. R. Deppe, R. Harding and D. Hoss, *Sozialdemokratie und Klassenkonflikte: Metallarbeiterstreik—Betriebskonflikte—Mieterkampf* (Frankfurt and New York 1978), p. 13.

17. Only about one-quarter of all SPD members aged 35 or under see themselves as part of a special Juso suborganisation; the others identify with the party directly. Within the active stratum, about half are employed while the other half are high school, college or university students, or apprentices. University students make up only seven per cent of total Juso membership, and only a minority of them are active. See Gerhard Braunthal, *The West German Social Democrats 1969–1982: Profile of a Party in Power* (Boulder, Colo. 1983), pp. 85–86.

18. As formulated initially by Michael Vester, 'Zur Dialektik von Reform und Revolution: Die Arbeitnehmer in der sozialistischen Strategie', in *Neue Kritik*, No. 34/1966, p. 20.

19. Axel Murswieck, 'Ende des Sozialstaats?', in Grube and Richter (eds.), *op. cit.*, p. 135.

20. *Ibid.*, p. 132.

21. Volker Granschow and Claus Offe, 'Political Culture and the Politics of the Social Democratic Government', in *Telos*, Vol. 53 (Fall 1982), p. 79 (italics in original).

22. Otto Kallscheuer, 'Philosophie und Politik in der deutschen Sozialdemokratie heute', in *Leviathan*, Vol. 11, No. 1 (1983), p. 17.

23. See, *inter alia*, Claudia von Braunmühl, 'The Enemy Within: The Case of Berufsverbot in West Germany', in *Socialist Register 1978*; Franz Hegman, 'Toeing the Line in West Germany', in *CAUT Bulletin*, February 1982; and *IMSF Informationsbericht Nr. 22: Berufsverbote in der BRD; eine juristisch-politische Dokumentation* (Frankfurt 1976).

24. Adam Przeworski, 'Social Democracy as a Historical Phenomenon', in *New Left Review*, No. 122/1981, pp. 54–55.

25. A dichotomy which is extended through several of the collected essays of Offe, *op. cit.*

26. Alan Wolfe, 'Has Social Democracy a Future?', in *Comparative Politics*, Vol. XI, No. 1 (October 1978), p. 114.

27. R.J. Dalton, S.C. Flanagan, P.A. Beck, *Electoral Change in Advanced Industrial Democracies: Realignment or Dealignment?* (Princeton 1984), p. 105.

28. Joachim Hirsch, 'Between Fundamental Opposition and Realpolitik: Perspectives for an Alternative Parliamentarism', in *Telos*, Vol. 56 (Summer 1983), p. 173.

29. Andrei Markovits, 'The Legacy of Liberalism and Collectivism in the Labour Movement', in A. Markovits (ed.), *The Political Economy of West Germany* (New York 1982), p. 176.

30. Willi Semmler, 'Economic Aspects of Model Germany: A Comparison with the United States', in *ibid.*, p. 48.

31. Claus Offe, 'The Attribution of Public Status to Interest Groups: Observations on the West German Case', in Suzanne Berger (ed.), *Organizing Interests in Western Europe: Pluralism, Corporatism and the Transformation of Politics* (Cambridge, etc. 1981), pp. 126–27.

32. Here see Semmler, *op. cit.*, pp. 41–46.

33. These examples are given in Jörg Huffschmid, 'Der Primat des Kapitals', in Grube and Richter, *op. cit.*, pp. 71–73.

34. Hirsch, *op. cit.*, p. 173.

35. Kenneth Dyson, 'Party Government and Party State', in H. Döring and G. Smith (eds.), *Party Government and Political Culture in West Germany* (New York 1982), pp. 77–100.

36. See Joachim Raschke, 'Einleitung', to J. Raschke (ed.), *Bürger und Parteien: Ansichten und Analysen einer schwierigen Beziehung* (Opladen 1982), pp. 10–16.

37. Claus Offe, 'Structural Problems of the Capitalist State', in Klaus von Beyme (ed.), *German Political Studies*, Vol. 1 (London and Beverly Hills 1974), p. 52.

38. On this, see Graf, 'Anticommunism. . .', pp. 196–203.

39. Hermann Scheer, 'Die nachgeholte Parteibildung und die politische Säkularisierung der CDU', in Wolf-Dieter Narr (ed.), *Auf dem Weg zum Einparteienstaat* (Opladen 1977), p. 167.

40. To be sure, much of this 'new', 'modern' appeal rested on certain well-tried themes and a nostalgia for the pre-*Modell Deutschland* days of the CDU State. On this, see Jeremiah M. Reimer, 'West German Crisis Management: Stability and Change in the Post-Keynesian Age', in N.J. Vig and S.E. Schier (eds.), *Political Economy in Western Democracies* (New York and London 1985), pp. 233–34.

41. Jutta A. Helm, 'Politics, Stability and Growth: West German Politics in Transition', in *Comparative Politics*, Vol. XVI (July 1984), p. 487.

42. Here see Susanne Berger, 'Politics and Anti-Politics in Western Europe in the Seventies', in *Daedelus*, Winter 1979, esp. pp. 30–33; Offe, *Contradictions. . .*, *passim*.

43. Klaus von Beyme, *Das politische System der BRD* (Munich 1979), p. 93.

44. Herbert Döring, 'A Crisis of the Party System?—An Assessment', in Döring and Smith (eds.), *op. cit.*, p. 213.

45. Jutta A. Helm, 'Citizen Lobbies in West Germany', in Peter Merkl (ed.), *Western European Party Systems: Trends and Prospects* (New York and London 1980), p. 577.

46. As formulated by Hirsch, *op. cit.*, p. 172.

47. Bernd Guggenberger, 'Bürgerinitiativen: Krisensymptom oder Ergänzung des Systems der Volksparteien?', in Raschke (ed.), *op. cit.*, pp. 196–197.

48. References to the 'Green Programme' here are based on: Die Grünen, *Das Bundesprogramm* (Bonn 1982); and Die Grünen, *Was wir wollen, was wir sind* (Bonn 1983).

49. Hirsch, *op. cit.*, p. 175.

50. Ernie Keenes, 'Deep Ecology and Political Economy: The Praxis of Green Politics', unpublished paper, Department of Political Science, Carleton University, Spring 1985, mimeo. p. 27.

51. Petra Kelly, interview in *Der Spiegel*, 11 March 1985.

52. Interview with Dirk Schneider, MdB, cited in Albrecht Rothacker, 'The Green Party in German Politics', in *West European Politics*, Vol. 7, No. 3 (1984), p. 111.

53. Rudolf Bahro, *From Red to Green: Interviews with New Left Review* (London 1984), p. 175.

54. *Ibid.*, p. 179.

55. *Ibid.*, pp. 183–84. Further see his *Elemente einer neuen Politik: Zum Verhältnis von Ökologie und Sozialismus* (West Berlin 1980).

56. Bahro, *From Red to Green. . .*, p. 117.

57. *Ibid.*, p. 179.

58. Offe, *Contradictions. . .*, pp. 244 and 246 (italics in original).

59. *Der Spiegel*, 20 May 1985, p. 18.

60. Reported in *ibid.*, pp. 31–32.

61. Bahro, *From Red to Green. . .*, pp. 229 and 132 *et seq.*
62. *Ibid.*, p. 175.
63. Quoted in *Der Spiegel*, 5 March 1985, p. 40.
64. Oskar Lafontaine, 'Der andere Fortschritt II', in *Der Spiegel*, 5 February 1985, pp. 77 and 79.
65. On this see the interview with Werner Sewing, published as: John Ely, 'Alternative Politics in West Germany', in *Our Generation*, Vol. 16, No. 2 (1984), p. 57.
66. See Rothacker, *op. cit.*, p. 112.
67. Interview with Willy Brandt in *Der Spiegel*, 5 March 1985, p. 31.
68. *Der Spiegel*, 5 March 1985, p. 37.
69. Reimer, *op. cit.*, p. 251.
70. Johannes Rau, 'Nährboden für rechtsautoritäre Kräfte? Die Grünen aus der Sicht der SPD., in J.R. Mettke (ed.), *Die Grünen: Regierungspartner von morgen?* (Reinbek 1982), pp. 188–89. This line of thinking reflects a persistent tendency, especially in the media, to write off the Greens as somehow authoritarian or fascistoid. It is echoed, e.g. by Jean Cohen and Andrew Arato, who assert that 'subverting existing forms of democracy in the name of a more democratic alternative is bound to have authoritarian consequences'. See their 'The German Green Party: A Movement Between Fundamentalism and Marxism', in *Dissent*, Vol. 31, No. 3 (Summer 1984), p. 330.

THE GREEN PARTY AND THE NEW NATIONALISM IN THE FEDERAL REPUBLIC OF GERMANY

Y. Michal Bodemann

> It is in the concept of hegemony that those exigencies which are national in character are knotted together; one can well understand how certain tendencies either do not mention such a concept, or merely skim over it. A class that is international in character has—in as much as it guides social strata which are narrowly national (intellectuals), and indeed frequently even less than national: particularistic and municipalistic (the peasants)—to 'nationalise' itself in a certain sense.
>
> Antonio Gramsci, *Selections from the Prison Notebooks*, p. 241

When the editors of the New Left Review asked Rudolf Bahro to explain why, of the major capitalist countries, only West Germany had produced an ecology party of any importance,[1] his answer was strangely evasive. While Bahro correctly identified the Greens as having a much broader base than ecology alone, he on the other hand not only failed to explain the astonishing rise of the German Greens but he also explicitly refused to acknowledge its peculiarly German characteristics. Although Bahro—who officially left the party at its convention in June 1985—is certainly not representative of overall Green sentiments, the lack of reflection on the peculiarly German nature of the Greens is widespread within and outside the party.

And the rise of the West German Greens is phenomenal indeed, in contrast to Green parties elsewhere: as late as 1973 or even 1974, there was not a single political observer who would have predicted the development of this party; even the movement in its pre-party stage had at that time only begun to emerge; in the federal elections of 1980, they still only received 1.5% of the popular vote, and yet in the federal elections of 1983, they nearly quadrupled their support to 5.6%, just above the forbidding 5% hurdle which no other small party had ever managed to surpass since the 5% law was passed in the fifties. The electoral success, moreover, by no means shows the whole picture. The positions which the Greens have been articulating—from measures against acid rain, nuclear energy, Pershing missiles, patriarchy or racism, to measures in favour of curtailing the power of the state apparatuses, in favour of alternative lifestyles, for grassroots and plebiscitary democracy, new directions in industrial production or solidarities with developing countries—all these positions have begun to find support far beyond the Green Party or its associated movements.

137

The most incisive impact in this regard certainly must have been the radical redirection of the SPD—at least in its outward presentation—from the politics of Helmut Schmidt's *Modell Deutschland* toward Willy Brandt's embrace—a near-deadly embrace for the Greens—of much of the Green agenda, after the SPD's electoral defeat in the 1983 elections. The Greens have had this strong impact for a number of reasons. Most of all, they are far removed from being a single-issue protest party, far removed also from being principally an ecology party as has sometimes been suggested[2] (e.g., Mewes, 1983). Instead, they are hegemonic in scope: their political concerns cover all aspects of society: they claim to speak on behalf of the mass of the population and society at large and both the *Realo* and *Fundi* factions in the party view themselves as the *anti-party party*—as radically different in world view, organisation and lifestyle.

The hegemonic scope of the Greens has not only had an effect on the Social Democrats from where many of their activists are drawn and where they have recruited many of their voters.[3] Even the Christian Democratic Parties, CDU and CSU, its Bavarian counterpart, have adopted pro-ecology rhetoric and to some extent at least, were forced to deal with nuclear, pro-peace and feminist demands. There is hardly any newspaper or magazine, from *Der Spiegel* to that of the influential automobile club, ADAC, a lobby for the auto industry, which has not been forced to deal with the key issues on the platform of the Greens.

The question must be asked, then, why is it that the Greens, with this hegemonic scope, have been able to articulate their positions so effectively, and that they have struck such a receptive chord? Their effectiveness is even more astonishing because some of the leadership comes out of the old, marginalised student movement including especially the ultra-left K groups; others are recruited from the educated to esoteric, often unemployed elements of the middle class,[4] or from progressive elements of the protestant church;[5] they do not fit into the hitherto established political spectrum of the West German republic and they only represent a narrowly delineated band of age cohorts.[6]

In what follows I will try to show that the Greens represent the confluence of a variety of historical forces and actors, many of which are of specifically German provenance, that these historical forces have brought their ideological baggage into the Green movement; and finally, that without this ideological baggage, the Green movement would hardly have been in the position to mobilise the broadly based political support which it actually enjoys—and which it enjoys despite so many and often self-inflicted odds.

Political parameters of the Federal Republic and its extra-institutional opposition
There are different conceivable beginnings for a history of the Green

Movement, and indeed some of its SPD and conservative critics have attempted to discredit it as a late product of German Romanticism or perhaps the *Wandervogel* movement at the turn of the century. (That this genealogy is not without justification will be shown later on.) In view of the fact, however, that no other German language or culture area (Austria, German-speaking Switzerland or East Germany) has produced a Green movement of comparable strength, I agree with some authors[7] that the history of the Greens is bound up most closely with the history of the Federal Republic, and that here is the logical starting point.

Brand *et al* point to the fact that in 1945 many traditional elements of German society, both in terms of capitalist or pre-capitalist production as well as in terms of the social structure had either been effectively destroyed or at least seriously weakened. The development of the West German republic is intimately linked to a particularly radical transformation of the forces of production: in no other Western country could the post-war technological development begin with a similar clean slate, since most of its old industrial infrastructure and the social and political institutions had been smashed either by Nazism itself or, in the course of the war, by its defeat.[8] The party system which subsequently emerged was based, in the case of the CDU/CSU, to a large extent on the churches, especially Catholicism—which was perhaps the single major institution to emerge, virtually unscathed after 1945; the SPD emerged on the ruins of the old labour movement, whereas the small Free Democratic Party (FDP) found its support in sections of capital: its reconsolidated smaller and big entrepreneurial elite.

All of these forces (which, especially through the CDU, allowed new career opportunities for the more 'pragmatic' elements of the old Nazi apparatuses) had the following characteristics in common—and defined the Federal Republic of Germany in these terms: (a) they professed a general modernising, universalistic, pro-industry outlook; (b) they were committed to an effective, centralised state structure with strong involvement in the state both in industrial production and a concomitant welfare system; (c) they accepted the division of Europe laid down at Yalta; and were therefore—the SPD hesitatingly at first—committed to participation in NATO at the cost of a unified German nation-state; and finally (d) all of these political forces in the early post-war period contained vocal dissenting minorities which were resolutely anti-Nazi and either pacifist, anti-capitalist or libertarian-democratic in outlook. Martin Niemöller, Heinrich Böll or former president Gustav Heinemann as well as many lesser known figures in the anti-Nazi resistance played an important role here. Brand *et al* have convincingly argued that these democratic-progressive elements were defeated around a number of important post-war debates in West Germany.

The first of these debates concerned the nature of the post-war economic order itself, and involved on one side the strong pro-labour and socialist forces in the churches, the SPD and even within the CDU at the time—and on the other, the pro-capitalist elements, strongly backed by the Allies. This debate culminated between 1950 and 1952 in the struggle for an effective workers' co-determination in industry. In the end, due to skilled manoeuvres in which Adenauer avoided a major capital-labour showdown, and despite some limited compromises, the objectives of the labour movement were defeated. And the defeat in the *Mitbestimmung* debate in significant ways defined the pro-Western, capitalist trajectory of the Federal Republic on one hand, and seriously weakened its socialist and progressive forces on the other.

The second key debate during the first half of the 1950s concerned the rearmament of West Germany. The anti-militarist element in this campaign found added support from those who recognised that by rearming the western part of Germany, the German division would become irreversible. Despite pervasive anti-militarist sentiments in the population at that time, the anti-rearmament campaign received only lukewarm and erratic support on the part of the leadership in the SPD, the unions and the churches who at the height of the Cold War feared to be pushed out of the dominant political discourse. Much like the earlier campaign for *Mitbestimmung* and the later struggles against nuclear armaments for the *Bundeswehr* (1957–8) and against the war measures act (*Notstandsgesetze*, 1968), these basic debates failed to establish within the existing party structures, any institutional space for dissenting socialist, left-nationalist, pacifist and left-libertarian forces which could have questioned the FRG's defining principles outlined earlier and which delineate the contours of the state itself.

At the same time, the state neither managed to neutralise these forces nor were they coopted by any of the existing parties or institutional building blocks of the West German republic.[9] These forces, marginalised or dissociated from their parent institutions—extra-parliamentary opposition (APO), became a commonly used term—remained partly free-floating and partly, in the Easter Marches for peace and the campaign for nuclear disarmament, developed very provisional outlines of new associative networks.

The Student Movement

Beginning in the mid-sixties, important changes took place in the political climate of the FRG. The Cold War began to abate; with the Grand Coalition of CDU and SPD, the SPD moved into the sphere of power; a new postwar generation appeared in the universities, the Civil Rights Movement in the US and the Anti-War Movement later on pointed to new forms of political confrontation and to broader global perspectives—all of which found the state quite unprepared and clumsy in its reaction.

In this new atmosphere, the role of the student movement which climaxed in the events of 1968 can hardly be overestimated. Any attempt to understand the rise of the Greens must appreciate the role of the German student movement which appears on one hand as the synthesis of the older extra-institutional opposition against the Nato and pro-capital principles of the FRG—indeed the opposition of the 1950s was reasserted here in the opposition against the *Notstandsgesetze* of 1968—on the other hand, the Student Movement emerged as an altogether new force in the sense that it mobilised and politicised new strata and class fractions of German society with explosive force.

These new and largely middle class elements in the student movement were shaped by the following experiences: *first*, the previous political experience of dissent was brought home again—and as a leitmotiv it accompanied the movement throughout: it taught that any political opposition from *within* the established institutional political context was doomed to failure; therefore, the opposition had to be 'extra-parliamentary'; *second*, the new political discourse of the student movement was not part of the older proletarian-socialist discourse and the invasion of Czechoslovakia in August 1968 blocked any such chance; while the movement, to be sure, did adopt some of its elements, it principally represented an attack against existing hierarchies in the universities, municipal and Länder or federal institutions; further, having no direct experience with Nazism, it lacked the anti-fascist combativeness of the extra-institutional opposition of the 1950s; it replaced the old anti-fascism with rebellion against parents and the formulation of new alternative life styles.

Third, the massive physical confrontation with state power left a deep impression on the student movements' perception of the state as an alien apparatus. It made it impossible for this generation to develop any positive identification with *this particular* German state; *fourth*, as a movement with a new political discourse, limited ties to immediate political models and no particular attachment to the West German state, the student movement and its successor groups began to scrounge in the ideological garbage heaps of pre-Nazi Germany: a search began for new national conceptions and alternative social paradigms; *fifth*, and of great importance: as in other Western countries, the demise of the student movement was also the beginning of the new women's movement which started in West Germany around 1971. The struggle around abortion legislation turned a movement limited to politicised women in the universities into a broader national movement. In marked contrast to the previous movements, it claimed to speak for *all* women and thus prefigured the hegemonic scope and the universalism of the Green Movement later on. It also produced for the first time independent female leadership which was to become so important in the Green Movement later on. And finally *sixth*, the demise of the student movement after 1968, its increasing dogmatism, ultra-leftist factional splits, the urban guerilla tactics of the *Rote Armee Fraktion* of Baader and Meinhof and other violence-oriented elements signalled to many not only the defeat of the 'extra-parliamentary' parameters of the movement, but also pointed to new beginnings: a 'movementist', non-institutionalised opposition, despite spectacular instantaneous successes was an easy target for the state machinery. A viable radical alternative to the existing state and its established institutions had to be sought within a cohesive institutional structure.

Citizens' initiatives and ecology

Whatever the shortfalls of the student movement might have been, in one sense it represented a significant breakthrough in contrast to previous extra-institutional initiatives which had all failed to accomplish their political goals: The student movement proved that extra-institutional opposition could be successful, albeit erratically and episodically; and there were indeed significant and lasting transformations of the universities; it did affect municipal politics here or there, and most of all, it provided the umbrella under which the political culture and the lifestyle of sectors of the new middle class could be transformed and could unfold. The discovery that individual citizens could effect change outside the parliamentary system was carried over to a new phenomenon, the *Bürgerinitiativen* (citizens' initiatives) which began to multiply very rapidly after 1968.

Most observers agree that the first citizens' initiatives saw themselves as loyalist, 'positive-constructive' critics largely in the ambience of the SPD and the relatively liberal climate which the SPD-led government provided in the early 1970s.[10] The early citizens' initiatives were localistic and single-issue oriented; to define them as entirely ecology-oriented, as some authors (e.g. Bolaffi and Kallscheuer) suggest, is incorrect. Apart from local ecology related issues (against nuclear plants, expansion of highways, energy conservation, deforestation, urban renewal and for expanded public transportation), the *Bürgerinitiativen* assumed advocacy for 'underprivileged' groups such as foreign workers, tenants, the sick, elderly, the 'Third World', or they attempted to develop better day care, youth centres, opted for new psychiatric care or opposed *Berufsverbote* and neo-Nazism.

In the early phase, from about 1969 to 1973, the *Bürgerinitiativen*, albeit spread throughout West Germany, were entirely spontaneous, local, and still largely urban middle class initiatives. After 1973, a perceptible shift occurred. Especially in light of the massive new public investments under the Schmidt government, in highways, nuclear plants, the proliferation of polluting industries and urban speculation, the ecology element in the citizens' initiatives became dominant; and the failure, moreover, of the local and federal governments to respond favourably to its loyalist critics increased the hostility of the movement to the state and its representatives. As Joschka Fischer, a leading spokesperson of the Greens in Hesse put it, the *Modell Deutschland* of Chancellor Schmidt was ensconced behind anti-terror laws, barbed wire, tanks, computers, special courts and maximum-security isolation jails.[11]

In this second phase, (1974–1977), the citizens' initiatives began to focus their opposition at three nuclear energy related mega projects: Wyhl in Baden-Württemberg, Brokdorf at the Lower Elbe, and Gorleben in Lower Saxony. In this critical phase, a number of essential features of the Green Movement emerged. First, the massive demonstrations and other opposition associated with these projects turned local initiatives into as yet loosely defined regional or federal organisations, for two reasons. Local activists came into closer contact with each other and began to communicate and form organisational linkages; and with that, the awareness grew that it was in the interest of all regions not to get stuck with nuclear plants: the localistic issue was being generalised into the demand that there be no nuclear power plant in X but also nowhere else.[12] Secondly, the opposition was no longer a middle class-based opposition but involved large segments of local farmers, civil servants, traditional naturalists or workers: it was a *popular* opposition which could no longer be branded, by the established parties, as 'communist infiltrated' or otherwise be blamed on marginal elements. Third, the de-localisation of this opposition on one hand, its shift from particular issues to *the issue in general*, and its character as a broadly based popular movement, independent from received ideologies, forced its as yet amorphous leadership to elaborate its own ideology. This ideology began to be articulated at the very point when the Greens began to organise as a party, culminating in their election to the European Parliament (1979) and several Länder parliaments.

The process of party formation, took shape in the third phase of the citizens' initiatives (1977–1980) in which the Greens emerged as an ever more sharply focused and distinct movement. It was the constitutive phase of the Green Party and at the same time a period of crisis for the movement at large. The Schmidt government, under the pretext of combatting the *Rote Armee Fraktion*, pushed for a massive increase in police power, and by encouraging confrontations between the protest movement and the police, there was an attempt to criminalise the movement as a whole. Thus, beginning in 1977, the violent confrontations forced a clear division between those—the so-called *Autonome Gruppen* and *Spontis*—who sought violent confrontation, and the vast majority of the movement which recognised that such confrontations were counterproductive—not least in terms of the popular image.

Precisely those groups which opted for passive resistance and insisted on non-violence were also the ones that formed the core of the Greens as a parliamentary party. By December 1979, with the missile debate in the

Bundestag, the Greens had also clearly moved away from the narrow issue of ecology; they returned to their origins and the *multiplicity* of concerns and now especially began to draw greater strength from the peace movement; the linkage between ecology and peace was provided by the issues of nuclear energy and nuclear armaments, especially as they were raised on the occasion of the Protestant church's convention in June 1981 in Hamburg. Around that time as well, the Greens' four principles: *ecological, social, grassroots democratic, nonviolent*, were given wider currency. The first decisive breakthrough was a respectable showing in the elections to the European Parliament in Strasbourg (3.2%) in 1979 and the subsequent Länder elections in Bremen, Baden-Wuerttemberg, Berlin, Lower Saxony, Hamburg, Hesse and Bavaria, which (except Bavaria with 4.6%) brought the party above the 5% hurdle, before the Federal elections in 1983 (5.6%).

The Greens in the left-right spectrum

With their election to the Federal Parliament, fifteen years after the heyday of the student movement, we have to ask where and how the Greens would fit, if they do at all, in the left-right spectrum of German politics. A straight answer is quite difficult as long as we focus entirely on the recent debates, notably the party congresses in 1984 and 1985. There appears to be a bewildering multiplicity of debates between ecosocialists and ecolibertarians, feminists and gays and lesbians, Christians and followers of the nature mystic Rudolf Steiner, national-romantic populists and authoritarian-reactionary conservationists, anarchists and green-reformist parliamentarians—and above all, between the *Fundis* and the *Realos*—between fundamentalists like Rudi Bahro or Petra Kelly who view parliamentary work as political conscience-raising, categorically reject alliances and political power and use the parliaments as a mere platform to air their views, and Joschka Fischer or Dany Cohn-Bendit from the *Realpolitik* faction who are willing to assume, as has happened especially in Hesse, political responsibility in an—albeit 'conflictual'—coalition with the SPD. It is important to see that the *Fundi–Realo* split is essentially not a left-right division because there are socialist fundamentalists like Jutta Ditfurth, Rainer Trampert or Thomas Ebermann[13] just as there are right-leaning realpoliticians such as Wolf-Dieter Hasenclever or Thomas Schmid, and the disagreements especially in the respective left factions clearly predominate over the common political perspective, as ecosocialists, or whatever.

Further, if we compare the Greens merely in ideological content with the established parties, we find some marked differences indeed: the Greens after all do subscribe to a no-growth philosophy, in contrast to both left and right in the established German political spectrum; they do practise forms of plebiscitary and grassroots democracy not found elsewhere on the Right or Left, and moreover they question the fundamental principles upon which the FRG has been founded and to which the

established parties all subscribe. Most important perhaps, the conservation-
ism and the ecology platform as a whole, so fundamental to the movement, are difficult to classify—and would hardly pass as leftist within the
traditional spectrum.

I would argue, however, that a number of key criteria do permit us to
view the Greens as an essentially leftist party 'of a new type'. First, the
citizens' initiatives drew heavily from, and incorporated, substantive
segments of the student movement. Most important in this respect was the
involvement of members of the ultra-left *Kommunistische Bund* (KB) who
initially appear to have attempted to subvert, but eventually joined the
Greens,[14] leaving the KB, or dissolving local cells altogether. These activists
in particular supplied badly needed political expertise to the initially
politically inexperienced local Green initiatives.

Secondly, the essentially leftist character of the Greens may be extra-
polated from the failure or success of various local proto-party platforms.
Bolaffi and Kallscheuer have argued persuasively that the early Green
Party platforms (1978–80) which at that time participated in local or
Länder elections remained unsuccessful where these platforms were
basically oriented towards right-wing conservationist voters.[15] Green
platforms were similarly unsuccessful, however, where they appealed to
exclusively ecosocialist and traditional leftist voters, as seen in Hamburg
and Hesse (1978) and Bremen and Berlin in 1979. A successful electoral
strategy in turn was based upon a firm centrist-ecologist base open to
ecosocialist and traditional leftist support. This strategy worked in the
1979 Bremen elections where the basically centrist *Bremer Grüne Liste*,
with marginal support from both the Left and Right beat the leftist
Alternative Liste; it worked in the elections to the European Parliament
in 1979 and similarly in Berlin that same year. The Berlin elections of
1981 once again demonstrated that the conservative oriented *Grüne
Berliner Liste* (0.3% of the vote) was no match for the AL, the official
representative of the federal Green Party in Berlin, with 7.2%.

A recent study (Müller–Rommel, 1984) also arrives at the conclusion
that the supporters of the Green Party, its voters, clearly view themselves
as being predominantly on the Left, and more so in 1983 than in 1980.
From that perspective, they appear as a leftwardly moved SPD; the party,
after all, from which the Greens have drawn many of their activists (Petra
Kelly being the most noteworthy example) and their passive supporters.
It would be highly misleading, on the other hand, to deduce from this that
the Greens are evolving towards a German version of a socialist party. The
German Greens are the specific product of the extra-institutional opposition
in the FRG and as such they *are* a party *sui generis*. I will attempt to
demonstrate this in the following sections.

TABLE I

Self-classification of Green voters and of voters of the established parties, within the left-right spectrum, in % (1982)[16]

Parties	CDU/CSU	SPD	FDP	GREENS
N	1081	660	266	193
left	0.2	4.3	1.2	8.8
centre-left	3.5	30.9	11.6	37.9
centre	35.5	49.1	61.2	38.3
centre-right	42.8	11.8	17.3	11.4
right	18.0	3.9	8.7	3.6
total	100.0	100.0	100.0	100.0

Current problems and future directions

In light of the enormous internal diversity and the contradictions within the Greens today, we must ask what the possible future direction of the party might be. Two issues seem of particular relevance in this regard: the question of party structure and organisation, and their overall programme, notably the relationship to and understanding of national German identity as one of the constitutive elements of the party. There is a widespread impression, as old as the Green Party itself, which suggests that the Greens are about to split into several opposing splinter groups. The recent party conventions, however—both the Hamburg convention of December 1984 and the convention at Hagen of 22–23 June 1985 demonstrate that this perception is false; suggested, however, by the strident polemical style in the Party. Despite or perhaps because of the multiple factionalisms—and certainly due to the diversities within the *Realo* and *Fundi* camps themselves—conflicts tend to become neutralised, critical issues are being skirted, and there is a clear tendency toward overall formal consensus or at least toleration of majority positions.

Faced with the constant threat of annihilation—dropping below the 5% hurdle and not receiving any election financing and parliamentary funding, and surely due to some basic consensus against the other parties, the Greens at the federal level have so far managed to stay united. Moreover, the ideological disputes at that level have never been fought to the bitter end. Characteristic for the conciliatory and mediative attitude of the party delegates is the wording of the following resolution, adopted by the Hagen party convention:

> Vis-à-vis parts of the fundamentalist wing, the federal convention of the Greens states: the Greens consider the entire breadth of parliamentary options, from opposition to single party government, as a self-evident range of parliamentary

participation. We reject a voluntary restriction to opposition alone, because this would mean that we would voluntarily leave the government to the political opposition.

This clearly pro-*Realo* stance, however, was in form at least counter-balanced by this message to the *Realos*, in the second part of the resolution:

Vis-à-vis parts of the real-political wing, the Federal convention states: striving for participation in power at nearly any price and as a supposed question of destiny for the Greens would amount to a useless check of fundamentalist dogmatism and is not acceptable for a Green politics which aims at the basic transformation of society.

In place of battling factional disputes, the conventions have demonstrated, as the conservative *Frankfurter Allgemeine Zeitung* put it, a flight into detail.[17] The make-up of the Greens, at the level of party delegates and similarly its representation in the federal and Länder parliaments is made apparent from the way in which one such detailed issue—laboratory animal experimentation—was dealt with: the convention defeated a resolution which called for the immediate total ban of such experiments—a *casus belli* which led Rudolf Bahro to leave the party at the Hagen convention. Instead, the convention accepted a moderate resolution which albeit supporting a moratorium, nevertheless agreed to a limited form of laboratory experimentation with animals for medical research.

Both the Hamburg and Hagen conventions took place before the background of a slump in precisely the social movements—ecology, peace, women's movement—from which the party draws its strength. This slump enabled the delegates, on the other hand, to focus on the organisational-structural issues which at present are most urgent: the question of the electoral platform for the future election, the question of the so-called 'Green structures': the question of rotation (of parliamentarians within a legislative period), financial compensation for work on the party executive (so far unremunerated) and in parliament (presently heavily tithed by the party); finally, the role of non-party members as candidates in elections. And both the slump in the movements as well as the sheer persistence of the party for more than five years has demonstrated that this party, not unlike others, is subject to the Michelsian law: there is a slow but steady development of a party bureaucracy and of party cadres, an evident production of professional politicians which have emerged as pragmatic centrists (sometimes dubbed the *Zentralos*), between the contending factions.

Yet, to draw inferences from the party's present performance at conventions or in parliament to the party tout court, or at the local and Länder levels or to view the *Realo–Fundi* split as a peripheral problem would be incorrect. For one, the *structural problem of the party* does not become fully apparent at the level of party conventions. It does appear, however, at the local level where elected Greens have to face their constituents, the *'Basis'*, or grassroots. Since the party prides itself in its 'movementist', non-structured, anti-authoritarian and non-bureaucratic character, it is also unable to define who its leadership and grassroots actually are and how these grassroots inform the party itself. Claus Offe and Helmut Wiesenthal, in an eloquent analysis of the Green's electoral defeat in the elections in North Rhine Westfalia[18] have argued that the failure to define the grassroots (and presumably the forms of communication between grassroots and party) allows those individuals who are in the Weberian sense *abkömmlich*, i.e., have sufficient time available to be politically active and be present at each and every local party meeting. But at the same time they are not representative of the Green electorate as a whole, and they have undue influence on the direction of the Party itself. These self-appointed representatives operate to the detriment of the mass of the Green electorate, and the central issues which that mass represents: the anti-nuclear, ecology, peace and womens' issues. In other words, peripheral concerns such as animal rights or the notorious resolution from the lunatic fringe which emerged in North Rhine Westfalia before the disastrous *Landtag* election, advocating the decriminalisation of sexual relations of adults with children are made to appear as dominant concerns and thus demonstrate that the Party is not in control of its own agenda. This *structural* weakness of the party—its uncontrolled and undefined (relationship to the) grassroots is supported by and reflected in the unquestioned tenet of the Greens, to be the advocate of minorities *per se*.

The 'New Nationalism'

A second reason why the *Fundi–Realo* split is important has to do with the fact that it raises the explosive issue of the German national identity. This split is a characteristically German phenomenon and a West German phenomenon in particular. As a German phenomenon, it echoes the reform-or-revolution debate in the SPD at the turn of the century; culminating in the SPD's support of Kaiser Wilhelm II's entering the war; but it also appears as a microcosm of the debate in the Federal Republic which I described earlier—the debate since the late forties between the established pro-Western forces on one hand and the extra-institutional opposition on the other; and the *Fundis* are here indeed that group which questions the foundations of the state most radically, whereas the *Realos*, willing to engage in compromise, implicitly also recognise (albeit not necessarily accept) the status quo.

The grave significance of this rejection of the foundations of the West German state by a large section of the Greens has been recognised quickly in France, including the nationalist French Left, who realise that any questioning of the status quo in Germany also challenges the entire post-war balance of power in Europe.[19] It was lastly because they dared to question the post-war order that the Greens became the leading force in the German peace movement. Their argumentation—not shared, to be sure, by the peace movement as a whole[20] runs approximately like this: The Palme Plan, i.e., a nuclear-free zone in Eastern and Western Europe, should be seen as a first step towards the full demilitarisation of that zone. From demilitarisation, however, it is only one more step to a parallel withdrawal of neighbouring countries from NATO and the Warsaw Pact respectively, and towards a neutral status for both East and West Germany; once both are neutralised, what would keep the two Germanys from forming a federation, as *Deutsche Gemeinschaft*, as Peter Brandt, for example, has argued[21]—a federation involving the 'Swedisation' of West Germany and the 'Yugoslavisation' of the GDR on the other?

It is important to see that in contrast to virtually all other post-war nationalist sentiments and re-unification initiatives, this is a decidedly Green-pacifist initiative with considerable support from the entire 'non-dogmatic' left, by individuals with outstanding socialist credentials.[22]

This is not the place for a much needed international discussion of the values or dangers of a German left nationalism *per se*; the question of the new nationalism, however, is important here because the Greens have broken one of the basic taboos of West German politics by lending legitimacy to the nationalist debate. In light of the fact that there is great popular appeal today for this reopening of the German national question and in light of the fact that, as I have argued, the Greens are not in full control of their own agenda, one must ask what could keep rightist-nationalist forces with substantial following from latching on to the Greens and elevating their ideas to a central issue within the Party?[23]

It must not be forgotten here that the Greens are the historical product of a *multiplicity* of forces, not just from the Student Movement and the Left, and that one of the bases of their strength, via the citizens initiatives, was the broad local support by farmers, artisans, workers and petty bourgeois elements in especially the ecology and nuclear issues. It must also be remembered that the right-wing conservationist Greens, to the right sometimes of the CDU[24] were an important element in the con-stitutive phase of the Greens as a party. The Greens, then, also consist of a significant mainstream-populist element; and what would keep these conservative elements from occupying greater space in the party itself? The party-grassroots relations are still undefined and thus open to a variety of wayward elements; and the party's tendency to patch over its ideological differences at the level of federal party conventions rather than resolving them, might easily lead to greater influence of rightist elements in the party itself.

Indeed, it is apparent that every single progressive-green issue has also generated its rightist corollary, often with 'völkische' or Nazi overtones, as outlined in the following chart:[25]

ECOLOGY	pollution-free environment; environmental preservation	pure soil	peasant	
			people and their land	LEBENSRAUM
		Heimat (home)		BLUT UND BODEN
PEACE	anti-NATO			
	nuclear disarmament	neutralism	reunification	
	demilitarised zone in East and West		the German Nation	VOLK
ANTI-STATISM	(against the centralised Leviathan-state)	decentralisation	regionalism/ communalism	GERMANIC 'TRIBES'
				racism, anti-Semitism
		(Eichberg Venohr)[26]		
WOMEN	full equality with men, achieved in part through	autonomous womens' space	biological/ psychological differences between men and women	glorification of motherhood 'female space' KINDER, KÜCHE KIRCHE
			'matriarchy' (Erler)[27]	

NO-GROWTH/ ANTI-CAPITALISM		ANTI-TECHNOLOGY
		ANTI-INDUSTRIALISM
		ANTI-MODERNISM
	(Bahro)	

While there are outright racist and reactionary ideologues who have, for example, used the ecology metaphor to express their racism against foreign workers[28] and where the *Volk* is 'polluted' by miscegenation with the foreign element, their influence has been restricted for the most to neo-Nazis and Rightists in the CDU/CSU. A far more attractive ideological perspective is surely that of the 'national-revolutionaries' who have been lumped with others into the New Right in the Federal Republic, but who might, in the eyes of many, actually pass as leftists of some sort. Peter Dudek, one of the keenest observers of this 'national-romantic populism'[29] has argued that the national-revolutionaries are particularly important not because they have borrowed from the new social movements, but rather, that the new social movements have borrowed many ideas from them. Whether this unidirectional position stands up to the facts or not, it is certainly correct that there is a great deal of communication and exchange of ideas between the new movements and the Greens on one hand, and the New Nationalists on the other, and the idiom of the latter is barely distinguishable from the language of the former. Consider, for example, the following statement by one of the leading figures of the national revolutionaries, Wolfgang Venohr:

> National liberation and anti-fascism cannot and should not be opposites. One must revive the German national pride. The note of surrender in the matter of German history must be torn up. The Long March through the consciousness of the German people must be of a national-revolutionary kind.[30]

The intellectually most brilliant and original figure among the national-revolutionaries is Henning Eichberg, a professor of political science at the University of Stuttgart, with a previous background in neo-Nazi groups and who from there shifted after 1968 to the national-revolutionary perspective, roughly in the tradition of the 'labourist' Nazi Otto Strasser who advocated the 'national liberation from the Versailles Treaty' and who split with the NSDAP in 1930.

Eichberg, an open admirer of the IRA and the ETA (one of the periodicals in which he writes bears the name *Wir Selbst*, a translation of the Irish Sinn Fein) is an ardent advocate of endangered peoples, and of political-cultural regionalism. He is opposed to 'state centralist industrial societies' which, as 'highly technological industrial systems colonise the peoples in the world, deprive them of their national and cultural identity' and in the form of the two superpowers, impose upon them the 'Vodka-Cola culture'. This 'industrial racism began in the holocaust of the Jews' and continues in the destruction of the Romanies, Inuit, and others.

Eichberg advocates a loose 'Federation of German Peoples' Republics', and is an outspoken opponent of the modern centralist state which in his view has abused the nationalist idea:

> Not only is Germany colonised as a whole, starting with the establishment of the allied military dictatorships of 1945, but within Germany there are internal colonies as well. (. . .) There is a straight line which leads back from the Little America of Bonn to National-Socialist fascism with its 'Gleichschaltung' of the regions and still further back to the Prussian-German Reich.[31]

An 'Independent Frisia', an 'Alemannic Free State', a 'Free Franconia', a 'Socialist Saxony' (part of the GDR; YMB) or a 'Tyrolean Republic' are therefore in his view not in contradiction to the national principle (of German identity), 'but only its logical continuation'.[32]

It is my contention that variants of these national-romantic ideas are widespread and they fall on fertile soil, especially because they are articulated in a leftist idiom and with no ties to neonazism, older versions of fascist leadership cults, authoritarianism or militarism. In support of elements of his position, then, Eichberg draws on such respected and largely leftist intellectuals as the writers Martin Walser, Hermann Peter Piwitt, Peter Schneider, as well as Herbert Achternbusch, Peter Brandt and Herbert Ammon—but numerous other intellectuals, left-liberals to socialists of various shades could be cited as well.

Gemeinschaft

What connects Eichberg and the other New Nationalists to significant tendencies in the Green Movement is their common attachment to the idea of Gemeinschaft—one of the most persistent and deeply rooted themes in German thought. Indeed, as I have attempted to show, the key themes in the new social movements—their autonomy and rationality notwithstanding—can all be traced back to Gemeinschaft themes: from ecology to *Heimat*, from peace and neutralism to German national unity, from anti-statism and small units to pseudo-tribal conceptions or *überschaubare Lebensräume* (Kaltenbrunner, in Eichberg, 1984), from feminism to the matriarchal hearth with much wool for communal knitting; and from anti-capitalism, with Rudolf Bahro, back to pre-industrial rural communes.

This Gemeinschaft—and implicitly anti-Western[33] sentiment is well illustrated, for example, in the following rumination by Manon Maren-Grisebach (1982), a leading member of the Greens whose baroque sentimentality cannot be adequately rendered into English:

> Western human beings live mostly unassembled (*ungesammelt*), their inner being confused—and yet, they want to find themselves. So we move closer together in co-op housing, in small groups at night, sitting on the ground (*erdhockend*) or on the grass, and like to be silent with each other (. . .) The circulation of life and that of death flow into each other in a greater circle, which includes all earthly (*erdhaft*) appearances.[34]

There are, however, not one, but two ways in which Gemeinschaft may be contrasted with Gesellschaft. In the first case, it is a view of Gesellschaft as the anonymous metropolis in which individuals are estranged from one another, in a society with neither heart nor soul—much in the way in which Georg Simmel, following Töennies, and later Max Weber, had conceptualised it, and also much in the way in which the young Engels first diagnosed it after his first encounter with the large industrial metropolis in Britain. In the second approach to Gesellschaft, however, the preponderant attribute is not estrangement, but class antagonism, and the abolition of such antagonism in a new Gemeinschaft. There is in

German culture a distinct tendency to dogmatic-abstract principles which end up being so lofty that they may be abandoned without much ado. One historical model for such a conversion is that of the early socialist Moses Hess who later in life decided that history is primarily the history of race (i.e. national) struggles, and only secondarily that of classes.[35]

A similar denial of the importance of class antagonisms—and the class component within the new social movements themselves has never been adequately reflected upon or analysed—is evident in the nonchalance with which some Greens view a federation of East and West Germany. The myth of the old Gemeinschaft is used once again to paper over the obvious (and multiple) contradictions within West German society.

The anti-progressive elements in Eichberg's and many more properly Green theories therefore, all their revolutionary trappings notwithstanding, are thus the dismissal of modernism—the move from anti-capitalism to a romantic anti-industrialism—and the denial of class and other internal antagonisms in favour of an apotheosis of the *Volk* as the historical subject, and whose *Gemeinschaft* character is suggested as a way out of estrangement (and class struggle),[36] as Dudek has very rightly pointed out.

It has been the main thesis of this paper that the Greens represent a fundamental, radical critique of capitalist society and of the modern state, and of German society and its state(s) in particular. It is therefore also unavoidable that the Greens have to address the question of German national identity. What remains uncertain, however, is whether the Greens' radical critique will continue to focus on the contradictions of capitalist society and its form of production, or whether in a new crisis of the party, it might not move away from this critique, embrace the myth of *Gemeinschaft* more fully, and pursue the idea of the German Nation. This latter course is all the more possible because, through no fault of their own, the Greens have been unable to become engaged in an *international* debate— they lack the internationalism of the early socialist movement—they are faced with a Social Democratic Party committed to their destruction, and they are viewed with scepticism by large segments of labour and the traditional left.[37] The encouraging words of the late Wolfgang Abendroth, one of the most distinguished German socialists, are therefore all the more significant. He writes:

> The old generation of the labour movement to which this writer belongs, should criticise [the Greens] with patience and tolerance. In all debates with the Greens, it should always be mindful of the mistakes which the labour movement itself had made, and it should therefore know that a young movement initially without tradition has to learn from their own experience. But most of all, it should never forget that this party, despite all its shortcomings, is one of its most important allies, not only in the struggle for peace and the preservation of Nature and the environment, but also in order to re-establish new starting points of political consciousness in the organisational sphere of the working class—a class still largely estranged from thinking autonomously-selfconsciously about itself.[38]

NOTES

1. Rudolf Bahro, 'From Red to Green', interviews with *New Left Review* (London, Verso, 1984).
2. Eg., Horst Mewes, 'The West German Green Party', in *New German Critique* 28 (1983).
3. Some of the most prominent activists previously from the SPD are Petra Kelly, and Ossip Flechtheim, a prominent political scientist at the Free University in Berlin; the study by Ferdinand Müller-Rommel, 'Die Grünen im Lichte von neuesten Ergebnissen der Wahlforschung', in Thomas Kluge (Hrsg.), *Grüne Politik. Der Stand einer Auseinandersetzung* (Hamburg, Fischer, 1984) is one of several that has pointed to the SPD origin of many Green voters. Other analyses come to the conclusion that voters vacillate back and forth between SPD and the Greens, and the Greens have recently drawn more voters from the CDU in some elections. Cf. e.g. Margrit Gerste's analysis in *Die Zeit*, overseas edition of October 12, 1984.
4. Among Bundestag parliamentarians, there is a striking number of journalists, schoolteachers and booksellers. One parliamentarian is listed as unemployed. See Müller-Rommel, *ibid.*, and John D. Nagle, 'The Greens in the Bundestag: A New Pattern of Leadership Recruitment', (ms., 1985).
5. Rudolf Bahro, *op. cit.*, p. 130 refers to the Hamburg *Kirchentag* of 1981 as an important rallying point for the new social movements. The important role of the 1981 *Kirchentag* especially for the new peace movement has been pointed out by K.-W. Brand, D. Büsser, D. Rucht, *Aufbruch in eine andere Gesellschaft. Neue soziale Bewegungen in der Bundesrepublik* (Frankfurt: Campus, 1983, p. 228).
6. Bernd Guggenberger, 'Zwischen Feldküche und Familientreffen', *Die Zeit*, (German edition of June 28, 1985) speaks of the Greens as an almost pure 'generation-party' whose formative period was the student movement of 1968 and who are today in their mid-thirties. Müller-Rommel, *op. cit.*, p. 129 shows that the majority of Green voters seem to be *below* that commonly accepted cohort, however, (58% of voters under 30 in 1982). Voters above 45 years of age in 1982 amount to little more than 12%.
7. Cf. K.-W. Brand *et al.*, *op. cit.* I have relied a great deal on this excellent and detailed analysis of the new social movements.
8. What did survive, apart from the Catholic Church, were most of the pre-war firms—I.G. Farben being the rare exception—which very quickly resumed their operations with most of its pre-war personnel. Moreover, on the ideological level, no real rupture had occurred, as is clear from the reports of many emigrés who found with amazement how Nazi ideology and antisemitism had survived the war and the post-war chaos.
9. The only party which did indeed support and partly help initiate these progressive campaigns was the KPD. The KPD, however, banned in 1956, failed to achieve significant support after its post-war re-emergence, and the Cold War did the rest to limit its mass potential, having it appear at the same time as the mouthpiece of the GDR in West Germany. See to this William D. Graf, 'Anti-communism in the Federal Republic of Germany', *The Socialist Register*, 1984, p. 179 ff.
10. Angelo Bolaffi and Otto Kallscheuer, 'Die Grünen: Farbenlehre eines politischen Paradoxes. Zwischen neuen Bewegungen und Veränderung der Politik', in *Prokla* 51 (1983), p. 15; Brand *et al.*, *op. cit.*, p. 85 ff; D. Rucht, *Planung und Partizipation. Bürgerinitiativen als Reaktion und Herausforderung politisch-administrativer Planung.* München (1982).

11. Joschka Fischer, 'Identität in Gefahr!', in Thomas Kluge, *op. cit.*, p. 26. A condensed version appeared in *Der Spiegel* 9, (1984).

12. Bolaffi and Kallscheuer, *op. cit.*, p. 66.

13. Thomas Ebermann and Rainer Trampert, *Die Zukunft der Grünen. Ein realistisches Konzept für eine radikale Partei* (Hamburg, Konkret Literatur Verlag, 1984), is a presentation of the eco-socialist position.

14. Anna Hallensleben, in Thomas Kluge, *op. cit.*, p. 157 ff. points out that some of the early Green tickets asked their members to sign a statement declaring that they were neither members of a neo-fascist nor of a K-group organisation. These groups feared that they were being infiltrated by the K-groups.

15. Bolaffi and Kallscheuer, *op. cit.*, p. 68 ff.

16. Source: Müller-Rommel, *op. cit.*, p. 133.

17. *Frankfurter Allgemeine Zeitung*, June 24, 1985, in their report from the Hagen federal convention.

18. 'Die Grüne Angst vorm "Reformismus",' *Die Tageszeitung*, May 31, 1985.

19. The commitment of the French Left to nuclear militarism is analysed by Diana Johnstone, 'How the French Left Learned to Love the Bomb', in *New Left Review* 146 (1984). Johnstone refers to the harsh rejection of the German Peace Movement in French nationalist terms by people such as André Gorz and Jacques Huntzinger. Regis Debray fits the same mould: 'I have always believed that France will once again carry the torch of revolution all over Europe. . . I cannot imagine any hope for Europe if it is not under the hegemony of a revolutionary France holding on to the banner of independence. Sometimes I even ask myself whether one day the entire mythology of the Germanophobe and our century-long hostility with Germany will be indispensable to save the revolution or to save even our national-democratic heritage.' Quoted in Dan Diner, 'The National Question in the Peace Movement—Origins and Tendencies', *New German Critique* 28 (1983), p. 107. Similarly, Mitterrand's patronising Bundestag speech in 1983 and his snubbing of the German peace movement only helped to exacerbate the lack of communication between the French and German Left. Petra Kelly in the summer of 1984 responded with a harsh attack against French nuclear policy, in nationalist terms as well. Too little attention has been paid to this emerging hostility between the French and German Left which has developed concurrently with the Green Movement and its questioning of the foundations of the West German state. See also note 20 below.

20. For example some of the signatories of the conciliatory 'Memorandum an die französische Linke', in *Die Tageszeitung*, May 15, 1984 which has not evoked much reaction in France. The memorandum, among other things, attempted to explain to the French Left why not all Germans are pleased to see French nuclear war heads pointed at West and East Germany. 'The prospect to be "reunited" on a pan-German battlefield of a conventional or nuclear war has led many Germans to recognise that their security interests are different from those of the two superpowers and in part also from those of the neighbours in East and West.' *Ibid.*, p. 9.

21. Peter Brandt and Herbert Ammon, (eds.), *Die Linke und die nationale Frage. Dokumente zur deutschen Einheit seit 1945* (Reinbek, Rowohlt, 1981).

22. Cf. the signers of the *Memorandum* cited above which includes a number of people from the left wing of the SPD and the unions.

23. The following episode from West Berlin in the spring of 1984 illustrates some of this: The *Berlin-Deutschland AG*, a working group that was to develop proposals related to issues concerning the two German states and Berlin, on behalf of the *AL* (Greens in West Berlin) decided to invite Henning Eichberg (see below) to present views of the so-called national-revolutionaries on regional-

ism and on the 'German Question'. His lecture was to be entitled, 'Where does the social-emancipatory content of the German question lie? On regionalism as anti-colonialism and its anti-state consequences.'

In a draft of their platform of May 1984, the *AG* pointed to the anomalies of the status of Berlin and the denial of civil and democratic rights to the citizens of West Berlin, on the part of the Allied powers in the city. The *AG* therefore came to the conclusion that 'in order to overcome the abnormal geographic-political situation of West Berlin, we must ultimately raise the question of German unity, and contribute to its solution. (. . .) Forty years after the war we believe the time has come to surmount the unconditional subordination of the European countries by the Soviet Union and the United States. (. . .) This requires of Germans that they accept the differing political systems (*Gesellschaftsordungen*) on German soil. They (have to) form a confederation of both German states, a "League of German Länder", based upon a peace treaty with the European neighbours, the United States and the Soviet Union, and based also upon the military non-alignment of the two German states'.

Most groupings within the *AL* as well as the pro-Green *Tageszeitung* reacted negatively to the *AG*'s invitation of Eichberg, and the *AL* refused official sponsorship. In a statement to the press, its Acting Executive declared, 'In the interests of the *AL* as a whole and in accordance with our political position, the Acting Executive recommends to the working group to be more sensitive on this question (danger of appropriation by the right) and to be more sensitive in relation to different orientations within the *AL*. The Executive considers cancellation of the event as necessary. For the *AL*, it is politically incompatible to be a forum for national-revolutionaries'. (Statement to DPA, July 5, 1984).

But the *AL* executive had no effective sanctioning mechanisms, and while the *AG* itself eventually backed off from officially sponsoring the lecture, it took place nevertheless.

Another illustration for the inability of the Greens to control its agenda is the emergence of the *Eco-libertarians*, officially set up in 1984. The eco-libertarians consider themselves anti-socialist, oppose social security and present themselves as a middle-class, *bürgerliche* current 'inside and outside the Green Party'. This current, which so clearly violates the *social* principle of the Greens, as one of its four basic principles, has demonstrated that new political orientations may enter the Green platform without being sanctioned by the party itself.

24. Eg., Herbert Gruhl, a former CDU deputy who founded the *Grüne Aktion Zukunft* and was the author of an influential book on ecological issues. *Ein Planet wird geplündert. Die Schreckensbilanz unserer Politik* (Frankfurt, 1975). A conservative CDU peace advocate is the journalist Franz Alt who has had a considerable echo in the conservative fringe of the Green Movement. (Alt, Frieden ist möglich, Munich/Zurich, 1983.)

25. It would be totally erroneous to deduce from this chart that there are firm tendencies in the Greens who have moved to *völkische* or even Nazi conceptions. This is merely to show that these connections can be drawn, have been drawn by critics of the Greens, and are, at any rate, highly suggestive. Cf. Arno Klönne, *Zurück zur Nation?* (Hamburg, Eugen Diederichs, 1985).

26. Henning Eichberg, *Balkanisierung für Jedermann? Nation, Identität und Entfremdung in der Industriegesellschaft* in Befreiung 19/20 (1981).

27. Gisela Anna Erler, *Frauenzimmer. Für eine Politik des Unterschieds* (Berlon: Wagenbach, 1985).

28. 'The inundation of Europe with Afro-asiatic immigrants is not only economical-

ly and culturally, but also ecologically absurd.' Quoted in Peter Dudek, 'Konservatismus, Rechtsextremismus und die "Philosophie der Grünen",' in Thomas Kluge, *op. cit.*, p. 95; Alfred Dregger and other conservatives in both CDU and SPD have used similar language.

29. Peter Dudek, *op. cit.*, and *idem.*, 'Nationalromantischer Populismus als Zivilisationskritik', in Wolf Schäfer, (ed.), *Neue Soziale Bewegungen: Konservativer Aufbruch in buntem Gewand?* (Hamburg, Fischer, 1983). as well as Sigrid Meuschel's essay, 'Für Menschheit und Volk. Kritik fundamentaler und nationaler Aspekte in der deutschen Friedensbewegung', in the same volume.

30. Wolfgang Venohr in Dudek, *op. cit.*, p. 29.

31. Henning Eichberg, 'Deutschlands Balkanisierung? Über die Nichtanerkennung der westdeutschen Bundesrepublik und über die nationale Frage als praktische Distanzierung vom Staat', ms (1984), p. 10.

32. *Ibid.*, p. 11 and Dudek in Schäfer, *op. cit.*, p. 30.

33. The anti-Western sentiment is surely the most disturbing element that has become visible in the new movements, and it derives partly from the fact that these movements are, to a significant extent, cut off from international debates. Dan Diner, *op. cit.*, p. 104 quotes the following from Thomas Schmid, a leading member of the ecolibertarian current in the Greens, published in the influential-chic *Freibeuter:* 'I cannot deny that I am also fascinated by that German proclivity for absoluteness, by that obstinacy and pigheadedness—to get to the bottom of the matter, also to get to the bottom of terror, not to stand still in the shallow waters of common sense, but to be deep, profound and mysterious. In contrast, Anglo-Saxon cultures have different premises, and various life styles can coexist. (. . .) Anglo-Saxon tolerance is a virtue, and we Germans mainly lack that tolerance. But there are negative aspects: to put up with everything, to remain on the surface, to reconcile everybody with everything—this amounts to shallowness!'

From there, it is only a small step to anti-Semitic imagery: 'There is nothing more homeless, hence nothing more rootless, nothing more like Ahasverus than capital. It chases around the globe searching for tax havens, low wage countries and a graveyard atmosphere for investments where it can fill its fat belly on foreign labour.' Hermann Peter Piwitt, 'Deutschland. Versuch einer Heimkehr', published in the leftist *Konkret* 11 (1981), cited in Diner, *op. cit.*, p. 102. Micha Brumlik has pointed to similar anti-Jewish conceptions in some of the feminist literature in West Germany ('Alt, Rinser, Jung u.a. Über den neuen christlich-feministischen Antijudaismus', in *Links* 181 (April 1985). One of Brumlik's chief targets in this essay is the writer Luise Rinser who in her youth wrote in admiration of the *Führer*, and who was the Greens' candidate for President of the Federal Republic, in 1984.

34. Manon Maren Grisebach, *Philosophie der Grünen* (Muenchen/Wien, 1982, p. 23.

35. Moses Hess, *Rom und Jerusalem* (New York: Bloch Publ. Co., 1945/1862).

36. Dudek in Schäfer, *op. cit.*, p. 27.

37. See, however, the very positive debate between socialists and Greens in Klaus-Jürgen Scherer & Fritz Vilmar, *Ökosozialismus? Rot-Grüne Bündnispolitik* (Berlin: Verlag Europäische Perspektiven, 1985).

38. Wolfgang Abendroth *et al.*, *Nicht Links—nicht rechts? Über Politik und Utopie der Grünen* (Hamburg: VSA-Verlag, 1983), p. 24.

THE 1980 AND 1984 US ELECTIONS AND THE NEW DEAL
An Alternative Interpretation

Vicente Navarro

'A main obstacle to change is the reproduction by the dominated forces of elements of the hegemonic ideology. It is an important and urgent task to develop alternative interpretations of reality. . .'

A. Gramsci, Ordine Nuovo, 1925

'They want you to despair. Don't. Change your lenses, and you will see many people where you saw none before.'

W. Guthrie, North American folksinger, 1936

I

CURRENT POLITICAL EVENTS IN THE U.S.: THE HEGEMONIC EXPLANATIONS

According to the most important agents of communication in the Western world, a political earthquake occurred on November 6th of 1984 in the US that is likely to have enormous implications for domestic and foreign policies. The Presidential election was widely interpreted as representing:

1. *An overwhelming victory for ultra-conservatism in the US, strengthening the conservative wave that is assumed to be in motion throughout the Western developed capitalist world.* Not only conservative and liberal, but even many radical authors, accepted this interpretation. For example, a leading radical in the US, David Plotke, warned the British Left in an article written shortly before the election that 'a Reagan landslide would provide the basis for consolidating a durable conservative regime [in the US] for the remainder of the Century.'[1]. This perception is echoed in many voices within the Western European Left that caution against moving Europe to the Left at a time when the ultra-right is strengthening its hold in the US.[2] President Reagan, empowered by what is defined as an 'overwhelming popular mandate', is perceived as virtually omnipotent. Many of the changes taking place in the economic, social and military policies of several Left wing forces in Europe are at least partially explained by this specific reading of the 1984 election.

2. *The end of the New Deal in the US, due to the collapse of the New Deal coalition and the discrediting of the Keynesian policies that sustained it.* Here again, we find broad agreement on this point

158

among conservative, liberal and even many radical authors.* Just to mention a few examples of this position:

- The radical journal *Mother Jones* interpreted the November election as a popular rejection of 'unreconstructed New Deal liberalism. The New Dealers deserved their beating'.[3]
- An economic correspondent for *The New York Times* portrayed the Democrats' 'ignominious defeat in November as. . . a resounding rejection of the New Deal creed of ever-more beneficient government programs that has dominated the Party for half a century'.[4]
- The liberal economist J.K. Galbraith referred to Keynesianism as 'obsolete'.[5]
- Everett Carl Ladd, from the liberal Urban Institute, explained the defeat of the Democratic Party as the result of Keynesianism running afoul intellectually.[6]
- Mondale's main pollster, Peter Hart, after reviewing the significance of his candidate's defeat, concludes that 'the forces that put together the Democratic New Deal coalition are dead. It is past history and indeed we are moving into a new era'.[7]

These are not solitary voices, nor solitary interpretations. They are the hegemonic ones, part and parcel of the new conventional wisdom.

3. *A strong anti-government mood in the country.* This mood is assumed to have been building up for some time and to explain Reagan's success in the 1980 election. People, it is said, are fed up with government, which is perceived—as the Republican Platform put it in 1980—as *the* problem.[8] In the Democratic primary of 1984, the two major candidates—Mondale and Hart—frequently referred to that popular mood and the need for the Democratic Party to learn the lesson of the 1980 defeat. In his acceptance speech to the San Francisco Democratic Party Convention, Mondale called for reducing the Party's commitment to an expansion of government's role in people's lives.[9] In the primaries, candidate Hart went even further. One of his favourite aphorisms was, 'To get the government off your back, [you have to] get your hands out of the government's pocket'

---

*Contrary to prevalent interpretations of US realities, American culture (and language) is highly ideological. There is a continuous redefinition of acceptable language in which unwelcome terms (and concepts) become recast in acceptable terms. In this article I use the American terms 'conservative', 'liberal', and 'radical' with the understanding that the term 'liberal' encompasses (using the British political equivalents) liberals and social democrats and the term 'radical' includes radicals, socialists, communists, and the radical branches of the social movements (e.g. feminist, ecology). I am also using the term 'Left' in a broad sense, as it is generally used in acceptable discourse, to encompass radicals as well as liberals. Only a small fraction of the American Left is anticapitalist.

—a slogan with a clear Reaganite ring to it, which triggered Senator Kennedy's remark that 'We don't need two Republican parties in this country.'[10] Actually, the 1984 Democratic Party Platform was the best indicator of how widely it is believed, among liberals and even radicals, that the lesson to be learned from 1980 is the need to reduce the call for government programmes and interventions in order to solve or ameliorate some of the major social problems that exist in today's US. Despite the fact that never before have liberal and even radical forces (such as labour, blacks and Hispanics, feminists, ecologists, gays) been as visible and active as in the 1984 Democratic Party convention (almost 50 per cent of all delegates, for example, were labour delegates), the platform approved at that convention was *the most conservative and non- (some could even say anti-) New Deal platform that the Democratic Party has had for a long time.*[11] As one example among many, the 1984 platform dropped the long standing commitment of the Democratic Party to a major, still unimplemented New Deal programme: the establishment of a national, universal and comprehensive health programme (NHP).* In its stead, the health section of the platform contained, as a major issue, the need to establish health cost controls and cut health expenditures as a way of reducing the federal deficit. The deficit became a major focus of Mondale's campaign. This abandonment of that commitment to a National Health Program was in response to the liberals' perception that, as David Mechanic, a leading liberal medical sociologist approvingly put it, 'the heavy hand of government causes more problems than it solves'.[12] Although radicals did not share this belief that government was *the* problem, many agreed with conservatives and liberals in perceiving the popular mood as anti-government. Two editors of *Socialist Review*, for example, lamented that 'most Americans accept Reagan's claim that social programs and welfare spending have gotten totally out of hand'[13] and that 'most Americans now believe that the economy performs better with less government intervention and. . . with reduced growth rates for social policy expenditures'.[14] And Dennis

---

*The American welfare state includes two types of social programmes: (1) New Deal-type programmes (the majority of which were established during the New Deal), including a) those that benefit the majority of the waged and salaried population such as Social Security, Medicare, College loan assistance and scholarships; and b) those that alleviate temporary hardship due to short-term job loss such as unemployment insurance; and (2) Great Society-type programmes including those directed at the most vulnerable sectors of the population, e.g. Supplemental Security Income, Aid to Families with Dependent Children, Food Stamps, Medicaid. The overwhelming majority of federal social expenditures go toward New Deal-type programmes. In the dominant discourse, 'New Deal programmes' is a code term representing all federal social expenditures.

Wrong, a leading member of the Editorial Board of *Dissent*, concludes a survey of the 1984 elections with the statement that 'Reagan's electoral victories strongly suggest that extension of the Welfare State, associated primarily with the orientation of the Democratic Party, has lost political appeal.'[15]

4. *A realignment of the American electorate, with the emergence of a new conservative majority, instrumentalised through the Republican Party*, a Party defined by J. Judis (one of the editors of the radical *In These Times*) as 'the most vital political force in today's US'[16] and the party that 'has shown increasing signs of becoming the governing party in the US'.[17]

5. *The validation of the success of Reagan's economic policies.* The Republicans are presented as the party of 'new ideas', responsible for the economic recovery of 1984. Supply-side economics on the one side and monetarist policies on the other are considered innovative and successful components of Reaganomics worthy of emulation by other countries (both developed and underdeveloped). Many European governments (including some left wing governments), inspired in part by the success of Reaganomics, are now pursuing monetarist and austerity policies. Bettino Craxi, the socialist Prime Minister of Italy, has lauded Reagan as an economic manager who knows how to create jobs, and various figures in the Mitterrand government have voiced similar enthusiasm for 'le miracle de l'emploi' brought by Reaganomics.[18]

6. *The urgent need for the Democrats to abandon the New Deal and other 'old ideas' and prepare new alternatives that lessen the government's role in the solution to our problems.* The Democratic Party's commitment to the New Deal and to what is known in Left wing circles as 'statism' is perceived to be the root of the Party's present crisis. This perception is not new. As I indicated before, it was reflected in the Democratic Party's interpretation of the 1980 defeat. It appeared clearly in the response of the Democratic-controlled Budget Committee of the US House of Representatives to the testimony of the President of the AFL–CIO, Lane Kirkland, on May 4, 1981. Kirkland, speaking on behalf of 13.5 million workers and for an *ad hoc* alliance of organisations representing the core of the Democratic coalition (the NAACP, the National Council of Senior Citizens, the National Women's Political Caucus, Americans for Democratic Action, and the Environmental Policy Center), urged an expansion of social expenditures. As T.B. Edsall reported, Kirkland's remarks met with sharp hostility from the Democratic leaders. Such antagonism toward the main labour leader from the 'left' political party would be inconceivable in any other Western democracy. Kirkland was accused of asking 'for more of the same, more

of the New Deal policies that have just been rejected overwhelmingly by the 1980 electorate'.[19]

Before moving on to analyse the evidence that sustains these explanations, let me first clarify that none of them (from the first to the sixth) is new. They have been present in all major media interpretations of each Democratic Party defeat. Every time a Democratic candidate has lost the election (McGovern in 1972, Carter in 1980, Mondale in 1984), the major media have interpreted that defeat as 'the End of the New Deal', 'the Collapse of the New Deal Coalition' and 'a popular mandate to reduce government's role in economic and social areas'. Actually, the collapse and 'end' of the New Deal is one of the most frequently announced events in American media. Only the end and collapse of Marxism is announced with greater frequency and vehemence (*Time* magazine has carried an article on the end of Marxism at least twice a year since 1975, and that average has increased lately to four times a year). Stanley Keller has eloquently shown how remarkably uniform the response of the major media has been to the defeats of Democratic candidates.[20] Let us focus, for example, on the 1980 Republican 'landslide', both because it is considered the starting point of the conservative wave that, according to David Plotke, will take us to the end of this century and because of its great similarities with the 1984 Presidential election.

The 1980 Presidential 'Landslide': How It Was Interpreted
In most media accounts of the 1980 Presidential election, the New Deal coalition also appeared very high on the casualty list. Stories in *Time*, *Newsweek*, *The New York Times* and *The Wall Street Journal* proclaimed its death. The only differeces were in the characterisation of the corpse. *The New York Times* defined it as 'collapsed',[21] *Time* as 'dismembered',[22] *The Wall Street Journal* as 'wrecked',[23] and *Newsweek* as 'shredded'.[24] The *National Review* summarised the prevalent reading of the 1980 Presidential election this way: 'It was the victory of an anti-New Deal coalition that really got rolling in 1968, when George Wallace and Richard Nixon between them put together a 60 to 40 landslide against the liberal candidate, H. Humphrey', and 'reached into all sections of the country when Nixon achieved his 49 state trouncing of George McGovern'.[25] Jimmy Carter, in this perception, was 'an aberration, historically considered',[26] whose Presidency was made possible by the Watergate scandals. The same media referred to Reagan's 1980 victory as 'stunning', 'decisive', a 'shocker', 'stupefying', 'roaring', a 'landslide', 'the most astonishing landslide in election history', the '80 quake', a 'tidal "wave",' and 'A Mt. St. Helen of disappointment and anger [for Democrats]'.[27]

The overwhelming message presented by the media was that Reagan's 'decisive' landslide was a vote and a popular mandate for conservatism. As the liberal Anthony Lewis of *The New York Times* put it, 'What happened in the 1980 election reflected a profound and general turn to conservatism in the country.'[28] Thus, an enormous ideological avalanche took place that was consciously reproduced by conservative, liberal and even many radical authors. Left wing weeklies such as *The Nation* and *In These Times* lamented that enormous conservative mandate, a mandate that has overwhelmed, confused and paralysed large sectors of the Left in the US for quite some time.

Forgotten or left aside in this ideological avalanche were the following facts:

1. *Reagan's share of the total potential vote (26.6 per cent) was the third lowest of any winning candidate since 1932.*[29] Reagan captured only a slightly higher percentage of the American electorate in 1980 than Ford did in 1976.[30] The difference between the Republican vote in 1976 (26.2 per cent) and in 1980 (26.6 per cent) was less than .5 per cent, hardly the basis for defining that victory a landslide in favour of conservative Republicanism. Actually, Reagan's share of the total popular vote (50.9 per cent) barely exceeded that of Jimmy Carter in 1976 (50.4 per cent). Fourteen of the twenty winning candidates in this century had done as well.[31] What liberals and radicals do not seem to realise is the bias of the US electoral system that clearly favours bipartisanism. Very small changes in electoral support produce large landslides in electoral results. For each percentage of the major party vote that Reagan won nationally, he won 1.64 per cent of the electoral vote and 1.56 per cent of the states.[32] In spite of the hyperbolic reporting, there was no landslide in 1980.

2. *Voter support for Reagan was very soft.* According to the Gallup post-election poll, 37 per cent of voters decided to vote for Reagan during the last week of the 1980 campaign.[33] Three surveys found that about 10 to 12 per cent made their decision on the very last day.[34] Actually, the commitment of voters to candidates in 1980 was unusually weak.[35] For example, in mid-October, only a few days from polling day, 43 per cent of Reagan's adherents among registered voters were 'more interested in voting against Carter than for Reagan',[36] which speaks more of the unpopularity of Carter than of the popularity of Reagan. On election day, a quarter of the voters indicated that they had voted for the 'lesser of evils' while only 6 per cent indicated they voted for 'the better of goods'. The ratio of the former over the latter was the highest for any election since 1952.[37] Moreover, in the Gallup Poll of popularity of Presidential candidates, conducted since 1952, Reagan emerged as the third least popular (after McGovern and Goldwater) of all the Democratic and Republican Presidential candidates since 1952. And among successful candidates, Reagan was the least popular of

all.[38] Contrary to what the press was saying, polls were showing that Reagan was the least popular winning candidate since 1952.

3. *The 1980 election did not reflect support for the Republican Party.* On the contrary, the popularity of both major parties, Democrats and Republicans, has been declining since the 1960s and continued to decline in 1980, the year of the alleged 'outstanding' Republican victory. In a 1980 *CBS/New York Times* poll, only 17 per cent of the public gave the Republican Party a 'highly favorable' rating compared with 25 per cent in 1970 and 34 per cent in 1967. An impressive decline in popularity! In the same year, only 28 per cent of the public gave the Democratic Party a 'highly favorable' rating, down from 35 per cent in 1970 and 42 per cent in 1967. In brief, we saw a decline of popularity of both major parties during the 1970s, particularly accentuated in the case of the Republican Party.[39]

4. *The Gallup Poll found no more voters describing themselves as 'right of centre' in 1980 than it had in 1976.*[40] In fact, Louis Harris polls have noted a decline since 1968 in the proportion of the electorate describing itself as 'conservative'.[41] Moreover, Warren E. Miller, reporting respondents' self-placement on the seven point liberal-conservative scale in the University of Michigan 1980 National Election Study, observed: 'Despite the swirl of controversy over the magnitude of the Nation's swing to the right, our data give little support to the view that there has been any dramatic change, at least since 1972. The proportion of self-declared liberals and conservatives has remained virtually constant, with at most a drift favoring conservative positions.'[42]

5. *Popular support for New Deal-type programmes (such as Social Security and Medicare) and Great Society programmes (such as food stamps and Medicaid programmes) remained undiminished.* All major polls in 1976–1980 (continuing to 1984) have shown vehement popular support for the core programme of the New Deal (Social Security), with 92 to 96 per cent of the population opposing cuts in this programme. Also, in 1979, 1980 and 1981, large majorities opposed cuts in federal aid programmes benefitting the elderly, poor, and handicapped; in general health programmes; and in federal aid to education.[43] Moreover, large majorities were in favour of expanding rather than reducing government regulations to protect the health and safety of consumers, workers and the environment.[44] Again, it is worth repeating that the evidence showing there was not a popular mandate to reduce social expenditures on either New Deal or Great Society types of programmes was overwhelming. The popularity of the most important New Deal programme—Social Security—was so solid that all candidates in 1980 felt obliged to

make the promise (later broken by President Reagan) that Social Security was here to stay and would not be cut. Considering this popularity of the major New Deal programme, the news of the death of the New Deal was not only premature but greatly overstated.

It speaks of the overwhelming power of the dominant ideology (and of the class interests it represents) that, in spite of the clear evidence that in the 1980 Presidential election there was neither (1) a move to the right by the American people nor (2) a popular mandate to carry out anti-New Deal and anti-Great Society policies, the two sides of the political spectrum—Republicans and Democrats—interpreted the 1980 elections in precisely the same way: a popular mandate to reduce government intervention, including social expenditures. Consequently, in March 1981, just a few months after the 1980 election, the Congress passed unprecedented anti-New Deal and anti-Great Society legislation. Senator Daniel Patrick Moynihan told his colleagues in the Budget Committee that, responding to the popular mood and mandate, 'We have undone thirty years of social legislation in three days.'[45] The vote for that undoing was unanimous, and included leading liberals such as Senators Moynihan, Gary Hart of Colorado, Howard M. Metzenbaum of Ohio and Donald W. Riegle, Jr., of Michigan. The liberal Democrats had read the 1980 election in the same way as their Republican colleagues. Gary Hart (rehearsing his short-lived bid for the Presidency in 1984) would later repeat one of his favourite themes, 'The failure of the liberal wing of the Democratic Party is that it has run out of ideas with its continued adherence to the New Deal.'[46]

The conclusion that Congressional leaders of the Democratic Party have drawn from the defeats of recent Democratic candidates (McGovern in 1972 and Carter in 1980) is that they need to abandon or soft pedal their commitment to the New Deal and other 'old ideas'. A detailed examination of these two defeated candidates, however, shows that neither could be called a New Dealer. McGovern (whose head of staff was Gary Hart) did not run his 1972 Presidential campaign on a New Deal platform, nor was he perceived as a New Dealer. He de-emphasised the expansion of social programmes, abstaining, for example, from calling for a National Health Programme. Actually, he was even perceived as anti-labour by large sectors of the union movement. Not only as a result of McGovern's stance on foreign policy issues but also because of his economic and social policies, labour, for the first time in many years, did not support the Democratic candidate. McGovern lost and Nixon won another 'landslide'. The evidence shows, however, that had McGovern campaigned primarily on New Deal issues, the Republicans would have suffered a resounding defeat.[47]

Carter, on the other hand, was elected in 1976 on a platform that included the expansion of New Deal programmes, such as the establishment of a National and Comprehensive Health Program and the expansion of Public Service Employment.[48] The reality of his term was quite different: none of these proposals was enacted. Actually (and contrary to what he promised), federal social spending as a percentage of GNP was reduced under Carter's Administration. For the first time in twenty years, social expenditures ceased their upward trend and actually started to decline.[49] The annual real growth rate of federal social programme spending was more than halved under President Carter from its levels under Presidents Kennedy through Ford. This growth rate, which was 7.9 per cent under Presidents Nixon and Ford, dropped to 3.9 per cent under President Carter.[50] Thus, Carter's defeat in 1980 can hardly be attributed to an expansion of New Deal programmes. In fact, it was Carter's failure to act on his stated commitment to these programmes that further contributed to the image of poor leadership he came to acquire in the latter part of his term and that explains in large degree his unpopularity in the 1980 election. The annual growth rate of social expenditures has further declined during the Reagan administration, to 1.5 per cent.[51] However, many of Reagan's most brutal attacks in social programmes had their origins in the Carter Administration. As Arthur Schlesinger has indicated, Carter was the most conservative Democratic President since Grover Cleveland.[52]

THE 1984 PRESIDENTIAL ELECTION: QUESTIONING THE HEGEMONIC INTERPRETATION

Not uncharacteristically, the defeat of candidate Mondale in the 1984 Presidential election was presented as (a) an overwhelming landslide for Reagan, (b) the outcome of a conservative mood in the country, (c) proof of the death of the New Deal and the collapse of the New Deal Coalition, and (d) a mandate to continue the anti-government policies carried out by Reagan in his first term. According to that interpretation, Reagan had indeed convinced the American people that Government was the problem, not the solution.

As in 1980, conservatives, liberals and even some radical voices interpreted the 1984 election in remarkably similar ways. And, once again, left and liberal forces felt overwhelmed and defeated. Forces within the Democratic Party immediately started a witch hunt, trying to finger those responsible for the loss of the United States to the Republicans. Two editors of *Dissent* accused the 'extreme' Left of causing the defeat of the moderate and 'reasonable' Left. Jeremy Larnor blamed the Jackson campaign for Mondale's defeat, claiming it frightened whites and drove them to vote for Reagan.[53] Along the same lines, Joseph Clark placed the blame with the anti-Vietnam war movement of the 1960s, supposedly responsible for discrediting Left wing positions in the US through their association with a communist movement—the NLF of Vietnam.[54] Although these accusations are extreme and not representative, they are nevertheless symptomatic of the Democratic response to the defeat; i.e. the search for culprits within the Left. The rise of ultraconservatism and the collapse of the New Deal is otherwise presented as an unquestionable fact.

Although the detailed analysis of people's opinions, popular moods and popular electoral behaviour has yet to be prepared, enough information is already available to enable us to question these hegemonic interpretations of the 1984 Presidential election. Just as the dominant interpretation of the 1980 election was wrong, the dominant interpretation of the 1984 election is equally inaccurate. Let me be specific and present information that questions each interpretation.

The Death of the New Deal: Once Again?

Regarding the alleged overwhelming wave toward conservatism, it is worth noting that only 6 per cent (just one per cent more than in 1980) of voters in 1984 indicated that they voted for Reagan because of his ultra-right and conservative philosophy.[55] They voted for Reagan primarily because they felt that the recent economic recovery (starting in late 1983) was benefitting them or was likely to benefit them in the near future. One has to remember that just a year and a half before the 1984 election, during the depression of 1982–83, Reagan was the most unpopular of the last six Presidents. None of the prior six presidents had sunk this low after just twenty-four months in office. As indicated by W.C. Adams, 'Reagan's scores declined so dramatically, they quickly reached the depths of those given Lyndon Johnson in 1968, Richard Nixon during Watergate, and Jimmy Carter after prolonged economic and hostage agony. This comparison alone ought to debunk the myth of the teflon president.' The unimpressive Reagan recovery after 1982 was the outcome of the economic 'recovery'. But, even with this 'recovery', Reagan's rebound in the polls from 35 per cent approval rating (January 1983) to 57 per cent (September 1984) was rather weak. Carter and Ford had enjoyed higher rebounds in the polls than Reagan.[56] It was the economic recovery (to be explained later) that led to that increase of electoral support for the Reagan Administration but not for the Republican Party. According to a Pen-Schoen Poll taken after the election, almost half of the electorate did not believe that the Republicans had proved they knew how to run the country. Also, two-thirds disagreed with the assertion that the country is best served by a Republican during times of serious economic problems and half suggested that Reagan's performance in office had not changed their opinion of the Republican Party. A plurality indicated that they would prefer to support a Democratic candidate for President in 1988.[57]

As for the so-called popular mandate to cut social expenditures, the exit polls on election day, as well as other polls, show very clearly that there was not popular support for Reagan's austere social policies. Polls carried out on election day (exit polls) found overwhelming support for both New Deal and Great Society programmes; 80 per cent of voters expressed support for equal or more social expenditures and only 15 per cent said they were for cutting funds for these programmes.[58] Moreover, favourable views of Great Society type of programmes increased between 1980 and 1984 according to *The New York Times/CBS News Poll:* The proportion of people saying that such programmes 'had made things better' rose from 31 per cent in 1980 to 41 per cent in 1984, while the percentage maintaining that these programmes 'had made things worse' fell from 21 per cent in 1980 to only 19 per cent in 1984.[59] And in January 1984, at the height of the debate about how to reduce the federal deficit, 95 per cent of those questioned in *The Washington Post/ABC News Poll* vehemently opposed any cuts in Social Security and 62 per cent opposed cuts in general social programmes while only 23 per cent opposed cuts in the defence budget.[60] Election Day referendums are another indicator of support for social expenditures. More pro-social than anti-social expenditure referendums were approved. Although California's rejection of cuts in welfare benefits was the most publicised, there were many other referendums that showed broad support for social expenditures.[61] The evidence is clear; the popular support for New Deal and Great Society programmes had not diminished on election day. The popular support for those programmes has been high and constant during all the years of the Reagan Administration. Poll after poll, year after year, the evidence is overwhelming. Let's start with 1981, the first year of the Reagan Administration. In the September 1981 Harris Poll, which asked respondents to identify specific cutbacks that were less preferable than 'not balancing the federal budget', the majority indicated that 'federal aid to the elderly, poor and handicapped', 'federal health programs', and 'federal aid to education' should not be cut.[62] In the February 1981 *Washington Post/ABC News Poll*, two-thirds of respondents, incidentally, agreed that 'the government should work to substantially reduce the income gap between the rich and the poor', precisely the opposite of what government policy was at the time and continues to be. Regarding government regulation, the October 1981 *CBS/New York Times Poll* found that 67 per cent of respondents wanted to maintain present environmental laws even at the cost of economic growth.[63]

Opposition to any reduction of government expenditures for the poor, elderly, and handicapped and for health services also extended to state and local governments' expenditures. For example, *The New York Times* reported on February 4, 1982[64] that a 1982 opinion poll (sponsored by the Federal Advisory Commission on Inter-government Relations) found that the public, if faced with the necessity to accept cutbacks in state and local government services, would prefer cuts in assistance to parks and recreation, colleges and universities, and streets and highways over aid to the needy. Only 7 per cent favoured cuts in services to the needy.

Thus, there is very strong evidence that people oppose any reduction of government expenditures for the handicapped, poor, elderly, and for health and education. Professors Carl Ladd and S.M. Lipset,[65] after reviewing available evidence, concluded that the same polls that found the public would like to reduce 'welfare' also found that they opposed cuts for the elderly and special education or services for blacks, the poor, the handicapped, or the needy. Also, they found that the majority of people continued to support the welfare state.

As to 1982, the second year of the Reagan Administration, the March 1982 CBS/New York Times Poll on priorities among alternatives to reduce the federal deficit found that the proposal to cut spending on programmes for the poor had less support (29 per cent) than proposals to reduce the size of income tax cuts (59 per cent) and reduce proposed spending on military and defence (49 per cent). People were asked: 'To reduce the size of the federal deficit, would you be willing or not willing to have the government reduce proposed spending on programs for the poor?' Only 29 per cent said they would be willing, while 63 per cent said they would not be. Even the most maligned of the transfer programmes, Aid to Families with Dependent Children and Food Stamps, were supported by 57 per cent of the respondents.[66] Similarly, one of the leading pollsters in the country, Lou Harris, indicated in 1982 that his polls since 'the end of [1981] have been showing that by a very large majority (84% to 12%), the American people do not want any rollback on the requirements of the Clean Air Act; that by 62% to 34% Americans would prefer military spending be cut before health programs; a huge majority, 75% to 22%, do not want cuts in Medicare or Medicaid; by 63% to 30% a majority opposes a ban on abortions'. Harris further added 'When people are asked whether to cut Medicare or defense, they vote to save Medicare by four to one; and when Medicaid is pitted against defense, it wins three to one.' He concluded: 'People all over the country have been profoundly shocked to find that the people running the country seem to be in favor of segregation, seem to want to abolish abortion and birth control, seem to want to abandon the poor and the elderly and the minorities. . . and that the American people [think] that America could well be systematically stripped of all its compassion for decency and humanity. . . but they are just beginning to get fighting mad about it. . .'[67]

During 1982, there was also a high and continuous support for government regulations to protect workers, consumers, and the environment. Regarding industrial safety, 75 per cent of the respondents in a nationwide poll indicated that they favoured keeping without weakening the current government regulations aimed at protection of workers against actual and potential damage.[68] Similar levels of support for social expenditures and for government regulations to protect workers, consumers, and the environment appeared in all major polls in 1983 and 1984.[69]

In summary, for many years, poll after poll has shown that the majority of Americans do not want cuts in social and health care programmes or in programmes for the elderly, the poor, and the needy. Nor do they want a weakening of the health protection of the worker, the consumer, and the environment. Also, and contrary to widely held belief, the majority of Americans favour *more*, not less, government intervention in supporting people's lives and welfare. For example, in the health sector, most Americans would be willing to pay even higher taxes if those taxes were spent on health services; feel that there is a need for national health insurance, which would require greater government intervention; think that the benefits of government regulation or the costs of medical services and drugs outweigh the drawbacks; and support federal control of doctors' fees, hospital costs, and prescription drugs.[70] And the size of those majorities has increased rather than declined during the Reagan years, forcing the influential *National Journal* to warn the US establishment that people are asking for 'creeping socialism'.[71] As John P. Robinson and J.A. Cleisman have written, the shift in popular opinion seems to be more in the liberal or anti-conservative direction since Reagan's election in 1980.[72] And Lipset, after reviewing all popular opinion polls, concluded that during all these years, 'most Americans remain more liberal (Left) than the President on economic, defense, foreign policy, and social questions'.[73] Even Senator Paul Laxalt, a close friend of Reagan and the Chairman of the Republican National Committee, noted 'the strange phenomenon that most Americans. . . are opposed to much of what the President supports'.[74]

On the basis of all this data, it is clear that (1) the level of popular support for New Deal and Great Society type of programmes has been and continues to be very high for the former and high for the latter; (2) there has not been a popular mandate to cut social expenditures—to the contrary, the mandate has been to maintain and even expand social expenditures and government social regulation and interventions; and (3) the defeat of the Democratic candidates in 1972 (McGovern), 1980 (Carter) and 1984 (Mondale) cannot be attributed to their very limited, even non-existent commitment to expand the New Deal and other forms of social expenditures.

The Collapse of the New Deal Coalition: Again?

As for the collapse of the New Deal coalition (labour and minorities), it is worth noting that the percentage of individuals from union households, blacks, Hispanics, Jews and the unemployed (the core of the coalition) who voted Democratic actually increased in 1984 over 1980. 53 per cent of union households, 90 per cent of blacks, 65 of Hispanics, 66 per cent of Jews, and 68 per cent of the unemployed voted for Mondale in 1984, compared with 48 per cent of union households, 85 per cent of blacks, 59 per cent of Hispanics, 45 per cent of Jews, and 51 per cent of the un-employed who voted for Carter in 1980.[75] If instead of union households (that includes families), we consider union members, then 57 per cent voted for the Democratic candidate.[76] And if we include AFL–CIO members (excluding the pro-Reagan teamsters), then 60 per cent of labour union members voted for Mondale. Some sectors of labour, like the steel-workers, voted Democratic 66 per cent.[77] The overall percentage of blue- and white-collar workers voting for a Democratic Presidential candidate was virtually the same in 1984 as in 1980. In light of these figures, the contention that the New Deal Coalition collapsed or that labour unions have abandoned the Democratic Party seem questionable. Moreover, while the Democratic Party lost the Presidential election, it did not lose in the many Congressional, state house and gubernatorial elections that were taking place at the same time. Nearly 65 per cent of all elective positions were won by Democrats in 1984, with the New Deal coalition playing an important role in these victories. For example, 63 per cent of the union-backed candidates for Congressional seats and governorships won.[78] Actually, the news of the evening on election day was the failure of Reagan's victory to carry other Republicans in on its coat-tails. The anger and frustration of the ultra-right was justified. As a leading figure of the ultra-right, Richard Viguerie, indicated, 'The 1984 election will rank amongst the all time greatest blunders in American politics because Reagan double crossed lower level Reaganite candidates.'[79] As The Economist noted, the November election was a victory for Reagan but not for the Republican Party: 'The US Congress, instead of becoming more conservative, turned out to be a bit more liberal.'[80] Equally important is the realignment of Democratic forces within the US Congress, with fewer conservative members occupying key positions than in 1980 or 1982. The powerful US House Budget Committee, for example, is now chaired by Representative W.H. Gray, a member of the Black Caucus—without doubt the most progressive caucus within the US Congress.[81] It is important to stress that these changes are not earth shattering. However, in the US, political progress is always measured in millimetres, not miles, and small changes make a difference. For example, they can make the difference between Congressional support for, or opposition to, assistance to the 'contras' in Nicaragua, or acceptance of, or resistance to, cuts in social consumption.

In the State Legislatures and Governorships, the Democrats continued to hold an overwhelming majority. In all those Democratic elections, the New Deal coalition (labour and minorities) continued to play a critical supportive role. Similarly, they have played a critical role in the last Municipal Elections in the US, in which there has been a shift towards the left (towards less conservative mayors) rather than towards the right.

Coleman Young in Detroit, Wilson Goode in Philadelphia, Tom Bradly in Los Angeles, Harold Washington in Chicago, Thurman Milner in Hartford, and Flynn in Boston, won because of labour-minority alliances. This labour-minority alliance also played a pivotal role in putting in the Democratic column the twenty largest urban centres of the US in the last Presidential election.[82]

It is difficult to conclude from all this data that the New Deal coalition has collapsed. The New Deal coalition is very much alive, and has recently broadened its base to include feminists and ecologists, two important mass movements in the US. Although conservative forces from both parties would like the American people to believe that the New Deal coalition is indeed dead, the reality is another matter. Actually, what we are witnessing in today's US parallels the situation in Western Europe: a shift within the Left or progressive parties, with movement to the Left in local municipal elections and a shift to the Right (explained by 'national and international economic and political imperatives') at the national level.

In light of the data presented so far, what needs to be explained is not the defeat of Mondale but rather the support that he received from the bases of the Democratic Party, of which the New Deal Coalition was a key one. Mondale's main campaign platform was to reduce the federal deficit by raising taxes. He even indicated that there was a need to reduce social consumption as a way of reducing the deficit, as if those social expenditures were responsible for the deficit. Despite evidence to the contrary (to be shown later), Mondale seemed to share the belief, expressed by pollster Daniel Yankelovich, that 'the growth of the welfare state imposes heavy constraints in the economy, while the slow growth of the economy chokes off the support the welfare state needs if it is to thrive'.[83] Although reduction of the deficit was the main issue in Mondale's campaign, only 5 per cent of the American people considered this to be an important issue[84] and only 12 per cent felt that Reagan was responsible for the deficit.[85] There is significant evidence that the American people are willing to pay higher taxes if these extra revenues go to provide social services for all the population, e.g., a National Health Programme.[86] However, they are certainly not willing to pay extra taxes to cover an abstract category, called 'the deficit'. In brief, Mondale did not run as a New Dealer, nor was he perceived as such. He was running *away from* the New Deal, not to be identified as such. *The New York Times* characterised his economic and social policies as 'bluntly conservative'.[87] In spite of this, the bases of the Democratic Party supported Mondale (1) out of party loyalty, (2) because many share the assumptions of the dominant ideology (see my remarks about the Democratic Platform) and (3) above all, because of a strong perception among the New Deal coalitions that Reagan was the most anti-labour and anti-minority President that the US had had during this century.

A final point of clarification. What I have said so far should not lead to the opposite conclusion that Mondale would have won had he made the commitment to establish a National Health Programme (or any other New Deal programme) a central issue in his campaign. To defeat an incumbent President is very difficult indeed in the US. Presidential patronage, as well as Presidential influence in creating economic, social and 'media events', cannot be underestimated. Only one president (Carter) out of the last ten has not been re-elected. It is particularly difficult to unseat an incumbent President when inflation and unemployment are perceived as declining, as happened in the 1984 election. But it is equally erroneous to believe that Mondale lost because of his non-existent commitment to the expansion of the New Deal.

The Ideological Creation of Events and Establishment of the New Conventional Wisdom

Previous sections of this paper have presented information that contradicts the major interpretations of the 1980 and 1984 Presidential elections that have been given by conservative, liberal, and even some radical authors. A very urgent question that needs to be addressed is why large sectors of the Left have accepted these dominant interpretations.[88]

One explanatory factor is the absence of a left wing mass movement in the US, and thus the nonexistence of a mass-based socialist or communist media. The dominant corporate media reproduce unhindered a whole set of symbols, messages, values and interpretations of reality that permeates all political positions, including those of the Left. Liberals and even radicals are easily absorbed in a terrain in which conservatives are dominant, not infrequently reproducing the same schemas and interpretations offered by the Right. The difference in their interpretation tends to be one of tone rather than substance. While the Right applauds, the Left laments. Otherwise, the interpretation is remarkably similar.

This situation has become doubly clear in the current conjuncture in which the ideological mean within the dominant corporate ideology has moved even further to the right. The best indicator of this is the adoption by ABC, a major news broadcasting corporation, of the ultra right wing journalist George Will as the 'centre' ('reasonable') moderator of the evening news on television, heralding the values of private property, social austerity and social Darwinism to the American population as they eat their supper and watch the news. There is little doubt that there has been a further move to the right by the American establishment, including its media.[89] Corporate media does not reflect popular mood and opinion. Rather, it contributes to create it, in accordance with the values of the dominant establishment forces that define the parameters of 'reasonable' discourse. In the same way that those dominant forces are not uniform, that 'reasonable' discourse is not uniform either. Diversity does exist—although within dramatically narrow boundaries. Socialist and communist views are rarely, if ever, presented in the major American media. The corporate dominant interpretations of reality are the ones reproduced and presented.[90]

To acknowledge this reality is not to deny the existence of diversity or to suggest that popular views are a mere reflection of views transmitted by the dominant media. As Gramsci indicated, the views of the working population are a synthesis of a matrix of views and practices, of which the dominant ones are important but not the only ones.[91] Those dominant views are measured against information absorbed from their own practice, which is frequently in contradiction with establishment perspectives. This explains the apparent paradoxes (referred to by some established figures as schizophrenic opinions) regarding popular views of reality.[92] For example, when people are asked their views about government in general, they will likely reply—reflecting the dominant views transmitted day after day and evening after evening—that we have too much of it. But, if instead they are asked about specific government programmes and interventions that affect them or affect others whom they know, then, the overwhelming response is one of support.[93] Similarly, if asked about their attitudes towards 'welfare' programmes, the response tends to be antagonistic, reflecting the mass media image of the welfare 'cheater'. However, if one asks for opinions about the main welfare programmes, without ever using the term 'welfare', people's response is quite different. The majority support those programmes.[94] Incidentally, when people are asked their opinion of 'socialism', the overwhelming majority respond negatively. But, if people are asked (as they have been by Hart Pollsters) whether workers, employees and community residents should control the enterprises located in their communities, the overwhelming majority answer that they should.[95]

In summary, the message that people receive from the top is contrasted with the message that people get from their own practice at the bottom. Both messages are important in shaping people's opinions. This situation explains why the working population never repeats mimetically what the establishment wants them to believe. Their own practice produces messages that frequently conflict with dominant ideology, making the working population receptive to alternative messages. Potential receptivity accounts for the narrowness in the diversity of the major establishment media.

It should also be pointed out that American establishment media create events that may or not correspond to reality. A clear example is the alleged anti-tax revolt that surfaced in California in 1978 with Proposition 13. Peretz has convincingly shown that there was no such anti-tax revolt.[96] Although the anti-tax Proposition 13 in California was successful, many other pro-tax referendums were passed at the same time but were ignored by the media. Instead, the establishment media focused on Proposition 13, trumpeting the anti-tax rebellion. It was that media campaign that was responsible for the subsequent rise in popular dissatisfaction with paying taxes. When the media event subsided, so did that anti-tax mood. Dissatisfaction with paying taxes has been remarkably constant, and is related more to the regressive nature of taxation than its overall levels (as I will explain later). Another media created upsurge was the increase of self-declared Republicans among the population after the 1980 election. The continuous trumpeting of the Republican 'overwhelming victory' created that upsurge, *after* the election, to be reduced again shortly after in 1981 and 1982.

In brief, American people tend to be rather consistent in their popular opinions (expressed through polls), including their sustained support for New Deal and Great Society programmes. A valid question that may be raised at this point is why, in 1984, they voted for a Presidential candidate who so clearly opposed these programmes. The answer to that question needs to be given at different levels. One explanation is that the overwhelming majority of US Presidents have been elected by a minority, not a majority of potential voters. And President Reagan, elected by a mere 29.8 per cent of potential voters in 1984 and 26.7 per cent in 1980, was no exception to this trend.

Still, the question may be asked again. How is it that so many people voted for Reagan despite the fact that they did not support his social policies? The answer to that question involves the nature of Western democracy and its profound limitations. The act of voting is based on a totalising interpretation of policy. In other words, in the act of voting (except in referendums), people are asked to vote for totalities, not for sectional choices. One votes either Republican or Democratic. But one cannot vote selectively, i.e., one is not offered the chance of voting for the many components of those policies (such as education, health services, transport, employment policies). The vote is everything or nothing. In Walter Lippman's words,

> We call an election an expression of the popular will. But is it? We go into polling booths and make a cross on a piece of paper for one of two or perhaps three or four names. Have we expressed our thoughts on the public policy of the United States? Presumably we have a number of thoughts on this and that with many buts and ifs and so on. Surely the cross on a piece of paper has not expressed them.[97]

Representative Democracy, on this view, is dramatically insufficient. It does not measure, nor does it reflect, the popular will on the many dimensions of public life. *Electoral behaviour and popular opinion are not synonymous.* Thus, there is not contradiction or schizophrenia involved in Reagan winning the election while the majority of the people (including his voters) have different and even opposite views on many and even the majority of Reagan's policies. The paradox of the last election—that the majority of the electorate seemed to be in disagreement with many of the

Reagan positions yet still the majority of those who went to the polls voted for him—is not incomprehensible. Voters chose Reagan primarily because they identified the economic recovery (and very much in particular the decline of inflation) with his policies.[98] It is understandable that the Right wing wants American people to believe that the vote was a vote for *all* Reagan policies. However, it is extremely important to point out that the evidence shows otherwise. Not only the polls, but the referendums show that the majority of the American population had not abandoned the New Deal, nor were they in favour of cutting social expenditures. There was not a popular mandate in 1980, nor is there one in 1984 for the anti-New Deal and anti-Great Society policies of President Reagan.*

II

ANALYSIS OF CURRENT REALITIES: THE CLASS BEHAVIOUR OF THE REPUBLICANS AND THE NON-CLASS BEHAVIOUR OF THE DEMOCRATS

The first section of this paper questioned the major hegemonic inter-pretations of the 1980 and the 1984 Presidential elections. In this section, I will focus on what has been happening in the US during this period. But first, an elementary truth needs to be restated: The US capitalist class is the most powerful capitalist class in today's world. In a truly Gramscian fashion, the interests of this class have been presented (and accepted) as the universal interests. Thus, to be anti-capitalist is perceived to be anti-American. Indicative of the power of this class to define the dominant discourse is the fact that, aside from references to the US as a middle-class society (a society in which the majority of Americans are supposed to be in the middle between the rich and the poor), the power category of class never appears in the media.† Consequently, the most powerful capitalist class on earth appears as non-existent, i.e., a 'silent' class. Very rarely are those 'on the top' presented, discussed, applauded or denounced as the capitalist class, a term that usually is dismissed as 'rhetorical', and there-fore an object of suspicion, i.e., for ideologues but not for serious people. The US capitalist class, however, is the most class conscious of all classes in the US. And the current leadership of the Republican Party represents the most 'class conscious' strata within that class. In the unrestrained pursuit of its interests, it has exhibited the most aggressive class behaviour

---

*Although this article focuses on domestic policies, there is similar evidence showing that American popular opinion does not support many of the major initiatives and assumptions of Reagan's foreign policy.

†It is interesting to note that more US people define themselves as members of the working class (48%) than of the middle class (43%).[99] The Establishment's media, however, never refers to the majority of the US population as working class. Rather, they define it as middle class.

that the capitalist class has shown since the beginning of this century. One of its most substantial class achievements has been the weakening of the base of support that government has provided to organised labour in its dealings with management. This has been accomplished through sharp reductions in unemployment insurance, through the complete dismantling of the public services job programme, through the weakening of the Occupational Health and Safety Administration, through the appointments of persons hostile to organised labour both to the National Labor Relations Board and to the Department of Labor, and through the reduction of social expenditures.[100] Similarly, Reagan's tax and economic policies have benefited primarily the capitalist and upper middle classes and have hurt the lower middle and working classes.[101] The Reagan leadership and the Republican Administration have followed an unprecedented aggressiveness in their class behaviour. To be rich is to be best in America.

The opposition party—the Democratic Party—however, does not represent any form of class behaviour.* Not even a semblance of class discourse appears. Even within some sectors of the radical left, class has been dismissed as a constraining and irrelevant category to be replaced by more meaningful categories. This situation is largely due to the lack of a mass socialist culture in the US, which makes radical intellectuals not only easily manipulated by the corporate media but also very receptive to the latest intellectual trends and fashions generated elsewhere, particularly in Europe. Let me elaborate on this. An extremely important debate in Europe in the 60s and 70s focused on the need for left-wing forces, whose political and economic instruments have always emphasised class behaviour (i.e., the working class party and the class-based union) to relate those parties and unions to new forms of social movements that do not have a class base or practice. The feminist, ecological and peace movements, for example, while having an anti-capitalist potential, do not base their *modus operandi* on class. Thus, there was indeed a great need for the European socialist and communist Left to break with class reductionism and expand and articulate its interventions with non-class social movements. A new theoretical production appeared within the European Left that emphasised the importance of these non-class based movements (such as the feminist, ecological, anti-nuclear and peace movements) as important agents of social transformation. Many US radicals borrowed and reproduced that problematic into the US. For example, one of the most influential radical authors in the US, Immanuel Wallerstein, wrote a review in an American journal, *Contemporary Marxism*, of the possibilities for social transformation in the developed capitalist world. He concluded that review with the

---

*I want to clarify that working class behaviour and anti-capitalist behaviour are two different things. Swedish labour follows class practices that are not anti-capitalist. See Ref. 102 for an expansion of this important distinction.

remarkable statement that the US is closer to profound changes than Western European countries, because the US Left is not stuck in class analysis and practices and because there is a large Third World population within the US and a strong US women's movement.[103] Wallerstein and other radicals seem to be unaware that, while there was a great merit for the European Left (heavily involved in class practices) to discover the non-class mass movements, the situation is precisely the opposite in the US—where there exist all types of non-class movements but no class-based political party (except the Republican Party) or union.* Actually, one of the most successful capitalist class interventions in the US was to outlaw any form of class behaviour on the part of its antagonist: the working class. The Taft–Hartley Act forbade American labour to act as a class and forced it to function as just another 'interest group'. No other Western capitalist country has faced this situation. This splitting of the working-class into different interest groups dramatically redefined all elements of political, economic and socio-cultural behaviours and possibilities. Class has disappeared from reasonable discourse; terms such as 'capitalist class', 'petit bourgeois', and 'working class' are dismissed as ideological. Instead, the new terms of political discourse are 'the rich', 'the middle class' and 'the poor', all defined in the area of consumption rather than in terms of the relationship of people to the means of production. Language, however, is not innocent. It does indeed reflect the power relations in society. The working class has been redefined in terms of biological categories (black, white, Hispanics, women, men, the aged) and in terms of consumption (rich, middle, and poor). The political, economic and social consequences of that redefinition of the working class into interest groups are enormous. And their importance for understanding today's US is great.

The disappearance of class from political discourse does not reflect, of course, any disappearance of classes from the American landscape. The category of class continues to be of undiminished importance in explaining the political behaviour of the US and of all its agents, including the social movements. For example, the gender gap in political behaviour, with

---

*Wallerstein's dismissal of class and his emphasis, instead, on social movements as the major agents of change explains his conclusion that the US is closer to profound changes than other 'western industrialised countries'. Past and current experience shows precisely the opposite. Among developed capitalist countries, no other country has more social movements and less class practices (by the dominated classes) than the US. And no other capitalist developed country has (1) a less developed welfare state, (2) a more-stable capitalist system and (3) a stronger capitalist class, than the US. As I will discuss later, those societies where the dominated classes follow class practices, have larger welfare states and more progressive legislation and programmes to benefit all sectors of the working population (including women and feminist rights) and better protection of occupational and residential environments than those societies, as in the US, where the dominated classes and forces do not follow class practices.

women voting more progressively than men, is in large degree due to the fact that women occupy the lower echelons of the working class (lower paid and less secure), making them more receptive than men to calls for social change. Without denying the enormous value of the feminist movement in changing popular attitudes, the material base upon which ideological messages are reproduced cannot be dismissed. Other countries without strong feminist movements are also witnessing changes in electoral behaviour of the sexes.[104] Moreover, several polls have shown that the gender gap in the US is caused more by women's response to economic issues rather than by issues considered to be women's issues, (such as abortion, gender related legislation, equal gender representation in political institutions).[105] In summary, while it is erroneous to view our reality only in terms of class, it is extremely wrong to ignore class as an important category of power and organisation that serves to explain the nature of our realities.

Class, Taxes and Social Legislation

Class practices are also important to an understanding of social policy in the US. Social legislation has been very different in those periods such as the New Deal, when labour operated as class, from periods like the 60s when labour operated as an 'interest group'. During the New Deal, social legislation (e.g., Social Security) benefited for the most part all sectors of the working class. The Great Society legislation of the 1960s, on the other hand, responded to 'interest group' behaviour and affected only the most vulnerable sectors of the working class (e.g., food stamps for the poor). An exception was Medicare which, while based on a biological criteria (age), benefited the majority of the population since everyone was a potential recipient. Thus Medicare could be considered as a New Deal type of programme.

During the last forty years the expansion of social expenditures has affected both types of programmes, although the overwhelming growth of these expenditures has been in New Deal type programmes. As shown in the last section there has been undiminished support for both types of programmes, although support for existing New Deal programmes is higher (95 per cent of the people) than for the Great Society programmes (68 to 72 per cent, depending on the programme). Given the current ideological avalanche, it is important to repeat that both types of programmes are popular, with 94 per cent of the population vehemently opposing cuts in Social Security, the key programme of the New Deal. This enormous support for Social Security did force candidate Reagan to promise the American people in 1984 that he would not cut Social Security benefits (although 46 per cent believe that he will).[106] Also, 62 per cent oppose cuts in social programmes for the aged, poor and disabled (although 65 per cent feel Reagan will cut them in his second term).[107]

These programmes are funded with taxes paid by wage and salary earners. Table I shows that while income taxes and very much in particular social security taxes increased during the period 1960–1984, corporate taxes declined dramatically during the same period (and very much in particular during the Reagan Administration, which halved them in its first four years).

TABLE I
Sources of Federal Revenues

Fiscal Year	Individual Income Tax	Social Insurance Tax	Corporate Income Tax	Excise, State and Other
1960	44.0%	15.9%	23.2%	16.8%
1965	41.8%	19.1%	21.8%	17.4%
1970	46.9%	23.0%	17.0%	13.0%
1975	43.9%	30.3%	14.6%	11.3%
1980	47.2%	30.5%	12.5%	9.8%
1984 (est.)	44.8%	36.8%	7.8%	10.5%

Source: Table 6.4, T.B. Edsall, *The New Politics of Inequality*, 1984, p. 212.

It is worth noting that preferential treatment for corporate America started under President Carter. In 1979, the business-backed Steiger-Hausen bill proposed a liberalisation of corporate depreciation allowances that translated into an annual $50 billion cut in corporate income taxes.[108] In brief, during the 60s and 70s there was a decline in tax revenues coming from corporations and an increase in taxes on incomes. That shift of revenues becomes even more significant when we analyse the increased differentials in taxes paid between wealthy and non-wealthy income earners:[109]

> Between 1953 and 1974, direct taxes paid by the average income family doubled, from 11.8 per cent of income to 23.4 per cent of income, while the tax burden of a family with four times the average income went from 20.2 per cent to 29.5 per cent, an increase of less than half. Between 1969 and 1980, social security taxes increased by 92 per cent. And since social security taxes apply to only the first $35,700 of wages, the major portion of this increase was on the non-wealthy. During the same period, corporate income tax collections fell 14 per cent, and capital rates were cut by 20 per cent.

Throughout this period, Corporate America has been paying increasingly less taxes and Working America more. This is the fiscal version of class struggle, a struggle that is carried out by the assumed non-existent capitalist class against the working class, whose existence is also denied and recycled as an 'interest group'. These anti-working class fiscal policies will be further strengthened in the new tax reform proposal put forward by the Reagan Administration. In this proposal, presented as Reagan's second social revolution, the limited progressiveness of the federal income tax is further reduced, flattening the tax structure most dramatically. Other regressive features of this proposal include taxing health, unemployment, and workers' disability benefits.[110]

This shift of fiscal responsibilities that favours the corporate or capitalist class is justified by conservative forces by the need to stimulate capital investment. The benefits for the corporate class, it is claimed, will eventually trickle down to the rest of the population. Even on its own terrain, however, this argument does not hold much credibility.[111] The US was one of the low performance economies in the 70s, in spite of very low tax burdens on capital (far lower than in Japan and West Germany, defined as good performance economies, who had the highest and second highest reliance on capital taxes).[112]

Apologetics aside, Capital paid less taxes and Labour more not because there was a systemic need for that to occur but rather because Capital was winning the war against Labour. Here it is important to clarify a much debated and misunderstood issue: the overall level of taxation. It is true that the total US tax level is relatively low compared with other countries. In 1974 it was 27.5 of GDP, placing the US 14th out of 17 major industrial capitalist nations. Only Switzerland, Japan and Australia had lower overall tax levels. But, if instead of looking at overall levels, we focus on levels of taxation by occupational groups, it then emerges that for an average production worker the US ranked 8th highest in the tax burden.[113] The American tax system is indeed highly regressive. This regressiveness is further highlighted if we look at what the average citizen gets in return for his or her taxes. The average European gets more from government than the US citizen does. For the most part, the European citizen gets health care, family allowances, better unemployment insurance, pension and disabilities, as well as many other social benefits that increase individual income. For example, in eight European countries, family allowances add at least 6 per cent to the wage income of the average household. In France, Italy, Austria and Belgium, family allowances increase wage income by over 9 per cent. The average American taxpayer, however, gets comparatively little from his or her taxes. A large percentage of taxes goes for military expenditures that return very little economic benefit to the average citizen. Let me add that during the Reagan Administration (in which military expenditures have increased enormously, social expenditures have declined, social security taxes have increased, and tax reforms favourable to upper incomes have been implemented), the average citizen has got even less from his or her taxes.

This measure of regressiveness explains why the average citizen feels under a heavy tax burden and strongly opposes increasing taxes. People are against increasing taxes and rightly so. They are not getting much in return. But, (and it is an extremely important *but*), they are willing to pay higher taxes if they are assured that they will benefit from them. This explains why:

(a) social security taxes (the ones that have increased most rapidly in the last ten years) are the least unpopular taxes,[114]

(b) the majority of Americans would be willing to pay higher taxes if they could be assured that those revenues would pay for services (such as a National and Comprehensive Health Programme) from which *all* citizens will benefit.[115] However, people are not willing to increase taxes to resolve the deficit problem. Their anti-tax sentiment is highly selective. Thus, it is wrong to state, as is always stated, that people are against paying taxes. How people feel about paying taxes depends on what they will get in return. It is as simple and logical as that,

(c) there is support for social expenditures and, within them, higher support for New Deal programmes (aimed at the whole population) than for Great Society programmes (aimed at specific populations).

In brief, the average US citizen is getting less in return for his or her taxes than the average citizen in major Western European countries, a situation that is in large degree explained by the highly skewed nature of the tax system of the US (falling heavily on the middle and low income levels of the working population) and by the huge proportion that military expenditures represent within federal government expenditures.[116] Since social expenditures are for the most part financed by taxes imposed on the working population, these transfers of government funds have not had a redistributive effect from the capitalist class to the working class. Rather, there has been a redistributive effect within the working population, with some sectors of the working class paying for others. This situation explains why Great Society programmes have been somewhat less popular than New Deal type programmes. They have frequently been used to divide the working class, pitting whites against blacks, men against women, young against old, the middle income families against low income ones and so on. The identification of the Democratic Party with the Great Society rather than with the New Deal has somewhat weakened the popularity of the Party. As Edsall has written,

> The formulation of mechanisms to reduce the divisions between these two sets of programmes (New Deal and Great Society), if not to integrate them, remains essential to the Democratic Party if it is to lessen this conflict within its own constituencies.[117]

This need to integrate both types of programmes is doubly important now given the decline of wages and family income of American workers, making them less enthusiastic about programmes that directly benefit only some sectors of the working class. In 1980 wages were 7.5 per cent below their peak in 1972 and lower than they had been at any time since 1967.[118] Median household income, measured in constant 1981 dollars, was 11 per cent ($2,440) lower in 1981 than in 1973.[119] Thus it is not surprising that it is more popular within the Democratic Party constituency to ask for a Comprehensive National Health Programme than for health programmes targeted at specific sectors of the population (like rural populations or the urban poor). The recovery of the Democratic Party depends upon recovering class practices as opposed to 'interest group' practices.

A last point needs to be made regarding the relationship between funding of social expenditures and the level of popularity of paying taxes. A further way of dividing the working class into interest groups is not only to divide the beneficiaries of social expenditures (e.g., food programmes, Aid to Families with Dependent Children) but also to divide the payers of those services. Large sectors of those social services are financed by way of tax exemptions, a highly regressive form of subsidising the welfare state, further contributing to the regressive nature of the taxation system and distribution of government services. For example, and unlike Europe, the US does not have a comprehensive health programme to cover the whole population; instead, we subsidise medical care expenses by means of tax exemptions. Similarly, we have no general programme of family allowances. Instead, we subsidise the expenses of child-rearing also by means of tax exemptions. In both cases, this approach is regressive, since a $1,000 tax deduction in either medical or child-rearing expenditures gives a higher-bracket family more tax subsidy than a low-bracket one. Here, again, to base the provision of services on tax exemptions rather than universal tax-based comprehensive programmes (as in Europe) serves to increase further the cleavages within the working population, the base for the Democratic Party.

In summary, the electoral history of the US shows that the Democratic Party has been more popular in periods when it has been perceived as the party of the entire working population, not just the party of its different components or interest groups. No other government has attained more popularity than the Democratic Administration during the New Deal. Franklin D. Roosevelt was by far the most popular President of the US. Under the New Deal, the working population fought for and won Social Security, Works Project Administration, the National Labor Relations Act, and enactment of a system of progressive taxation (low for the working class and high for the wealthy)—all programmes and interventions that actually or potentially benefited the whole working population. One of the missing pieces was a National Health Programme, dropped by New Dealers because of opposition from the insurance industry and medical profession. From Roosevelt to Johnson, the outcome of Presidential elections has been directly related to how the population perceived the candidates vis-a-vis the New Deal. Witness Goldwater's dramatic defeat because of his stance against Social Security.

Class practice rather than interest group practice is what has put Democrats in power. Let me stress here that this situation is not unique to the US. Countries like Finland and Sweden, where parties are perceived to have clear class practices, have higher rates of electoral involvement, higher voter turnout, and more extensive welfare states than those that don't have these practices.* Indeed, societies in which the political and economic instruments of labour are perceived as class instruments have lower income inequality between the top and the bottom layers, a higher percentage of GNP allocated to social expenditures, a higher level of overall progressive taxation, and lower unemployment.[120] It is in those countries in which class practices within the working class do not exist and in which labour operates as one more interest group (highly divided into different subgroups, each one looking out for its own), that we find a depoliticisation of the population, with low voter turnout and a fragmentation of politics.[121] This is precisely what is happening in today's US.

The lack of polarisation of US politics and the conventional wisdom that parties have to move to the centre to attract the middle class are producing a depoliticisation of American life, with increasing disenchantment toward the two major political parties. In 1980 between 60 and 70 per cent of the population (depending on the problem area) indicated that they really did not perceive much of a difference between the two major parties.[122] The abandonment of the New Deal commitments in 1984 also led *The New York Times* to editorialise that the differences between the two parties were uncomfortably narrow.[123] It is not surprising then, that in 1980, 40 per cent of Americans defined themselves as independent, followed by 37 per cent as Democrats and 24 per cent as Republicans,[124] a considerable increase in the number of independents and dramatic decline in both Democratic and Republican Party adherents. More than a realignment, what we have seen in the US is a dealignment from the two major parties. This abandonment of the New Deal commitment and the similarity between the two parties has also led to an increase in the number abstaining from electoral politics. The US has the highest abstention rate in the Western world;[125] 50 million eligible citizens did not register in 1984 and 35 million of those who registered did not vote. Of these 85 million non-voters, 46 per cent consider themselves independent, 80 per cent are white, 83 per cent have a high school education or less, 72 per cent are between 18–44 and 50 per cent are between 18–29 years of age, and 32 per cent live in the South.[126] Another characteristic of US politics is that the working class votes less than the other classes. In 1980 77 per cent of

---

*Working class practices appear when there is one major union formation which unites labour and a political party which represents labour.

white-collar professionals voted compared with only 44 per cent of blue-collar workers. This class abstentionism hurts the Democrats more than the Republicans.[127] Wolfinger and Rosenstone have shown that those who vote include more Republicans than the entire potential electorate.[128] Its importance appears clearly when one considers that in 1984, if the blacks, Hispanics, the unemployed, the low-income workers (below $12,500), and people with less than a high school education would have voted in the same percentage as those who earn $35,000 and above, and if their voting behaviour remained the same as those in the low income group who voted, Mondale would have won.[129]

The declassing of American politics and absence of class polarisation, together with the recycling of politics through interest groups, has thus led to depoliticisation and abstentionism, particularly among the lower echelons of the working class who do not see much meaning in their electoral participation. The experience both in this country and abroad shows that the class polarisation of politics (which in the US happens within the Republican Party but not within the Democratic Party) is a condition for active democratic participation. The realisation of an expanded welfare state, centred around the New Deal, has as a prerequisite the political polarisation of the Democratic Party and the development of class practices and discourse.

III

SOCIAL EXPENDITURES AND THE DEFICIT: THE IDEOLOGICAL DEBATE

Having analysed in the previous section where government revenues come from, let us now look at where these government expenditures go. Since 1979 there has been an enormous shift from social to military spending, with the dramatic growth of military expenditures in large degree made possible by a reduction in social expenditures. The US military budget increased from 5.2 per cent of the GNP in fiscal year 1980 to 6.6 per cent in fiscal year 1985, to 7.3 per cent planned for fiscal year 1988. Moreover, interest on the national debt, which results mainly from past and present military outlays, has gone up even faster. Added to military spending, the two together rose from 7.2 per cent of the GNP in fiscal year 1980 to 9.9 per cent in fiscal year 1985, and will rise to 10.5 per cent of the GNP in fiscal year 1988 on the basis of Reagan's optimistic projection of lower interest rates.[130] Social expenditures (including Social Security, Medicare, other Social Insurance, and Medicaid), on the other hand, declined from 11.2 to 10.4 per cent of the GNP in the period from 1981 to 1985. Expenditures for natural resources and infrastructure, incidentally, also declined from 1.6 to 1.2 per cent of the GNP, and the total grants to state and local governments dropped from 3.3 to 2.7 per cent.[131] The US

Council of Economic Advisors refers to such shifts of resources as 'absolutely unprecedented', and its 1984 report recognises that 'the reduction of domestic outlays financed by general revenues is thus slightly more than sufficient to balance the increase in defense spending and interest costs. . . One implication of the very substantial reduction in non-defense spending is that it permits an increase in defense spending without an equal increase in tax revenue'.[132] The same report indicates that by 1989, the current Administration proposes cuts from the pre-Reagan peak of 28 per cent for water and navigation projects; 32 per cent for mass transit and 70 per cent for sewage treatment. In the same year (1989), the combined dollar costs of interests and the military in 1989 prices will be $686 billion dollars, which will amount to a fiscal charge of $2,766 per capita or $11,065 per family of four.[133] Excluding Social Security and other earmarked trust funds, military and related expenditures will repre-sent 65 per cent of the 1989 fiscal budget.[134]

It is important to indicate that in spite of the stated position of the Reagan Administration that government is the source of our problems and that the large size of government expenditures is at the root of the sluggishness of the US economy, the actual size of the public sector—measured by federal government expenditures—has increased as a percent-age of the GNP. Discounting inflation, the federal government plans to spend 30 per cent more in 1985 than it did in 1980.[135] This growth has been due in considerable degree to the unprecedented growth of military expenditures, which is primarily responsible, along with the tax cuts (that have favoured the corporate class and the upper middle class), for the large federal deficit.

Regarding the deficit, there is a need to clarify several points. One is that, contrary to what the current Administration states, the growth of social expenditures (of the Great Society variety) is not the primary cause for that deficit. According to the Administration, 'programmes such as Medicaid and Food Stamps have become a major source of persistent deficits. . .'[136] As The New York Times editorialised, 'It takes a lot of nerve for an Administration that is calling for a $758 billion budget and a $92 billion deficit to blame its trouble on $11 billion in food stamps and $18 billion in Medicaid. That makes the unskilled and the unemployed not merely victims but villains.'[137]

As part of the well-orchestrated campaign aimed at making people believe that Great Society and New Deal programmes are responsible for the deficit, a scare has been created about the apparent insolvency of Social Security. David Stockman put it quite clearly in an Atlantic inter-view in which he indicated that the purpose of that scare was 'to permit the politicians to make it look like they are doing something for the beneficiary population when they are doing something to it, which they normally would not have the courage to undertake'.[138] As further clarified by Stockman, the Social Security 'crisis' responded not so much to the needs of the beneficiaries but rather to the need to shift funds to reduce the deficit.[139] Social Security recipients are supposed to contribute to resolve the budget deficit, which is not of their doing, but rather, the result of growing military expenditures and cuts in income and corporate taxes that have primarily benefited the corporate and upper middle classes.[140]

Another point meriting clarification concerns the argument that the growth in government and social expenditures is responsible for the slow-down of the economy. The international experience, however, denies that.

TABLE II
Government Spending and Gross Domestic Product, 1973–1979

Country	Annual Growth Rate of Government Spending as Percentage of GDP, 1973–81	Government Spending as Percentage of GDP, 1981	Average Annual Growth Rate 1973–1981
Japan	6.6	34.0	3.2
Italy	4.2	50.8	3.0
France	3.3	48.9	2.8
W. Germany	2.3	49.3	2.4
UK	1.8	47.3	1.6
US	1.6	35.4	2.6

Source: R. Kuttner, *The Economic Illusion*, 1984, p. 191.

Table II, shows that other economies with a larger annual growth rate of government spending as percentage of GDP during 1973–81, and higher government spending as percentage of GDP in 1981, had a higher annual growth rate for the period 1973–81 than the US. Similarly, Table III shows that countries with the largest government social expenditures (as percentage of the GDP) for the period 1978–1983 had better economic indicators (unemployment and economic growth) than the US. Other available data show that a low level of taxation, a regressive form of taxation and restrained public spending is not, as current conventional wisdom indicates, the key to economic performance. Quite to the contrary. Japan, Italy and France had the best growth rates during 1973–81. They also had the most rapid growth of public spending.

TABLE III
Unemployment, Economic Growth and Social Expenditure

Country	Unemployment*	Economic Growth**	Social Expenditures***
Australia	9.5	1.8	12.8
Austria	4.2	1.8	24.1
Belgium	14.9	1.5	32.6

TABLE III (contd)
Unemployment, Economic Growth and Social Expenditure

Country	Unemployment*	Economic Growth**	Social Expenditures***
Canada	11.1	1.6	15.5
Denmark	10.6	1.6	29.0
Finland	6.2	3.8	23.3
France	8.2	1.8	23.8
W. Germany	7.8	1.5	26.4
Italy	10.0	2.1	22.7
Japan	2.6	4.3	12.5
Netherlands	14.0	0.7	29.1
Norway	2.8	2.5	21.0
Sweden	3.4	1.5	31.9
Switzerland	0.4	1.5	9.4
UK	13.1	1.1	19.0
US	8.4	1.8	15.0

* Unemployment: Standardised rate of unemployment as per cent of the labour force in the fourth quarter of 1983.

** Average annual growth of GDP 1978–1983, in per cent.

*** Public expenditures for health, social and welfare services as per cent of GDP in current prices in 1981.

Source: G. Therborn, 'The Irreversible Welfare State', Conference on the Future of the Welfare State, 1984.

The End of Social Keynesianism and the Victory of Military Keynesianism

Another position that needs to be questioned is the interpretation of the current recovery of the US economy (on the heels of the deepest recession since the Great Depression) as an outcome of the successful supply side and monetarist interventions that, presumably, have characterised Reaganomics. David Plotke warned American liberals and radicals, back in 1980, not to dismiss supply side economics. As he put it, they may not be a joke.[141] More recently, several Socialist governments in Europe have defended their policies of austerity (including large cuts in social expenditures) as necessary steps to revitalise their economies, following the successful Reagan economic model. It speaks of the enormous power of current hegemonic ideology that Reagan policies are perceived as half monetarist, half supply side. It was a perceptive conservative, ex-Prime Minister of France, Barre, who in the pages of *Le Monde*, warned his fellow conservatives not to let their ideological blinkers interfere with their understanding of the Reagan policies.[142] Barre advised his counterparts to pay attention not to what was said but rather to what was done. Reagan's policies were and are following Keynesian policies to the letter. The stimulation of the economy through (1) public expenditures, (2) tax cuts and (3) deficits constitute the textbook practice of Keynesianism. Supply side practices have been indeed a failure and a joke. The theory that tax cuts would lead to higher savings and higher investments proved to be wrong. Investments actually declined sharply between 1980 and 1983. McIntyre has shown that the corporations that received higher tax benefits during the Reagan Administration (which were supposed to stimulate investments) were the ones that invested less. They used those tax cuts to increase their profits, but not their investments. From 1980 to 1983, business investments declined by 9 per cent, while the costs of federal tax subsidies to corporations increased by 41 per cent.[143] During this period, the supply side incentives did not cause businesses to invest, because there was slack demand for their products. Regardless of tax benefits, businesses did not increase investment when existing plants were operating at 60 per cent of capacity and customers were not buying. The recovery was triggered by the huge demand stimulated by a $200 billion deficit and $600 billion in military expenditures, a demand-side recovery facilitated by the politically motivated decision of the Federal Reserve Board allowing, in mid 1983, real interest rates to fall.[144] All US Presidents (with the exception of Carter) have stimulated the economy one year prior to the election. Increased capital investment came later, when businesses saw the resumption of consumer demand.[145] It is important to realise that the deficit would not have been less stimulating to the economy (1) had the tax breaks benefited the working class and lower middle class (rather than the corporate class and upper middle class) or (2) had the government's extra-expenditures been social expenditures rather than military expenditures. What we have under Reagan is a corporate-military Keynesianism rather than social Keynesianism. But it is Keynesianism nevertheless.

Another misconception, related to the previous one, also reproduced by liberal and even radical authors, is that Reagan is anti-government, i.e., his Administration is stuck in Nineteenth Century economic theory. David Plotke, for example, refers to Reagan's success in convincing the population of the merit of his anti-government policies.[146] The Chicago School theorist, Friedman, however, is not the organic intellectual of this Administration. Reagan is following the most active government interventionist policies of all post-World War II Presidents. His Administration has gone far beyond mere Keynesianism. Through military expenditures, the Reagan Administration is reshaping and guiding the nature of the US economy. To pour 1.5 trillion dollars in military expenditures in the US economy in five years is not a minor matter.[147] It is having an enormous impact on the economy, and this impact is not an unplanned one.[148] As explicitly indicated by the current Secretary of Defense, Caspar Weinberger, a welcome effect of the unprecedented growth of military expenditures is the re-industrialisation of the American economy.[149] This re-industrialisation is taking place under the direction of the US Department of Defense, defined by Sheman and Wood as the 'largest planned economy in the world outside the Soviet Union'.[150]

In light of all this evidence, to continue defining Reagan's policies as aimed at reducing the role of the federal government in our economic, political and social lives is to indulge in apologetics, not rigorous analysis. The Reagan Administration has significantly changed the role of government and other branches of the State by quite dramatically increasing the interventionist and repressive character of the State. As stated by H. Salvatori, a key member of the 1980 Reagan Transitional Team,

> In the history of man everyone has talked about expanding rights, having more and more freedom. But we have found that if you let people do what they want to do, you have chaos. We can't restore moral values, that's hopeless. What we have to do is restructure society, set minimum standards of respect and order. Frankly, we need a more authoritarian state.[151]

The Reagan Administration has indeed followed that blueprint. There have been many government interventions to constrain and diminish personal and individual freedoms. Witness, for example, recent Congressional approval of an unprecedented intervention in the realm of academic freedom. According to recent legislation, a local school district implementing a desegregation plan shall not be eligible for Federal funds if 'secular humanism' is taught in its classrooms. 'Secular humanism' is not defined in the legislation. Rather, the local school districts are responsible for determining whether they are teaching it. In the views of many of those districts 'secular humanism' includes the teaching of erotic themes in literature; the emphasis in American history courses on unequal distribution of wealth; Darwin's theory of evolution; reduced attention in curriculums to the values of family, patriotism and God; and the prevalence in schools of an 'atheistic philosophy' that is at war with the principles of a 'Christian nation'.[152] Indeed, what we are witnessing today is what the late Nicos Poulantzas referred to as 'the further development of the authoritarian state'.[153] Another characteristic of this authoritarian state is its corporatisation, i.e., the establishment of public policy outside the normal democratic process. Policy is defined by para-governmental bodies (such as Presidential commissions) that include powerful interest groups whose interests need to be taken into account. Thus, the major 1981 amendments to the Social Security Act were brought about by a Commission that 'brought together significant parties outside of normal congressional processes'.[154] These commissions further centralise state power, diluting the process of democratic participation.

In brief, Reagan's policies have not diminished state intervention in people's lives. Rather, they have further changed (and quite dramatically at that) the nature and form of that intervention. While formal ideological debate occurs at the level of 'market versus government' interventions, reality continues to show that the real issue in the US today is who dominates the state—and for whose benefit. Government interventions increased enormously in 1980–84, benefiting primarily the corporate and upper middle classes. It speaks of the overwhelming dominance that those classes have over the means of information, ideological reproduction and legitimation that those class interests are continuously presented as the American interest and that the terms of its discourse (and interpretations of reality) have been widely accepted even by its adversaries. Today's debate is taking place on the terrain defined by the reactionary strata of the corporate class, with the left (broadly defined) for the most part accepting the arguments and terms of that discourse.

The Future: What Needs to be Done

It seems clear from the previous analysis that the solution for the Democratic Party at the national level is not to move to the right (further abandoning the commitment to the New Deal) but rather to the left (expanding on that commitment). The conventional wisdom that the Democratic Party needs to move to the centre (the moderate expression to refer to the right) in order to attract the middle class is the primary reason for its recent defeat. It further confirms the similarity between the two parties, increasing voter abstention on the part of critical sectors that the Democratic Party needs if it wants to win. I have already shown that if the lower echelons of the working class had voted in the same percentages as other sectors, Mondale would have won. As could have been predicted, Mondale's clear move to the right did not capture right wing voters, nor did it stimulate registered but unmotivated voters. They did not perceive enough differences between candidates to vote for Mondale.

It would be erroneous to conclude from this analysis that the solution demands proposals for the establishment of programmes aimed primarily at these lower income groups. This approach would only strengthen the perception of 'interest group' politics and would be exploited by the corporate class. The solution is to develop programmes that benefit all members of the working population, including those groups. In other words, there is an enormous and urgent need to resurrect the class practices of the New Deal.

An Example of a New Deal Programme: A Comprehensive and Universal Tax Based Health Programme

Let me give an example of what I mean by this emphasis on a New Deal programme. There is today a large problem in the health care sector of the US. By whatever health indicator one can think of (infant mortality, low birth weight, life expectancy, etc.), the US indicators do not compare favourably with other countries. And the situation is even deteriorating in many important areas. For example, the decline of infant mortality has slowed down since 1981.[155] This is a result, among other factors, of the 1979–1982 recession and also of the reduction of social expenditures, a reduction that affected primarily but not exclusively the low income groups within the working class. The cuts under Carter and very much under Reagan have affected both Great Society programmes (such as Medicaid) and New Deal programmes (such as Medicare). Those cuts were carried out with bi-partisan support, following a non-existent popular mandate. As I have shown before, the majority of people opposed those cuts. In 1984, the reduction of social expenditures (including health expenditures) was one of the top three issues in the country about which the majority of people expressed concern.[156] This reduction of social expenditures further enlarged the number of people who did not have any form of private or public insurance coverage. In 1984, this figure went up to an impressive 38 million people (nearly 20 per cent of the total population), the largest number and largest percentage of uncovered population in any Western developed society.[157] Moreover, 100 million Americans do not have catastrophic insurance coverage. If they have to face a major health care expenditure, they are in deep trouble. The inability to pay for health expenditures is one of the main causes of bankruptcy in the US. This problem of coverage also affected the majority of the population who had some form of coverage, since the most common form of coverage is not comprehensive and still requires substantial payments by the patient. In the US 27 per cent of all medical expenditures are still direct payments by the patient compared with only 8.4 per cent in Sweden, and 5.8 per cent in Great Britain.[158] The concern for lack of or limited coverage goes side by side with concern for high costs. Here again, in 1984 the high cost of health care was one of the top three concerns for the majority of the US population.[159] Not surprisingly, the majority of Americans want major changes in the health care system. And the percentage of people asking for profound changes is increasing, not declining. In 1983, for example, 50 per cent of polled Americans indicated that 'fundamental changes are needed to make the health care system work better', and another 25 per cent felt that 'the American health care system has so much wrong with it that we need to completely rebuild it'. These percentages increased in 1984 to 51 per cent and 31 per cent respectively.[160] In a 1984 *ABC News–Washington Post* poll, an unprecedented 75 per cent of the respondents indicated that 'the government should institute and operate a national health program'.[161]

The problem, however, is not lack of resources. The US spends 10.8 per cent of the GNP on health services.[162] The problem is the channels (i.e., the institutions) through which those resources are being spent. Indeed, the problems of insufficient coverage and high costs are rooted in the private, for-profit character of American medicine. US government programmes are publicly financed but privately delivered, and the waste is plainly overwhelming. According to a US Senate Committee, the amount of waste in the publicly financed and privately delivered Medicaid programme is equivalent to the total cost of the British National Health Service, with the Medicaid beneficiary incidentally, receiving fewer benefits than the average British beneficiary.[163] In light of the current anti-statist fashion that exists in large spectrums of the Left, it is important to clarify that an international analysis of health services shows that those countries with government control of the funding and administration of health services have better coverage, lower costs, better distribution of resources, and higher popular satisfaction with health services than those that have large for-profit private sectors in the health services (like West Germany, France and the US).[164]

This point bears repeating in light of current cost containment federal policies that focus primarily and almost exclusively on regulating the prices of the hospital services, i.e., fixed amount of payment for diagnostic (DRGs) without actually touching directly on (1) the organisation, planning and delivery of health services or (2) on the overall size of the for-profit sector, the group primarily responsible for the predicament of our health care services. This sector has grown considerably in the last few years due to the massive involvement of for-profit hospital chains in the delivery of health services, an involvement that has been facilitated by federal policies and programmes such as Medicare. As *The Economist* recently indicated, 'Ironically, for-profit hospital chains owe much of their current prosperity to Medicare, the federal programme to help pay the medical costs of old people. . . Medicare provides about one third of the revenue of the average hospital but around half the revenue of for-profit hospital chains.'[165] For-profit hospitals are able to screen the most profitable patients and diagnostics competing with very favourable conditions with voluntary and public hospitals who are less able to screen their clinical cases.

As in other sectors of the economy, the government pays for but does not actually control the private delivery of health services. These payments are tantamount to a huge subsidy to the for-profit activities of the health sector, which includes not only for-profit hospitals but also payments to professional fees and other forms of payments to private professionals and independent contractors, pharmaceutical companies, medical suppliers, and related activities that exist both in the for-profit (investor owned hospitals) and the 'non-profit' sectors (the private, the voluntary and the public institutions). The size of this for-profit sector has been estimated by Maxwell to range between 44 and 88 per cent of all health care expenditures in the US.[166] *It is the size of this sector that is at the root* of the current crisis of health services, in the US, characterised by an enormous growth of expenditures on the one side (e.g., Medicare spending rose from 1 billion in 1966 to $66 billion in 1984) and the limited benefit coverage offered by those health programmes (e.g., the aged still pay, directly and out of pocket, 42 per cent of their health bill).

Foreign experience clearly shows that in order to control the costs of health care and to be able to expand the health benefits to the whole population, the government will have to do far more than control the price of the services provided by the hospital per diagnostic. It will have to intervene actively in the planning, organisation, regionalisation and delivery of health services, making sure that people's needs and not business and professional profits are the primary determinants of the funding and organisation of health care. Profits and health needs rarely coincide. The majority of Americans agree on this point. They want government intervention not only in the funding but also in the delivery and organisation of health services. This popular demand is not unique to the US population. In all Western developed societies, national health programmes have been the most popular programmes established after World War II by Labour and Social Democratic governments. Even Mrs Thatcher has not dared to dismantle Britain's National Health Service, and the Labour Party has gained popularity when it has appeared as the defender of the NHS. As Harold Wilson once put it, 'The National Health Service has been the crown of the Welfare State. . . and the very temple of our Social Security.'[167] No other programme within the welfare state has been as popular as a comprehensive and universal health programme.

This international reality has not yet touched the American Democratic Party. In the last election, only Jesse Jackson spoke of the need for a National Health Programme, and he did not emphasise it to any serious extent. However, such a programme would have helped his candidacy to break its image of representing only the black constituency. Aggressive support of a National Health Programme would have helped to link Jackson with the aged, the unions, and other elements of the rainbow coalition he wanted to establish. His support for a National Health Programme was perfunctory, however, a mere item in his list of social programmes, without recognition of the critical role that such a programme could play in the majority of people's lives. He was perceived more as a Great Society than a New Deal politician. And while Jackson's influence was major and positive, he missed an opportunity to put the most important New Deal programme at the centre of his campaign. This practice is not unique to Jackson. Among the Left, there is an unawareness of the critical and enormous importance that health care plays in people's lives. The funding of a comprehensive and universal health programme should be based on different but highly popular interventions, including:

1. changed priorities within the health sector, not only through incentives but also active government interventions. The current reliance on highly technological medicine is neither good medical care nor good health care. Although high technology curative medicine has a role to play, it should not be the dominant form of intervention.

The state of North Carolina, for example, has about the same number of deliveries per year as Sweden, but twice as many low birth weight babies and neonatal deaths, due to poverty and malnutrition. In 1978-79 there were only 30 ventilator-equipped neonatal intensive care unit beds in Sweden compared to 60 or so in North Carolina, where even further expansions are now proposed.[168] It would be cheaper and more humane to provide food and other social services rather than curative technology. The *laissez faire* approach to medical care enables and stimulates a sophisticated technological approach to medical problems, but does not serve well as a broadly based preventive approach capable of diminishing both the problems and the need for expensive technology. In summary, there is a need to shift the priorities away from hospital, curative, personal, and highly technological medicine towards preventive, community, environmental, occupational and social medical and health care interventions. This shift of priorities will not occur by continuing reliance on the for-profit private sector. It requires an active government intervention and active popular participation;

2. a shift of resources within the public sector, away from the military and back to social expenditures, reversing a trend that threatens the survival of the US population. According to the 1986 Reagan budget proposal, the military budget will have further increased a staggering 239 per cent by the year 1990. These funds are spent, in official rhetoric, to make American children more 'secure' from external enemies. Meanwhile, from 1980-1985, during the Reagan Administration, more American children die from poverty than the total number of American battle deaths in the Vietnam War. Till 1990, 22,000 American babies are estimated to die per year because of low birth weight. Poverty is the greatest child killer in 1985 in the affluent US. None other than President Eisenhower indicated that 'The problem in defense is how far you can go without destroying from within what you are trying to defend from without.'[169] Here again, we find that Americans do support the reversal of this trend, with shifting of resources from military to social and health expenditures. 46 per cent of Americans felt that the government spends too little in social services (including health).[170] The level of popular support for health expenditures is much, much higher than the level of support for military expenditures;

3. increases in the level of taxation of the corporate class and upper middle class, a level that has declined dramatically and is even imperiling the functioning of the US economy. The overall size of tax cuts aimed at the corporate class was $220 billion in 1984.[171] The entire federal costs of a comprehensive health programme were estimated by the Carter Administration to be $20 billion for 1984,

less than 10 per cent of the revenues lost to the federal government because of cuts for the wealthy.[172] A Comprehensive Health Programme has to be redistributive, based on authentically progressive revenues. It should increasingly rely on general revenues rather than social security taxes. This reliance on general revenues would also allow for shifting revenues among sectors. This is particularly important in light of the demographic transition, which is usually presented as a major reason for the rise of health expenditures. To have more elderly means to have more health consumption. The absolute and percentage growth of the elderly is presented as one of the reasons for the crisis of the Western systems of health care. Due to the repetitiveness of this argument, let me clarify that:

(a) the enormous growth of expenditures in the US Federal Programme for the elderly, Medicare, for the period 1978 to 1982 was not caused by an increase in the numbers of elderly. Neither the number of elderly patients nor their utilisation of health services increased during that period. The major cause of that growth of expenditures was price inflation; i.e., the price of hospital and medical services that benefit providers and suppliers but not the patients;

(b) the same demographic transition leads to fewer young people, with a freeing up of education, transportation and recreation public funds that could be shifted to health services. For example, the OECD Secretariat has shown that the estimated saving for public education in the seven major industrialised countries, due to the demographic transition, could ensure a 0.7 per cent annual growth of real social expenditures until 1990, more than sufficient to cover the expanding demands of the elderly in health services;[173]

4. government funding, administration, and management of the health care services and institutions, with active worker and community participation in the running of these institutions. Himmelstein and Woolhandler have documented the ideological biases of most cost control measures that are being researched in US, and that are being implemented by the US government. All of them implied a cut of benefits to the working population. A progressive agenda will have to focus on cost controls that enlarge these health benefits and further empower the patient and potential patient population, i.e., the citizenry. These authors estimated that if the US would have had a national health insurance in 1983, it would have saved the US population $38.7 billion annually ($29.2 billion in health administration and insurance overhead, $4.9 billion on profits, and $4.6 billion on physicians' income). If the US would have a national health service, the US population would save $61.9 billion ($38.4 billion in

health administration and insurance overhead, $4.9 billion in profits and $18.6 billion in physicians' income). Complete nationalisation of the health services, with nationalisation of the drug and supplies industries would save $85.3 billion dollars (one third of all health expenditures). And most importantly, those savings would occur while expanding rather than reducing the health benefits for the whole population.[174]

All of these points bear repeating in light of current arguments about the crisis of the welfare state, which attributes that crisis to either the demographic transition or to the growth of public expenditures assumed to be out of control. Documented reality shows otherwise.

Will That Change Occur?

The major problem that the progressive forces are facing today in the US is not that we have the most reactionary President since the beginning of the century in the White House. This Administration is doing what it was appointed to do. It is remarkably predictable and consequent. The problem that we face is the increasing abandonment by the Democratic Party of the New Deal, with Left forces within and outside that Party in a state of demoralisation and paralysis. This is the gravest danger that we face in the US. I want to make it clear that I am not minimising the enormous importance of having a less reactionary President in the US. However, it is important to recognise that change- progressive change- could take place, even with Reagan in the White House. Remember that a whole set of progressive legislation and programmes was enacted in the 70s (such as EPA, NIOSH, OSHA and many others) while conservative Republicans were in the White House. Behind each one of those programmes, there was a lot of agitation and struggle, sweat and tears. Democracy is not only the act of voting but also the act of mobilising, organising, and exerting social pressure. As Gramsci kept saying, 'The vote gives you the right but not the power.' And history has proved it. Behind each electoral achievement, behind each progressive piece of legislation, behind each progressive government programme, there has always been a history of struggle and mass mobilisations. This is where the Left should be. This is not to imply that mobilisation struggles and electoral politics constitute two separate and non-convergent roads. Quite to the contrary. While for the Right electoral politics serve to demobilise the population, for the Left the mobilisation is the main motor of electoral politics. Never has the Left achieved a major legislative victory without mass mobilisations.[175]

Here a key point needs to be raised: the nature and agencies of these mobilisations and political *praxis*. Indeed, there is a strong current within the US Left, including its radical versions, that dismisses class as a meaningless category for social and political action. Many radical left-wingers are adding their voices to the growing chorus singing farewell to the working class. A new orthodoxy has been established within large sectors of the New Left, in which new positions are being solidified into a new set of postures and cliches, with summary dismissal of alternative left-wing positions as outmoded, passé, dogmatic or unrealistic. Much of this new orthodoxy is influenced by the writings of Gorz[176] and Touraine[177] from France, Laclau and Mouffe[178] from the UK and Stanley Aronowitz in the US.[179] Their farewell to the working class is accompanied by a note of mourning for the Marxism that they once claimed as their own. Their recent self-identification as *neo*-Marxists enables them to (by using the *neo*) establish a safe and respectable distance from the main body of Marxist *praxis*. Their *neo*-Marxism, however, has now quickly become *post*-Marxism.

Without denying the diversity in these various post-Marxist positions, there are, however, some elements of their analyses that are similar. One is the assumption that, because of the evolution of national and inter-national capitalism, the working class has been diminished, splintered and/or dissolved during the period since World War II. Because of this situation, the working class is considered to have diminished in import-ance as an agency for change. In its stead, new social movements based on race, ethnicity, gender, sexual preference, ideological and peace concerns have emerged as the new agents for change, with greater potential for radical politics than organised labour. Class politics have been replaced by coalition politics, in which different groups, concerns, and interests come together within a coalition in which there are no hierarchical relation-ships. No one group is more important than another.[180] According to one proponent of coalition politics, what is needed in the US is for 'Hispanics, Native Americans, the poor, women, gays, lesbians, liberal progressives and radicals to join forces to resist sweeping repression and economic conservatism'.[181] In this scenario, class loses its key importance as an analytical and political category. And Marxism becomes obsolete, a 'hang up' that keeps the Left stuck, stunting its development. Thus, the problem in the Left is thought to be that while 'many progressives have on the theoretical and rhetorical level moved beyond this basic tenet of orthodox Marxism, it is still retained at the level of practical politics'.[182] For others it is not only Marxism, but the very concept and practice of Left politics that are obsolete. As one of the editors of *Dissent* suggested recently, 'Perhaps the Left/Right distinction itself is becoming obsolete as a way of understanding politics and political possibilities.'[183]

It is important to clarify that all these positions assume, of course, that the practice of the US Left (at least in the recent past) has been a class practice and that Marxism has been the theoretical orbit in which the US Left has moved. Anyone even vaguely familiar with the US scene, how-ever, can see that both assumptions are profoundly wrong. The US Left has not followed class practices for quite a long time. And for the most part, the US Left, including its radical components, has been and continues to be profoundly anti-Marxist. Indeed, the US Left has primarily followed the type of practice that the post-Marxists now propose, i.e., 'coalition politics' within a constantly shifting pattern of alliances. Indeed, what those theoreticians of the neo-New Left are advocating is but a recycling of the old 'pluralist-interest groups' theories that have been the dominant form of political discourse and practice in the US for many years. The emergence and importance of social movements in the US—the main trademark of US political behaviour and mass mobilisation—are a direct consequence of the absence of class-based practices by the dominated classes. The centrality of social movements in the US as forms of political and social mobilisation is more reflective of the backwardness of US politics (i.e., the absence of class instruments of struggle by the dominated classes and strata) than its assumed vanguardism (i.e., an achievement that other societies can emulate). It is this backwardness that explains why the US has a less developed welfare state (e.g., nearly 12 per cent of the US population does not have any form of health coverage), fewer social and economic rights for women (e.g., the average maternity leave in the US is four weeks, compared with six months in Sweden and eight months in Finland), and less protection for workers and the environment (e.g., Swedish workers have an important voice in hiring and firing occupational physicians, a right unheard of in the US); also, the US allows far larger levels of toxic substances in the air than the majority of Northern European countries where the dominated classes follow class practices.[184]

Class practice on the part of the dominated classes continues to be of paramount importance to respond to the always present class practice of the dominant class. This is not to deny the enormous importance for the Left to be sensitive to forms of exploitation other than class exploitation, nor to ignore the importance of establishing coalitions with strata outside the working class. But in any class society, class relations determine and organise the other forms of exploitation. This is overwhelmingly clear in the US. For example, how races relate to one another depends in large degree on the relative position of the races within a class matrix in which the capitalist class is the dominant force. In the steel mills of Baltimore, for example, the place of the worker within the hierarchical labour process in the mills was determined until the middle 60s by the race and ethnicity of the worker. Foremen were Italians, Poles were coal workers and Blacks were sweepcleaners. Divide and conquer was and continues to be the practice of the dominant class. This reality cannot be ignored by the dominated class. The operational meaning of this awareness is not, however, the mere aggregate of the demands of each component of the 'people'. Class practices are not the aggregate of 'interest group' politics. And New Deal programmes are not the mere aggregate of Great Society type of programmes. This was, incidentally, the main problem with Jesse

Jackson's 'rainbow coalition'. Without minimising the very positive role of the Jackson Presidential campaign, still, a major weakness of that campaign was its emphasis on Great Society type of demands, with heavy emphasis on the rights of Blacks without providing enough linkage with other components of the working class.

Class Disintegration or Class Recomposition?

Another assumption of the neo-New Left is that the weakness of the Left reflects the 'shrinking' of its classical constituency—the working class. This is the explanation given for the decline of the unions and of the Democratic Party in the US. The redefinition of the working class and its re-structuring is not a unique US phenomena, however. Most Western capitalist developed societies have gone through a similar reorganisation of the working class. And, as Therborn has shown, in the majority of these countries (except the US and the UK), the left-wing electorate increased rather than declined during the years that the restructuring of the working class was taking place.[185]

Similarly, other countries facing similar changes in the working class have seen an increase rather than a decline in the percentage of the labour force that is unionised. In Canada, for example, the percentage of the civilian labour force that was organised increased in the 1963–1983 period from roughly 30 per cent to 40 per cent, at the same time that the percentage of organised workers declined in the US from 30 to 20 per cent.[186] This decline, incidentally, cannot be explained by lack of popular support for unionisation. 75 per cent of all workers agree that unions improve the wages and working conditions of workers,[187] and that level of popular support has increased rather than declined during the Reagan years.[188] Thus, the decline of the unions and the assumed decline of the Democratic vote cannot be traced primarily to changes within the working class. It has to be rooted in the instruments of that class.

A main cause of the weakness of the unions is their corporativist practices (i.e., each union looking out for itself and its own constituency) and their limited democracy. Their lack of class behaviour, compounded by the absence of a political instrument (i.e., a labour party), has left the working class very weak and unable to resist the enormous class aggression shown by the capitalist class since 1978. Regarding democracy, it is worth noting that 50 per cent of the US population believes that most union leaders no longer represent the interests of the workers in their unions.[189]

The situation is not entirely bleak, however. Changes are occurring, many in the right direction. For example, for the first time in the post-war period, the executive committee of the AFL–CIO has reversed its long-standing commitment to defence expenditures. Moreover, it has in its leadership individuals who explicitly refer to themselves as socialists. Also, the AFL–CIO leadership has recently taken steps towards breaking the corporativist practices of the US unions by (1) discouraging competition among unions for new members; (2) linking work-related struggles with struggles and demands outside the workplace; (3) trying to organise the unorganised, including the unemployed; (4) supporting class demands with nationwide appeal, such as the establishment of a national health programme; and (5) becoming actively involved in the Democratic Party, playing a critical and key role in the selection of the Presidential candidate and trying to actively influence the development of its programme.

Since the early 70s, there has been a shifting pattern of coalition within the Democratic Party. Contrary to the message put forward by the Right and even large sectors of the Left, the New Dealers have not been in hegemonic positions in the Democratic Party since the late 60s and early 70s. The new dominant coalition appears in the new forms of discourse that the Democratic Party adopted in the last elections. The new message was the articulation of the need for *compassion*—(the *noblesse oblige* attitude of the enlightened upper classes towards the 'have-nots') with the call for *modernism* (social engineering and government efficiency attractive to the new professional-technical strata). On the basis of the call for compassion, charitable impulses and moral calls for the 'haves' to be mindful of the 'have-nots' become the centre-piece of political programmes. On the basis of the call for modernism, social and economic problems are converted to technical and managerial interventions to get the economy back into proper working order. In both messages, the issues of power in general and class power in particular disappear. The call for class solidarity, social justice and anti-corporate policies has been put in storage or simply thrown out as part of an outdated discourse that (like the New Deal) needs to be transcended.

In light of this reality, what needs to be explained is not so much the defeat of non-existent New Deal candidates—McGovern, Carter and Mondale—but rather the alliance of the working class with the Democratic Party in view of the weakening commitment to the New Deal by the Democratic Party and the increased similarities between the two major parties. It has been during the 70s and 80s that the enormous growth of political abstentionism by the population in general and the working class in particular has taken place. This political marginalisation is symptomatic of a growing awareness of the impossibility for change, accompanied by a cynical view of the establishment. The lack of trust in the major establishment institutions in the US on the part of the majority of the population, a phenomenon that President Carter referred to as 'malaise', peaked in the 1978–80 period (the politics of austerity years), to be further augmented in the 80s to reach in 1982 the highest point ever of lack of popular confidence in the major establishment institutions.[190] It was also during this time that large sectors of labour started discussing the need for the establishment of a Labour Party. The re-election of Reagan slowed down that process. Also, the active involvement of AFL–CIO in the Democratic Party (supporting Mondale in 1984, once Kennedy indicated his wishes not to run), and the likely shifting of conservative Democrats to the Republican Party, contributed (for the time being) to sidetrack that much needed debate. It is unlikely, however, that a new party will be established while the Republicans are still in power. A new party, if established, is likely to emerge from a substantial split in the Democratic Party while it is in power. The difficulties in establishing a new party are enormous: hence, the continuing alliance with the Democratic Party, and labour's calls for the Democratic Party to change. However, the much needed radicalisation of the Democratic Party is not taking place. Quite to the contrary. Witness, for example, the defensiveness of the Democratic Party leadership towards the accusation of being the party of 'interest groups', the code term used by the establishment to define labour.

To recognise this situation is not to say that there is no room for change within the Democratic Party or that all work within that Party is a waste of time and energy better invested in establishing a new Party. There is a need to work both within and outside the Democratic Party, via all forms of participation, organisation and mobilisation to re-establish a Left wing space and historical block including a broad coalition of forces, centred around labour, struggling for the further expansion and redefinition of democracy, initiated in the New Deal and still far from completed. The New Deal was not the accomplishment of a Party or of President Roosevelt. It was the fierce struggle of the working population that pushed and pressed that Party and that Administration towards the establishment of the bases for the American Welfare State. This New Deal, rather than co-opting and integrating the working class, further empowered it, which explains the hatred of the ultra-right for those programmes. As Huberman concluded in his moving history of the US working class:

> The common man and woman must not forget the New Deal. It was a valuable experience. It gave the workers and farmers a sense of their own power. They learned that in order to be able to get any of the things they wanted they had to organize both politically and economically. And today, when the New Deal is rapidly becoming a memory, they must remember that lesson. They must redouble their economic and political activities. They want jobs and peace. They must take the initiative in getting them. And they will learn through their struggle that jobs and peace are attainable only under a system or production for use, not for profit.[191]

The enormous popularity of the New Deal even today shows that the majority of people have not forgotten it. But there is an enormous ideological avalanche aimed at making people forget past struggles for democratic rights and the achievements those struggles won. It is because of this situation that there is an urgent need for the Left to demystify and denounce that ideological avalanche and present alternative interpretations to the dominant and hegemonic ones. As that great American—Woody Guthrie—told us once, we have to change our glasses to see light where they want us to see darkness, to see hope where they want us to see despair and to see possibilities for change where they want us to get trapped in the shifting sands of continuous pessimism.

NOTES

1. D. Plotke, 'Reagan's American Dream', *Marxism Today*, November 1984, Vol. 28, No. 11, p. 20.
2. J. Borja, 'El futuro de la izquierda' (The Future of the Left), *El Pais*, December 28, 1984.
3. D. Osborne, 'Democrats Need Hart and Soul', *Mother Jones*, Vol. X, No. 1, January 1985, p. 60.
4. A. Crittenden, 'The Democrats' Economic Vacuum', *The New York Times*, January 27, 1985, Business Section, p. 1.
5. J.K. Galbraith and N. Salinger, *Almost Everyone's Guide to Economics*, Bantam Books, 1979, p. 15.
6. E.C. Ladd, 'The Reagan Phenomenon and Public Attitudes Toward Government', in L.M. Salamon and M.S. Lund (eds.), *The Reagan Presidency and the Governings of America*, The Urban Institute Press, Washington, D.C., 1985, p. 230.
7. E.C. Ladd, 'Interview with Peter Hart', *Public Opinion*, December 13, 1984.
8. GOP (Republican) Platform for 1980, The Republican National Committee.
9. Mondale's acceptance speech, Democratic Convention, San Francisco, 1984.
10. Cited in F. Siegel, 'Emil Oestereicher (1936–1983), Notes on Neo-Liberalism', *Telos*, No. 59, Spring 1984, p. 172.
11. W. Weaver, 'Democratic Platform Shows a Shift From Liberal Positions of 1976 and 1980', *The New York Times*, July 22, 1984, p. 20.
12. D. Mechanic, 'The Transformation of Health Providers', *Health Affairs*, Spring 1984, p. 65.
13. D. Altman, 'A New Barbarism', *Socialist Review*, Vol. 15, No. 1, January/February 1985, p. 9.
14. D. Plotke, 'Reaganism and the Problems of Special Interests', *Socialist Review*, Vol. 15, No. 1, January/February 1985, p. 18.
15. D. Wrong, 'The End of Ideology', *Dissent*, Spring 1985, p. 147.
16. J. Judis, 'Reflections on 1984', *In These Times*, November 21–December 4, p. 11.
17. J. Judis, 'Republicans Surge While Democrats Drift', *In These Times*, May 22–28, 1985, p. 2.
18. R.B.D. Boff, 'Perspectives', *In These Times*, May 15–21, 1985, p. 12.
19. T.B. Edsall, *The New Politics of Inequality*, W.W. Norton, New York, 1984, p. 145.
20. S. Kelley, *Interpreting Elections*, Princeton University Press, Princeton, 1983.
21. *The New York Times*, November 5, 1980.
22. *Time*, November 17, 1980.
23. *Wall Street Journal*, November 5, 1980.
24. *Newsweek*, November 17, 1980.
25. *National Review*, November 18, 1980, p. 1434.

26. *Op. cit.*, p. 1453.
27. The quoted words and phrases come from (in order of quotation) *The New York Times*, November 5, 1980; *The Washington Post*, November 6, 1980; the *Los Angeles Times*, November 5, 1980; the *Chicago Tribune*, November 6, 1980; the *Wall Street Journal*, November 5, 1980; cover David Broder et al., *The Pursuit of the Presidency*, 1980, Bantam Books; *The New Orleans Times*, November 11, 1980; *The Washington Post*, November 6, 1980 and the *Chicago Tribune*, November 6, 1980.
28. A. Lewis, 'Tidal Wave', *The New York Times*, November 6, 1980.
29. S. Kelley, *op. cit.*, p. 169.
30. S. Kelley, *op. cit.*, p. 169.
31. *Ibid.*
32. *Ibid.*
33. E.C. Ladd, 'The Reagan Phenomenon and Public Attitudes Toward Government, *op. cit.*, p. 224.
34. The Gallup Poll post election survey, the ABC News Election Day Poll and the NBC–Associated Press Election Day Poll, cited in S. Kelley, *op. cit.*, p. 171.
35. University of Michigan 1980 National Election Study, cited in S. Kelley, *op. cit.*, p. 170.
36. *Time*, November 3, 1980.
37. University of Michigan 1980 National Election Study, cited in S. Kelley, *op. cit.*, p. 172.
38. Gallup Poll release for October 18, 1980 cited in S. Kelley, *op. cit.*, p. 173.
39. E.C. Ladd, 'The Reagan Phenomenon and Public Attitudes Toward Government', *op. cit.*, p. 223.
40. Gallup Poll release for November 13, 1980.
41. ABC–News–Harris Survey release for November 11, 1980.
42. Cited in S. Kelley, *op. cit.*, p. 185.
43. For a detailed analysis of opinion polls (on social expenditures and government regulations) for the period 1976–1983, see V. Navarro, 'Where is the Popular Mandate? A Reply to Conventional Wisdom', *International Journal of Health Services*, Vol. 13, No. 1, 1983, p. 169.
44. *Ibid.*
45. T.B. Edsall, *op. cit.*, p. 17.
46. Interview with Gary Hart, E.C. Ladd, *op. cit.*, p. 228.
47. S. Kelley, *op. cit.*, p. 123.
48. D.L. Bawden and J.L. Palmer, 'Social Policy: Challenging the Welfare State', in J.L. Palmer and I.V. Sawhill, *The Reagan Record: An Urban Institute Study*, Ballinger Publishing Co., Cambridge, 1984, p. 184.
49. D.L. Bawden and J.L. Palmer, *op. cit.*, p. 184.
50. *Ibid.*, p. 214.
51. *Ibid.*, p. 214.
52. Cited in D. Wrong, *op. cit.*, p. 147.
53. J. Larner, 'Four More Years: Comments and Opinions', *Dissent*, Winter, 1985, p. 9.
54. J. Clark, *op. cit.*, p. 8.
55. 'Special Issue: Analysis of the 1984 Election', in G. Hall, 'Reagan's "Political Realignment" Did Not Show', *Political Affairs*, December 1984, p. 5.
56. W.C. Adams, 'Recent Fables About Reagan', *Public Opinion*, October/November 1984, p. 6.
57. M.J. Pen and D.E. Schoen, 'The GOP as Majority', Op-ed. pages, *The New York Times*, February 6, 1985, p. A23.
58. G. Hall, *op. cit.*, p. 5.

59. R. Pear, 'People Responding to *The New York Times/CBS News Poll* Last Month Had a More Favorable View of Great Society Programs Than People Questioned in 1980', *The New York Times*, Sunday, December 16, 1984, p. E3.

60. B. Sussman, ' "Reagan's Popularity High Although Policies Are Questioned", Discussion of *Washington Post/ABC News Poll* on Popular Views on Federal Budget Issues', *The Washington Post*, January 20, 1985, p. A1.

61. G. Hall, *op. cit.*, p. 5 and 'Analysis of US Election Propositions', *The Economist*, November 10–16, 1984, pp. 30–32.

62. S.M. Lipset, 'Poll After Poll After Poll After Poll Warns President on Programs', *The New York Times*, January 13, 1982, (editorial page).

63. 'Poll Finds Strong Support For Environmental Code', *The New York Times*, October 4, 1982, p. 30.

64. 'Polls Show Reaction On "Aid" To Poor Differs From The Attitude On "Welfare" ', *The New York Times*, February 14, 1982.

65. C. Ladd and S.M. Lipset, *The United States in the 1980s*.

66. 'Reagan's Budget Found Evoking More Concern', *The New York Times*, March 1982.

67. 'Pollster Says Opposition To Reagan Mounting', *The Nation's Health*, July 1982, pp. 1–2.

68. Public Opinion Round Up 97–3, September 11, 1981, Democratic Study Group, Washington, D.C., 1981.

69. V. Navarro, 'Where is the Popular Mandate?', *op. cit.* Also, Opinion Roundup, *Public Opinion*, October/November, 1984, pp. 26–27.

70. Gallup Poll, August 1979, quoted in *Health Law Newsletter*, No. 105, January 1980, p. 1 and Harris Poll 1979, quoted in *Medical World News*, January 7, 1980, p. 9.

71. W. Schneider, 'Public Ready For Real Change in Health Care', *National Journal*, 3/23, 1985, p. 664.

72. J.P. Robinson and J.A. Fleishman, 'Ideological Trends in American Public Opinion', *The Annals of the American Academy of Political and Social Sciences*, March 1984, p. 56.

73. S.M. Lipset, 'Feeling Better: Measuring the Nation's Confidence', *Public Opinion*, April/May, 1985, p. 57.

74. Cited by S.M. Lipset, *op. cit.*, p. 57.

75. 'Portrait of the Electorate', *The New York Times/CBS News Poll*, *The New York Times*, November 8, 1984, p. A19.

76. B. Keller, 'Unions Reassess Mondale Support', *The New York Times*, November 9, 1985, p. A21.

77. G. Hall, *op. cit.*

78. B. Keller, *op. cit.*

79. G. Hall, *op. cit.*, p. 4.

80. *The Economist*, *op. cit.*, p. 25.

81. 'New Budget Chairman: An Unswerving Fighter', *The New York Times*, January 5, 1985, p. 7.

82. L. Kramer, 'A Lot of Big Cities Joined Washington in Fritz's Column', *The Washington Post*, January 20, 1985, C5.

83. D. Yankelovich, 'When Reaganomics Fail, Then What?', in L.M. Salamon and M.S. Lund, *The Reagan Presidency and the Governing of America*, The Urban Institute Press, 1985, p. 251.

84. G. Hall, *op. cit.*, p. 5.

85. Penn and Schoen Associates, *The Carter Analysis*, February 1984.

86. V. Navarro, Where is the Popular Mandate?', *op. cit.*

87. *The New York Times*, September 11, 1984, p. A24.

88. Exceptions within the Left are *Monthly Review* and *Political Affairs*. They have not reproduced the hegemonic interpretation of the 1980 and 1984 elections.

89. To explain the further move to the right see V. Navarro, 'The Crisis of the International Capitalist Order and Its Complications for the Welfare State', *International Journal of Health Services*, Vol. 12, No. 2, 1982.

90. B.H. Bagdikian, *The Media Monopoly*, Beacon Press, 1983.

91. A. Gramsci, *The Ordine Nuovo Selection From The Prison Notebooks*, International Publishers, 1978. Also G. Therborn, *The Ideology of Power or the Power of Ideology*, Verso Books, 1982.

92. R. Blendon and A. Altman, 'The Case of Health Reforms: Americans' Schizophrenia', *The New England Journal of Medicine*, October 1984.

93. V. Navarro, 'In Defense of the American People: They Are Not Schizophrenic', *International Journal of Health Services*.

94. *Ibid.*

95. Complete Hart Poll Results, published in *Common Sense*, pp. 16–17, September 1, 1975. Also, quoted in Bender, M., 'Will the Bicentennial See the Death of the Free Enterprise?', *The New York Times*, January 4, 1976, p. 27.

96. P. Peretz, 'There Was Not A Tax Revolt', *Politics and Society*, 11 (2):231, 1982.

97. W. Lippman, *The Phantom Public*, Harcourt, Brace Publications, 1925, pp. 56–57.

98. M.J. Pen and D.E. Schoen, *op. cit.*

99. 'Opinion Roundup, Social Class', *Public Opinions*, October/November 1984, p. 21.

100. T.B. Edsall, *op. cit.*, p. 229.

101. D. Lee Bawden, *The Social Contract Revisited: Aims and Outcomes of President Reagan's Social Welfare Policy*, The Urban Institute Press, Washington, D.C., 1984, and M. Moon and I.V. Sawhill, *Family Incomes: Gainers and Losers*, in J.L. Palmer and I.V. Sawhill, *The Reagan Record*, The Urban Institute Press, 1984, pp. 317–346.

102. V. Navarro, 'The Determinants of Social Policy: The Case of Sweden', *Journal of Health, Health Policy and Law*.

103. I. Wallerstein, 'The USA in Today's World', *Contemporary Marxism*, No. 4, 1982, pp. 16 and 17.

104. Cited in G. Therborn, 'The Prospects of Labor and the Transformation of Advanced Capitalism', *The New Left Review*, No. 145, 1984, p. 29.

105. Cited in R.S. Beal and R.H. Hinckley, 'Presidential Decision Making and Opinion Polls', *Annals of the American Academy of Political and Social Sciences*, March 1984, p. 80.

106. Washington Post–ABC News Poll, *The Washington Post*, January 20, 1985.

107. *Ibid.*

108. R. Kuttner, *The Economic Illusion*, Houghton Mifflin Co., 1984, p. 53.

109. R. Kuttner, *op. cit.*, p. 189.

110. A. DeCormis, 'Reagan: A Tax Reformer?', *The Guardian*, June 1985, p. 8.

111. Editorial, 'The Need for Tax Reform', *Monthly Review*, November 1984, p. 1.

112. R. Kuttner, *op. cit.*, p. 187.

113. *Ibid.*, p. 190.

114. Percentages of Harris Poll respondents who felt taxes were too high, by type of tax, 1969–1978, in Peretz, P., 'There Was No Tax Revolt', *Politics and Society*, 11 (2):231, 1982.

115. V. Navarro, 'Where is the Popular Mandate?', *op. cit.*

116. Jack A. Meyer, 'Percentage Distribution of Federal Outlays', Table 6, 'Budget Cuts in the Reagan Administration. A Question of Fairness', in D. Lee Bawden (ed.), *The Social Contract Revisited*, Urban Institute Press, 1984, p. 42.

117. T.B. Edsall, *op. cit.*, p. 39.
118. E. Boorstein, 'What is Ahead: The US Economy', *op. cit.*, p. 36.
119. *Ibid.*, p. 195.
120. T.B. Edsall, *op. cit.*, p. 197.
121. *Ibid.*, pp. 145, 146 and 147.
122. E.C. Ladd, 'The Reagan Phenomenon and Public Attitudes Toward Government', *op. cit.*, p. 223.
123. Editorial, 'Happy Days Are Here Again', *The New York Times*, August 26, 1984, p. 20E.
124. E.C. Ladd, *op. cit.*, p. 222.
125. A. Manatos, 'US Voter Turnout: Now World's Worst', *The New York Times*, Op-ed. page, December 1, 1984, p. 23.
126. 'Analysis of the 1984 US Elections', *Daily World*, December 27, 1984, p. 110.
127. T.B. Edsall, *op. cit.*, p. 184.
128. R. Wolfinger and S. Rosenstone, *Who Votes?*, Yale University Press, 1980, pp. 109–110.
129. 'Left and the Elections', *The Guardian*, November 21, 1984, p. 3. According to *The New York Times/CBS News Poll* 'Portrait of the Electorate', November 8, 1984, p. A19, unemployed workers voted 68 per cent for Mondale. This group comprises 8 per cent of all adults, but only 3 per cent of those who voted in 1984. Voters earning less than $12,500 went for Mondale by 53 per cent; they comprise 28 per cent of the adult population but only 15 per cent of the 1984 electorate.
130. Cited in V. Perlo, 'People vs. Profits', *Daily World*, May 18, 1985.
131. G.B. Mills, 'The Bridges: A Failure of Discipline', Chapter 4 in J.L. Palmer and I.V. Sawhill (eds.), *The Reagan Record*, An Urban Institute Study, 1984, p. 122.
132. V. Perlo, 'Analysis of the 1984 Economic Report to the President of the Council of Economic Advisors', *Daily World*, March 1, 1984.
133. *Ibid.*
134. *Ibid.*
135. 'Government and the Economy', in S. Bowles and R. Edwards, *Understanding Capitalism*, Harper Row, New York, 1985, p. 247.
136. *The New York Times*, February 14, 1982.
137. Editorial Page, *The New York Times*, February 14, 1982.
138. Cited in E. Boorstein, *op. cit.*, p. 170.
139. *Ibid.*, p. 172.
140. *Ibid.*, p. 172.
141. D. Plotke, *Marxism Today*, *op. cit.*, p. 17.
142. Cited in Seccion Economica, *El Pais*, October 1982.
143. R. McIntyre, 'The Failure of Corporate Tax Incentives', *Multinational Monitor*, Vol. 5, Nos. 10 and 11, 1984, pp. 3–11.
144. R. Kuttner, *op. cit.*
145. *Ibid.*, p. 54.
146. D. Plotke, *op. cit.*
147. M. Davis, 'The Pathology of Reaganomics', *The New Left Review*, No. 149, 1985, pp. 45–65.
148. M. Davis, 'Late Imperial America', *The New Left Review*, No. 143, 1984, p. 6.
149. Cited in J.M. Cypher, 'Rearming America', *Monthly Review*, 33 (6):15, 1981.
150. H. Sherman and J.L. Wood, *Sociology, Traditional and Radical Perspectives*, Harper and Row, New York, 1979.
151. Quoted in 'Reagan Policy in Crisis', *North American Congress on Latin America Report*, 15 (4):10, 1981.
152. J. Knight, 'This Government is Off Our Backs? Academic Freedom is Wicked',

Op-ed. page, *The New York Times*, February 9, 1985, p. 23.
153. N. Poulantzas, *State, Power and Socialism*, Verso Books, 1978.
154. M.N. Zald, 'Political Change, Citizenship Rights, and the Welfare State', *The Annals of the American Academy of Political and Social Sciences*, May 1985, p. 65.
155. S. Shapiro, 'Sociodemographic Risk Factors in Infant Mortality and Low Birth Weight', Health Policy Forum, Harvard University, October 15, 1984.
156. J. Shriver, 'The Most Important Problem', Gallup Rep., 1984, 220–221:28-9.
157. 'Number of Uninsured Americans Increases', *Medical Care Review*, Summer, Vol. 41, No. 2, 1984, p. 72.
158. 'Direct Payment by Consumers in 1975, Excluding Voluntary Insurance', Figure 4–4 in R.J. Maxwell, *Health and Wealth: An International Study of Health Care Spending*, Lexington Books, 1981, p. 65.
159. D.E. Altman, 'What Do Americans Really Want?', *Health Affairs*, Fall 1984, p. 139.
160. Louis Harris and Associates Inc., in the 1983 Equitable Health Care Survey.
161. W. Schneider, 'Public Ready for Real Change in Health Care', *National Journal*, 3/23, 1985, p. 664.
162. R.M. Gibson, K.R. Levitt, H. Lazenby and D.R. Waldo, 'National Health Expenditures, 1983', *Health Care Financing Review*, Winter 1984, Vol. 6, No. 2, p. 1.
163. Cited in J. Steele, 'How US Doctors Bleed the Government', *Guardian* (London), August 30, 1976.
164. V. Navarro, 'The Public/Private Mix in the Funding and Delivery of Health Services: An International Survey' (in process).
165. 'Profitable American Hospitals', *The Economist*, May 18–24, 1985, pp. 82-83.
166. R.J. Maxwell, *Health and Wealth. An International Study of Health Care Spending*, Lexington Books, 1981, p. 68.
167. H. Wilson, The House of Commons, Vol. 629, London, Hansard (Fifth Series—1960), p. 190.
168. R.J. David and E. Siegel, 'Decline in Neonatal Mortality 1968-1977: Better Babies or Better Care', *Pediatrics*, 1983, 71:531-540.
169. These figures and quotes are from *A Children's Defense Budget. An Analysis of the President's FY 1986 Budget and Children*, Children's Defense Fund, 1985.
170. 'Public Favors Cutting Defense, Retaining Social Programs', *The Gallup Report*, March 1985.
171. 'The Winners and the Losers Under Reaganomics', *UAW Washington Report*, September 4, 1981, pp. 2-3.
172. 'The Estimated Costs for a National Comprehensive Health Program', US Department of Health and Human Services, 1980.
173. G. Therborn, 'The Irreversible Welfare State', *op. cit.*, p. 24.
174. D. Himmelstein and S. Woolhandler, 'Cost Without Benefit: Bureaucracy and Entrepreneurialism in US Health Care', (in press).
175. V. Navarro, 'The Nature of Democracy in the Core Capitalist Countries: Meanings and Implications for Class Struggle', *The Insurgent Sociologist*, Vol. X, No. 1, Summer 1980.
176. Gorz, *Farewell to the Working Class*, Pluto Press, 1982.
177. A. Touraine, *Le mouvement ouvrier*, Fayard, Paris, 1984, and Movements Sociaux D'aujourd' hui, Les editions Ouvriers, 1982.
178. E. Ladau and C. Mouffe, *Hegemony and Socialist Strategy. Towards a Radical Democratic Politics*, Verso Books, London, 1984.
179. S. Aronowitz, *Crisis in Historical Materialism*, 1984.
180. A representative article of this position is C. West, 'Reconstructing the American

Left: The Challenge of Jesse Jackson', *Social Text*, Winter 1984/1985.

181. P. Pierce, 'What Price Unity', *Democratic Left*, Vol. 13, No. 1, 1985, p. 10.

182. *Ibid*.

183. D. Wrong, 'The End of Ideology', *Dissent*, Spring 1985, p. 149.

184. To compare several countries in terms of (a) health coverage, see V. Navarro, 'An International Perspective on Health Care: Learning From Other Nations', Proceedings for the Select Committee on Ageing, May 1, 1985, US House of Representatives; (b) Womens' Rights, see April issue of *Economic Notes*, Labor Research Institute, 1985; and (c) Environmental Rights, see *The State of the Environment in OECD Member Countries*, 1979: OECD, Paris, 1980.

185. G. Therborn in J. Curran (ed.), *The Future of the Left*, Polity Press, 1985.

186. *The Changing Situation of Workers and Their Unions*, A report by the AFL-CIO Committee on the Evolution of Work, February 1985, p. 11.

187. *Ibid.*, p. 8.

188. 'Decline in Support for Unions May Have Ended, Poll Says', *The New York Times*, May 19, 1985, p. 13.

189. The Changing Situation of Workers and Their Unions, *op. cit.*, p. 9.

190. S.M. Lipset, 'Feeling Better: Measuring the Nation's Confidence', *op. cit.*, p. 9.

191. L. Huberman, *We, The People: The Drama of America*, Monthly Review Press, 1947, p. 351.

THE AUSTRALIAN LEFT: BEYOND LABOURISM?

Peter Beilharz

A decade ago it was popular to argue that the two major parties in Australia were no more different than Tweedledum and Tweedledee. This kind of thinking, if it can be so called, fed on a traditional refusal among the Australian Left to take seriously the problem of labourism. This refusal has now, in the eighties, returned with vengeance, as farce. Many on the Left are now subservient to the very Labor Party which they had earlier derided. Labor itself has developed in particular corporatist directions. Many on the Left have seized on these developments as offering a new beginning, beyond dogmatism, beyond clichéd militancy, beyond ultra-leftist rhetoric and headbanging. But there is little prospect that any of this will lead beyond labourism. In the Australian case as in the English, labourism encompasses a pragmatic politics where the essential focus is on concrete demands of immediate advantage to the working class and organised labour. Labourist politics in Australia, as in England, of course takes place on, and accepts, the terrain of capitalist social relations.[1] Yet labourism has a magnetic effect on the Australian Left, and this is a tendency which has been strengthened over the last ten years.

In 1972 the Whitlam Government came into office. The conservative ice age was ended; this was the first Federal Labor Government to be elected in Australia since the post-war reconstruction period. The response on the Left was euphoric, even among those who were less than enthusiastic at the prospect of what came to be called 'technocratic labourism'. The common argument on the extra-Labor Left was that this Government had effectively been summoned by capital to do its bidding, to do what the conservatives had been unable to do: to rationalise the economy, modernise the polity and regulate and control the union movement. The Whitlam experience was, however, cut short by vice-regal intervention; the Left was now forced to re-evaluate its often cavalier detachment from the world of Labor politics. By the time the conservative Fraser Government was ousted by the Hawke Government in 1983, many Leftists had shifted their perspectives to the extent that they were prepared to become willing servants of this labour movement. The Labor Party and Labourism itself have long provided the central focus for the Australian Left; much of the Left had thus returned to its historic home, in and around the Labor Party. The Hawke Government was elected on the basis of a prices and incomes Accord, a pact which had earlier been formed between the ALP and the Australian Council of Trade Unions (ACTU). Many of the Left have enthusiastically embraced this new situation as one offering great potential for change in a socialist direction. Guilt produced by an earlier abstentionism seems to have resulted in an overwhelming desire to be where the action is. Yet socialist politics in Australia seems thereby to have become ultimately little more than defensive of labourist tenets.

Ten years ago it seemed plausible enough to argue, as Winton Higgins did in *Socialist Register* 1974, that the Australian Left and indeed the Communist Party were shaping up for a great future. The Labor Party has since changed; as the mark has shifted, so has the Left around it. Today the influence of the Communist Party is at an ebb; it has just experienced its third major split since 1963. Having disgorged its Maoists in that year and its pro-Soviets in 1971, the CPA split again in 1984, this time at least in part over the question of where the action was—with the ALP, or independent of it? Ironically, then, those who railed bitterly against technocratic labourism under Whitlam are now busily embracing its corporatist extension in the Hawke régime. Others who were arguing for a coalition of the Left in the seventies have not changed their tune; their political positions have been structured by the dominance of labourism across these years, the difference now being that the ALP is given a more central place in this 'coalition'. Some points of continuity emerge, then, though clearly much has also changed. Political discourse in Australia, as elsewhere, has shifted right, and the Left has followed this shift. In this context the question to be asked of Australian socialism is whether it can indeed pass beyond labourism, or even fulfill its aims. Some would argue that it can, or perhaps already has, passed from labourism to social democracy, however interpreted. Others might argue that, in these times, the problem is rather even to achieve labourism, in order to surpass it. For while the record suggests that many of Labor's victories in Australia have been pyrrhic, labourism still dominates political life for those who are committed to the struggle for socialism. This essay begins to survey some of these problems.

The Context: Australian Politics Shifts Right

The aura of reform still adheres to the Whitlam years. Whitlam's Government had some striking motifs; it had a cosmopolitan disposition, by Australian standards, it had a European ambiance, in the sense that its policies and image were urbane, meritocratic in social policy, expansionist in economic policy. It introduced a major social reform in Medibank, a compulsory and universal national health insurance scheme. It encouraged the growth of the welfare state and it specifically encouraged the public service to be a pacesetter in wage levels. Unemployment, rather than inflation, was now regarded as the primary problem facing the Australian economy; the containment of prices rather than labour costs was seen as the policy priority in the early Whitlam years. While no real social contracts of any·substance were negotiated between the ALP and the ACTU in these years, the Whitlam Government did seek control over prices and incomes through referenda, which were unsuccessful. This programme of gentle reform was disrupted not once but twice by conservative refusals to pass Labor's supply bills in the Senate (a prerogative peculiar to the Australian rendition of Westminster). The first refusal in 1974 prompted a double dissolution of Parliament and a joint sitting of both houses of Parliament, which momentarily overcame the Liberal programme of obstructionism. On the second occasion, in 1975, the Governor-General, Sir John Kerr, circumvented the problem by precipitating a constitutional crisis, sacking Whitlam and his Government and installing Fraser, the leader of the Liberal Party, as caretaker Prime Minister pending a yet further election. The atmosphere of incompetence and sundry scandals surrounding the Whitlam Government, together with the conservative conspiracy to eject it from office, together resulted in Whitlam's final defeat at the polls. The experience left indelible marks on many in the ALP; it seemed to confirm the popular slogan of the time, that they had gone 'too far, too fast'.

Since the dismissal some of the Left have produced a kind of mythology around these events and its central Labor characters; as Peter Wilenski has argued, the Whitlam period was the closest Australia had got to an experience like that of 1945 in England.[2] Certainly some Labor supporters like Patrick White and Manning Clark look back on the period with moist eyes; as Xavier Herbert put it, in less nostalgic prose, the events had proved what bastards Australians really were. The extra-Party Left shared this distress, and not only because of its hostility to vice-regal relics like Kerr or haughty graziers like Fraser; there were mass demonstrations, even arguments for a general strike. The representatives of technocratic labour emerged, after all, as being superior to the forces of Australian conservatism. This was indeed a judgment well based. Certainly the Whitlam experience was something less than flawless; that its last budget had already initiated the process of spending cuts to be extended by the incoming Fraser Government ought to have been edifying for the Left. The Whitlam Government had made some preliminary gestures in the direction of gradualist reform at the very moment when the present economic crisis was making its first real effects felt; the Whitlam project thus accentuated the fiscal crisis of the Australian state, prompting the slide away from Keynesianism towards monetarism in economic policy.[3] The Fraser Government substantiated this shift, if unevenly; it established a Razor Gang to extend further spending cuts, it elevated the issue of inflation as the most urgent policy priority, it highlighted labour costs over price increases, and introduced punitive industrial relations legislation. It restored the *status quo ante* in social policy, dismantling Medibank, the symbolic core of the Whitlam era. Its programme of cuts, however, was less radical in some sectors than parts of the Left may have imagined; the parallel with Thatcherism here was more rhetorical than real.[4]

Bob Hawke, ex-leader of the ACTU, had in the meantime entered Parliament and replaced Bill Hayden as Leader of the Labor Opposition. The unceremonious dumping of Hayden in favour of the charismatic leader was symptomatic of the growing importance of electoralism in the Party. Hawke had for some time been possessed by an image of national reconciliation and consensus.[5] His populist credentials stood him in good stead: he led the ALP back into office in 1983. Fraser stepped down as Leader of the Liberal Party; the Party conducted a *post mortem* into its second defeat in eight years, coming to the conclusion that they had not been sufficiently conservative. The report of the Commission of Inquiry, *Facing the Future*, argued that the Liberals had a credibility problem: they spoke the language of monetarism, but the policy basis of their practice was insufficiently different from that of Labor. The solution was self-evident—Liberal policy had to be more consistently aligned with its conservative or reactionary rhetoric.[6] The Liberal Opposition, since, has developed a policy advocating further cuts in government spending, large-scale privatisation, cuts in real wages and so on. At the same time, however, the Hawke Government has been stealing its thunder; so that the Shadow Treasurer, Mr Howard, a leader of the Liberal 'dries', has been obliged to express a begrudging admiration for the achievements of Hawke's Treasurer, Keating. The Liberal Party has then clearly moved to the right, and has expressed its wish to move further in that direction in the near future. The bipartisan commitment to Keynesianism characteristic of the post-war period has been decisively rejected; thus the spectacle in which Marxists, in Australia as elsewhere, have become Keynesians. But Labor has also shifted right, and taken the broader Left with it.

Labor Shifts Right: The Hawke Era

Whereas the imagery drawn on by Whitlam was Fabian or social democratic in nature, Hawke's identity draws more on images of the labourist past, garnished with the ideology of consensus. In particular, Hawke claims an affinity with Curtin, Labor leader during the war.[7] The choice of association is less than apposite; H.C. Coombs, for example, has argued that the parallel is concocted, that Curtin was a real reformer,[8] while Rob Watts has shown that even this reformism was somewhat less than thoroughly committed to principles such as equity.[9] The Curtin Government operated very much within the field established by 'new liberalism'[10] —this in itself would seem to be suggestive of the distance between Hawke and Curtin. The Left, in any case, has seen the election of the Hawke Government on the basis of the Accord as representing a new beginning,[11] opening new opportunities, formalising, as it allegedly does, the rights of unions in political decision-making processes. The argument over the Accord is essentially one about potential; so that many Leftists would argue that while the Hawke Government is up to the same old tricks, the Accord itself offers new and real possibilities for socialist politics.

The Accord is essentially a wages/prices deal in conception, though it has in fact functioned in such a way as to actually involve wage restraint in exchange for tax cuts and social wage increases. As a political document the Accord is a masterpiece of ambiguity: it offers all things, effectively, to all men (women still do not register much on the instruments of Labourist politics). The Accord is a document which facilitates several quite distinct interpretations, and it is this which explains the diversity of argument over the question of its *potential*. The pragmatic subtext in the Accord rests on its bottom line, indicating a commitment to centralised indexation. The introduction to the Accord, in comparison, offers a rather more ambitious project, vitiating this bottom line, in its conception of the objective of full employment as a long-term goal.[12] The most ambitious subtext in the Accord is yet more ethereal, being manifest in its claim that poverty can be abolished[13] (via mechanisms unseen; the implicit and mistaken presupposition presumably being that poverty and unemployment are coextensive). The Accord also claims to address the question of equity,[14] yet this problem is clearly beyond the scope of a wages deal based on indexation, which leaves the question of income distribution and relativities untouched. The further problem emerges, that the different subtexts of the Accord bear no necessary relation to each other, are written in without guarantee; so, for example, the Accord's proposition to restructure taxation progressively and to shift away from indirect taxation, a clause clearly inserted at the behest of the ACTU, floats freely in the text, unsecured by mechanisms which might guarantee its implementation. The document called the Accord, then, contains at least three, largely independent subtexts—a bottom line, concerning wages, an intermediate level, addressing issues like taxation and health and safety, and a maximum programme, involving claims like the abolition of poverty. All these claims are constructed within one central project: economic recovery. Rather than specifying conditions of interrelation between these programmatic levels, the Accord issues merely in a pretentiously entitled list of 'mechanics of implementation', which reduce to the construction of an Economic Planning Advisory Council (EPAC) and a Prices Surveillance Authority and a commitment to extending the current information base.[15]

In terms of practical results it has been the lowest common denominator—the wages/prices deal—which has become the effective reality of the Accord. Yet the fact that the Accord contains other claims and projections allows some socialists to argue that here is a deal to which the Labor leadership can be held, and not only in its minimum requirements. The most significant arguments here relate to the provisions in the Accord for industry development policy and long range planning arrangements, which have been picked up both by major unions like the Metalworkers and enthused over by left Labor academics. This is one crucial source of debate on the Australian Left, which will be returned to later.

The Accord, this wages/prices deal between the ALP and the ACTU, was broadened into a *de facto* tripartite deal at the National Economic Summit held in April, 1983. The Summit was a brilliantly orchestrated, and televised, public relations coup, which effectively developed the Accord into the basis of a tripartite deal by extracting capital's consent to the arrangement. The Summit brought together a massive cast of representatives from the three major power blocs in Australian society, business, labour and government, as well as a smattering of others who spoke from positions less powerful and influential. Welfare, for example, was represented at the Summit, but its voice was ignored—its pleas for the recognition of the pressing needs of those who were suffering most in society fell on deaf ears.[16] The central *motif* of the Accord—that economic recovery could best be facilitated by a wages/prices deal—now emerged again as the central *motif* of the Summit. Treasurer Keating, speaking immediately after Bruce McKenzie, the welfare representative, set the agenda for the Summit by returning the focus to the *real* issues—the relationship between business and unions, prices and incomes, and the size of the deficit.[17] The Summit finally culminated in the issuing of a communiqué which consolidated the Accord by securing the *post facto* consent of business to its basic proposals.

The simple point is that such radical potential as might arguably exist within the Accord has not been realised.[18] Partly this is so because of the very nature of corporatist or tripartite arrangements. The net effect of the Accord has been that profits have been increased, while via indexation the wages of better-placed workers have been more-or-less maintained. Some stronger unions, for example in oil and in construction, have managed to do deals outside of indexation, while smaller unions like the Food Preservers and furnishing trades have been bludgeoned into accepting its limits. Lower paid public servants have highlighted the internal contradictions within the Accord by arguing for increases outside indexation in order to maintain the parity between public and private sectors which the Accord also claims to provide for. The Hawke Government has seen this general pattern of events as accurately representing the potential of the Accord—its object, as we are frequently told, is to bring Australians together, to soothe away the contradictions of class relations and difference (at the expense of those excluded from its arrangements).

The Accord has been implemented within a process which has seen the consolidation of the right-wing economic programme foreshadowed but barely enacted by the Fraser Government. The Hawke Government has actually initiated policies of economic deregulation the likes of which Fraser had only contemplated: it has deregulated the banking system, allowing foreign banks into the domestic economy; it has floated the dollar,[19] prompting speculation both of the monetary kind and of the political kind, that Australia's economic path is leading towards third-worldisation.[20] Meanwhile the Hawke Government has been revealed to have a foreign policy well to the right of previous Labor Governments,[21] and has drawn little substantial inspiration from the policies of its sibling in New Zealand. While it has established Medicare, child of Medibank, it has funded it in an anything but adequate way, it has refused to actually restructure the health care system or to confront the power of the Australian Medical Association, and it is driving those who can afford not to queue into the arms of the private insurers.[22] It has argued for the re-introduction of the tertiary education fees abolished by Whitlam and it has privileged the private school system over the public, contrary to Labor policy. It has developed an obsession with the size of government deficit and with being seen to please business. It has argued very forcefully for retrogressive changes in the taxation system, and has moderated these arguments only in the face of overwhelming opposition from the Labor State Governments, the unions and other non-business interest groups (this was one occasion on which the union movement argued that preferred Labor policy would jeopardise the Accord). It has used Labor's own 1984 National Conference in order to override branch level opposition to uranium mining and to further marginalise the Left within the ALP (though some would argue that the Left's marginality is self-inflicted). It has at this same Conference formally shifted its own economic platform further to the right.[23] It has reneged on its somewhat less than radical proposal to increase welfare benefits to 25% of average weekly earnings. It has systematically avoided addressing the fact that three of fifteen million Australians at least live in poverty or on benefits. Both Hawke and Treasurer Keating have publicly tongue lashed welfare lobbyists who have sought to draw public attention to these issues, substantiating the worst fears that there is now to be an authorised representative of the public interest—the Hawke Government— which cannot, in principle, be disagreed with. This Caesarist touch has prompted some to draw analogies between the regimes and personalities of Mussolini and Hawke.[24] Such analogies are bent: the problems are different, and contemporary arguments about corporatism throw more light upon them than such fanciful parallels.[25] But these are issues which have barely been registered by the Australian Left, many of whom have fallen into either celebratory or antagonistic positions on fairly predictable grounds.

The Left Shifts Right, or Consolidates

How could the Left draw inspiration from any of this? The answer can best be rendered in terms of arguments about the potential embodied in Labor Governments in general and in the Accord in particular. The Left within the ALP has drifted with this tide, arguing typically in terms of the 'potential' of the Accord, as has that part of the CPA which split in 1984, eventually to form the Socialist Forum. Some Left Labor politicians have argued that the Accord could function even as an Alternative Economic Strategy of sorts;[26] at the same time other Labor politicians have argued that the present Government would do best to return to the socialist tradition within labourism.[27] These responses in different ways raise questions about what labourism in Australia traditionally has stood for, and what it means today. The problem is essentially the same one, as the labourist tradition still today dominates Left Labor thinking.

Different parts of the ALP have of course struck up rather different positions over the question of socialism and Labor. Until recently the most radical faction, the Socialist Left, was dominated by old socialists whose views were often indistinguishable from those of older communists, and whose influence rarely extended into the Parliamentary Labor Party. They had a clearer set of policy priorities over questions in the Middle East than within Australia; it is now generally conceded that their arguments helped establish the irrelevance of socialism in Australia. New blood within the Socialist Left has produced a fairly dramatic change over the past two years. These newer, younger Socialist Leftists are less given to Stalinoid dogmatism and more predisposed to technocracy. They now have Cabinet representatives in State Labor Governments like Cain's in Victoria, but remain more marginal within Federal Government.[28] Like those who remain in the CPA, the new Socialist Left are given to supporting the Accord and simultaneously arguing for the extension of welfare. But their views hold relatively little sway within the inner sanctums.

The centrist or Fabian current in the ALP, its guiding theoretical 'conscience', has now mobilised in the newly-formed Centre Left faction,[29] which claims to function as a moderator between the Left and Hawke's power base in the Right (largely to the latter's advantage, apparently). Given the dominance of the labourist tradition within Australia, it would seem reasonable to expect that it would be the gradualist politics of social justice which have held the theoretical roost. The hegemony of this position can be detected in the ongoing, if somewhat less than enthusiastic, debate about Labor's Socialist Objective. The ALP's formal commitment to the Socialist Objective has never been as forthright as that in Clause Four of the British Labour Party's Constitution. Since 1921 the Socialist Objective has been qualified by the rider that socialisation was appropriate only where necessary to prevent exploitation or the antisocial use of the instruments of production.[30] Clearly the presupposition here is that exploitation is accidental to capitalist production, the result of bad will on the part of evil men; the argument indicates the fundamentally populist nature of labour thinking in Australia.[31] This imprecision notwithstanding, attempts have been made to dilute the Objective yet further; the arguments that have been put in this direction are reminiscent of Gaitskell's, for the primary motivation is that even 'socialist' rhetoric is an electoral liability, that language can easily be 'modernised', the old connotations sloughed off and social democratic intentions still be adhered to.[32] Some Party socialists merely negate this case; other socialists like Bob Connell within the Party and Agnes Heller from outside it have put stronger cases for the maintenance of a socialist identity.[33] While socialists like Heller have made much of the idea that socialist arguments *must* be democratic, indeed that socialism ought best be canvassed as radicalised democracy,[34] other defenders of socialism have often tended to manipulate murkier arguments about an allegedly strong distinction between the social democratic tradition and that of democratic socialism. Some unreformed reformists within the Party argue that Labor ought see itself as social democratic, in the Bad Godesberg sense, and argue that the Whitlam experience can best be understood in this light.[35] Others, more concerned with maintaining socialist credentials, insist that *democratic socialism* is more powerful a nomenclature; this is the terminology used by the Centre Left of the Party in its odd ideological moments. The argument of course reduces to the proposal for parliamentary socialism, with the *caveat* that the process of transition 'of course' involves more than that.[36]

The language of socialism, however contrived, has little to do with Labor practice, and when it is used it is often inauthentic. The Socialist Objective, even as it stands, is light years away from present Government concerns. Socialist argument within the ALP is typically rhetorical, and usually private. And when it comes to a socialist programme rather than a socialist objective, the result is again either posturing and irrelevant or pragmatic and ill-considered.[37] And yet people persist in expecting great and indeed socialist things of the ALP, arguing, for example, that the Accord could somehow lead forward to socialism. The fundamental issue, oft-avoided, here, is the difference between the Labor Party and Labor Governments. It may be possible to argue that the Labor Party is wedded to *some* conception of socialism, but the record of Labor Governments suggests a different story. And yet those who enthuse for the socialist potential of the Accord always seem ultimately to presume that Labor Governments will, at the very least, be well-disposed to union-led initiatives in the direction of socialism. The will-to-socialism does not inhere in the ALP; yet those who argue for the Accord as an AES-type strategy must ultimately presume that Labor can become a vehicle for a committed Left wing parliamentary majority with such a will and an appropriately revolutionary policy package.[38]

It is this situation which has in the past led Australian socialists into

'independent' Left parties like the Communist Party. Yet given the in-
effectivity of marginal politics in Australia and the hegemony of labourism, the smaller Left parties have always been to some degree structured
by labourism. The Communist Party is probably the best example here, for
despite its occasional fits of sectarianism, it has often tended to function
as though it were the Left wing of the Labor Party. Frontism is a strong
current in its history, indeed popular frontism and social fascism are
expressive of its two basic moods, reflecting its fundamental ambivalence
toward labourism: we need the Labor Party, but it spurns us yet; we
support it, yet it betrays us.

Winton Higgins has indicated, if unwittingly, the enthusiasm for
Althusserian Marxism among the young revolutionaries who came to the
Communist Party in the early 70s. The Althusserians arrived from the
desert, so to speak, and they were armed with theory. In some ways
their arrival was timely, for apart from an early entente with Gramsci the
CPA was not oversupplied with the theory which was gripping European
intellectuals.[39] This was the period before the recognition that there was
a crisis in Marxism; so it could easily be argued that the theory-practice
relation had lain undeveloped because of an absence of good theory. It
followed that an immense theoretical revolution was a necessary prerequisite to good practice. This is not the place to offer a general assessment of the effect of Althusser in Australia; suffice it to say that the
results were mixed, that some young Marxists around the journal *Intervention* put Althusser to good use, in developing a political economy of
Australian capitalism,[40] while elsewhere the effect was foreclosure,
sclerosis and involution, culminating in the identification of Marxism with
Althusser and prompting, in the eighties, disappearance into Francophilic
anti-Marxism.[41] In his *Socialist Register* paper, however, Higgins radically
overstated the impact of Althusserian Marxism,[42] to the extent of suggesting general CPA leadership sympathy with these arguments.[43] What
Higgins' case overlooked—and the point is of course made easily in hindsight—was that outside radical intellectual circles, the new arguments, if
accepted at all, were assimilated into the existing communist wisdom of
frontism. The fact that Poulantzas, for example, had directed much of his
energy against the frontist tradition was of no import within the rank and
file of the Communist Party. It was the Eurocommunist element in
Althusserianism which took seed, as it complemented an ongoing tradition;
its revolutionary element found no ground, particularly after the defeat
of Whitlam. The 'coalition of the Left' policy developed in the late sixties
may have fed on radical sources, but came to depend ultimately, again, on
the Labor Party. The reception of Gorz's 'revolutionary reforms' and
Holland's AES-type strategy likewise needs to be located in this context;
these arguments, regardless of their own potential, were read through the
frontist grid which was necessarily labourist. Thus, for example, major

communist unionists like Laurie Carmichael could enthuse for Holland's arguments knowing but not acknowledging that in the absence of a vital Communist Party in Australia, the role of vanguard would fall by default into the lap of. . . the Labor Party.[44]

Within the CPA, then, the revolutionary rhetoric of the late sixties and early seventies has finally given way to a sensible pragmatism. The change can indeed be seen in its rhetoric. John Sendy has observed, for example, that the period of 'ultraleftism' was so fulsome that the CP's 1974 Congress political document used the words *revolution* and *revolutionary* no less than 54 times in nine pages.[45] Even during this period, however, central figures in the Melbourne leadership were making much ado about Engels' aside concerning the obsolescence of barricades in order to promote the cause of parliamentary socialism.[46] The argument was drifting towards social democracy, if in the traditional sense; it is very likely now the case that 'democracy' is the magic word, the associations again being traditional rather than innovative.[47] Eurocommunist arguments were well received in this environment, particularly in Melbourne, because they facilitated this process of pragmatising socialism. Leading communists in Melbourne had been heading in this direction at least since the early seventies; viewed retrospectively, what is surprising about the 1984 split is that these liquidationist tendencies took so long to surface. In April 1984 twenty-three leading members of the Victorian CPA announced their collective departure, at least partially in response to what they viewed as abstentionist tendencies over developments like the Accord.[48] Some who stayed within the CPA clearly saw the split as premature, for the 'Prospects for Socialism' debate canvassed within the Party since 1982 had already produced strong arguments for liquidation of the Party. The most recent communist manifesto, *Towards Socialist Renewal in Australia*, indicates a general commitment to the idea of a new socialist party.[49] What all this seems to suggest is that the dispute between the CPA and those who departed reduces to the terms and conditions of fellow-travelling with the Labor Party. While the CPA remains committed to an alliance of independents, those who now form Socialist Forum eschew independent party forms and policy, and avoid the prescription clause of the ALP by refusing themselves party identity. The Forum's *Statement of Identity* could be said to read like an argument for social 'democratic *agitprop*, though it also suggests an openness which has not generally characterised the communist tradition in the past. The Forum's generalised endorsement of the Accord is suggestive of something else.

Unfortunately the animosities between those who left and those who have stayed in the CPA seem to be sufficient to prevent a debate of the kind which has occurred in Britain in, around and over *Marxism Today*. The CPA's equivalent, *Australian Left Review*, has become, on occasions at least, so pluralist as to be almost meaningless, or at least self-contradictory, combining new-look graphics and sometimes punky arguments with the views of old-timers, side by side. The CPA can, for example, simultaneously publish feminist anti-Marxism in *Australian Left Review*,[50] and punctuate the Letters columns of its weekly *Tribune* with complaints from its pro-Soviet elders. While feminism has a strength and attraction which Marxism today cannot rival, its new hegemony has been achieved largely through displacement rather than an open exchange of ideas about, say, class and social movements. Debates over strategy or policy have thus barely begun within *Australian Left Review*. While the Sydney CPA have produced usefully temporal arguments about the reform of the taxation system,[51] and argued that the Accord itself needs reforming,[52] the Socialist Alternative Melbourne Collective associated with the Melbourne CP has furthered debate by producing a pamphlet on Socialist Melbourne, 2000 AD.[53] It can be observed, with some irony, that these arguments about a marvellous socialist Melbourne not only seem to reflect classical utopian views, but also retread the path of local communist utopianism; Ralph Gibson, for example, had already anticipated a *Socialist Melbourne* in a 1951 CPA pamphlet. Clearly the dates needed adjusting. Those whose memories reach back this far could also observe that the Socialist Forum is a kind of second coming, and wonder whether the new Forum might follow the direction of its namesake, into the mainstream of the Labor Party.[54] Here, then, can be witnessed the limits of a process of returning to local traditions, or recalling the ghosts of the Australian past.

Some attempts have also been made to stimulate argument on the Left by highlighting ongoing debates in England. Clearly the arguments advanced in *Marxism Today* have a strong attraction to younger sections of the Communist Party. Unfortunately, however, some of this argument has been derivative in a crippling way. In the document *Socialism in Australia —toward Renewal?*, a dossier including Australian communist arguments and those of Stuart Hall and Beatrix Campbell, David McKnight, for example, argues in effect that Australian problems *are* English problems. While drawing attention to some very real problems facing the Australian Left—the growth of social movements largely outside the Left, for example—McKnight argues as though the real problem centres on developing 'Thatcherist' tendencies in the Liberal Party, as though the ALP leadership has been unaffected by such tendencies.[55] The argument is that Thatcher is novel, as though Hawke were not; Hawke, indeed, on this view, is Callaghan.[56] The Liberal Shadow Treasurer is castigated for free market rhetoric, while Labor's Keating somehow remains immune. The Accord is dealt with only in terms of its allegedly socialist potential. The specific differences between Britain and Australia are here eclipsed; the arguments raging in Britain are applied mechanically rather than creatively. The specific nature of *labourism*, as a major concern, once more eludes scrutiny.

Beyond the mainstream Left, sects like the Spartacists of course vehemently oppose labourism.[57] The International Socialists, lacking the strength of their British counterparts, are still waiting for world revolution to beat a path to their door.[58] The Socialist Labour League, in Australia as elsewhere, relies on catastrophist economics and exclusivist dialectics for its mass appeal.[59] More significant but still peripheral parties like the Trotskyist Socialist Workers Party and the pro-Moscow Socialist Party of Australia have struck up an unprecedented alliance against the Accord: they have swum through the proverbial river of blood separating Stalinists from Trotskyists to clasp hands, midstream, against class collaboration-ism.[60] This collaboration itself raises controversial issues about the precise relationship between Stalinism and Trotskyism; it is clear that on this occasion at least the two are united in their pro-Sovietism.[61] The SWP's pro-Sovietism has also been manifest in its role in the peace movement, where its entrism helped to precipitate a major split within the newly-founded Nuclear Disarmament Party.[62] In any case, these new-found allies in the SPA and SWP have together argued that the Accord is to be understood in traditional terms as a capitalist attack on the working class movement, which they of course offer to lead, now in tandem, to the barricades. Yet, simultaneously, both parties must still acknowledge the centrality of the ALP, as they do.[63] It is of course quite possible to be allied to Sovietism and labourism at the same time. The question of the status of the Soviet Union remains largely undebated on the Left; rather the stock positions are merely struck up. In the mid-seventies arguments within the CPA had divided, with some like Eric Aarons arguing a Deutscherist position, that the Soviet Union was 'socialist based', while those allied with *Intervention* had argued for the 'transitional' category in the manner of Mandel.[64] Today there seems to be an unstated consensus that Eastern Europe functions as bad publicity for the Left, but there is no real debate over the nature or lessons of the experience of Soviet-type societies. This remains a major limit on the peace movement in Australia.[65] It seems to be reflective of a residual Sovietism in terms of images of the future, one which is entirely compatible with the populist and fabian traditions.

The trade union movement remains closely allied to Left labourism and communism. With the exception of a few unions allied with the SWP/SPA or with the remnants of Maoism, most unions and indeed the ACTU are locked into the Accord, arguing simultaneously that the Accord can have a minimum function of preventing further ALP leadership perfidy and a maximum function of opening new possibilities, especially with reference to saving jobs via the development of industry policy. Tra-ditionally militant unions like the Metalworkers have taken on and develop-ed the notion of industry development policy from the Accord in their document, *Policy for Industry Development and More Jobs*.[66] In the

Foreword to the AMFSU plan, Laurie Carmichael argues that full employment can be restored through a programme of first, expansionary macroeconomic strategies; second, a programme of redistribution of tax and wealth; and third, effective industry strategies including modernisation, expansion via increased exports and tripartite decision-making. Nixon Apple's introduction to the plan then clarifies its basis in the ideology of endless growth, the logic of economic recovery being one in which nominated industries would be developed first for local consumption, second, sequentially, for export, while the third step in the process would involve the withdrawal of Government support from successful firms and the reallocation of resources to the next set of industries selected for development.[67] The logic at work in the plan itself is Keynesian and masculinist. Full employment is not problematised as full (male breadwinner) employment; feminists could readily lay the charge that the proposal is one of jobs-for-the-boys. Problems like poverty and welfare are given summary treatment,[68] as the essential motor here is the 'trickledown' economics of reluctant collectivism, structured upon the logical chain that industry policies produce growth which produces increased employment which produces decreased inequality.

The Metal Trades Union plan is an impressive indicator of the union shift away from the old combination of revolutionary rhetoric and wages-and-conditions militancy. It arguably provides a policy for economic recovery, which Australian capital itself has sought but been unable to achieve. Yet, in a sense like the Lucas Combine Plan, it has simultaneously inspired outsiders but has achieved no substantial results in its own terms. Perhaps there is a pattern here; Sweden also seems to attract more admiration outside its own boundaries. Business in Australia in any case has offered a rather less interventionist view of industry policy,[69] and it seems to be the case that this view is rather closer to that of the present Government. As with the Accord, policies like those articulated by the Metal Trades Unions have been identified as a focal point for intervention. In the absence of a vigorous Labor Government neither would seem likely to have any visible impact on the socialist agenda; despite these policy initiatives, labourism in Australia remains largely inert.

Arguments over the Accord and Corporatism

All these developments have served to elicit theoretical debate over corporatism and the future of socialism. Regrettably, relatively little such debate has occurred within or between Left groups. So much of the Left is complicit in the Accord that it seems unable to argue reasonably over its nature. Obviously people are likely to be defensive of a project they have sponsored, argued for, defended against opponents on the right. And the argument can always be put, and sometimes is, that the Accord is better that nothing, that a system of ongoing wage indexation must be more reliable than an erratic mess of collective bargaining arrangements, and so on. Yet the Left's complicity ultimately seems to be more awkward than this; as the *Australasian Spartacist* observed, the CPA is likely to be less than critical of an arrangement which it helped plan,[70] while other groups like the Political Economy Movement have also acknowledged the difficulty of critically assessing proposals which they have played no small part in forming.[71] Similarly, there is no shortage of ALP members who are privately critical of the Accord and what it symbolises but who cannot speak out for fear of being construed to be anti-Labour. What this has meant is that such debate as has occurred has taken place between Left academics. Two broad positions have emerged in the debate over corporatism in Australia. Some like Clegg, Dow, Boreham and Higgins have argued that the Accord offers new directions for socialists, particularly in the direction of what they call *political trade unionism*; others, associated with the journal *Thesis Eleven*, have argued that recent developments not only foreclose on the possibilities for socialism in Australia, but must also serve to foreclose the scope of discourse about the future of socialism.

The central source of dispute here, in a sense, is the question whether Sweden offers a possible road to socialism in Australia. Clegg, Dow and Boreham argue that corporatist arrangements facilitate socialist development by allowing union politics to shift generally economic interests to specifically political ones, such as the claim to participate in the planning process. They argue that a robust capitalist economy with high growth rates and high standards of living is *incompatible* with capitalist social relations. Displacement of decision-making procedures to tripartite bodies is therefore potentially progressive: trade union energies can thus be progressively channelled into political unionism, facilitating the process of democratic class struggle.[72] Clegg *et al* thus argue with Korpi[73] and Higgins and Apple[74] that the class representation of labour and capital is necessary both for economic recovery *and* for the transition to socialism: the premise is that recovery can be managed in such a way as to shift power decisively to the working people and their families. Social contracts can, then, in a sense be turned against themselves; a 'war of position' can be waged from within the bastions of bourgeois society. The process of democratic class struggle can allow unions to use tripartite mechanisms to prevent the losses inflicted on them by previous social contracts. Clegg *et al* argue that, in the Australian case, these principles or possibilities are obscured by the rhetoric of consensus; the important point, for their case, is that the Economic Planning Advisory Council can open up the hitherto privatised decision-making processes of capital, indeed that tripartite mechanisms like EPAC can benefit *all*, including those who are excluded from the labour-capital relationship, even if they don't know it.[75]

Higgins has argued a similar position, though in a more cautious manner;

his arguments in defence of political trade unionism are less explicitly related to the Australian situation. Higgins puts a very strong case for the view that the real potential of Accord-type arrangements is that they provide openings for outside voices in the development of industry policy. His is a pragmatism of a sensible, rather than snivelling, sort: the argument is that historically the Left in Australia has always lost the credibility stakes, because it has too often fallen victim to the temptation of empty sloganising, when it could have been developing an independent alternative policy of its own. The way forward for socialists is to produce more concrete and credible—and therefore radical—policies to deal with immediate electoral problems, to win more votes and then to educate 'public opinion' and win it around.[76] Higgins and Clegg et al alike, acknowledge the poverty of parliamentary socialism; in common, they effectively shift primary political responsibility for social change onto the shoulders of the trade union movement, though the argument remains Swedish inasmuch as it presumes an at least well-disposed Left government. Theoretically, Keynes and Kalecki are summoned here as approving authorities.[77] The essential proposal, then, is that political trade unionism can allow the Left ultimately to pass through labourism and enter a social democratic phase, in the Swedish rather than German sense. As Higgins puts it, the Labor Party has been trapped for too long in labourism; the extra-party Left can help push it further, not into becoming a socialist party but into becoming a party with some credible socialist policies.[78]

Beilharz and Watts have contested this case and its practical logic in defending the Accord. They pick up Triado's argument, that the problem with corporatist arrangements is that they represent producer-groups at the expense of the citizenship principle; consequently the Accord necessarily results in the political exclusion and disenfranchisement of those who are already economically powerless.[79] In this way tripartite arrangements may be held to benefit those who actually enter into them, but they cannot be presumed to have universally beneficial effects. On this view, then, the rhetoric of consensus is no mere tactical accretion on corporatism, but is rather a significant part of its baggage. As Triado argues, the novelty of corporatism is that it furnishes the institutional means to mediate the demands of functional interest groups in capitalist society, with the aim of developing an administrative consensus over resource allocation, investment planning, industry restructuring and so on within an over-riding conception of the 'national interest'.[80] Inasmuch as it involves the incorporation of dominant class interests or interest groups, corporatism has no socialist telos; it emerges as a form of crisis-management, the limited strategic potential of which reflects the general balance of social forces. The general balance of forces, for these critics, is something less than favourable: business is not yet a force for socialism, and neither is the Hawke Government, but nor can trade unions reasonably be expected to function as political vanguards. Historically trade unions in Australia have been immersed in the culture of labourism;[81] experiences like the New South Wales Builders Labourers foray into ecological politics in the seventies are the exception to the labourist norm. As Frenkel and Coolican have shown, trade union militancy in Australia has no specifically political base;[82] consequently it is unreasonable to expect Australian unions simply to break out of this mould and emerge as fluent speakers of Swedish. It could reasonably be expected, rather, that the Australian labour movement will be somewhat selective in what it partakes of this smorgasbord: for while unionism in Australia *is* political, its politics are those of labourism. This is not to say that we ought not to hope for better, but rather to ask for realistic hopes. It is also to ask that arguments for alternative policy be viewed within the real constraints which surround them.

As Triado observes, it is worrying that corporatism has elicited so little debate on the Australian left, given its pertinence to recent events.[83] Some have argued as though the use of the category corporatism is itself a device of foreclosure, that others wish to sidestep the nature of the problem simply by naming it.[84] The major arguments outlined above would seem to suggest the contrary—that the problem remains to explain the nature of recent developments and their potential. What seems to be occurring, rather, is that debate has not progressed far because those politically or organisationally close to the Accord do not really want to talk about it. It is in this regard that we may speak of the negative political consequences of corporatist arrangements—for these arrangements not only disenfranchise the powerless, they also effectively silence parts of the Left involved in their formation, and threaten to vaporise their critics. This is the sense in which critics of corporatism would advance the view that rather than repoliticising social arrangements, corporatism *depoliticises* Australian society in general and the Australian Left in particular. No longer, for example, are there cases advanced for even an Alternative Economic Strategy; the Accord has filled its place. Most of the Left seems in fact to have bought into the 'politics' of consensus. But the enthusiasm for strategy cannot of itself generate socialism.

Labourism and the Impasse of the Left

Into the eighties, then, labourism has consolidated its hold on the politics of Australian socialism, within this rightward ambit. Within the Labor Party arguments about socialism are rarely heard, unless in the guise of arguments about the Accord. The Fabians do not seem to argue much, not even among themselves. The Communist Party, which historically has vacillated between foreign inspirations and local sources, has largely left behind its Soviet and Chinese residues, drawing closer through the *via Italiana* to the labourist tradition itself. As Alastair Davidson noted in closing his history of the Communist Party, the vicissitudes of CPA history were largely due to the fact that it thought the Russian Revolution was entirely relevant to Australian history: but it was not.[85] The traditions of the later Comintern did become assimilated to some extent with local traditions; but looking outwards, because of internal failures, the search for the holy grail continued. If it can be argued that the CPA and the Socialist Forum have now returned, more or less, to an Australian orbit, then it ought also be acknowledged that this has been achieved at a high cost: the dependence on imported overseas arguments has been transcended at the cost of finally *declaring* its faustian pact with labourism in Australia. Further, this shift 'into the mainstream' has been consolidated at the very moment when the mainstream itself is shifting right. Australian Trotsky-ism, which has always been derivative,[86] has also been drawn practically toward labourism, even if it claims publicly to be repulsed by it. Maoism is in tatters and the smaller Left groups remain essentially irrelevant, and aggressive proportionately to their irrelevance. The old New Left which emerged in the late fifties has dispersed,[87] in some cases into the Labor Party; its main legacy lives on in Melbourne in the journal *Arena*, which has become a major independent institution on the Left. There are no comparable filiations in Sydney, where Marxism is now distinctly un-fashionable and radical politics has been beaten from pillar to post—the Althusserians, who may have been off the track but who *did* contribute to the improvement and vitality of debate in the seventies, have disappeared. The theoretical debates which raged between humanists and Althusserians, over Marx, over Chile, have long since dried up; the differences which brought about the 1984 split in the Communist Party remain essentially unaired. The debate over corporatism has barely taken off, presumably because too many of the Left are too closely involved to engage in self-criticism. Yet the debate around corporatism ought to be central, not for its own sake, but because it raises for consideration a whole series of central issues which need to be analysed, about the future of socialism, about the nature of trade unions and parties, about the adequacy of class analysis, about the necessity and nature of alliances, about masculinity and Left strategy, about the future of the welfare state and so on. But these are of course bad times; disillusion is rampant on the Left, or illusion; nihilism is fashionable, as is narcissism, and privatisation; and the dull compulsion of everyday life of course affects Leftists too.

The broader dimensions of theoretical argument in Australian Leftism reflect these facets of life in the eighties; they might also be said to reflect the cleavage in theoretical interests which informs the Left. Two major tendencies can be identified. The first, formed around labour history and revived in the seventies by political economy, hovers around labourism as its immediate focus. Ironically, perhaps, the renewed crisis-tendencies of capitalism in the seventies represent a double blessing for many Leftists:

their arguments, apparently suspended by the post-war boom, emerged again, correct, and improved through the use of Althusserian theory, but *saving*, thereby, these people from the task of addressing *politics* in anything other than a revolutionary way. The second tendency, which is often more marginal, has fixed on ideology and culture as primary interests, again often at the expense of politics other than the personal. Certainly the Left has been much drawn to the idea of a dominant ideology, and class analysis here intersects with culturalism, to the extent that radical Australian sociology has only just begun to address the questions raised earlier and elsewhere about the same.[88] It can also be observed that the Left has long laboured under the delusions of populist ideology, identifying conservative figures like B.A. Santamaria or Fraser or Murdoch as the source of the problem, or blaming the local or American secret police for ongoing conspiracies rather than considering the question why most Australians might be indifferent to arguments about socialism. Certainly there can be no space for arguments about magical political solutions to the impasse of the Australian Left; but the legacies of economism and ideologism remain inhibitors as far as the process of developing a specifically political discourse is concerned. Indeed, it would seem reasonable to argue that a more specifically political discourse might have the function of mediating between existing discourses. But in Australia, as elsewhere, there seems to be a proliferation of more or less hermetic radical languages which has continued unabated since the seventies.[89] This is not to suggest that there can or ought be a unitary discourse or master language; indeed, the principle of difference and the separation between strategic and theoretical interests is in some ways vital.

What this means is that while both theoretical and strategic renewal has begun, Australian socialists are not yet facing a new beginning in any generalised sense. There is no clear sense of a socialist project on the Left. The Accord may or may not last; it is quite possible that the Hawke Government will lose office before the Accord might come to grief. The Left would seem likely to remain structured by recent developments. The Accord would seem now to be a Labor motif; like Whitlam's Medibank, it will be ready for a comeback, as Labor's generative framework for crisis-management. Whether corporatist arrangements lead in the direction of social democracy or merely consolidate labourism, the future represents a sobering challenge for socialists in Australia. A generalised recognition of this situation and the responsibilities it raises would itself pose a first step in the direction of its resolution.

NOTES

1. See further R. Miliband, 'Socialist Advance in Britain', *Socialist Register* 1983, p. 107 ff. The peculiarly Australian configuration of labourism is detailed by

W. Higgins, 'Reconstructing Australian Communism', *Socialist Register* 1974, 151 ff, and P. Love, *Labour and the Money Power* (Melbourne University Press, 1984).

2. P. Wilenski, 'Reform and Its Implementation: The Whitlam Years in Retrospect', in G. Evans and J. Reeves (eds.), *Labor Essays 1980* (Melbourne, Drummond, 1980), p. 41.

3. B. Catley and B. McFarlane, *Australian Capitalism in Boom and Depression* (Sydney, APCOL 1981); B. Head (ed.), *State and Economy in Australia* (Melbourne, Oxford 1983).

4. See especially G. Elliott, 'The Social Policy of the New Right', in M. Sawer (ed.), *Australia and the New Right* (Sydney, Allen and Unwin 1982).

5. J. Hagan, *History of the ACTU* (Melbourne, Longman-Cheshire 1981), p. 452.

6. Liberal Party of Australia, *Facing the Facts: Report of the Liberal Party Committee of Review*. (1983).

7. See for example the references to, and quotations from, Curtin peppered throughout B. Hawke, *National Reconciliation. The Speeches of Bob Hawke* (Sydney, Fontana 1984).

8. H.C. Coombs, 'John Curtin: A Consensus Prime Minister?', *Arena* 69 (1984).

9. R. Watts, *The Light on the Hill. The Origins of the Australian Welfare State 1935–1945*, doctoral thesis, Melbourne University 1983; 'The ALP and Liberalism 1941–1945', *Thesis Eleven* 7 (1983); 'The Origins of the Australian Welfare State', in R. Kennedy (ed.), *Australian Welfare History* (Melbourne, Macmillan 1982).

10. See especially the work of Watts, and see T. Rowse, *Australian Liberalism and National Character* (Malmsbury, Kibble 1978).

11. This view has been presented in Britain by B. Hindess, in 'Bob's Bon Accord', *New Socialist*, January 1985.

12. ALP–ACTU, *Statement of Accord* (ACTU, n.d.), pp. 1–3.

13. *Ibid.*, p. 7.

14. *Ibid.*, p. 4.

15. *Ibid.*, p. 16.

16. See *National Economic Summit Conference: Documents and Proceedings* (Canberra, AGPS 1983), Vol. 2, pp. 18–21; Beilharz, 'The View from the Summit', *Arena* 64 (1983).

17. *National Economic Summit Conference. Ibid.*, p. 21 ff.

18. See for example C. Bulbeck, 'The Accord: The First Two Years', *Thesis Eleven*, forthcoming; and see G. Singleton, 'The Economic Planning Advisory Council', and R. Stewart, 'The Politics of the Accord', in *Politics* 20/1 (1985).

19. See for example P. Keating, 'Opportunities for Investment and Corporate Finance in Australia', *Australian Foreign Affairs Record* 56/2 (1985).

20. See for example T. Wheelwright, 'The Dollar is Down, the Debt is Up and the Government is Out to Lunch', *Australian Left Review* 92 (1985).

21. 'The Strategic Basis Papers', *National Times*, March 30, 1985, clarified this tendency; and see B. Hayden, *Uranium, the Joint Facilities, Disarmament and Peace* (Canberra, AGPS 1984).

22. P. Wilenski, *ibid.*, p. 43; P. Beilharz and P. Moynihan, 'Medibank: Monument or Mausoleum of the Whitlam Government?', *Thesis Eleven* 7 (1983).

23. For detail, see for example, *Tribune*, July 3, 1985.

24. See for example K. West, *The Revolution in Australian Politics* (Ringwood, Penguin 1984) cf. P. Beilharz and R. Watts, 'The Discovery of Corporatism', *Australian Society*, November 1983.

25. See especially B. Jessop, 'Corporatism, Parliamentarism and Social Democracy', in P. Schmitter and G. Lehmbruch (eds.), *Trends Toward Corporatist Inter-*

mediation (Beverly Hills, Sage 1979).

26. P. Steedman, *Full Employment is Possible. The Accord—A Framework for Economic and Industrial Democracy* (Canberra, June 6, 1984); and see generally P. Beilharz, 'The Left, the Accord and the Future of Socialism', forthcoming in *Thesis Eleven*.

27. A. Theophanous, 'Back to Basics, says the Left', *Age*, July 5, 1984.

28. T. Colebatch, 'Cliches, not Logic, behind Condemnation of the Left', *Age*, March 9, 1985; K. Childs, 'The New Socialist Left', *Age*, November 15, 1984. It has been suggested that their hand can be seen in the Victorian ALP policy document *Social Justice, Age*, March 7, 1985. If this is true, there is little to be impressed by: the document is, like the Accord, lacking any real rigour or adequate mechanisms of implementation.

29. See for example B. Hayden, *The Implications of Democratic Socialism* (Melbourne, Fabian pamphlet 16, 1968) and 'The Contemporary Implications of Democratic Socialism', in G. Evans and J. Reeves (eds.), *Labor Essays 1982*, and even B. Hawke, 'Fabianism and Labor Policy', in *National Reconciliation: The Speeches of Bob Hawke*.

30. See *Labor Essays 1980*, p. 157.

31. See Love, *Labour and the Money Power*.

32. See Gareth Evans' papers in *Labor Essays 1980* and in B. O'Meagher, *The Socialist Objective* (Sydney, Hale and Iremonger, 1983).

33. B. Connell, 'Towards a Socialist Program', in *The Socialist Objective*, and *Socialism and Labor. An Australian Strategy* (Sydney, Labor Praxis, 1978). A. Heller, *Why We should Maintain the Socialist Objective* (Kooyong, ALP, 1982).

34. F. Fehér and A. Heller, 'Class, Democracy, Modernity', *Theory and Society* 12 (1983).

35. See for example Gareth Evans, *ibid*.

36. B. O'Meagher, Introduction to *The Socialist Objective*.

37. Connell, in *The Socialist Objective*.

38. See R. Kuhn, 'Alternative Strategies: Left Nationalism and Revolutionary Marxism', *Journal of Australian Political Economy* 12/13 (1982).

39. See A. Davidson, *Antonio Gramsci. The Man, His Ideas* (Sydney, ALR, 1968). Davidson had in fact also introduced Althusser to Australians: see his 'Althusser: Marxism Old and New', *Arena* 19 (1969). The young Althusserians were apparently less than taken with Davidson's views; Grant Evans criticised them in *Intervention* 2 (1972), while Higgins overlooked Davidson's contribution in his *Socialist Register* article.

40. See especially K. Rowley, 'Pastoral Capitalism', *Intervention* 1 (1972); J. Collins, 'Immigrant Workers in Australia', *Intervention* 4 (1974).

41. See for example *Beyond Marxism? Interventions After Marx* (Intervention, 17, 1983).

42. See for example T. O'Lincoln, *Into the Mainstream: The Decline of Australian Communism* (Sydney, Stained Wattle, 1985), p. 143 ff.

43. Higgins, 'Reconstructing Australian Communism', p. 179 ff.

44. L. Carmichael, 'A Peoples' Program', *Intervention* 9 (1977), and A. Game and R. Pringle, 'Reply to Carmichael', *Intervention* 10 (1978).

45. J. Sendy, *The Communist Party. History, Thoughts and Questions* (Melbourne, CPA History Group, 1978), p. 28; and see generally his *Comrades Come Rally!* (Melbourne, Nelson, 1978).

46. For example, B. Taft, 'Marxism is Open Ended', *Australian Left Review* 83 (1983).

47. Cf. Fehér and Heller, *ibid*.

48. *Statement by 23 Members of the Victorian State Committee of the CPA,* April 17, 1984; and see 'The CPA Split: Renewal or Dissolution?', *Thesis Eleven* 9 (1984).

49. CPA, *Australian Socialism: A Proposal for Renewal* (Sydney, 1984).

50. See for example J.J. Mathews, 'Putting Women First', *Australian Left Review* 84 (1983).

51. L. Aarons, *A Case for Radical Tax Reform* (Sydney, CPA, 1984).

52. *Socialist Perspectives on Issues for the Eighties. CPA 28th National Congress* (Sydney 1984), p. 5.

53. Socialist Alternative Melbourne Collective, *Make Melbourne Marvellous* (Melbourne, CPA, 1985).

54. A. Barcan, *The Socialist Left in Australia* (Sydney, APSA Monograph 2, 1960). And see *Fabian Newsletter* 24/4 (1985, Melbourne).

55. D. McKnight, 'Rethinking Socialism in the 80s', in McKnight, editor and publisher, *Socialism in Australia—Towards Renewal?* (Sydney, 1985), p. 3.

56. McKnight, p. 10.

57. *Australasian Spartacist*, March 1985.

58. See for example O'Lincoln, *Into the Mainstream.*

59. See for example D. Freney, *The Socialist Labour League—Moonies of the Left* (published by the author, 1982); N. Beams, *A Stalinist Liar Unmasked—A Reply to Denis Freney* (Workers News Pamphlet, 1983).

60. *Manifesto of Social Rights* (Strawberry Hills, n.d.); *Joint Statement of the Socialist Party of Australia and the Socialist Workers Party* (1984); A. Pha, *ACTU Policies on Unemployment* (Sydney, SPA, n.d.); A. Pha and J. Mc-Phillips, *The Crisis, the Accord and Summit Communique* (Sydney, SPA, n.d.). SWP, *The Struggle for Socialism in the Imperialist Epoch* (Sydney, Pathfinder, 1984).

61. *Joint Statement of the SPA and the SWP*, 9f, 4.

62. See for example *Tribune*, May 1, 1985; K. Cooke, 'Confusion in the Peace Ranks', *Age*, May 28, 1985; K. Mansell, 'Making Sense of the NDP Split', *Tribune*, May 29, 1985.

63. *Joint Statement of the SPA and SWP*, p. 7 ff.

64. O'Lincoln, *Into the Mainstream*, pp. 128 ff, 154. The debate had other points of significance, signalling as it did both the attraction of the Althusserians to the revolutionary legacy of Trotskyism, and the affinity between Deutscher's views and those of the frontist-Eurocommunist lineage.

65. See Mansell, 'Making Sense of the NDP Split'.

66. Metal Trade Unions, *Policy for Industry Development and More Jobs*, (August 1984).

67. *Ibid.,* pp. iii, xvi.

68. *Ibid.,* p. 197.

69. A. Jolley, *Towards the Regeneration of Australian Manufacturing* (Melbourne, Victorian Chamber of Manufacturers Research Discussion Paper 14, 1984).

70. *Australasian Spartacist*, March 1985.

71. See for example the editorial to *Journal of Australian Political Economy* 17 (1984).

72. S. Clegg, G. Dow and P. Boreham, 'From the Politics of Production to the Production of Politics', *Thesis Eleven* 9; Dow, 'The Case for Corporatism', *Australian Society*, November 1984.

73. W. Korpi, *The Democratic Class Struggle* (London, Routledge & Kegan Paul, 1984).

74. W. Higgins and N. Apple, 'How Limited is Reformism?', *Theory and Society* 12 (1983).

75. Clegg, Dow and Boreham, p. 27.
76. Higgins, 'Response to Questionnaire on Social Democracy', *Thesis Eleven* 7, p. 134.
77. See for example, Clegg, Dow and Boreham.
78. Higgins, 'Why do we need a Left Party?', *Tribune*, August 8, 1984.
79. J. Triado, 'Corporatism, Democracy and Modernity', *Thesis Eleven* 9; Beilharz and Watts, 'The Discovery of Corporatism'; Beilharz, 'The View from the Summit'; Beilharz and Watts, 'Tories in Labor Drag?', *Australian Society*, May 1984; Beilharz and Watts, 'The Accord and Morals', *Australian Society*, February, 1985. Related but different arguments have been put by feminists, for whom exclusion is a lived reality: see inter alia D. Blackman, 'Women and The Accord', *Australian Left Review* 89; A. Game and R. Pringle, 'From Here to Fraternity—Women and the Hawke Government', *Scarlet Woman* 17 (1983) and P. Hall and B. Preston, 'The Accord—What's in it for Women', *Scarlet Woman*, 17–20. A. Game, 'Affirmative Action: Liberal Rationality or Challenge to Patriarchy?', *Legal Service Bulletin*, December 1984.
80. Triado, p. 40.
81. See Hagan, *History of the ACTU*.
82. S. Frenkel and A. Coolican, *Unions Against Capitalism?* (Sydney, Allen and Unwin, 1984).
83. Triado, p. 33.
84. See for example Hindess, *ibid;* R. Curtain, 'Abstaining and Complaining', *Australian Society*, March 1985; M. Burford, 'Interpreting Socialism', *Australian Society*, March 1984.
85. A. Davidson, *The Communist Party of Australia* (Stanford, Hoover, 1969), p. 183.
86. See the survey in Melbourne Revolutionary Marxists, *A Call for The Revolutionary Regroupment of the Australian Left* (September, 1975). On the meanderings of Maoism, see for example E.F. Hill, *Reflections on Communism in Australia* (1983); J. Herouvim, 'Politics of the Revolving Door—The CPA (ML)', *Melbourne Journal of Politics*, 15 (1983–4).
87. Barcan, *op. cit.*
88. See *inter alia* T. Irving, 'Radical Political Science', in D. Aitken (ed.), *Surveys of Australian Political Science* (Sydney, Allen and Unwin, 1985); D. Austin, *Australian Sociologies* (Allen and Unwin, 1984).
89. See for example *Interventions Beyond Marx*, cf. Connell, 'Marxists and Anti-marxists', *Intervention* 18; and see the Local Consumption Series, as well as G. Gill, 'Post-Structuralism as Ideology', *Arena* 69 (1984).

August 1985

LYRICAL ILLUSIONS OR A SOCIALISM OF GOVERNANCE: WHITHER FRENCH SOCIALISM?*

Mark Kesselman

The demise of French socialism in the current period occurred on June 13, 1982, barely a year after the Socialists' electoral triumph.[1] The government's *plan de rigueur* signalled the abandonment of its ambitious attempt to initiate a radical form of social democracy in France. Unlike Hegel's owl of Minerva, this time theory preceded practice. For years, French intellectuals had been proclaiming the end of socialism—when they were not equating socialism with the gulag. The extent to which rightist ideological hegemony and the near-absence of socialist theorising contributed to the government's conservative shift cannot be determined. But the feebleness of leftist intellectual activity, as well as the lack of pressure from the left, including trade unions and social movements opposed to statism, militarism, chauvinism, and class inequality, was doubtless significant. More influential in the short run was the failure of the government's attempt to radicalise social democracy.

The government's initial approach was itself a compromise with the objective, announced in the *Projet Socialiste* adopted in 1980 by the Socialist Party (PS), of achieving a rupture with capitalism. France was unique among major capitalist democracies because its two major left parties, the French Communist Party (PCF) and PS, continued to proclaim that socialist transformation necessitated the abolition of capitalism. In 1981, however, the Socialist–Communist government (in which the PS was by far the dominant partner) judged that economic stagnation, unemployment, and the damage wrought by decades of conservative rule precluded seeking radical change at the outset. Instead, the governing coalition sought to liberalise French society as well as sponsor structural reforms and redistributive measures to foster the kind of social democratic class compromise prevalent in Northern Europe.[2] The most immediate goal was to revive the stagnant French economy. Borrowing Keynesian techniques from social democratic practice, the government sharply increased transfers on grounds of social equity, and in order to boost aggregate demand and stimulate investment, employment, and growth. However, rather than create a virtuous circle of growth, the first phase provoked a vicious circle familiar from similar socialist attempts in Chile

---

*I am deeply grateful for suggestions from Amrita Basu.

and Portugal in the 1970s: much of the increased purchasing power went for imported goods. The result was to increase France's international trade deficit, exacerbate inflation, weaken the franc, drain currency reserves—and bring France to the brink of economic chaos.

The *plan de rigueur* signified abandoning the attempt to achieve rapid growth through state intervention. But it also signified abandoning the goal of radical change. The new priorities were to control inflation, reduce budget and international trade deficits, and rationalise French capitalism. In the process, the government curtailed social welfare programmes, sanctioned massive layoffs, and curtailed proposed democratic reforms within industry, local government, and the state bureaucracy. The impact of Socialist rule was cruelly described by one faction of the PS: 'Far from demonstrating the left's capacity to direct social change in a desirable fashion, five years of left government. . . have obscured and devalued socialist prospects.'[3] Public opinion polls that charted changing political attitudes between 1980–84 found that 'socialism' displayed the greatest decline in popularity.[4]

Socialist Party leaders describe the shift in 1982 very differently. They argue that harsh realities compelled the left to relinquish 'lyrical illusions' (in the words of PS First Secretary Lionel Jospin). Rather than pursue an impossible—and irresponsible—dream, the left should confront the most pressing problem: the need for economic modernisation in order to improve France's international economic competitiveness. The next section describes the bedrock change in French Socialist theory and practice from 'lyrical illusions' to a 'socialism of governance'. The new approach could be described as '(capitalist) economics in command': by some alchemy, socialist goals were transformed into the quest to perfect France's capitalist economy. The focus here is on the PS because of the party's central role in defining the ideological agenda of the left. The PS assumed this position during the 1970s, a product of its increasing political prominence, the decline of the PCF, and the rightward shift among intellectuals.

The Dialectics of Desocialisation

Especially when judged by the deflationary, neo-liberal policies pursued by other capitalist democracies in 1981, the French Socialist government's first-year balance sheet is extremely impressive. The government substantially increased social transfers, including family allowances, rent subsidies, and pensions; introduced a fifth week of paid vacations, a large increase in the minimum wage, retirement at age sixty, and a one hour reduction in the working week; and sponsored far-reaching reforms of the industrial relations system, local government, criminal justice, and electronic media. The most distinctive reform, going beyond social democracy as it had evolved since the 1950s, was a considerable enlargement of the public industrial and banking sector: nine large industrial firms and most private banks were nationalised.

The first year's reforms changed many aspects of France's political economy. But rather than generating a demand by progressive social movements for further democratisation, the opposite result occurred; a variety of privileged social forces, supported by rightist political parties, mounted determined resistance (what the French term neo-corporatism). The reason was that the reforms marginally eroded the position of privileged groups, thus provoking their anger, yet failed to mobilise support among less advantaged groups—women, workers, immigrants—to offset rightist opposition.

The Socialist government was not only isolated from social movements but squarely opposed many of their goals and tactics. For example, it quickly antagonised the ecology movement by refusing to modify France's heavy emphasis on nuclear power. When immigrant workers launched strikes to protest against management's highly repressive tactics in the automobile industry, Prime Minister Mauroy direly warned of the damage to the French economy. In 1985, I asked one of Mitterrand's more leftist associates whether he thought that a cause of the government's difficulties was the low degree of left mobilisation. He replied, 'As Minister of the Interior, I could hardly approve of that kind of activity.' By its statist approach, the Socialist government reinforced a traditional socialist image that antagonised its own social base and led many intellectuals to reject socialism.

Linked to its statism, the Socialist government emphasised an economic approach to socialism which emphasised productivist values rather than fostering democratic and solidaristic goals. Yet the government's failure in the economic sphere was dramatic: it derived from the fact that France's state-stimulated expansion was not followed by a widely-predicted international economic revival in 1981–82. Rather than the French economy securing an early lead in supplying expanding international demand, French exports fell during the worst worldwide recession since the 1930s (at the same time that French imports were soaring). When currency reserves were nearly depleted in early 1982, the Socialist government was forced to choose between imposing severe protectionism and a steep devaluation—which would have necessitated withdrawing from the European Monetary System and would have provoked international capitalist opposition—or adopting a deflationary course.

The *plan de rigueur* adopted in 1982 departed from traditional austerity by including provisions for vocational training programmes for redundant workers, early retirement for workers in depressed industries, and social sector employment programmes (what the government termed the 'social treatment of unemployment'). The lowest paid workers were excluded from the wage-price freeze. Plans went forward to implement reforms passed in the first year. But in other respects, the 1982 measures and others sponsored in later years were part of the stop-go deflationary arsenal familiar elsewhere: measures to lower business taxes, shift income from labour to capital, stabilise or reduce public sector employment, and lower income taxes for those in top brackets. The new turn spelled an end to grandiose visions of *socialisme à la française*. Henceforth, the government's first priority was to rationalise French capitalism. The Socialists' new discourse suggests the distance travelled since the *Projet Socialiste* advocated a rupture with capitalism.

The Socialist government has sought to sponsor a fundamental re-structuring of the French left's ideology. Gone are attacks, characteristic of PS publications, congresses, and public statements through 1981, on the exploitation, profiteering, and irrationality inherent in capitalism. Instead, the government argues that the major problem facing France is the need to modernise the productive apparatus—which is described as backward and inefficient, but never as capitalist. In the past, the government argues, the French relied unduly on the state, whereas they need to engage in greater competition, risk-taking, and private entrepreneurial activities.

As early as September 1982, in a speech that the Elysée described in advance as having 'national significance', François Mitterrand stated that *socialisme à la française* was not his 'bible'. In a TV interview the follow-ing year, he defended the legitimacy of gaining a large personal fortune, if it was not based on inheritance or financial speculation, and he praised the profit principle. He called for national unity to replace class struggle: 'Conditions have emerged permitting a class armistice and class peace. . . Thus, class struggle is not my goal; I hope that it ends.'[5] Jean Daniel, editor of the *Nouvel Observateur*, suggested that, as a result of Mitterrand's remarks, 'the entire [Socialist] philosophy of governance must be revised. . .'[6]

Mitterrand argued that the burden for modernising the French economy falls on the left because, when in power, the right failed 'to understand or persuade others that henceforth French grandeur must consist of our successfully competing on foreign economic and commercial battlefields. [The right] did not prepare France for this competition'.[7]

The Socialists always prided themselves on being in the vanguard of progress. But modernisation assumed even greater importance in 1984 when newly appointed Prime Minister Laurent Fabius made it one of two axes of the government's overall policy. '[We must] modernise to wage the battle for full employment. . . Any genuine improvement in employ-ment depends on growth; durable growth requires a solid productive apparatus, able to export and hold its own in domestic markets; and any solid productive apparatus must be modern. . .'[8]

Fabius asserted that modernisation will fail if it is defined as exclusively technological and economic. 'Economic modernisation cannot succeed without modernising social relations.' Yet he defined social modernisation in an economistic and conservative fashion as the process by which all social forces reflect together 'on how social progress can contribute to competitiveness and growth'.[9]

Socialist Austerity

What is distinctively socialist about an approach that reduced health and unemployment insurance benefits, reduced purchasing power in 1983–84, and failed to reduce France's substantial income inequalities? The simplest, if least satisfactory, answer was provided by Lionel Jospin when he was asked this question in a TV interview: 'Because it is sponsored by socialists.'[10]

Former Prime Minister Pierre Mauroy defended the government's new stance since 1982 as necessary to digest the substantial reforms of the first year: 'Governments which have sponsored as deep a transformation as we have cannot maintain a constant pace of change. Periods of social peace are indispensable. . . The revolution is never permanent. If social change is to be durable, it must be intermittent.'[11]

For Mauroy, the approach adopted in 1982 represents a pause in a continuous process of social change. Others, however, assert that the shift is both permanent and salutary. Jean Daniel argues that the Socialists' ideology became ossified as a result of electoral exigencies. 'Ideological renewal within the left was suppressed by the necessity of allying [with the PCF]; otherwise, the left might not have reached power.' By having to govern for a long period, the Socialists 'will be forced to reach new conclusions; in fact, they already have'.[12]

Many Socialist leaders echo Daniel. They suggest that, in the past, after sponsoring a spate of reforms, the French left was quickly forced from power. Thanks to their 1981 electoral victory and the political institutions of the Fifth Republic, the Socialists gained control of the commanding heights of the state for at least five years. As a result, they had both the opportunity and necessity to adopt a longer term perspective and to assume responsibility for the conduct of the entire nation rather than merely defend the less advantaged. Mauroy suggests that the left must go beyond sponsoring reforms in order to 'demonstrate that it has the capacity to administer an industrial society'.[13] Illustrative of the Socialists' 'new look' is that Mauroy uses the term 'industrial society' and thereby wholly avoids the very real and difficult issue for socialists of how simultaneously to administer a capitalist society and transform it in a socialist direction.

To govern for a durable period (gérer la durée as Mitterrand often described it) has meant a sharp change in orientation. Gérard Delfau, a Socialist Party leader, suggests that the Socialists must choose whether 'to seek immediate gains for workers or to assure their longer-run interests by representing the entire nation'.[14] Mitterrand also illustrated the change when asked in an interview why he defended socialism so little: he replied that he was no longer the head of the Socialist party but of the entire French nation, with its diverse ideological currents.[15]

Lionel Jospin described the Socialists' transformation best when he suggested that the process consisted of a shift from a 'socialism of opposition' to a 'socialism of governance'. In Jean Daniel's words, '...The resistance of stubborn reality, the practice of power, and the confrontation with constraints have provoked a dramatic conversion from the fantasy of revolution to a responsible social democracy. . .'[16]

The economic crisis has played a primordial role in the transformation of French Socialism. Socialist leaders argue that they underestimated the gravity of the crisis and failed to grasp the fragility of France's economy. They now argue that economic stagnation in France, intense international economic competition, and rapid technological change have reduced the possibility of engaging in any reforms that are not designed to improve France's economic position. As Jospin describes it, the Socialists must relinquish their 'lyrical illusions' and 'intellectual arrogance', for 'Reality has brutally reminded us that the laws of economics exist. . . We must accept that modifying economic realities is a slow process, that political will [the French term is 'voluntarism'], while necessary, has its limits; and that our policy choices may produce negative consequences.'[17] Jospin reifies the laws of capitalist economics, and apparently assumes that the only alternative to 'lyrical illusions' is the grim realities of the dismal science.

It should come as no surprise that, in the current Socialist vision, when capitalism is mentioned, it is praised. For two Socialist scholars, writing in a journal linked to the Rocard faction, '. . . The market is the most effective instrument yet devised for producing wealth, innovation, and the global improvement of living standards. . . A rupture with capitalism should no longer be the central objective of French socialism'.[18]

Prior to 1981, French Socialists asserted that they sought a third way between social democracy and Soviet socialism. Within several years, François Mitterrand was describing the model, which he termed the society of the mixed economy, as a third way between ultra-liberalism and collectivism. 'The society of the mixed economy is French society as it is presently emerging, through the coexistence of two powerful independent, yet complementary, sectors.'[19] When he was asked whether the mixed economy was a strategy for achieving socialism, his answer was evasive and unsatisfying: 'The coexistence of the two types of society will be long. It corresponds to an evolutionary stage of Western economies when progressive forces are in power. When conservative parties gain office, they seek to remove the obstacles preventing concentrated capital from becoming dominant.'[20]

What, then, is the meaning of socialism in the current period? According to Jacques Julliard, 'It is common knowledge that Fabius has buried socialism. . . The real question, the only interesting one, is what will replace it. And on this score nothing has yet emerged.'[21] The recent crop of books by Socialist leaders do not fill the gap.[22] Typically, they argue that socialists have learned about the necessity of achieving economic efficiency while retaining a commitment to equality, solidarity, and social justice. For example, 'Socialism is an attitude, an approach. Distributing power, broadening access to responsibilities. . . while seeking as much as possible to involve workers.' In a similar vein, socialism is 'the struggle so that people exercise mastery over their destiny, the ceaseless struggle against inequalities, and the defence of human rights'.[23] These accounts are vague about the specific content of equality, the appropriate strategy for achieving it, and its relationship to the traditional goal of socialism: democratising control of production and the state.

As is well known, the PS is highly divided by factional strife. The position described until here commands agreement from three of the party's four major factions: the Mitterrandistes', under Jospin, and the Mauroy faction sponsored the 1982 shift; Michel Rocard argues, quite reasonably, that the party's orientation is belated vindication of his own position in the party's internecine struggles. The major critique of the dominant orientation within the PS derives from Centre d'Etudes et Recherches Socialistes (Ceres), often described as the left wing of the party. In public pronouncements, Ceres leaders barely conceal their contempt for the party's position. In private conversations, they are even less restrained.

Contrary to what one might expect, Ceres does not criticise the fact that the Socialist party and government have embraced the logic of capital. According to Ceres, socialism is simply not on the agenda in the current period. The real problem is that the government has not grasped that the principal danger is multinational corporate (primarily United States) domination of France's economic and political destiny.[24]

According to Ceres, the major political-economic cleavage in France pits the interests of most French people against 'the forces of decline— those who place their class interests ahead of France, those who accept submission to the capitalism of multinationals, the dissolution of France, the vassalisation of France. . .'[25] Yet in this situation, the Socialist government lacks a project to stem France's decline. The only possible approach is to couple protectionist measures with vigorous state actions to foster growth and develop France's industrial base. Ceres identifies three major priorities in the current period: national independence, economic growth, and a democratised society (with emphasis on the first).[26]

Ceres proposes to substitute a vibrant conception of the 'modern republic' for the discredited socialist ideology. Ceres leaders believe that the image of the modern republic evokes the kind of broad-based national-ism that was at the origin of the Third Republic. Education Minister Jean-Pierre Chevènement, Ceres leader, is fond of quoting Jules Ferry on the need for civic virtue (and he has ordered that civics instruction be made compulsory in primary schools). Chevènement has advocated the value of 'republican elitism' to instill the love of competition, initiative, and excellence as a way to revitalise France.

This brief review suggests the theoretical sterility of debate within the PS; there is precious little creative socialist analysis outside the PS either. The PCF, which has obtained less than fifteen percent of the popular vote in elections during the 1980s, advocates a majoritarian mass movement to force a shift in economic decision-making. The PCF proposes replacing capitalist criteria of short-term profitability by socially-oriented criteria of decision-making at all levels of production.

According to the PCF, priority should be assigned to investments that maximise employment and economise on capital, as opposed to the present situation, in which wages are treated as a cost of production.[27] The PCF accords heavy emphasis to workers' direct intervention to re-shape decision-making criteria; and it emphasises the need to concentrate investments in France, rather than further weaken the French economy through investments abroad.

There has been relatively little interest in the PCF's new approach, probably because the party has lost credibility as a result of its electoral decline, erratic strategic shifts, sectarian attitude since 1984, and refusal to question democratic centralism. With a few noteworthy exceptions, there have been no independent left analyses of French socialism.[28] This situation merits separate analysis, for it points up the general conservative shift in France.

The Sound of Silence
On July 26, 1983, Max Gallo, novelist, essayist, and official spokesperson for the Socialist government, published an article in *Le Monde* lamenting the absence of leftist debate concerning the government's project to modernise France.[29] The following day, *Le Monde* journalist Philippe Boggio analysed the reasons for 'the silence of left intellectuals'.[30] Was the government's isolation a result of intellectuals' disappointment with the government's conservative policies? Quite the contrary. According to Boggio, intellectuals suspected the government of complacency toward the Soviet Union and toward communism. The Union of the Left alliance was seen as a pact with the devil; the PS was regarded as blind, cynical, or opportunist with respect to the greatest threat to liberty in the twentieth century.

The torrent of articles replying to Gallo and Boggio in the next weeks suggested that there was no single cause of intellectuals' discontent with the government. The debate helps illuminate the crisis of socialist theory and practice in France.[31] First, it is noteworthy that there were few critiques of the government from the left, an illustration of how far the balance has shifted to the right within French political culture. Second, many intellectuals echoed Boggio in their opposition to the USSR, communism, totalitarianism, and the PCF. Why is anti-communism stronger in France than in comparable nations?[32] The major reason is probably that it represents a backlash, amplified by the print and electronic media, that follows a period in which (in Régis Debray's cruel phrase) it was chic to be on the left. The memoirs of intellectuals like Edgar Morin and Emmanuel LeRoy Ladurie reveal the depth of bitterness that developed among intellectuals who resigned or were expelled from the PCF.[33] It is ironic that the very factor that impressed leftists outside France as increasing the possibility of radical change—the Union of the Left alliance— was viewed with dismay by many French intellectuals. (In this connection, one needs to appreciate the widespread bitterness that developed on the left following the breakup of the alliance in 1977, and the disgust with the behaviour of both the PCF and PS in the late 1970s.)

Third, intellectuals' reservations regarding the Socialist government involved a complex of factors going beyond opposition to communism. In a prescient article written years before Gallo's appeal to intellectuals, Diana Pinto analysed the 'hidden conflict' between French intellectuals and socialism.[34] She identified three shifts in intellectuals' attitudes during the 1970s which produced a sceptical stance toward socialism. First, intellectuals repudiated the Marxist paradigm in theory and 'actually existing socialist' practice. André Glucksmann illustrates the most extreme (and sectarian) rejection of Marxism and the discovery of totalitarianism; Claude Lefort and Cornelius Castoriades, more temperate (albeit one-sided) variants.

Second, the decline of anti-Americanism. The initial impetus derived from French intellectuals' fascination with the peace movement, new left, and other social movements. Gradually, they shifted from viewing the United States as intellectually vacuous and reactionary to dynamic, pragmatic, and pluralist. The third change involved a rethinking of France's own history. Intellectuals began to challenge the stereotype of France as representing a revolutionary vanguard in world history. Revisionist attitudes developed toward France's revolutionary past.

Intellectuals' reservations about socialism were reinforced by the French Socialist experience after 1981. They were disturbed by the Union of the Left alliance and believed that the Socialist government adhered to an archaic conception of socialism, as symbolised, for example, by the government's emphasis on the need for nationalisation. Most left intellectuals were sympathetic to Michel Rocard and the 'deuxième gauche', which were in a marginal position within the PS and government. Intellectuals often considered the Socialist government's slogans and rituals somewhat ridiculous, for example, Mitterrand's post-inauguration visit to the Panthéon, or Minister of Culture Jack Lang's ostentatious refusal to visit the annual festival of American films at Deauville. Rather than suggesting a more appropriate socialist project, however, intellectuals theorised about the impossibility or undesirability of global social projects, or remained silent. The climate of intellectual opinion in France helps explain the Socialist government's turn to 'realism' in 1982.

What Was To Be Done?

One cannot condemn the Socialist government for its preoccupation with economic efficiency, competitiveness, and growth. However, it can be faulted for its naivete, inconsistency, and lack of preparation in confronting the economic crisis. The Socialists reached office, in considerable measure, because of their telling critiques of the right's failure to appreciate the gravity of the crisis, the dilapidated state of French industry, and France's growing dependence on international capitalism. Yet it appeared that the Socialists did not believe their own campaign rhetoric.

The Socialist Party proved incapable of translating its ambitious promises into concrete policies. It was an electoralist party as well as an agency adept at passing legislation and directing day-to-day administration. (The PS was the most entrenched party at the level of urban government.) But there was a link missing between the torrent of laws passed in the first years and the specific administrative application: the capacity to stimulate a broad movement to achieve the party's overall goals. The problem may be rather that the PS lacked a global socialist strategy and programme. President Mitterrand was fond of recalling that most of his 110 point electoral platform had been voted into law. Yet, judging from public opinion polls, a majority of the French believed that one of the principal reasons for his unpopularity (he received the lowest rating of any Fifth Republic president) was that he failed to keep his promises.

The Socialists have proved unable to develop an adequate social vision. They shifted from an abstract call for a rupture with capitalism, to Keynesianism plus nationalisations, before adopting the right's deflationary and rationalising policies. It is hardly surprising that their turn to *rigueur* proved unpopular, for it 'neglected the preoccuaptions of solidarity, social transformation, and democratisation which are the core—and the honour—of the left'.[35]

The Socialist movement failed to resolve the complex dilemma of how to achieve substantial reforms of capitalism while avoiding economic disruption from capitalist resistance. Initially, Socialist rhetoric oscillated between attacking the 'privileged caste' and cajoling capitalists to invest. Soon, however, there was a shift toward seeking to bolster capitalist confidence and profitability. In his declaration of general policy, Laurent

Fabius argued that 'the essential responsibility for modernisation falls on private firms. They deserve the support of the entire country. I have always believed that the left was best qualified to reconcile private enterprise and the nation'.[36]

In 1981, the French left confronted a situation quite familiar to other left movements in Western Europe: social democracy was forged from the attempt to sponsor step-by-step transformation within the structure of opportunities and constraints offered by liberal democratic institutions. Under these conditions, pressures to deradicalise are legion.[37] Given decades of social democratic experience elsewhere, it is surprising that the French Socialists were so ill-equipped, both theoretically and in their governing practice. Although French Socialists had long been disdainful of Northern European social democracy, they quickly succumbed to conservative constraints on reaching office. By glossing over their capitulation through references to a 'socialism of governance', the PS ignores the need to develop a synthesis involving both opposition and governance. At the same time, French Socialists justify their retreat in a way that is uncannily reminiscent of social democracies elsewhere: the need for the socialist movement to be concerned with immediate problems of living standards and employment, the need to be responsible and mature, the need to represent broad national interests rather than merely workers' interests, and the imperatives posed by the international economy.

The real question is not whether enormous obstacles constrain the possibility of achieving radically democratic change: it would be utopian to deny the difficulties involved in following a socialist path. But what counts is to exploit whatever latitude for manoeuvre exists despite harsh realities. Concretely, did the situation confronting the Socialists in France dictate as conservative a response as they developed?

Take the relationship between rationalising the productive apparatus and democratising relations of production. The Socialist government assumed that the two goals were basically incompatible and chose to subordinate democratising productive relations to the need for industrial modernisation and technological innovation. However, this definition of the situation is rooted in an earlier era of Taylorised production. In the current period, the character of technological change points to a more complex relationship: at the shopfloor level, the new technology requires high levels of skill, polyvalence, initiative, and judgment, in brief, the transcendance of Taylorism. At the community and global level, overall economic efficiency may be enhanced by democratic planning, collaboration among social forces, and the ability to adapt rapidly and exchange information. The micro-electronic revolution creates possibilities for radical changes in social relations, which, thus far, are barely developed in theory or tested in practice.

The silence (or opposition) of intellectuals and the weakness of social movements inhibited socialist change in this domain. For the absence of vibrant debate on the left deprived the Socialist movement of inspiration, concrete proposals, critical support, and visions of radical alternatives, leaving it vulnerable to rightist ideological, political, and economic onslaught. The right incorporated newly emerging social demands for flexibility, individualism, and autonomy into a neo-liberal project dismantling the welfare state and reconstructing capitalism. Yet the new themes are not inherently incompatible with socialism—they first erupted, after all, in the social movements of the late 1960s—and in fact could be the basis for a modern, decentralised, participatory socialism. However, this left approach required an ideological vision that intellectuals failed to provide, and a vigorous social movement that was lacking.

The timing and sequence of reforms is relevant to understanding the dialectic of desocialisation. The boldest reforms could probably only be launched in the grace period following the Socialists' election, when there were high popular expectations and extensive support for the left. Yet the government chose to make its first priorities an increase in social transfers (which soon proved economically destabilising) and a sweeping decentralisation of French administration. Neither reform involved democratising the centrally important arena of productive relations. And neither, however desirable it might be, was framed in a way to stimulate a spiral of mobilisation for additional change. By their content, as well as the statist manner by which they were proposed and implemented, they served to demobilise.[38] Very quickly, the government's grace period ended and conservative opposition burgeoned.

In private conversations, two Socialist cabinet ministers offered opposite assessments of the first months. When, in the fall of 1981, I questioned the strategy chosen and suggested the need for more radical, democratising reforms at the outset of Socialist rule, I was admonished by one leading Socialist to be patient. Each phase of reform would come in its own time: first, social transfers and decentralisation to consolidate support; next, nationalisation to create the instruments for socialist economic planning and, eventually, more radical change. However, events proved that the cycle of change was diametrically opposite. According to the second minister with whom I spoke, the first months of Socialist rule were critical. And, rather than the state of grace being a cause for rejoicing, it was a disaster, since it signified a passive condition of watchful waiting and scepticism rather than active support forged through struggle. He cited a series of by-election results in January 1982, at which the left suffered a decline of support, as a turning point. At a cabinet meeting days after the elections, the cabinet was polled on its reactions to the elections. Pierre Mauroy, the confident, reassuring Prime Minister, and most of his colleagues, minimised the importance of the results. However, the minister confided, Mitterrand agreed with his own pessimistic assessment that the results signified that the Socialists had lost popular confidence and were on a downward slide of support, which spelled the end to the phase of audacious reforms.

Conclusion

Rarely have conditions seemed as propitious for moving in a democratic socialist direction as they were in France in 1981. The French Socialist experience suggests the disturbing possibility that democratic socialism, broadly defined as collective appropriation and direction of the means of production, political decision-making, administration, and community, is indeed a 'lyrical illusion'. How else can one explain the failure of widespread social mobilisation in support of democratic socialism in 1981, the indifference or opposition of so many intellectuals, and the government's retreat beginning in 1982? What lessons for socialist theory and practice emerge from the failure of French socialism?

Three dilemmas appear critical in explaining the conservative outcome beginning in 1982; all three need to be overcome if democratic socialism is to have a future. First, the balance of political, economic, social, and ideological forces within France hindered radical change. Right wing political parties recovered quickly from their electoral defeat to mount effective opposition to Socialist policies. Despite the Socialists' political victory and passage of the nationalisation reform, the bulk of the French economy remained in private hands. Despite governmental blandishments, private investment stagnated. Further, while progressive social movements were weak, privileged social forces were well-organised and soon took to the streets (and highways) to defend their interests. In the ideological sphere, best-selling books extolled the virtues of the conservative revolution (in the United States) while there were no analyses of how to achieve the socialist vision. Given these constraints, it is unthinkable that the Socialist government would have ventured further into the uncharted terrain of democratic socialist change.

Second, the international capitalist system rapidly punishes national policies that do not respect the rules of the (capitalist) game. The French economy is so tightly integrated into the world capitalist system that, unless the left demonstrated its ability to out-perform the right, according to criteria of capitalist rationality, living standards would decline, unemployment rise, and opposition snowball. The Ceres faction of the PS urged protectionist measures, to provide a respite from foreign competition for French industry. This might have been a possibility—but only if adequately prepared and backed by strong popular support, conditions which were absent.

Third, the French left did not take the full measure of the first two constraints. It was initially utopian, by underestimating the gravity of the situation, and then defeatist, in that it allowed constraints to dictate policy. Thus, although France's margin for quantitative redistributive measures was narrow, given the stagnation of the world economy, other kinds of reforms might have been initiated. At the extreme, what are usually described as obstacles and constraints might be converted into opportunities for a revitalised socialist project. For example, in recent years the link appears to have been severed between investment, technological change, growth, and full employment. Investment has begun to displace both labour and capital, an unprecedented situation which can impose heavy costs and yet make possible extraordinary progress. Without a drastic change in patterns of employment and wage relations, the third technological revolution can increase unemployment and strengthen tendencies toward a dual economy and society. However, a creative socialist project would incorporate the vast possibilities provided by this development of productive forces in order to reorganise production, reduce work-time, and develop new extra-work community-based activities.

The Socialist government demonstrated that it could overcome constraints and promote progressive change. While the industrial relations and decentralisation reforms are far from radical—they help to modernise French society and bring France closer to other advanced capitalist nations—they illustrate well how to translate stirring slogans into concrete practice. However, the Socialist government failed to demonstrate this capacity where it counted: in democratising relations of production. Thus, if the government cannot be held responsible for failing to achieve socialist transformation, by abandoning lyrical illusions and developing a socialism of governance it helped discredit the attempt to forge a democratic socialist path.

NOTES

1. When 'socialist' is capitalised, it refers to the French Socialist Party or government; when it is used in lower case, it refers to those (whether within or outside the party) committed to socialism.
2. For a description, see my 'Socialism Without the Workers: The Case of France', *Kapitalistate*, no. 10/11 (1983), pp. 11–41. The Socialists did not openly admit that they aimed to develop a form of social democracy in France until the following year; until then, social democracy was an epithet for the French left.
3. Ceres, Rapport Introductif, 14ème Colloque (Paris, 1985), p. 10.
4. SOFRES, Opinion Publique 1985 (Paris, Gallimard, 1985), p. 100.
5. *Le Monde*, September 17, 1983.
6. Jean Daniel, 'L'heure des intellectuals', *Le Débat*, no. 27 (December 1983), p. 169.
7. Interview in *L'Expansion*, no. 249 (November 16, 1984), p. 63. However, one should avoid a Manichean vision on this score. See Alain Vernholes, 'La Rigueur dans la demonstration', *Le Monde*, April 2, 1983.
8. *Le Monde*, July 26, 1984.
9. *Ibid.*

10. *Le Monde*, October 23, 1984.
11. Pierre Mauroy, *A Gauche* (Paris, Albin Michel, 1985), p. 45.
12. *Le Matin*, December 31, 1984.
13. Mauroy, *op. cit.*, p. 15.
14. Gérard Delfau, *Gagner à gauche* (Paris, Robert Laffont, 1984), p. 79.
15. *Libération*, May 10, 1984.
16. *Nouvel Observateur*, May 31, 1985.
17. *Le Monde*, August 27, 1983.
18. Alain Bergounioux and Gérard Grunberg, 'Perspectives pour une gauche libérale', *Intervention*, no. 11 (Jan.–March 1985), p. 90.
19. *Libération*, May 10, 1984.
20. Interview in *L'Expansion*, no. 249 (November 16, 1984), p. 65.
21. *Nouvel Observateur*, June 14, 1985.
22. See, among others, Delfau, *op. cit.*, Max Gallo, *La Troisième alliance: Pour un nouvel individualisme* (Paris, Fayard, 1984), Jacques Mandrin, *Le Socialisme et la France* (Paris, Le Sycomore, 1983), Mauroy, *op. cit.*, Louis Mermaz, *L'Autre volonté* (Paris, Robert Laffont, 1984), and Jean Poperen, *Le Nouveau contrat socialiste* (Paris, Ramsey, 1984).
23. The first quotation is from Gilbert Orsoni, 'Le socialisme, moyen de diffusion des pouvoirs, *Le Monde*, July 5, 1985; the second, from Bergounioux and Grunberg, *op. cit.*, p. 92.
24. See Mandrin, *op. cit.*, the Ceres journal *En jeu*, and the contribution to the preparations for the PS 1985 Congress at Toulouse by Christian Bataille and others, 'Un projet contre le déclin', *le poing et la rose*, no. 112 (May 1985).
25. Didier Motchane, 'Un Projet contre le déclin', *En jeu*, no. 23 (1985), p. 9.
26. Bataille, *op. cit.*
27. Philippe Herzog, *L'Economie nouvelle à bras-le-corps: Economiser le capital pour libérer les hommes* (Paris, Messidor-Editions Sociales, 1984).
28. See the special issue of *Les Temps Modernes* on 'La Politique économique de la gauche en question', no. 441 (April 1983), Michel Beaud, *Le Mirage de la croissance*, 2 vols. (Paris, Syros, 1983/95), and Alain Lipietz, *L'Audace ou l'enlisement, Sur les politiques économiques de la gauche* (Paris, La Découverte, 1984).
29. Max Gallo, 'Les intellectuels, la politique et la modernité', *Le Monde*, July 26, 1983.
30. Philippe Boggio, 'Le Silence des intellectuels de gauche', *Le Monde*, July 27–28, 1983.
31. Also see Emile Malet, ed., *Socrate et la Rose: les intellectuels face au pouvoir socialiste* (Paris, Editions du Quotidien, 1983), Jean-Marie Domenach, *Lettre à mes ennemis de classe* (Paris, Seuil, 1984), and Edgar Morin, *Le Rose et le noir* (Paris, Galilée, 1984).
32. See Pascal Delwit and Jean-Michel Dewaele, 'The Stalinists of Anti-Communism', in Ralph Miliband, John Saville, and Marcel Liebman, eds., *Socialist Register 1984* (London, The Merlin Press, 1984), pp. 324–48.
33. See, for example, Edgar Morin, *Autocritique*, 2nd ed. (Paris, Seuil, 1975) and Emmanuel LeRoy Ladurie, *Paris-Montpellier, PC-PSU 1945–1963* (Paris, Gallimard, 1982).
34. Diana Pinto, 'Le socialisme et les intellectuels: le conflit caché', *Le Débat*, no. 18, (January 1982), pp. 4–10.
35. Beaud, *op. cit.*, vol. 2, p. 93.
36. *Le Monde*, July 26, 1983.
37. See, for example, Adam Przeworski, 'Social Democracy as a Historical Phenomenon', *New Left Review*, no. 122 (July–August 1980), pp. 27–58, Przeworski, 'Material Interests, Class Compromise, and the Transition to Social-

ism', *Politics & Society*, vol. 10, no. 2 (1980), pp. 125–53; and Claus Offe and Helmut Wiesenthal, 'Two Logics of Collective Action: Theoretical Notes on Social Class and Organizational Form', in Maurice Zeitlin, ed., *Political Power and Social Theory* (Greenwich, Conn.: JAI Press, 1980), vol. 1, pp. 67–115.

38. See my 'The General's Revenge: French Socialism and the Fifth Republic', *Telos*, no. 55 (Spring 1984), pp. 125–37; and 'The Tranquil Revolution at Clochemerle: Socialist Decentralization in France', in Philip G. Cerny and Martin A. Schain, eds., *Socialism, the State and Public Policy in France* (London, Frances Pinter, 1985).

THE GREEK EXPERIENCE*

Michalis Spourdalakis

The October 1981 Greek election which climaxed the Panhellenic Socialist Movement's 'short march to power' was justifiably greeted with widespread enthusiasm by the left in the West. PASOK's victory not only terminated over half a century of right-wing rule (including a brutal seven year dictatorship) but also followed the socialist victory in France in the midst of the Reagan–Thatcher–Kohl reaction, thus disproving at least momentarily the mythology of a right-wing resurgence. Nor did this pleasant Greek surprise end with one term in power. In June 1985 PASOK won another decisive victory, and the renewal of its mandate seems to show that socialist governments need not be a mere interlude to right-wing rule in this era of chronic capitalist crisis. Now that the Greek Socialists are comfortably into their second term (with even the opposition admitting that they are there to stay), it is time to examine the record of PASOK in office. This is what this short article intends to do. After some brief reference to the period of PASOK's 'short march to power', we will examine the economic, labour and social policies of Papandreou's Government; its foreign policy; the changes it brought about in the hydrocephalous Greek state apparatus; and finally, the nature of the opposition to its rule.

PASOK's 'Short March to Power'
The Panhellenic Socialist Movement appeared on the Greek political scene in 1974, in the immediate post-junta period. It was established by activists from the mid-sixties and especially from the anti-Junta resistance who had gathered around the charismatic personality of Andreas Papandreou, in addition to a number of radical and Marxist groups and individuals which the dictatorship had brought to life. It was the expression of the social radicalism which resulted from the peculiar economic development of the country during the two decades following the war. It was a radicalism, as the mid-sixties social unrest had indicated and as the opposition to the Junta regime proved, of the political alliance between the old social strata (simple commodity producers and the peasantry),

---

*I am grateful to Leo Panitch for his constructive criticisms and vital editorial assistance as well as to Helga Stefanson, who took great pains to make my English printable.

which had been squeezed out of the socio-political picture and the new social strata to which the recent economic development had given birth (i.e. the urban working and new middle classes of the disproportionately large service sector). The latter had been located mainly on the sidelines of the political process of the country until this point.

It was the volume and dynamics of the radicalism of these strata in combination with the subjective weakness of the other parties, particularly those on the left, which made PASOK the spokesman par excellence of Greek radicalism and contributed to its unprecedented short march to power (it progressed from 13.5% of the popular vote in the 1974 election, to 25.3% in 1977, to the victorious 48% in 1981, and in the 1985 election, while in power, it lost two percentage points for a 46% electoral win). PASOK made its entrance on the Greek political scene with a 'Declaration of Principles' which explicitly went beyond the problematic of Western European social democracy.

During its 'short march to power' however, a spectacular modification of its programmatic intentions took place. The Movement's former strategic goals of 'ceasing the exploitation of man by man' and 'human liberation' introduced in its founding Declaration. were replaced between 1977 and 1981 by such objectives as 'narrowing the gap between different income groups', and 'generating a self-supporting national development' which was supposed to reduce the 'uneven distribution of income' by overcoming 'the peripheral development' of the country. The initial effort to connect the goal of an independent foreign policy with a socialist strategy was attenuated and replaced by a moderated version of the Movement's initial policy of complete withdrawal from both NATO and the EEC. Furthermore in its 'Governmental Programme', with which PASOK took power in 1981, its initial plan to get rid of US military bases was absent and the need to negotiate their 'compartmentalisation' was put forward. PASOK's controversial moderation during its march to power can be further witnessed in relation to its original promises of 'nationalisation' and 'socialisation' of various economic sectors. The post-1981 PASOK has avoided any commitment to nationalisations, 'since they cannot guarantee democratic control by the people' and since the Greek state already controls major sectors (i.e. energy, transport, banking). Instead it has committed itself to an extensive programme of 'socialisations', which are defined in vague terms like 'employee participation in the administration' of the socialised companies. Finally another important link in PASOK's chain of moderate and compromising discourse lies in its conception of social classes. While in 1974 the Movement's descriptive reference to classes was enough to promise the potential development of its policies along class lines, the party which finally entered the echelons of Greek state power in 1981 made its references to society exclusively along the lines of the distinction between 'privileged' and 'underprivileged'.

But these modifications in PASOK's initial and dynamic radicalism are not the only things which cast doubt on the Movement's socialist promise. While in its founding Document the Movement undertook to make 'the principle of democratic procedure' its living organisational practice, during the seven years following 1974, PASOK became a prime example of an undemocratic, even authoritarian organisation. Controlling intra-party opposition by administrative means, Papandreou established a centralised organisation in which everything revolved around the omnipotent leader and his inner circle. Taking advantage of the popular appeal of his charisma and the lack of a democratic party structure, 'Andreas', as the people of Greece prefer to call him, has become the alpha and the omega of PASOK's political existence.

It is important to bear in mind that from the very beginning, PASOK has insisted that it is not a social democratic party. The party still advertises its commitment to 'the structural change of society', and still claims, at least rhetorically, that 'Marxism is [its] method of social analysis'. In fact, its overall discourse does sustain some anti-imperialist overtones. Moreover it has constantly—although to a lesser degree in the past four years—criticised social democracy and it has avoided an official affiliation with the social democratic Socialist International. The question of PASOK's nature therefore, is a complex one, which goes beyond the scope of this article. What is important however, is to keep the Movement's development in perspective when we examine its practice as the first Socialist Government of Greece.

From Keynesian Hopes to the Austerity of Despair
When only a few months before the 1981 election PASOK announced its 'Governmental Programme', or its 'Contract with the People', there was little disagreement that the document bore only a passing resemblance to the party's 1974 declaration. That earlier declaration's vague but radical strategic goals of 'social liberation' as the prerequisite for 'national independence', meaningful 'democratic procedures' in and outside production and 'elimination of the exploitation of man by man' had been replaced by the goals of 'autonomous economic development' and the simultaneous overcoming of 'recession and inflation' In its first economic statement as a Government, PASOK put forward a set of neo-Keynesian measures for the accomplishment of these goals. Production was to be stimulated through the strengthening of middle and low incomes, as well as through a 'new policy' of incentives for productive investment. Price controls were to be implemented for 'basic products and services', in addition to a close scrutiny of public investment and expenditure with a parallel effort to eliminate widespread tax evasion. 'Problematic companies' (companies in debt), were to be rationalised and 'structural changes' were to be made in the public sector so that decisive control of

the activities of the monopolies would be achieved. For the latter, the 'socialisation of strategic sectors of the economy' was seen as necessary, although some of the weaker industrial sectors, such as the pharmaceutical and armaments industries, were put under state control.

These were, with the possible exception of the latter case which was put on the back-burner, the economic policies of the first year of *allage*.[1] Almost immediately after its victory, Papandreou's government, using the pre-existing corporatist labour practices of the Greek state and a watered down version of its programmatic promise for 'automatic income adjustment', introduced a wide range of income increases in both the private and public sectors. There was an overall 3% increase in real incomes, which although not sufficient to cover the losses of the previous years (a net real loss of 5.5% in the 1979–1981 period) did amount to real relief, especially for those in the low income brackets.

However, it was not long before the shortcomings of these 'demand-side' economics became apparent. Within a year, Papandreou himself admitted that the Government's policies had not brought the expected results. On the contrary, the economic policies of the first Greek Socialist Government were creating more problems than they had been intended to solve. The stimulation of demand, which had been undertaken primarily through legislative wage increases, did result in increased demand. This however was not translated into overall increases in domestic production, but rather into increased imports. Domestic producers had tried to offset their higher wage costs by increasing prices. However, due to the already high level of inflation in the country (25–26%) and to the open nature of the Greek economy, this simply tended to encourage people to buy the relatively inexpensive imports. The dependent nature of the Greek economy combined with EEC limits on import controls, served to ensure that the Greek Government could do little to stop this process. In fact the open nature of the Greek economy also tended to retard domestic investment in capital equipment, which might over time have helped to meet that increase in demand without price increases. This is because domestic producers would not have time to recover their capital investments without first being beaten by foreign competitors. Finally, any attempt to meet demand increases by means of increased exploitation was simply not on the agenda. The post-electoral enthusiasm and popular confidence ('PASOK in government, the people in power', the government's main electoral slogan) hardly constituted the right political atmosphere for wage restraint. In fact, when in some cases intensification of production was attempted, labour mobilisation cut it short very quickly —there were 6.5 million hours lost to strikes in 1982, compared to 3.5 in 1981.

Thus the attempt to 'stimulate the economy' by manipulating its demand side, failed. Investment trends continued to show a negative flow

(4.5%). Even the Government's astonishing (given its previous attacks on multinationals) direct political intervention in 1982 to create incentives primarily for foreign capital did not generate the expected response. Finally, the Government's hopes to exploit the country's (and PASOK's own) traditionally good relations with the Arab world, and in this way to attract investment, proved fruitless. There was a lot of talk and very little action. The international economic situation (recession in the West and a decrease in oil prices) had made not only Arab but also other foreign capital, apprehensive.

After its first year in power, confronted with this situation, the PASOK Government made a 180° turn, adopting the internationally 'fashionable' economic policies associated with monetarism. With these new policies, the much desired recovery was now to be achieved not through the stimulation of demand but through: a) the reorientation of the country's production towards exports and the improvement of the country's competitiveness; b) exchange measures such as the devaluation of the drachma; and c) the reduction of production costs through a wage freeze.

The new measures were however more than the mere product of the contradictions of the 1981–82 policies. They were also a result of the long standing effects which the new international division of labour had had on the dominant commercial fraction of Greek capital. Greek shipping capital, which had in the post-war period enjoyed a prominent position in the world's sea transport industry, was reaching its limits both because of emerging protectionism and the world economic recession. Therefore policies which would promote a more competitive, export-oriented resource and manufacturing industry in Greece were in their interests. Such an economic orientation would at least develop a basis to compensate for the markets lost abroad as well as open up new opportunities for their stockpiling of surplus.

The general catastrophic results of monetarism and the politics of austerity are well known. Greece was not about to become an exception. The wage freeze in combination with the high inflation rate not only ate away at workers' incomes but also reduced demand, which in turn further stalled investment activity in local industry. The result was that unemployment jumped from 2–3% to more than 8%[2] in eighteen months. The expected private investment flow did not take place on schedule since the recession continued and memories of the radical tone of the Government party were not conducive to investors' confidence. In addition, the drachma devaluation, undertaken on the premise that it would assist exports and help to control imports, was not yielding the expected results because of the character of Greek imports (73% of which are food and consumer goods) and also because of the economy's slow adjustment to the new export-oriented industrial policy. The currency devaluation had further exacerbated both the fiscal deficit and the foreign debt. The deficit jumped by 148% to 12% of GNP, while the foreign debt rose from $5.9 billion to $8.5 billion or to one third of GNP.[3]

This picture started to alter in the year prior to the 1985 election. Due to a slight improvement in the international economic situation and the appeal of the Government's 'realism' to investors, the economic climate improved. On the foreign investment front, the Government made several breakthroughs, not only in economic agreements with the EEC countries, but also with Arab capital. But the Socialists' biggest coup in the field of foreign investment was the economic agreement which they made with the Soviet Union regarding the exploitation of Greek bauxite reserves, which are the richest in Europe. This was the largest foreign investment ever made in Greece and the terms of the agreement are to an unprecedented degree beneficial to Greece. As the *Economist* put it, it is a 'dream agreement', given the dismal situation in the international aluminium market. Moreover, after the failure to stimulate major industrial investment, the Government turned to medium-small productive capital, virtually abandoning (though not consistently across the board) the so-called unproductive sector (trade, services, transport). At the same time, by means of forced labour concessions, the socialists put forward an extensive plan to rescue those enterprises in economic trouble.

The result of these economic policies was a new economic picture. In 1984 there was an increase of 2% in economic growth—as opposed to 0.3% in 1983—to which the primary sector was one of the major contributors (thanks to the EEC policies previously much criticised by PASOK); inflation was carved down to 18.5% and expected to fall by another 2% in 1985; there was a significant increase in exports (5.5% compared to -0.8% in 1983) with a simultaneously slower increase of imports, which made the prospect of financing the debt seem somewhat more promising. At the same time, however, unemployment continued to grow and labour was constantly asked to tighten its belt further.

The recently published five-year economic plan, as well as Papandreou's opening statement to the new Parliament in the Summer of 1985 made it clear that the Socialists' economic orientation and priorities would not change at least in the near future. The Government would continue to act in a 'realistic' fashion to attract foreign investment, forgetting its previous grandiose plans for inter-state agreements with selected countries. The focus was to be upon private direct foreign investment as had been exemplified by the trips of Government officials to the US and the Middle East. Furthermore, the rather generous public expenditures of the first year of the Socialist administration was to be further 'rationalised'. And finally, the long standing problems of productivity and competitiveness of the Greek economy were to be solved through labour's 'responsible participation' in established tripartite corporatist bodies which would guarantee 'social peace' with wage concessions.

Controversial Labour Policies

The Socialists inherited a markedly corporatist labour relations system in which compulsory government mediation and other direct involvement in trade union procedures were the rule, and free collective bargaining and open/democratic trade union structures the exception. PASOK did not appear to be disturbed by this heritage, and it carried out the arbitrary replacement of the leadership of the National Federation of Labour with party faithfuls. Ignoring the hypocritical outcry of the right and neutralising the initial objections of the Communist Parties through cooptation, PASOK thereby took over the system and carried on the customary undemocratic practices. Papandreou's Government hoped that by influencing in this way the national and (in many cases) the regional leadership of the trade union movement, it would not only be able to extend its influence among the working class, but also to mobilise support for its labour policies.

During the first year of the Government, PASOK did not in fact need to exert much extra effort to legitimise its labour policies. In addition to the wage and pension increase which came as part and parcel of its initial Keynesian policies, the Government put forward a number of laws which were at the time justifiably considered pro-labour. There is no doubt that some of these measures, despite the patronising rhetoric which came with them, were unprecedented. Lockouts became illegal, the possibility of the 'legal' prohibition of strikes was eliminated, labour's right to organise was solidly protected, and finally a number of scarcely pre-existing labour benefits (e.g. holidays, pensions, maternity leave, unemployment insurance, etc) became legally guaranteed. The legitimacy accorded to the Government in the eyes of the unions was bolstered by the effective support which both Communist Parties also provided to the new administration.

By mid-1983 however, the Government's change in economic policies towards austerity came to be accompanied by diametrically different labour policies. The Government decided to abandon its policies of inclusion and consensus and pursued policies of exclusion and coercion. Cynically pointing to the real problem of low productivity in the public sector, the Socialists introduced a law which in effect banned the right to strike in the public sector, but which had little to do with improving productivity. Ironically, they called it 'socialising the means of production'. It was the kind of law, as many liberal observers in Europe noted, which not even Mrs Thatcher had dared introduce in her first term. The real significance of this initiative, however, can be seen only in the light of a fuller understanding of the Greek public sector.

First of all, the public sector in Greece extends well beyond the usual activities of Western capitalism. It encompasses almost 90% of the financial sector, all land and air transport, all communications and even some segments of heavy industry. Second but not less important is the fact that the public sector represents the most radical expression of trade unionism in the country. Consequently, qualitatively different labour relations in this sector could in effect set the limits and the pace of labour demands throughout the entire country. Furthermore, since the sector is very much tied to the activities of private capital, such new 'labour relations' would improve the 'investment climate'.

The opposition and especially the left seemed confused by these actions and accused the government of being 'contradictory' and of oscillating between pro-and anti-labour policies. However, in spite of appearances, the differences in the Government's two-faced policies on labour are not contradictory nor have they arisen as a result of confusion but are complementary to and fully consistent with the Government's overall economic policies.

An important aspect of the 'supply-side' economics that the Socialists decided to adopt as their main economic policy instrument after their first year in power, is the reduction of labour costs. The PASOK Government is doing this in a rather skilful manner which minimises its political costs. In the private sector, wage concessions are to be left to the market mechanism, which, given the growing threat of unemployment, works effectively as a disciplinary device. In fact, the Government (very much contrary to other Western governments), not only does not miss any opportunity to advertise the rate of unemployment but it seems that the various departments and the Prime Minister himself 'compete' as to which can quote a higher rate.[4] This tactic has been successful, if we can judge from the reduction of labour unrest as well as from the open wage concessions actually secured in the private sector (particularly in businesses which were under the special 'rescue plan' of the Government).

In the public sector, however, where the unions are strong and tenure is granted to employees as a long standing practice, the Government chose a head-on collision with labour. Moreover, using the otherwise reasonable argument of striving for 'a more efficient public sector', the government's efforts to legitimise its direct disciplinary actions against public sector workers are having devastatingly divisive effects on the labour movement. Those frustrated private sector workers who have been laid off and those young university graduates who have never been employed have not only come to believe in the Government's initiatives but have also gradually started to see 'privileged' civil servants as the enemy. It is not difficult to imagine what paralysing effects such conditions have had on labour militancy, especially since this objective bitter reality is combined with the incapacity of the left opposition to put the Government's labour policies in perspective and oppose them effectively.

Thus PASOK's labour policies are of a piece with their overall economic policies. Using the well-known tactic of the carrot and the stick for private and public sector employees respectively, Papandreou's Government has managed to discipline labour and create an 'environment of social peace' (with a few scattered exceptions) and a 'moderate political climate'. It is an achievement which has been applauded by such international organisations as the IMF and the OECD. Of course for how long the Greek working class will be willing to put up with Papandreou's policies still remains an open question. It seems that the answer will depend not only on the general political climate and the policies of the left parties in opposition, but also on how much and how fast the trade union movement, especially in the traditionally militant public sector, can free itself from the near-sighted politics of the tacit PASOK–Communist alliance and rekindle its former innovative militancy. Last October's trade union mobilisations against the government's economic policies of wage restraints can possibly be interpreted as a step in that direction.

A Unique Foreign Policy

In its brief life in opposition, PASOK had adopted a radical rhetoric regarding the country's foreign policy. The Movement had developed its foreign policy as an extension of its understanding of the country's political economy, which, as we have seen, it formulated along the lines of dependency theory. Thus PASOK saw the USA, NATO and the 'West' as the causes of the 'Greek tragedy', and put the struggle against these forces at the top of its political priorities. Although in its 1981 governmental programme, the high pitched tone of its anti-imperialist policies (i.e. oust the American bases, withdraw from NATO, cancel membership of the EEC) had been considerably softened, there was still a strong sense that many of these promises would be implemented.

More than four years of socialist foreign policy have been enough to disappoint these expectations. Although maintaining part of his rhetoric, especially during the 1985 electoral campaign, Papandreou has managed to undertake policies diametrically opposed to those contained in his party's original plans. The Socialists reached an agreement with the Americans which, in spite of the government's claims, extends and guarantees the American military presence in the country.[5] Furthermore, in exchange for the maintenance of the 7:10 ratio of US military assistance to Greece and Turkey, PASOK's government will continue to respect the Rogers Agreement which fully reintegrates the country into NATO's strategic plans in south-east Europe. The highlight of this turn-around in PASOK's foreign policy is the decision to purchase an enormous amount of military equipment (100 aircraft of which 70 will come from the USA and the rest from France, tanks and sophisticated surveillance devices). This sale (which the Greek press hailed as 'the purchase of the century') not only perpetuates the country's military dependence upon the USA and NATO, but because of enormous cost also opens the gate for very unpleasant financial consequences.

There is no doubt that Papandreou's 'anti-American', 'anti-NATO' pronouncements generated a hostile attitude from the Reagan Administration and it is clear that great pressure has been applied. But the Government has too often gone overboard to accommodate US interests—for example the voluntary inclusion of the demilitarised parts of the country into NATO defence plans and the acceptance of US operated AWACS. The most disturbing facet of all this, is that what remains of the anti-American, anti-NATO governmental attitude is being used as a means of obtaining US help in securing the country's eastern border in combination with a chauvinistic—and even racist—rhetoric against the enemy: Turkey. As this rhetoric has been systematically used for internal consumption, it has allowed the Government to continue to increase the military budget at the expense of social services and has in turn helped to justify the 'need' for the maintenance of 'social peace' and a 'moderate political climate'.

Given all of the above, it is fair to claim that the Socialists' foreign policy has not changed much from that of its right-wing predecessors. In addition to defence policy, it did not take PASOK long to realise the oversimplifications contained in its previous analysis of the EEC. Thus, not only has the country's loyal membership in the Commission continued, but it has also taken full advantage of its grants, particularly those given to the primary sector.

At the same time it is also important to note that, to its credit, the PASOK Government has not fallen into the fashionable Cold War rhetoric of the other socialist parties in Europe. In fact other aspects of the Government's foreign policies have contributed to giving PASOK and its leader considerable legitimacy among the Western left. For example, Papandreou's anti-nuclear rhetoric and his active participation in the 'peace initiative of the six'—though from the outset doomed to failure—has undoubtedly contributed to the dilution of the Cold War atmosphere on the continent. PASOK has also been a supporter—although a suspiciously uncritical one—of the PLO and the Arab countries, particularly those with so-called militant governments (i.e. Libya, Syria, Iraq). Finally, much to the dismay of the Reagan Administration, the socialists have maintained good relations with the Soviet Union and the other Eastern European countries. Papandreou refused to sign the EEC's Cold War document which condemned the Soviet Union following the KAL incident; it mediated in the negotiations for transforming one of the private shipyards into a servicing station for the Soviet fleet in the Mediterranean; it has been provocatively silent on the Afghanistan issue; and finally it has gone so far as to be a very strong supporter of the Jaruselski regime, calling it 'the best thing that ever happened to Poland'.[6]

However, if we are to understand the material base and the limitations of such controversial policies, some light must be thrown on the motivating forces behind the Government's initiatives and silences in the formation of the country's foreign policy. Papandreou's good relations with and open support for the countries of the Soviet bloc must be attributed to: a) Greece's traditionally good trade relations with the Comecon countries (almost 10% of Greece's exports), which remained strong even under the Junta; b) the growing interest of Greek shipping capital during the last twenty years in expanding its activities in these countries;[7] c) the effort both to attract Soviet investment (as in the case of the bauxite agreement described above) as well as accommodating the ventures of other Greek capital, like the recent undertaking of huge projects in the Soviet Union by Greek construction companies. Finally, and probably most importantly, these policies must be seen as an effort to neutralise any effective opposition from KKE, (the Communist Party), which dominates the political space to the left of PASOK. So far, the practice has in fact been successful, if we can judge from the KKE's habit of taming its response to strike activities whenever these coincide with positive Governmental gestures to Soviet policies. Still, these reservations about PASOK's foreign policy should not lead to a dismissal of its positive aspects. Greek socialists are undoubtedly an oasis in the European desert of Cold War and this should not be forgotten.

The Socialist Record on Other Fronts

In spite of the criticisms, there is no doubt that the Greek Socialists have introduced a number of positive reforms and progressive social programmes. As examples, we can cite the liberal reforms in family law and in the legal framework regarding the overall position of women in society, which although watered down in their final version due to church pressures, are definitely a step forward. The introduction of civil marriage, the relaxation of divorce laws, the abolition of the archaic laws on dowry and marital contracts and the legal recognition of the right of women to enter into a contract without the consent of their husbands are some of the most significant reforms in this area. In addition, the Government's vocal support for equal pay for equal work, though far from implementation, is a promising step in the right direction.

In addition, the Papandreou Government confronted the opposition of the academic establishment and introduced extensive educational reforms (especially in post-secondary institutions) which both in form and in content, whatever their shortcomings, opened the doors for greater participation on the part of both students and junior staff. Similarly brushing aside the threats of the medical establishment, the Socialists are actively trying to fight their way through the countless private medical plans and are working on the introduction of universal medical and pension coverage. At the level of administrative reforms, the Government came forward with the implementation of its long-standing promise of political decentralisation and extended the jurisdiction of local and municipal authorities, thus creating a favourable legal framework for mass participation. (It is of course not surprising that due to the country's undemocratic political tradition, which was anything but conducive to mass participation, such participation is far from evident up to this point.) Finally, among the Socialists' positive measures has been the recognition of the World War II Resistance Movement, as well as the compensation of the veterans involved. This latter may not appear so important to outsiders but there is no doubt that this amounted to a strategic slap in the face to the considerable anti-communist forces in the country. In fact in light of the strength of the anti-communist propaganda in Greece since the time of the civil war, PASOK, despite its shortcomings, limitations and perversions must be credited with having re-established the legitimacy of socialist language in the country's political discourse.

Many of those in the ranks of the 'radical opposition' consider these reforms—especially in the context of the Government's latest warnings of the 'need for consolidation and expansion of the welfare state'[8]— nothing but part of the capitalist 'modernisation' of the country. Even if one agrees with this criticism, it is difficult to agree with its unspoken assumption that truly radical social reforms will appear spontaneously. Deep structural changes do not grow on trees and any thoughts along these lines can be nothing but ultra-leftist pipe dreams. PASOK's reforms might indeed have given the potential to the class struggle to move to a higher plateau where gains could be more substantial, if appropriate changes in Greece's stifling state structure had accompanied them. Unfortunately, these changes have hardly been forthcoming.

PASOK and the State Apparatus

If there is one area in which the PASOK Government has surpassed the fears of even its most bitter critics, it is in the pattern of state administration. PASOK's presence in the edifice of Greek state power has promoted a general tendency toward authoritarianism in the central state apparatus— very similar to the one described by Nicos Poulantzas in his last book. Political parties are portraits in miniature of the societies which they have chosen for their social project, and PASOK is no exception. For those familiar with Papandreou's internally hierarchical and centralised party, the Socialists' record on this front did not come as a surprise.

In spite of gestures and rhetoric to the contrary, we have witnessed over the past four years an unprecedented centralisation of state power. The new municipal democratising structures are unused and effective power remains in the top central state apparatus which has become if anything even more distant from popular control. Parliament has faded into the background of the configuration of the Greek state and immense power is being concentrated in the Prime Minister's hands. PASOK's backbench MPs have actually been prohibited from asking questions in the House and Papandreou has distanced himself from parliament. Three members of PASOK's executive (the famous 'troika') decide on major Governmental policies and the cabinet, for 'efficiency reasons', has recently shrunk to only 19 members, of which one ministerial portfolio is held by Papandreou himself and three others are ministers 'under [i.e. reporting directly to] the Prime Minister'. Also, Papandreou's controversial decision last spring to reform the constitution and remove Karamanlis (whose charisma and national appeal undoubtedly made him the other major pole of power in the Greek political configuration) from the Presidency and replace him with someone of Papandreou's own choice, was designed to further promote and consolidate the tendency towards one-man rule.

Far more ominous in fact has been the Socialists' continued exclusion of certain sectors of the Governmental edifice from democratic control. In the name of 'efficiency' and/or 'neutrality', PASOK has systematically exempted the military, the diplomatic service and the Justice department from parliamentary or public scrutiny. This is especially troubling since Papandreou's Government has surpassed its immediate predecessor in the scale of state coercion practised in certain areas. The heavy-handed policing of strikes, the increased surveillance of places where young people congregate, the crack-down on punks and the constant harassment of gays, are some striking examples of this depressing picture.

In general the Socialists have added a new dimension to the Greek political culture—the technocratic definition of politics. Traditionally orthodox governmental efforts to fill bureaucratic positions with party faithfuls[9] have now been accompanied by a rationale for patronage appointments which stresses the unique 'expertise and competency' of the appointees who can therefore by definition deal effectively with the country's problems. Of course, given the actual extent of patronage (based largely on party membership) this practice can be seen as the mere continuation of the tradition of clientelism.

Also, in these past few years of socialist administration we have witnessed a further inclusion of the institutions of civil society into the policies and the logic of state activity. The systematisation of corporatist practices in the trade union, cooperative and students' movements are living examples of this tendency. Every expression of civil society (political, cultural or otherwise) in the last few years has been pushed towards expression only within the strict framework of the party system's logic and the centralised practices recognised by it. This is the case not only when independent political or cultural initiatives want to gain legitimacy, but also so if they do not want to find themselves excluded by coercion from the terrain of their activity. The crack-down on an independent anti-fascist political initiative in November 1984, the virtually forced imposition of party allegiance in the labour, women's and students' movements, the partisan criteria for subsidising the artistic community are only some cases in point.

Of course, the Greek state has a long history of illiberal practices. In addition, the state in the Greek social formation carries a particular weight in the articulation of social relations. It is the state and not civil society which has been proved the arena par excellence in which the social classes articulate their presence and secure their reproduction. For this reason, the main thrust of the practices described above is neither unusual nor totally new.

In the reality of power, PASOK has translated its initially loose definition of 'participation' to mean participation of the experts in the state apparatus. It is this technocratic definition of participation which not only allows the agents of the new middle class (i.e. highly educated and specialised professionals) to take a step into the apparatus of power, but also contributes to the decomposition of the social strata which were traditionally nourished by right-wing nepotism on the fringes of the state structure.

Socialist policies are also accompanied by a rhetoric which promises a 'rational solution to problems', which in turn is to be achieved through 'meritocracy' and the promotion of 'fair chances in all spheres of public life'. Thus, all the complaints about 'inequalities' cannot develop fully into a protest which will touch the structural causes of the problems. Every evil is now understood as a product of mismanagement or in-competence, and all sicknesses are magically transformed into symptoms. The Socialists in power have adopted an a-historical fetishistic attitude *via-à-vis* state power.

The Opposition

The story of PASOK in power constitutes a long chain of broken promises and dashed hopes. It is therefore only natural to expect the growth of opposition and turbulence. However, this is far from being the case. The Greek socialists ran the last electoral campaign with unusual confidence and won the election with an ease unprecedented for a party which has been in power in a period of deep crisis. Much of this is to be credited to Papandreou's capacity for neutralising critics. But it should also be attri-buted to the weaknesses of the prospective opposition.

The 1981 electoral result was as much a defeat of the right (New Democracy) as it was a victory for PASOK. The 1985 election was nothing but a repetition of the 1981 situation. After finding itself for the first time outside of state power, New Democracy has experienced great difficulty in appearing in any united fashion. In reality, the dominant right-wing party is deeply divided between a fraction which favours modernisation along Keynesian lines and political development along the lines of 'modern liberal democracy', and another which is clearly more

conservative and maintains a discourse reminiscent of pre-1967 clientelistic and monarchist practices. It is a deeply rooted division that the
frequent changes in the party's leadership are not capable of solving. In
fact recent resignations indicate that the long overdue cleansing of internal
differences in the party may soon lead to a major split. Thus, it will be
some time before this party overcomes its problems and becomes a threat
to the present Socialist dominance. Meanwhile, these problems are reflected in New Democracy's opposition. Its criticisms of PASOK have been
inconsistent, scattered and very much dependent upon the character and
the mood of its leader at the time (New Democracy has changed leadership
three times in the past four years).

In spite of the problems with its policies, and contrary to its disastrous
record while in power, the dominant right-wing party still managed to
fight a tough electoral battle during the last election. It trailed behind
PASOK by only five percentage points, and it proved that the right is far
from dead as was often maintained or implied by the Government and the
rest of the left. To contribute further to the organisational and political
plight of New Democracy however, Papandreou's Government has very
skilfully picked on its most conservative elements and has effectively kept
alive the 1981 atmosphere of polarisation which identified New Democracy
as the nation's number one enemy. Not only does New Democracy not
pose any threat to the Socialists but in fact its actions have been conducive
to keeping them in power.

If the incapacitation of the right-wing opposition seems rather comfort-
ing, the inarticulacy of the left cannot help but generate feelings of
depression. To begin with, KKE (orthodox), the most significant left wing
rival to the Government, has not managed to put forward a comprehensive
opposition to PASOK. In spite of its organisational militancy and effectiveness, its opposition has been limited and scattered. It usually focuses on
the day-to-day issues with an emphasis on the Government's foreign
policy—especially the part referring to the relation to NATO and to the
USA. On other issues, KKE presents a schizophrenic image, since it
simultaneously welcomes some of the Government's policies and criticises
some of the others for 'not going far enough'.

Furthermore, KKE can be and has been easily manipulated by the
skilful leadership of PASOK whenever it has attempted to step outside
the boundaries of 'constructive opposition' and increase its militancy.
Trapped in its self-imposed obligation to support Soviet diplomacy,
KKE has put itself on a self-neutralising course. Phenomena such as
abandoning oppositional activity when the Government makes a positive
gesture to one of the Soviet bloc countries or when its representatives
are included in the corporatist initiatives of the Government, are not rare.
Many critics of the party—both on the left and right—have talked about
their suspicions of a secret 'moratorium' of peace between KKE and the

Government. The truth or falsity of this speculation is irrelevant since it is the internal/structural limitations of the party which themselves make it incapable of confronting a left-wing government in an imaginative way. The ten per cent decline in the party's electoral appeal in the last election (9.89%), which is its first electoral setback since its legalisation in 1974, is but a further case in point of the party's sorry situation. These problems of KKE have been met with unusual (for that party) internal criticism from its membership, especially after its electoral losses in the last election. Of course this internal criticism has been confronted with well known Stalinist methods. A growing number of the rank and file as well as middle level functionaries have been expelled or forced to resign from the party.

On the other hand, the record of the KKE (Interior) in opposition has not been any more impressive. KKE (Interior) originated in the 1968 split of the Greek Communist party. The latter, due to its underground status, had to maintain two politbureaus, one of the exterior, which resided in Eastern Europe, and one of the interior, which stayed in the country. The split came as a result of the dispute between the two bureaus as to which was to have the last word on the Party's policies. After the split, the interior lost the battle, in spite of its relative size, to become the major representative of the Greek communists, abandoned the orthodox path, and developed along Eurocommunist lines which were fashionable at the time. This party confronted the government's policies with the strategy of 'critical support' (especially during the first year of socialist rule when the party was overwhelmed by PASOK's popularity). The result was a lack of focus in its policies. It oscillated between enthusiastic support for the Government's reforms and 'disappointment' with PASOK's broken promises. After 1982, with the change in the Government's policies and given its dismal showing at the polls, KKE (Interior) launched an attack on the Government. This attack however, did not develop into the formation of comprehensive policies—only the jargon (often workerist) and the tone have changed, and they do not carry conviction. Furthermore, its seventeen year history of reformist policies, and lack of an industrial working class base, along with its limited resources and its miniscule and periodic parliamentary presence (the party had no members in the 1981 parliament and only managed to win one seat in the last election) have set the limits for its support and effectiveness.

What does make this party interesting, however, are its differences from the (orthodox) KKE. Apart from not being slavishly pro-Soviet, the Party of the Interior has also embraced (albeit somewhat opportunistically) the political concerns of the 'new social movements'. With the exception of its loose links with the Eurocommunist parties, the KKE (Interior) does not have any restrictive internationalistic commitments and its structure is, at least in theory, more democratic. For these reasons it has become by default the point of political reference for the independent left, which for the moment is concentrated around numerous theoretical publications. In fact the existence of these groupings has been recognised as the main reason for its survival. The party in fact promised to open its organisation to incorporate them, in an effort to develop an alternative strategy for the left. This is something that radicals in the country are watching with great anxiety since under the current difficult conditions of the Greek left it is the only present hope for the development of a truly radical and effective alternative to PASOK and its controversial reforms.

Given the weakness of the party alternatives, the greatest challenge to PASOK's Government initially came from within the party itself. The apparent gap between the party's politics in opposition and its actual practice in government soon shocked many party militants. In 1981, there was of course widespread optimism among the radical wing of PASOK which often went beyond the rank and file recruits to the civil service and up to the ministerial portfolios. This radical enthusiasm lasted at least for the first year of the Socialist administration and was expressed in direct interventions of party people in Governmental policies and initiatives. Soon however, this spontaneous scrutiny of the government by its own party ran up against the reactions of the departments which were primarily manned by technocrats. Such party interference in the government had to end and it was in fact halted by the successful manoeuvres of Papandreou and the top layer of the party's leaders. To begin with, through internal rallies and conferences there has been a conscious effort to convince the rank and file that the interference of the party in Government policies could be detrimental to the effort of the Government to present itself as a 'government of the whole nation' and not as a partisan one. Then there was a mass recruitment of all top party functionaries into the Government. This co-optation had its intended effects not only because it reduced the volume of the party's voice but also because it took away any autonomous existence that the party might have had, since those members who joined the Government remained as members of the central collective bodies of the party. Today, there is virtually no one in PASOK's party strucuture of any significance who does not occupy some top position in the Government. There has emerged an identification of party with Government but not the other way around.[10] Thus, PASOK's own party organisation has been forced into hibernation and is activated only for electoral purposes. In those few cases where internal reactions to Government policies have continued to be voiced, PASOK's leadership has reacted in its favourite manner—by ostracising the opposition. The events of the 10th Session of its Central Committee in August 1983 and the manipulation of the membership's participation in its First National Congress in May 1984 make a strong case for the inability of the extra-parliamentary party organisation to become the Government's conscience or to influence its policies in any substantive way.

The obvious requirement for the expression of opposition is a structured forum which functions democratically, and PASOK in its eleven-year history has destroyed even the possibility of this. This should not be taken to mean that PASOK has completely destroyed its entire left wing. On the contrary, the left wingers of the party have gathered around the newly formed Ministry of Youth, where they have been given some autonomy, a disproportionately large budget and very well defined tasks incapable of having any effect on the government's major policies. In this way, the leftists of the party have found 'an oasis', as they admit, 'in the desert of Greek politics', while at the same time their existence creates an alibi for the Government's controversial initiatives. Moreover, it must be said that the tight control of the party by Papandreou and his close associates, and the concentration of power which they have managed to achieve both in and outside the Government, have led to adverse reactions on the part of some liberal members of PASOK, a number of them in ministerial posts. The absence of a political base to their criticisms has led however to their isolation and final resignation from the party. Their major contribution to the opposition was nothing more than the feeding of right-wing propaganda for a few weeks. Thus, in the foreseeable future, PASOK has nothing to fear. The admirable manoeuvrability of its leadership, the disgust in collective popular memory for right-wing rule and most importantly the state of affairs in the parties of the opposition are an insurance that the Socialists are not going to face any serious challenge—at least at the political level—to the general direction of their policies.[11]

PASOK's latest electoral success and continued governmental strength may rekindle the hopes of many in the West who seek to establish viable alternatives to right-wing governments in today's crises. The Greek Socialist experience is not something to dismiss lightly. But in a more fundamental sense PASOK's record speaks as much to socialist failure as it does to electoral survival. Indeed, the very association of its radical/socialist and participatory rhetoric with economic policies of austerity and profoundly undemocratic party and state practices may do more harm to the credibility of a democratic socialist promise than we might like to admit as we deal with the minimalist immediate concerns of our day-to-day defensive struggles.

NOTES

1. 'Allage' (= change) has been the main slogan of PASOK since the 1977 electoral campaign. In the past few years it has had a tremendous impact on the political discourse of the country, since thereafter all parts of the political spectrum started to use it. However, it is PASOK which has managed to put forward the most convincing definition of the term and become finally the 'Government of *allage*'.

2. The figure is only indicative, as in addition to the shortcomings of the techno-cratic measurement of unemployment and the traditional Greek aversion to systematic statistical research and analysis, there is disproportional under-employment in the country due to the swollen petty commodity production and the seasonal nature of tourism which occupies a dominant place in the Greek political economy.

3. *The Greek Economy in Figures: 1984* (Athens: Electra Press Publications, October 1984).

4. In his speech to a conference of European and American economists, A. Papandreou said about the problem of unemployment in Greece: 'Of course the figure 8% is a conservative figure. I believe that 9% or even 10% is closer to reality.' Summer 1983.

5. Many observers have claimed that the agreement resembles the one signed by the Philippines. Basically the agreement guarantees the presence of the US bases for five years and then further negotiations are anticipated.

6. As a result of some of these policies, Western leftists have often made the mistake of exempting PASOK from the criticism applied to other European social democratic governments. For example see J. Petras, 'The Rise and Decline of Southern European Socialism', *New Left Review* No. 146.

7. For an excellent analysis of the orientation of Greek shipping capital see M. Serafetinidis *et al.*, 'The Development of Greek Shipping Capital in Greece', *Cambridge Journal of Economics Antitheses* No. 5 (in Greek).

8. From A. Papandreou's Speech to the new parliament, *To Vema*, June 23, 1985.

9. While important but secondary in the high positions, party loyalty is a must for the middle and low range bureaucrats. The phenomenon of 'green guards'—as they are sarcastically called in the country—may very well be understood as a modern expression of the long tradition of clientelistic patterns. Now however, it is articulated in the instrumentalist arguments of PASOK's political discourse.

10. This practice of the Greek socialists has misled some observers to talk about the beginning of a one party state. For example see Roy Macridis, *Greek Politics at the Crossroads: The Socialist Experiment* (Athens: Euroekdotike, 1984). (Also in English.)

11. In fact M. Evert, a prominent member of New Democracy had to admit publicly after last summer's election that 'we are in for a long opposition'. Interview in *To Vema*, July 14, 1985. We get the same flavour from analyses of the electoral results of PASOK's major left wing rival, KKE.

AUTHORITARIANISM, DEMOCRACY AND THE TRANSITION TO SOCIALISM

James Petras

Introduction

The issue of democracy cannot be discussed independently of political and social context. Eighteenth century democratic revolutionaries, as well as 19th and 20th century anti-colonial revolutionaries, liberal democratic and contemporary socialist practitioners have at one time or another supported varying degrees of democracy or authoritarianism according to the political context. While some writers have espoused the notion of supporting democracy everywhere and at all times, in practice this has proven to be an untenable position, leaving the way open to a number of unsatisfactory solutions which include: (1) proclaiming the principle democracy and divorcing it from practice, (2) redefining democracy to include authoritarian practice, (3) invoking vague juridical formulas to cover immediate *ad hoc* expediencies and then revoking them when the situation becomes manageable, (4) specifying a set of contextual circumstances in which democratic freedoms can be suspended for a specific time frame for particular sets of transcendent political reasons. It is sheer demagoguery devoid of historical substance simply to wave the flag of democracy at every point and place in history—particularly in periods of large scale, long term changes from one social system to another. On the other hand, it is a perversion of democratic sensibility to make a virtue of historical necessities, to extend and institutionalise authoritarian practices beyond the particular context in which they were evoked and to claim that the new autocratic polity represents a higher form of political governance.

The celebration of 'democracy' has become a major canon in the new orthodoxy of new liberals and older ex-radicals. Fulsome and uncritical praise is lavished on electoral processes, and stinging invective on any regime—no matter what its security status—is reserved for those which fail to measure up. Postures of indignant agitation are struck in the face of any who would suggest that there are profound class and historical issues that necessarily enter into the debate on the relation between democracy and socialism.

What is most perverse is that the 'rediscovery' of liberalism (an 18th century doctrine) is presented as the latest discovery in political thought, transcending '19th century Marxist orthodoxy' and purporting to describe

268

a new post-Marxist era. Accompanied by bromides about the inadequacy of historical materialism, the discussion focuses on the uniqueness of politics, the absolute autonomy of culture and the centrality of discourses. At a time when western market economies have been experiencing a decade of stagnation and close to 30 million unemployed, western intellectuals are proclaiming the all-round efficacy of the market—to the point of hyphenating it to socialism. As the real-existing market economies regress toward continuing crises and mass unemployment, western intellectuals have become even more determined to attack 'statism' in the name of non-existent idealised versions of the market. The real class constraints and historical issues that impinge on the relationship between democracy, authoritarianism and socialism have been obscured.

This paper will consider the issue of socialism and democracy in two contexts: (a) in the Third World and (b) in the socialist bloc. In the Third World two historical experiences will be discussed: (1) the relevance of democratic socialism in the transition from authoritarian-military to democratic regimes; (2) the relevance of authoritarian and democratic practices in the transition to socialism. In our discussion of the socialist bloc we will discuss alternative reform strategies to the dilemmas of bureaucratic centralism; we will focus on the emergence of neo-liberal market and technocratic alternatives to democratic socialism. The problems of democracy and socialism posed in the Western world revolve around a different set of issues involving essentially the failure of the western social democratic parties to create alternatives to capitalist dominated class structure and political institutions. The latest round of social democratic regimes, particularly in Southern Europe, have gone further in the direction of promoting neo-liberal policies than their Northern neighbours and their policies actually erode some of the positive reforms of the welfare state. But that is for another discussion.

My choice of topics reflects a concern with major *contemporary* processes that are *relevant* to the discussion of democracy and socialism. More specifically, a number of third world countries, in particular several in Latin America—are in the process of 'redemocratising': moving from authoritarian military dictatorship to democracy. The relationship of democracy to socialism is central to that debate; yet the discussion has heretofore focused on other dichotomies: between democracy and dictatorships, civilian and military regimes, human rights abuses and civil rights, creditors and debtors. All the issues implied by these dichotomies are important and indeed have immense bearing on the democratic transition. But the larger socio-economic context within which the transition to democracy is acted out and more fundamentally the political-economic order and conditions within which democracy can be consolidated is not considered. The second topic chosen for discussion reflects the process of transition to socialism as it was attempted in Chile and Jamaica, and is being attempted in Nicaragua. Two sets of position are rejected: the first sees the transition to socialism as an immediate extension and deepening of all democratic freedoms to all social actors; the second sees the transition to socialism as a period of prolonged one-party revolutionary rulership involving democracy of a 'new kind'—usually a sort of non-democratic form of representation through state-aligned mass organisations. We reject both perspectives: for failing to specify the context and boundaries, conjuncture and political actors, within which democratic and authoritarian practices take place, and the relationship between them. More specifically, our perspective criticises the proponents of democracy everywhere and always, for failing to develop a 'security' policy—for failing to specify the appropriate political, military and social policies capable of sustaining the social regime against its enemies (indeed the criticism can be extended to include a failure to recognise the nature and scope of the opposition and the consequences of their action). With regard to the proponents of popular democracy, the issue of democracy is subsumed within a national-security meta-physic: the exceptional circumstances of direct threats is extended, the number of enemies is constantly enlarged and the emergencies become norms; democracy is registered as a luxury, impugned as a lower form of political organisation, redefined to include authoritarian centralised rulership. My contention is that specified boundaries for authoritarian practice are necessary accompaniments to the transition to socialism; just as democratic practice must create an adequate political-defensive framework before and during the process of socio-economic transformation.

The third choice of topics reflects the major changes occurring in the socialist bloc countries and attempts to interpret the meaning of those processes using two distinct concepts: liberalisation and democratisation. The former describes what is the ascendant tendency within the reform movements—the implementation of changes increasing the scope of the market, the role of technocrats and the margin for socio-economic in-equalities. The contrast between liberalisation and democratisation is central to understanding certain Communist countries' integration into the world market and the limits of change from the point of view of democratic socialism. The growth of democratic trends within the socialist bloc is perceptible, incremental, and reversible; to the degree that liberalisation both increases political space and social inequality it creates a contradictory future in which the deepening of the democratisation process could become a defining issue. The discussion of the relationship between democracy and socialism is not only of academic interest but has important practical consequences in shaping struggles, movements and societies in the coming period.

From Authoritarianism to Democracy: The Relevance of Democratic Socialism

The basic problem in the transition from an authoritarian regime to democratic rule is that it contains built-in constraints which severely strain the capacity of the newly elected regime to consolidate the new political institutions, leading to a new round of popular mobilisation and the recurring phenomenon of military authoritarianism.

Reaching agreement with the military and their US backers (private and public officials) democratic politicians uphold the continuity of (1) the senior military officer corps—its school, programmes, recruitment procedures, etc.; (2) the payment of the external debt; (3) the existing distribution of wealth, property and taxation. In this context, 'economic recovery' impels the democratic regime to extract surplus from the lower class, seek new foreign loans to offset current payments, limit fiscal and structural reforms to a minimum. The result of the 'democracy of compromise' between the right wing authoritarian military and the liberal democratic forces is a *democracy* whose *socio-economic content reflects the continuities with the previous regime.* The government of *liberal democracy* acts as a *funnel* for overseas bankers. It remains a *component* within an authoritarian state structure, and a *broker* between different competing 'interest groups' (trade union officials, grain exporters, farmers, industrialists, etc.). The democratic regime's commitments to the bankers and the state structures preclude it from taking substantial and tangible measures to meet the claims of its mass electorate, leading to alienation, and increasing conflict. The cumulative effects of popular disaffection can result in the regime increasing the role of the military and police in the political system.

Several popularly elected regimes in Latin America illustrate the dilemmas of the liberal version of 'redemocratisation'. Prior to taking governance, the US backed military regimes were in deep crisis: between 1975 and 1984, the gross external debt had increased by 300 per cent; interests and profits had increased by 566 per cent; the per capita GDP was a negative 2.2 per cent per year in 1981–84.[1] Inflation sky-rocketed from 50 per cent per year in 1976–81 to 175 per cent in 1984. As capital flows declined and interest and profit repatriation increased, there was a net outflow of 23 billion dollars from Latin America. In most countries, real income had declined precipitously, from 20 to 50 per cent over the decade. The military and its Washington backers had bequeathed to the democratic regime highly polarised societies with deteriorating economies and standards of living, which were at the same time squeezed by debt. The massive capital outflows necessitated new financing and the entrance of the International Monetary Fund with its class selective 'austerity measures' designed to shift the whole burden of recovery on wage and salaried earners, social programmes, public owned enterprises and the local market. The combined impact of producing large export surpluses and the continual drain through debt payments led to massive civilian popular protests throughout Latin America. The military and their US backers were totally discredited; without support from any significant political sector, they turned toward negotiating with civilian politicians. The eventual return to electoral systems was, however, based on the agreement by the incoming civilian regimes to honour their debt payments, to preserve military prerogatives, to exclude radicals from power. The cases of two of the earliest democratising countries in the region is instructive regarding the disastrous consequences which these compromises have in consolidating democracy. In 1981, Fernando Belaunde became President of Peru and immediately acceded to meeting its financial obligations while increasing military spending to accommodate the outgoing military. In addition, a programme of economic liberalisation was adopted, in line with the prescriptions emanating from Washington. These policies have produced the worst socio-economic crises of the century. GDP fell by 11 per cent in 1983. Per capita income fell by 13.3 per cent between 1981–1984. Manufacturing output declined by 20 per cent during the first three years of the liberal-democratic regime. Unemployment and underemployment reached an unprecedented 63 per cent of the economically active population. The social polarities and increasing misery resulting from 'real existing liberalism' had several political consequences. First, Shiny Path (Sendero Luminoso) guerrilla group gained considerable support throughout the highland interior. Secondly, the military was summoned by the Belaunde regime to repress it, resulting in the worst human rights abuses in decades (4,000 civilians killed, jailed, disappeared). Thirdly, the government party liberal democrats plunged to being the fourth party in the recent elections, receiving about seven per cent of the vote. Finally, the combined social democratic (46 per cent) and left-socialist (21 per cent) vote covered over two thirds of the electorate. The Peruvian experience demonstrates the inefficiency of liberal realism which attempts to consolidate democracy primarily through meeting the claims of the banks and the military. The newly elected social democratic APRA president, Alain Garcia, in his first pronouncements acknowledged as much when he stated that Peruvian development and reconstruction could not begin without some sort of moratorium on debt payments. There remain serious doubts, however, over whether Garcia and the APRA regime will have the political will to follow up the Presidential rhetoric with concrete measures. The transition from military to democratic politics in Bolivia follows a similar pattern. The democratic regime of Siles Suazo (which included liberals, social democrats and pro-Moscow Communists) initially attempted to follow IMF prescriptions, pay past debts, and preserve military perquisites. The consequences were equally catastrophic. Per capita fell by 25 per cent between 1981–

84; inflation soared to 3,000 per cent by 1985, while annual interest payments soared to 400 million—an amount which if invested in Bolivia would stimulate income, jobs and productivity. The political consequences were massive general strikes by labour and the peasants, leading to the temporary suspension of debt payments and the increasing reliance of Siles on the military to retain political control. The political environment created by the liberal regime's policies have been propitious to the growth of new military intrigues and a new round of military coups is not unlikely.

The new-elected Alfonsin government in Argentina came to power facing the same debt problem as the other elected regimes, but with a discredited and much weakened military and a massive popular mandate to straighten out the economic mess left by Alfonsin's predecessors.

The government of Raul Alfonsin is instructive on the pitfalls of 'negotiated democracies'. While Alfonsin initially talked of a 20 per cent budget cut in the military, in fact a recent study cites a continued arms build-up. As part of their 'political realism', the Radicals (liberal-democratic party) attempted to avoid confronting the military establishment's role in the mass torture and disappearances by handing the investigation over to. . . the military. The massive popular outcry over the military tribunal's predictable exoneration of all military officials forced Alfonsin to accept a new civilian Tribunal. As the Tribunal proceeds and accusations mount, the military has returned to conspiratorial plots against the regime. As the liberal regime answers to its democratic constituency, the conditions agreed to with the military unwind; to the degree that the Alfonsin regime fails to heed the democratic electorate in pursuit of its agreements with the bankers and military, it increases the level of discontent. This is clearly evident in the area of economic policy. Alfonsin promised increases in income for wage and salaried groups to permit them to recover the levels of the mid-1970s. These promises, however, are not compatible with his agreement with the IMF requiring huge export surpluses to service the foreign debt. As long as Argentina's liberal-democratic regime abides by its agreements with the international bankers, the external debt will consume 50 per cent of export earnings and six to eight per cent of the GDP. The real decline in wages under Alfonsin has already provoked several major labour conflicts and more are in store. Between the bankers and the military squeeze on the one side and the human rights, labour and salaried groups on the other, the negotiated electoral change secured by liberal democracy is in tight straits. After attempting to mediate between labour and the IMF on June 14, 1985 Alfonsin announced a drastic economic shock programme acceptable to the IMF: an indefinite freeze on wages, prices, and public sector tariffs, a new currency (the austral), and a commitment to stop printing money. The Alfonsin government lacks the administrative machinery to control prices and its external obligations will require it either to borrow or print money—reigniting the inflationary spiral and squeezing labour. The initial support by over eighty per cent of Argentinians (including labour) for the plan indicates their desperation, and the continuing political capital of Alfonsin. Nevertheless, the programme's commitment to meeting its external obligations at the expense of local consumption and investment will eventually erode support.

Let us be clear: we are for redemocratisation. The problem is not *democracy in the abstract* but the *particular commitments* and policies that specific sub-sets of politicians undertake in the process of assuming government and ruling. Commitments to meet the obligations of overseas bankers are not compatible with fulfilling the social claims of labour and the promises to business of economic recovery. The continuity of the military institutional structure and high military spending is a constant constraint on the elaboration and implementation of consequential redistributional policies.

Reallocating income toward revitalising and modernising local productive facilities and recovering labour's standard of living requires a new framework for politics; one that recognises the indivisible linkage between political and legal changes and the institutional and structural transformations needed to sustain popular electoral support for durable democratic institutions. Long-term legitimacy of the elected regime depends on a moratorium on foreign debt payments. This is so, first, because the debt was contracted by an illegal military regime; assuming the debts of the illegitimate regime supports a degree of continuity and proximity that weakens the beliefs of the electorate in the authenticity of the democratic change. Secondly the legitimacy of the regime is based on its effectiveness in *reversing* the patterns of economic relations: reallocating resources *toward* the domestic economy and away from the overseas bankers. The persistence of previous patterns of outflow of payments can only lead to the erosion of the democratic regime: the political change will be seen as so much effluvia amidst the continual economic bloodletting.

The inability thus far of the supporters of the democratic transition to consolidate democracy belies the stage theory of democracy on which they base their strategy: the first stage is 'liberal democratic' and therefore to be led and controlled by moderate forces. Subsequently—an unstated time frame—'democracy' will evolve socio-economic policies to deal with pressing problems. This approach overlooks the compromise and links between the liberals and the state, liberals and the bankers, and the liberals' own commitments to sustain themselves in office as 'brokers' among diverse interests. The commitments assumed by liberals in power define the future trajectory. The institutional and international continuities from the past define the parameters of 'realism'. A realism that empties representative institutions of substantive politics and leads to large scale popular defections, the growth of extra-parliamentary activity, the resurgence of militant struggles and the civilian liberal invitation of a greater military presence. The authoritarian-democratic cycle makes another turn. . .

In all the newly democratising nations, there exists a vast mass movement opposed to the existing military regimes, the policies of the banks and of the IMF. They have been the victims, not the beneficiaries, of these policies. While there are important socio-economic differences among the opposition, the great majority, particularly wage and salaried workers and employees and small business people, are in favour of shifting resources from overseas payments and military salaries and procurement to investment in locally-owned productive facilities, social services and local consumption. These social forces and their interests coincide with the pragmatic position of the region's socialist movements. The strength of the socialist forces varies from country to country: in Bolivia the labour movement is second to the military in effective power. In Peru, the left (The United Left Coalition) is the second electoral force in the country. In Argentina, the situation is much more complex, as the major political opposition to the government is the Peronist movement, which retains many of the authoritarian right-wing leadership of the recent past. Thus, while socialist movements are better situated than the current liberal regime to carry out systematic reforms, they still confront the formidable enmity of the military, divisive internal rivalries and, in the case of Argentina, a meagre presence in a labour movement still controlled by 'populist' labour bosses. Nevertheless, socialists and labour have, in some instances, been successful in pressuring liberal regimes to limit debt payments, even if none of the regimes until now has followed the socialist lead in declaring a moratorium on debt payments. Even out of government, the socialist presence through continual struggle has modified the conditions under which the original liberal-military transition to democracy was effected.

To return to our basic question, the issue of the transition from authoritarian regime to democracy indicates the relevance of socialism: in order for democracy to be consolidated and the alternating democratic/authoritarian cycle to be shattered, a series of measures which go beyond liberal reform politics are essential, and those measures are embodied in a democratic-socialist perspective which involves the dismantling of the authoritarian military apparatus and the reallocation of resources from the banks to the local economy.

Authoritarianism, Democracy and the Transition to Socialism

In discussing the relationship between democracy and the transition to socialism it is essential to distinguish three distinct but inter-related contexts that have a bearing on this question: establishing the *foundation* of the new social system; initiating the process of *institution-building*; creating the sources of *participation* and legitimation. Each one of these moments defines the limits and possibilities of democracy: premature extension or delayed implementation of democracy can have disastrous results. For example, the exploitation by the opposition of democratic institutions led to the military intervention and US destabilisation of the Allende Government, preventing it from laying the foundations for a socialist transition. A not too dissimilar process occurred earlier in Guyana and later in Jamaica. On the other hand, the failure to promote democratic institutions subsequent to the foundation period, has adversely affected democratic development among many of the Communist bloc countries.

The two strands of socialist transition—the libertarian and authoritarian —and the problems that they embody can be best observed in the experiences of Chile under Allende and Jamaica under Manley, on the one hand and Cuba under Castro on the other.[2]

In the case of Chile and Jamaica, consequential efforts were made to redistribute land, income and political power through extensive national-isation and expropriation of plantations, mines and industrial enterprises. New mass popular organisations were created and with varying degrees of effectiveness began to play an active role in making decisions affecting the workplace and community. In the international sphere, both regimes turned toward the non-aligned movement, took an active role in the struggle against imperialism and took the leadership in the struggle for a new international economic order providing more equitable relations between the industrialised and Third World countries. These structural changes at the national level and the international realignments, however, took place within a shell of institutional forces and arrangements which were fundamentally opposed to them. In both countries, the police and security forces were subject to imperial influence and funding; democratic officers and conscripts were purged or retired (in Chile the socialists participated in these retirements in order to pacify the right) providing the right with dominant control over the state apparatus. Most senior civil service bureaucrats retained their ties with their previous patrons among the foreign and domestic rich, blocking effective implementation of programmes. Capitalists, bankers and merchants protected by the state apparatus sent money abroad illegally, hoarded, sold on the black market, organised thugs to attack civilians—in a word, violated the law with impunity—given the benign attitude of the class-biased state. Parliament-arians and party opponents violated custom and reason by blocking any legislation permitting the basic operation of the constitutional system. The violence and conflict mounted and the opposition operated to under-mine the popularly elected regimes. The Socialists failed to recognise the challenge to their democratic mandate and to assert their latent and overt authority and powers: to strengthen democratic officers and purge rightists in order to re-establish law and order; to strengthen executive power and temporarily recess parliament in order to pass essential budgetary measures; to institutionalise and provide resources to the newly elected popular workplace and community councils to implement legislation. By not restricting democratic participation to those who would destroy it (and who eventually did) and not deepening it for those who were its primary defenders, the libertarian socialists undermined the transition to socialism. It is ironic that today the major lesson drawn by many liberal-left commentators is that Allende and Manley went too far and too fast, and that they should have sacrificed major sectors of their programme to continue in office. This superficial interpretation overlooks the tremendous energy and support which the original changes engendered and which sustained the regime: mass movements of the increasingly class conscious and organised workers and poor cannot be turned on and off like a tap.

The major issue was that the changes in civil society were not accompanied by structural changes in the state: the issue is less the rate or even the scope of socio-economic change, but the coordinated shift in the organisation of state power. In fact, greater changes in state power would have allowed for a more measured tempo in social transformation. While it is beyond the scope of this discussion, increasing confrontation with the US required decreasing dependence on its financial and commercial networks. It is not good revolutionary strategy to retain vulnerability and increase militancy. The failure of Allende and Manley to secure the foundations of a new state to facilitate the gradual socialist transition, their continuation of the politics of capitalist pluralism when the bourgeoisie itself had adopted a more intransigent authoritarian mode of class warfare was fatal. The basis for real and effective pluralism existed on the foundations of the new state and mobilised social forces.

In the case of Cuba, the process of socialist transition was dominated by the confrontation with the US. The period of direct military intervention required a suspension of civil liberties, the centralisation of political power and the close coordination of civil associations by the state. Having successfully defended the revolution from imperial attack, the rulers of Cuba substituted temporary into permanent features of the society: state-party inter-lock became a positive feature of Cuban socialism. The exceptional and necessary conditions which originally evoked the particular measures of centralisation and authoritarian control were turned into 'virtues' and built into the basic conception of socialism. The exclusion of imperialist and capitalist restorationists was extended to limit democratic debate among socialists over issues of forms of representation, economic development strategies, market and plan, etc. The conflation of an exceptional time of military threat and long-term political development, of imperial enemies and socialist critics has led to the stabilisation of an egalitarian, but authoritarian political system. The ineffectiveness and unresponsiveness of this system led in the 1970s to some constructive, but limited, reforms with the introduction of competitive municipal elections.

In summary, the libertarian and authoritarian trends embodied in these three experiences illustrate the problem of establishing the boundaries between democratic and authoritarian practices in the transition to socialism.

In order to develop a perspective on the problem of the inter-relationships of democratic and authoritarian practices it is essential to analyse each one of the above mentioned historical moments to establish the conditions and therefore boundaries which guide the utility of each practice.

Establishing Foundations: The Authoritarian Imperatives

It is common knowledge that privileged property groups have not allowed themselves to be divested of their property, simply because a majority of the population is in favour of it. Nor have military rulers and the police apparatuses peacefully abandoned lucrative political offices to democratic regimes intent on dismantling the repressive machinery and prosecuting the criminal, corrupt and venal amongst them. And the US (and to a lesser degree Europe) has not readily conceded having client regimes displaced by insurgent democratic movements intent on developing a non-aligned policy. In our time, revolutions which are profoundly social, democratic and national in content have occurred only in the Third World and they have occurred in contexts of intense social, political and continuing military confrontation against a coalition of domestic military and civilian elites and their US backers. The conditions under which the political transformations occur favour the emergence of politico-military structures, organisations and discipline. The *implantation* of the new social regime reflects two processes: the mobilisation of the beneficiaries of the trans-formation and displacement of the adversaries. In summary the *trans-formation process* is a military-political *struggle* in which *resistance* and *repression* are the two major activities around which the two conflicting sides mobilise. Political victory establishes the basis for *foundation-building:* the establishment of a new productive system, social order and constitution establishing the institutions and procedures within which participation will occur. The process of foundation-building involves profound political and social polarisation, intense conflict, frequent resort to force as neither the displaced forces nor the newly established democratic regime share a common set of values, interests or political framework to resolve their differences.

The codification of the revolutionary transformation embodied in the new constitution defines the new structures of authority and repre-sentation. The openness of the channels for participation and the effective-ness of the operation of the new institutional order are dependent on the degree of military security—as national survival dominates all other political realities. Continual military confrontation, particularly the conflict between an aspiring revolutionary democratic regime and an interventionist world power, requires the subordination of civilian economy to the military, democratic institutions to military mobilisation. The introduction of authoritarian measures is a direct result of the military conflict, which defines the scope and form of democratic participation. The conditions under which military definitions of political reality can be considered legitimate must from the beginning be defined as *exceptional circumstances*. Furthermore the *suspension of democratic rights should be clearly admitted* and defined as reflecting a specific situation. These conditions are necessary in order to prepare the groundwork for democratic rulership immediately upon the lifting of the *military emergency*.

Institutionalising the revolution at a time of military confrontation presents special problems. The imperatives of the military context define the relations between leaders and followers in centralist terms. Military forms of rulership, the acquisition of supplies through requisitions, conscription of labour power for defence purposes, the mobilisation of transport, leads to a strengthening of central authority rather than democratic give and take between leaders and followers. The organisational structure of society is largely inhabited by defence rather than representative political organisations. Where the latter do exist, their energy and time become absorbed by the defence issues.

Yet for all the difficulties that military security *necessarily* imposes on an emerging democratic regime it is absolutely essential that *political boundaries* be *established* and *respected;* boundaries that clearly distinguish between those political and social forces defending the old regime and those backing the new; between those who defend the country from the military aggression of the great power and those who do not; between those who defend the new foundations and those who do not. *Boundaries* serve basically two essential functions—restricting participation of those who would destroy the new regime and permitting it to those who accept the new regime but may differ on policy, institutional practices, etc. *Boundaries* are crucial in the process of democratisation in *recognising* differentiation of interests in the post transformation period and *avoiding amalgamation:* the lumping together of democratic critics with the enemies of democracy.

Pluralism, namely the toleration and affirmation of different viewpoints and interests within the new social system is thus built upon the establishment of the new foundation, its institutionalisation and codification.

With the end of military confrontation and politico-military warfare, civil society should begin to gain ascendancy over military-defence organisations. The basic problem in socialist transition is precisely the difficulty in this process of conversion from the period of foundation building and defence with its authoritarian structures to the period of institutionalisation of democratic pluralism. The differences between the American Revolution and Civil War and the contemporary social revolutions in the Third World are not over the initial periods of authoritarianism—both processes engaged in very similar repressive processes with their internal enemies. Rather the difference is over the process of *conversion* and the *establishment of boundaries:* the American revolutionary leadership recognised the *time limited* nature of repressive measures and more or less delineated the group to be excluded from effective participation (to be sure numerous non-loyalists were also excluded from full participation including women, blacks, Indians, immigrants, etc.). Within the new boundaries (an independent republican nation-state based on private property) full participation was granted to debate and discuss the policies of the new regime. In contrast, in the post-revolutionary period the socialist regimes operate with 'elastic' boundaries: post-revolutionary policy critics are assimilated to counter-revolutionaries; the period of authoritarian rule is extended beyond the period of foundation and defence and *becomes the norm* rather than the *exception.* The differences in context between a period of struggle for survival and a period of peaceful development, between foundation-making and institutionalisation are conflated: the language of politics is violated and the imagery of permanent war is evoked. The *politics of amalgamation* is introduced: dissent and debate in the post-revolutionary period is subsumed with the military activities of the counter-revolution, serving as a pretext for continuous repressive measures.

The revolutionary socialists' incapacity to distinguish the necessary authoritarian measures of the foundation-defence phases from the subsequent periods is rooted in the relations between the two periods. Twentieth century socialist revolutions have exhibited two basic weaknesses: an inability to convert the movements of transformation into institutional configurations independent of central authority; an inability to consolidate the transformations and establish the boundaries for the free play off politics, combining a unitary government with pluralist participation. The ideological expression of this aberrant behaviour is the abstract generalised conception of the revolutionary classes and their social interest. By conceiving of *The* Working Class and *The* Peasantry and of their *Historic* Interest, the different and competing post-revolutionary classes and strata, their specific sets of immediate interests are obscured. Abstractness and Historicism serves to justify Monolithism.

In fact the passage from authoritarianism rooted in the imperatives of fondation-building and defence to the institutionalisation of pluralist democracy is blocked at several points. In the process of foundation-building, the agencies to establish the foundations are constricted to a limited group within the leadership which substitutes itself for the organised participation of social forces. This *substitutionism* legitimates the leadership (who become the 'founding fathers') but constricts the role of the beneficiaries/protagonists of the transformation process. An elected constitutional convention is more appropriate for defining the basic features of the new social system than the genius of leadership. Secondly the process of institutionalisation is decisive for the development of democracy. The absence of autonomous civilian institutions, the incorporation and predominance of military defence institutions from the previous period into the centre of the new institutional universe, the removal of institutions from the control of the protagonists of change through a 'state-centric' conception of institutionalisation, and the blurring of the boundaries between roles and actors in the previous authoritarian military with the institutional phases, all coverage to reinforce the extension of authoritarianism into the new institutional process. An alternative democratic conception envisions the proliferation of autonomous civilian organisations, the subordination and diminution of the role of military-defence organisations, societal control and direction of the new institutions independent of the state, and the demobilisation of military and dismantling of the repressive measures. These measures create favourable terrain for the emergence of a pluralistic socialistic state.

Purposeful blurring of boundaries is the hallmark of authoritarian government: the boundaries between phases, actions and actors. Deliberate *specification of context* and immediate objectives, undermines the authoritarian impulse toward amalgamation, and provides the basis for moving from constraints to free expression.

Pluralism, Democracy and the Socialist Transition

The term 'pluralism' has been used and abused in many different contexts in discussing the issues of socialism and democracy. Pluralism refers to the existence of a variety of competing interests, ideas, policies among a variety of political forces each seeking to influence decision-making structures. Many conservative and liberal ideologies however associate pluralism with a *specific* set of socio-economic interests in a *given* social order with a *particular* distribution of political power. For Liberals and Conservatives the presence of capitalist property owning groups defending property interests, profits, etc., with private control of the media and political machinery subject to the unequal distribution of economic resources, defines the minimum conditions for discussing 'pluralist politics'. Unfortunately many socialists agree with this view and commit two opposing types of errors. Authoritarian socialists lump capitalist-defined conceptions of pluralism with the generic type and repress all expression ('If that's pluralism we are against it'). Libertarian socialists concede the conservative-liberal conception, permit property groups to dominate strategic sectors of the economy and society, thus exploiting their position to destroy democracy. The authoritarian response by failing to distinguish between a notion recognising a plurality of interests within collectivist society and the ideologically-loaded capitalist conception of pluralism, contributes to the homogenisation of society and the installation of a monolithic political regime. In the authoritarian setting, political conflict is transferred to a series of interest groups located in the bureaucratic interstices of society. The socialist adaptation of the liberal conception of pluralism has led to several efforts to incorporate capitalist cooperation in the transition to socialism. Chile under Allende and Jamaica under Manley made efforts to induce private capital to cooperate in the economic development of the country. In both cases, capital responded by massive illegal and legal transfers of capital, running down plant and equipment, and working in tandem with international capital and the United States to destabilise and erode the popular base of the democratic-socialist regime. Subsequent to the downfall of the socialist regime, the self-styled conservative upholders of pluralist democracy supported a military dictatorship in Chile and an authoritarian conservative parliamentary regime in Jamaica.

A more realistic conception of socialist pluralism is evidenced in the efforts of the Nicaraguan government to fashion a political framework for socialist transition.[3] The transformation of the state apparatus, the initiation of dynamic public and cooperative sectors and the rapid growth of autonomous (or semi-autonomous) mass organisations has provided the foundations for an electoral process involving a broad range of competing social groups, interests and programmes. The most essential positive aspect is that the democratic civilian organisations are debating issues and programmes during a period of military defence and infusing the process of institution-building and foundation-making with the pluralist ethos. The reaction of the counter-revolutionary forces has taken two forms (1) to ally and subordinate themselves to the policy of the US imperial state as armed mercenaries, (2) to penetrate the political arena in order to weaken the foundations and institutional framework upon which the new social order rests. Their strategy is to manipulate the notion of pluralism to include bourgeois control of the strategic institutions of political decision-making (media, state) and economic development (public enterprises). Unwilling to accept the new social and political parameters of pluralist participation, the bulk of the Nicaraguan bourgeoisie has rejected participation and begun to disinvest and run-down production— engaging in a self-fulfilling prophecy: creating the conditions they claim to have sought to avoid, namely an economy with a growing public sector. The Nicaraguan experience with pluralism and socialism highlights several issues: (1) that democracy and socialism are possible in the process of institution-building and even during periods of military defence; (2) that the boundaries between dissent and armed subversion can be drawn effectively thus preserving political freedoms at the same time as defending the new social foundations of the regime; (3) that the fundamental issue for capital is neither political participation nor economic opportunities (assured by the Sandanista government) but political power, and specifically the balance of power in the state; (4) that the anti-democratic, anti-economic behaviour of the private sector cannot be separated from an analysis of the international political-economic context in which it operates. The massive and direct intervention of the US imperial state, providing subsidies to cushion economic losses and providing alternative sites for investors to relocate their operations, sustains the willingness of the private sector to risk rejecting the pluralist rules of the game. For the Sandanistas, the alternative to socialist pluralism is to follow the path of the Southern European Socialists: of sharing political power with the bourgeoisie in order to obtain economic cooperation, and in the process lose political control and popular support without securing any substantial increase in economic production or social improvements in the lives of the poor.

Given this international setting and the behaviour of the capitalist class, socialist transitional strategies must fashion a notion of pluralism that does not count on capitalist cooperation if they hope to preserve the democratic process. If individuals or groups of domestic capitalists happen to agree to abide by the rules of the game, the pluralist system can accommodate them. Depending on how the US-Contra-Nicaraguan war proceeds, the pendulum may swing toward more authoritarian or democratic practices; while the exigencies of survival are paramount and may evoke centralised and authoritarian measures, the principle that these are exceptional measures and the norm of autonomous democratic institutions should be upheld. The issue is not the particular measures which the revolutionary regime takes at a particular moment in time but the direction toward which it is moving.

Neoliberalism: Bureaucratic Centralism Alternative to Democratic Socialism

The current impasse in the development and expansion of the productive forces in the Socialist bloc countries has led in some countries to a number of significant reforms and new policy initiatives. These changes have far-reaching effects in the economic structure, social order and perhaps political system. The reforms include the emergence of clearly expressed alternative economic programmes defining new mixes of private, public and cooperative ownership; wide discretionary powers for local managers above and beyond those previously delegated by central planners; proposals to introduce participation and discussion by workers assemblies at the workshop level concerning managerial decisions, production targets and the conditions of work; the increasing influence of local municipal authorities and their capacity to shape the governance of local communities. These reforms all suggest that the 'totalitarian' imagery of socialist society is no longer valid in capturing the growing proliferation of 'semi-autonomous' interest groups, decision-making centres and levels of power. There appears to be a two-tiered system of power: at the highest levels concerning decisions of international importance and relating to the general direction of society, power is concentrated among a small elite; at the middle and lower levels, there is a growing proliferation of interest groups, embodying a variety of social, regional sectoral, ethnic interests competing for power.

Critical to defining the nature of the current developments in the socialist countries is the level of analysis that one chooses to focus on. The level of reform at the *micro* level suggests substantial movements toward greater degree of participation, debate and discussion; while at the *macro* level discussion and participation is limited to a select group of actors, some of whom favour and others oppose the process of 'decompression'—the liberalisation of political and economic life.

The micro-processes which evidence changes toward new forms of participation are at the workplace and in local government. At the workplace, greater responsibility for production, working conditions and discipline, payments, product selection, introduction of new technology has begun to emerge. At the municipal level, local authorities are assuming greater authority and responsibility for health, education, public and other services. The proximity of local authorities to their immediate constituency and the growth of civic awareness has led to municipal politics becoming an area for increased citizen criticisms and claims.

While these micro changes at the workplace and municipalities represent an important new departure and open new vistas for a democratisation process, they have to be located within the macro-framework. Changes at the micro level reflect policy formulated at the national level: the micro level is where dissent and disagreements are possible. While the local organs may propose, it is the national elite that disposes. The boundaries of power, authority and decision-making may be in flux—and one may say that at the local level they have been enlarged—the general direction is still for the political directorate to establish the spheres of decision-making.

The process of enlarging decision-making among local authorities is in part a result of the impasse of over-centralisation and in part the growth of local capacities for assuming responsibility. Basically, it reflects the delegation of power by the central authorities to units to implement policies and decisions more efficiently at the local level. However while the initiative may have originated at the top, the assumption of responsibility and autonomy of action has created a momentum of its own. This has led to the growth of rather complex relations with the centre, including a certain degree of bargaining with the central authorities. The reversability of these processes is real, yet when the shifts result in more effective operations, this becomes unlikely.

The shifts toward decentralised decisions and local authority have a tendency to consolidate and create new coalitions. These alliances embody new orientations among the working class, intelligentsia and segments of the Party. New concerns among workers and managers with improving performance, rewarding skills and upgrading employment categories (rejection of 'dirty work') coincide with the central authorities' concern with the growth of discontent at the workplace. In this regard, the predominance of liberal party officials allows for the implementation of concessions to deflect conflict and to increase the sources of information to allow for the efficient operation of an increasingly more complex technological society.

In summary, at the middle levels, interest differentiation and interest group politics are increasingly competing with, displacing and operating through the long-standing authoritarian bureaucratic structures. Competing social groups—intellectuals, technocrats, political cadres, new generations of young workers become the sources and embodiments of these predemocratic movements and groupings. They are both 'in' the system sharing its gains in material well-being and belief in its ideological foundation and 'out'—retaining a belief in the need for continuing reform and redefinition of the relationship between an all-inclusive state, individualism and the autonomy of social organisation.

A major motif in some socialist bloc countries is 'reform'—and the major trend within the reform currents is *liberalisation*. For historical-structural reasons, as well as for reasons within the present ideological conjuncture, liberalisation has been far more significant in defining the content and direction of the reforms than the democratic tendency. In this regard, it is important to recognise the very distinct characteristics of the two tendencies and not to confuse them. Liberalisation essentially involves measures to open the economic system to greater private initiative and responsiveness to market demands and needs. It encourages and promotes wage and income differentials, attacking the statist-egalitarian-employment security syndrome as an inefficient constraint on modernisation. Democratisation involves measures taken to increase popular decision-making and involvement in the processes in which societies decide on basic priorities and public policies.

Several contradictory developments within the collectivist countries have contributed to the emergence of reform politics. The dynamic growth of extensive development has created the basis for intensive forms of development. Yet the needs of intensive expansion (new technology, overseas markets, complex organisation, greater flows of information, more flexible and responsible management and labour force, the increasing demand for quality goods) are incompatible with a rigid bureaucratic centralist system organised for quantitative targets with a semi-skilled or unskilled labour force. While the contradictions of dynamic growth created the conditions for reform, the particular direction of reform (liberal-market as opposed to democratic-socialist planning) was the result of political decisions and the particular mobilisation of bias embodied in the new ascending social forces gaining hegemony in socialist societies. Liberalisation is *par excellence* the ideology of upwardly mobile skilled professionals (collectivist yuppies?). Managers, intellectuals, and technocrats favour the shift to decentralised-market policies because they provide greater opportunities, mobility, consumer goods, economic rewards and social authority as well as greater economic rationality. For the party leadership, liberalisation allows them to maintain political power and prerogatives while decentralising economic decision-making and responsibility. The hope is that reform will lead to gradual depoliticisation of socio-economic issues implicit in the partial separation of political and economic spheres. Over the medium run, this is seen as a way of allowing the state to appear as a 'neutral' arbiter between conflicting interests, in a fashion not too dissimilar from the role ascribed to the state (by its ideologists) in capitalist society. With the introduction of liberal reforms, the political elite hopes to shift the focus to the operation of the market, and consumer. In this perspective, the managerial strata become responsible for socio-economic claims, while the Party's control over political decisions, organisation and structure are not affected. The separation of the political and economic spheres results in the growth of liberal economics and, in modified form, the continuation of authoritarian politics. These precise structural advantages are the important reason why the regimes efforts at self-reform take the form of liberalisation rather than democratisation. A second basic reason is that there are significant strata especially among intellectuals, skilled workers in growth industries, farmers in fertile regions adjacent to major metropolitan areas and others who ultimately benefit from the replacement of bureaucratic-egalitarianism by the market mechanism. Substantial social forces who developed their skills and received higher educational training within the centralised collectivist framework, now feel that it has outlived its usefulness. For them 'state socialism' was a period of primitive accumulation creating the basis for 'market socialism'—with greater individual mobility through the extension of market opportunities.

Democratisation emerging from a movement of working class solidarity represents a top to bottom shift in power in contrast to the intra-elite power-sharing characteristic of liberalisation processes. While liberalisation optimises market behaviour, democratisation increases the participation of labour in the planning process. While both liberals and democrats may favour decentralisation, liberals favour devolving power from the party to the new technocratic-managerial elite while democratisation favours increasing the role of self-management councils in setting planning and development priorities. Prior to the initiation of reform, liberals and democratic socialist share a common platform of opposition to the bureaucratic-authoritarian system. With the introduction of the reforms, the convergence gives way to divergences. When the liberal reforms threaten segments of the working class on particular issues (job security, unemployment) bureaucratic centralists can occasionally pick up some support from labour.

Liberalisation gives a major impetus to the economy both in terms of opportunities for a greater degree of personal choice of consumer goods, services and after-hours employment. This creates a broad basis of legitimacy. However, deeper integration into the market and the growing inequalities that accompany the introduction of the new economic mechanisms create new sources of discontent among young workers (not absorbed by the cost-efficient firms) and regions with underdeveloped or backward enterprises (textiles, mines, infertile farming zones) etc. Moreover, over-exuberant insertion into the world market (particularly over-dependence on overseas borrowing, excess zeal in importing capital goods which have few prospects of generating export earnings, etc.) can lead to severe payments crises and even submission to IMF prescriptions. Market induced crises can further polarise market socialist societies. Thus while the democratisation process is substantially weaker than the liberalisation trend, the socio-economic consequences engendered by the latter may provide the basis for the revival of democratic socialism. This is not a matter of wishful thinking. The liberal reforms are producing a degree of relaxation of central controls, experimenting with limited forms of worker co-participation, and introducing more pragmatic criteria for evaluating the success or failure of the new economic mechanisms. The 'liberal shell' may provide both the political space and the contradictions which may hasten the democratisation process.

Chinese Neoliberalism: The Technocratic Alternative to Socialist Democracy[4]

The current Chinese leadership is very adept in using the language of Western modernisation doctrine with all of its classless rhetoric for its neo-liberal development strategy. The neo-liberalism espoused by the regime and celebrated by the West speaks of a 'flexible system' yet fails to specify the common conditions which might allow all the social groups in China an equal share of the benefits. In fact, the regime is militantly and inflexibly opposed to any discussion or practice that smacks of egalitarianism. The new boundaries and priorities that define the parameters within which the new flexibility operates are not specified. In particular, as the regime moves away from the plan and egalitarianism, it is creating new rigidities imposed by the differential impact of the market on different classes, economic sectors, regions, households, etc. Favourable economic location, high soil fertility, access to state credit and overseas capital are differentially distributed and affect the capacity of different groups to seize opportunities and bend the flexibility of the system to their favour.

Neo-liberal policymakers have adopted a technocratic theory of social change and economic development, muting and then discarding the previous notions of class struggle. Neo-liberals have combined an exaggerated emphasis on increasing production through maximising income differentials, with new management techniques and work processes, to redefine work-place relations. The result has been a greater degree of managerial control over employment and the terms of employment. As central planning gives way to the market and as managerial and entrepreneurial authority extends over the economy, labour incomes increase at the expense of security of employment. However, the evolution of managerial authority toward greater influence within a market-based economy is in conflict with the central ideological foundations of the social system which explicitly define the workers as the owners of the means of production. By making the future development of economy and society depend upon the productivity and efficiency of a new managerial dominated system, the regime undermines the previous ideological basis for challenging the new system. The new regime has fashioned 'pragmatic' ideology to legitimate the new forms of workplace organisation. It claims practice (pragmatism) not 'theory' as its criterion for truth. Measures of 'success' are basically the immediate impact of policy on production in particular social settings. Regime ideologists omit discussion of the effects of current policy on long term, large scale institutional developments which provide support for local level/short term private activity. The massive infrastructure developments sustaining current activity were based on long term, large scale collective activity. The demobilisation and individualisation of agrarian units weakens the capacity to sustain these activities. Unless the State assumes the activities organised by the collective units, the infrastructure will deteriorate and ultimately affect the local/private producers: private affluence differentially distributed cannot coincide for long with the poverty of public sector activity. The restricted perspective and short-term results that characterise 'pragmatic' policymakers prevent them from taking account of the long/middle terms effect of increasing social inequality and its potential for political and social polarisation. The structural changes in the internal organisation of the social order are accompanied by increasing intimate relations between local upwardly mobile groups and overseas counterparts in multinational banks and corporations, and can lead to the fragmentation of the society and economy. Externally-integrated dynamic sectors increasingly obtain a disporportionate sector of national income while underdeveloped local enterprises vegetate at the margin of the economy.

The centrality of the market can lead to dramatic short term increases in economic productivity; but to the degree that the market and the enterprise determine the allocation of economic resources and the terms for upward social mobility, political institutions (State, Party, Ideology) will become increasingly auxiliary or marginal to the operation of society. The dissolution of political control over the economy and society can lead to market and class determinants, based on income, economic power and control.

The previous bureaucratic centrally planned economy and its ultra voluntarist ideological accompaniment contributed to the rise of 'pragmatism' in several wyas. First the bureaucratic centralists separated the long range goal of a classless society from a policy of gradual and visible improvement in the availability of goods. Secondly, they equated increasing consumption with 'bourgeoisification', adopting a 'market' or circulationist concept of class—(rather than defining class in terms of productive relations). Thirdly they made virtues out of necessities: the austerity and constraints which necessarily accompany initial accumulation, revolutionary warfare, economic boycotts and foreign intervention were translated into a false vision of socialism. The Maoists failed to separate the different phases of revolution, capitalist development and external relations. This led them to conflate all phases and promote a policy of permanent mobilisation in which reality was altered or exaggerated to sustain the ideology. The result was the separation of the ideology from reality, and the subsequent manipulation of ideology as a 'mobilising tool'. Permanent mobilisation of the labour force against vague or fictitious political objects and in the absence of any tangible material improvements led to political and perhaps physical exhaustion. De-politicisation or privatisation was accompanied by an almost exclusive focus on immediate tangible material improvements. The devaluation of ideology led to the transfer of loyalties to those political leaders and policies who promised tangible results.

The conflation of the different phases of the revolution led to the notion of permanent class struggle. While Mao did make a distinction between contradictions among the people (non-violent) under socialism as opposed to the contradictions of capitalism, in practice he followed a different approach engaging in massive and violent struggles against rich peasants, 'capitalist roaders', (Party members) and other elements of post-revolutionary society. The technique of amalgamating all differing perspectives into a reviled counter-revolutionary category was intended to draw on the negative emotive feelings of the labour force toward the new adversaries. These campaigns were orchestrated to maximise state-centred economic accumulation and to eliminate political-factional opponents. The result was disruption of the productive process and social organisation and disorientation among the labour force—as previously highly-regarded comrades were castigated and removed from office. Thus the notion of 'permanent revolution' came to lack any positive reinforcement: neither increased political control by labour, nor increasing improvement in income. Constant mobilisation against subjectively defined enemies without concrete and clear positive consequences leads to cynicism and withdrawal from politics. The conflicts over development strategies in the post-revolutionary period were of a qualitatively different sort to those that appeared in the earlier revolutionary period. The foundation of the new economy and the new state provided the basis for a *new socialist pluralism*, in which differences were unavoidable and open debates necessary to sustain political and social commitments. *The incapacity of the Chinese leaders to recognise the new foundations as a boundary within which debate, discussion and controversy could flourish led to the extension and deepening of the previous military-political monolith conception of political organisation.*

In summary, indiscriminate use of Marxist ideology to describe very disparate aspects and phases of economic and political development led to its losing any cognitive value and political relevance to development. Ideology became the subjective expression of a voluntarist elite increasingly divorced from the everyday interests of the masses.

This context of an ideological vacuum explains the relative success of the contemporary Chinese pragmatists. Applying their neo-liberal agenda, they short-circuit debate by acting first and theorising later. Specifically by appealing to labour's immediate direct interests for material improvement, they have recognised a vital aspect of Chinese reality that previous leaders downplayed or ignored. The Chinese leadership's appeal to 'facts' and empiricism attracts people who were constantly mobilised in ill-defined campaigns against nebulous adversaries with no visible material pay-offs. The 'facts' in question are concrete—opportunities for greater income by self-induced efforts. The regime is less clear in spelling out what the consequences of these 'facts' are for social equality and political power over time. This ahistorical, asocial, apolitical, amoral approach does not seem to the population to be another ideological deception: one can count one's chickens, pigs, tractors, television sets. Yet the emerging pattern of polarised development is creating a structure in which a few will have greater opportunities than others. The previous regime's tortuous construction of a socio-historical reality based on real and fictitious subjects as struggle and sacrifice was largely divorced from the day to day productive-economic activity that is characteristic of post-revolutionary China. People work to increase their standards of living. They struggle to obtain work, control the conditions of work and to improve their income. The past regime constantly evoked images of the past (Yenan), of international and obscure intra-elite struggles—substituting these images for the immediate interests of the labour force. The current regime has re-cast the world in imagery more relevant to the producers: instead of history of struggle, it emphasises the present of increasing consumption; instead of international conflict, it stresses increasing international exchanges; instead of intra-elite struggles, it emphasises national development. In this perspective of peace and progress through hard work and education, the regime has left out any discussion of the mechanism to ensure social justice. At best, the regime postulates a vague diffusion or trickle down effect from the rich to the poor. To the extent that it has discussed equality, it has equated it with the austerity and poverty of the previous period, thus avoiding discussion that might combine growth and equity, liberalisation and democracy.

The current Chinese leadership's counter position of 'practice' to 'theory' is a false one. The current regime has a 'theory'—unstated and perhaps implicit. It argues for the transformation of China through a coalition of wealthy farmers, technocrats, managers of growth industries, foreign capital and national Party leaders. Through these social and political agencies, the regime is stimulating the diffusion and application of new technology and reinforcing the tendencies toward new forms of private concentrated capital accumulation. The policy of deliberately favouring the 'strong' is epitomised by the slogan 'get rich', yet not all agrarian or industrial classes are in a position to accumulate and expand, least of all at the same rate.

Nor is it clear that 'practice' was absent from the previous regime: its practice, however, was to observe a different set of facts than those observed by the current regime and to act on them in a different manner. The alliance between the old cadre/political bureaucracy and the poorest layers of the labour force was linked to a system which preserved political prerogatives of the party machine in exchange for maintaining minimum standards and security for all. Their conception of socialism was of an authoritarian-egalitarian system which repressed both free expression and individual mobility. The current regime's conception reflects the entre-preneurial aspirations and upward mobility proclivities of substantial sectors of the agrarian and intellectual population. Its neo-liberal approach is oriented toward promoting growth through individual and household accumulation and differential economic payments. The attempt by the regime to deny the 'practice' of its predecessors is a means of avoiding any serious discussion of its policy, particularly those aspects that present potential conflictual areas for debate (namely the positive results of large scale collective efforts, job security, food subsidies, etc.).

The style of debate presented by the current regime—self-evident truths, bland assertions of success, revision of history including distortions of the past and evasions of the present—are reproduced in the West, eager to celebrate China's move toward dismantling the collective system of production. The very notion of 'practice' (so ambiguous and unwilling to recognise multiple dimensions and layers of social reality) central to the current regime is associated with a *single dimension;* growing production, increasing goods, affluent individuals. Both the texture and substance of the written and spoken word are reminiscent of the late 19th century in the West. Qualitative aspects of production relations are subsumed in quantitative indicators of growth: the growth of managerial autonomy and enterprise earnings are emphasised while labour's subordination to the market and the managerial ethos is ignored. The growth of consumer goods and their availability to a broader public is emphasised while improvement of social services and particularly the disparities in access to these goods and services are rarely considered. The upwardly mobile new affluent classes are presented as models of the society. Liberalisation is creating new areas of power, privilege and status differentiation. The regime's promotion of the Chinese Horatio Algers, like its counterparts in earlier US history, is a powerful myth which probably does attract and energise vast groups of the poor who seek to emulate their path to affluence and success. But the resultant individualism and rampant competitiveness leads to social fragmentation. The absence of large-scale collective units could create serious problems in the maintenance and expansion of essential power grids, dams, rural infrastructure and natural resource development, most of which are far out of reach of private groups or household units.

Finally, class conflicts at the local level and expressions of sporadic individual resentments by those who are displaced, by-passed, and marginalised, in a word who have lost relative to the upwardly mobile groups, represents a new reality which can only increase with time. The 'pragmatists' may believe their own myths that trickle down economic development benefits everyone but historical experiences elsewhere argue otherwise. The blanket condemnation of egalitarianism as remnants of the 'Maoist', 'dogmatic' past and the trumpeting of the virtues of entre-preneurship cannot obscure some troubling new developments: increased earning for some farmers and merchants is creating pressure on salaries of urban wage earners; increasing dependence on the market creates a highly differentiated peasantry; cut backs in state subsidies adversely affects low income families. Wealth in family households can only expand by extending production and exploiting non-household labour. The deepening of the current tendencies in the economy will produce new class formations, and in time new class conflicts on a more extensive and prolonged basis may occur.

Conclusion
The struggles for socialism and democracy are inextricably linked. As we

have argued earlier, the consolidation of democracy *requires* the conscious intervention and mobilisation of socialist forces. The problems of re-democratisation in the Third World cannot be solved through electoral contests that are premised on the continuation of military power and the dominance of development agendas by international banks. The problems in the real existing socialist countries are no less acute. The experiments by the state bureaucrats and their technocratic advisors with 'market socialism' may gain them some popular support and breathing space, but new class differences and economic problems (unemployment, inflation, debt) threaten to ignite a new round of social conflicts. Historical development over past decades has demonstrated the enormous vitality in the struggle for socialist democracy, a history which has infrequently been written. One example: the social history of the Chilean social movements and their experience with direct democracy during the Allende years has yet to be written. In the contemporary context, the most singular event is the Sandanista effort to combine social transformation and free elections under war-time conditions.

The theory and practice of democratic socialism embodied in the Sandanista experience of defence and political pluralism provide socialist theorists and activists with a wealth of new ideas concerning the opportunities for transcending real existing liberal and Stalinist versions of authoritarian politics. It is precisely the attractiveness and relevance of revolutionary democratic socialism to millions—East and West—which has precipitated Washington's sustained aggressive military and economic campaign to destroy it and Moscow's effort to co-opt it.

NOTES

1. The data in this section are drawn from Enrique V. Iglesias, 'Reflections on the Latin American Economy in 1982'; ECLA Economic Projections Centre, 'Latin American Development Problems and the World Economic Crisis', in *CEPAL Review* No. 19, April 1983, pp. 7–50, 51–84; and CEPAL, *Preliminary Overview of the Latin American Economy During 1984*, No. 409/410, January 1985.

2. For Jamaica during the Manley Government see Michael Kaufman, *Jamaica Under Manley. The Limits of Social Democratic Reform* (London: Zed Press, 1985); Fitzroy Ambursley, 'Jamaica: The Demise of Democratic Socialism', *New Left Review* 128 (July–August), pp. 76–87; and Richard Bernal, 'Jamaica: Democratic Socialism Meets the IMF' in Jill Torrie, *Banking on Poverty* (Toronto: Between the Lines, 1983), pp. 217–240.
    For Chile during the Allende period see Barbara Stallings, *Class Conflict and Economic Development in Chile 1958–1973* (Stanford: Stanford University Press, 1978), particularly Chapters 6 and 9; Juan Espinoza and Andrew Zimbalist, *Economic Democracy: Worker Participation and Chilean Industry* (New York: Academic Press, 1978); Gabriel Smirnow, *The Revolution Disarmed: Chile 1970–1973* (New York: Monthly Review Press, 1979); and James Petras and Morris Morley, *The US and Chile* (New York: Monthly Review Press, 1975).

For Chile during the Pinochet years see Alejandro Foxley, *Latin American Experiments in Neo-Conservative Economies* (Berkeley: University of California Press, 1983), Chapters 3–4, pp. 40–113; and NACLA, *Chile: Beyond the Darkest Decade* Vol. XVII, No. 3, September–October, 1983, pp. 2–26.

For Cuba see Sandor Halebsky and John Kirk, *Twenty-five Years of Revolution 1959–1984* (New York: Praeger, 1985); and Arthur MacEwan, *Revolution and Economic Development in Cuba* (New York: St. Martin's Press, 1981).

3. For Nicaragua see Henri Weber, *Nicaragua: The Sandanist Revolution* (London: Verso, 1981); Carmen Deere and Peter Marchetti, 'The Worker-Peasant Alliance. . .', *Latin American Perspectives,* Spring 1981, pp. 40–73; and 'Electoral Process in Nicaragua', Report of the Latin American Studies Association Delegation to the November 4, 1984 General Election.

4. For China see the special issue of *World Development,* Vol. 11, No. 8, edited by Neville Maxwell and Bruce McFarlane. The following articles were particularly useful:

    —Mark Selden, 'The Logic—and Limits—of Chinese Socialist Development'.

    —Thierry Pairault, 'Chinese Market Mechanism: A Controversial Debate'.

    —Bruce McFarlane, 'Political Economy of Class Struggle and Economic Growth in China 1950–1982'.

    —Richard Kraus, 'Bureaucratic Privilege as an Issue in Chinese Politics'.

AN OPEN CONSPIRACY: CONSERVATIVE POLITICS AND THE MINERS' STRIKE 1984-5

John Saville

A convenient starting point for the chronology of the Tory offensive against trade unionism is the publication by the *Economist* in 1978 of the final report of the Ridley committee on the nationalised industries. This report was part of the preparations which the Thatcher shadow cabinet were making in anticipation of a return to a parliamentary majority at Westminster. During the previous years Conservative politicians and businessmen in general had become acutely aware of the strengthening of trade union defences in most areas of industrial life, and in particular the two successful miners' strikes in 1972 and 1974 had exercised a powerful and lasting influence. The mass picket of the Saltley Coke Works in February 1972—which closed the gates and effectively determined the outcome of the strike—was never forgotten by the miners, the Conservative Party and the police; and it was followed, two years later, by another miners' strike which persuaded Heath to appeal, unsuccessfully, to the electorate. These events badly scarred Conservative interests in the country, and the development of reactionary ideas, and reactionary organisations, was greatly encouraged; and it was after the fall of the Heath government in 1974 that the extreme Right in the Conservative Party began to develop further organisations and support groups. There were already a number of well-established bodies in the field such as the Economic League, Common Cause, IRIS, with many years of experience, including the services of some right-wing trade unionists, and there were a number of ideological bodies which provided sophisticated materials for what was to become the new Toryism. The most influential of these was probably the Institute of Economic Affairs which went back to the late fifties. The most prominent of the new organisations was the National Association for Freedom (NAFF) an umbrella group for an assortment of Conservative reactionaries. Its initial establishment was a response to the killing of Ross McWhirter by the IRA in December 1975, and its original Council was composed of industrialists and politicians including Norman Tebbitt, Rhodes Boyson and Peregrine Worsthorne. The working brains behind NAFF were Robert Moss and Brian Crozier: Cold War warriors who were fanatical supporters of American foreign policy and specialists in Latin American affairs, including Chile. From the time of its establishment until the Tory victory in the summer of 1979 NAFF was involved in a growing number of anti-trade union actions; and it encouraged or started a series of smaller pressure groups with particular limited aims of their own but all with a specific anti-working class content.[1]

The central problem for the propertied interests, and their representatives, has always been the trade union movement, the organised power of the working people. The Labour Party has never worried the ruling groups in Britain in the way that has been the case with trade unionism, and during the second half of the nineteen seventies the details of what was needed to be done in order to curb, contain and if possible destroy British trade unionism had been much discussed and generally agreed upon. It was all set down in the Ridley Report, leaked to the *Economist* and published on 27 May 1978. The *Economist*'s headline was 'Appomattox or Civil War', and it suggested in its introduction that it was likely to cause 'a humdinger of a row'. But there was no row; and it became the blue-print for the Thatcher government when it came to office. Almost every detail of its recommendations have been followed in the legislation of the past five years.

The *Economist* noted that what it was offering to its readers was the final report of the Conservative party's policy group on the nationalised industries. Its summary began by reference to the Conservative commitment that each nationalised industry should achieve a set rate of return on various definitions of capital employed; and it continued with a number of recommendations about management; the scope for privatisation; and a strong argument for the end of statutory monopolies in the public sector. The most significant parts of the Report related to the labour side of nationalised industries. The concept of wage comparability was rejected, and the basis for wage settlements was a combination of the manpower situation in the industry and the vulnerability of society to a strike. Where industries 'have the nation by the jugular vein' the Report said 'the only feasible option is to pay up'. And so the Report, following its own logic, classified industries into three categories of vulnerability. The most vulnerable group were sewerage, water, electricity, gas and the health service. The second, intermediate group were railways, docks, coal and dustmen; and the least vulnerable group were other forms of transport, ports, telephones, air transport, and steel. While the ideas and recommendations of the main Report were important, and have indeed served as guidelines for the legislative and industrial policies of the Thatcher government, the real nub came in an annexe prepared by Ridley and some of his co-authors. They addressed themselves to central questions: how to counter any 'political threat' from those who could be regarded as 'the enemies of the next Tory government'. They anticipated a major challenge from a trade union over a wage claim or over redundancies, and since it might occur in a 'vulnerable industry'—such as coal, electricity or the docks—with 'the full force of communist disruptors' it was necessary to be clear about the strategy to be followed. Accordingly they elaborated a five point scheme which the *Economist* summarised as below:

- Return on capital should be rigged so that an above-average wage claim can be paid to the 'vulnerable' industries.
- The eventual battle should be on ground chosen by the Tories, in a field they think could be won (railways, British Leyland, the civil service or steel).
- Every precaution should be taken against a challenge in electricity or gas. Anyway, redundancies in those industries are unlikely to be required. The group believes that the most likely battleground will be the coal industry. They would like a Thatcher government to: (a) build up maximum coal stocks, particularly at the power stations; (b) make contingency plans for the import of coal; (c) encourage the recruitment of non-union lorry drivers by haulage companies to help move coal where necessary; (d) introduce dual coal/oil firing in all power stations as quickly as possible.
- The group believes that the greatest deterrent to any strike would be 'to cut off the money supply to strikers, and make the union finance them'. But strikers in nationalised industries should not be treated differently from strikers in other industries.
- There should be a large, mobile squad of police equipped and prepared to uphold the law against violent picketing. 'Good non-union drivers' should be recruited to cross picket lines with police protection.

The Ridley plan began to be inserted into the Statute Book within a year of the Thatcher government taking office. The Tories were much assisted by the decline of manufacturing and the growth of unemployment, leading to a marked weakening of the bargaining power of labour through the fears of job losses. The appendix to the Ridley report had emphasised the deterrence to strike action by 'cutting off the money supply' to the strikers and making the unions finance them. Accordingly on the 15 April 1980, the Social Services minister, introduced the Social Security (No 2) Bill. Most of the clauses of this Bill were concerned with what Patrick Jenkin called 'reducing the prospective growth of the social security programme'; but Clause 6 was in a different category. Strikers were not entitled to claim benefit but their dependants were. The Tories and their sophisticated expositors like the *Economist* had long argued that social security payments made to the wives and children of men on strike, or the dependants of women on strike, gave strikers an additional ability to resist, extend and prolong a dispute. The amounts involved were, in fact, small in relation to the total expended on benefits[2] but they were far from unimportant in respect of those involved in any one strike. What Clause 6 of this new Bill did was to reduce by amounts between £12 and £16 the total of benefit payments made to wives and dependants. In the miners strike it was almost always £16 that was deducted, and for a couple with no extra resources that meant £6.45 a week to live on with Child Benefit of an extra £2.75 for each child under eleven years of age. Any additional income—from a wife's part-time job—meant a corresponding reduction in benefits or no benefit at all. The reduction was to apply to trade unionists and non-unionists alike, and it also applied to anyone out of work as a result of a trade dispute at his or her place of work; and it applied to lock-outs by employers. Strikers without dependants have always been debarred from social security payments although it was sometimes possible—never very easy—to prove an 'urgent need'. Under the new rules introduced by Clause 6 no payment whatsoever would be given to single strikers, whatever their circumstances, so that, to give an example, a single woman striker living with an elderly mother on supplementary benefit would have to survive on her mother's income.

One of the alleged purposes of Clause 6 was to force trade unions to give strike pay, but even where pay was given, the striker's family would still be worse off under the new regulations in that there would be deductions of at least £4, and in many cases the loss would be higher. But the main reason was clearly defined by the Secretary of State. He accepted that the new regulations would 'save money to a modest extent, but that is not its main concern. The government was elected, amongst other things, to restore a fairer bargaining balance between employers and trade unions. Clause 6 represents one of the steps to that end'.[3]

The establishment of 'a fairer bargaining balance' between Capital and Labour in the open market is at the centre of the industrial relations policies of the Thatcher government. In the nineteenth century the Poor Law Amendment Act of 1834 was the definitive legislation which ensured that for all groups of labourers below the minority of organised skilled workers the 'free' market operated for the whole of the nineteenth century; and the free market simply means that those with the power to hire and fire set the terms on which pay and conditions shall be fixed.[4] In Thatcher's Britain the situation is, of course, very different. For many decades there has been a slow but increasing accumulation of protective legislation of many different kinds; and any attempt to achieve a 'free' market, in which the worker is more or less at the disposal of the employer, which was the nineteenth century situation, is a much more difficult and inevitably more protracted exercise. But large rivers have small beginnings, and a number of significant advances have been registered. Clause 6 of the 1980 Social Security Act was to make the daily lives of strikers with families much more difficult. What was next required was legislation to curb trade union activity in general, and to weaken the constraints upon employers in the working conditions they provide. This dismantling of the restrictions upon employers in the matter of wages and working conditions is one important thrust of the Thatcherite legislation since

1980; a second has been to frame legislation in terms that often require interpretation by the courts. The judges and their courts are still widely believed to be impartial in their adjudications; and so they may well be in some areas of the law, but emphatically not in labour legislation. The history of the courts during the past two centuries has shown a consistent political bias against radicals in general and trade unions in particular, and while the majority of the British public appear to accept the neutrality of the judicial system in all its respects—and the public in this important respect has always included the leadership of the British Labour Party—it is not true that the courts show an even hand between Capital and Labour. It is not just that the sanctity of property relationships form the major premises of judicial thinking and decision-making, but the historical record makes it abundantly clear that magistrates and judges, at all levels of the judicial system, share the common prejudices of the middle and upper classes. So it was in the days of Chartism; in the late 1860s; in the decade of the eighteen nineties; in the General Strike; and in our own day in the well-publicised judicial hostility towards the 1984–5 miners' strike.[5]

The recommendation of the Ridley Report—to cut off 'the money supply' to strikers was now achieved; and the next step was to introduce as much restriction as possible upon trade union activity, including the vulnerability of union funds through court action. These objectives were central to the two Employment Acts of 1980 and 1982. The first Employment Act of 1980 removed legal protection for certain types of sympathetic industrial action, and most forms of 'secondary' industrial action now became unlawful. In these cases the employer can now obtain an injunction against the union, and sue for damages. The Act also made substantial changes in the law of picketing and in the conditions for the closed shop; and it gave the Employment Secretary the right to issue Codes of Practice, and to revise existing codes. Hitherto Codes of Practice had been prepared and issued by the conciliating body, ACAS. The Employment Secretary in 1980, James Prior, issued draft Codes of Practice in early August 1980 on picketing and the closed shop with comments to be received by 10th October. The TUC refused to make representations. Failure to observe any provision in a Code of Practice would not in itself make anyone or any body liable for prosecution; but the Employment Act itself laid it down that courts of law and industrial tribunals should take into account such provisions that were relevant: an invitation to employers to prosecute. Section 16 of the Employment Act had already drastically restricted the legal immunity for peaceful picketing, and the Code of Practice set out in detail what was involved. The most far-reaching change was the limit placed on the number of pickets. The wording of the draft regulations—adopted unchanged in principle in the final Code—is worth reproducing, since it not only sets out clearly the changes in the nature and character of picketing, but describes the involvement of the police and the courts in more direct ways than ever before:

30. 'The number of pickets at an entrance to a workplace should, therefore, be limited to what is reasonably needed to permit the peaceful persuasion of those entering and leaving the premises who are prepared to listen. As a general rule, it will be rare for such a number to exceed six, and frequently a smaller number will be sufficient. While the law does not impose a specific limit on the number of people who may picket at any one workplace, it does give the police considerable discretionary powers to limit the number of pickets in any one place where they have reasonable cause to fear disorder. It is for the police to decide, taking into account all the circumstances, whether the number of pickets in the particular case is likely to lead to a breach of the peace.

31. The police will often discuss with the picket line organiser what constitutes a reasonable number of pickets in any one case. But it should be clear that if a picket does not leave the picket line when asked to do so by the police, he is liable to be arrested for obstruction either of the highway or of a police officer in the execution of his duty if the obstruction is such as to cause, or be likely to cause, a breach of the peace.'

The second part of the Code of Practice considered the closed shop, with provisions which made it very difficult for unions to establish new closed shop agreements, and which encouraged the weakening or the break-up of existing agreements.

There were a large number of clauses in this 1980 Employment Act which further weakened the position of workers in respect of their general conditions of work or in the matter of dismissal. Thus, maternity rights were seriously weakened; burden of proof by workers of unfair dismissal was made much more difficult; and compensation rights for unfair dismissal were severely eroded or abolished. These represented only the first instalment. The second stage came with the Employment Act of 1982. This put further limits on the right to strike; it made more certain that trade unions and trade unionists would be taken to court by employers, and that individuals would face prison sentences; and it provided means whereby trade union funds could be mulcted for damages for 'unlawful' industrial action, or for contempt of court. Many of the provisions of the Act were phrased in such a way as to allow the Courts to adjudicate and decide on matters crucial to trade union activity. It is necessary again to underline this particular point. While this 1982 Employment Act was specific about a number of changes proposed, all adverse to the unions, many of the new restrictions being imposed were not clearly defined and required interpretation by the Courts. So, for example, an employer could go to the Court asking for an injunction (in Britain) or an interdict (in Scotland) banning a particular industrial action, and the injunction would prevent action until the Court had pronounced; and that could be months. Failure to obey the Court order could lead to fines or imprisonment for contempt of court, and in the case of a union it could lead to an order for the sequestration of funds.

By 1983, then, the political and legal framework within which the trade union movement operated had changed dramatically as a result of legislation by the first of the Thatcher administrations. There were restraints upon industrial action that in a number of ways were more severe than any the union movement had experienced since the Trade Union Act of 1906 repealed by the Taff Vale decision; and although this for the Tory government was the beginning, and certainly not its conclusion, much had already been achieved before the electoral victory of the Thatcher administration in the summer of 1983.

*   *   *   *   *

The miners were the obvious target for the Thatcher administration as the Ridley Report had emphasised. Although the miners' union was much shrunken in numbers it was cohesive and disciplined and it was in a key sector of the economy. Moreover, the most important development inside the National Union of Miners had been the political shift to the Left during the nineteen seventies, symbolised by the election of Arthur Scargill to the presidency of the Yorkshire miners in 1973, then of Mick McGahey as vice-president of the National Union in the same year, and finally, in December 1981, of Scargill as president of the NUM, in succession to Joe Gormley, and with a decisive vote of just over seventy per cent.[6]

The NUM from 1974 had operated within a national agreement—the *Plan for Coal*—agreed and signed between the National Coal Board, the NUM and the government. During the sixties coal had been rapidly displaced by oil, and in theory by nuclear power; but the great rise in oil prices in 1974, as well as the miners' strike of that year and the return of a Labour government, led to a major reversal of previous policy. Henceforth coal was to be a major component of Energy policy and in particular as the principal source of electrical power generation. The current production of coal in 1974 was 117 million tonnes and the *Plan for Coal* projected an output of 135 millions by 1985 and 170 millions by the year 2000.[7]

This programme meant a much increased level of investment. It was assumed that about two million tonnes a year would be lost due to the physical exhaustion of coal seams, and that to reach the new targets additional capacity of about four million tonnes a year would have to come on stream. It must be noted that the estimates for future demand were already, in 1974, above realistic levels; and in 1977, especially because of the unexpected and falling demand for energy, the coal targets were revised downwards. There were two main reasons for this decline in demand: one was the vigorous and successful efforts at energy conservation, and the second was the quite sharp decrease in the rates of economic growth in many parts of the world economy.

What the TUC, the Labour Party leadership (at any rate in its public pronouncements) *and* the NUM have never come to terms with is the high politics of energy supply. Reducing dependence on coal was already a firm option before 1974 and the cheapness of oil underpinned all the other factors involved. When there occurred the sensational rise in oil prices in 1974 the politics of energy suddenly became much more intense. On the one hand the level of oil prices made coal the obvious alternative: hence the *British Plan for Coal*. But 1974 was also the second occasion when the NUM had exhibited the industrial muscle it possessed and for the political Establishment—much broader in its membership than the Conservative Party—a further narrowing of energy resources upon coal was greatly to be feared, given the actual and potential militancy of British miners.

The components of the Energy Establishment are at the same time complementary and competitive with each other. They are represented by powerful business interests whose relations with the Departments of Energy and Trade and the Cabinet Office are close and intimate. At the centre of the Energy Establishment in Britain is the Central Electricity Generating Board (CEGB) with enormous assets of nearly forty billion pounds: the largest electricity undertaking in Europe and probably the world. Its present chairman, formerly head of the Atomic Energy Authority (AEA) is Sir Walter Marshall, appointed by Mrs Thatcher, and a single-minded advocate of nuclear power. He is known for his advocacy of the Westinghouse Pressurised Water Reactor, and is also a supporter of the policy of privatisation. Linked with the CEGB are other parts of the public sector such as British Nuclear Fuels who own the Sellafield re-processing plants. The other main component of the nationalised sector is, of course, the National Coal Board whose main consumer is the CEGB and with a chairman, Ian McGregor, also appointed by Mrs Thatcher. We now have at the head of the electricity supply monopoly and the coal mining monopoly two men who are in favour of nuclear power, the run-down of the coal industry, and the privatisation of the profitable parts of each industry.

In the private sector of energy there are first the oil companies, immensely powerful and with strong political clout. Obviously it is a central interest of the oil companies to encourage dual capacity—oil and coal—in the electricity generating stations in Britain, and in this important matter they have been successful: as the 1984–5 miners strike demonstrated. But the oil companies have other interests, and in particular the opening of the British market to cheap imported coal. After 1974 the oil multinationals invested heavily in coal mining and they are now much involved in the international coal trade, including that from South Africa. The other major part of the energy grouping are the engineering and building firms who contract for power stations of all kinds and, for deep sea drilling equipment and platforms. These include a clutch of very large electro-engineering enterprises such as GEC, and civil construction companies of the size of Woodrow Taylor and Wimpeys. All these groups, in both the public and private sectors, have special relationships with particular departments in Whitehall, and these include, beside those of an obvious technical or commercial nature, the Ministry of Defence and the Foreign Office. What is involved, it must be emphasised, are economic interests with assets of billions of pounds. There are, inevitably, many cross-currents within and between the various interests within this large umbrella of energy, and competition is often fierce. The new cross-Channel cables from France which will begin carrying nuclear-generated electricity in the autumn of 1985 are a case in point. When the existing cables are fully operative electricity generation will be the equivalent of a power station of the size of the planned Sizewell plant; and the French are now pressing very hard for further supplies to be taken. This kind of diversification in energy supply will not only reduce dependence upon any one group of workers including the power supply workers; and it will have the specific result of further reducing the British demand for coal, and that means the jobs of British miners.[8]

*   *   *   *   *

It will now be appreciated that the basic facts of the energy situation had long been in the making when the Thatcher government took office; but that government came with specific objectives: the attack upon trade unionism being at their head. Anti-union legislation together with rapidly increasing unemployment would take care of the union movement in general; but the miners were a special case, with an industrial power that carried strong political implications as 1974 had so clearly demonstrated. The war with the miners must begin but the ground for battle had to be chosen with care, and if conditions were not propitious then a tactical withdrawal was in order. Thus it came about that in February 1981 the Thatcher government executed a much-publicised retreat from a confrontation with the miners. Early in the month the NUM had met Sir Derek Ezra, the chairman of the Coal Board. There was a complicated discussion, the details of which are still unclear, but the miners' leaders emerged with the news of large scale closures and job losses. Joe Gormley was still president and the NUM executive, with Right and Left in total agreement, passed a unanimous resolution giving the Government seven days before a strike ballot would be organised. Miners all over Britain began to take unofficial action and it immediately became obvious that a ballot would result in a majority for action. The miners also received what would seem to be firm pledges for sympathetic action from a range of unions including the steelworkers, the railwaymen and the seamen. The Government, which had at the outset taken up its usual attitude of non-interference in industrial disputes, moved quickly. The Energy Secretary, David Howell, brought forward a meeting with the NUM and the Coal Board, and the Government agreed to provide further investment. John Biffen agreed at the time that the Cabinet had given in to 'industrial muscle'; and so did the country. Three and a half years later, towards the end of the miners strike, on the 11th December 1984 and speaking on Channel Four News, David Howell accepted that the retreat in 1981 was 'entirely' a matter of tactics: 'Neither the Government nor I think society as a whole was in a position to get locked into a coal strike. . . In those days stocks weren't so high. I don't think the country was prepared, and the whole NUM and the trade union movement tended to be united on one side.' These were the days, it must be recalled, before McGregor ran his scythe through the steel workers; before the stark incompetence of the Labour leadership had been fully revealed during the General Election of 1983; before years of unemployment had eaten into the morale of working people; and before the anti-union legislation had made its serious impact upon union activity.

In the three years leading up to the coal strike of 1984 the situation changed substantially, and in every way detrimental to the position of the miners. The 1980 Coal Board Act required the NCB to break even by 1983-4, and although the Government made its tactical retreat in early 1981, the pressure for actual and potential closures continued unabated. In January 1981 the Yorkshire Area of the NUM—Scargill was president and Jack Taylor vice-president—had held a ballot asking for a general agreement that action should be taken in order to stop closure of any pit except on the grounds of geological exhaustion. It was a ballot on general principle and not in relation to any one pit closure. The Yorkshire Area campaigned carefully and won an 86 per cent vote; and while it attracted little national attention, no doubt it was a factor that the Government took into account in the subsequent months. But the history of national ballots in the next couple of years was less satisfactory. Gormley announced his retirement in the early autumn of 1981 and Arthur Scargill was elected president of the National Union in December 1981. While he was still president-elect there was a dispute over a pay claim. The NCB offered 9.5 per cent, and the executive took the matter to a national ballot. This was in January 1982, and was the occasion when Gormley, still in office, published his opposition to strike action in the *Daily Express*. The membership voted 55–45 per cent against strike action.

Gormley's departure from the NUM more or less coincided with the retirement of Sir Derek Ezra from the Coal Board. He was replaced with Norman Siddall as caretaker chairman for a year. It was in this period that occurred the second national ballot defeat in October 1982. The main issue was again pay and national conference had already begun an overtime ban. The national ballot, however, linked the pay claim with the question of pit closures. It was obvious in retrospect a tactical mistake to run the two issues together, and the ballot produced 61 per cent against action with 39 per cent in favour. Yorkshire, which in the previous national ballot had voted 66.5 per cent in favour now dropped to 56 per cent in favour. The third lost national ballot came in the following spring. In March 1983 the Tynawr Lewis Merthyr pit (near Pontypridd, South Wales) was scheduled for closure, and the South Wales area voted for strike. The Scottish Area voted to support South Wales, and the Yorkshire Area Council also voted by 73 votes to 2 to back South Wales. Scargill called an emergency meeting of the executive committee and argued that Rule 41 should be invoked whereby individual areas may call strikes if the national Executive committee sanctions them. The Right wing on the EC argued that the question of the closure of Lewis Merthyr was a national issue, and a ballot was accordingly held. When the votes were counted they reproduced the figures of the previous autumn, with 61 per cent against strike action. Even Yorkshire, which continued to vote in favour, showed only 54 per cent, a drop of two per cent on the previous figure. Just over a fortnight after the votes were announced, Mrs Thatcher announced the nomination of Ian McGregor as chairman of the Coal Board. The coal crisis was moving nearer. After her victorious general election of the summer of 1983, when allocating the positions in the government, Mrs Thatcher is reported to have said to Peter Walker: 'I want you to go to Energy. We're going to have a miners strike.'

McGregor took office on 1st September 1983, and almost immediately began to talk about the need to eliminate what he described as uneconomic output. The definition of 'uneconomic' is discussed in detail below. There was a final pay offer for this year at just over five per cent, and an emergency national conference of the NUM imposed an overtime ban which began on October 31st. It was linked with the campaign against pit closures. The previous summer, just before McGregor came to office, the NUM annual conference had unanimously passed a resolution opposing not only 'pit and works closures, but all reductions in manpower', and the EC was given the power to conduct a national ballot on the issue if and when it was deemed appropriate.

The overtime ban caused many local difficulties and disputes, especially in Scotland and Yorkshire. And then on March 1st 1984 the Yorkshire Area of the NCB announced the closure of Cortonwood. Five days later, at a national meeting with the three mining unions—NUM, NACODS and BACM—the NCB gave notice that there was to be a cut in capacity of four million tonnes and that a third of this was to come out of the North-Eastern area.[9]

It is necessary to underline the importance of Cortonwood. It was a pit that was understood to have at least a further five years of life, and men had been transferred into it from other pits until two weeks earlier. The decision to close down Cortonwood was therefore quite unexpected, and although the Yorkshire NCB insisted that the matter was not decided in London but was a regional decision taken in the circumstances of the requirement to reduce output, it was certainly fully in accord with national strategy. The appointment of McGregor had been an unmistakable signal that a confrontation with the miners was now to be seriously considered: the problems were the matter of timing, and the required provocation. And it is in the context of 'provocation' that Cortonwood is important. Pits were already being closed down in Scotland, South Wales and other peripheral areas. The *Scotsman* (7 February 1984) noted that the Scottish Area Director of the NCB, Albert Wheeler, had in the previous thirteen months reduced the number of Scottish pits from 15 to 9 with only one new colliery coming on stream in the future; while South Wales had no new pits to set against their closures. The Coal Board could have completely closed down both South Wales and Scotland—as indeed is broadly their intention in the future—without touching the heart of the miners' union in the central mining districts. Yorkshire has 60,000 miners, out of a national total of 180,000; it has a militant leadership; and it was, and in most ways still is, Scargill's home base. With Nottinghamshire it was the powerful centre of the industry. Yorkshire had to be broken. Scotland and South Wales could remain on strike for five years, and the NCB and Whitehall, could and would have forgotten that there were miners still living in those parts; and the shortfall in output would have embarrassed no one. If the Government was to break the power of the National Union of Miners, Yorkshire had to be involved from the beginning.

The NCB timing for the closing down of Cortonwood was, of course, carefully calculated from their side, and it was right;[10] but it was certainly not propitious for the miners. No national strike of coal miners will choose to begin at the outset of spring when, with the summer coming along, consumer demand for heat and light will be moving downward to its lowest levels of the year; and coal stocks at this time, following the injunction of the Ridley Report and underlined by the events of February 1981, were at a high point. In the 1981 crisis they had been 37 million tonnes; by the spring of 1984 they were 57 million. Moreover, during 1983 oil imports had been quite sharply increasing, and power stations were being prepared for an increasing use of oil firing. This was an issue on which Glyn England, chairman of the CEGB, had shown strong disagreement with the Government, and his contract was not renewed. He was replaced in 1983 by Sir Walter Marshall who began right away to talk about the excessive dependency upon coal. There were some interesting developments in this area. During the nineteen seventies all the major power stations were made much more self-sufficient than they had been previously, and they also developed a greater flexibility in their use of fuel. Drax in South Yorkshire for instance, is listed as a coal-fired power station yet it has one oil turbine; and in the 1970s the Ferrybridge 'C' plant was provided with a hydrogen pipe line and with chemical and oil storage facilities.

The timing was also right for the Government when they looked at the internal situation of the NUM. The miners had a president who could not be cajoled or bought off. Scargill was incorruptible; he was also inflexible on the issue of pit closures and job losses, and since the government were never going to be interested in serious negotiations, Scargill's obduracy might work in their favour. Now this could not be assumed as anything but one option at the beginning of the strike, for there were many imponderables, above all the range of support that could be forthcoming from other sections of the trade union and labour movement. But at the beginning of 1984 the Government could assess favourably their appreciation of the internal problems the NUM leadership faced. The failure of the national ballots of November 1982 and of March 1983 had deeply worried the NUM leadership. In the March ballot only 19 per cent of Nottinghamshire miners had voted for strike action, with 18 per cent in Leicestershire and 12 per cent in South Derbyshire. There were problems too in the militant areas. South Wales had been severely shaken by the lack of support for what had become a national campaign over the threatened Lewis Merthyr colliery. Welsh miners had travelled all over Britain to argue for support for South Wales. They were well received everywhere, including Nottinghamshire and the Midlands; but their reception stopped short of support in the national ballot. When the strike call was made in March 1984 some Welsh pits had to be picketed out; but once out, and it was a matter only of days, South Wales remained solid until the very last days of the year's strike. But the Midlands were very different, and their poor response to the national ballots meant that no one could predict how the Midland coalfields would react to a call for strike, and if they joined the strike, how long they would last. Traditions are very persistent, and 1926 still cast very long shadows. But just as important as these internal problems of the NUM was the stark, bitter fact that large sections of public opinion did not believe the miners had a viable case against closures; and public opinion, in this context, certainly included large numbers of manual workers. The constant re-iteration of the inefficiency of the nationalised industries, to which the labour movement had reacted hardly at all, had shaped 'commonsense' attitudes. In the case of the mining industry the Minister of Energy, Peter Walker, was making continuous reference to what he said was a subsidy of £1,334 million for the year 1983–4, or roughly £130 per week for each working miner. The fact that it was a wholly misleading statement was not emphasised by anyone in the year leading up to the strike. There was no serious discussion of the so-called 'uneconomic' arguments. Why therefore should there be any questioning of the Government's arguments condemning the 'subsidy' to an industry that in many parts was 'uneconomic'? Moreover, the miners' union had long co-operated in the closing down of collieries on a large scale, so why should Scargill now adopt a wholly intransigeant attitude in the nineteen eighties? The consequences of pit closures upon communities was a fairly new argument, at least at a national level, and that could be understood; but this aspect of the miner's case was greatly overshadowed by the widespread belief that the industry was 'uneconomic' and that contraction had to be accepted. This problem is discussed in some detail below, but let it be said at this point that the failure to analyse these 'uneconomic' arguments was a major weakness of the miners' own position, and a massive indictment of the Labour Party, whose understanding of the issues in energy matters was to be proved notably inadequate. There was, therefore, a great deal of prejudice against the miners before their strike began, and there was never a national effort to explain their case during the strike.

* * * * *

The sequence of events which provided the immediate reasons for the strike began, as noted above, with the announcement by George Hayes, the South Yorkshire NCB director, that Cortonwood was going to close. This was on March 1st. Five days later, on March 6th, at a National Consulvative Council meeting the NUM were told that the Coal Board was looking for a four million tonne cut in production in 1984–5 and that this would involve 20,000 jobs. On the 8th March, at an executive committee meeting of the NUM the Yorkshire and Scottish areas asked for official strike agreement under Rule 41. The NUM has two rules under which strike action can be sanctioned. The first is Rule 41 whereby any area can ask the EC for permission to engage in an area strike; and the second is Rule 43 under which a national strike can be sanctioned only after a ballot of the whole membership.[11] At the March 8th meeting there was a motion for a national ballot but it was not in fact voted on—although about a dozen members present had spoken in favour of a national ballot— and only three members voted against action under Rule 41. Scotland and Yorkshire therefore obtained their constitutional sanction, and their strikes began on Monday 12 March. This is what the Left had wanted the previous year, but they had been forced to accept a national ballot. On this present occasion their strategy was based on certain crucial assumptions. The first was that the area strikes would have a domino effect upon other areas, and that mass picketing would be the means whereby a national strike would come about. The events of 1972 and 1974 were deeply imprinted upon the consciousness of mineworkers, and the great solidarity picket of Saltley was never far from their minds. In 1984, it was other miners who had to be picketed, not workers at power stations, or the docks, or transport undertakings, although that would also be necessary. Immediately for Yorkshire miners it was adjacent Nottinghamshire, Derbyshire and Lancashire that were working, and they poured over the county boundaries. This was the first, and necessary, part of a successful strategy: a complete national stoppage. The second was the looked-for solidarity of other groups with the miners: workers on the railways, in the steelworks, and on the docks: those who had offered firm support in 1981, the threat of which had forced a retreat on the Government. And the third part of a strategy that would achieve success, although it was much less emphasised than the industrial action, was the political support the miners could reasonably expect from the labour movement in general, and, no doubt they also hoped, from the political leadership of the Labour Party. But none of these matters turned out the way that was being counted upon, and what is remarkable about the miners' strike is not that it was defeated but that it took a year to achieve that defeat.

The first major problem was the disunity within the NUM, and the twenty per cent of miners who continued working throughout the whole year. There could be no denying the seriousness for the miners' leadership of the fact that important areas continued to work throughout the year's strike. In 1926 most of Nottingham went back by the end of August; now, in 1984–5, in the absence of a national ballot, they continued working from the first day. The question of the national ballot will not be discussed here except to underline the obvious: that it was an albatross round the neck of the NUM leadership, and the refusal to have a ballot was used effectively by all the enemies of the miners. It also confused some sections of their well-wishers.

The second problem was one that might have been more clearly appreciated than it apparently was at the outset. The police had also been seriously disturbed by the events of 1972—which included Saltley Gate, the Shrewsbury pickets and the Pentonville Five—and they began to centralise their activities on a national basis. The constitutional position has been that the police force in England and Wales is divided between 43 areas and their administration controlled by a tri-partite arrangement between the Home Secretary, the Chief Constable and the local Police Authority or Committee. The six metropolitan County Councils, excluding London, constitute Police Authorities, while in the ordinary County Councils there are Police Committees made up of two-thirds local councillors and one third magistrates. Police Committees deal with staffing, including the appointment of Chief Constables, equipment and general costs, and their remit is 'the maintenance of an adequate and efficient police force'. The Chief Constables are responsible, under the 1964 Police Act, for the direction of the local police force on operational and policy matters. The Home Secretary has a strong central role, with defined powers on certain questions, but in times of crisis, he will have the dominating position. The Home Secretary has always had this ability to act in a centralising way in critical times throughout the modern period of British history, from the 1790s to the present day.[12] In the day to day affairs of the police H.M. Inspectors of Police report direct to the Home Secretary on the efficiency of all authorities.

That is the constitutional position, but the reality is somewhat different. There has been a steady movement especially in the past decade towards increased centralisation and changes in the practice of policing. Northern Ireland has exercised a powerful influence during the last twenty years or so, and the growth of para-military groups within the existing police forces has been a marked feature of this period; developments within the police forces themselves and which are not subject to the lay authorities who theoretically, in the last resort, control these forces. The most important single administrative change has been the establishment of the National Reporting Centre whose existence was hardly known about until a statement was made on 18th March 1984 in connection with its role in the miners' strike.[13] The Centre was first established in 1972 as a response to the Saltley picket and other events of that year. It was an organisation which brought together all the Chief Constables of England and Wales, and the Controller is always the current president of the Association of Chief Constables (ACPO). At the beginning of the miners strike in March 1984 this was David Hall, the Chief Constable for Humberside who later stated that at the very beginning of picketing in Nottinghamshire—which began on the first day of the strike—1,000 officers had been mobilised from different police forces in the country. Within the first month, and in consultation with the Home Secretary, 8,000 police had been mobilised from all but two of the Constabularies in the country. Most of the police used came from the Special Patrol Groups whose establishment had been a feature of the 1970s: groups trained in the use of firearms and in the techniques of riot control with appropriate equipment. The work of the National Reporting Centre is not controlled by the lay authorities nor is there any reporting back except to the Home Office. It is in fact a strategic command for a nationally organised riot force which can be directed to any place in the country and which is especially important in industrial disputes. Without the National Reporting Centre's co-ordinating activity the policing of the 1984–5 miners strike would have broken down, and since its control is ultimately that of the Home Secretary, a strike-breaking Government such as the Thatcher administration has now a powerful para-military organisation at its disposal, with no lay control, either from local authorities or from the House of Commons. Only the Labour front bench at Westminster seemed to be unaware that the fiction of police neutrality could no longer be accepted.

The third problem the miners faced was the single-mindedness of the Thatcher government in its determination to be rid of the troublesome Miners' Union. Grunwick, Eddie Shah at Warrington, the trampling down of the Steelworkers by MacGregor had shown the way, and the anti-Trade Union legislation was now on the Statute Book; there was widespread cautiousness if not demoralisation among trade union leaderships; and it was time for what undoubtedly would be a serious physical confrontation with the miners. It was to prove a good deal more difficult than the Government and the Coal Board must have assumed at the outset. McGregor himself, with a notorious record of union-busting in the United States, proved under pressure to be weak and incompetent;[14] the solidarity of the miners and their families was truly remarkable with the role of the women in the coalfields being outstanding; and although the national support of the TUC and the Labour Party leadership, and especially of the latter, was to be a good deal less than half-hearted, what was impressive was the extent and range of support for the miners from very wide sections of the British people and from the labour movement in particular. But for the Thatcher government, there was only one real problem, namely, that the miners would settle on terms which would represent at least a partial victory, and which would therefore not meet the central aim that the Government had set itself: the destruction of the industrial and political effectiveness of the NUM. So long as the miners refused to settle, and the strike continued, all the Government had to do, in conjunction with General Winter and General Hardship, was to continue to pour money in the conduct and continuation of all the measures which were being taken against the miners, and victory would come in the end. The amount of money expended was irrelevant; public spending could go on and on, and the strike having started must end only in a miners' defeat. The Government came close several times to failing in their objective of total victory. It was this inflexible intransigeance of the Thatcher government that was not wholly appreciated by the NUM, and as far as can be judged from their published statements, not at all by the Labour leadership. There was no financial cost too great for the miners to be destroyed, and the Government spent money without restraint: most particularly on the large scale police operations, and on the oil firing of the power stations. The cost was in billions of pounds, but for the Tories it was worth every billion. By comparison, the Falklands episode, so important for the Thatcher electoral victory in 1983, was but froth. The defeat of the miners was seen as an important victory of the capitalist State, and it was rejoiced in by the world of business. No indication of the power of Capital over Labour was better illustrated than this stark confrontation between the miners and the coercive forces of the British State.

There was a fourth problem that again was not fully appreciated or appreciated at all during the early weeks of the miners strike; and that was the failure of workers in other key industries to support the miners by industrial action. We leave aside the relations between the TUC General Council and the NUM on which there is a good deal to be said on both sides; and there was support from members of ASLEF and the NUR. But there was no movement from power station workers, a large number of whom were organised by Frank Chapple; no help from the steelworkers, with a weak leadership and a membership that was described as 'shell-shocked' from McGregor's butchery of the previous three years; and there was no stopping the increasing amounts of imported coal. It came mostly from Poland, West Germany and the United States, with smaller but also growing amounts from South Africa. Belgian and Australian miners and dockers gave practical support to the British miners, but from Scotland southwards, right down the east coast of England and along the south coast, the unregistered ports outside the Dock Labour Scheme were never busier. The coal flooded in, and the local port and transport workers must have earned nearly as much extra pay as the thousands of policemen drafted into the mining areas whose earnings rocketed. The Ridley Report had suggested the need to recruit 'good non-union drivers', and the willingness of lorry drivers to go through picket lines remained an unpleasant feature of the whole course of the miners' strike; the Transport Workers Union could do nothing about it. It should be noted that a quite common argument to pickets from transport workers referred to the large numbers of miners who were still working. It was, without question, a hypocritical argument by many, but the twenty per cent of miners who worked throughout created much confusion, and certainly much excuse by strike-breaking workers in other industries.

The miners did not, therefore, have the support of the working class in an organised sense. There was no possibility that the electricians union, the EEPTU, would offer solidarity with the miners; but a concerted one-day stoppage of all the registered docks, the railways, and the steel works would have been a serious warning, and a week's solid strike in sympathy with the miners might have forced the government into a serious bargaining stance. Let it be said that such concerted action was never likely, and in the crisis of the year-long strike the leadership of the unions related to mining and the coal industry, whatever their individual opinions, were unable to bring their members into supportive action. There were exceptions, among them certain regions of the railways,[15] and dockers, but it must be recognised, as a reflection of the present state of political consciousness of working people in Britain, that national support in an organised sense was lacking. There was very large-scale support from outside the mining communities, much greater than in 1926; and this was not only due to a good deal more pronounced material affluence. There was a very considerable groundswell of support throughout the labour movement in Britain, and its support was maintained throughout the years' struggle. In 1926 the largest amount of money for the miners came from Soviet trade unions, whereas in 1984–5 home based support was the most important component of every kind of aid, by a very long way. But the dockers illustrate the point being made here. There were two national dock strikes. The first was called on the 9th July 1984 after coal had been unloaded at Immingham for the British Steel Corporation by non-registered dock labour. The strike was undoubtedly a serious threat to both the NCB and the Government, but it was ended by a compromise formula which conceded a good deal to the union but which in any case had to be accepted because of the growing pressures from dockers in unregistered ports and especially at this time, from Dover. The second dock strike began on 24 August after the British Steel Corporation's decision to un-load coal at Hunterston (in Scotland), again using non-registered labour. All twelve dock labour scheme ports in Scotland were on strike, and most in England, but the non-registered ports on the East Coast, and in particular Dover and Felixstowe, continued working (as did all the many small wharves up and down the east coast which were importing coal as fast as they could). At Felixstowe the average wage of 1,532 employees in 1983 was £13,507, and when a strike vote was taken for this second strike only 5 out of 900 voted in favour. The second dock strike ended on 19 September[16] having failed in its basic objectives.

*   *   *   *   *

What could have been done? Was there ever a possibility that the miners' strike could have been won, given the determination of the Thatcher government to defeat the miners at any cost, and given also the failure of other trade unions to provide effective solidarity action? There were, as indicated above, several occasions when the NCB in particular looked in a relatively weak position and when the pressures upon the Government appeared to be growing. McGregor himself was proving notably incompetent and unconvincing in his presentation of the NCB case, and we now know, from what has later been revealed after the strike was over, that there were at times serious disagreements between him and the Energy Secretary.[17] The last major talks of any weight and import began with a vote by NACODS (National Association of Colliery Overmen, Deputies and Shotfirers) which produced 82.5 per cent in favour of a national strike. NACODS, whose role in the pits was crucial, a withdrawal of their labour would mean a complete national stoppage of work, had no tradition of striking and this vote was unprecedented. On the 3rd October NACODS and the NCB went to ACAS (the National Conciliation body), and talks continued throughout most of October. There were one hundred and thirty-seven hours of talks in all and before a settlement was agreed NACODS insisted that the NUM were included. The latter, however, refused the new closure procedure which represented a number of concessions on the part of the NCB, and NACODS alone signed; and withdrew their strike notices. Had the NUM also signed, both sides would without doubt have claimed a victory, in that the NUM would have accepted a closure procedure, and the NCB would have conceded a good deal more than they started with. Most important, of course, the NUM would have remained a powerful force in the industry. It is now generally agreed that the failure of these talks was the last occasion when some sort of settlement which did not involve the defeat of the NUM was practicable. In the month following, much helped by financial bribes from the NCB, some 16,000 men returned to work. At the time, it must be emphasised, the situation did not look clear cut. In an article in *Tribune* on 5 October Colin Sweet, director of the Centre for Energy Studies at the Polytechnic of the South Bank, made a quite favourable assessment of the miner's situation in the strike; and Sweet is a well-informed and sensible commentator. He laid considerable emphasis in this article on the decline in coal stocks and on the difficulties of both importing and using foreign coal supplies. What most observers underestimated was in fact the ability to import coal at dozens of small ports and improvised wharves along the east and south coasts, and the technical ability of those in charge of the power stations, with the willing co-operation of the power workers, to produce record levels of electricity. Without the co-operation of the power workers with management the output of electricity could not possibly have been maintained, and most commentaries on the miners' strike failed to appreciate the crucial contribution to the Government's victory that was being made by the workers in the generating plants.[18]

Whether the NUM leadership *could* have settled even at this late date in the strike—the end of October 1984—is a big, and crucial question. Arthur Scargill and his colleagues had evoked enormous sacrifices from their members on the clear understanding that they were fighting for jobs for their communities and against all closures. The issues, as the leadership of the NUM had made abundantly plain from the very beginning of the strike, were straightforward, and uncompromising. But, and it is a major qualification, the assumptions made at the commencement of the strike had not been fulfilled. Twenty per cent of miners had worked throughout; there had been no effective solidarity from other unions; and the Labour Party leadership had publicly and very obviously stood to one side. It would have been very difficult for the NUM leadership, especially Scargill, McGahey and Heathfield, to settle on terms that were less than the claims with which the strike had begun; but is that not always the situation in strikes? Is it not rare for workers to win strikes outright, and not all that common for a settlement to be agreed which includes concessions on both sides? The quarter of a century after 1950 was an unusual period in the history of capitalism. It was a time when unions did improve quite substantially their bargaining position, backed by some statutory legislation. But the boom years had ended in 1973, and the growing crisis in the seventies had led into the election of a rampant trade-union busting government led by Mrs Thatcher; and everything that had been done by the government since its election in the summer of 1979 had confirmed the spirit and the letter of the Ridley Report. It is true that the Labour leadership in Parliament had displayed a quite extraordinary incompetence, and a remarkable lack of urgency in the face of a government bristling with anti-labour and anti-union attitudes that had been translated into anti-union legislation. While therefore it would have been politically difficult for the miners' leaders to have advocated a settlement at the end of October 1984, had they done so, it would have left the NUM, in the short and medium run at any rate, strengthened and not weakened. The Union would have been in a much stronger position to deal with the special problems of Nottinghamshire and the other smaller areas which continued working during the strike; but above all, it would have demonstrated, for the benefit of the whole labour movement, that the bitter hostility of much of the media, the large scale and persistent harassment by the police forces, and the notorious bias of the judiciary, at all levels, could be met, and overcome. A settlement at this time would have borne witness to the power of industrial workers backed by a remarkable range of support groups within and outside their own communities. It would, further, have been evidence, if additional evidence was needed, of the pusillanimity of the Labour leadership when confronted with the vicious hostility of the conservative Establishment, and of the feebleness of policies dictated by the ups and downs of the opinion polls.

But a settlement was not made, and the miners went on to defeat, an outcome that was not wholly the product of what may be described as the 'high politics' of the mining dispute. The NUM failed dramatically, for example, with the media and this cannot be accounted for entirely by the known bias and political prejudices of much of the national press or the TV companies. The organisation of publicity from the NUM headquarters in Sheffield was nearly as inefficient as that of the national Labour Party from Walworth Road during the 1983 General Election. Planning the day-to-day publicity and propagandist campaigns is not for amateurs; it requires specialist experience of journalism, radio and TV; and the full-time officials of unions should not be expected to act as part-time public-relations experts. The classic example of how a strike should be run took place in September/October 1919 when the National Union of Railwaymen and other railway unions were on strike for nine days.[19] It was the first modern industrial dispute in which both sides used the mass media for the presentation of their case. The Union Executives authorised the Labour Research Department to take charge of the publicity for the whole strike; and remarkably successful it was. Lloyd George called the strike an 'anarchist conspiracy'; and all the daily press, with the exception of the *Daily Herald*, explained to their readers how public opinion was totally against the strikers: 'a little band of conspirators who forced their duped followers into a strike against the whole nation' said the *Daily Express*. What the Labour Research Department achieved with their nation-wide publicity was first a rapidly growing support among manual workers for the case they presented and then a much wider sympathy among other sections of the population. But—and it is a crucial qualification—the railwaymen in 1919 had a case, and it was presented intelligently and clearly to the whole nation. And what was the case the miners presented throughout the whole year of their strike from March 1984? The answer is that whatever case the miners had, it came across in a confused and wholly inadequate way. Arthur Scargill himself played two roles. The first, which he did brilliantly, was the union leader of a strike. His first responsibility was directed to his own members: the encouragement to their commitment, and the upholding of their morale. In this crucial respect Arthur Scargill may very properly be compared with Arthur Cook. They both identified with their members in a remarkable and unusual way, and for the extraordinary moral stamina the miners and their families displayed throughout the year of the strike Scargill can rightly claim to have been the most important single influence. He was for the English miners on strike what the 'FED' was for South Wales.[20] The role of a charismatic trade union leader, central though it is to the conduct of a strike, cannot however easily be transferred to that of spokesman to the public at large; and what the NUM never assembled was a group of dedicated specialists in public relations who for twenty-four hours each day would be concerning themselves with the presentation of the miners case on radio, in TV programmes, and through the press. A big and complicated business, and how many were there at the NUM headquarters concerned solely with such publicity? But while efficiency in presentation is crucial, the prior question to be asked is the nature of the case to be presented. Here, it must be said, there was a political vacuum which the Labour Party above all failed to occupy, but they were not helped by the inadequacy of the arguments the NUM themselves were marshalling. It was only in the second half of the strike that the economic arguments of the NCB, and the large-scale inadequacy of their accounting procedures, were subject to sustained criticism. It must be said that even when the materials became available the NUM leadership all failed to present adequately what was a very powerful case against the Coal Board and the Government. Only in Scotland, in the last stages of the strike, was there a serious attempt to put across the economic case against the NCB.

Analysis of the misrepresentations of the economic position of the coal mines of Britain, and of the consequences of closure, was undertaken by academics outside the NUM and the Labour Party. It began with Andrew Glyn, of the University of Oxford, whose work was published by the NUM in the autumn of 1984 but whose arguments were hardly ever used by Arthur Scargill and other spokesmen for the miners. Then came the analysis of Scottish mining by George Kerevan and Richard Saville around Christmas 1984, and there was later a study by a group at Aberystwyth of some aspects of the South Wales position. In January 1985, the journal *Accountancy*, published a devastating critique of the accounting methods of the National Coal Board by five academic accounting specialists, including David Cooper, Price Waterhouse Professor of Accounting and Finance at UMIST and Tony Lowe, Professor of Accounting and Financial Management at the University of Sheffield.[21] What all these studies added up to was a total reversal of the Coal Board's position on the so-called 'uneconomic' pits, and a complete rejection of the general arguments used by the Government in their claim that there were sound economic reasons for the closing of pits.

These are three parts of the problem overall that have been selected for comment, although what is given below is no more than a summary of detailed economic and accounting analyses that are in the public domain, and, it should be added, are comprehensible to the lay reader. The first relates to what is sometimes called the social audit of the industry—the social and economic costs of closing a pit or pits compared with the costs of keeping the pit or pits working. All the data used in the various analyses were taken either from the published accounts of the National Coal Board or from the Report of the Monopolies and Mergers Commission on the National Coal Board which was published in June 1983 (Cmnd 8920). The point was made by Glyn and the Accounting specialists that some of the NCB data could only be considered approximate, although the basic generalisation and conclusions were not affected; but it is worth noting that one must assume that since some of the financial details were not defined as would be expected of a commercial organisation, the Coal Board themselves were basing their judgments on data that were not as precise as would normally be required in commercial decision-making. Glyn took the NCB's data for the 103 pits for which the NCB showed what they described as 'operating losses' and set against these 'losses' the economic costs of closure. These latter included redundancy pay for the miners who left the industry, and the revenue therefore also lost in tax; the cost of unemployment pay and social security for those 'new' miners who would have been taken on in place of the older men if the pits had not closed; and the unemployment pay and social benefits that would be paid, as well as the tax that would be lost, of those outside the pits who lost their jobs as a result of pit closures. Glyn estimated that for every 100 jobs lost in the mines there would be about 87 lost elsewhere—around 25 in the NCB and the remainder in the supplying industries. If all these economic costs of closure are added up then for the 29 weeks of 1983/4 before the overtime ban 'while 103 pits are shown as reporting losses over the period in not one case would closure have benefitted Government revenue'.[22]

The second part of the problem, however, is that the definition of the so-called 'operating losses' by individual pits are themselves a product of faulty, incorrect and indefensible accounting procedures by the NCB. The most convenient analysis is in the article in *Accountancy*. Here Professor Cooper and his colleagues examined in close detail the colliery profit and loss account—the F 23—upon which the NCB base their decision-making for investment, their estimate of future profit and loss, and their public statements about closure. The F 23, the authors said bluntly, was 'fundamentally flawed' in terms of the purposes for which it was used *viz* to justify pit closure decisions; and they then proceeded to explain why the F 23 'does not provide a sensible basis for debate on pit closures'. Their analysis may be conveniently illustrated by the case of the pit whose threatened closure was the immediate cause of the strike: Cortonwood. Briefly, what they showed was that the NCB arrived at a figure of loss by setting operating costs against net proceeds, a reasonable method it would seem until it was appreciated that within the figure of operating costs the NCB included items which by no stretch of any commercial imagination could be included in current operating costs. Thus, compensation for surface damage and subsidence was included: costs which it should be noted would continue whether the pit was kept open or closed. Similarly, the cost of redundancies and early retirements were included within current operating costs although again these costs would remain if the pit was closed. The conclusion arrived at about Cortonwood was that whereas in 1981/2 the NCB F 23 showed a loss per tonne of £6.20 the true figures were that the pit would have contributed a positive income of somewhere between £2.49 and £5.45 per tonne. And the authors imply—they are cautious in their statements—that the analysis for 1983-4 would show results in the same way. This is what Glyn had already shown in his earlier pamphlet: that if the items are removed from the debit side that cannot seriously be allocated to operating costs then the NCB in fact made an operating profit in the year prior to the strike.[23]

A few months after the strike ended another acountant published his analysis in the *Guardian*. This was Emile Woolf and the interesting thing is that Mr Woolf did not appear to be familiar with the literature mentioned above. His data were worked out independently from the NCB accounts and are presented below. It was clear from his article that Mr Woolf was shocked at what he discovered in the NCB accounts. They were, he wrote, 'a supreme masterpiece in the art of obfuscation. Even if Sherlock Holmes had held a Masters degree in Accounting he would have found his powers of sleuthery stretched to the utmost in finding his way through this particular maze of artfully presented decoys'.[24]

Woolf began by referring to Peter Walker's repeated statement that the taxpayer had subsidised the coal industry by £1,334 million during 1983–4 or roughly £130 per week. What everyone naturally assumed from these figures was that the Coal industry was making losses of this order. When Woolf analysed the figures he found that £459 million represented the costs of the contraction already imposed on the industry—including redundancy payments and increased pensions to those who had left the industry more than 10 years earlier—and in no rational calculation could these costs be included under the heading of 'operating costs' which should refer only to current costs of mining. As Woolf noted hundreds of millions of pounds which related to the costs of contraction in the past were being included in the figures to justify contraction in the future: 'surely one of the most blatant instances of the proverbial self-fulfilling prophecy ever uttered from an ostensibly authoritative source'.

Woolf then continued to analyse the remaining £875 million of the original £1.3 billion. 'This represents the deficit grant paid by the Government to the NCB to cover its reported losses for the year. Surely that is bad enough, some might say.' But of this £875 million deficit no less than £467 million represented interest charges, almost all of which were paid by the Coal Board to the Government and were largely the result of the closure programme imposed upon the industry by the Government. So the Government created, in Woolf's words, 'a mountain of debt for the industry' in respect of its contraction and then blamed the industry for not being able to meet the interest charges. There were other items analysed by Woolf including the payments for subsidence compensation, the costs of which nearly doubled in 1983–4 over the previous year and also including further 'social costs' of past closures. Again these payments have nothing to do with operating costs. Here is Emile Woolf in conclusion:

If the Secretary of State is really interested in the cause of the £1.3 billion burden on the taxpayer quoted at the beginning of this article the answer is simple. It is made up of the closure, redundancy and early retirement payments already sub-totalled at £634 million; subsidence claims of £245 million; and interest paid to the government £402 million. By any objective measures the coal industry, based on its audited accounts (as adjusted for distortions) appears to be operationally viable.

And Woolf ended in obvious surprise that the NUM had not used this material and this sort of analysis during the strike: 'Who was advising the Miners?' he asked.

There is a third part of the problem: a matter that is so simple and at the same time so crucial for the economics of the coal industry: the price at which coal is sold in Britain to the Central Electricity Generating Board. Just over 70 per cent of coal mined in Britain is sold to the CEGB. The price is determined by complex negotiations which obviously have a major impact on the published accounts of the coal industry, since the level of prices will affect the apparent profitability or apparent loss-making of the NCB. Professor Cooper and his colleagues noted that current prices to the CEGB were above the international spot price at Rotterdam but the economics of imported coal are complex and obviously depend, among other factors, on exchange rates which have shown to be wildly fluctuating in the most recent years. But what is firm is the fact that coal is sold to the CEGB at something like 40 per cent below the cost of oil with equivalent heat output; that the CEGB have been instructed by the Government to raise their own prices to consumers at well above the inflation rate and have therefore made very large profits; and that if the NCB charged the CEGB at 20 per cent below the cost of oil—instead of about 40 per cent—the additional revenue for the NCB on 1983-4 would have been more than £1,500 million;[25] and Peter Walker's mythical taxpayer would have been in credit without any other adjustments being required to the NCB's balance sheets. And since it is now appreciated that the NCB's balance sheets are shot through with accounting mistakes—all biased against the mines and above all against the miners—the removal of Government restraints on pricing would show a coal industry which was wholly viable.

Throughout the year's strike the presentation of these basic truths—the lies and distortions of the case against the Coal industry by the Government and the NCB—was almost wholly absent; and the British public were left in ignorance concerning the facts of one of their basic industries. While there is no doubt that the NUM ought to have appreciated very much more clearly the devastating arguments that could be used in support of their claim of no pit closures—a demand that was wholly justified—the major responsibility for the failure to instruct and educate public opinion, and to expose the constant misrepresentations of Government spokesmen, and above all the Prime Minister, was upon the Labour leadership at Westminster. There was however a political vacuum around the coal strike, as there was in 1926. In part, as with the NUM, it must be presumed to be ignorance. The research facilities organised directly by the NUM are few, and apparently it never occurred to them to put the matter out ot contract either with left-wing academic specialists or with capable organisations such as the Labour Research Department; or with both. And the same appears to have been true of the Labour Party. Its front-bench spokesmen were quite inadequately briefed, and offered none of the serious critique that was being made outside Westminster during the closing months of the strike. Nowhere in *Hansard* is there to be found a sustained analysis of the economic and accounting practices of the Coal Board, and of their massive misrepresentations. And this is scandalous and indefensible. Here we have the Labour Party in Parliament, trying desperately to offer a coherent position and platform to the country, yet without anything approaching a comprehensive policy for energy, and allowing the Tories to get away with economic mayhem against the mining industry. This is not just a matter of sustained prejudice against Arthur Scargill, although that played its part; but it raises very serious questions about the absence of sophisticated research available to the Labour leadership. We have on evidence an article on the economics of the miners' strike by the Shadow Chancellor, Roy Hattersley, published in the *Observer* on 21 October 1984. Mr Hattersley is not one of the lightweights in Labour's Shadow Cabinet; his speeches in the Commons are well prepared and are usually more solid and interesting than those of his Leader. But this *Observer* article showed that Hattersley had only half of the answer, and the absence of the other half meant that his case against the Government was muted and lacked any real biting edge to the argument. 'We must assume' he writes 'that Cortonwood is a classic uneconomic pit. . .' But as the analysis above has shown we must assume nothing of the sort. At the time Hattersley was writing his article Professor Cooper and his colleagues must have been working on theirs, or likely enough, they had already finished it because it was originally planned to publish in the December issue of *Accountancy* and only the intervention of the NCB held up its publication until the following month.[26] Hattersley got his social audit figures right, but his understanding and analysis of the NCB's accounts was only half of the complete answer; so, for example, he assumed that even when interest payments and compensation for subsidence were taken out of the deficit side of the balance sheet for Cortonwood it still left a loss of £5.5 per tonne; while Professor Cooper shows that there was in fact a positive contribution from Cortonwood to the operating profits of the NCB.[27]

If the Labour Party at the top cannot organise when in Opposition access to independent research which can take apart the obfuscation, lies and misrepresentations that are encapsulated in so many official documents and statements, what chance have they in office of understanding what the British Establishment is about, let alone of bringing them to account? There is, however, another dimension to the politics of Labour which the miners' strike also demonstrated: the dimension of courage. During the strike Thatcher and her colleagues played the issues of the ballot, and especially of the violence on the picket line, to their fullest extent; and the Labour front bench were unwilling to meet the Government head-on. There was a major failure of nerve on the part of Kinnock and his colleagues. As the *Guardian* remarked towards the end of the strike the historian of the future will not go to the pages of *Hansard* for a detailed commentary on the strike because it was not in fact a matter of serious concern for the House of Commons: measuring concern by the number of columns relating to the strike in *Hansard*. This was not quite fair to the Labour backbenchers, some of whom showed considerable tenacity in their attempts to bring the strike before the House of Commons; but it most emphatically does apply to the Labour front bench. During the first ten weeks of the strike, after which the House was on holiday for a fortnight, there was no debate on the strike initiated by the front-bench Labour Opposition. David Owen, the leader of the SDP, who expressly stated that he wanted the miners to lose and who throughout exhibited his conservative attitudes in general, said on May 17 that

> once again we should be going on holiday without having had a debate on the miners dispute. In view of the fact that the Opposition, who control totally the opportunities for debate, have not seen fit to allow a debate, will the Leader of the House give a promise to those of us, on both sides of the House I think, who feel that there should be a debate that he will initiate a debate in Government time immediately after the holiday if the Leader of the Opposition has not plucked up enough courage to have a debate?[28]

Earlier in the same day Kinnock had asked for debates on the effect of the abolition of the GLC on the Arts; on the European Community; and on the New Ireland Forum: all important subjects but none as central for British politics as the miners' strike. It was, as noted earlier, the fears about the issues of violence and the national ballot that paralysed the Labour leadership. They believed that these were significant vote-gatherers for the Tories and that the way to remain in a reasonable position in the public opinion polls was to ignore the issues as far as that was possible, and to take up a traditional law-and-order attitude when these matters could not be side-stepped. Kinnock very early in the strike, made a statement that clearly exhibited his political nervousness:

> Will the Prime Minister understand once and for all that I condemn, and always have condemned, violence in pursuit of industrial disputes, even when it occurs among people who feel impotent in the face of the destruction of their jobs, their industry and their communities?

That was on March 13th 1984. On the 5th April Kinnock replied to a statement by Eldon Griffiths, spokesman for the Police Federation, and one of the large band of thorough-going reactionaries in this Parliament, in respect not of the miners' strike but concerning a different matter: 'The honourable gentleman' Kinnock said 'stated that I made an attack upon the police. That has never been true, is not true, and never will be true. . .'[29] When a debate was initiated on policing and civil liberties in the miners strike it came from a Labour back bencher who obtained it under Standing Order No 10, the usual way backbenchers attempt to get a discussion of urgent matters. The debate opened with Allen McKay, the Barnsley West MP, making a moderate speech which was largely an attack on policing methods. The Home Secretary replied, concentrating mainly on picket violence, and he was followed by Gerald Kaufman, the shadow Home Secretary who supported the right of people to work during a strike and who agreed that they were entitled to police protection: 'We know that in Nottinghamshire in recent weeks the presence of the police has often been welcomed by local residents. This is my response to the Right Honourable and learned Gentleman's challenge to me. Will he join me in condemning any excesses by the police?' Neil Kinnock was not present at this debate.[30]

31 July 1984 was Opposition Day in the House of Commons: when the Opposition chose the subject of the main debate. The miners' strike had now lasted twenty-one weeks: it filled the newspapers and the TV screens and since Parliament was to adjourn the next day for over two and a half months—to reassemble on Monday 22 October—it might have been thought it would be politically appropriate for the Opposition to lead a debate on the miners' strike in general, or on civil liberties and the strike—a matter which was causing much public concern—or on the need for a comprehensive energy policy and the place of coal in that policy. Instead, Kinnock avoided what the Labour leadership still regarded as potentially very damaging to their political image, as reflected in the opinion polls, and settled for a long resolution condemning the general economic, industrial and employment policies of the Thatcher government; and in his opening speech Kinnock made only a brief reference to the miners' strike towards the end of what he said. It was a poor speech by the not very high standards of this Parliament, and it was followed by Thatcher who taunted Kinnock with his silence on the issues of the ballot and mass picketing and who talked at some length about 'uneconomic' pits. The rest of the Labour members who spoke—including Michael Foot and Benn—concentrated entirely upon the miners' strike, as did most of the few Tories who intervened. But no Labour speaker discussed the misleading accounts of the NCB and it was Enoch Powell who referred to the 'crucial failure of management in the industry that set the train of events on foot'.[31] Hattersley summed up for Labour in a speech that inevitably had to relate to the general terms of the resolution. He began with a well-constructed attack on Thatcher, and certainly made a better speech than Kinnock; but once more the crucial issues of the strike were not debated. The Chancellor of the Exchequer concluded for the Government, and on the next day the House went on holiday for nearly three months.

*   *   *   *   *

It was violence on the picket lines that most inhibited the Labour leadership and determined that the strike should not be central to their Parliamentary strategy and performances. There was a great deal written about the violence in the miners' strike throughout the whole year and there was a good deal of discussion, and evidence, of police provocation. But just as the Labour leaders could not understand the gross distortions in the NCB accounts, with the result that they had no substantial answer to the 'uneconomic pits' argument, so they took the violence on the pickets as the media presented it. The Labour movement outside Westminster, or many parts of it, were acutely aware of police provocation, and police violence, and there were many protests, in the Labour and Liberal press, and from the back-benchers in the Commons.[32] But without the authority, and the persistent statement of that authority, coming from the Labour Front bench the impact upon public opinion at large was noticeably marginal. In the months that have followed the ending of the strike the evidence of police action has accumulated, and in no incident has there been more revealing detail made public than in the case of the supposed riot at Orgreave: a day of violence which probably more than any other single incident convinced large sections of British opinion that the miners were guilty of mindless violence. It is now (mid August 1985) known to be quite untrue, and a fabrication of the police supported by the mendacious media.

Towards the end of May 1984 convoys of coke from Orgreave—a coking plant—began to move to the steel works at Scunthorpe. On the 29 May there was a mass picket of some 7,000 and a large number of arrests. On the next day Arthur Scargill was arrested on the early morning picket. The pickets continued and then, on the 18 June there occurred one of the classic police 'riots' in modern British history. It was, as already noted, not seen as such at the time, and Orgreave became a synomyn for violence on the picket line.

The trial of most of those arrested at Orgreave began in mid-May 1985; by the end of June the prosecution case was crumbling fast. What really happened at Orgreave was revealed in great detail during the 48 days of the trial and summarised in an impressive article in the *Guardian* on August 12th 1985 by Gareth Peirce, a solicitor who acted for a group of the defendants. The day began with men arriving from 6 a.m. on for the picket. They were escorted by the police to an open field. They stood around in the sun 'talking and laughing. And when the coke lorries arrive, you see a brief, good humoured, and expected push against the police lines; it lasts for 38 seconds only'.

These words were written by Gareth Peirce and she was describing incidents in the key exhibit in the trial: video film made by the police themselves and shot from behind the police lines. The film was not put in as evidence by the prosecution; it was a demand from the defence. The police had surrounded the pickets in the large field. There were battalions of police in riot uniform, some with short shields, some with long. Further away were large numbers of mounted police and in another place, police with dogs. Then the police riot began. The long shield groups opened their ranks and the mounted police galloped through. There were repeated cavalry charges followed by attacks from the riot police on foot. It lasted for three hours. As the senior police officer at Orgreave had stated before June 18th, if there was to be a battle, he wanted it 'on my own ground and on my own terms'. And this is what he achieved. Some missiles were thrown at the police, after the police had attacked, and about noon on that day defensive barriers began to be erected against further police onslaughts:

> You hear on the soundtrack 'bodies not heads' shouted by one senior officer, and then see junior officers rush out and hit heads as well as bodies. . .
>
> One senior officer, who said that it was the first time he had seen horsemen riding at people with batons drawn, was asked at the trial whether people might throw missiles out of terror to repel attacks by mounted officers, he said, 'No, that never occurred to me'. Another officer conceded that the purpose of the horses and the short-shield officers was to terrify; if miners did not disperse when they were run at by the police, then they were eligible for arrest. This was the view of the law expressed by the last junior officer to give evidence before the riot trial was finally jettisoned by the prosecution.

But this was not how events of this day were seen on TV screens that same night. The TV news—which Channel was not specified by Gareth Peirce—'reversed the order of the footage available to show men throwing missiles and then police charging. . .' and this was the line pursued by the police witnesses at the trial, completely contrary to the clear evidence of their own film. Orgreave, let it be said again, has remained in public memory as an especially violent example of the miners' violence on the picket line.

The account of Orgreave by Gareth Peirce has begun to be documented from other sources: a year after it happened. The evening of the day that the *Guardian* published Ms Peirce's article Gerald Kaufman, the Shadow Home Secretary, asked Leon Brittan to make available the police film of Orgreave. But why did the Opposition spokesman on these matters have to wait for Gareth Peirce to publish her article? Kaufman said he was deeply disturbed by the revelations in her article, but why was he not disturbed very much earlier? Or are his sources of information so meagre that this was the first time he had learned of the provocation and brutality at Orgreave? Either way, whether he knew or whether he was in ignorance, it reflects very sadly on the Labour leadership, and confirms their miserable record on policing and civil liberties.

*   *   *   *   *

The conduct of the Parliamentary Labour Party during the miners strike can only be described as unprincipled, and lacking, not only in integrity, but in plain commonsense. The strike was a provocation; that was widely said in the Commons by speakers from the Labour side; and it lasted a year. The Labour Party in Parliament were given the opportunity to begin a serious educational campaign to explain the politics of Thatcherism in the context of the miners' strike. Of course to do this they needed a comprehensive energy policy, which they had not got; they would be required to understand how the NCB and the Government were falsifying the annual accounts of the coal industry, and this was not appreciated because someone or some group within the Labour Party apparatus had not recognised the problem; and third, it would have required political courage to withstand the lying propaganda of most of the media, and the Labour leadership were regrettably short of courage. But it could have been done, as the GLC leadership showed for most of their period of office. A major opportunity has been lost, both in the matter of the viability of a nationalised industry and in the difficult questions of policing and civil liberties. This last is especially important, for the course of the miners' strike witnessed a steady accumulation of arbitrary powers by the police. Much has been learned from the experience of Northern Ireland; the training manual prepared by the Chief Constables and entitled Public Order, Tactical Options is a guideline for para-military operations;[33] and during the year's strike the police were in effect allowed by the courts to re-write the law. 'If' says Gareth Peirce 'they encounter a situation in which they wish to disregard the law, they no longer feel inhibited from doing so'. The Labour Party allowed these things to happen without effective protest on their part; and to bring the police once again under popular control in the future is therefore made much more difficult. Moreover, it is a mistake in our kind of society, with our traditions, to categorise bodies such as the police as a single reactionary mass; and by failing to sustain a continuous criticism of police actions, the Labour leadership signally failed to support the liberal or less reactionary minorities within the police forces themselves. The momentum therefore remains with the hard-line reactionaries, of whom there are many.

The courts during the miners' strike followed the general line of Government policy, and they invented new sets of rules which caused a remarkable extension of the civil common law—that is, law made by the judges and not by Parliament.[34] The new interpretations, and the judgments handed down, were always against the miners and their unions; and the courts thereby continued their long tradition of hostility to the popular organisations of ordinary people. In times of social peace the issues do not arise, but in crisis—an upsurge of trade union activity on a large scale, as in the 1890s, or the run-up to the General Strike of 1926 and the Strike itself, or the 1984–5 miners' strike, the Courts can always be expected to do their duty to the propertied interests the preservation of which provide the inarticulate major premiss in their judicial analysis and thinking. We live in a period when the world system of capitalism is experiencing serious difficulties; when even in affluent societies such as Britain the social and political conflicts between classes are sharpening; and when the most reactionary British government in the 20th century has set in train a swingeing attack upon welfare facilities, civil rights and trade union organisation. The problem for the Labour leaders is that they were brought up to believe that consensus was for ever, and they are not well equipped, or not equipped at all, for the harsher times that lie before us. If their attitudes during the miners' strike are repeated in the future, then political democracy, and democratic rights and procedures, are in serious danger.

NOTES

1. *A State of Siege* (eds. J. Coulter, S. Miller and M. Walker, Canary Press, 1984), pp. 4–15.
2. C. Jones and T. Novak, 'Welfare Against the Workers. Benefits as a Political Weapon', in H. Beynon (ed.), *Digging Deeper. Issues in the Miners Strike* (Verso, 1984), pp. 87–100. See also the comments by Stan Orme, *Hansard*, 5th Ser. Vol. 982, Cols. 1064–1069 (15 April 1980).
3. Patrick Jenkin in *ibid.*, Col. 1053.
4. The recent discussions on the labour process have shown how certain groups of workers have manipulated their working conditions somewhat to their advantage. For an example of the recent writing on these matters, Frank Wilkinson (ed.), *The Dynamics of Labour Market Segmentation* (Academic Press, 1981).
5. The detailed history of judicial prejudice has not yet been written. For recent writings on the subject, J.A.G. Griffith, *The Politics of the Judiciary* (Fontana, 1981); P. Hain, *Political Trials in Britain* (Penguin, 1984).
6. Most of the details of Scargill's career, and the internal history of the NUM in the 1970s, are taken from M. Crick, *Scargill and the Miners* (Penguin, 2nd ed., 1985).
7. The most useful compendium on the background to the miners' strike is H. Beynon (ed.), *Digging Deeper* (1984).
8. For details of the Energy Establishment, C. Sweet, 'Why Coal is Under Attack: Nuclear Powers in the Energy Establishment' in H. Beynon (ed.), *Digging Deeper*, pp. 201–216.
9. M. Crick, *Scargill and the Miners*, Ch. 6.
10. Cf. the *Sunday Times*, 20 May 1984: 'There are good reasons for thinking that the timing of the dispute, and the choice of battleground on which it has been fought, was deliberately engineered by the Government so that it could take place on the Government's terms.'
11. Rules 41 and 43 are printed in full in an Appendix to M. Crick, *Scargill and the Miners*, pp. 161–2.
12. Before the establishment of modern police forces, in the 1830s, the Home Secretary always co-ordinated and controlled the military who were regularly used in riotous situations; and in critical domestic situations the Home Secretary has continued to act in a co-ordinating capacity until the present day.
13. The most useful account of the National Reporting Centre is in an article of that title by Martin Kettle, in *Policing the Miners' Strike* (eds. B. Fine and

R. Millar, Lawrence and Wishart, 1985), pp. 23–33.

14. For McGregor's record as a union-buster in the United States, D. Reed and O. Adamson, *Miners Against the Strike 1984–1985. People versus State* (Larkin Publications, 1985), pp. 100–106; *Morning Star*, 7 February 1985.

15. It would be politically very important to have a complete record of the NUR's actions during the strike, as well as those of other unions. There were some areas of the NUR who adhered to the traditions of solidarity. Cf. the statement by Roy Butlin, secretary of the Coalville (Leicestershire) NUR branch, quoted in A. Callinicos and M. Simmons, *The Great Strike. The Miners Strike of 1984–5 and Its Lessons* (Socialist Worker, 1985), p. 121: 'My members at Coalville have not moved any coal by rail in the Leicestershire coalfield for 35 weeks. There were times in the long summer months when we seemed to be the only trade unionists doing anything. We're in the middle of a working coalfield, but we've been holding back half the production from Leicestershire. Virtually every pub and Club [in Coalville] has barred us. Of the 19 Labour councillors, 13 are scabs and two are the wives of scabs'. Butlin was speaking in December 1984.

16. Reed and Adamson, *Miners Strike 1984–1985*, pp. 44–5, 53–4.

17. The matter was widely discussed in the press during the years' strike, and after. See for an example, *Guardian*, 29 July 1985.

18. There were exceptions, but the generalisation as a whole was, unfortunately, to stand.

19. P.S. Bagwell, *The Railwaymen* (Allen and Unwin, 1963), pp. 392–5.

20. H. Francis and D. Smith, *The Fed: a history of the South Wales Miners in the twentieth century* (Lawrence and Wishart, 1980), esp. Ch. 1.

21. The article was due to be published in the December 1984 issue of *Accountancy*, but the NCB intervened: *Guardian*, 28 November 1984.

22. Andrew Glyn, *The Economic Case Against Pit Closures* (NUM, Sheffield, 1984), 25p; p. 6.

23. 'The conclusion must be that the Government cannot be said to be subsidising the production of coal. Sales of coal, even in the present depressed conditions, are practically enough to pay the miners and for the other inputs actually used to produce the coal including a proper level of depreciation. The general state of the industry's finances cannot be used to justify in any way the NCB's pit closures programme', Glyn, *Economic Case*, p. 3.

24. Emile Woolf, 'Digging holes in the NCB's accounts', *Guardian*, 10 July 1985.

25. A. Glyn, *Economic Aspects of the Coal Dispute*, quoted in G. Kerevan and R. Saville, *The Economic Case for Deep-Mined Coal in Scotland* (NUM, Scotland, 1985), p. 23.

26. See note 21 above.

27. 'That mine [Cortonwood] would, at least in 1981/2, have contributed between £2.49 and £5.45 per tonne to NCB operating performance (on 1984 assumptions'): T. Berry, T. Capps, D. Cooper, T. Hopper and T. Lowe, 'NCB Accounts —a mine of misinformation?' *Accountancy*, January 1985, pp. 10–12.

28. Hansard, 5th Ser. Vol. 982, Col. 507 (17 May).

29. *Ibid.*, Col. 1109 (5 April).

30. *Ibid.*

31. *Ibid.*, Cols. 287–9 (31 July).

32. The *Guardian* throughout the miners strike published numerous letters alleging police violence; as did the left wing press. There are many references to police harassment and violence in the various chapters in Fine and Millar, *Policing the Miners' Strike*.

33. The manual is discussed in the *Guardian* article by Gareth Peirce; and will undoubtedly feature prominently in the future debates in the Commons. Some

extracts are given in the *Observer*, 21 July 1985.

34. See the articles by Nick Blake and Louise Christian in Fine and Walker, *Policing the Miners' Strike*.

July–August 1985

REFLECTIONS ON THE MINING STRIKE

Richard Hyman

Judgments on the course and implications of the miners' struggle should not come easily. For some on the left, no doubt, the 'lessons' of the dispute were to hand, pre-packaged, almost from the outset: predictable derivations of a more general political 'line'. Yet major historical events rarely mesh precisely with prior analyses and formulae. Often they call for difficult, even painful, revisions of our preconceptions.

No socialist can fail to acclaim the courage, determination and resourcefulness of the women and men in coalfields across Britain in the year-long fight to defend their jobs and communities. Endurance on this scale is without historical parallel. The odds ranged against the miners were likewise unprecedented: an arrogant and vindictive government; a paramilitary police force established by stealth and unaccountable for its often brutal conduct; a judicial system systematically hostile to the strikers and their union; agencies of public 'welfare' thoroughly subordinated to the repressive purposes of the state; press and television largely dedicated to distortion and abuse. After the retreats and demoralisation of the first five years of Thatcherism, sustained resistance against such obstacles and such deprivations offered an inspiration which—even in defeat—has enriched us all.

But celebration alone is not enough. For all the brave initial denials, the outcome was a crushing defeat, mitigated only partially by the positive and perhaps enduring achievements of those twelve months in transforming social relations in the striking communities and the broad movements of support. To come to terms with the sources and significance of this defeat we must move beyond uncritical applause. At the same time, little is learned if our assessment rests merely on simplistic charges of external betrayal. The contribution of the TUC and Labour Party leadership was at best inadequate; but who expected otherwise? Unless we focus critically on the conduct of the strike itself we may serve the myth-makers, but do not assist those centrally involved in the strike who, being human, cannot claim infallibility.

And yet. . . How can an outsider in the comfort of academic security venture any criticism of the strategies and tactics of comrades who struggled with such amazing fortitude against the harsh challenge to their whole social existence? And what insights can in any case be offered from the sidelines, when so many of the combatants themselves have by now debated at length the key issues arising from the conduct of the strike? Now that the myriad tendencies and factions have defined their several contributions to the long post-mortem, is anything new to be said; and if so, can it expect a hearing?

If 'scientific socialism' is more than a vacuous slogan it entails a critical understanding of the articulations between concrete and abstract, particular and general. Most analysis to date has involved argument, often polemical, around immediate tactical questions. How far can such debates be linked to broader and more persistent problems of relevance to socialists? If the post-strike assessment is to involve more than a private settling of accounts within the coalfields and the NUM, with outsiders acting merely as partisans or spectators, some generalisation beyond the specific points of contention in the strike's aftermath must be attempted.

First, though, to survey the main areas of immediate controversy. Three questions clearly predominate: the avoidance of a ballot; mass picketing and the role of 'violence'; and the character and objectives of the dispute as a whole. Some of the arguments were raised at the very outset of the conflict; others surfaced in the summer of 1984, often in coded form, as it became evident that the prospects of victory were receding and the miners were in danger of debilitating isolation; many more were voiced publicly only with the return to work. Underlying this process was the gradual and incomplete exposure of a hidden agenda of political division, only partially related to the dispute, within the NUM left. However naive the attempt, it seems worth reconsidering these controversies as issues of importance in their own right, before addressing an alternative set of underlying problems.

        *   *   *   *   *

'It has been like a monkey on our backs. Everywhere we've gone we've had to answer the question of the ballot: not the strike and the issue of jobs and nuclear power—the ballot.'[1] Its overpowering symbolism haunted the controversies within the union itself, in the broader labour movement, and among 'public opinion' more generally. The refusal to hold a national ballot provided the central rationale or pretext of those sections of the NUM who rejected all calls to join the strike, of workers in other industries reluctant to offer support, and of hostile politicians and commentators. Conversely, among strike activists, 'the ballot developed into a sort of virility symbol'.[2] Those not on strike had no right to vote other miners out of their jobs; those infected with the disease of 'ballotitis' were clearly hostile, or at best half-hearted, towards the strike; to refuse 'to be constitutionalised out of a defence of our jobs'[3] was the one worthwhile test of commitment to the defence of the industry.

The manoeuvres which avoided a ballot at the NUM Executive in April 1984, and the confirmation of its rejection at the subsequent Special Conference, can be readily understood in the light of the experience of the previous two years. In January 1982 the press, abetted by retiring President Joe Gormley, had conducted an intensive campaign against a national strike over pay. The outcome—only a month after Arthur Scargill's personal electoral triumph—was a 55 per cent vote against a stoppage. In October the same year, over 60 per cent opposed a strike when the two issues of the new pay claim and resistance to pit closures were linked. The result was the same in March 1983, when South Wales called for national backing in opposing the closure of Tymawr Lewis Merthyr colliery. Even before this triple rebuff, there was a view on the left that a national ballot on the issue was futile: 'those with jobs were not keen to jeopardise them while those who had experienced closures in the past resented being called on to strike for pits which had not supported them when their pits were closed'.[4] The ballots of 1982-3 reinforced the view that areas not directly threatened by closure should have no veto over action by those that were. Hence the strategy of co-ordinated local action under NUM rule 41, rather than formal national action under rule 43.

Yet the earlier defeats compounded the hazards of such a course of action. Union democracy was made a major—perhaps *the* major—issue, for it could be suggested that the national leadership was out of step with the majority of the membership and desperate to avoid putting their representativeness to the test. Given the Executive's willingness to organise the earlier polls, the belated discovery of a principled objection to balloting over 'other men's jobs' smacked of opportunism. The decision in October 1983 to call a national overtime ban over wages—avoiding the need for a strike ballot—could be seen even by sympathetic observers as a manipulative tactic,[5] anticipating the use of the Presidential authority in April 1984 to rule out of order the call for a national vote. Of course the Gormley era had seen even greater deviousness on the part of the NUM leadership; but the left professes higher standards. In appearing anxious to escape the control of the majority of the membership, the NUM leadership exposed their own legitimacy to predictable challenge. How effective a challenge became only too clear as the strike proceeded.

Ironically, a major source of the whole problem was that strike activists agreed with their opponents in treating the ballot issue as a matter of principle. Both sides endorsed the simple equation: to oppose the strike is to support the ballot; to support the strike is to oppose the ballot. A national vote was demanded by enemies of the strike, and for that very reason should be resisted. 'Putting a minus where the bourgeois puts a plus': an understandable reaction, examples of which can be found throughout the history of the socialist movement; but often tactically disastrous.

True, those within the NUM who demanded a ballot *were* against the strike. And those outside the union who took up the call were typically concerned to discredit the striking miners or at least their national leaders. For such critics, balloting and democracy could be presented as synonymous. Thus the provocative interventions of Jimmy Reid[6] not only personalised NUM policy under the label of 'Scargillism' (thus ignoring the powerful rank-and-file basis for the leadership position on all contentious questions) but also rested on a fetishism of the individual ballot as the expression of 'institutions and traditions of representative parliamentary democracy'. Such homilies were scarcely calculated to impress striking miners, whose whole struggle was directed against the anti-social policies of a government whose arrogance is sustained by the workings of 'representative parliamentary democracy'. Nor should it be necessary in any forum of the left to rehearse at length the argument that the ballot-box is not the be-all and end-all of trade union democracy. Not primarily because of the machinations of the Tory press: Fleet Street poison did not prevent Scargill's record majority in his election as NUM President; and in any event, if socialists cannot combat the influence of the media then we may all as well abandon the struggle. Far more fundamentally: an essential principle of trade unionism is the *active* involvement of members in *collective* discussion and decision-making, with the maintenance of internal relationships through which leaders can be *continuously* accountable to those they represent.[7] In itself, the individual ballot is an inferior procedure which privatises decision-making: a passive, formalistic and episodic mechanism which provides no real basis for positive membership control.[8]

Yet it is evident that in practice the internal procedures of most trade unions fall far short of the ideal of active collective initiative. The enthusiasm for the ballot-box expressed in similar terms by Reid and Thatcher exerts considerable popular appeal, because it appears to offer a simple solution to what are genuine problems of trade union democracy. The alienation of so many trade unionists from their own unions, which they perceive as distant, bureaucratic and unresponsive structures, creates the ingredients for the appeal of Tory populism. If members want the opportunity to ballot, leaders and activists disregard this at their peril.

In the case of the NUM, moreover, 'ballotitis' has far deeper roots. Among workers for whom social existence outside work was so often an extension and complement to collective relations in the mine itself, the pithead ballot was as much a public as a private act. The complex inter-play of individual judgment and mutual dependence which underlay the labour process at the coalface surely contributed to the traditional emphasis on balloting before commencing—and often ending—large-scale strike action. Within the county associations which established the Miners' Federation a century ago, 'policy decisions had to be confirmed on a wide range of questions by lodge ballots'. Their historian explained that 'the rules of the miners' unions and indeed their whole conception of democratic procedure laid it down that before a strike was called there must be a ballot vote of all union members'. In 1915, moreover, the miners' leaders sought to prescribe that the Triple Alliance should require a two-thirds majority in a ballot of affiliated unions before calling a joint strike: this in a body which represented, in the eyes of so many of the ruling class, a vehicle for insurrection.[9] 'The traditions of all the dead generations. . .' Of course times have changed. Social relations both above and below ground have altered dramatically. The redundancy payment scheme directed at older miners has transformed the age structure of the labour force, half of whom were not directly involved in the stoppages of the early 1970s and doubtless care little for the practices of former decades. Yet as revolutionaries half a century ago discovered, 'trade union legalism' can exert a powerful influence which it is hazardous to disregard'.[10] One may view with cynicism the motives of some of those who appealed so vociferously to the sanctity of rule 43; but there is little reason to question the sincerity of many who demanded that the NUM leaders, directing what was in all but name a national strike, should observe the provisions of their own rulebook.

Could a ballot have succeeded; and if so, would the minority have accepted the verdict and joined the strike? We can only speculate. Pointing to the evidence of five opinion polls among miners, all of them showing substantial majority support for the struggle, Crick concludes that 'the ironic thing is that had the NUM held a national ballot in the first few months of the strike, the Left would almost certainly have won it'.[11] At the time the polls were viewed with some scepticism by activists, the more paranoid regarding them as a conspiracy to tempt the NUM into a ballot defeat. Certainly there is a difference between expressing an opinion to a pollster, and participating in a decision which will actually determine policy. Yet the achievement of NACODS in September in winning over 80 per cent backing for a strike reinforces the evidence that a campaign by the NUM could have succeeded. Timing would clearly have been important. An assessment written in the first weeks of the strike stressed the need for time to overcome initial doubts and hesitation: 'just as Mrs Thatcher chose to her own advantage when to have a General Election. . ., so the NUM may best be served by delaying its national ballot over strike action, as support builds up and gains a momentum of its own on the basis of campaigning in the interim'.[12] The April Conference, with its amendment to rule requiring a simple majority for a national strike, could have been central to such a campaign. Instead it took the fateful decision against any ballot.

A successful ballot campaign could have been a potent symbol of legitimacy, not only in presenting the union's case to the world outside, but also in its internal relations. To refuse a national ballot on the grounds that it might be lost was to concede, in effect, that many of those actually on strike participated unwillingly. It also enabled 'working miners' to deny the charge of blacklegging: in the absence of a duly constituted national stoppage they were observing the local democratic decision not to participate in other areas' disputes. Had a ballot majority destroyed this argument, would miners in areas like Nottinghamshire have scabbed regardless? Nobody knows; but it would have been immensely easier for strike supporters at branch and district level to win the argument. An account of the strike which applauds the leadership decision on this issue provides unwitting evidence for the contrary view: 'in most Nottingham-shire pits, those working felt they were scabbing but they also thought it would only last a few weeks until a national ballot either brought them out or ended the strike in Yorkshire'.[13] In other words: a national strike vote would have removed all ambiguity as to the status of the dispute in the Midlands coalfields, allowing a clear appeal not only to the demands of solidarity but also to the verdict of the union's own constitutional machinery. It was this essentially *pragmatic* rationale which was rejected out of hand by those who made opposition to a ballot a spurious question of principle.

*   *   *   *   *

The same reflex reaction of turning on their head all arguments of right-wing politicians and their media supporters—in effect allowing the enemies of the NUM to determine its policies in reverse—seemed to condition approaches to picketing. Again, principle and pragmatism interacted in ways which were perplexing and almost certainly damaging.

The miners' struggles against the Heath government created two contrasting images of picketing. One was of a lone NUM picket holding a placard at a railway bridge: a symbolic barrier which the drivers on the line below refused to cross. The other was the closure of the Saltley coke depot, when 10,000 Birmingham engineers marched to reinforce the miners picket line. The latter brought Arthur Scargill to national prominence; and arguably, it was a mythologised vision of the 'Battle of Saltley Gates' which inspired the emphasis on mass picketing in 1984. Picketing can assume many forms.[14] It can aim to encourage existing workers to join a strike, or prevent the use of substitute labour; to stop the entry of components and raw materials or the removal of finished products. It can take place at the site of a strike, an associated workplace, or a 'third party' more distantly related to the dispute. It can be a symbolic gesture, a means of 'peaceful persuasion', or a more forceful method of barring movement. The co-ordinated deployment of mobile mass pickets had been a key tactic of Yorkshire activists in the unofficial struggles of

1969 and 1970 and the subsequent official national action: 'we launched from the coalfield here squads of cars, minibuses and buses, all directed onto predetermined targets, with five, six, seven hundred miners at a time'.[15] In 1984, many must have hoped for an action replay.

Such hopes were illusory for three main reasons. Firstly, the miners' triumph at Saltley was for the police a trauma which they spent a dozen years preparing to exorcise.[16] In 1984 the new *de facto* national police force took the class war seriously: to the miners' numerical presence they responded with even greater numbers and far superior hardware, together with trained battle-readiness. At Orgreave the miners looked for a repeat of Saltley, while the police were committed to have a very different outcome. The consequence was a series of mediaeval engagements in which the miners were first physically trounced and then subjected to an ideological battering with the aid of selective newsreel footage.

Of course the media image of 'picket line violence' did involve grave exaggeration and distortion. An early assessment in the *New Statesman* described 80 per cent of picket lines as 'orderly, if brusque'.[17] In the majority of cases only small bodies of pickets participated.[18] And in the few occasions when mass picketing erupted into violent clashes, the explanation—discreetly ignored by the media—was typically provocation or brutality on the part of police and working miners.

Nevertheless the question remains: were such episodes, and their treatment in the media, a predictable consequence of the strategy of mass picketing? And if so, does this cast doubt on the advisability of such a strategy? The nature and function of a mass picket are at best ambiguous. Viewed most charitably, the numbers may be a gesture of collective solidarity and commitment, a moral support for those spokesmen who seek to persuade another group of workers (drivers, non-strikers) from crossing the line. But the latter, confronted by the sheer weight of numbers, may feel themselves subject to intimidation rather than peaceful persuasion; and indeed, many participants in a mass picket may take it for granted that if reasoned argument fails, the veto of force is the logical alternative. The mass picket can thus constitute a seductive short cut to convincing fellow-workers of the merits of the strikers' case. And built into the social dynamics of picketing in force can be an escalation of abuse and violence; a process which baton-happy police may intensify but do not necessarily initiate.

There can be little doubt that the early picket-line confrontations turned the divisions between Yorkshire and Nottinghamshire into an unbridgeable chasm; just as the later clashes at Ravenscraig destroyed any vestigial possibility of unity between miners and steelworkers. Much more generally, mass picketing allowed the *methods* of the strikers to overwhelm their *objectives*. It does not require a deep study of media sociology to realise that picketing aggro will prove more newsworthy than pit closures—even without a government anxious to mould the terms of the debate. 'The Government may fear the industrial power of the miners, but it calculates that so long as the issue can be displaced from the industrial sphere into the political sphere, it can be treated as a problem of law and order—the defence of the right to work against mob picket violence—and all the powers of the authoritarian populist consensus can then be enlisted on the Government's side. The public can be rallied much more easily in defence of the social order than in defence of the market order.'[19] It is important to stress that the evolution of the conflict scarcely required active state initiatives in news management: 'both the image and the reality of worker against worker have been given to the government on a plate'.[20] The paradox of the mass picket is that what is superficially a symbol of strength and unity can become in practice a force for impotence and division.

*   *   *   *   *

'To save pits and jobs, and to stimulate and revive Britain's battered economy, the NUM calls for the expansion of our industry in line with the Plan for Coal objective of up to 200m tonnes output per year. . . The miners have no choice but to oppose pit closure plans. Alongside workers in all of Britain's once-proud basic and manufacturing industries, we will fight—not just for ourselves and our families, but for the entire nation—and the future.'[21] In one sense, the objectives of the strike were clearly defined. In another, they were deeply ambiguous and remained so throughout the dispute. The NUM demanded a radical revision of production targets, in line with the most favourable of the scenarios envisaged in the 1974 Plan for Coal; a massive programme of investment in coal-getting and coal-using facilities; and an end to all pit closures on economic grounds. But to what extent did these demands represent maximum aspirations, the agenda for a long-term propaganda campaign; or bargaining objectives which might, as negotiations proceeded and the balance of forces became clearer, be modified and diluted; or an irreducible minimum on which no compromise could be contemplated? To approach this question from another direction: what would have counted as victory for the miners? A reprieve for Cortonwood, Polmaise, Herrington, Bullcliffe Wood and Snowdown? The withdrawal of the 6 March proposals? Guarantees against future cutbacks? Commitment to expansion? MacGregor's dismissal? Thatcher's resignation? No union engaged in struggle can afford to spell out its 'bottom line'; but in this dispute the limits of what was acceptable, as opposed to ideally desirable, remained more than ordinarily obscure. And this almost certainly obstructed the NUM in presenting its case to a wider audience.

Opposition to pit closures was itself open to a variety of interpretations.

'Economic' justifications for closure could be rejected on principle; or it could be argued that, empirically, the economic evidence did not support a closure programme. 'Opposition' could mean, minimally, a refusal to agree to closures; more actively, campaigning to keep pits open; support for pit-by-pit resistance; or an all-out stoppage.

'No pit closures unless through exhaustion' was a major demand in the revived radicalism in the NUM in 1970,[22] and conference commitment to this policy was achieved in 1972. But throughout the 1970s the union continued to acquiesce in such closures. Initially at least, this was in the context of the expectation of overall expansion set out in 1974.[23] Circumstances were transformed by three developments apparent in the latter 1970s but more starkly highlighted under Thatcher. The first was the escalating level of unemployment and the associated collapse of traditional industries in which energy use was high; the twin consequences were a slump in demand for coal and the elimination of alternative job opportunities in many mining areas. Secondly, world trade in coal became more competitive; and the pursuit of a 'strong pound' in the early Thatcher years created a price advantage for imported coal. Thirdly, the NCB's goal of concentrating production in new 'super-pits' employing advanced technology implied that even substantially increased output in the 1990s would be no guarantee against serious job loss.

The issue of pit closures was thus increasingly explosive as the 1980s approached; and the Thatcher government lit the fuse. The Ridley report of 1978, and the Coal Industry Act of 1980, prescribed that mining should conform to Tory norms of profitability. In February 1981 a wave of spontaneous strike action forced the NCB to withdraw its projected acceleration of closures—but only temporarily. The appointment of Ian MacGregor in 1983, after he had crushed the steel unions and slashed the labour force by half in only two years, signalled the approaching confrontation. The announcement of Cortonwood's closure, followed by the national plans to cut 20,000 jobs, proved that government and NCB were now ready for the clash.

Yet when provoked into a battle by the enemy, it is particularly important to define the terms of the struggle: certainly if the aim is to appeal for support to a wider public. So was the NUM objective merely to halt the *escalation* of a piecemeal programme of 'economic' closures which had been tolerated, though with individual instances of more forceful resistance, through the decade since the 'Plan for Coal'? Or to implement for the first time the union's long-standing policy, and veto such closures altogether?

Many of the pronouncements of the NUM leaders suggested that now, after the years of concession and compromise, the policy of 'no pit closures unless through exhaustion' would finally be enforced. A heroic stand, but was this in principle a winnable demand? In at least three respects, mobilisation of broad support was inhibited.

Firstly, in appearing to counterpose to 'MacGregor's butchery' the absolute principle of no economic closures the NUM encouraged the image of a clash of rival 'extremisms'. *Was* the union arguing that no pit should be closed while coal could still be raised without undue risk of life and limb, whatever the cost of its extraction? Seeming equivocation on this issue gave the government and the NCB a valuable propaganda advantage. Moreover it seems possible that opposition to economic closures as an abstract principle diverted the NUM from critical attention to the detail of the NCB's economic arguments. How far the limited success of the NUM in propagating its case should be blamed on media hostility or its own inadequate presentation is a matter of some controversy.[24] But certainly there seems to have been no serious effort to develop a critique of the NCB's economic analysis *before* the long-awaited attack in March 1984. Andrew Glyn's systematic critique was indeed published by the union,[25] but not until October 1984; and little sustained use seems to have been made of it. Other studies by sympathetic economists[26] received even less dissemination. Nor was the evidence by academic acountants that the Board was systematically distorting its figures[27] deployed with particular vigour. To confront the specific content of the NCB's economic rationale would of course risk conceding that in certain circumstances economic considerations could in principle justify closure. Even if—as Glyn argued—the economic evidence supported the continued operation of all the threatened pits, circumstances could alter. But given the need to mobilise popular support, the risk surely deserved to be taken.

The second problem in defining the *principle* of 'economic' closures as the central issue of the struggle is that this fails to encompass questions of no less fundamental importance. One is that jobs can be lost *without* pit closures, as a result of restructuring of production and technological innovation. 'Coal *and* Dole' could well represent the NCB's preferred scenario. Another is that pit closures may be viewed as an inevitable feature of an extractive industry, since exhaustion may occur or extreme geological difficulties make continued operation impossible. Yet this entails that 'economic' arguments will often concern, in effect, not *whether* but *when* a given pit shall close.[28] The announcement of Corton-wood's imminent closure provoked the explosion because its future had so recently been 'guaranteed' for the next five years. But this still implied its closure in 1990: on grounds, presumably, acceptable to the NUM.

In an eloquent survey of the dispute, Raphael Samuel argued that 'the coal strike, when its ethical issues are addressed, appears as the contest in which economics is assembled on one side, humanity and compassion on the other'.[29] Pit closures, he emphasised, must be assessed in terms of 'the waste of human resources, the undermining of cultural autonomy. . . the destruction of a whole heritage of non-transferable skills'. Moving from the individual effects to the social, 'the closure of "uneconomic" pits creates "uneconomic" communities'. These are arguments of crucial importance; on any humane criteria of social accounting, the NCB's 'hit list' of 'uneconomic' collieries is totally indefensible. And yet: what Samuel calls 'the hidden injuries of social change' are as real, and presumably as traumatic, when pits close through exhaustion or because operation is no longer possible within acceptable margins of safety. If the most fundamental issue is the social and economic viability of communities *above* the ground, overriding stress on the continued operation (at *any* cost?) of the pits underneath unduly restricts the terrain of argument. Greater emphasis on the social costs of closures—whatever their cause—and proposals for counteracting policies could have assisted a more broad-ly based social and political campaign.

This leads to the third issue: would any settlement of the strike short of the NUM's maximum objectives have been an acceptable outcome? And if so, was such an outcome attainable? And would a greater apparent readiness to pursue a negotiated settlement have assisted in winning support? 'No compromise' was clearly a powerful slogan among strike activists. The years of Gormley and his predecessors were seen as a time when the union was all too ready to meet the NCB at least half way though the members' interests required a more unyielding stance; Scargill personified a more resolute approach. Yet what George Woodcock once called the 'shoddy, shabby compromise' can stem from very different sets of motives. On the one hand it may reflect an overriding commitment to peaceful agreement as against militant struggle: an approach which in-evitably leads to the emasculation of any radical challenge to capitalist priorities. On the other hand, however, compromise may stem from a realistic assessment of the prevailing balance of forces: if the odds are un-favourable, half a loaf may be the best attainable result.

Resistance within the NUM to 'sell-outs' had its counterpart within the government and the NCB: those who insisted that the miners must suffer an unqualified and humiliating defeat. But 'traditional' members of the management team were willing to contemplate a negotiated settlement, and even within the government there was probably some support for compromise. While refusal to compromise—like the refusal to ballot—appeared to some as a question of principle, the very fact of participating in negotiations implied a preparedness to modify some elements in the NUM position. What might a negotiating strategy have entailed? In the light of the issues raised earlier and the actual agenda of the various sets of talks between NUM, NCB and intermediaries, four major items may be suggested. Firstly, a re-assessment of the grossly misleading accounting practices whereby the NCB defines pits as uneconomic. As already indicated, the NUM did little to expose the Board's vulnerability on this score. Secondly, a definition of the method whereby the social costs of a proposed closure could be set against the claimed economic savings. Because the union insisted on its absolute opposition to economic closures, the possibility of a case-by-case process of cost-benefit analysis was not systematically addressed. Thirdly, a radical revision of the wholly inadequate colliery review procedure. This was of course a major element among the demands pursued by NACODS in October 1984, though the NUM opposed such a course until the strike was nearing its end. Fourthly, the necessity for the NCB to provide resources for economic and social rehabilitation when pits are closed *for whatever reason*. While individual miners receive redundancy payments well above the average for industrial workers, the amount allocated by the NCB to meet social consequences of collective job loss is a derisory gesture. This is surely an urgent matter for trade union intervention.

To negotiate on these issues, however, implies acceptance that the NCB will indeed continue to close pits on 'economic' grounds—not necessarily by admitted right, but through simple superiority of power. Though precisely this tacit recognition of political reality underlay NUM actions in the preceding decade, in 1984 this position was expressly rejected. The consequence was that negotiations were dominated by face-saving efforts to maintain this principle intact: for example, by devoting major energy to identifying a 'third' category of pit closures located uneasily between 'economic' and 'exhaustion or safety'. Was this the best method of defending miners' interests? For some NUM leaders, perhaps, the negotiations were in any event conducted reluctantly as a response to external pressure, since any agreed outcome would inevitably involve compromise on the central rationale of the strike.

The content of a hypothetical negotiated settlement—as with all other speculative scenarios for the strike—must be subject to considerable argument. But by all accounts, what the NCB was willing to concede in June 1984 would have been far preferable to what the NUM strove in vain to achieve in February 1985. The agreement which for a time seemed likely after TUC involvement in September, followed shortly by the NACODS strike ballot, caused anguish in the columns of the *Economist*. Usually reliable sources suggest that Thatcher's fervent prayer was that Scargill would refuse; and so it was. A 'fudge' at that time would presumably have involved a (temporary) withdrawal of the five closures and the March document; a significantly strengthened review procedure; and agreement to discuss further the principles involved in the closure issue. Nothing, indeed, would have been firmly resolved—any more than had been by the miners' victory in 1981. But the NCB—and hence the government—would have been seen to have retreated substantially in the face of determined resistance. Both industrially and politically, the whole labour movement would have gained a massive boost. And miners would have resumed the guerilla struggle against closures with heightened morale.[30]

The 'all-or-nothing' approach which rejected such an outcome could reflect one of three possible assumptions. First, that a sufficiently determined movement of industrial resistance could force NCB and government into a complete reversal of policy. This gravely exaggerates the power of even a united NUM, and neglects the decisive changes since 1972 and 1974: a far more ruthless Tory government, a far more effective state apparatus. Second, that whatever the limitations of industrial struggle in a single industry, the miners' action would inspire a broader political movement which would overturn Thatcherism and create the environment for the NUM to achieve its objectives. Such a view totally misreads the political climate: in particular ignoring the degree of passive working-class assent to the government's economic project, in the absence of an alternative perceived as credible; and the obsessive refusal of the Labour Party leadership to support 'unconstitutional' challenges to the 'legitimate' government. The political resonance which the strike generated was in many respects remarkable; but apart from a relatively narrow constituency of committed support, the dominant response of sympathisers was charity rather than solidarity. The third possible assumption was that the struggle, even if defeated—and perhaps, *particularly* if defeated—would radicalise miners and inspire even more vigorous campaigns in the future. All the evidence supports the diametrically opposite viewpoint. Early in the strike, one writer commented that 'Mr MacGregor has long admitted that his task of running down the steel industry was made easier by the long strike that preceded it which robbed the steelworkers of their stomach for a fight. The government is hoping for a re-run'.[31] There can be no serious doubt that this has indeed occurred. Peter Jenkins predicted all too accurately, a few weeks before the return to work, that 'the reality at the end of the strike will be that the balance of power has shifted decisively from union to management. . . In the new circumstances the closure programme is likely to be more radical and more costly in jobs than the programme put forward at the beginning of the dispute last March'.[32]

In short: the policy of 'fighting to the finish' extended the sacrifice and deprivation of the strike to its anniversary; intensified the divisions within the union, turning thousands of strikers into reluctant blacklegs; encouraged the NCB and government into a new phase of intransigeance resulting in the return to work without a settlement. The aftermath has seen several hundred victimised strikers still unemployed; the acceptance by the NUM of precisely the same pay offer rejected in autumn 1983; and a mood of demoralisation which the continuing militant rhetoric of some NUM leaders cannot conceal. Management at area and pit level displays a ruthless assertiveness unknown since nationalisation: a new disciplinary approach to workers, the removal or restriction of many of the customary facilities for trade union representation. The attempt to claw back the concessions made to NACODS in the autumn (resisted with determination) is one sign of the transformed balance of power. Another—as Jenkins anticipated—is the announcement of far more drastic proposals for closures and job loss. Tory confidence after the humiliation of the NUM may well lead to yet more radical attacks on coal industry financing, quite possibly followed by the first steps towards privatisation.

*   *   *   *   *

I am aware that many of these arguments parallel what are by now familiar elements in a debate initiated within the 'Eurocommunist' tendency of the CPGB. For most protagonists in this controversy, however, there is presumably a hidden agenda rooted in fundamental divisions which transcend the specific issue of the coal strike. The outside observer is led to suspect that many of the conclusions drawn concerning ballots, picketing, or the public presentation of NUM objectives, derive from long-standing orientations towards a 'broad democratic alliance' rather than reflecting a distinctive analysis of the politics of trade union struggle.

To this extent, my own concern is distinctive: on the basis of the preceding discussion of NUM strategy and tactics, to address more general problems of trade union organisation and action. The analysis, it should be stressed, is exploratory and tentative. Three issues are considered: the tension between organisation and action at local or sectional level on the one hand, and national or class level on the other; the role of force in relation to consent; and the nature and significance of leadership in working-class movements. Though the theoretical status of each of these issues is clearly distinct, their practical implications intersect considerably.

It is commonly argued that the scope for democratic control in organisations or societies is inversely related to the size and heterogeneity of the constituency. The main themes of Michels' interpretation of mass working-class organisations—the existence of irresistible pressures towards oligarchic leadership and membership apathy—are widely accepted even by those who reject aspects of his argument.[33] Conversely, active participatory democracy is often considered to require, as an essential prerequisite, either close day-to-day interaction among members or else a strong sense of collective identity and cultural affinity. Hence Turner's hypothesis that effective internal democracy in trade unions is confined to organisations 'exclusive' in their membership composition.[34] Such arguments, as was notoriously the case with Michels, are often marked by an extreme fatalism. Yet even if 'iron laws' are rejected as simplistic and exaggerated, it is difficult to deny that such writings identify genuine *tendencies* within organisational politics: the more extensive and differentiated the interests encompassed within a unit of organisation, the less the likelihood of constituting a cohesive collective actor; hence the greater the obstacles to rank-and-file initiative, or even effective leadership accountability to the membership.

Yet the cohesion which stems from a common particularistic situation and interest is frequently the obverse face of sectionalism and parochialism. Internal unity founded on *differentiation* from the wider working class can well generate disunity and division in external relations. Moreover, what can be achieved through local or sectional struggle is constrained by the broader framework of productive relations; even militant particularism is politically accommodative.[35] Hence the traditional definition of the socialist objective as the integration and harmonisation of workers' diverse experiences and aspirations to form a united class struggle. Throughout the history of modern working-class organisation, then, can be seen a constant counterpoint between the goals of rank-and-file autonomy and self-activity, as against disciplined and cohesive mass action. Notions of 'democratic centralism' have at times been posed as the resolution of this contradiction; but their meaning in practice has never been clear.

The power of localism is a universal theme in accounts of mining trade unionism. 'Men herded together and hardened in the pits were made to feel the oneness of their interests, and they gave it full expression in a marvellous and very elaborate system of fraternities, mutual aid, solidarity and co-operation.[36] Collective organisation among miners has always been rooted in the organic cohesiveness of the colliery; formal trade unionism at the level of the whole coalfield and beyond has been a more artificial and hence more vulnerable construct. Without this potent local collectivism, mining unionism could not have displayed its amazing resilience; yet the divergence of local interests has been a constant obstacle to national unity. Throughout the history of trade unionism in the coalfields, failure to respect sufficiently the strength of local claims to self-determination has led to fractures and secessions. The NUM itself is only a partial transformation of the explicit federalism on which national organisation was based for over half a century before 1944. It remains, in Allen's words, 'a *de facto* federation of semi-autonomous county unions disguised as areas of a national union'.[37]

Patterns of struggle—despite dramatic instances of massive national confrontation—have for the most part reflected and reinforced a predominant localism. The exceptional level of strike activity in the 1940s and 1950s—at one point, mining accounted for three-quarters of all stoppages recorded in Britain—was the product of a multiplicity of small and usually short-lived actions, largely connected with the piecework payment system. Will Paynter, perhaps the major architect of the national day-wage system of the 1960s, denounced the divisive effects of piecework and was no less critical of the associated tradition of small-scale unofficial militancy.[38] His arguments were out of tune with the new mood of rank-and-file assertiveness; the call to respect the union's national integrity read like a simple affirmation of the authority of a national leadership committed to a 'constructive' partnership with the NCB. The left-wing advance within the NUM during the 1970s commenced, necessarily, with challenges which were fragmented, partial and unofficial. Without the anti-leadership eruption of 1969 and 1970 as a foundation, the successful national movements of 1972 and 1974 would surely have been impossible. More fundamentally still, the miners' historic struggle to control the conditions of their work—a struggle necessarily rooted in the particularities of each separate pit and seam—may be seen as the elemental force from which more generalised assertions of collective interest and aspiration are derived.

Yet in retrospect it is clear that Paynter expressed one element in the contradictory relationship of unity and discipline, autonomy and division. The circumstances which generated the broad-based struggles of the early 1970s proved exceptional. The production bonus system, the final achievement of the manoeuvrings of the embattled right-wing leadership, re-created the scope for decentralisation and fragmentation. From the mid-1970s the number of small, short strikes in mining rose rapidly (against the trend in most other industries); while the historic regional contrasts in geology were once more translated into sharp divergences in conditions of employment.[39] The widening gap in material circumstances was clearly expressed in NUM politics. In February 1974, when every area of the union had voted for the strike,[40] Nottinghamshire had registered 77 per cent support as against 90 per cent in Yorkshire; in March 1983 the respective percentages were 19 and 64.

'Area by area will decide, and in my opinion it will have a domino effect': the strategy enunciated by McGahey at the outset of the strike[41] recalls the means by which action was spread in 1969 and 1970. But then the context was a growing homogeneity of discontent, justifying optimism that the example of militants in one area would inspire members elsewhere; while in 1984 the dominant motivation was essentially pessimistic: since the more favoured areas would never vote in favour of strike action, the initiative must be taken without them. Yet in a struggle which became 'more about community than class',[42] the consequence was to reinforce the divisive effects of localism. The refusal of a ballot appears here in another guise: 'it implicitly cut across the long-established principle of national unity, national decisions and national action'.[43] In this sense, the importance of a ballot lies not in its questionable virtue in enfranchising miners as individuals, but rather in its force as a symbol of national integration, a ritual affirmation of unity of purpose. In the event, action under rule 41 evolved precisely as the rule prescribes: a series of area stoppages conducted largely autonomously and following very different rhythms in the various coalfields. Faced with a ruthless adversary exceptionally well prepared for battle, the NUM conducted an unco-ordinated campaign which exposed and accentuated its internal divisions.

*   *   *   *   *

The 'domino' tactic of escalating area action bears directly on the role of force and consent in the dispute. How was the strike to be spread from one coalfield to another? The issue of picketing, discussed previously in terms of the confrontation with state power and the management of publicity, is again the central question. From the first days of the dispute there was a powerful rank-and-file initiative to deploy flying pickets: in Scotland and South Wales, from striking pits to those initially holding back; in South Yorkshire, into the neighbouring counties of Lancashire, Derbyshire and Nottinghamshire. The outcome was of course very different: almost total closure of the Welsh and Scottish coalfields, but only limited support in the Midlands.

To some extent the explanation is straightforward. South Wales and Scotland were 'marginal' coalfields highly vulnerable to future closure programmes; initial reluctance to join the strike was in part a consequence of the earlier failures of other areas to support them when *they* were fighting closures. The central coalfields, by contrast, were far more secure. In addition, localism doubtless had some influence: colliers were more likely to respond favourably to pickets from their own area than to 'foreigners'. Yet the question then arises: what is the function of a picket which those picketed are not predisposed to respect? On this point, comment on and during the strike is often equivocal. Callinicos and Simons, whose sole criticism of the strategy of mass picketing is that it was pursued with insufficient vigour, are contemptuous of those—such as Notts general secretary Henry Richardson—who questioned the use of flying pickets. 'It never dawned on him that rank-and-file Yorkshire miners might make better ambassadors in Nottinghamshire than full-time officials. . . If the Nottinghamshire area council had called on its branches to hold canteen meetings where flying pickets could put their case, the outcome of the vote [i.e. the local Notts ballot] could have been very different.'[44] The use of pickets as 'ambassadors' was indeed pioneered by the South Wales area in its campaign against closures the previous year, when delegates were sent to every colliery in Britain. But the question of numbers is of qualitative significance. Ambassadors by the dozen are perhaps conceivable; in hundreds strains credulity.

To present the issue starkly: what happens if persuasion fails? Admit defeat, or employ more forceful methods? With mass picketing, the force of argument can readily become the argument of force. Was this intended from the outset? Those who regarded Notts as hopelessly corrupted by latter-day Spencerism presumably set little faith in the dispatch of ambassadors to canteen meetings. On this view, the central coalfields were deaf to persuasion and would join the strike only if physically prevented from working. Were the Notts miners in fact a hopeless case? And if so, was force an appropriate alternative to persuasion?

The solid support from Nottinghamshire for the strikes of 1972 and 1974 clearly owed much to the particular constraints which the new standard pay rates imposed on an area with earnings traditionally well above the national average; the area incentive scheme detached economic militancy from the broader community of interest within the NUM. Yet local orientations in the past decade have proved deeply contradictory. On the one side can be seen the votes in the ballots of 1982 and 1983, when support for strike action was less than half the national average; or the Tory successes in the 1977 Sutton-in-Ashfield by-election, and in 1983 in the new Sherwood constituency with its ten collieries. But against this can be set the evidence of militancy which transcends sectional economism: notably the campaign to reduce the retirement age to 55, if necessary through a national strike. There was extensive evidence of advances by the left in this traditionally right-wing area, with election successes for lodge officials and area executive positions, a trend sustained by the victory of Henry Richardson as broad left candidate for area secretary in 1982.

Favoured by geology and economics, the county had less than any other to fear from MacGregor's butchery. To persuade the local miners that government policies ultimately affected their own interests, and that resistance could prove effective, would have been an immense task. Nevertheless, at the outset of the dispute 'the coalfield was split and incredibly volatile'.[45] Picket-line confrontations helped resolve the contradictory politics of Notts miners towards an outcome which fatally divided the whole strike movement. 'Scenes of violence—often more akin to football "aggro" than political violence—turned mining communities against the strike. . . Locals came out to bait the pickets and cheer their men into work. Nottinghamshire miners' leaders. . . are convinced that they could have close to a majority in their area for a strike, but for the violence depicted on TV.'[46] The rhetoric of 'scabs' and 'bastards', while a totally understandable reaction to those who refused to join the strike (and who in many cases were soon to seek deliberately to provoke the pickets), conveyed the message that dialogue was useless. The escalation of antagonism which resulted was to create a radical, and perhaps irreconcilable polarisation within the union. One consequence in Nottinghamshire was a 'rank-and-file revolt' in which incumbents were displaced by 'working miners' at branch, area council and full-time officer level. After the progress achieved in the previous decade, the left has been eclipsed—perhaps for a generation.

Whether different tactics by the strikers might have won the consent of the majority of Notts strikers is unanswerable. Whether failing this consent it was appropriate to seek to close down the coalfield by force of numbers raises different issues which have historically been the focus of controversy among socialists. At the most general level: it is common to define the normal condition of capitalist society as a war between classes, and military metaphors abound in the rhetoric of the left. Most schools of socialism have been anti-militarist as regards relations between states, but anti-pacifist in domestic politics. The dominant assumption has always been that no ruling class will abandon power willingly: oppressive social relations must be overthrown, and in the process there may well be casualties. Yet most socialists have refused to glorify violence, and have been suspicious of the dehumanising logic that coolly insists that 'you cannot make omelettes without breaking eggs'. Rosa Luxemburg's attitude to revolutionary violence is exemplary: 'a whole world has to be overturned, but any tear that could have been avoided is an accusation'.[47] Hence the familiar maxim of British socialists a century ago: 'peacefully if we may, forcibly if we must'.

Yet socialist discussion of violence has primarily concerned the revolutionary overthrow of the established order and its defenders, and the treatment of reactionary social strata within a post-revolutionary society. Responses to the institutionalised violence inherent in the routine social relations of 'stable' capitalist societies involve far more problematic issues. Thus terrorism as a political tactic is in general unacceptable: a method which short-circuits the task of winning mass support for resistance. Apart from very exceptional circumstances (an occupying regime, or a ruling class perceived in similar terms), random violence by a dedicated minority alienates the majority of the population and allows the authorities to harness their support for a defence of the social order. Gramsci's distinction between a war of manoeuvre and war of position is obviously relevant here: under 'normal' conditions there exists a dense network of (materially based) ideological linkages between the working class and the institutions of bourgeois society. To unravel this network requires a delicate, protracted, but if successful cumulative effort. By contrast, an insensitive challenge to key principles of the taken-for-granted social relations of capitalist society will prove self-defeating. Thus 'picket-line violence' served as a potent mechanism for the ideological marginalisation of striking miners.

The classic socialist debates on violence refer to conflicts between, not within classes. Yet within the working class there exists a multiplicity of differentiations of function and condition, from which stem divisions of interest which inevitably affect labour action. The proletariat can be *empirically* constituted as a class only at the moment when it abolishes the circumstances of its oppression: the notion of class unity is otherwise an abstraction from an array of divergent particularities which are often appraised subjectively in antagonistic form. What then determines the boundaries of potential common struggle? What groups can in principle be won to solidarity, at least over certain issues, and which must be regarded as incorrigibly hostile? And what formulation of issues and choice of tactics will most probably attract rather than repel possible allies?

These questions set the controversy over mass picketing in a broader context. Unless fellow-workers are regarded as by some means open to reasoning and conviction, the very notion of class politics is futile. Aggressive physical confrontation between worker and worker is the frustrated (and often altogether understandable) symptom of an argument which is already lost. Its effect may be to consolidate one's own forces but to confirm those confronted in their role as enemy; while for those not engaged in the immediate conflict, the merits of the violence itself rather than the precipitating issues will dominate reactions. Several commentators have remarked on the paradox that while the resistance at Greenham Common inspired many of the women whose collective support and initiative were vital for the endurance of the strike, the principles of the peace movement had little resonance in the conduct of the pickets. Beatrix Campbell explored the contrast:

> Inescapably the sight of the picketlines echoes the sight of blockades at Greenham Common. Women and men who've joined picketlines at pits and depots have received none of the training in non-violent direct action which the peace movement demands to discover its members' fears and strengths, to discover the best way of coping with violence. Sit down, comes the advice. Hold on to each other. Step back, consider how you feel, how the land lies, how the balance of forces is matching up. Make sure you can see what's going on and that you can handle what's going on. Experience shows the unnerving futility of a big crowd lurching up to the gates, pushing and shoving with the police. Today they always win. The worst thing you can do is to stay on your feet: that way you can't see anything and you are at your most unstable.
>
> Some men have instinctively resisted speculation on the sort of tactics the miners might borrow from Greenham Common. Some are mesmerised by the idea, but interject with the proviso: 'but would miners lie down, could they?' It's as if lying down is something inherently threatening to the virility of class warriors. Is this more important than the recognition that the infantry charging the cavalry from its trench simply leads to broken heads?[48]

Subsequently, Campbell emphasised the need to distinguish illegality from violence: non-violent law-breaking is central to the Greenham women's action.[49] Likewise, under recent Tory laws most non-aggressive forms of picketing would represent unlawful action: but their perception by those picketed and by the broader working class might be very different. Ultimately, perhaps, the use of force may be inescapable: the closed shop, for example, is necessarily a coercive institution. But force deployed as a substitute rather than a complement for consent is always alienating. It is clear that the left must explore far more intensively than in the past the contradictions inherent in the traditional macho notions of 'industrial muscle', and the possibility for learning from theories of non-violent resistance. What forms of industrial action are best suited to winning the consent of those whose support is ultimately essential for success? Pursued seriously, the necessary debate will be long and painful.

*   *   *   *   *

There will be many for whom all such arguments are beside the point.

> Models of trade union behaviour which do not account for the rank and file are bound to mirror the tabloid obsession with leaderships. . . Nationally, the NUM found its hand forced by the Yorkshire area, which itself voted for the strike against the advice of its full-time officers. . . For the Yorkshire miners, pit closures were never an issue for balloting. 'We're not letting those bastards in Notts vote our men out of a job.' . . . Similarly with the picketing. The Yorkshire area executive decided on a policy of picketing only their own pits, with only six men to a picket. But the miners surged over the borders into Notts. I don't suppose for the minute that, if Scargill and Heathfield had stood in the middle of the A1, the Doncaster miners would have stopped trying to get into Nottinghamshire.[50]

All this is true, but the issue of leadership cannot be simply dismissed on that account.

The left has long been somewhat schizoid about leadership. With good reason: as that brilliant polemic *The Miners' Next Step* so powerfully demonstrated, there is indeed a 'bad side' to leadership. Leaders often develop vested interests, adopt an 'official' viewpoint with conservative connotations, substitute their own personal expertise for the collective initiative of the membership. Yet few socialists endorse the thorough-going rejection of leadership expressed by the South Wales militants in 1912. Ironically, their successors who castigated the failings of 'trade union bureaucrats' commonly insisted on the elite role of the revolution-ary vanguard party. Both elements in this contradictory amalgam have tended to mystify the empirical working class: union officialdom persistently betraying a membership which is in essence combative and class-conscious; the party constantly pursuing the correct initiative to release the masses' revolutionary zeal.

Any adequate conception of leadership must focus not primarily on leaders as such—whether depicted as reactionary bureaucrats or exemplary revolutionaries—but on the *relationships* between leaders and members. A recent discussion of strike strategy expresses this point with clarity:

> *Above all, the successful strategist has to display qualities of leadership.* The job of *mobilising, developing* and *directing* the power necessary to win strikes lies first of all with the obvious natural leaders, the shop stewards and the full-time

officers. Workers sometimes shy away from the idea of leadership. It often suggests the idea of generals ordering soldiers about in an army. Trade unions are not like that. But in any trade union at any time the experience of different people is different. The shop stewards should, on the whole, by the very fact that they have taken on the job, be more committed to the goals of the union than many members. They will have been more involved in union issues and negotiations. Whilst they must always do their best to involve the membership they should have more far-sighted and informed views. Their greater experience and knowledge must be put at the disposal of the members. The same goes even more for full-time officers.

This is not to say that the membership should automatically accept and act on the views of their representatives. Far from it. In the end, the members and not their representatives must make the decisions. Members will then be able to make up their own minds with greater awareness and understanding of the issues. In other words, *what we need in unions is democratic leadership,* and that means building up a good two-way relationship with members over time, trying to involve them in all decisions, trying to get their participation in union matters, arguing and discussing with them, trying to build up new activists, but remembering always that the members are the union.[51]

Leadership involves the ability to assess the constantly changing balance of forces, and to evaluate the likely outcome of different initiatives and responses. It may entail arguing for militant action when the members are reluctant, or urging caution when they are militant. It requires an ability to end strikes as well as to begin them. And not least it depends on the constant exchange of information and argument without which reasoned and democratic collective decisions are impossible.

'We are not of those who place implicit reliance upon leadership and who consider that the sole duty of the rank and file is blindly to trust that leadership, but at the same time we must emphasise that any group of trade union leaders withdrawn from industry, given the opportunity to study the detailed problems with which their membership is faced, should have the courage to lead.'[52] Arthur Horner's remarks in the aftermath of the General Strike remain applicable today. One comment on the leadership of the 1984–85 strike rejects the suggestion 'that the miners were badly led. Certainly, mistakes were made. But the weaknesses complained of are inseparable from the strike's strength, and from the fidelity of the leaders to the sentiment of the lodges and villages'.[53] But if the rank and file should not blindly trust their leaders, nor should the same failing operate in reverse. Another of Arthur Horner's comments is apposite. Contrasting the quiet reception of his own speeches to the enthusiasm evoked by Arthur Cook, he relates that Cook 'would electrify the meeting. They would applaud and nod their heads in agreement when he said the most obvious things. For a long time I was puzzled, and then one night I realized why it was. I was speaking *to* the meeting. Cook was speaking *for* the meeting. He was expressing the thoughts of his audience, I was trying to persuade them. He was the burning expression of their anger at the iniquities which they were suffering'.[54]

Horner did not present this assessment as a criticism of Cook. Neverthe-less, the issue could have been raised in 1926: did leadership require the telling of uncomfortable truths, a realistic appraisal of the balance of forces, the advocacy of tactical retreat rather than protracted grinding defeat? Certainly such questions are relevant to an assessment of 1984–85. The media have been rightly attacked for their personalisation of what was often termed 'Scargill's strike'. Nevertheless, it is clear that the NUM President exerts a personal charisma over many rank-and-file members, particularly in Yorkshire; and that the relationship displays some features of a personality cult. And a style of oratory reminiscent of Arthur Cook—telling the audience what they want to hear—reinforces this intense popular appeal. Yet is populism enough? In faithfully expressing the feelings of the young, militant activists—'reared in a folk culture that mythologised the 1970s strikes'[55]—was the task of strategic leadership abdicated? To have proposed different tactics to those spontaneously initiated by the rank and file, to have recommended terms falling short of the miners' justifiable demands, would have invited unpopularity and perhaps rejection. But had the risk been taken, might the outcome have been very different?

The experience of the strike brings to the fore the fundamental issue of the nature of trade union democracy. What is the role of leadership? How can the dangers of elitism and manipulation be avoided, without succumbing to mere subservience to the short-term enthusiasms of the most vocal sections of the membership? How can the inevitable uneven-ness of function and experience be fused within a collective relationship in which all contribute to a common initiative? There are no simple answers; but in its present embattled state, the labour movement cannot afford to evade the questions.

NOTES

1. Striking miner quoted in Huw Beynon, ed., *Digging Deeper*, Verso, 1985, p. 7.
2. George Bolton (Vice-President, Scottish Area NUM and Communist Party chair) in 'The Miners' Strike', *Marxism Today*, April 1985, p. 24. This comment contrasts with Bolton's argument in an earlier round-table discussion: 'while we could have held a ballot during the strike, what would that have achieved, it wouldn't have solved the problem, it wouldn't have stopped the pit closure programme'.
3. Mick McGahey quoted in *The Times*, 7 March 1984. According to Kim Howells, this expression was widely used in South Wales during the previous year.
4. V.L. Allen, *The Militancy of British Miners*, Moor Press, 1981, p. 302.
5. Çf. Jonathan Winterton and John Rentoul, 'Confronting the New Technology', *New Statesman*, 20 January 1984.
6. 'Only a Ballot Can Pave the Way for a Miners' Victory', *Guardian*, 16 September 1984; 'What Scargill Means', *New Society*, 17 January 1985.
7. For an elaboration of this argument see Peter Fairbrother, *All Those in Favour*,

Pluto, 1984.

8. It is a familiar point that 'representative parliamentary democracy' was original-
    ly advocated as a *curb* on popular political control by that arch-conservative
    Edmund Burke.

9. R. Page Arnot, *The Miners: a History of the MFGB 1889–1910*, Allen and
    Unwin, 1949, p. 374 and *The Miners: Years of Struggle*, 1953, pp. 176–7; P.S.
    Bagwell, 'The Triple Industrial Alliance, 1913–1922' in Asa Briggs and John
    Saville, eds., *Essays in Labour History 1886–1923*, Macmillan, 1971. Ironically
    it was the Railwaymen under the right-wing leadership of Jimmy Thomas who
    most strongly opposed the ballot principle.

10. By another irony it was the most prominent communist activist in the Miners'
    Federation, Arthur Horner, who insisted in the period of 'class against class' that
    revolutionary trade unionists must appreciate the depth of ordinary members'
    respect for rulebook prescriptions. For Party leaders in the early 1930s, 'Horner-
    ism' was a more threatening deviation than Trotskyism.

11. Michael Crick, *Scargill and the Miners*, Penguin, 1985 edn., p. 108.

12. Ben Fine, 'The Future of British Coal', *Capital and Class*, 23, Summer 1984,
    p. 80.

13. Alex Callinicos and Mike Simons, *The Great Strike*, Socialist Worker, 1985,
    p. 78.

14. For a detailed analysis see Peggy Kahn, Norman Lewis, Rowland Livock and
    Paul Wiles, *Picketing*, Routledge, 1983.

15. Arthur Scargill, 'The New Unionism', *New Left Review*, 72, July–August 1975,
    p. 10.

16. The study by Kahn (at the time a close associate of Scargill) and her colleagues
    made this clear in advance of the strike.

17. 'Last Stand or Orderly Retreat', 23 March 1984, p. 9.

18. *Great Strike*, p. 53.

19. Andrew Gamble, 'This Lady's Not For Turning', *Marxism Today*, June 1984,
    pp. 13–4. The 'right to work', one notes, applies to non-strikers, not those
    unemployed or threatened with the dole.

20. Mick Johnson, *New Statesman*, 8 June 1984.

21. Arthur Scargill, *Sunday Times*, 11 March 1984.

22. Allen, *Militancy*, p. 169.

23. Following the June 1974 *Plan for Coal*—essentially an outline scenario—a
    tripartite study by the NCB, NUM and Department of Energy produced two
    reports. The final document argued that with increased output targets 'the need
    to close pits on economic grounds should be much reduced', but continued that
    'inevitably some pits will have to close as their useful economic reserves of coal
    are depleted'. The whole controversy over 'what the *Plan for Coal* really meant'
    was arguably an unproductive diversion throughout the strike.

24. See in particular the exchange in the *Guardian* between Patrick Wintour (20
    May 1985), Nell Myers (3 June 1985) and John Torode (11 June 1985).

25. Andrew Glyn, *The Economic Case Against Pit Closures*, NUM, 1984.

26. E.g. George Kerevan and Richard Saville, *The Case for Deep-Mined Coal in
    Scotland*, mimeo, 1985.

27. Tony Berry, Teresa Capps, David Cooper, Trevor Hopper and Tony Lowe,
    'NCB Accounts: A Mine of Mis-Information?', *Accountancy*, January 1985.

28. In practice, 'economic' and 'non-economic' factors may be hard to disentangle—
    as, for example, in identifying when 'exhaustion' is reached.

29. 'A Plan for Disaster', *New Society*, 7 March 1985.

30. 'What was on offer was by any standards a remarkable breakthrough against
    one of the most rigid alliances of government and management since the 1926

General Strike. If Arthur Scargill had grabbed a deal then, and had put it to a ballot of his members, it is difficult to see how Mrs Thatcher could have sold the outcome to her supporters as anything less than a damaging retreat' (Ian Aitken, *Guardian*, 16 November 1984).

31. Victor Keegan, *Guardian*, 30 June 1984.
32. *Guardian*, 13 February 1985.
33. Robert Michels, *Political Parties*, Hearsts, 1915.
34. H.A. Turner, *Trade Union Growth, Structure and Policy*, Allen and Unwin, 1962.
35. This point has been regularly made in historians' discussions of 'Labourism', and is central to Huw Beynon's identification of 'factory consciousness' as the over-riding basis of shop steward militancy (*Working for Ford*, Penguin, 1984 edn.).
36. F. Zweig, *Men in the Pits*, Gollancz, 1948, p. 163.
37. *Militancy*, p. 283.
38. *British Trade Unions and the Problem of Change*, Allen and Unwin, 1970.
39. Before the overtime ban, the average weekly bonus in the highest-paid areas was around £100, four times the level in the lowest-paid. Variations between individual pits were even greater.
40. Only the colliery officials recorded a majority against (61 per cent); the lowest support in a geographical area was Leicestershire's 62 per cent.
41. *The Times*, 7 March 1984.
42. Raphael Samuel, 'Friends and Outsiders', *New Statesman*, 11 January 1985, p. 15.
43. Hywel Francis, 'NUM United: a Team in Disarray', *Marxism Today*, April 1985, p. 30.
44. *Great Strike*, p. 49.
45. *Ibid.*, p. 78.
46. Walter Pond, 'Last Stand or Orderly Retreat', *New Statesman*, 23 March 1984. One may note that even despite the polarisation against the strike, it still obtained 26 per cent support in the area ballot—significantly above the figure a year before. And Notts miners respected the national overtime ban to the end of the strike.
47. Quoted in Tony Cliff, *Rosa Luxemburg*, IS, 1959, p. 26.
48. 'The Other Miners' Strike', *New Statesman*, 27 July 1984, p. 10.
49. 'Politics Old and New', *New Statesman*, 8 March 1985.
50. John Field, 'Labour's Dunkirk', *New Socialist*, April 1985, p. 12.
51. John McIlroy, *Strike!*, Pluto, 1984, p. 9.
52. Arthur Horner, *Communism and Coal*, CPGB, 1928, p. 214.
53. Raphael Samuel, Gareth Stedman Jones and Stuart Weir, 'Thatcher's Moscow', *New Socialist*, April 1985, p. 3.
54. *Incorrigible Rebel*, MacGibbon and Kee, 1960, p. 72.
55. Field, 'Labour's Dunkirk', p. 13.

CAPITALISM OR BARBARISM: THE AUSTRIAN CRITIQUE OF SOCIALISM*

Andrew Gamble

1. The impossibility of socialism

In recent years there has been renewed interest in the debate about the feasibility of socialism. This has been prompted by reflection on the experience of the economies of 'actually existing' socialist societies, but also by the challenge to social democratic policies and institutions in advanced capitalist economies which has come from the New Right.

As evidence has accumulated about the inefficiencies and internal problems of the planned economies the idea of central planning has become discredited among socialists. Many socialists now advocate the use of markets and rejection of the 'utopian' elements in Marxism, especially the notion that a socialist economy can do without markets, without money, and without a specialised division of labour.[1] Other socialists have questioned the importance of public ownership as a key objective, arguing that control over enterprises can be achieved in a variety of ways.[2] Other socialists have pointed to the limited appeal of socialism to many workers and have questioned whether the working class has ever had an interest in replacing capitalism by socialism.[3]

Wracked by internal controversy over the feasibility of socialism socialists have also had to confront the arguments of an increasingly assertive and confident New Right. A central theme of New Right writing is that socialism as it is conceived by socialists is impossible in principle and totalitarian in practice. Many New Right ideologists also assert that there is no half-way house between freedom and totalitarianism. Social democracy and all other forms of government interference with market outcomes lead directly to full socialism and a return to barbarism or at least a retrogression to lower forms of civilisation. This idea was captured in the title of Hayek's best-known book *The Road to Serfdom*, published in 1944. Social democrats often took the lead in attacking this notion

*This article is based on a paper given to the Conference of the Centre for Socialist Theory and Movements, University of Glasgow, April 1985, which was organised on the theme 'Has Socialism a Future'. I am grateful to the Conference organisers for the invitation to give a paper and also to many of the Conference participants, in particular Leo Panitch, David Baker, Gordon Johnston, Phil Wright, Mollie Temple, Arthur MacEwan, and Philip Sharpe, for discussion of the themes of this paper. I also wish to thank Ralph Miliband for his comments on an earlier draft.

since it struck at the heart of their political practice and beliefs. Anthony Crosland could write confidently in 1956:[4]

> No-one of any standing now believes the once popular Hayek thesis that any interference with the market mechanism must start us down the slippery slope that leads to totalitarianism. This was an implausible enough view, in a British context, even when it was first advanced; it has been thoroughly discredited now that we have experienced a decade of varying degrees of government control, with no sign of weakening of our democratic fibre.

In the same optimistic vein he claimed:[5]

> It constitutes a major victory for the Left, the significance of which is grossly underestimated by those with short memories, that the majority of Conservatives today would probably concede the right, indeed the duty, of the State to hold itself responsible for (1) the level of employment, (2) the protection of the foreign balance by methods other than deflation, (3) the level of investment and the rate of growth, (4) the maintenance of a welfare minimum, and (5) the conditions under which monopolies should be allowed to operate. This is a far cry from the obscurantism of the Tory party twenty years ago.

These victories of the Left have been rapidly overturned in the last ten years and there has been a strong revival of the ideological case against all forms of socialism. *The Road to Serfdom* was suddenly in demand again and was reprinted twice in 1976. In the midst of the greatest world economic crisis since the 1930s it was the critics not the apologists of capitalism who were forced onto the defensive. In the 1970s the institutions and policies of social democracy were defined as the reasons why the capitalist economy was plunged into recession. In response socialists of all persuasions have been forced to re-examine their basic beliefs and to ask themselves, is socialism desirable and if so is it feasible? Is it possible to organise an industrial society on socialist lines?

These questions have revived interest in the earlier debate about the feasibility of socialism which raged in the 1920s and 1930s. The initial challenge was made by the Austrian economist, Ludwig von Mises, in a paper written in 1920.[6] This was subsequently elaborated in two books.[7] Mises belonged to the Austrian school of Menger, Wieser, and Böhm-Bawerk; Hayek studied under him. Menger was one of the pioneers of marginalist analysis and subjective value theory, but the Austrian school had always been distinctive from marginalism elsewhere by the vigour of its prosecution of the ideological struggle against socialism.[8] Böhm-Bawerk had attempted to demonstrate that *Capital* was logically flawed, and that Marxism had no scientific basis.[9] Mises now attempted to extend this by demonstrating that socialism was impossible. Any attempt to establish a socialist economy would fail since it did not grasp the complex basis of modern society:[10]

Without economic calculation there can be no economy. Hence in a socialist state wherein the pursuit of economic calculation is impossible, there can be—in our sense of the term—no economy whatsoever.

Mises was influenced by Max Weber who also criticised socialists on the grounds that they misunderstood how a modern society based on market exchange and a specialised division of labour worked. Weber's 'proof' that direct democracy was impossible complemented the attempt by Mises to demonstrate that a socialist economy was impossible.

Hayek later emphasised that what Mises meant was not that socialism was literally impossible but that economic calculation as it was understood by economists was impossible in a socialist economy. A socialist state might be established but its organisation of production would be much more inefficient and wasteful than that of a capitalist economy. Mises always insisted that his book on *Socialism* was a scientific inquiry not a political polemic, but he never let this hinder the flow of his invective. He claimed that the masses had been duped by socialism because of their ignorance and their inability to follow difficult trains of thought, and bitterly attacked Marxism. This was a doctrine which denied logic and though it proclaimed the inevitability of socialism, prohibited enquiry into how a socialist society might be organised. Instead it encouraged dreams of 'bliss and revenge' amongst the ignorant and the poor. It was the most radical of all reactions against the reign of scientific thought over life and action established by rationalism. Indeed in his original paper Mises speculated that the disappearance of rational economic calculation under socialism would lead to the disappearance of rational conduct altogether as well as rationality and logic in thought itself. This was because historically, he claimed, human rationality had been a development of economic life and Mises doubted if it could survive if divorced from it.

Mises set out to remedy the omission of the Marxists by asking whether socialism was possible and what principles of organisation it would establish. Underlying the bombast and the Spenglerian pessimism Mises deployed a closely reasoned argument against socialism. Like all the Austrian school he was a champion of subjectivist marginalist economics. He rejected the historical school in economics (in which he included Marxism) because it was unable to see any of the 'permanent economic problems' which are independent of the historical framework.

Austrian economics is an attempt to analyse these 'permanent economic problems'. The most important is scarcity. In every society there is an endless variety of wants but only a limited quantity of means available for satisfying them. Some way of ranking wants and allocating resources becomes necessary. The solution is found through the subjective theory of value. This asserts that the only value which a good has is the significance which it has for an individual. Individuals can be supposed to rank all goods and services in terms of their own set of personal preferences. These subjective preferences of individuals are expressed through monetary valuations or prices, and this makes possible exchange. Central to Mises' argument is that the existence of money and exchange makes possible a specialised division of labour and rational economic calculation. Prices are established by economic agents making valuations of goods and services and calculating how best to spend their incomes so as to satisfy all their wants.

Economic calculation will be rational if economic agents are able to gain the greatest possible amount of satisfaction at the smallest possible cost to themselves. The economy as a whole will be efficient when the greatest possible amount of satisfaction is generated from the resources that are available. This sounds metaphysical, and it is, but the practical implications are extremely important. For rational economic calculation has been defined in terms of money and markets. Only if there is a system of flexible prices and free market exchange for all goods and services will individuals have any possibility of giving practical expression to their subjective preferences. The economic principle for the Austrians means economising resources—using resources in the most efficient way possible to satisfy human wants. The only way of knowing whether a resource is being used efficiently or wastefully is to see whether its price is determined by market forces of supply and demand, which means by numerous daily individual valuations.

A great edifice is constructed from these *a priori* reasonings. Mises argues that in a modern society based on a complex division of labour exchange is only possible using the medium of money. Calculations in kind rather than in money might be possible for consumption goods but not for capital goods. Without money and prices how could means of prduction be valued? There would be no means of knowing whether any particular piece of work was necessary and whether resources were not being wasted in producing it. This is capitalism's great advantage:[11]

> Under capitalism the economic principle is observed in both consumption and production. . . in this way arises the exactly graded system of prices which enables everyone to frame his demand on economic lines. The scale of values is the outcome of the actions of every independent member of society. Everyone plays a twofold part in its establishment, first as a consumer, secondly as producer.

Under capitalism says Mises decision-taking, economic calculation, and planning are all decentralised. Under socialism they are centralised; any prices if they exist are arbitrary and unrelated to individual preferences. Hence rational economic calculation is impossible. Only capitalism ensures that the economy is run on rational lines. Socialism aspires to carry humanity forward to a higher stage of civilisation; in practice it will lead to a retrogression to barbarism. For Mises the choice was not socialism or barbarism but capitalism or barbarism. Socialism was unrealisable because capitalism is the only feasible system of social organisation based on an advanced division of labour:[12]

> If capitalism has succeeded in maintaining itself in spite of the enmity it has always encountered from both governments and the masses, if it has not been obliged to make way for other forms of social cooperation that have enjoyed to a much greater extent the sympathies of theoreticians and of practical men of affairs, this is to be attributed only to the fact that no other system of social organisation is feasible.

Mises also gave no comfort to those socialists for whom markets no longer hold any terrors but who baulk at endorsing private ownership of capital, and advocate some form of market socialism. This keeps the market as a method of allocating resources but abolishes most forms of private ownership of the means of production. This will not solve the problem says Mises. Private ownership of the means of production is absolutely necessary for rational calculation. This is because the market and its crucial function of forming the prices which allow every individual to make the calculations that in aggregate maximise human satisfactions, cannot be separated from the existence of private property. The principle enshrined in private property is the freedom of capitalists, landlords, and entrepreneurs to dispose of their property as they see fit. Only if they are free in this way will 'true' prices be formed for factors of production. For Mises capitalists seek to maximise their profits by serving consumers wishes and no adequate replacement for them exists.

2. The socialist riposte

Mises' challenge was certainly not ignored. The most common response to the Austrians was to dismiss their whole argument by rejecting the assumptions on which marginalist analysis was constructed—its doctrines of scarcity as the economic problem and value as subjective preferences. But some socialist economists chose to meet the challenge on the marginalists' own terrain. Accepting the definition of the economic problem as scarcity and therefore the marginalist definition of rational economic calculation, a number of economists set out to show that Mises was mistaken. Rational calculation was possible in a socialist economy.

From the outset 'socialist economy' was defined in a particular (and extremely narrow) way. As Schumpeter later summarised it,[13] the term meant an economy in which control over means of production and over production itself was invested with a central authority. Whether this authority was organised as a democracy or as a despotism was immaterial. The question with which the debate was concerned was simply whether such an economy, in which private ownership of the means of production

and direction of the production process had been replaced by state ownership and state direction, could be organised on rational lines. Could it set
prices in Mises' sense?

In attempting to show that it could the socialist economists were able
to draw on work by two leading anti-socialists, Barone and Pareto. Barone
had demonstrated in work done before Mises' essay that the different
institutional character of capitalism and socialism made no difference to
the fundamental logic of economic behaviour.[14] That remained the same.
Provided individuals were still given incomes, and allowed to spend them
freely, and prices were set by the resulting forces of supply and demand,
rational economic calculation and allocation of resources could be shown
to be feasible.

Mises had conceded that consumption might be organised rationally
under socialism by this means, but had vehemently denied that production
could be. This was because centralised ownership of all productive enterprises would prevent the establishment of genuine, i.e. market-determined,
prices for factors of production. Socialist economists such as Oscar Lange,
H.D. Dickinson, F. Taylor, and A.B. Lerner, set out to show that he was
mistaken.[15] Lange in particular developed a powerful argument that just
as a central authority in a socialist economy could create a market for
consumer goods by crediting all citizens with independent incomes which
they were allowed to spend freely, so the central authority could establish
a central board to set prices for capital goods to which enterprises would
then be obliged to respond. The prices that cleared the market and
promoted economic development would be discovered through practical
experience of planning, a process of trial and error.

Socialist economists were able to show that just because a socialist
economy had abolished private ownership of the means of production this
did not prevent it organising the economy by means of prices and markets
so as to permit rational economic calculation at all levels, and to ensure
efficient allocation of resources between competing uses. Most of those
who have commented on the debate have concluded that the socialists
overwhelmed their opponents.[16] Schumpeter, who was trained in the
Austrian school, had no doubt in the 1940s that socialism was feasible.
He even thought it was inevitable. What he doubted was whether it was
desirable.

The socialists' victory in this debate, however, was a strange one. As
Mario Nuti has noted,[17] what they showed was that capitalism was possible
without capitalists. For the proof that rational economic calculation was
possible under socialism meant accepting that the only institutional
change socialism introduced was change in the legal ownership of enterprises and the degree of centralisation of economic power. But in order to
ensure economic efficiency such a socialist economy had to retain or
reintroduce money, prices, and markets, hence commodity production.

In this way a greater part of the Austrian case had to be conceded. A modern industrial society was impossible to organise without specialised division of labour and commodity production. Many Marxists like Maurice Dobb strongly criticised the approach of Lange and others on the grounds that socialism meant the abolition of wage labour and commodity production not their indefinite continuation.[18] Max Weber's iron cage was not the inescapable future of all individual societies.

3. The road to serfdom

With the enlargement of public sectors and public responsibilities in many countries after 1945, the old argument about capitalism and socialism was relegated to the 'end of ideology'. The reality many argued was mixed economies, cooperation between government and industry, and considerable interpenetration of state and economy, and the use of markets and planning not as rival but as complementary mechanisms of coordination.[19]

The Austrian school was unimpressed, however, by the claims of Keynesians and social democrats that it was state involvement in modifying the workings of markets that was responsible for the great surge of capitalist growth in the 1950s and 1960s. Mises never recanted his hostility to all forms of state intervention, and the neo-Austrian school inspired by him in the United States became more and more extreme in its view of all forms of taxation and state regulation.[20]

It was, however, Hayek who was most important in developing the Austrian critique of socialism and whose work became so influential during the great new surge of anti-socialist and anti-interventionist doctrines when the moment was right for them again—in the 1970s.

Hayek made an important contribution to the debate on socialism in the 1930s when he edited *Collectivist Economic Planning*. From the start he struck a different note from Mises by arguing that the main objection to socialism was not that it was impossible but that it was impractical. Hayek wanted to demonstrate that on theoretical grounds socialism must be less efficient than capitalism; less efficient both in terms of maximising 'welfare' and in increasing productivity and social wealth. He therefore argued that 'in a society which is to preserve freedom of choice of the consumer and free choice of occupation central direction of all economic activity presents a task which cannot be rationally solved under the complex conditions of modern life'.[21]

Hayek has greatly expanded on this theme in his writings since 1945, but until recently his arguments were not widely understood or discussed. Hayek no less than Mises has enjoyed polemic and has been an extremely active propagandist for the New Right. From the beginning he saw himself as a crusader against socialism: 'Insight into the economic problems of society turned me into a radical anti-socialist.'[22] The central theme of all his writings is that socialism is a tissue of illusions: 'Surely it is high time for us to cry from the house tops that the intellectual foundations of socialism have all collapsed.'[23]

This rallying call is accompanied by a series of sweeping assertions in the grand Austrian manner. On the moral side, claims Hayek, it has been shown that socialism destroys the basis of all morals, personal freedom and responsibility; on the political side it leads 'sooner or later' to totalitarian government; on the material side it greatly impedes the production of wealth and may actually cause impoverishment. Socialist hopes he says have now all been shown to be illusions; hopes for a great leap in productivity under socialism; hopes for a just distribution of income; hopes for the abolition of the wage system; hopes for a new managerial ethic. All have been revealed says Hayek to be without foundation because they run counter to the 'complex conditions of modern life'.[24]

All these unsupported assertions echo the themes of *The Road to Serfdom* but in the forty years that have elapsed since it was published Hayek has become much more optimistic about the future of capitalism. Socialism he now believes reached its high tide in 1948. Since then it has steadily lost its intellectual appeal and has been abandoned by the masses. The main reason for this is the example of socialism in action presented by the Soviet Union. This has opened many intellectuals' eyes, argues Hayek, to what socialism must mean in practice; an organisation of production not more but much less productive than private enterprise; instead of greater social justice a new arbitrary order of rank; and instead of political emancipation a new political despotism.

Hayek in this kind of polemical vein is dismissed by many socialists as just another Cold War ranter. But this can lead to the substance of his critique of socialism or more accurately, collectivism, being overlooked. This critique is based on the way in which knowledge arises and is used in society.[25] In a highly interdependent industrialised society knowledge is dispersed because possession of it everywhere depends on special circumstances of time and place. One implication is that knowledge is always imperfect, while another is that only a market system can hope to utilise the knowledge that is dispersed throughout society efficiently. Markets are necessarily imperfect, however, because the distribution of knowledge and therefore the calculations of individual agents are imperfect. But, argues Hayek, however imperfect the market may be it must be more efficient than any attempt to centralise knowledge through a central planning board as envisaged by Lange. Knowledge cannot be gathered in that way without loss. No body of planners can ever have the same degree of knowledge as the mass of economic agents in their wide variety of locations and circumstances.

This conception of the role of knowledge in markets allows Hayek to reformulate Mises' objection to socialism:

> Rational calculation in a complex economy is possible only in terms of values or prices. . . these values will be adequate guides only if they are the joint efforts, such as the values formed on the market, of all the knowledge of potential suppliers or consumers about their possible uses and availability.[26]

What is novel about Hayek's critique of socialism is that it cuts away the ground from the elegant formal demonstration by Barone, Lange, Lerner and others of the possibility of rational economic calculation under socialism. Hayek has little time for neo-classical equilibrium models because they assume that perfect information about past, present, and future economic conditions is available to all economic agents. With such an assumption it is possible to demonstrate that a socialist organisation might be superior to a capitalist economy in creating the conditions for perfect competition. Hayek argues however that the assumptions made in equilibrium models are only analytical devices and are seriously misleading if taken as conditions which are realisable in actual economies. Uncertainty and imperfect knowledge are necessary features of all economies and this makes markets role as a discovery process far more important than their contribution to the achievement of general equilibrium in an abstract model of the economic process.[27] The great strength of the Austrian tradition in economics is the strength it gives to some at least of the actual institutional characteristics of capitalism. Hayek's case against socialism is that a command economy will always be less efficient than a market economy in using information about wants, costs, and the availability of resources to produce the goods and services that the society needs.

4. Actually existing socialism

Hayek's case against socialism is theoretical rather than empirical but he believes that the experience of the Soviet Union confirms his theory. Recent writing on the feasibility of socialism is focused directly on interpreting the experience of actually existing socialist societies. The judgment has been overwhelmingly adverse. A host of writers including western analysts of the Soviet economy like Nove and Wiles as well as leading intellectuals and dissidents from Eastern Europe such as Brus, Bahro, and Selucky, have amassed evidence about the waste, inefficiency and low productivity of Soviet type economies compared with their capitalist rivals.[28] They have shown how shortages, bottlenecks, and misallocation of resources are persistent features.

This literature has buried the old assumption, still commonplace in the 1950s, that the Soviet economy would eventually outperform western capitalism. In the 1980s it is the dependence of the Soviet economy on capitalist countries for much of its new technology, its inability to grow enough food for its own needs, and the well-publicised imbalances between production and consumption, which have helped form the dominant contemporary image of the Soviet economy and by extension of socialism itself, as a relatively backward, and relatively inefficient mode of socio-economic organisation.

The character of the Soviet type of economy is now much better understood; so too are its strengths and limitations. From the commencement of the First Five Year Plan the Soviet economy was transformed into a command economy geared to rapid industrialisation. All decisions on investment, output, employment, and resource allocation were determined centrally with a limited use of the price mechanism in the distribution of consumer goods and in labour markets. A command economy was successful in promoting industrialisation and remains successful in preempting resources for the defence sector, but it has been much less successful in pursuing a wide variety of goals and developing a balanced, flexible and efficient economy.

The most widely canvassed solution to the problem of the centrally planned economies has been greater decentralisation. In the Soviet Union and several Eastern European countries and currently in China there have been experiments aimed at giving greater autonomy to enterprises by introducing incentives for managers and workers, and relying more on prices and markets to coordinate and monitor the behaviour of enterprises. The literature on command economies of the Soviet type tends to support Hayek's view that a centralised system will only be more efficient than a decentralised one if it has a single objective to which all others can be subordinated.

The socialist project has not emerged unscathed from these debates. The earlier debate between Mises and Lange became focused on whether capitalism was possible without capitalists. The socialists may have 'won' that debate but only by accepting that very little would be changed in a socialist society except the legal form of ownership. Many socialists at the time were sympathetic to those Marxists, such as Maurice Dobb, who refused to accept the terms of this debate and who argued that socialism was a genuine and higher mode of production not just a modification of capitalism, and that its essence was central planning.

It is this claim that Hayek's theory of markets and the dispersion of knowledge seeks to destroy, while the evidence on the actual performance of command economies appears to confirm that central planning does have serious flaws and can offer no easy solution to the problems of resource allocation. The lesson which many socialists have drawn is that the only feasible socialism is a socialism which accepts that scarcity is the economic problem and therefore accepts the need for rational economic calculation as neo-classical economists understand it. This makes markets indispensable.

This conclusion is buttressed by the view that there are a limited number of ways of organising an economy. For Nove the choices are between central planning, markets, and self-sufficient communes. Lindblom offers a longer and more interesting list,[29] but the point is the same. There are a limited number of modes of social organisation, and therefore definite limits to the kind of socialist economy that can be envisaged.

5. Full Communism and feasible socialism

Many socialists have become unsure about the feasibility of socialism. This has been noted by socialism's critics. Norman Barry has written:[30]

> What is disturbing about contemporary socialists is that they seem to reject both central planning and the market mechanism yet suggest no alternative that meets the minimum demands of economic rationality.

Assar Lindbeck in his critique of the economics of the New Left has also argued that socialists have to choose between markets and bureaucracy: 'The more strongly we are against bureaucracy the more we should be in favour of markets.'[30]

Many socialists find the choice unappetising. This would not surprise the Austrians who always accused socialists of being impractical utopian dreamers, unable to confront the realities of modern social organisation and the difficulties they posed for implementing socialism. The dilemma for socialists is a real one. If the earlier debate was about whether it was possible to conceive of capitalism without capitalists the new debate is whether it is possible to conceive of socialism without markets.

Central planning no longer commands the support it once did among socialists. The identification of socialism with central planning which was so encouraged by the Soviet experiment in the 1930s is now sustained more by the writings of anti-socialists than by socialists themselves. The superior productivity and prospects for growth of capitalist economies compared to those in the Soviet sector has been conceded. In world historical terms capitalism remains the most advanced mode of production. No other mode of production has yet managed to surpass it.

This has led many socialists to reconcile themselves with the market on the grounds that it is preferable to central planning. The market has been rehabilitated as a neutral tool of coordination. It is pointed out that market systems need not always be private enterprise systems. Markets can be separated from capitalist institutions as Lange and Dickinson always maintained and used as instruments of planning. In this way a balance can be struck between market and plan. But there is little doubt that it is markets and market relations which predominate. This is now identified by many socialists as more socialist than the alternative. As

Selucky summarises it, any consistently non-market economy must by definition be 1) centralised, 2) run by the command plan, 3) controlled by a handful of planners rather than by workers themselves, 4) based on manipulation of producers by the planning board.[31] Many socialists agree with Selucky. A non-market economy is non-socialist because it is not decentralised. Only a decentralised economy can sustain a democratic polity, and only markets can secure decentralisation.

Such views are rejected by some socialists because they appear to conflict with an ideal of 'full communism', an economy in which commodity production, wage labour, money and the state, have all been abolished. Marx and Engels consistently refused to draw up 'utopian' blueprints of how socialist societies might be organised, but there are certainly many hints in their writings as to the kind of society they hoped might one day emerge.[32] They never suggested, however, that the conquest of scarcity or the overcoming of the division of labour would be practical options for a new socialist regime. Marx also argued in *Capital* that the 'realm of necessity' could not be abolished under any mode of production.

Socialists have sometimes got themselves into an unnecessary tangle by supposing that because one of the conditions for capitalism is commodity production their duty as socialists is to oppose every manifestation of it. But commodity production can take numerous forms and play quite different roles in different social formations. There is no reason why socialists should resist the use of markets *in a socialist society* to solve many of the economic problems of resource allocation which arise from scarcity. Failure to acknowledge the role markets can legitimately play leads to proposals for the curtailment of demand by placing direct controls on the range and variety of goods and services to be made available for consumption.

Recent Green critiques of industrialism have helped to discredit the notion that 'abundance' is either a possible or a desirable goal,[33] but they have also unintentionally breathed new life into some of the ascetic and puritan traditions in socialism, which have always disapproved of many of the contemporary forms of mass consumption and popular culture.[34] This new emphasis on scarcity rather than abundance as the setting for socialism also strikes a deep chord in the revolutionary tradition.

War communism between 1919–20 was supported with real enthusiasm by many of the Bolsheviks because it offered a speedy transition to an economy without money and without commodities. The ideal of a revolutionary regime preaching egalitarianism and practising austerity, presiding over a centralised economy and placing revolutionary virtue above material rewards, has many echoes in revolutionary societies, from the Committee of Public Safety to the Cultural Revolution.

Alec Nove ridicules the idea that these short-lived regimes offer any prospect of a transition to a new and higher mode of production. His feasible socialism has no such end in view. It is simply a socialism which could be achieved 'within the lifetime of one generation'. Implicitly he takes his stand with the Austrians. Full communism or anything approaching it that tries to get rid of markets is doomed to failure because it disregards important and permanent features of reality—that there is scarcity; that human beings are acquisitive and aggressive, and that knowledge cannot be centralised. Like the Austrians Nove believes that markets are the inevitable and permanent feature of any industrial society. Any attempt to do without them completely will end in ruin.

Yet Nove's conclusion—that there is nevertheless a 'feasible socialism' would be quite unacceptable to the Austrians. His book is a persuasive restatement of the argument that capitalism is possible without capitalists. He envisages a legal structure for 'feasible socialism' that recognises the following economic agents: centralised state corporations such as banks and utilities; socialised, i.e. self-managed enterprises; cooperative enterprises; small-scale private enterprises; and individuals. The reason why private ownership of larger enterprises should be ruled illegal in this type of socialism is left vague. The Austrian case is that any form of market socialism will be inferior to capitalism because it will undervalue the role of 'entrepreneurs' in making markets function properly as processes of discovery of new needs, new products, new jobs and new technologies.[35]

6. The impossibility of capitalism

There does not yet exist a detailed critique of the arguments of either Nove or Hayek. There are many *a priori* rebuttals which simply take elements of full communism as the standard by which existing societies can be assessed. Full communism however is as unattainable as perfect competition and seriously misleading as to the kind of problems that would dominate economic organisation in a socialist society. But important though Nove's and Hayek's critiques of socialism are, and necessary though it is for socialists to treat these arguments seriously and to learn from them, the debate on socialism need not be confined to the ground chosen by its opponents—whether capitalism is possible without capitalists.

Three strands in socialist thinking about socialism need developing.

i. Economic calculation

Socialists have always objected to a model of 'rational' economic calculation that finds nothing wrong with such 'irrational' outcomes as poverty in the midst of wealth, famine in the midst of plenty, and unemployment in the midst of need. But they have often underestimated the difficulties of defining alternative methods of economic calculation which would permit wider social needs to be met while still economising resources. Socialists object to money and commodity production for two main reasons; firstly because they distort and conceal the process of exchange, resulting in structural and cumulative inequalities; and secondly because there are important needs that cannot be identified or satisfied through choices made by individuals in markets. In the first case under a regime of commodity production exchange takes place behind the backs of the producers. Michael Barratt Brown has suggested that in a socialist economy it might be possible for dated labour inputs to be used alongside money prices to create a standard for assessing the fairness of exchange and public and open criteria for determining distribution and investment.[36] Such a system would involve a considerable extension of popular participation in decision-making. Extending democracy in this way would not replace markets or money for the bulk of economic coordination but would be intended to create a mechanism for settling some of the major questions about the direction of the economy.

A second socialist argument against commodity production focuses on the way needs are defined and expressed. Socialists have long argued that social forms of satisfying needs that do not take the form of commodities such as health care are possible and desirable in many fields. The socialist idea of community means finding ways to institutionalise popular control over the economy in order to create a fairer society and one based on the more active consent and participation of its members. Commodity production tends to destroy whatever communities exist because it intensifies individual, regional, national, and international competition. The more commodity production has expanded, the more individuals' need for sociability, emotional intimacy, and personal integration has been frustrated. The psychological and social costs of unrestrained commodity production require the imposition of limits on markets and the development of non-commodity forms of production and distribution.[37]

ii. The concept of mode of production

Central to the socialist critique of all theories that justify the capitalist economy is that implicit in commodity production itself is the possibility of an alternative rationality and an alternative way of organising the economy. This is denied by the Austrians and the market socialist critics of planning because they employ such an abstract and ahistorical analysis. Central planning is an easy target to demolish, but they go on from there to assert that there is an inescapable choice between 'bureaucracy' and 'the market', and that choice of the market option necessarily involves accepting money and prices and commodity production, in short capitalism without capitalists. This is nonsense. Markets and bureaucracies are not permanent universals which remain unchanged through history. They have always to be understood through the roles and functions they perform in particular societies and different modes of production. A better distinction than between markets and bureaucracies is between centralised and decentralised systems. Many capitalist market societies turn out to be highly centralised. One major current of opinion on the Left has always held that socialism can only be achieved if it can bring about a real decentralisation of power. On this view the problem is not the choice of the method of allocating resources but how to empower the poor, the disadvantaged, and the oppressed and the propertyless in a world economy which increasingly denies the possibility of local autonomy and in which the logic of capital accumulation is the major constraint on all political decision-making and choices.

Nove asks us to imagine a 'feasible' socialism in which the crucial element in existing power relations, namely the power of the owners of private capital has been removed. He is silent as to how that might be brought about. Given the power of private capital in existing capitalist societies the issue of the role of the market and planning are quite different from what they would be in a society in which this class of owners had been dispossessed. Alec Nove's feasible socialism is like an airship that has escaped its moorings. It looks very elegant up in the sky but there is no way its intended passengers can clamber aboard. Nove makes strong criticisms of the Labour party's alternative economic strategy, yet his own blueprint would involve more radical changes than anything the Labour Left has ever proposed. He never discusses the feasible means by which his feasible socialism might be achieved.

The value of the Marxist concept of the mode of production is that the relative merits of markets and bureaucracy cannot be discussed independently of particular social formations with their own distinctive configurations of class power and political organisation and their own set of problems and contradictions.

The variety of markets and bureaucratic behaviour even within one social formation is, in any case immense. In any conceivable socialist economy there are certain to be commodity forms and markets and money. Though they have drawbacks they have undeniable advantages over bureaucratic forms in many areas. The key question is not whether markets can be dispensed with but the social and political context which defines how they are used and whether they contribute to a centralised or decentralised structure of power. Existing 'command' economies and 'market' economies both tend to centralise power rather than to diffuse it.

iii. The feasibility of capitalism

There is a third objection to the Austrian critique of socialism. Some of the Austrians voice it themselves. Schumpeter asked, 'Can Capitalism survive?' and answered his own question. 'No, I do not think it can'.[38] On closer examination it is not socialism that may be 'impossible' but capitalism. When 'actually existing capitalism' rather than the 'full capitalism' of the economics textbooks is analysed what is apparent is how dependent markets are on non-market conditions to survive at all. Free economies are discovered to need strong states, stable families, and adaptive and intergrative cultures. Bureaucracy and 'politicisation' are inseparable from modern capitalism because of the expansion of the state's many roles and responsibilities. Lindblom has pointed out that even in developed capitalist economies the bulk of social activities are not organised through markets.[39] There exist many areas of experience and exchange outside markets and rational economic calculation.

One of the paradoxical contributions of the Austrian tradition is a recognition of the limits and frailty of markets and therefore implicitly of the possibility of alternative forms of calculation and economic organisation. Within the capitalist economy new sectors are constantly emerging that are not subject to the market. There is a double process at work in capitalism; constant pressure to expand markets and commodity production, hence ever greater individualisation of needs and penetration of capital into new areas; but at the same time constant pressure for non-market agencies to support and sustain the process of capital accumulation by carrying the political, ideological, administrative, as well as ideological 'deficits' it constantly generates.

The New Right project starts from the assumption that capitalism has never properly been tried as a means of organising the economy. While many socialists wish to see actually existing socialism rid of commodity forms many New Right adherents wish to see actually existing capitalism rid of non-commodity forms. This sets up serious tensions within New Right thinking, in particular between neo-liberal and neo-conservative strands.[40]

Few socialists any longer reject markets absolutely. The positive aspects of markets, particularly their role in helping to decentralise power and place controls on bureaucracies has become more widely recognised. But socialists have no need to capitulate to the Austrian critique. The acknowledgement that markets have limits and that there are many ways in which exchange is organised apart from commodity production remains a crucial starting point for thinking about socialism. The existence of non-commodity forms of exchange despite their many problems and imperfections means the existence of institutions which routinely determine needs and allocate resources other than through commodity production and the atomisation of producers and consumers. One implication is that socialism would only become truly 'impossible' if the New Right project were ever to be fully realised. For if all non-commodity forms within existing capitalist societies were abolished, socialism would become inconceivable even as utopia. Even utopias are constructed from elements of practical experience. Since capitalism is unable to universalise the market and commodity exchange, socialism continually reappears as a possibility within capitalist forms. Capitalism itself makes socialism feasible. But it does not bring it any nearer.

NOTES

1. Two influential recent works are A. Nove, *The Economics of Feasible Socialism*, Allen & Unwin, 1983; and G. Hodgson, *The Democratic Economy*, Penguin Books, 1984.
2. J. Tomlinson, *The Unequal Struggle? British Socialism and the Capitalist Enterprise*, Methuen, 1983.
3. David Selbourne, *Against Socialist Illusion*, Macmillan, 1985.
4. Anthony Crosland, *The Future of Socialism*, Cape, 1956, p. 343.
5. Crosland, *ibid.*, p. 342.
6. Ludwig von Mises 'Economic Calculation in the Socialist Commonwealth', reprinted in F.A. Hayek, (ed.), *Collectivist Economic Planning*, Augustus Kelley, New York, 1935.
7. Ludwig von Mises, *Socialism: an Economic and Sociological Analysis*, Cape, 1936. His book on Liberalism, first published in 1927 was translated and republished as *The Free and Prosperous Commonwealth*, von Nostrand, 1962.
8. This was particularly true of the second generation Austrians who were confronted by the rise of mass socialist movements.
9. E. Böhm-Bawerk, *Karl Marx and the Close of his System*, Orion, New York, 1949.
10. Mises, 'Economic Calculation in the Socialist Commonwealth', p. 105.
11. Mises, *Socialism*, p. 120.
12. Mises, *The Free and Prosperous Commonwealth*, p. 85.
13. J.A. Schumpeter, *Capitalism, Socialism, and Democracy*, Allen & Unwin, 1950.
14. E. Barone, 'The Ministry of Production in the Collectivist State', in Hayek (ed.), *Collectivist Economic Planning*, Augustus Kelley, New York, 1935.
15. Among the many contributions to the debate see in particular, B.E. Lippincott (ed.), *On the Economic Theory of Socialism*, University of Minnesota Press, 1938; H.D. Dickinson, *The Economics of Socialism*, OUP 1939. A review of the debate from an Austrian perspective is provided by K.I. Vaughn, 'Economic Calculation under Socialism: the Austrian contribution', *Economic Inquiry*, October 1980, pp. 535–554. This contains a useful bibliography of books and articles.
16. See the judgments by Schumpeter in *Capitalism, Socialism and Democracy*, and C. Lindblom, *Politics and Markets*, Basic Books, 1977.
17. Mario Nuti, 'The Contradictions of socialist economies: a Marxian interpretation', *Socialist Register 1979*.
18. Maurice Dobb, *Political Economy and Capitalism*, Routledge & Kegan Paul, 1937. *On Welfare Economics and the Economic Theory of Socialism*, CUP, 1969.
19. Crosland, *The Future of Socialism*; A. Shonfield, *Modern Capitalism*, OUP, 1965.
20. See the writings of Murray Rothbard. A survey of neo-Austrian economics can be found in A.H. Shand, *The Capitalist Alternative*, Wheatsheaf, 1984.
21. F.A. Hayek, *Collectivist Economic Planning*, p. 202.
22. F.A. Hayek, *New Studies in Philosophy, Politics, Economics, and the History of Ideas*, Routledge & Kegan Paul, 1978, p. 306.
23. *Ibid.*, p. 305.
24. A survey of Hayek's ideas is provided by Norman Barry, *Hayek's Social and Economic Philosophy*, Macmillan, 1979.
25. F.A. Hayek, 'The Use of Knowledge in Society', in *Individualism and Economic Order*, Routledge & Kegan Paul, 1948.
26. F.A. Hayek, *New Studies in Philosophy*, p. 303.

27. See the discussion by Barry and by Vaughn.
28. Nove, *The Economics of Feasible Socialism*; P. Wiles, *Economic Institutions Compared*, Blackwell, 1977; W. Brus, *The Economics and Politics of Socialism*, Routledge & Kegan Paul, 1973. R. Bahro, *The Alternative in Eastern Europe*, Verso, 1978; R. Selucky, *Marxism, Socialism, and Freedom*, Macmillan, 1979.
29. Lindblom, *Politics and Markets*, pp. 105–6.
30. Barry, *Hayek's Social and Economic Philosophy*, p. 182.
31. R. Selucky, 'Marxism and Self-management', *Critique*, 3, Autumn 1974.
32. See Bertell Ollman, 'Marx's vision of communism', *Critique*, 8, Summer 1977, pp. 4–41.
33. Most trenchantly by Hans Magnus Enzensberger, 'A Critique of Political Ecology', in *Raids and Reconstructions*, Pluto, 1976.
34. See Bahro and also P. Baran and P. Sweezy, *Monopoly Capital*, Penguin Books, 1968, Ch. 10.
35. See I.M. Kirzner, (ed.), *Method, Process, and Austrian Economics*, Lexington Books, 1982.
36. M. Barratt Brown, *Models in Political Economy*, Penguin Books, 1984.
37. James O'Connor, *Accumulation Crisis*, Blackwell, 1984.
38. Schumpeter, *Capitalism, Socialism and Democracy*, p. 61.
39. Lindblom, *Politics and Markets*, Ch. 8.
40. This theme is taken up by several contributors to Ruth Levitas (ed.), *The Ideology of the New Right*, Polity, 1985.

ECONOMIC PLANNING IN MARKET ECONOMIES: SCOPE, INSTRUMENTS, INSTITUTIONS*

D.M. Nuti

1. Scope

The appropriate balance between 'plan' and 'market' has been debated *ad nauseam* in relation to the USSR, Eastern Europe and China, while for capitalism it is the only question still debated today when capitalist planning is discussed at all. Yet the answer to this question is relatively easy.

The experience of Soviet-type economies shows that the most determined attempts at centralised control of the whole economy through direct command and detailed physical allocation lead to elemental spontaneous processes which can be no less anarchic than those of pure capitalism. Instead of establishing social control over accumulation, Soviet-type economic and political centralisation leads to an over-accumulation bias, which at first yields fast growth but then persists well past the exhaustion of labour reserves and causes falling utilisation of plant and excess demand for labour and intermediate inputs. Systemic commitment to price stability prevents excess demand for labour and goods being translated into higher (or high enough) prices; shortages and queues ensue, disrupting the supply system and aggravating the built-in microeconomic inefficiency of the centralised system; cycles appear, as retrenchment from over-accumulation is forced upon central powers by domestic and external constraints, or as popular dissatisfaction with economic performance is dealt with by alternate bouts of liberalisation or further centralisation. It is clear that economic planning should go no further than major macroeconomic variables while markets should be allowed to determine detailed output structure and relative prices by the actions of competing firms unencumbered by central controls, while taxes and subsidies can be used to convey to firms public choices about environmental protection, desirable patterns of income distribution and any other relevant factor neglected by markets.

At the same time the experience of capitalist economies has shown that the sphere of markets should go no further than output proportions and relative prices (with the same provisions for public preferences),

---

*This paper was presented at the Conference organised by the *Cambridge Journal of Economics* in Cambridge, 26–29 June, 1985, on the theme 'Towards New Foundations for Socialist Policies in Britain'.

while only economic planning might control major economic variables, to prevent some or all of the macroeconomic evils: unemployment, stagflation, inflation and external imbalance on a large scale. In the macroeconomic sphere markets can make any kind of expectations come true if widely held, or they can act perversely (e.g. lower wages possibly lowering the level of labour employment through adverse feedback on demand), or 'turbulently' (as officially recognised by British government circles when sterling recently plunged to dollar parity). Even when they do work, markets often are much too slow or incur economic and social costs which cannot be tolerated. Increased reliance on markets is a poor response to macroeconomic imbalances.

The lesson of Soviet-type and British-type economies, therefore, is that economic planning should cover no more and no less than macro-variables such as employment, aggregate income, investment share and its broad allocation, public consumption and criteria of income distribution, the balance of international payments flows for trade and capital; while markets should cover no more and no less than the structure of output (by sectors and enterprises) and relative prices; with policy instruments, instead of direct orders, being used to make markets fit with the plans. This view is firmly rooted in the socialist tradition, from Dobb to Nove, and the controversies from 'right' and 'left' seeking to stretch the scope respectively of market and plan beyond these limits can now be regarded as settled, in view of the recent spectacular failures of both Soviet-type overstretched planning and British-type over-stretched markets. Macroplanning with micro-markets is the current model of the Hungarian economy, which has so distanced itself from the Soviet model as to request, in recent negotiations with the EEC (though now stalled) the incorporation in a treaty of the statement that Hungary now has a market economy, satisfying the requirements of GATT. It is also the model towards which China and Poland are striving and, at least in the view of Gorbachov's boldest interpreters, so is the Soviet Union. With the addition of workers' self-management and group ownership, it is also Yugoslavia's basic model.

Once we have settled the question of the appropriate scope of market and plan, however, we are not much wiser as to what we should actually do. This type of macroeconomic planning is indistinguishable from ordinary public policy, of the kind theorised for instance by Tinbergen and Johanssen: the government 'objective function' is maximised for levels of desirable targets obtained by means of policy instruments (fiscal and monetary policy, public enterprises, direct controls), up to the point where the trade-offs between targets in the government preferences are the same as, or closest to, the trade-offs obtainable through alternative policy-mixes. If this is not how it is, it is how it should be. What is the difference, then, between this and, say, Nove's 'feasible socialism'? How could the failures of public policy in economies intermediate between the Soviet and British types, which are no less conspicuous than the failures of central plans and competitive markets, be suddenly avoided just by sticking the label 'planning' or 'socialist planning' on public policy?

It can be argued that the difference between traditional public policy and economic planning is one of degree, and that quantitative difference makes for qualitative change in both character and performance. Economic planning, especially socialist planning, will have a longer time horizon, a different ranking of targets and of the relative degree of their fulfilment (for instance, it will attach greater importance to employment than to price stability), will employ policy instruments to a greater extent than the ordinary public policy of a non-socialist government, as well as use a model of the functioning of the economy with features borrowed if not from Marx, Kalecki and Keynes at least from Pigou, Malinvaud and Drèze, instead of Friedman, Lucas and Sargent. This is a plausible view and certainly there is, to say the least, much room for improvement in public policy management everywhere. But there is not yet a significant success story, let alone a consistent success record, for this kind of planning either East or West. By and large, the macro problems of unemployment, stagnation, inflation and external imbalance have persistently proven to be almost intractable, targets being either conflicting or otherwise beyond the reach of policy instruments within the accepted range. From the evidence so far available we must conclude that, unless something new happens in the world, or is brought into the theoretical picture, economic planning as 'active' public policy cannot be expected to perform the miracles that 'less-active' public policy does not perform, that 'feasible socialism' à la Nove has already come and gone, and there is not much hope for the future of socialism as economic performer. At times of tranquillity there would seem to be not much to choose between markets and plans because they both work, whereas at difficult times we can only trade-off the drawbacks of plans with the drawbacks of markets, also with little to choose between them.

So, a more positive and optimistic outlook requires the introduction of new policy instruments and new institutions to match the ambitions of economic planning and of socialist values. It is true that in the last twenty five years a fair amount of institutional innovation has taken place in both major systems. In capitalist countries this has taken the guise of indicative planning of the French type, neocorporatist social pacts and modifications of the work contract. In socialist countries parallel innovation–apart from the reform moves to drive their economies away from the command model—consists of Yugoslav type self-management, GDR-type vertically integrated firms, and performance-related compensation schemes. All these developments fall outside the range of conventional public policy instruments, except as part of the catch-all category of 'qualitative' instruments, and are aimed at attacking the intractability of macroeconomic problems. All these new institutions are perfectly harmless; unfortunately, they are also not very effective.

Indicative planning was supposed to provide a transparent, consistent and consensual picture of future developments, to which all would conform out of self-interest; but the participants in this exercise often cheated; even when they did not cheat, their views about the future could not be well summarised by single-valued and firm expectations, and even if they all agreed on a possible and desirable scenario they could not agree on their own individual part in it; planning contracts were never real contracts; stabilisation plans, i.e. ordinary public policy measures, took over from indicative planning, followed by even more conventional drastic austerity measures. Neocorporatist pacts were short on implementation and turned into unilateral gifts by the workers. Proposed and implemented changes in the work contract range from the introduction of wage indexation at times of accelerating inflation to its abolition when inflation decelerates, from synchronised collective bargaining to tax-based wages policy, from work-sharing (i.e. the collectivisation of unemployment) to Weitzman's proposal for replacing wages by a variable share in the revenue of their enterprise. All these labour contract modifications amount to devices to hold down real earnings without being seen to do so; as workers can only be cheated once, all the time imaginative new tricks have to be invented to keep wages low.

On the socialist side, Yugoslav-type self-management seems more the result of (and dominated by) group ownership, a form of property which has no known justification, than a direct attempt at workers' participation in decision-making. There is no doubt that self-management can make a very valuable contribution to the planning environment through greater economic democracy and can be a tangible counterpart of economic concessions in a social pact; it is still an open question, however, whether self-management can have a positive direct impact on economic performance. Vertical integration of GDR firms has reduced the informational and organisational problems of its centrally planned economy to the size of a sector but has no particular virtue in the Hungarian-style economy; moreover, the flexibility exhibited by the GDR economy is more likely to come from the umbilical cord linking it to the FRG rather than from its vertical industrial structure. Performance-linked formulas for the determination of earnings bestow rewards or punishments mostly on workers who have not had any responsibility and therefore deserve neither.

Newer policy instruments and newer economic institutions than these will have to be devised to support the high ambitions of socialist planning (the discussion of necessary *political* preconditions for planning—East or West—goes beyond the scope of this paper). The suggestions and reflections that follow are tentative and incomplete thoughts, put forward in the brainstorming spirit of the Cambridge Conference.

2. *New instruments*

The intractability of macroeconomic problems such as unemployment, inflation, foreign payments deficits, is due primarily to the pervasive presence of a network of conflicts between different persons, classes and groups (or even between coexisting roles of the same persons, classes and groups). These conflicts have three frequent characteristics:

(i) the dispersion, variability of roles and anonymity of the large number of agents involved in the conflict (e.g. I would sacrifice some of my wage if, as a result, fewer people were unemployed but only if a number of other people did too; nobody is signalling this intention and neither do I; even if all of us like-minded people got together we would have to find a number of willing firms and negotiate with them the terms on which our wage sacrifice is transformed into higher employment; too many agents are involved);

(ii) the inter-temporal nature of most conflicts, which introduces the possibility that the best resolution of a conflict might involve a sequential and therefore uncertain settlement of conflicting interests, which is not implemented because of that uncertainty. (Those of us willing to sacrifice our wage levels to reduce unemployment have got together and negotiated mutually acceptable terms with a number of firms; but since we are sacrificing our wage now and the increase in employment will come some time later, and the delivery of later larger employment is uncertain, in the circumstances we will not sacrifice our wage levels.)

(iii) the actual pay-offs of alternative strategies encourage a non-cooperative stance by partners in conflict (e.g. it is in the interest of firms not to employ in the future people they would not otherwise wish to employ, whether or not I and my well-meaning friends have sacrificed current wages for that purpose).

Neither markets nor plans are good at resolving these conflicts, familiar from literature on prisoners' dilemmas, isolation paradoxes, moral hazard, etc. In order to resolve these conflicts, markets would need multilateral, inter-temporal, contingent contracts, of a kind and on a scale that has proven—so far—uneconomic or inconvenient to stipulate, let alone enforce. Planners cannot resolve these conflicts either because policy instruments affect mostly the present, unconditionally with respect to possible settlements of conflicting interests between a large number of parties.

It is conceivable, however, that a new class of policy instruments be used by planners: namely, *future contingent instruments* (FCIs), i.e. legally binding unilateral commitments, on the part of the government, to adopt at a future given date or dates a given instrument of economic policy (say, a tax or a subsidy), and/or given parameter or parameters for that instrument (or package of instruments), conditional on a given state of the economy (say, a given level of employment, or the growth rate of income); such commitments would be irrevocable within a specified period of time, with a guarantee that they would not be nullified by subsequent offsetting measures within the time specified. Within this time limit such commitments could be binding for successive governments, much as any government is already bound, for instance, by the national or international debt incurred by its predecessors.

At present there is only one rudimentary instrument of this kind, namely indexation (for instance, of government's loans, or wages in the public sector, or tax thresholds) with respect to the price level. This is equivalent to the choice of a numeraire different from money, whereas the proposed range of FCIs could be linked to any index of macroeconomic performance.

The advantages of the proposed instruments are:
(i)   the replacement of uncertain expectations about government future intentions, which often nullify the effectiveness of current measures, by firm beliefs (as firm as beliefs in the state can be, at any rate, when its commitments are backed by the judiciary and are no longer changeable at the whims of the executive);
(ii) the possibility of adopting not just a present policy stance but a firm time pattern of policy measures, designing a path towards a configuration of macro-variables by the government. The path need not be inflexible, for alternative courses can be announced, contingent on the value taken by exogenous as well as endogenous variables;
(iii) the provision by the government of a guarantee of last resort in the case of social pacts containing conditions about the value of macro-economic variables, with a pre-announced set of measures designed to reward adherence to such pacts.

Let us suppose, for instance, that the government wishes to raise investment and employment, while workers would be willing to sacrifice wages but are distrustful of the uses to which their forsaken wages will be put by their employers. The government can guarantee this kind of pact by effectively indexing, through tax concessions, the lower level of wages to the rate of unemployment, simultaneously announcing that in a given number of months (equal to the expected average lag between investment outlay and employment) a capital tax will be levied also geared to the future unemployment rate unless this is on a preannounced target consistent with the reinvestment of the wage cuts. (A similar proposal put forward in 1983 by Fitoussi and Nuti in Italy raised interest in Trade Union circles). Alternatively, the government could announce that next year in the event of unemployment reaching a critical level it would immediately step in with a given large-scale public works programme; this might by itself restore investors' confidence and lead to an improvement that might make that intervention unnecessary; this is not just an ordinary announcement effect, since it is reinforced by the envisaged binding nature of government commitments.

It might be interesting to compare this type of policy instrument with the apparently similar framework of Debreu's general equilibrium model with intertemporal and contingent markets. Debreu-type contracts are private, bi- or multilateral and contingent on a state of the world (i.e. they are devised to eliminate not market uncertainty but environmental uncertainty) whereas FCIs are public, unilateral intertemporal promises, contingent precisely on macroeconomic features of market uncertainty.

Unilateral commitments, like unilateral disarmament, make cooperative strategies much more attractive if they can be made *contingent* on concomitant commitments by other conflictual partners as well as on external events, with a strong guarantee that the contingency clause will be respected if the contingent event is lagged. Thus, for instance, the classic prisoner's dilemma would be satisfactorily resolved if the validity of a prisoner's confession could be made conditional on a similar confession by the other prisoner.

In international relations we could imagine a country unilaterally committing itself to freer trade conditionally on acceptance, by its trading partners who take advantage of its new liberalism, of stiff protectionist measures if payments flows are seriously disrupted. If this type of commitment spread the chance of concerted reflation would greatly improve.

Because of their unilateral nature, such commitments do not require the prior agreement of a large number of potential contractual partners, yet the spreading of such types of commitments can facilitate the stipulation of a multilateral pact with private as well as public parties. For instance, the declaration by a city that the territory within its limits is a nuclear-free zone—such as is sometimes made—is an irrelevant moral stance of no consequence; but, if a city makes a unilateral commitment to make its territory a nuclear-free zone conditionally on a city of proportional size in the potential enemy country also being made a nuclear-free zone and a number of cities in both countries make this conditional unilateral commitment in pairs, bilateral disarmament will be all that much nearer. By the same process, conflictual parties (private as well as public) could make progress towards a pact even if the object of the contract (as in the example of peace) is indivisible; while if the object is divisible the reciprocal acceptance of conditional unilateral commitments will fulfil the contingent condition and lead to immediate improvement.

It would be naive to expect miracles from this range of policy instruments, though clearly they avoid the limitations of more conventional instruments in dealing with multi-party, intertemporal and contingent conflicts. New institutions will also be needed, in the strict sense of public agencies with separate legal personality undertaking policy tasks different from the production of ordinary goods and services.

3. New institutions

The main problem areas in the macroeconomic performance of market economies are unemployment, low income growth and external payments deficits. (Inflation is not half as bad as is widely believed and, in any case, if the other three problems are reduced it should be possible to control inflation through incomes policy and FCIs, if monetary policy does not suffice.) New institutions (i.e. public agencies) are therefore needed to deal with employment, investment and international trade. Let us imagine that three new public bodies are set up: the National Employment Corporation, the National Investment Corporation and the International Trade Corporation. What features must they have to contribute significantly to employment, growth and external balance?

First of all they would have to operate *through the market*, i.e. buying and selling and renting and letting and lending and borrowing, instead of issuing prohibitions and commands; otherwise the well-known drawbacks of the Soviet-type model would rear up. It follows that they should not have the structure of Ministries, they should have a profit and loss account (though they may receive grants from the state budget), and they should not have the monopoly of whatever they do (which would interfere with the efficiency of markets and also reintroduce the drawbacks of centralised planning).

Second, they should act *directly* on the level of employment, investment and trade, because their existence is justified by the inadequacy of *indirect* instruments of intervention.

Third, they should not involve an open-ended commitment (such as that incurred by health services in modern welfare states) and their responsibility should be, respectively, that of maximising additional employment, investment and net exports (or volume of trade) over and above what would have occurred without their intervention, within the budgetary constraints of their net revenues, plus own endowment when they are set up and recurring grants from state budget (grants could follow the pattern of FCIs, i.e. be indicated in advance by the government contingently on the performance of the economy in these crucial areas). The three corporations should therefore not be bound to the fulfilment of preset targets, unless they accept this responsibility in negotiations with the government on the amount of resources entrusted to them. These principles already narrow down very considerably what these corporations could do:

The *National Employment Corporation* would hire workers at the minimum national wage for each skill and occupation and rent them out to firms at the best competitive rate (whether lower, or temporarily higher) they can obtain in the market; if there is no demand for the services of some of its workers it can rent them out free of charge to Local Authorities. Any firm hiring workers at a rate below the going wage from the NEC is forbidden to lay off any other workers, so that NEC workers are the 'margin' for firms. In this way the marginal cost of labour to firms is lowered without lowering the average wage, thereby avoiding perverse feedbacks of labour cost on demand. The same result would be obtained with a wage subsidy on additional employment under the same restrictions on firing and on a given budget on a first-come first-served basis; but the subsidy would have to be preset and would not respond to market conditions as frequently as under the proposed arrangement. The NEC could be given, as well as a basic budget, an amount per worker hired corresponding to cost of unemployment to the government (forsaken income tax as well as unemployment subsidy per worker). The scale of NEC operations is dictated by its government grant, as well as by its own ability to rent out workers on good terms. The actual additional employment generated by NEC would be visible and countable; its cost per worker (net of unemployment cost) would be monitored and regarded as its performance indicator, though changes in this indicator would be related to changing external circumstances or scale of operation and supplemented by direct scrutiny of NEC activity. (Something resembling this institution has been suggested in Italy under the label 'Labour Service' in policy discussions, but with a vague mixture of functions ranging from job creation to job brokerage, neither of which are vested in the corporation proposed here.)

The *National Investment Corporation* would be a cross between military procurement agencies in capitalist countries and Soviet-type Machine Tractor Stations. Like military procurement agencies NIC would have a budget out of which to acquire equipment, through tender or negotiated purchases in the market, in this case plants expanding productive capacity of any good or service. Like MTS of Soviet memory, NIC would then rent plant out or sell it to firms or individuals at whatever rental or sale price can be obtained in the market. NIC would specifically be forbidden to operate plant itself, which would alter drastically the nature of its activities, the size and required expertise of its staff; though of course NIC could recommend (but not automatically obtain) that a public enterprise should be set up especially for that purpose (and indeed the possibility of this happening would enable NIC to obtain a better price in the market for the rental or sale of the plant). To avoid duplications, NIC would announce its plans in advance, indicating clearly whether these are intentions or firm commitments. NIC performance would be judged by its profit, or loss, relatively to the total resources with which it is endowed and also to the scale of its capacity creation. If the switchover to the proposed system is made from a command economy, NIC should replace *all* centralised investment other than public infrastructure.

The *International Trade Corporation* would act as an additional import-export company, empowered to enter long term contracts with both domestic and foreign companies (or even foreign governments in the case of trade with centrally planned economies or developing countries), as well as undertake international borrowing and lending as necessary. It has often been said that planned trade expansion, not protectionism, is the best way to cope with external constraints, but, in spite of the like-minded attitude of several countries, the institutional machinery for expanding trade in a planned fashion is lacking. ITC would import goods on long term contracts, for cash or barter, sell them domestically at spot prices (or, if it can, also on long term contracts); order and buy goods domestically for export, either to obtain currency to pay for its imports or to balance barter exchanges. Dealing in lots of commodities, it could act as broker in multilaterial and intertemporal barter. Its trading pro-grammes would be announced for future years, so that capacity for export could be especially developed and contracted, or domestic capacity expansion slowed down to absorb planned imports. Domestic sales of imported goods would be at competitive prices whatever the international price paid by ITC, so nobody could complain of dumping practices; even if ITC undersold domestic producers it would do so having announced its intentions in advance, to give domestic producers the time to soften the blow. ITC performance would be judged by its profit, or loss, relatively to the total resources with which it is endowed, and to total turnover and net exports. By and large this Corporation would be like a Soviet-type Import-Export company, except for the important differences that it would not have the monopoly of international trade, it would act on its own initiative following market signals in an effort to raise the volume of trade and (if possible) net export earnings instead of executing a trade plan, and it would deal in several commodity groups.

If the scale of operation of the envisaged corporations was too large for a single unit, more than one could be set up, with the same criteria. The corporation(s) in each area of responsibility would therefore pursue directly one each of the three most elusive targets of planning in market economies. The envisaged machinery would allow government and the public to monitor the costs and benefits of the pursuit of each policy objective, avoiding both the undershooting typical of capitalist economies using ordinary instruments of public policy, and the costly overshooting typical of the socialist economy using central planning. Moreover, the full cost of the realisation of public policy targets can be revealed (over and above the cost of indirect policy instruments attributable to them in the state budget and other public sector accounts), in a way which is not revealed in centrally planned economy where prices used for aggregation are not market clearing prices and priority sectors get a preemptive claim on deliveries equivalent to an infinitely expandable budget (Kornai's 'soft constraints'). Looking at costs, the public might decide to lower their sights and choose to trade-off targets in favour of a different mix.

It may be difficult to envisage the operation of an economy in which uch 'residual' state intervention directly acts on crucial macro-variables; ut it is even more difficult to envisage how an economy without at east the first or the second of these institutions can hope to conduct conomic planning instead of just taking pot shots at macro-targets with he conventional instruments and institutions of economic policy. This s perhaps not that important for capitalist economies, where by and arge people have almost given up the notion of planning and therefore here are no expectations to be disappointed. It is, however, very import-nt for socialist countries, which have been making repeated attempts at reeing themselves from the strictures of the command system but expect of markets—regulated as they might be through policy means—the delivery of macropolicy goals which markets can very rarely deliver; in their case, he discovery of the failures of markets and the inadequacy of usual olicy means may drive them back to the command system (as indeed has lready happened repeatedly, as witnessed by the frequency with which ttempts at reform are introduced and gradually withdrawn).

4. Transition

Even if the planning model sketched here, or any other model of planning n any economic system, were to be universally recognised as the best of ll possible models, it would not follow at all that the transition from the xtant model to the ideal one would be smooth, costless or even desirable.

The changeover to a new economic system is most likely to occur at a time of crisis, i.e. the new system (especially if markets are activated in command economies) is most likely to operate in the least favourable conditions, especially in the possibly weak form in which a new system may have to be introduced. The changeover is also likely to be paralleled by the rise to power of new political groups and, therefore, the simultaneous affirmation of pent-up aspirations previously repressed, which are bound to compete with standard macroeconomic targets. Large redistributional claims are likely to be put forward and it may be political-ly necessary to validate them in order to retain newly found power. Fear of change might lead to a drain of resources (people, skills, but above all liquid capital).

The broad implications of these circumstances are fairly clear but the empirical and theoretical study of them is nonexistent. The political movement favouring the introduction of macroeconomic planning in the market economy or the marketisation of a command economy will need, ready on the eve of taking power, if not an actual plan at least an insti-tutional blueprint, complete with draft legislation, as well as fingertip command of information about the state and the trends of the whole economy and its external connections. Impatience can be ruinous and, initially, only modest improvements in the achievement of desired targets can be expected, announced and implemented. The normality of everyday life will have to take priority over long-term targets. Redistribution will have to be achieved by redeploying wealth, not through the distribution of paper claims unmatched by goods in the market. Political concessions having a low resource cost will have to be granted instead of acceding to costly aspirations. Steps to stem capital flight will have had to be taken in anticipation of taking power (because the same anticipation will be shared by financial circles). External supply sources and outlets both in finance and trade relations may have to be partially switched if a substantial systemic change is envisaged; alternative partners then must be available, already committed to expanded relations preferably by earlier contingent agreements.

It is a most disheartening law of contemporary political and economic history that no political movement favouring systemic change (whether wishing to introduce planning in a capitalist economy, or—like Solidarnosc —wishing to marketise the command system while retaining macroeconomic control) has ever got anywhere near power having the slightest idea of how to proceed afterwards, let alone with an institutional blueprint or a plan. (Only *total* marketisation is a simple, effectively self-implementing move with the total abolition of central control). And if any such political movement took power tomorrow anywhere in the world it would not be in any better position than its failed predecessors. This is why it is most important to discuss as widely and in as much detail as possible not only the uncharted territory of feasible socialisms, but also the feasible paths that might lead there.

THE POLITICS OF NEW TECHNOLOGY*

Frank Webster

'. . . the unfortunate thing is that at present the word "progress" and the word "Socialism" are linked inseparably in almost everyone's mind. . . the Socialist is always in favour of mechanisation, rationalisation, modernisation. . .'

George Orwell, *The Road to Wigan Pier*, (1937).
Harmondsworth: Penguin, 1967, p. 176.

'. . . intellectuals must affirm outright, without qualification or hesitation progress is a lie. Only then will people be able to think, say, and act upon what they already know, without fear of isolation, ridicule, or repression. Responsible intellectuals. . . must struggle in their own realm to gain legitimacy for worker resistance to progress. They must change the terms of debate and extend the range of respectable discourse in order to insure that those who choose to resist need never act alone.'

David F. Noble, Present Tense Technology, Part Three, *Democracy* 4(3)1983:87.

Introduction

A recent article explains how one of the most militant workforces in the country, car workers at British Leyland's Longbridge plant, came to have its spirit of resistance broken. There are several reasons: the failure to mobilise members in response to the sacking of the union convenor late in 1979, the aggressive management tactics of Michael Edwardes, mass unemployment, the combativity of the Thatcher government. . . However, what the authors of this *New Society* piece single out as 'the real turning point' was the introduction of new technology which forced on the unions 'flexibility' by deskilling jobs, massively increasing output, and introducing an electronic information network called Machine Monitoring System that resulted in much greater surveillance of individual employees.[1]

The BL unions offered no significant opposition to the robots, computer numerical control systems and electronic supervision technologies that brought this into being because, say Scarbrough and Moran, 'new technology enjoys an important status as an inherently progressive force in society. Few if any trade unions. . . are willing to risk the accusation of being "Luddites" in relation to technology'. It was this 'mystique of technology' that the Longbridge management was able to exploit to overcome labour resistance to innovations that would seriously undermine

*Thanks to Keith Lambe and Ralph Miliband for their criticisms of earlier drafts of this article.

385

the power of the shopfloor.

The unions scarcely stood a chance. So ensnared in the ideology of 'technological progress' were they that 'Even the shop stewards on the Works Committee—notable for their communist sympathies—sought to protect it (new technology) from the plant's industrial relations problems'. And what option did they have given the fact that the 'alternative plan' put forward by the stewards' combine in the 1970s 'had made massive investment in new production facilities the centrepiece of its approach'? Not surprisingly, 'when the investment actually materialised at the plant in 1980, the unions could hardly stand on their heads and oppose its introduction'.

*   *   *   *   *

The Longbridge episode focuses a recurrent dilemma for the Left: how can it reconcile an attitude towards technology which regards it as inherently progressive with the fact that it is used and is being used as a weapon against labour? The urgency of finding a resolution to this puzzle can hardly be overstated since we are living through a period of particularly intense technological change. Computer communications technologies are the leading edge of this movement, but it also includes genetic engineering, nuclear power and biotechnology. Indeed, technological innovation is today a privileged means of effecting social, economic, and even political change and until the Left establishes a clear and confident technology policy it will be condemned to dithering, to wringing its hands at the results of technological adoption which favours the powerful while helpless to resist its implementation because it is approving of the 'progress' the technology itself represents.[2]

It is in response to this situation that this article sets out to:

— examine the Left's perception of technology and explain why it impairs resistance to changes that favour capital.

— argue that if the Left wants to influence changes decisively it needs to reconceive technology in a way that allows it to understand adequately the key role of technology in attempts to restructure relations so that capital might escape recession and, as important, to appreciate the influence social relations have had on the development of technologies currently being introduced.

— urge that the Left should thoroughly politicise technology and technological innovation, from the point of application back to origination, and in so doing to develop and implement socialist priorities and procedures to guide technological change.

*   *   *   *   *

The Left's perception of technology

The dominant assumption of the Left is that technology is neutral and consequently amenable to use or abuse depending on who exercises political power. Thus while capitalism might abuse technology in service of private interests and market injustices, the arrival of socialism will lead to positive use of technology for the community as a whole.

This attitude is evident in much Left thinking. It is present in the writing of Marx and Engels where they rage against capitalist misuse of machines to exploit working people, but foresee a time when these same technologies can be 'transformed from master demons into willing servants'.[3] It is prominent in the Labour Party which argues that a Thatcher government 'is the worst possible background for the adoption of new technology', though directed by Kinnock it 'could create a historic stage in the development of a socialist caring society'.[4] And it received perhaps its classic statement in Harold Wilson's 1963 'white heat' speech which, contrasting Tory and Labour policies, offered voters 'the choice between the blind imposition of technological advance, with all that means in terms of unemployment, and the conscious, planned, purposive use of scientific progress'.[5]

This emphasis on the malleability of technology co-exists with the equally widespread conviction that a certain amount of technology is a prerequisite of socialism. Drawing on Marx's view that socialism would be viable only after the 'struggle for necessity' (for food, shelter, clothing. . .) had been won, and endorsing his assertion that the capitalist stage of development preceded socialism not least because by 'revolutionising the instruments of production' it would secure a material basis for socialism, there is on the Left a presumption that some degree of technological uptake is essential to lay the foundations for a new order.

This outlook results in what might be called an inheritor approach to technologies pioneered by capitalism. There are no qualms about taking over capitalist technologies because technology is amenable to socialist application, though they are also a precondition for socialism since there cannot be any satisfactory politics while people are hungry, naked, or in general want.

These principles evoke a paradox which bedevils the Left: technology is supposed to be susceptible to political manipulation, yet it is, in a real if unspecified sense, prior to social and political relations, since without a technological infrastructure life is governed by a raw and ungenerous nature. The presumption here, at one and the same time, is that while technologies are determined for good or ill by social and political decisions, imperatives of technology adequate to satisfy basic needs determine social and political relations.

There are a number of consequences of this tradition of thought. A major one is that it leads to vacillation towards technological innovation.

It could scarcely be otherwise given the Left's conviction that technology of itself is aloof from politics. Moreover, since technology is also essential for laying the basis for socialism, socialists can hardly rebel against its introduction. They can thunder against its misapplications, but they cannot be against the technology itself because come socialism it will be used advantageously. This is surely the reason for the undercurrent of celebration of capitalism's dynamism that runs through *The Communist Manifesto*.

An upshot is regular condemnation of 'mindless Luddites' by many on the Left when vigorous opposition is voiced towards technological innovation (it goes without saying that this is a favoured refrain of the Right)—*viz* Wilson's *cri de coeur* that 'there is no room for Luddites in the Socialist Party'[5] and, more recently, Jimmy Reid's denunciation of opposition to pit closures as 'Luddite' and thus 'thoroughly reactionary' since it fails to 'view modern technology as a liberating force'.[6] Equally common is a resigned feeling of 'inevitability' to changes spearheaded by technology though they are recognised by the Left as damaging to their cause. The overall result is that resistance to change favourable to capital is disarmed.[7]

A second consequence is that, if technology is essential for the socialist enterprise and if it can be inherited from capitalism, then to what extent are we to submit to the social relations, and the quality of those relations, that the technology imposes? This is a particularly acute question when set against the technologies associated with large-scale manufacture and bureaucratic organisation which characteristically result in workers feeling alienated, bored and demeaned. If one accepts the view that technologies are simply efficient means of guaranteeing output which yet impose themselves in particular divisions of labour and authority relations, then are we resigned just to accept them? If we do, and much of the reasoning of the Left leads one to this conclusion, then what is the attraction of socialism for ordinary workers and where have the socialist ideals of egalitarianism and an end to alienation gone?

A third consequence, related to the second, revolves around the popular socialist notion that a decrease in the working day is an assured route to socialism, and that this can be achieved by application of technology which allows at once increases in production and reductions in time spent at work. This is a theme well known to socialists, one found in the writings of Marx and Engels themselves, and most recently espoused by André Gorz.[8] It does allow the Left to retain the idea that technology, though developed by capitalism, is neutral, and to acknowledge that, whatever the social system, it imposes unpleasant conditions on workers. Its resolution is delightfully straightforward: apply still *more* technology so that what Gorz calls the 'sphere of autonomous activity', and others call leisure, can be massively extended.

However, what this must then encounter is the serious problem concerning the extent to which technology *per se*—the technology which is essential for socialism though created by capitalism—can lead to socialism. And this is not a frivolous issue given the deluge of futurist comment projecting precisely this—material plenty without the need to work, a Leisure Society awash with goods and services that are abundantly available to everyone—'without the long-awaited revolution of the proletariat'.[9] Socialists, for long accepting as a truism that technology is crucial for socialism, without stipulating just how much it shapes social arrangements, cannot complain when conservatives steal their fire by discovering in new technology the possibility of 'socialism' without political change because the technology will effortlessly take us to the 'affluent redundancy' of an 'Athens without Slaves'. Neither can socialists respond with vigour to technological innovations in the here and now that enforce leisure on working people so long as they conceive of socialism as a technologically supported idleness.

*   *   *   *   *

Present tense technologies

If ambivalence and hesitation are endemic to the Left's traditional perception of technology at a time when it can least afford to be indecisive because we are undergoing the most rapid technological transformation in history, what is a more adequate way of seeing? This should entail switching from conceiving of the abstraction TECHNOLOGY to stress that technologies exist in particular machines and objects that perform particular functions. It is important to move away from the unwordly perception of technology currently held because, paradoxically, it is by starting with a generic notion which is thought to be subject to use or abuse that, turning to the substantive, the Left finds itself encumbered by a theoretical legacy that makes it incapable of responding cogently and confidently to specific technologies. If we can focus attention on what David Noble calls 'present tense technologies',[10] we can shift from what is an unreal yet incapacitating debate towards an analysis of what technological changes practically represent and thereby towards a forthright programme of response.

The point is that no-one is or can be against TECHNOLOGY since TECHNOLOGY does not exist. Given the ubiquity of technologies—and virtually nothing we do in our lives, from the mundane (writing letters, shaving, telephoning) to the spectacular (flying across Europe), is performed without them—it may well be that an all-encompassing category is useful as a shorthand way of communicating, but it is an unfortunate by-product that the generality of the term TECHNOLOGY means that debates about its social meaning are frequently conducted at an unreal level. It is rather like using the term SOCIETY: no-one can be against

SOCIETY because this term is so diffuse; move down to particulars, however, to *this* social relation rather than *that* one, and very different conclusions may be drawn.

Technology and capitalist restructuring

Moving to the more concrete, we should acknowledge first of all that the primary rationale for technological change is to restructure British capitalism that it might better compete internationally. Amid a profound recession, the search is on to find an escape, and reorganisation of production processes, manufacture of new products, and revised market strategies are axiomatic to this endeavour. The thrust of capital's effort is to take on board new technologies of various sorts, cheapen and/or improve production and distribution, and thereby capture an increased share of foreign markets.

Technology is at the very forefront of this strategy of 'increasing competition' and 'restoring profitability' and it is a major reason why unions and their 'restrictive practices' must be broken since they represent at least potential obstacles to smooth and rapid adjustment. This is a message with which we are all familiar, one which Mrs Thatcher, backed by lavish propaganda campaigns in schools and media, voices in any and every speech which calls for 'rewarding entrepreneurs', 'hard work' and support for 'sunrise' industries which will supply the 'jobs of tomorrow'.[11]

Technology is, in short, at the heart of the Thatcherite political offensive,[12] and if the Left persists in appealing to its neutrality and holding to the 'progress' of advances in the 'productive forces', then assuredly it will be without a serious response to the assault.

But this is exactly what the Labour Party continues to do. Rejecting Thatcher's commitment to *laissez-faire* development of new technology (which in practice the Tories do not altogether abide by), Labour insists on the need for state planning of innovation. This does distinguish it from the Conservatives, yet it shares their impulse to introduce Information Technology in order to rejuvenate a market economy. Indeed, its criticism of Thatcher *et al* is that they are not proceeding with technical innovation quickly enough compared to our major competitors. Thus John Smith MP, shadow industry spokesman:

> We've been taking a long hard look at the UK's industrial future and we've come to the clear conclusion that the key to industrial renewal is the rapid application of high technology. Our criticism is that it's not going fast enough.[13]

This is also the reasoning that we find in the TUC which urges that Britain responds to the 'challenge' of IT by being 'in the vanguard of technological change', so as to grasp 'the unique and unparalled opportunity. . . for Britain to improve its economic performance and also its competitiveness in world markets'.[14]

The differences between the Labour and Conservative parties come down to the former's assertion that state orchestration is the best means of coping with the latest 'technological revolution' and its faith that a well-disposed state can distribute technology's bounty, which will be secured by making Britain's economy more competitive than that of other nations, to the less privileged.

These are by no means insignificant differences between the parties and there is not the least doubt that a Labour administration would be more appealing to socialists, but it is necessary to appreciate fully the implications of Labour's approach to technology. In its acceptance of IT as a means of 'industrial renewal' as fast as is possible it is acceding to the terms set by the international market. It scarcely makes a secret of the matter. Mr Callaghan said as much late in 1978 when he averred that it was time Britain 'woke up to microelectronics', because if it did not 'and other major industrial countries' did, then 'the prospect for us will be one of stagnation and decline'.[15] Since then, Callaghan's words have been repeated in one form or another by innumerable Labour representatives. The Tories are more curt, but the message is the same: 'Automate or Liquidate'.

Labour of course assumes that technological innovation is neutral, that there has been a 'discovery', and government should seize the opportunities presented. Following this logic, there can be no anxiety in steering technological changes on lines befitting the international market. Quite the contrary, Labour is enthusiastic to get on with the job, wanting to mobilise all state resources to hand that we can more effectively compete in the struggle for market share. And within all of this, it presumes, technology stands aloof, the preserve of politics being restricted to distributing the unprecedented wealth that follows from a revitalised 'Britain Inc.' thanks to rapid adjustment to the 'microelectronics revolution'.

But it is demonstrably the case that a technology policy guided by the principles of the market shapes the sort of technologies that are produced and applied. One consequence, for instance, is that many jobs are de-skilled and demeaned (and many others made redundant) because the principle underpinning the design and application of *this* technology rather than *that* one is 'how can we best the French, Japanese, Germans or Americans?' (and all these nations are operating on the self-same lines) and axiomatic considerations here are cheapening the costs of labour, controlling the labour process more effectively, and increasing the output of saleable goods and services. Another is that the technologies which get manufactured are those that are marketable rather than those that are socially needed (for example, in 1980 Thorn-EMI's chairman candidly opined that his company's 'decision to withdraw from medical electronics was [because] there appeared little likelihood of achieving profits in the foreseeable future';[16] for another example, where was the mass market for personal computers before the torrent of 'IT awareness' commercials convinced anxious parents that they were an investment in the educational and employment prospects of their children?). Still another consequence is that funding for research and development from which emanate as yet unimagined technologies is directed towards projects with commercial potential rather than communal application—witness the £350 million Alvey programme to pioneer 'fifth generation computers' which is explicitly tied to corporate goals.[17]

The outcome of Labour's presumption that conditions prevailing on the international market have no influence on the technology itself (the political variables being only the speed of uptake and distribution of the beneficence of growth) is that it is resigned to the 'inevitability' of accepting and indeed encouraging particular technologies whatever they might do to the workforce, unions or the number of unemployed. Given the fact that the advanced capitalist economies, entrapped in slump, 'are all looking to new technologies as the panacea'[18] for capital's woes, Labour's assumptions place it in an impossible situation. Compelled to manage technological innovation on terms set by the international market, yet operating in the name of socialism, it must find itself imposing and stimulating changes which militate against its core constituencies and political ideals.

Technologies embody social values
Following from this, it is necessary to emphasise that technologies have not dropped out of the skies, though this is the implication of media portrayals of that weird and wonderful galaxy 'Silicon Valley'. They have been produced in social contexts where they have been subject to the values and priorities of particular groups which, in discernable ways, get embodied in these technologies. To make this sort of statement seems to upset people, many of them on the Left who, sensing the presence of 'philosophical relativism',[19] insist that this is to reduce technology to a figment of the mind. It is nothing of the sort. But it is to assert, against those who proclaim that technology is amenable to use or abuse, that things are not nearly so straightforward because, in a constituted technology, social values have been incorporated. This is certainly not to say that, in different circumstances, we cannot use the technologies created by capitalism. The fact of the matter is that, being in the world, we have to make use of what is available and few artifacts are so determining that they cannot be put to some alternative uses. It is simply to say that, because technologies are practical products of the social world, they are shaped by that world and this limits the malleability of any technology that might be inherited.

Let me give a few examples:

— Houses are artifices in which to live, find protection from the weather, rear one's children, and accommodate one's belongings. But can anyone believe that these are 'just places to live?' Can anyone who has ridden through a town on a bus or train, from the city centre through the suburbs and beyond, be unaware of the values that have been incorporated into the architecture of homes? And can anyone be unaware of the intrusion of class inequalities into this housing (size of buildings, garages, location, brickwork, gardens, proximity to work etc)? Reflecting on the values that are manifest here can socialists be blind to the enormous difficulties that 'inheritance' of such technologies presents for an egalitarian order? Come socialism who will get the palaces in Bishop's Avenue, Hampstead, and who will be living in the council houses of Neasden?

— Cars are one of the commonest technologies today: in the USA there were 122 million registered automobiles, one for every two persons, in 1980, with 87% of households owning a car and over half possessing two or more. They are a means of carrying people and things from one place to another, but they are much more than a 'technical' transport device since they incorporate a multitude of social values such as family size, use of and attitude towards finite natural resources (they are highly wasteful of energy), tolerance of injuries and fatalities and enormous expense imposed on health services (in 1981, 50,000 people were killed in car accidents in America), status and style (the Porsche, Mini, Mercedes. . .), modes of living and of work (home in the suburbs away from the place of work).

Perhaps above all, the automobile embodies a value which is opposed to provision of public transport and favours individual provision of the means of mobility. It is worth stressing that the boom in the private motor car on which so much of the economic success of the fifties and sixties relied, the coincidence of the dismantling of much of the railway network, and the hidden subsidy from the taxpayer for provision of roads, reflect a deep-seated aversion in our society to the creation and maintenance of a public transport system. And it should be added that this is a value reflected in a particular technology despite the fact that it is extraordinarily hard to see anything but the necessity of owning a car in many parts of Britain nowadays because buses and trains are woefully inadequate in large part as a result of the development of the private motor car.

No-one would claim that a change in social relations would overnight abolish the car. But it is equally absurd to pretend that the car is but a neutral technology which, if abused in the here and now (driven too fast, driven under the influence of alcohol, driven often unnecessarily), will be taken over unchanged in a different order. It will certainly be used, and used in some ways differently, but over time it will also change technically as it is shaped by changed values and priorities.

— Much has been written in recent months about the Strategic Defence Initiative (commonly referred to as Star Wars), which aims to produce a system of computers and communications, co-ordinated with beam weapons, tied together by the most advanced space technologies. Costs are scarcely estimable, though early in 1985 President Reagan requested nearly $4 billion for initial programmes and $30 billion for the first five years funding, and full costs are put at many times that. The Strategic Defence Initiative is but the most dramatic instance of the trend towards 'electronic warfare'—everything from AWACS (airborne warning and control systems), battle-field communications, 'smart weapons', radar-seeking missiles, electronic countermeasures and counter-countermeasures, the militarisation of space, the launch, guidance and operation of nuclear weapons, to worldwide military communication networks—that characterises modern military and security affairs.

As constituted these technologies incorporate values of distrust, paranoia, and aggression in their design as means of surveillance and destruction of people within and outside particular nations. No doubt there are some alternative uses to which might be put the plethora of Command, Control, Communications and Intelligence systems strung around the globe, but surely the hope and conviction of socialists is that in a different regime most if not all will be redundant, unusable reminders of a totally different and repugnant way of life.

— Numerous commentators, but most of all Harry Braverman and more recently David Noble,[20] have described ways in which the development of factory and office technologies have been shaped by an overriding distrust of the worker. Nowhere in the twentieth century have investors or engineers seriously considered creating machinery which might ennoble work. Throughout, the aim has been to maximise output while minimising the role of the worker who threatens, as a human being who is unpredictable, as an economic cost, and as someone with contrary interests, to interrupt that pursuit. This is a value that has been incorporated into much technical and technological organisation of modern industry (in the 'factory office', in assembly line manufacture) and consequences of its relegation of the quality of the employee's life have been that workers have had imposed on them routine, mindless, fragmented and soul-destroying tasks.

Information Technology

The coinage of the term Information Technology (IT) to indicate a trend towards the convergence of telecommunications and computers has been accompanied by all manner of speculation about the things that it might do. Invariably commentators present us with a list of the 'choices' now on offer. Barry Jones gives a typical formulation:

> Technology can be used to promote greater economic equity, more freedom of choice, and participatory democracy. Conversely, it can be used to intensify the worst aspects of a competitive society, to widen the gap between rich and poor, to make democratic goals irrelevant, and to institute a technocracy.[21]

This posing of choices thanks to IT follows from the insistence of reviewers, Left and Right, that 'being just like any other technology, IT is intrinsically neither good nor bad. Everything depends on how the country adapts itself to using information technology'[22] which 'really is neutral'.[23] From such a presupposition the language of choice is irresistible.

These presentations are impossible to reply to because they refer persistently to abstractions rather than to substantive technologies. The question whether one is for or against technology can only be answered in the affirmative in this formulation—who can oppose something which allows free choice? But a meaningful response can only be attained at the level of specific technologies; at the level of *this* technology performing *this* function for these *ends* because it is here that technologies exist. Moreover, continuously asserting at a rarefied height that IT provides choices here, there, and everywhere, paradoxically restricts real choice because it diverts attention from analyses of the realities of the introduction and development of information technologies which would enable meaningful decisions to be made.

Let us focus on a number of substantive contexts into which computer communications technologies are being introduced that profoundly influence their form and content.

(a) *Corporate Requirements*

Above all other factors should be emphasised the large, predominantly transnational, corporations that are the major outlets for IT systems which account for the bulk of 'electronic office' technologies and computer networks. The advanced capitalist societies, domestically and internationally, are dominated by oligopolistic corporations that have particular and pressing informational needs to which a variety of IT responds. They require co-ordination and organisation over wide geographical boundaries and it is through new information and communication systems that these dispersed enterprises can be more effectively managed.

They recognise the role of IT readily enough: witness Westinghouse Corporation (1983 revenue $9.5 billion) which says it straight, announcing that in 1981

An integrated worldwide strategic planning process was put in place, linking products and country planning efforts. A global communications center is being established to provide timely and detailed information for every part of the world. This centralization of planning and intelligence will give Westinghouse a competitive edge in the worldwide deployment of its resources.[24]

Or listen to Mr E. Bradley Jones, president of Republic Steel, who describes the emergence of 'geo-economics' as 'a way of saying that the trading nations of the world are stepping up their intermingling of resources, man-power, technology and capital', a process which blurs national boundaries and demands the movement of capital and information 'with growing ease and speed', calling for computer communications networks to facilitate the production of such things as the Ford Escort which is assembled in three countries from parts made in nine.[25]

It could be supposed that the 'discovery' of IT and its harmonious fit with the requirements of corporate capital are coincidental, but this would have great difficulty in accounting for the practical implementation of computer communications technologies in service of increasingly centralised yet simultaneously dispersed organisations. Without the likes of Citicorp's transnational banking and financial interests calling for 'a completely integrated market place capable of moving money and ideas to any place on the planet in a matter of seconds' there scarcely would be moves afoot to establish an Integrated Services Digital Network that would enable high speed switching of digital circuits between subscribers across nations. It would be folly to ignore the profound influence capital has had both on the designers and manufacturers of these technologies (which, in turn, having a keen eye on the most lucrative markets, have throughout oriented their products to the deepest purses) and on the creation of communications policies premised on market principles.[26]

Any assumption that available technologies just happen to accord with the needs of capital would be hard pressed to explain how they are being developed to facilitate what has been called the 'productive de-centralization'[27] that is a feature of an emerging 'new international division of labour', by which is meant the decentralisation of production around the globe and inside individual countries by increasingly centralised corporate concerns that can monitor and instruct from distant locations small and isolated units (e.g. plant is located in the Far East or Caribbean and/or on the metropolitan fringes such as Southern Ireland and Scotland where labour is cheap and poorly organised).[28]

In addition, as data networks emerge they take on specific characteristics. Drawing together information about natural resources, financial conditions, political circumstances, labour supply and so on, the boom in data bases and on-line information services in recent years has overwhelmingly indicated the values of the international market. The rise and rise of 'information factories' from Reuters, TRW, Quotron, Dun and Bradstreet, ITT, IBM and Dow Jones and the predominantly economic and financial data they harvest and sell are traceable directly to the requirements of advanced capitalism. It is not only that the commodities these concerns trade in are specific to corporate interests (what would socialists want to know about the value of the yen in real time? what would socialists care about Wall Street fluctuations as they happen?), but also that they are priced way out of the range of socialists' pockets (for example, the services offered by Reuters to 400 or so brokers and bankers cost an estimated £1,250 subscription plus £600 per month).

It is, in sum, the need of corporate capital to monitor and manage its affairs which requires particular types of computer communications technologies and this receives a willing answer from profit-hungry IT manufacturers and servicers. This is the only way to make sense of the world's leading telecommunications corporation which advertises that 'At AT&T it is gospel that business strategy dictates system design'. And it is from this set of social relations that emanate most problems associated with electronic funds transfer, transborder data flows, and questions of national sovereignty being undermined.[29]

(b) From Taylorism to Social Taylorism

The character of present day technological innovation might be better understood by sketching pressures that have been exercised throughout the development of corporate capitalism. A striking feature of the twentieth century has been the search for better control of its operations by the corporation, an endeavour that has increased in ambition as the company has spatially advanced and penetrated deeper into the fabric of social life. It has resulted in the spread of more calculative, methodical and deliberate ways of conducting social and economic affairs, and it has led to life being more consciously and systematically regulated, more distinctly *managed*, than in the past.[30]

The major applications of this control originated and still are found in the sphere of work where F.W. Taylor's 'Scientific Management' instigated what business guru Peter Drucker sees as the real 'information revolution' because it recognised that careful observation and analysis of labour processes, followed by precise planning, could lead to more effective control of the workforce and leaps in productivity.

If Taylor commenced and put a name to what is recognisably modern management practice within the plant, and if his strategy placed a novel emphasis on information gathering and manipulation to effect it, then technology soon emerged as Taylorism's primary expression in the highly automated assembly lines and associated unskilled labour of Henry Ford's factories since the design of such forms of production made manifest Ford's knowledge of car manufacture and how to make it least reliant on employees by building skills into the machinery and line.

The search for control was neither restricted to the factory nor, from a later date, the office where IT facilitiates the 'Fordism of white collar work'. Another important area has been documented by Chandler[31] where he traces the merger in America of mass production and mass distribution as corporations grew in scale and vertically integrated, thereby replacing the play of market forces in the area of distribution with control by the 'visible hand' of 'managerial capitalism' which became responsible for co-ordinating, overseeing and assessing manufacture and distribution under one management roof.

'Managerial capitalism' soon found pressing the impulse to control affairs beyond the workforce and the distribution of produce. It is not only that the application of calculation was unlikely to stop short of such a crucial stage as selling, but also that mass production of itself required mass consumption and continuity of production could not be assured if this was left entirely to customers' whims.[32] For these reasons, by the second decade of the century procedures were developed to rationalise selling. Spearheaded by the auto industry, modern marketing was pioneered to try to assure sales of cars, clothing, cigarettes, processed foods and the like.[33]

Important aspects of this marketing were installment selling, used-car trade-ins, annual models and eye-catching packaging (the imperatives of selling palpably influenced the technology),[34] and advertising and market research, the former to dissemble information, the latter to amass details of income, life-style, buying preferences etc. that could be scrutinised the better to manage consumers. There is a fascinating literature from the twenties and thirties advocating 'scientific' methods of research 'in discovering the public's wants and reactions to particular products',[35] the techniques of which enormously stimulated the development of 'the electric sorting and tabulating machines'[36] made by International Business Machines that were the forerunners of modern computers and IBM. Relatedly, advertising required mediums and quickly established dominance in radio and later television, with profound consequences for programming and the rapid spread of receivers,[37] as a means of 'entering the homes of the nation through doors and windows, no matter how tightly barred, and delivering its message audibly through the loudspeaker wherever placed'.[38] In turn, there came about an acute need for accurate ratings to measure television's and radio's reach as an important facet of market research.[39]

This application of Scientific Management first in the workshop, then to the expanding corporation, and finally to the consumer can appropriately be called Social Taylorism, the extension of Taylorism throughout society. It is certainly the case that the garnering of information, and planning by management on the basis of what is gathered together, has grown enormously this past fifty years.[40]

Applied to the 'information revolution' through which we are allegedly living, it persists in an emphasis on applying new technologies to sell more effectively. Now, with the greater range and versatility of video, cable and satellite television, advertising and audience monitoring are rendered still more sophisticated. Far-sighted managements are turning to these new media to promote their cause further, to burrow themselves still deeper into the texture of society. According to the J. Walter Thompson Company, cable TV offers 'new or improved advertising opportunities':[41] for example, test marketing, direct response advertising, placing of advertising within specialist channels, home shopping services, sponsored programming, 'informercials'. What the new media allow is more advertising, more specific and targeted advertising to particular groups. And it also offers closer than ever monitoring of the audience. Thus AGB, Britain's biggest market researcher, which amongst other things meters television viewing for BARB (Broadcasters Audience Research Board), 'is already envisaging the day when the street interview, even telephone questioning, will be a thing of the past. Through its Cable and Viewdata company, it has a national sample of 550 homes, which it quizzes through special viewdata sets. Apart from instant judgment on commercials, it can stretch into other media fields, like the respondents' magazine readership'.[42] The same company's *Peoplemeter* has recently been introduced into the United States as a means of more precisely monitoring TV viewing (meters can show when a TV is switched on, *Peoplemeter* aims to discover whether viewers are actually watching).[43]

As an example of this strategy to control consumers, let us look at one of the world's major advertising agencies, Saatchi and Saatchi (S&S). The business of S&S is to develop and perfect the techniques of selling required by corporate capital. To this end it is 'continually examining the results of research to bring [it] closer to the heart of what makes consumers tick— their wants, needs, desires, aspirations'.[44] S&S is devoted to 'market research, attitude and image surveys, and new product testing' and to strengthen its observational capabilities it has just bought Yankelovitch, Skelly and White, a firm of social research analysts headed by an acclaimed statistician and social forecaster.[45]

S&S monitors people with a particular client in mind, transnational corporations, the needs of which are leading to 'pan-regional and world marketing emerging at the heart of business strategy'. Recognising their dominance of the world economy and drawn by their billion dollar advertising expenditure, S&S believes that in future 'research will be conducted to look for similarities between countries, not to seek out differences', that *global marketing* will require advertisers to find a formula for commercials 'so deep in its appeal that it can transcend national borders previously thought inviolate'.

Though global, this remit demands still more exact surveying of consumers, a capacity to recognise that 'there are probably more social differences between Midtown Manhattan and the Bronx, two sectors of the same city, than between Midtown Manhattan and the 7th Arrondissement of Paris'. What will be required is 'analysis of all demographic, cultural and media trends', so marketers 'can survey the world battlefield for their brands, observe the deployment of their forces, and plan their international advertising and marketing in a coherent and logical way'. S&S thus offers clients the prospect that people will be known on a world scale, so that what they will be allowed to know can be most effectively managed.

S&S is all in favour of new technologies provided they are founded on commercial principles. Thus it argues that the BBC's licence should be limited and funds collected from private benefactors, and it is bullish about cable's prospects 'as an advertising medium [because of] its ability to attract audiences through selective programming aimed at more clearly defined groups than the mass audience of the major networks. Multinational advertisers with a specific target audience in each country will be able to reach their target segment through a cable channel concentrating on their specific interest'.

All this, yet S&S aspires to be more than an advertising agency. Realising that 'as multinational corporations grow in size and complexity so the marketing, organisation and strategic problems which face them become more closely linked', it has consolidated by moving into management consultancy (advisory work in strategic planning, employee recruitment and training etc.) and marketing services (sales promotion, public relations, corporate image etc.), intent on supplying, in the words of the *Financial Times*, 'everything a company may need for its internal—and external—communications'.[46]

This suggests that the spread of Scientific Management goes beyond coordination of the dispersed corporation, more intensive marketing of products and observation of customers, all requiring IT to allow the gathering, assessment and dissemination of information. Further changes in corporations, above and beyond growth, concentration and spatial relocation, have impelled them, as part of the planning procedures essential to the retention and advancement of their position, to enter into what can only be described as the Scientific Management of political life itself.

Michael Useem[47] finds reason for this in a shift from 'managerial' to 'institutional' capitalism, by which he means that the economy is dominated nowadays not only by large corporations, but also that these are more interconnected than ever before. A result is a 'consciousness of a generalized corporate outlook' (p. 5) guided by an 'inner circle' of corporate leaders that has led to the 'political mobilization of business' (p. 150) over the past decade or so.

In this way capitalism has become more cohesive and better equipped to have its views represented in politics and has taken steps to ensure that this influence is systematised and regularised. In the days of the modern state, with widespread political regulation and considerable significance applying to governmental decisions, advanced capitalism has acknowledged the need—and with institutional capitalism has developed the basis—for effective and consistent political representation. Information and IT are key requirements of effecting this political mobilisation of business.

One dimension is the spate of corporate and advocacy advertising that has emerged in the commercial media and another is the boom in sponsorship which will be increasingly important as a means of subsidising communications technologies. These are attempts to continue the unrestricted activity of business by image manipulation, but they pale when compared to the more directly political representation of corporations. On the one hand, this is evident in their recognition that 'better communications' within and without the organisation are a means of getting their own way—and the mushrooming of PR companies, the cultivation of media contacts, executive grooming for TV appearances, in-house video productions and the like express this. On the other hand, it is apparent in corporate involvement in politics itself. The unrelenting growth of the business lobby and full-time lobbyists within Westminster, with their indices of 'opinion leaders', computerised files on MPs and their colleagues, constant stream of press releases and targeted leaflets is testament to this. But still more significant is the intense support for and influence on pro-business parties themselves. Corporate conviction that politics must be better managed than before has been expressed not only in substantial support for and donations to conservative political parties, subsidy of pro-business 'think tanks', and more vigorous participation in politics by the CBI. It has also been witnessed in the development within the polity itself of business procedures.

One can point to the ways in which S&S by its forays into the elections of 1979 and 1983 has bridged a traditional gap between politics and business by applying its expertise as a 'communicator' gained in selling products to selling politicians. American politics are the epitome of this process of week in week out polling of the electorate, and computer analysis of patterns and past practices, so that candidates can be better 'packaged',[48] but S&S are an index of the way politics here has been changing to become a matter of 'selling' ideas and 'delivering' votes, a sign that Scientific Management has entered politics itself.

S&S's campaign tactics and strategy are well known: the careful calculation of people's attitudes and the moulding of candidates around issues so identified, the daily polls, the targeting of posters, elocution lessons for Mrs Thatcher, meticulous selection of clothing and grooming of hair, pre-arrangement of 'photo-opportunities' and media 'events'. . . A corollary of this advertising mentality in politics is the excessive concern for secrecy that characterises the Thatcher government.[49] Another is the diminution of politics as a 'public sphere': the avoidance of serious political debate and exchange of ideas and principles and their replacement with slogans, image manipulation and news management.

It is important to stress that it is this consolidation and extension of Taylorism that drives the 'information revolution'. This is especially so because people are easily wrong-footed by talk of 'choice' in a 'new era' heralded by innovative technologies. If we place the power, interests and motives of corporate capitalism at the centre of developments and applications we depict a very different scenario—and appropriate reaction to—the 'Knowledge Society' which futurists, Left and Right, suggest is a radical break with the past.

Arguing that a crucial context for take-up of information technology now and in the past is the search for increased corporate control, and that this impinges on the technologies themselves, is an important factor in retaining and sustaining hostility towards capitalist changes that are so often announced as 'technical progress'. One way of illustrating this is to point out that a good many of these technologies without corporate capitalism are worthless. Who on the Left could find use for S&S's data bases and market profiles; for the customised software housed in the headquarters of transnational corporations; for the 11,000 hours of TV soaps rumoured to be held in a vault in Texas awaiting the establishment of cable in Britain? Are socialists not disturbed by the accumulation of creditworthiness files on buyers which results from the spread of plastic cards (Access, Barclaycard, Visa) and is a major motive for Marks and Spencer's recent incursion into this area since it gives 'invaluable feedback and data concerning individual customers, their needs and their purchasing power'[50] and will better allow future marketing efforts?

A retort might be that these are aspects of IT's applications, that they represent the 'software' which is socially skewed, but that the 'hardware' is what the Left can inherit because it is both valuable and malleable. There is of course some truth in this view, and I would not want to suggest that technology should be approached in manichaean terms of useful/useless, but it is important to grasp that values do intrude into the hardware itself. For example, the technologies that Taylorism has pioneered in factories and the work patterns they impose surely cannot be acceptable to socialists. Neither can the 'growth at all costs' (to people, the environment) mentality that they express be endorsed. Again, it is striking that so much IT for the home is an enhancement of the television monitor, itself developed, as Raymond Williams has observed,[51] as the 'box in the corner' to accord with the 'mobile privatisation' of modern family life. Video cassette recorders, TV games, home computers, satellite broadcasting and cable services all consolidate what has been an enormous commercial success, the television, and in so doing they perpetuate the move towards privatisation that is characteristic of consumer capitalism and, indeed, express materially the plans of corporate designers. As a recent *Campaign* feature put it, new technologies for the home represent a shift to 'Fortress Britain', a further withdrawal into the domestic sphere, equipping it with quantities of durables and pulling up the drawbridge on the world outside[52] (though communications facilities will enable the centralised observation of these isolated dwellings). While there are very important debates to be conducted about whether this hardware is to be programmed commercially or from public funds, there is another issue, less openly acknowledged, which questions whether the styles of life embodied in the technologies are to be encouraged by socialists. Would not socialists want to defy a technological trend which compartmentalises each family unit? Would we want to encourage the working from home via computer terminals which is on the horizon for many people, especially women? Would we not wish to reconstitute technologies that reflect and encourage more communal values?

(c) *The Priorities of the IT industry*

Kevin Robins and myself have described elsewhere the IT industry,[53] so here I can state briefly that it is a fast-growing business, dominated by an oligopoly of multi-billion dollar transnationals at the head of which are IBM and AT&T, that is rapidly changing amidst intensive competition over markets, standards and product innovation between these giants which increasingly offer proprietary ranges of complementary and compatible technologies. Though their focus is mainly on computer communications systems for the office, the IT industry is so vast and is so rapidly integrating and converging that very many enormous corporate bodies in media, telecommunications, electronics, computing and information supply are entering the arena to struggle for mastery over the emerging 'information grid'.

These IT corporations work on a number of assumptions. One is that they are answerable to no-one but their shareholders (and not much to the bulk of these) whose priority is profit maximisation. In pursuit of this goal all the major companies have identified business users as the most likely to offer a satisfactory return on investment. Fulfilling a policy of servicing the most lucrative markets in order to achieve the best possible profit has significantly influenced the technologies that have emerged. To believe that computer communications for business users, far and away the most sought after market, are neutral developments is untenable given the prioritisation of this area by the manufacturers and their clients.

The reality is that these are systems developed to 'serve the inter-corporate needs for which they were designed'.[54] Computer terminals in banks and travel agencies, communications networks linking company sites, data processing centres and the like have been pioneered, produced

and marketed for identifiable social needs, those of commercial enterprises, and it is surely reasonable to suggest that a different constituency
and different manufacturers might produce different technologies. It is
only by closing our minds to the possibility of alternative technologies
that we can assume as uncontentious the results of the stress of IT corporations on the 'electronic grid' within and between offices and thereby
resign ourselves to displacement of staff, increased machine pacing of
work, and concentrated power of the already powerful.

(d) IT for the Military and Police

Military and police agencies have a keen interest in information. IT offers
them the opportunity of handling more information more effectively,
and they are big spending organisations (military procurement expenditure
in Britain was about £8 billion in 1984-85). In light of this, there should
be no surprise that IT manufacturers all have substantial commitments to
produce equipment and software to meet the needs of these organs of the
state. Though precise figures are hard to come by, NEDO recently declared
that 'the UK electronics industry's single biggest customer is the Ministry
of Defence'[55] and there is widespread agreement among analysts that
military sales on average account for about 20% of corporate revenue in
the business.[56] At the higher levels companies such as British Aerospace
get around half their income from the Ministry of Defence, but no IT
corporation of significance got less than £25 million from the Ministry
in 1981-82 and Ferranti, GEC and Plessey occupied the top category of
'over £100 million'.[57] More pertinent, 70% of these contracts are non-
competitively allocated and are often at the cutting edge of technological
advance, making them especially attractive to IT corporations. A recent
report that the Commons Public Accounts Committee has 'no way of
knowing what proportion of the £5,000 million spent by the Ministry of
Defence on non-competitive contracts is being paid out in legitimate
expenditure and how much is spent on inflated bills with items disguised
to boost profits' (Guardian, 13 May, 1985) does nothing to diminish that
attraction. Indeed, the military demand provides a constantly renewed
energy for ever more sophisticated computer communications technologies—any system is outdated before it is completed—and thereby a
reliable outlet for IT manufacturers.[58]

The outcome is the creation of mind-boggling military technologies[59]
and an apparently inexorable growth of increasingly integrated police
computer networks and data banks, local, regional and national.[60] Readers
will not require a rehearsal of the dangers these technologies carry in
international affairs and at home, dangers of confrontation and warfare
and erosion of civil liberties. The least that one can say is that much of
the IT for the military and police is devoted to surveillance of the 'enemy'
within and without (spy satellites, telephone interception, 'bugs', con-

struction of dossiers on 'subversives' and so on), and that, amid the economic crisis, social upheaval and restructuring through which we are living, a strategy of strong state/free market[61] leads easily to opposition to government policies being equated with subversion.

What could socialists want with these technologies? With their illiberal values of spying and prying these surely cannot be seen as worthy of inheritance. It has been suggested that at least some elements of police data networks are worth saving, for example files on missing persons and stolen vehicles. I could concede this were the systems publicly accountable, but with two provisoes. The first is that to talk in this way is to overlook the motive for and context of their introduction which places to the fore the policing function as one of containing social unrest in often highly charged political and industrial circumstances (thus during the miners' strike entries on the Police National Computer's Stolen and Suspect Vehicle Index jumped 50% as police logged miners' cars used for picketing). The second, related, is that the idea that technology can be salvaged underestimates how much the design of these systems, especially the software which is the biggest expense, is customised in ways that make it difficult to put to other purposes.

*   *   *   *   *

The Politicisation of Technology

What this discussion amounts to is that the Left should stop asking what TECHNOLOGY can do and concentrate instead on what particular technologies are doing and why they are doing it. We should focus on technologies in the here and now so we may show how they can serve powerful interests and how their origin and application are shaped by those interests. A stress on 'present tense technologies' is a prerequisite for strengthening the resolve of those who often have good reason to oppose 'progress', yet are shaken in their actions by insistence on technology's neutrality and beneficence. This idea seems wilfully blind to the fact that many of the Left's problems emanate from and/or are exacerbated by technological innovations that displace employees, boost the speed of work, deskill labour, increase the national and international dominance of corporate capital, threaten global stability still more than it is already threatened, heighten surveillance and facilitate the dissemination of ideas and values from and favourable to the powerful. We on the Left should try to change our own and others terms of reference about technology, we should insist on a different type of debate, that those weakened by its applications can resist without feeling that they are cranks.

But how should we effect this? A straightforward and grandiose response is that a socialist policy for technology would not be so different from a socialist policy towards the economy, welfare or class, in that it would seek to apply socialist criteria of egalitarianism, community and support for the working class. Nonetheless, it would differ radically from previous and present socialist policies by applying socialist principles *to* technology instead of treating technology as an autonomous and a social phenomenon which gives off 'wealth' that can be distributed in a variety of ways. In other words, a socialist technology policy would insist that socialism does *not* stop at the door of a room occupied by experts who in time create manifold 'goodies' which are then passed to the outsiders. Socialism enters that door, does its utmost to make known to the widest possible public what is going on inside, and tries to impose its priorities on the technologists and their produce.

Suggesting this, we are able to see that a problem for the Left is that it is forced to respond to technologies already constituted. While it is important to lay bare the interests represented in these completed technologies, the Left should also be arguing that the processes by which modern technologies are created, research and development projects, require politicisation and debate so that priorities established before the production of technologies are open to scrutiny and influence. At the moment the controllers of R&D funds, those who decide to back one idea rather than another and thereby set the agenda for consideration of tomorrow's technologies today, are of two kinds, corporate capital and state agencies. The sums they invest are prodigious: for example, between 1977–82 IBM spent $8 billion on R&D, ITT spent $5 billion from 1978–83, and Bell Labs (of AT&T) in 1982 alone spent $2 billion on its 25,000 research staff, while in Britain the Ministry of Defence in 1983 disposed of half of all the government's R&D funds (and the state provided 50% of all the nation's R&D spending).

No-one can be under the illusion that these projects, at the point of origination of technologies, are not influenced by particular values and beliefs. Just a glance at the heated debates within companies and government departments over research priorities gives the lie to that. A task of the Left is to enter the debate about technological innovation at this early stage. There is certainly room for it *now* in the area of state expenditure, given that so much of it is channelled through publicly owned, though scarcely accountable, institutions such as universities and colleges. Doubtless such a proposal would be met with outraged cries that academic freedom and the scientific enterprise are threatened, but a socialist strategy on these lines would be doing nothing other than make explicit what has happened for over a century and what the present government is undertaking with special vigour since it feels that the inadequate response of higher education to capital has contributed to its demise. If, taking a leaf out of Thatcher's book, the Left can move towards imposing its criteria for technologies at the point of initiation and origination, to present at this stage its notions of need, quality of work, and modes of leisure, then it will have moved far from the inheritor approach to received technologies, towards one which regards them as expressive of social relations.[62]

Such advocacy is concerned, of course, with a socialist policy for technology which is long term. A much more pressing question is what to do with the technologies that are here now and with which any socialist enterprise must come to terms. Socialism will not start with a clean sheet and it will be compelled to use technologies already in place. Still more to the point, socialists have to make clear their policies on technologies now being applied, so it is important to outline the contours of a socialist technology policy that is relevant to present conditions.

This is territory that the Left has not yet charted—and a priority should be to commence this task—and I can only suggest a few landmarks, but, perhaps most prominently, socialists should mark their willingness to support resistance to technologies, introduced in the name of 'progress' because they increase 'productivity' and 'efficiency' at the expense of 'competitors', which make redundant, deskill or increase the pace of work for employees. Socialists should unhesitatingly back the victims of technological changes wrought by capital and they must refuse the temptation to qualify their support by whispering, for example, that 'though we support printers in their struggle against media corporations which are endeavouring to reduce their numbers, nowadays they are an anachronism —under socialism we'll be using the most advanced printing technologies ourselves and they don't require printers, but we'll give compensation enough to allow the dispossessed to enjoy a life of leisure'.

It is this sort of reasoning, which subscribes to an underlying, apolitical, process of technological progress, that gravely weakens efforts to combat the increased control of capital being effected in the here and now. The only acceptable socialist policy should be support for the opponents of technologies which do them down and an insistence that the socialist endeavour will extend to a radical revision of technological adaptation and the production of technologies themselves.

A related principle should be a willingness to refuse technologies that are inimical to socialist ideals. Most socialists appear to regard rejection of new machines as some sort of blasphemy, at best a yearning for a mythical yesterday, and at worst an assault on rationality itself. But what is wrong with refusing the products of electronic warfare? Is it irresponsible to reject the generation of energy by nuclear fission? And is it madness to suggest that Britain has far too many motor cars and the ambition to have one (or more!) in every house is materially wasteful, antisocial, and damaging of the countryside? Is it absurd to say that Concorde—beautiful engineering though it undoubtedly is—is a waste of resources, material and human, and should long since have been abandoned? And is it foolish to claim that high-rise accommodation for families is unacceptable to socialists, and the only sensible socialist policy is to urge the demolition of such buildings?

A socialist technology policy would not banish current technologies just because they have been created by capitalism. To argue that socialists should beware the fiction that technology is neutral is not the same as endorsing the nonsense that capitalist technologies can be rejected out of hand. What it should insist upon, however, is a suspicion of capitalist technologies, a preparedness to change or even to reject them, and an insistence that the criteria for their adoption will be socialist priorities rather than technical wizardry.

More positively, a socialist policy towards technology would feel an impulse to adopt an ecocentric outlook which is intensely suspicious of the technocratic mind that urges unlimited 'growth' and the 'technical fix' as solution to problems.[63] A high priority for socialist technologies would surely be that they are not ecologically or socially damaging: that they conserve energy and wherever possible favour using renewable resources such as wind, sun and wave rather than coal and oil; that they are non-polluting of the environment; that they encourage the craft elements of labour rather than provoke an intense division of labour in the name of efficiency of output. . .

It is very likely that such measures will be less 'efficient' than current technologies, but socialists should be able to resist too rapid an acquiescence to the pressure for 'more' at least cost. One major way of doing this is to discuss and thoroughly debate what socialist needs are and how they are to be ranked. Here it is important to remind ourselves that, in a capitalist society, need is determined by the saleability of an object and provided on the basis of ability to pay. Socialists would obviously want to change this, but they are still left with the imperative of deciding upon what would be needed by a socialist society.

It seems rare for the Left to consider need as a problem for socialism. Concerned overwhelmingly as they are with deprivation and injustice, socialists have an impulse to shout out for radical redistribution of what is available and the creation of still more to be shared in the future. It is the same perception which regards committed ecologists with suspicion: too often these appear to be people who, already having well-paid and secure jobs, good homes and affluent lifestyles, want to restrict what working class people have and aspire to have. Against this, however, it has to be conceded by socialists that the ecologists' emphasis that in contemporary Britain almost the whole population lives in a condition of 'post-scarcity', living in ways far beyond elemental needs of food, clothing and housing, is valid. Acknowledgement of this demands that we socialists ask ourselves and one another what is needed by socialism.

Socialists should insist that high on their list of needs are not only finished goods (carpets, fridges and the like), but also the quality of work experience and social interaction, a clean environment, and aesthetic pleasure, and meeting these needs might well be at the expense of an accountant's measure of efficiency. The establishment of socialist priorities here would throw up no end of difficulties of, for example, matching rewarding work with required level of output, but at the least it should allow us to jettison the futurist (dis)utopia of robotised production leaving people to indulge in purposeless idleness in an electronic Cockaigne.

In deciding upon socialist needs the question must be posed: does fulfilment of them cause injustices or create impediments to the socialist enterprise? For example, would satisfaction of requirements for certain foods or beverages have a deleterious effect on the economies of the Third World? If it does, then the damage caused must be put into the balance to help gauge the weight of particular needs, and it may be that, in the light of such considerations, socialists would decide that certain needs cannot be met.

This relation between socialist needs and the means of satisfying them is a vexed one with which technology is intimately linked. Under capitalism the meeting of market-defined needs characteristically breeds alienation for the worker who is compelled to endure machine-paced and unskilled labour. Any socialism worth its salt would reject both these ends and means, but it could still be forced to face difficulties of reconciling its socialist goals and the means of meeting them. For instance, if one accepts that household refuse must be collected (it could be possible to arrange for individual disposal via a sewage-type system or even incineration), it is reasonable to argue that this task is inherently unpleasant (dirty, with dangers of infection). Therefore, runs a familiar anti-socialist refrain, alienating work (and inequality) is assured by the technical imperative of removing garbage. This does not have to be the case. For the limited number of jobs that are deemed essential and unpleasant, a socialist society would surely want to do two things. First, it would set to in order to produce technologies that make the task less onerous; second, it would propose to introduce a form of 'communal service' by which each citizen is obliged, for a period of their lives, to undertake such duties.

Finally, socialists might wish to break with technologies that lead to users being overdependent, by favouring the production of machines which, if less exotic, can be repaired with minimal training. This advocacy is to point to the ways in which many modern technologies, even those performing rudimentary tasks (for example, coffee grinders, typewriters, lawn mowers, food mixers), defy home repair because they are consciously designed that way (examples are legion, ranging from automobiles to televisions, and everyone is familiar nowadays with proprietary warnings not to attempt one's own repair). A socialist technology policy, deliberately aimed at giving maximum authority to the individual and minimising reliance on experts, would surely urge that this 'technological illiteracy' is combated by developing machines that are easily repaired when things go wrong.

There are other priorities socialists might wish to establish as criteria for the acceptance and guidance of technology—technologies that reflect communal rather than private living (e.g. public rather than private transit systems), technologies that encourage decentralisation rather than concentration of power. . .—and my comments are only a start. They are, however, a necessary stage in the development of a socialist policy which is genuinely applicable *to* technology.

NOTES

1. H. Scarbrough and P. Moran, 'How New Tech Won at Longbridge', *New Society,* 7 February, 1985, pp. 207–209.

2. On the ambivalence of trade unions, see K. Robins and F. Webster, 'New Technology: A Survey of Trade Union Response in Britain', *Industrial Relations Journal* 13(1) 1982:7–26.

3. F. Engels, *Socialism: Utopian and Scientific* in L. Feuer (ed.), *Marx and Engels: Basic Writings on Politics and Philosophy,* Fontana, 1971, p. 145.

4. Labour Party, *Microelectronics: A Labour Party Discussion Document,* Labour Party, 1980, pp. 24, 38.

5. H. Wilson, *Labour and the Scientific Revolution,* Labour Party—Report of the 62nd Annual Conference, Scarborough, September 30–October 4, 1963.

6. J. Reid, 'What Scargill Means', *New Society,* 13 October, 1984, pp. 91–93; cf. J. Winterton, 'Computerized Coal: New Technology and the Mines' in H. Beynon, (ed), *Digging Deeper: Issues in the Miners' Strike,* Verso, 1985, pp. 231–243; S. Bradshaw, 'The Impact of High Technology on the Politics of Mining', *The Listener,* 25 April, 1985, pp. 2–4.

7. See K. Robins and F. Webster, 'Luddism: New Technology and the Critique of Political Economy', in L. Levidow and B. Young (eds.), *Science, Technology and the Labour Process, vol. 2,* Free Association Books, 1985, pp. 9–48.

8. A. Gorz, *Farewell to the Working Class: An Essay on Post-Industrial Socialism,* Pluto Press, 1982.

9. C. Evans, *The Mighty Micro: The Impact of the Computer Revolution,* Gollancz, 1980, p. 208.

10. David Noble's important essay, 'Present Tense Technology', appeared in three parts in the journal *Democracy* during 1983 (Part 1 in vol. 4<1>:8–24; Part 2 in 4<2>:70–82; Part 3 in 4<3>:71–93. It is to appear as a book, *Present Tense Technology,* San Pedro, California: Singlejack Publications.

11. See for example Mrs Thatcher's speech at the opening ceremony of the *Information Technology '82 Conference,* Barbican Centre, 8 December 1982. Press Office: 10 Downing Street, December, 1982.

12. Cf. D. Dickson and D. Noble, 'By Force of Reason: The Politics of Science and Technology Policy', in T. Ferguson and J. Rogers (eds.), *The Hidden Election: Politics and Economics in the 1980 Presidential Campaign,* New York: Pantheon, 1980, pp. 260–312.

13. J. Smith interviewed in *Computing,* April 18, 1985, p. 18.

14. TUC, *Employment and Technology,* September, 1979; TUC, *Congress,* 1979.

15. J. Callaghan, *Prime Minister Announces Major Programme of Support for Microelectronics,* Press Office: 10 Downing Street, 6 December, 1978.

16. Thorn-EMI, *Report and Accounts,* 1980, p. 4.

17. *A Programme for Advanced Information Technology: The Report of the Alvey Committee*, Department of Industry, HMSO, September, 1982.
18. G. Locksley, 'Europe and the Electronics Industry: Conflicting Strategies in Positive Restructuring', *West European Politics* 6(2) 1983:129.
19. H. and S. Rose, 'Radical Science and its Enemies', in *Socialist Register 1979*, p. 324.
20. See H. Braverman, *Labor and Monopoly Capital: The Degradation of Work in the Twentieth Century*, New York: Monthly Review Press, 1974; D. Noble, *America by Design: Science, Technology, and the Rise of Corporate Capitalism*, New York: Oxford University Press, 1977; D. Noble, *Forces of Production: A Social History of Industrial Automation*, New York: Knopf, 1984.
21. B. Jones, *Sleepers, Wake: Technology and the Future of Work*, Brighton: Wheatsheaf Books, 1982, p. 254.
22. P. Marsh, 'Britain Faces Up to Information Technology', *New Scientist*, 9 December, 1982, p. 638.
23. M. Laver, *Computers and Social Change*, Cambridge: Cambridge University Press, 1980, p. 10.
24. Westinghouse Corp., *Annual Report 1982*.
25. Quoted in *New York Times*, 11 October, 1981.
26. Citicorp is quoted in *Financial Times*, 10 May, 1982. The standard work on the relation between corporate capital and telecommunications policy is D. Schiller, *Telematics and Government*, New Jersey: Ablex, 1982. Illustrative of this relation is Citicorp's offer to business customers that they can 'communicate with Citibank offices around the world through *our own private financial telecommunications network*', (emphasis added) (in a Citicorp advertisement published in *Financial Times*, 17 January 1985); L. Else, 'Oil Majors show natural reserve in DP exploration', *Computing the Magazine*, 14 March, 1985, pp. 12-13 describes the leading role of oil giants Shell and BP in the Information Technology Users' Standards Association (ITUSA), a policy of which is to exert pressure on governments to produce IT standards 'in an acceptable and timely form'.
27. P. Mattera, *Off the Books: The Rise of the Underground Economy*, Pluto Press, 1985, Ch. 7.
28. See F. Webster and K. Robins, *Information Technology: A Luddite Analysis*, New Jersey: Ablex, 1986, Part Three.
29. The AT&T advertisement appears in the *New York Review of Books*, 9 May, 1985, p. 5; on general issues see the seminal work of Herbert Schiller, for example *Information and the Crisis Economy*, New Jersey: Ablex, 1984; 'Informatics and Information Flows: The Underpinnings of Transnational Capitalism', in V. Mosco and J. Wasko (eds.), *The Critical Communications Review. Vol. 2: Changing Patterns of Communication Control*, New Jersey: Ablex, 1984, pp. 3-29.
30. See K. Robins and F. Webster, 'Information, Television and Social Taylorism', in P. Drummond and R. Patterson (eds.), *Television in Transition*, British Film Institute, 1985.
31. A.D. Chandler, Jr., *The Visible Hand: The Managerial Revolution in American Business*, Cambridge MA: Harvard University Press, 1977.
32. See R. Williams, 'Advertising: The Magic System', in R. Williams, *Problems in Materialism and Culture*, Verso, 1980, pp. 170-195.
33. D. Pope, *The Making of Modern Advertising*, New York: Basic Books, 1983.
34. E. Rothschild, *Paradise Lost: The Decline of the Auto-Industrial Age*, New York: Random House, 1973; A.P. Sloan, *My Years with General Motors*, Sidgwick and Jackson, 1965.

35. John Watson, founder of behaviourist psychology and vice-president of J. Walter Thompson Co., in his foreword to H.C. Link, *The New Psychology of Selling and Advertising*, New York: Macmillan, 1932, p. viii; cf. J. Rorty, *Our Master's Voice: Advertising*, (1934). Reprinted New York: Arno Press Inc., 1976; S. Ewen, *Captains of Consciousness: Advertising and the Social Roots of the Consumer Culture*, New York: McGraw-Hill, 1976.

36. H.C. Link, 1932, *op. cit.*, p. 248.

37. E. Barnouw, *The Sponsor: Notes on a Modern Potentate*, New York: Oxford University Press, 1978.

38. F.A. Arnold, *Broadcast Advertising: The Fourth Dimension, Television Edition*, New York: Wiley and Sons, 1933, pp. 41–42.

39. D.L. Hurwitz, *Broadcast 'Ratings': The Rise and Development of Commercial Audience Research and Measurement in American Broadcasting*, University of Illinois at Urbana-Champaign, Ph.D. thesis, 1983. Ann Arbor, MI 48106: University Microfilms International.

40. See E. and S. Ewen, *Channels of Desire: Mass Images and the Shaping of American Consciousness*, New York: McGraw-Hill, 1982.

41. T. Syfret, *Cable and Advertising in the Eighties*, J. Walter Thompson Co., 1983, p. 30.

42. A. Thorncroft, 'Dawn of the Instant Reaction', *Financial Times*, 28 March, 1985.

43. J. Fierman, 'Television Ratings: The British are Coming', *Fortune*, 1 April, 1985, p. 53.

44. All quotes are from Saatchi and Saatchi Compton Worldwide, *Review of Operations*, 8 December, 1983; Saatchi and Saatchi Company plc, *Chairman's Review and Financial Statement 1984*; Saatchi and Saatchi Compton Worldwide, *Review of Advertising Operations 1984*; Saatchi and Saatchi Company plc, *Review of Consultancy and Research Operations 1984*.

45. See D. Yankelovitch, *New Rules: Searching for Self-Fulfillment in a World Turned Upside Down*, New York: Random House, 1981.

46. *Financial Times*, 29 November, 1984.

47. M. Useem, *The Inner Circle: Large Corporations and the Rise of Business Political Activity in the US and UK*, New York: Oxford University Press, 1984.

48. See R. Perry, *The Programming of the President: The Hidden Power of the Computer in World Politics Today*, Aurum Press, 1984; J.C. Spear, *Presidents and the Press: The Nixon Legacy*, Cambridge MA: The MIT Press, 1984; K.H. Jamieson, *Packaging the Presidency: A History and Criticism of Presidential Campaign Advertising*, New York: Oxford University Press, 1984; J. McGinniss, *The Selling of the President*, Harmondsworth: Penguin, 1970.

49. See M. Cockerell, *et al., Sources Close to the Prime Minister: Inside the Hidden World of the News Manipulators*, Macmillan, 1984.

50. *Observer*, 25 November, 1984; cf. D. Burnham, *The Rise of the Computer State*, Weidenfeld and Nicolson, 1983.

51. R. Williams, *Television: Technology and Cultural Form*, Fontana, 1974.

52. 'Fortress Britain': The Sudden Death of the Big Night Out', *Campaign*, 2 September, 1983, p. 23; compare Nippon Electronic's promise to 'make home a comfort haven', a 'treasured sanctuary', where 'boredom is unheard of' thanks to 'remote-control video recorders, giant 60-inch video screens. . . air conditioners that gauge the temperature automatically, stereos that remember your favourite music, appliances that do more so you do less, even home security systems to safeguard these valuables. Eventually even computers will be part of this scenario, controlling your environment and freeing your time further for other leisure pursuits', *NEC's Universe*, Tokyo: NEC, 1982, p. 5.

53. See Webster and Robins, 1986, Ch. 7 (note 28).
54. Tobin Foundation, *Structural Issues in Global Communications*, Washington DC: Tobin Foundation, 1982.
55. NEDC (National Economic Development Council), *Policy for the UK Electronics Industry, Review 1982/83*, Electronics Economic Development Committee, NEDO, April 1983, p. 7.
56. M. Brzoska, 'Economic Problems of Arms Production in Western Europe— Diagnosis and Alternatives', in H. Tuomi and R. Väyrynen (eds.), *Militarization and Arms Production*, Croom Helm, 1983.
57. *Statement of the Defence Estimates*, Cmnd. 8951-1, 1983, p. 38.
58. See M. Kaldor, *The Baroque Arsenal*, London: André Deutsch, 1981.
59. A useful overview is given by Frank Barnaby, 'Microelectronics in War' in G. Friedrichs and A. Schaff (eds.), *Microelectronics and Society: for better or for worse*, Oxford: Pergamon Press, 1982, pp. 243–272.
60. See D. Campbell, 'Society Under Surveillance', in P. Hain (ed.), *Policing the Police, Vol. 2*, Calder, 1980, pp. 63–150. Two illustrative instances of this trend are: a Metropolitan Police recruitment advertisement which says members 'can rely on a very sophisticated computer-based information network which copes with much of the hard work behind the scenes', (*Observer*, 28 January, 1985), and *Computing*, (14 February, 1985) which tells readers that 'while the creation of a national police force looks unlikely. . . the skeleton of a national police information network is already in place'.
61. A. Gamble, 'The Free Economy and the Strong State', *Socialist Register 1979*, pp. 1–25.
62. See B. Young, 'Reconstituting Technology: Chips, Genes, Spares', *CSE Conference Papers*, 1979, pp. 119–127.
63. D. Pepper, *The Roots of Modern Environmentalism*, Croom Helm, 1984, Chs. 2–4.

A FEASIBLE SOCIALISM?*

Roland Lew

Is socialism a contemporary issue? Judging by what one reads in the newspapers, by the general climate of opinion and by the heavy spread by the media, the answer would appear to be 'no'. People certainly talk about socialism, but only in order to denounce or discredit it. 'Authentic socialism' is a dangerous utopia or at best an illusion. 'Actually existing socialism' is a nightmare. The recent experience of socialist governments in Western Europe, proves that socialism is a sham, since they cannot or will not avoid adopting a harsh economic liberalism. Yet here we have one of the leading figures in Soviet studies proposing a 'feasible socialism'. A writer who specialises in the economics of the USSR and the Eastern bloc and who has never been noted for his support for socialism now puts forward his own version of socialism. One's first impression—though, given the present anti-socialist climate, perhaps it is merely a hope—is that the author is coming to the aid of at least a certain socialism. The favourable comments made by Perry Anderson in his latest book tend to strengthen that impression: 'In a work of luminous freshness and clarity, common sense and good humour, analytic logic and empirical detail, Nove has put to rest a century of unexamined preconceptions and illusions about what might be on the other side of capital, and awoken us to our first real vision of what a socialist economy, under democratic control, might look like.'[1]

On a second reading, one begins to have doubts. It is only natural that an intellectual who was born in Russia and who is presumably familiar with controversies on the left should continue to take an interest in socialist problems. He rejects Marx's conceptualisation, but gives his reasons for doing so and his argument is coherent. It is obvious from his earlier writings on the Soviet Union that he also rejects the results of the Soviet experiment. In his book on socialism, he simply summarises his earlier views; the reasons for his rejection of the Soviet Union are obvious and are supported by well documented arguments. But it is by no means self-evident that we have to accept that what he has to say has anything to do with a socialist vision.

*Alec Nove, *The Economics of Feasible Socialism*, London, George Allen and Unwin, 1983.

414

I. WHICH SOCIALISM?

Critique of Marx

The author's starting point is a harsh critique of Marx which is central to his whole argument: 'It is my contention that Marx had little to say about the economics of socialism, and that the little he did say was either irrelevant or directly misleading' (p. 10). According to Nove, everything that Marx said, directly or indirectly, about socialism is unacceptable; his main complaint appears to be that Marx is illogical, unrealistic and takes no account of the complexities of the modern world. The disappearance of the market and the withering away of the law of value, which are central themes in Marx, will lead to the despotism of centralised planning and to the power of despots. The only hope for a 'free association of producers' lies at the level of individual factories. The extension of self-management to the whole of society is inconceivable. The interests of the 'associated producers' vary from factory to factory. The assumption that there can be a spontaneous harmony between the interests of all workers and that local interests can merge into a general interest is a hollow dream that has nothing to do with the harsh realities of life. It is in fact more than a mad dream; it is a religious projection. It is all the more far-fetched and senseless in that there is and always will be such a thing as scarcity, not to mention selfishness and other aspects of social life. Hence Nove's sceptical comments about the 'golden age of abundance' which 'removes conflict over resource-allocation. . . a communist steady-state equilibrium. . . Then there is no reason for various individuals to compete, to take possession for their own use of what is freely available to all' (p. 15).[2] The abundance which was to have led to the emergence of the New Man still eludes us. Resources are not unlimited, and there will always be conflict, or even pitched battles, over scarce commodities, all of which leaves little room for illusions as to man's goodness or generosity. There is no good genie to distribute everything bounteously; it is more a matter of managing a real world that is both complex and uncertain.

These are the main arguments advanced to prove that political economy —in other words the management of relative scarcity—will continue to apply under socialism. For Nove and many other writers, the claim that the law of value will wither away under socialism—an argument used by Marx and most, but not all, Marxists, though Lenin appears not to accept it—lies at the heart of the Marxist utopia and it is this which makes it so unrealistic. 'The evident need to calculate, evaluate, devise criteria for choice between alternatives, at all levels of economic life' (p. 20) means that the law of value will pertain under socialism. Marx is further criticised for ignoring use-value and concentrating on exchange-value in his explanation of capitalism. The latter concept is bound up with the conditions of production, and Marx emphasises production at the expense of circulation. Marx's minimisation of use-value leads him to under-estimate the role of the market and to ignore the interests of consumers. In that sense, the Soviet planners are simply following the example set by their great forebear. In short, 'Marx had little that was relevant to say about computation of costs under socialism (and implied that under full communism costs would not matter anyhow)' (p. 27). When Marx does intervene in the debate, he does so with his famous and woolly theory that under socialism, economic life will be transparent. But as Nove reminds us, transparence becomes an opaque mirror when the '12 million identifiable different products' (p. 33) manufactured in the USSR get in the way. The vast range of tasks to be performed and the range of available skills mean that 'some hierarchy and subordination are inescapable in organising production' and there is therefore a need 'for a realistic. . . assessment of the role and limits of democratic procedures in economic decision-making' (p. 50).

Similarly, it is essential for there to be a state which rises above individual interests. Market regulation and a certain degree of competition are essential because *ex ante* regulation is impossible. Real needs cannot be determined before the market has been diagnosed, unless of course consumers are forced by drastic means to accept certain products for their limited needs. Nove is thinking here primarily of the Soviet experience, which he knows very well. Does, then socialism have any meaning? It does, if by socialism we mean that accidents of birth or fortune should not confer excessive privileges upon anyone. And 'feasible socialism' is certainly meaningful: it means 'a state of affairs which could exist in some major part of the developed world within the lifetime of a child already conceived' (p. 197). Realism, a sense of reality and a sense of proportion provide the leitmotif of Nove's book and many of his common-sense remarks remind one of the best features of the Anglo-American tradition.

A Negative Example: 'Real Socialism'
The same sober tone and the same spirit of synthesis characterise the chapter on the Soviet Union. Marx provided the negative theoretical model; the USSR provides the negative practical example. The Soviet Union is taken as a negative example because the fortunes and misfortunes of its concrete experience demonstrate the need for a market, and the urgent necessity to relax the grip of centralism—the absurd centralisation of millions of decisions—and to encourage various categories of citizens to take the initiative as both producers and consumers.

It is possible to establish 'a close connection between the rejection of the market and the system of upward managerial responsibility' (p. 82). The collectivisation of agriculture was 'a disastrous course' (p. 85). Although it cannot be denied that the living standards of the peasantry have improved since the death of Stalin, this has not put an end to alienation. Farmers are better paid, but the farms are still large and those who work them are still poorly motivated. The economic situation has to be improved; basic principles may even have to be radically revised. Essentials that cannot be obtained legally are obtained 'by other means'; this applies, for instance, to the constant and delicate problem of how to obtain inputs (raw materials) for industry. The result is the 'second economy', which is now an essential part of economic life. The logic of the Soviet system of production obviously demands the restoration of market relations. According to Nove, this is both an economic truth and an economic necessity; the regime's attempts to conceal that fact do nothing to help economic activity or the needs of consumers and citizens. Conversely, 'the existing price system renders necessary the existence of the central apparatus' (p. 101), and that in turn means that those who control that apparatus must have power and privileges.

This unreasonable and sometimes irrational system does not, however, result from the direct application of the principles of socialism and, certain features aside, it has nothing to do with the work of Marx. Nove is not unaware of the need to take into account the impact of specifically Russian features and of the historical context: 'the despotic political past; the weakness of spontaneous social forces (which partly explain the rise of despotism and are partly explained by it); economic and social backwardness, and the way in which these elements were reinforced by Leninist politics and the exigencies of civil war and "socialist construction" ' (p. 112).

Nove also assesses the attempts at reform in other 'real socialist' countries and describes the specificities of Yugoslavia, Poland, China and Hungary. He concludes that the least unsatisfactory reform was that instituted in Hungary in 1968. Despite its many faults, it represents a step in the right direction: market elements are being reintroduced; centralisation is becoming more flexible; prices reflect economic realities to a certain extent; factories and especially farmers are allowed a certain initiative. Nove contrasts the caution and moderation with which reform in Hungary has been implemented with the adventurism of Poland's economic plans in the seventies and with the over-decentralisation of Yugoslavia's self-management.

Having made these critical remarks on both Marxist theory and the practical experience of real socialism, the author devotes two chapters to his positive views, to 'his' socialism, and makes a fairly classic distinction between the transition to socialism and the socialist phase in the strict sense of the term.

I am discussing Nove's conception of socialism, but he himself discusses the economics of socialism. He writes as an economist but his comments take him far beyond economics in any strict sense and lead him to elaborate a whole vision of society, as we can see from his frequent remarks about ideology, the new man and contradictions. That of course is perfectly legitimate. Socialism is even less reducible to political economy (accumulation, investment, relations between different sectors) than capitalism. There is much more than that at stake, namely the future of the societies concerned.

II. TRANSITION AND SOCIALISM IN ONE COUNTRY

Nove's concern for realism leads him to think of socialism within the context of a single nation. He is well aware that 'socialism in one country' was one of the great slogans of the Stalinist period and was closely associated with Stalin himself,[4] and Nove's use of it at times sounds deliberately provocative. Stalin was certainly a realist, but only in the sense that he believed in *Realpolitik*. His vision of the construction of socialism in the USSR, however, was so unrealistic as to be aberrant. Presumably Nove is not in fact being provocative but simply rejecting the 'far-fetched fantasy' of 'universal, worldwide socialism' (p. 155). Even if we accept the most favourable hypothesis, this lies in the distant future. In the meantime, we have the more prosaic task of dealing with the real world. And the real world means nation-states. Nation-states will not go away and their existence therefore determines the various national experiences of socialism.

As far as the developed world is concerned, Nove's comments are often founded in the British context. One sometimes has the impression that the old tradition of insularity and the feeling that there is something specific about Britain are more important than the realism he constantly evokes to justify his project for socialism in one country.

Whatever the starting point may be—developed capitalism, real socialism or underdevelopment—a period of transition is inevitable. In that respect, the author belongs to the classic socialist tradition from which Stalin departed when, in 1936, he decreed that the USSR had suddenly but definitely entered the socialist era. For several decades the official communist movement throughout the world gave up thinking about the transition to socialism and left the task of continuing the classic tradition to isolated currents (Trotskyism) and individuals.

Nove's analysis of the transition from developed capitalism to socialism at times seems closer to the critiques made of the left of the Labour Party in Britain, of the Chilean experience under Allende or even of a certain *gauchisme* than to any positive or credible theory of transition. Several paragraphs are devoted to defending the idea that the key to transition lies in an increase in productivity rather than in the redistribution of wealth (p. 156 f). Redistributive programmes simply result in an equal distribution of poverty and are in no sense a step towards socialism. This is true and, in my view, a fairly classical position, provided of course that we ignore the propaganda value of redistribution for the labour movement. Such egalitarian programmes alienate the middle classes from the regime and can lead to disaster, as in Chile (p. 156). Making a larger cake is more important than dividing up the existing cake (p. 159). A wages policy which could restrict excessive wage claims without introducing strict price controls would remove many problems, and particularly the threat of a return to the black market.

Within the general framework of 'socialism in one country', Nove argues for an open economy and rejects the notion of autarky. Similarly, he regards drastic import controls as highly dangerous (p. 162). Such policies, which are supported by the Labour left, are simply unrealistic and would lead to a shift to the right (p. 165). The alternative would be to give in to the temptation to do away with elections and to adopt the logic of a 'people's democracy' backed up by a 'socialist' militia and police force. That would certainly protect the regime from the consequences of its failures, but it would be a terrible price to pay, and Nove rightly concludes that it would lead to the negation of socialism.

According to the classical model, the transitional period involves a certain socialisation of the economy. Nove departs from this schema by suggesting that the economy should remain open: 'Since there would be a mixed economy, with a large and important private sector, market forces must be allowed to function, and not be disrupted by a combination of price controls, import restrictions and material-allocation' (p. 165). Does the socialisation of the economy mean nationalisations? Here again, the author takes the view that whilst nationalisation itself can easily be achieved, its aims are not easy to realise. Capitalists can certainly be dispossessed, but it is rather more difficult 'to divert the profits from private appropriation to the public purse' (p. 167). The third objective of nationalisation—'serving the public good rather than making private profits' (p. 167)—is still more problematic and implies the introduction of criteria for efficiency in nationalised industries. Whilst the nationalisation of water services (p. 168) is not unpopular, the same cannot be said of many other services. Their 'duty, purpose and function' (p. 170) have to be taken into account so as to counter-balance the frequently narrow and selfish interests of workers in the nationalised industries. Noting that 'the interests of the producers and the consumers are not identical and can conflict' (p. 172), Nove then turns to his *bête noire*: irresponsible trade unions and British trade unions in particular. He calls for a trade union movement which can rise above short-sighted sectional considerations (p. 172).

At the other extreme, nationalised industries 'must be responsive to the users' needs, operate economically and with technical efficiency, reflect government policy where this affects them, and, last but not least, they must associate their employees with the decision-making processes, so that they have some real sense of "belonging", some pride in quality and achievement' (p. 173). All this is fine, but is it any more realistic or any less vague than the 'wild imaginings' of the 'dogmatists' whom Nove constantly attacks? The author himself does not seem very convinced. He ends with the rather sceptical comment that this 'will require great efforts by all concerned' (p. 173). By rejecting the idea of a 'recipe for a transition to socialism' (p. 175) he then restricts the scope of his comments still further. Nove often seems to attenuate his suggestions in an attempt to make the emphasis he places on the harsh realities of life more acceptable. Thus, whilst he accepts that hierarchy should continue to exercise its prerogatives, he also recommends 'the introduction of elements of workers' participation' (p. 175), but such vague formulae can do little to reassure workers who are all too accustomed to being dispossessed of their rights. The suggestion that 'a moderate socialist government' (p. 175) should cooperate with the employers' organisations but that cooperation 'might be conditional upon some restriction on distributed profits' (*ibid*) is even less reassuring. This really is rather vague. Nove claims that 'so much would depend upon a whole series of "unknowns" ' (*ibid*), both at home and abroad, but in fact the argument is all too familiar. What Nove is describing is not a transition to socialism and the dispossession of the capitalists, but a variant on social-democratic politics. He takes us back to a period which seemed to have gone for ever: to the period when social-democracy tried to implement at least part of its programme and was not simply content to apply the policies of its right-wing adversaries, as it does today.

Having said that, the entire discussion revolves around a 'simple' situation in that it is premised upon the existence of advanced capitalism and of a democratic tradition. Whilst we may not enjoy abundance, we certainly do not face the extreme scarcity endured by the vast majority of nations and we do not live in a socio-historical context for which social democracy is an alien idea.

Nove concedes that political change *may* be the key (p. 178), though 'political change' is rather a euphemistic way of describing what is in fact a real conflict of social interests. The transition from capitalism to socialism would involve, and would be dominated by, an anti-capitalist process. To say that it would not be a peaceful process is an understatement, but Nove has nothing to say about this. His desire to avoid discussing these harsh realities and the possible ferocity of class antagonisms is quite understandable, but is it realistic, coming from an author who is so determined to be a realist? By arguing that 'the most vicious conflicts sometimes occur not between but *within* the classes, over a wide variety of issues' (p. 19), he simply avoids the issue. Conflict within classes is certainly one of socialism's greatest problems, but that does not alter the fact that conflicts between classes are of primary importance, as is perfectly obvious from the spontaneous comments that managerial elites in Peking, Moscow, New York, or anywhere else for that matter, make about peasants and workers. Faced with a choice between the authoritarianism of real socialism, not to mention the Soviet dissident Yanov's advocacy of 'the reinforcement of hereditary privilege, and the enforcement of social discipline' (p. 179), and the democratisation of the planning system, Nove obviously opts for the latter solution, but precisely how 'planning with market elements' can be implemented remains to be seen. Broadly speaking, the answer would appear to be a Hungarian-style reform: 'first to relax the control of the party and state over agricultural production, and, secondly, to allow the creation of industrial and service co-operatives. . . This implies competition: competition for labour, which would have greater freedom to decide for whom to work; competition for customers' (pp. 180–181). This in its turn implies the possibility of failure and therefore the need to penalise failure.

Nove's solution may well be possible, or even reasonable,[4] but it remains very vague. Surely there is an obvious contradiction between his discussion of economies that have for decades been bogged down in absurd but enduring management systems and the suggestion that 'the creation of small autonomous units, especially co-operatives, would be the most urgent and most acceptable first step' (p. 182). Can the effects of Stalinist and post-Stalinist periods be undone by such cautious reforms? Whilst Nove quite rightly refuses to accept demonological explanations for developments in the Soviet Union and whilst he does display a welcome sobriety, he cannot, and presumably does not wish to, deny the magnitude of the tasks involved in transforming the Soviet system.

Nove devotes considerable space to the poor countries, a term which refers both to the 'developing countries' and to the 'real socialist' countries, but he makes it quite clear from the outset (p. 154) that here we are discussing a process of modernisation rather than socialism or even a transition to socialism. In fact this section, even more so than the rest of the book, offers a critique of leftist perspectives rather than constructive proposals.

Whole pages are devoted to refuting the concepts of unequal exchange and dependency (Frank, Amin, Emmanuel), and the concept of autarky. Nove's approach leads him to the conclusion that 'a Third World country which seeks to develop under socialist auspices will clearly have to face the fact of dependence on foreign trade. In many instances it will be a growing dependence, as its import requirements increase' (p. 189). The panacea is 'a mixed economy' (p. 193). Quite aside from its specific functions, planning may also, as G. Myrdal noted, have a mobilising function. Caution and realism are the watchwords: 'agricultural co-operation is a desirable aim, but *in no circumstances* should it be enforced upon an unwilling peasantry. . . As Engels said a hundred years ago, it is essential to proceed very carefully and patiently' (p. 193). Unfortunately, his Soviet disciples tend all to often to forget this common-sense advice.

Private firms. . . co-operatives. . . market regulation. . . the central role of the state. . . Nove himself wonders whether it might not be more appropriate to describe this as 'state capitalism' (p. 193). Is it socialism? 'If socialism is seen as requiring industrialisation, then obviously the requirements of capital accumulation will occupy a high priority (p. 195). Nove is perhaps too ready to describe as 'socialist development' all those features of the brutal accumulation of capital which many Third World countries dress up in a socialist terminology which is even more hollow and threadbare than that used to disguise the commodity known as 'real socialism'. It is quite true that we are not talking about Scandinavia (p. 195) and that it may be a question of fighting for survival. If survival is the issue, peaceful and cautious solutions may not be adequate to the scale of the challenge or to the monstrosity of what is happening as poverty and underdevelopment increase throughout the world.

Feasible Socialism

These then, are the elements and perspectives which Nove uses in his final chapter on 'feasible socialism'. By 'feasible' he means a socialism which could be achieved within the lifetime of a child already conceived 'without our having to make or accept implausible or far-fetched assumptions about society, human beings and the economy' (p. 197). It is unreasonable to hope for abundance. On the other hand, it has to be assumed that 'the state will exist; indeed it will have major politico-economic functions. The state cannot be run meaningfully by all its citizens, and so there is bound to be a division between governors and governed' (p. 197). The verdict is quite clear, as is the assumption that there must be 'a multiparty democracy, with periodic elections to a parliament' (p. 197). The market and competition are also important elements in Nove's socialism.

Nove then goes on to examine in detail the workings of his society and makes some interesting comments on the different kinds of enterprises that will exist within it. Enterprises should be as small as possible to allow real participation on the party of the producers. Some must of necessity be larger because of the need for economies of scale. He therefore envisages a whole range of enterprises including centralised state enterprises, state-owned enterprises (with a management responsible to the workforce), co-operatives, small-scale private enterprises and even freelance self-employed workers (p. 200). Competition will continue to exist, but there will be no 'wasteful' individual competition. Private enterprise will be mainly confined to individuals, but entrepreneurs will be able to employ a few people (p. 207).[5] However, 'be it noted that there is no provision for any class of capitalists; our small entrepreneur *works*. There is then no unearned income arising simply from *ownership* of capital or land' (p. 207). Whereas the sections on transition are ambiguous, there is here a challenge to the logic of capital (or private capitals). Planning will establish ground rules 'determining the share of total GNP devoted to investment, as distinct from current consumption, and this in turn would affect the rules that are made to ensure adequate savings' (p. 208). The proposed system requires 'prices that balance supply and demand, that reflect cost and use-value. This does *not* exclude subsidies whenever these are considered to be socially desirable, or where external economies are significant (public transport. . .)' (p. 210). Profits will still be made, but they will not be appropriated by capitalists. Even under socialism, there will still be a division of labour because the Marxist vision of abundance is a utopia (p. 214). Nove does, however, qualify this somewhat abrupt comment, which is quite alien to the socialist tradition. He restricts the division of labour to 'functional necessities', and does not preclude the possibility of jobs being rotated insofar as that is possible. Although inequality will still exist and will lead to wage differentials determined by supply and demand of skills, it will be kept to a minimum. References to responsible trade unions and to the active participation of at least a minority of the working population indicate that Nove's vision is inspired by the socialist tradition, even if it is not utopian: 'We must expect any meaningful self-management to alter the worker's frequently passive or negative attitude to work.' (p. 221) If that is possible, why should it not be possible to make the other transformations which the author regards as utopian? Here, he in fact briefly entertains an idea which he rejects elsewhere, namely that the behaviour characteristic of specific contexts at a specific time cannot simply be projected on to a different context. This is of course an idea that is basic to socialism, and we will return to it later.

Nove soon returns to his usual approach. The exchange of commodities will continue to play an important role in foreign trade, and even in trade between 'socialist states' (p. 224). He then devotes some stimulating pages to 'the economic role of democratic politics'. He describes how democratically elected assemblies 'would adopt, amend and choose between internally consistent perspective plans for the economy as a whole' (p. 226). Although he does return to the old tradition of democratic socialism, many of his remarks justify the question which he himself asks: 'Is it socialism?' (p. 227). And when he asserts that 'the danger one foresees is not of a vote to "restore capitalism" ' (p. 229), it is difficult not to conclude that he is indulging in wishful thinking. This comment is based upon the recent experiences of Czechoslovakia (1968) and Poland. It may well be accurate, but Nove does underestimate external pressures and the strength of capitalism at the international level. In fact, the whole book takes little account of the international dimension, a point to which we will also return.

Nove ends with a veritable profession of faith: 'at least the socialism here presented should minimise class struggle, provide the institutional setting for tolerable and tolerant living, at reasonable material standards, with a feasible degree of sovereignty and a wide choice of activities for the citizens' (pp. 229–230). This is a humane and a humanist vision, but is it realistic? It is more reformist than revolutionary and it is designed to improve and adjust the real world rather than to revolutionise it. Nove makes the point himself: ' "Permanent revolution" can be a disaster, as China's cultural revolution has shown. It disorganises, impoverishes, confuses. But permanent vigilance, *permanent reform* will surely be a "must" ' (p. 230). Nove has finally stated the underlying theme: 'permanent reform'. But is that really an alternative?

III. SOCIALISM WITHOUT REVOLUTION

Nove's book on socialism has a number of strengths. It is written by a man who has a socialist culture—and that in itself is rarer than one might think—and he avoids many of the usual clichés. It is written without bitterness, and even with a certain humour. In many ways, it is very attractive. But, as Perry Anderson notes, it is mainly of interest in that it is 'the first central work of the post-war epoch for and about socialism that is clearly written from outside the Marxist tradition'.[6]

The author has the considerable advantage of having a detailed professional knowledge of the experience of 'real socialism', and he approaches his subject with sobriety, eschewing all grandiloquence. His work thus represents a challenge to the way Marxism dominates socialist theory and certain socialist practices. It is a challenge that has to be taken up. Nove's defence of market socialism cannot be ignored. Although most thinkers and activists belonging to the socialist tradition would of course regard it as a heresy, this conception has to be included in the socialist debate. A number of Nove's comments and suggestions are pertinent and can only stimulate an open honest debate on socialism. But having said that, we have to question both Nove's 'realism' and the notion that his work provides a description of a possible socialism.

Unrealistic Realism
There is one notable absence in Nove's work: the real environment. The world in which we live is of course made up of nation-states. But if we ignore the effect of international realities, we are being as unrealistic as those who see everything in terms of world socialism. In that sense, the world-system approach adopted by Immanuel Wallerstein is more realistic, even if it is highly debatable and has already been challenged.[7] Without wishing to accept all the views of Wallerstein and his followers, it has to be admitted that the capitalist system has considerable vitality and that

it is a pervasive system. Although Anderson praises Nove's book, he also criticises it for being unrealistic. Nove's vision of socialism fails to take into account internal and external anti-socialist pressures: 'Nowhere is there any sense of what a titanic political change would have to occur, with what fierceness of social struggle, for the economic model of socialism he advocates ever to materialise.'[8] In other words, 'What has disappeared. . . is virtually all attention to the historical dynamics of any serious conflict over the control of the means of production, as the twentieth century demonstrates them.'[9]

We do not have to go back to outdated Stalinist notions to point out the obvious: capitalism would resist the anti-capitalist process with all its might and at every level, national and international. Nove assumes that, provided that we take into account all the economic, social and psychological constraints, we can peacefully get on with the task of building socialism and that no external pressures will be brought to bear. That in itself is a somewhat unrealistic assumption.[10] Unless, of course, this socialism is so novel that neither the non-socialist countries, the authoritarian and centralist 'real socialist' countries nor the capitalist countries will find it objectionable. Nove's socialism would have a system of planning, but it would also have a market, a hierarchy, an army and a national territory. It would not disrupt the international consensus. It might well annoy its neighbours, but they would certainly not find it intolerable. Nove's socialism in fact looks like a rehash of the old social-democratic model, the only difference being that it takes into account certain realities that the old model did not deign to consider and that it attempts to answer problems that the old model did not have to face. This non-revolutionary vision of transformation is certainly far removed from that of socialist utopias, so much so that it looks more like an attempt to reform and humanise capitalism rather than a possible form of socialism. After all, in Nove's model, capitalism still exists during the transitional period. It is only during the socialist phase, which is reached by some mysterious *salto mortale*, that the capitalists disappear. Nove might well agree with that point, but he would presumably argue that his 'reformist' society would lead to a better standard of living and would make it possible to build a more just society. But we can immediately object that there is nothing realistic about dreaming of a reformism that is at once cautious and audacious, especially not at a time when capitalism is becoming more barbaric and represents an affront to human dignity. Can we really speak of realism, when Nove claims that the underdeveloped countries will have to embark on the transition to socialism armed only with their own resources, that each country will have to get by as best it can? Where does that leave Bangladesh, black Africa, or even China, with its population of one billion? It is Nove's very insistence on being realistic that makes his proposals so unrealistic. The economics of 'feasible socialism' may mean more than 'socialism without Marx'; they may even mean 'socialism without socialism'. Nove's reasonable approach and his rational, or even rationalist, tone belie his undoubted socialist convictions and make even the possibility of socialism seem unlikely.

As we have seen, he has nothing, or nothing specific, to say about the break with capitalism (or bureaucracy in the 'real socialist' countries). It is only in the chapter on socialism that the capitalists disappear. Prior to that, Nove makes no direct attack on capitalism. He assumes that in the Eastern-bloc countries, the system will spontaneously reform itself. He argues that in the Third World, the issue is modernisation rather than socialism. Whatever the situation, there is no mention of conflict. The issue is always avoided. Perhaps this simply reflects the author's fears about the possibility of revolutionary violence. The logic of revolution can of course lead to the negation of socialism, even if it is disguised as socialism. The experience of history leaves no doubts on that score. But the same experience quite clearly teaches us that unless we face the fact that there is a conflict of interests, no real change is possible, nothing can be done to improve the position of the majority, and still less can be done to promote human dignity.

Nove is the author of a number of well-documented studies of the class nature of the Soviet regime and of the characteristics of its ruling elite.[11] But, curiously enough, he has nothing to say about those issues here. He is certainly aware of the selfish individual interests of the ruling elite, yet he simply remarks that a desire for survival might stimulate a desire for reform on its part. The elite may well opt for reform, as certain elements within it presumably realise that sometimes it is necessary to change much in order to change nothing. But elites usually display a stubborn, if not violent, desire to retain their privileges and are very much aware that their interests are not those of the majority. They also display a propensity to use force and at times extreme force to preserve their frequently excessive privileges. To restrict the argument to recent years; reforms in Eastern-bloc countries have often gone hand in hand with repression, and economic liberalisation has often led to a hardening of the regime. Both the elite and the masses have found that conflict is the only stimulus to change and, in certain circumstances, the only thing that opens up channels of communication. The fact that the masses came to the fore in varying degrees in China, Hungary and Poland did a lot to stimulate economic reforms. But even though it is widely recognised within the Soviet Union that there must be economic changes, the desire for change comes up against the intertia of the state apparatus and the masses show little desire to challenge it. Even if they are stimulated by pressure from below, reforms tend to ensure the continued survival of a system of domination which is incarnated in social forces that are determined to defend their own interests. All this has little to do with Nove's vision of the transition to socialism. It could, however, be said that in the East the authorities are developing more sophisticated ways of running their societies. The brutal, despotic methods which characterised earlier phases (such as the Stalin period in the USSR) are giving way to methods which are certainly authoritarian but which are more skillful in that privileges are negotiated in exchange for concessions. And the louder the protests from below, the greater the concessions. In other words, the social struggle—the class struggle—still manifests its effects in various ways.

George Orwell, that avowed enemy of totalitarianism and supporter of democratic socialism, was more realistic about this than Nove. He knew that any change which altered the basis of class privilege in a country like Great Britain would not be a peaceful affair and opined that 'the London gutters will have to run with blood'.[12] One does not have to have a taste for violence to see that the stakes are too high to allow for peaceful solutions. Nove himself places too much emphasis on the fact that human beings will always be selfish not to understand this. He admits that non-capitalism in fact means anti-capitalism (or anti-bureaucratism in the Eastern-bloc countries) and that it involves conflict, in other words a harsh and probably violent struggle. He is right to hope that errors can be avoided and that the birth pangs of the transitional period can be mitigated, but if he believes that conflict can be avoided, he has to abandon any hope for socialism. He would do better to revive the best aspects of the liberal tradition, defined in its traditional Anglo-American sense (and not in the sense that Reagan uses the word), or to return to a certain social-democratic vision, though it is far from certain that that vision still possesses any credibility.

We spoke earlier of 'socialism without socialism'. The irony is quite in keeping with the ironic and at times off-hand remarks which the author makes so often (especially towards the end of the preface written for the French edition). It is almost as though he wanted to distance himself from his own book, as though he was aware that his 'realism' undermines his socialist vision. Perhaps he realises that his project can be implemented only because it is so innocuous or, alternatively, that it cannot be implemented because it is not sufficiently motivated. Nove is obviously fascinated by the problem of socialism and by the adventures and mis-adventures of the Russian revolution. But he is also a specialist in Soviet affairs, a serious and well-informed analyst, and a sober, detached scholar. He therefore concentrates on reality as it is and reaches the sombre conclusion that whilst progress may be possible, a different society is unthinkable. He argues, for instance, that if human beings are selfish in one context, they will always be selfish. If he believes that socialism is dead, he should say so openly. The passion, the devotion, the intelligence and the terror which socialism has inspired deserve more than a passing salute, a fashionably dry realism and a few offhand comments.

IV. THE PROBLEMATIC OF SOCIALISM: THE OLD AND THE NEW

Given that Nove does discuss the problematic of socialism seriously, we cannot avoid the questions he raises. Is the only alternative to his proposals a return to the 'stupid' or 'intelligent' forms of dogmatism he denounces so tirelessly? Are a stateless society, abundance and world socialism really so many dangerous mirages? One cannot jettison so many aspects of the old socialist project quite that easily. I have tried to show this by bringing out the difficulties and contradictions involved in Nove's project. But it may be more useful to stress the positive aspects of the major themes of socialism.

We can begin with abundance, the theme with which Nove quite rightly opens his argument. The problems of abundance and scarcity legitimately dominate the whole debate over socialism. No one can deny that abundance is unlikely to exist in the near future. It is possible that abundance would have harmful effects. I think that mankind would happily take that risk. But rejecting the idea that lies behind the notion of abundance implies rather more than admitting that scarcity is inevitable. It implies denying a possibility that has existed ever since industrial capitalism first revealed its potential: the possibility that the human condition could be improved to a degree that would have been unthinkable in any previous period of history.

This brings us to the heart of the problem: the concrete possibility of a massive improvement in the human condition. In other words, industrial capitalism meant that it was possible to find a practical solution to the evils of the past. It was no longer a matter of bringing heaven down to earth, as it had been in Feuerbach's day; the point was to recognise that industry had reshaped the world and that the world now held the solution to the 'curses of the past'. Before the industrial period, it had been impossible to imagine a world in which necessities could be widely available. There was no need to define the terms of the argument strictly; what was certain beyond any doubt was that there could be infinitely more, that things would be infinitely better.[13] The potential for at least relative abundance meant that individuals could be more equal and that they had a greater right to happiness in this life. The whole socialist tradition saw the development of society in terms of an expansion of its potential. As Nove himself notes, 'It was quite proper for Marx in 1880 to attack Malthus and to stress how great are the still unused resources of the earth' (p. 17). It will of course be objected that overpopulation is now a serious problem throughout the world and that relative scarcity at least is obviously going to be with us for a long time to come. That is undeniable, but it does mean that there is no basis for socialism. By observing what was really happening in certain countries, and especially in England, the early socialists came to the conclusion that the industrial age had opened up radically new and previously unthinkable possibilities for human liberation. In other words, poverty was not inevitable. Does a century's hindsight mean that we have to add anything to that? We have to add that the industrial age also has a dangerous potential. But that has in fact always been the other side to the socialist tradition, with its slogan of 'socialism or barbarism'. That slogan shows how far the capitalist industrial movement, or in other words the industrial reality of the nineteenth-century world, could be seen as a threat to the human race. There are two sides to the socialist vision of the industrial world: it has the potential to liberate mankind, but society has first to be mastered. All this is well known, but it tends to be forgotten. It is often forgotten that socialists have always taken the view that historical analysis is itself a historical phenomenon and that they have always rejected 'naturalist' explanations of society. Nove's book reflects the ambiguities of the period in which we live. No one would deny that the modern world contains horrifying possibilities. But at the same time, there is a tendency to think that it *inevitably* generates such fearful evils that there is no possibility of radical liberation and that society is governed by *inexorable natural laws*. We have replaced the fates of the Ancient World with a new sense of fatality.[14] It is as inexorable as ever and seems to preclude the possibility of creating a society that might be radically better than that of the past. A radically better society would be one which could free the majority from poverty, submission and oppression. We are now infinitely richer than we once were (in the West, at least), but it is generally accepted that, more than ever before, we are *of necessity* a threat to ourselves and to our environment. Fate and natural laws apply to all, and they are no less rigid or demanding than the laws of God. And, as in the Ancient World, anyone who defies fate provokes the wrath of the gods. We simply have to submit to the gods, to heaven or to their earthly representatives. Economic laws are inexorable, and scarcity is man's lot. To say that this takes us back to the pre-socialist or even the pre-Enlightenment period would be an understatement. It brings us back to the present day, to the daily press in Paris, London or Peking, to the eternal litanies about the harsh realities of economics, the inevitability of inequality, and the inescapable constraints of the economy. The general diagnosis is not wrong, and it is quite true that the modern world does pose serious threats to mankind. It is the explanations that are phantasmagorical. What is worse, they represent a form of ideological manipulation. It is both absurd and socially inevitable (in terms of individual interests) to argue that abundance is impossible because there is no limit to the things we can desire and then to conclude that scarcity will therefore always be man's lot. And it is equally absurd to claim that the existence of scarcity means that there can never be a truly egalitarian society and that there is no hope of mankind ever being anything but selfish and acquisitive. To argue that we must accept that this is impossible (the ideological tune of the moment) or that we can only make minor improvements which leave the existing structures of society largely intact (Nove) is not a realistic acceptance of the immense problems facing the modern world. It is tantamount to bowing to the invasive power of capitalism. To claim that our present situation is the outcome of natural and not social objective forces really does mean putting capitalism in command and making it the master of ideology, if not the master of our very minds. I have quoted Nove's argument to the effect that selfishness and acquisitiveness are an eternal part of human nature. A lot of other writers probably accept this view, and it is probably true that it represents the popular consensus. But unless we accept social ills as something natural, no one can argue that this will always be the case. Even if abundance is impossible, no rational person can prove that we are therefore objectively condemned to live in an unequal, oppressive and alienating society. To claim that societies which have the potential of our societies must *of necessity* be flawed in that way is a religious or, to be more accurate, an ideological argument. But it is quite true to say that there are no limits to the social desire to sustain a social logic which makes inequality and oppression seem natural and inevitable. The socialist tradition rejects the view that the 'density' of societies is governed by 'natural' laws and quite rightly argues that societies are historical, that the rise of capitalist industry contains within it a new potential, as do the demands which social groups raise and the forms of action which they develop. The socialist tradition is based upon the conviction that it is objectively and materially possible to create a new society, that the mobilisation of the human will (militant action on the part of the dispossessed) can provide an answer to mankind's most pressing problems. This is more than a mobilising myth *à la* Sorel and more than a form of science fiction (a utopian vision rather than a utopia), even though they too are important elements of the socialist tradition. The fact that such a society may never exist, or that it may exist only in a very distant future, that the hopes of the early socialists who, like everyone else thought in terms of their own lifetimes and not in terms of geological eras, will not easily be fulfilled does not invalidate the ideas which lie at the heart of modern socialism. And it certainly does not invalidate Marx's ideas. The rise of industrial capitalism and the social changes it generated helped to popularise ideas that first emerged with the Enlightenment: it was possible for human beings to have a different destiny.

The millenarianism, the religious vision of redemption and the mystical elements which ran through and clung to the socialism which emerged from this new vision of history and which influenced militant forms of action are less important than the obvious and unprecedented fact that industrial society and all the social concepts it implied meant that the question of liberating mankind was no longer a hollow dream or a poetic fantasy about going back to the golden age: it had become a concrete problem. It was certainly an infinitely difficult problem, infinitely more complex than the whole socialist tradition believed it to be. But it has to be remembered, and this is something which is all too often forgotten, that the socialism Marx conceived was a synthesis of the theoretical and practical elements that were available to him. It seemed at that time that socialism would emerge quite naturally from a relatively uncomplicated capitalism. It seemed that socialism would be easy to construct.[15] It was based upon productive forces which were much more limited than those we know today, but it also reflected a more restricted range of needs, a stronger communal tradition, a lesser degree of capitalism and, it has to be said, a lower tolerance of mass barbarism. The past is dead and gone. We have to live, think and act with the effects of history. The history with which we must live is the history of the development of capitalism and, whatever Marx may have thought, it is far from having exhausted its potential for expansion. The realities of history have given the lie to that argument, and no one can deny the fact. Whilst capitalism or the modern industrial system has developed to a remarkable degree, its harmful effects are also greater than ever before. It has a capacity for all the most modern forms of modern violence, an ability to suppress and a constant tendency to create extremes of wealth and poverty on both a national and an international scale. As the theoreticians of totalitarianism knew only too well, there is such a thing as modern barbarism and even if we do not identify it with capitalism, it is undoubtedly part of the modern world. Barbarism is simply one aspect of a world that has been reshaped and invaded by the values of the West and its industrial logic. Taking this situation into account is one thing, but turning the problem of abundance into a bogeyman is another thing altogether. If we accept that the constraints of social life are inescapable, then we have to admit that the improvements we are proposing can never be made.

In his introduction, Nove comments that 'I am aware that human acquisitiveness is a force which cannot be ignored, which indeed must be harnessed in the search for efficiency' (p. 7). The tone is very reminiscent of Hobbes' suggestion that there must be some force to tame the intrinsic evils of human nature. Even if we introduce a greater balance of powers and increase public accountability, this implies that we must accept that someone must have authority over the majority. We thus legitimise something which will become authoritarian or even despotic.

This much is obvious from the value that is attached to the particularly threatening institution of the state. Much as Nove may mock the old programmes for a stateless socialism, and much as he may argue that the absence of any state can lead to the worst forms of despotism, he cannot deny that statism too has its dangers. How can anyone fail to see that the most brutal societies of the twentieth century have arisen when the state has been granted excessive powers and when power has been handed over to the state or to an omniscient head of state? If the state, nationalism and selfishness are always to be with us, even in attenuated form, we can only conclude that more horrors lie in store.[16] Rather than refusing to accept the obvious, we should, rationally but boldly, take into account the complexity of a world which no longer permits the simple hopes and solutions we inherited from the past. Of course we cannot do away with the state or with nations by waving a magic wand. We should, however, remember that in Mao's China the extension of the rights of the state went hand in hand with the restriction or even the abolition of the rights of the individual. Nor should it be forgotten that Soviet society is, in its present form, very legalistic. We have only to look at a rapidly developing capitalist state like Singapore or at certain impoverished Third World countries to see what state despotism means. Even in Europe (and the US), calls to roll back the state mask the insidious growth of a state that is all the stronger for being less visible but more pervasive. The ruling class has always longed for the day when citizens would internalise the view that the system is legitimate. Rather than accepting the state as something inevitable, we have to think of at least provisional ways to prevent the spread of statism and to allow individuals and collectivities to take more initiative and power. It is at this level that Nove and others have many interesting and stimulating comments to make. But putting all these good ideas into practice means that we have to think against the state and mobilise against the state. In other words, the word revolution is still on the agenda, even if it does strike fear into some hearts.

We have to learn from the past. We have to weigh up the risks of the inevitable destabilisation that a revolution would produce. We have to face the question of money, of the market and of the hierarchy of skills realistically and unflinchingly. We have to take a realistic view of the withering away of the state. And I would point out in passing that the socialist tradition is not quite so blind to all these questions as is sometimes claimed. Time and time again, socialists have proclaimed that socialism must allow people to develop their skills and must not lead to uniformity,[17] that during the transitional period and even during the first phases of socialism there will be certain inequalities because there will be no such thing as abundance.[18] But if inequality persists and does not disappear, and if hierarchy is still similar to the one we know today, we cannot speak of socialism or even of an improvement in the human condition. As Marx said in a rather different context, that kind of socialism is simply old night soil.[19]

This brings us to the question of the immutability of human nature, which is merely the obverse of the abundance argument. Abundance is impossible because men and women are what they are: egotistic, self-centred creatures. Once we accept this argument, we reject the problematic of socialism. If nothing can really change, if there is room for only minor improvements, the world will always be a jungle in which man fights man. A whole host of thinkers have used a vast range of arguments to prove that we need a society or a regime that can control or bridle man's animal instincts. It is often argued that we need an authoritarian power to defend the common interest against the rapacity of individual instincts, or that we at least need some authority to restrain the excesses of a zoological being who, his pretentions notwithstanding, is still very close to his animal origins—and indeed that he is a particularly unpleasant animal. It was against this very argument, which has been central to the thinking of societies of all periods, that the Enlightenment and the socialist tradition which derives from it rebelled. The new world which the thinkers of the eighteenth century foresaw was not a world of large scale industry. In many ways it was similar to the world the *Encyclopédistes* glimpsed when they published volumes of plates showing ingenious but primitive artisan techniques. The world they wanted to see offered new possibilities and a new framework for the analysis of man's relationship with the outside world. They believed of course that new environments produce new forms of behaviour. We could now add that new environments can produce either negative or positive changes. If the historical environment deteriorates, behaviour will also deteriorate. But nothing is immutable. On the contrary, the twentieth century has seen rapid changes in ethics and value systems all over the world. The die has not been cast. If it had been, it would be pointless to discuss socialism, even in speculative terms. The critical tradition which became an influential current of thought after the Enlightenment was not mistaken when it saw human liberation in terms of a dialectic between reciprocal changes in the human environment and in human beings themselves.

The terms in which the problem is now posed are obviously not what they once were. Our task has become more difficult and we have to revise radically our outdated and simplistic ideas. The task may be more difficult and more complex, it may take longer than we once thought and it may lead to unexpected results, but none of this removes the urgent need to get down to it. Unlike Nove, who believes that we can construct a form of socialism by using elements of the real world as it now is, I believe that we have to find a path to a different future by critically examining both past and present, even if it is true that the road to liberation is a long road. Perhaps the task will never be completed. But it is still the only task worthy of mankind. This is the heritage left us by the socialist tradition and by Marx himself. In that sense, we still have to construct socialism *with* Marx and with the socialist tradition.

NOTES

1. Perry Anderson, *In The Tracks of Historical Materialism*, London, Verso, 1983, p. 100.
2. Cf. p. 60: 'It seems also that to assume away personal selfishness, acquisitiveness, competitiveness is far-fetched.'
3. It was in fact Bukharin who created and theorised this problematic.
4. Ernest Mandel replies at length to Nove's criticisms in Chapter 10 ('Is Socialism really Possible, Necessary, Desirable') of his forthcoming book on socialism, *Marx's Theoretical Heritage: Restating the Case for Socialism at the End of the Twentieth Century*. Mandel tries to demonstrate that 'market socialism' can only lead to the restoration of capitalism. On the other hand, he argues that a democratically centralised marketless socialism is both practicable and necessary. Ultimately the debate centres upon the role of the market in social development rather than upon the need for a market as such. Mandel follows the majority socialist tradition in arguing that the market must eventually wither away. According to Nove, the market will be central to the activity of socialist society, but it will not have the role that it has under capitalism.
5. In his reply to Nove, Mandel accepts that it might be possible (or useful?) to have individual enterprises under socialism. In recent years, the People's Republic of China, which once banned practically all private economic activity, has begun to allow individuals to own property on a small scale. Individual private enterprise is restricted to areas in which there are serious shortages (of restaurants, hairdressers, etc.). This sector is still limited but it is developing very rapidly and larger enterprises which employ people outside the family are beginning to appear.
6. Anderson, *In the Tracks. . .*, p. 101.
7. For a selection of material by Wallerstein's followers and his critics, see Christopher K. Chase-Dunn, (ed.), *The Socialist States in the World-System*, Sage Publications, 1982. Cf. Roland Lew, 'Problématique du "socialisme réel": à propos de quelques publications récentes', *Revue des pays de l'est*, (Brussels), no. 1, 1984.
8. Anderson, *In the Tracks. . .*, p. 102.
9. *Ibid.*, p. 103.
10. According to Anderson, Nove's book is characterised by 'a typically utopian abstraction of actual historical reality and its empirical field of forces' and his socialism is 'located in thin air' (*ibid*). There is something of a contradiction between these criticisms and the earlier favourable comments.
11. Including a very interesting study entitled 'The Class Struggle of the Soviet Union Revisited', *Soviet Studies,* no. 3, July 1983, pp. 298–312.
12. George Orwell, 'My Country Left or Right', *The Collected Letters, Essays and Journalism of George Orwell,* London, Secker and Warburg, 1968, vol. 1, *An Age Like This,* p. 539; Cf. 'The Lion and the Unicorn', vol. 2, *My Country Left or Right,* pp. 56–109; Simon Leys, *Orwell ou la haine de la politique,* Paris, Herman, 1984.
13. In his recent 'The Controversy about Marx and Justice', Norman Geras discusses different possible meanings of 'abundance' in Marx. He concludes that the term cannot refer to an unlimited abundance, which is truly impossible (a continent for everyone). For Marx, 'there is abundance relative to some standard of reasonableness which, large and generous as it may be possible for it to be, still falls short of any fantasy of abundance without limits', N. Geras, 'The Controversy about Marx and Justice', in *New Left Review,* 150, March–April 1985, pp. 82–83. Mandel adopts a similar position in his reply to Nove.

14. Cf. Nove's comment (p. 8) to the effect that modern society's problems relate to the industrial process as such.

15. Cf. Richard Adamiak: 'All the early nineteenth-century socialists are confident that such a system, socialism, is not only feasible, but simple to operate and requiring no coercion'; 'State and Society in Early Socialist Thought', *Survey* vol. 26, Winter 1982, p. 11.

16. Nove often cites Trotsky to justify his argument, but when it comes to the eternal characteristics of human beings, he makes somewhat dubious use of his supposed ally. Thus, "Man is by nature a lazy animal", said Trotsky in 1920. 'He can also be lazy in 1983, and quite probably in 2020.' (p. 19). Nove is referring to *Terrorism and Communism*, in which Trotsky calls for the militarisation of labour. That text is very different from both Trotsky's anti-Bolshevism of the pre-1917 period and from his anti-Stalinism of the post-1923 period. What is more important, the views Trotsky held in 1920 could not have led to what he understood by socialism. It may well be true that someone who had only recently rallied to Bolshevism may have felt the need to exaggerate somewhat. It may also be true that the cruel civil war period introduced a note of hysteria. But that is no justification for accepting this hyperauthoritarian vision as a common sense view. There is a vast difference between the Trotsky of 1920, who came very close to what was to become the Stalinist position, and Trotsky the anti-Stalinist. Whether or not his views are consistent is another matter altogether. The striking thing about the 1920 text is that it is so ahistorical and so metaphysical, presumably because it was written in response to the urgent needs of a brief period of civil war. This makes the argument even more untenable: centuries of history are invoked to justify a difficult position which he held for only a few months before accepting the common sense solution of NEP.

17. The recent debate within political philosophy over the issue of equality and justice is a reminder that according to Marx the aim of a socialist or communist society is not to enforce egalitarianism via a process of levelling down. On the contrary, individuals must be allowed to develop their different and unequal capacities. It could even be said that Marx belongs to the 'individualist tradition', to, that is, the tradition which sees the liberation of the individual as the criterion by which any social change or reform is to be judged. Collective emancipation therefore means the liberation of all individuals. Marx has little in common with those 'socialists' who would place collective rights over those of the individual.

18. Nove is not unaware of this. He hides behind Trotsky to defend the idea that a market is a necessity. But Trotsky was not simply the leader of the revolutionary opposition. In 1922, he was a war leader; in 1932 he was an exile. In 1922, he defended NEP, a policy which he himself had recommended in vain in 1919. In 1920 he called for the militarisation of the economy and later produced an indefensible theoretical justification for that policy.

19. An egalitarian programme is not a guarantee of egalitarianism. As a realist, Nove will have no difficulty in agreeing with that. He will no doubt also recall that in the young state of Israel, wage differentials were very similar to those which he proposes for his socialist society (roughly one to three). That egalitarianism did not simply reflect the young state's objective situation; it was a value which was actively promoted.

MARX, THE PRESENT CRISIS AND THE FUTURE OF LABOUR*

Ernest Mandel

I

For several years, the *political* thesis that human emancipation can no longer rely on the 'proletariat', the class of wage labour, has been increasingly buttressed by economic arguments. Some posit that wage labour is receding rapidly from its position as the main sector of the active population, as the result of automation, robotisation, mass unemployment, growth of small independent business firms, etc. (Gorz, Dahrendorf, Daniel Bell, Hobsbawm).[1] Others state that there is no future for mankind (and therefore for human emancipation) as long as 'classical' industrial technology and thence 'classical' wage labour are maintained at their present level because such a situation would lead to a complete destruction of the ecological balance (Ilitch, Bahro, Gorz).[2] The present crisis is therefore seen not as a typical crisis of overproduction and overaccumulation. It is seen as a fundamental change of structure of the international capitalist economy, with a long-term fundamental shift in the weight, cohesion and dynamic of wage labour, at the expense of that class, as a 'crisis of the industrial system'.

Can this hypothesis be verified empirically? If not, what is the meaning and what are the long-term potential consequences of growing structural unemployment, which, in and by itself, is an undeniable phenomenon? If yes, what is the explanation of the phenomenon of the supposed 'decline of the working class' as an objective phenomenon? What are its potential economic consequences?

II

Empirically, the *basic* trend which is statistically verifiable is that of the growth of wage labour on a world scale, and on all continents, and not that of its absolute or relative decline. If one looks at the ILO statistics, one can see this at first glance. When I say basic trend, I mean of course not three-months or six-months variations, but 5 or 10 years averages. Even since the beginning of the present long economic depression, for

---

*This paper was initially delivered to a colloquilem 'The Future of Human Labour' organised by the Institute for Marxist Studies at the Vrise University, Brussels, February 14–16, 1985.

example since 1968 or since 1973, this remains the predominant tendency.

The verification of this tendency implies a series of conceptual precisions:

(a) That one does not reduce 'wage labour' to 'manual labour in large-scale industry' (Marx's definition of the 'total worker', der *Gesamt-arbeiter*, in *Capital I*, and in the unpublished section VI).

(b) That one defines 'wage labourers' (proletarians) in the classical way as *all those who are under economic compulsion to sell their labour power* (excluding thereby only those managers and high functionaries who have high incomes which allow them to accumulate sufficient capital to be able to survive on the interest of that capital).

(c) That one does not reduce the proletariat to productive workers but includes in it all unproductive wage-earners who fall under condition (b), as well as all unemployed who do not become self-employed (see Marx's *Capital*, Rosa Luxemburg's *Einführung in die Nationalökonomie* and the general concept of the 'reserve army of labour').

(d) That one gives an objective and not a subjective definition of the class of wage labour (class in itself); i.e. that one does not make its existence dependent on levels of consciousness.

This implies, among other things, that wage labour in agriculture (e.g. India) and in the so-called 'service industries' is wage-labour to the same extent as wage labour in mining and in manufacturing industry. With that criterion the statistical evidence that we are still witnessing a growth and not a decline of the 'world proletariat' is undeniable. The total number of non-agricultural wage-earners in the world today is somewhere between 700 and 800 million, a figure never attained in the past. Together with agricultural wage-earners, it reaches 1 billion. This is confirmed by the following data even concerning the imperialist countries:

Changes in annual civilian employment of wage earners
(annual average 1973–1980)

Norway	+2,5%
Portugal	+2,5%
United States	+2,2%
Australia	+1,1%
Italy	+1,1%
Denmark	+0,8%
Japan	+0,8%
Austria	+0,3%
France	+0,2%
Belgium	0,0
United Kingdom	−0,1%
West Germany	−0,2%

(ILO, Le Travail dans le Monde, Geneva, 1984)

There remains the problem of the relative decrease of wage labour employed in the largest capitalist factories, i.e. of a relative deconcentration of labour accompanying a further concentration and centralisation of capital. This has been the tendency since the beginning of the present slump in the imperialist countries, not in the semi-industrialised ones and not on a global scale, where concentration of labour continues to advance. Whether in the metropolis this is only a conjunctural phenomenon like the relative decline of the so-called 'old' industrial branches before large-scale plants appear in 'new' branches, or whether it has become a long-term trend, remains to be seen. We will have to wait at least till the 1990s before we are able to draw definite conclusions in that respect.

III

The short-and medium-term impact of full scale automation or robotisation on total employment (the number of wage-labourers employed) has been practically nil till the beginning of the seventies (taking into account shifts of employment between branches, which are of course very real), and remains modest today and for the foreseeable future. Recent OECD studies predict that between now and the nineties, robotisation will cut somewhere between 4% and 8% of all existing jobs *in the West* (and between 2 and 5% of all existing wage jobs on a world scale).[3] It does not add how many new jobs will be created in the industrial branches producing robots and automatic machines. Predictions vary wildly between the 'optimists' and 'pessimists' in that regard. But even if we follow the most pessimistic predictions according to which the number of new jobs created in these new industries will be negligible, the total number of wage-earners employed will still constitute the overwhelming majority of the active population till the end of the century (between 80 and 90% of the population in the West, Eastern Europe and the USSR).

So there is no objective ground for speaking of a 'decline of the proletariat' in an objective sense of the word.[4]

This does not mean that one should underestimate the dangerous potential of long-term mass unemployment. This has basically two causes in the capitalist countries:

(a) The decline of rates of growth during the long depressive wave, rates of growth which fall below the average rate of growth of productivity of labour (third technological revolution).

(b) The impossibility of the economic system absorbing population growth into employment under these same circumstances, all other things remaining equal.

In addition, we have to take into consideration the precise effects of robotisation on specific branches of industry which have played a key role in the organisation and strength of the working class and the labour movement, e.g. the automobile industry in the United States and Western Europe. Here, the prospects are threatening and should be understood before it is too late (as has been unfortunately the case in the steel and ship-building industries).

The consequences of growing long-term structural unemployment (in the West: from 10 millions around 1970 to 35 millions today and 40 millions in the mid-eighties) are a growing fragmentation of the working class and the danger of demoralisation, already visible in certain sectors of the proletarian youth (e.g. black youth and Spanish-speaking youth in the USA and in certain regions of Great Britain),[6] who have *never* worked since they left school and are in danger of not finding jobs for many years to come.

Japanese socialists[7] have tried to study the effects of new technologies especially on the automobile industry. Also stressing qualitative aspects of the changes (loss of skills, increase in accidents, emergence of new layers of workers and of skills etc.), the authors find a reduction of shop floor workers of around 10% at the most highly 'robotised' automobile plant in Japan, Nissan's Myrayama Plant, between September 1974 and January 1982, accompanied however, by small increases in white-collar personnel. Even the Japanese 'company unions' seem worried by these developments, 'life-long employment' still the rule in Japan notwithstanding (*Japan Economic Journal*, February 21, 1984).

IV

The only serious answer to the growth of massive structural long-term unemployment during the present long depression is a radical international reduction of the working week without a cut in weekly pay: the immediate introduction of the *35-hour week*. This means the spread of the existing work-load among the whole proletariat without loss of income (12% of unemployment can be suppressed by every worker working 12% weekly hours less), and with obligatory additional hiring and the reunification of the working classes torn apart by unemployment and fear of unemployment. This should be the central strategic short-term goal of the whole international labour movement, in order to prevent the relationship of forces between Capital and Labour from being changed in a serious way at the expense of Labour. The longer-term perspective is the 30-hour week.

All considerations about 'national competitiveness' and 'enterprise profitability' should be abandoned in favour of that absolute social priority. One could easily prove that from a global and international—not single firm— point of view, that this is also the most economically rational solution. But of course capitalist 'rationality' *is* single-firm based 'rationality', i.e. *partial* rationality, which leads more and more to *overall* irrationality. The disastrous political risks of massive unemployment, both nationally and internationally, do not need to be stressed.

Marx was unequivocally clear on both issues: the beneficial effects of a radical reduction of the working week without reduction in pay, and the need for international solidarity of labour to substitute itself for 'national' (or regional, or local, or sectoral, or even one-corporation) solidarity between workers and capitalists.

It is sufficient to quote Marx's *Adress* (Inauguraladresse) *to the Working Men's International Association* (First International):

> Past experience has shown to what extent the neglect of the fraternal links which should tie and inspire the workers of different countries to firmly stand together in all their struggles for emancipation, is always punished by the common failure of their unconnected attempts (Marx–Engels–Werke volume 16, pp. 12–13, my translation—E.M.).

And in his quarterly report on the activity of the General Council of the WMIA, Marx wrote:

> And even its national organisation easily leads to failure as a result of the lack of organisation beyond national boundaries, as all countries compete on the world market and mutually influence each other. Only an international union of the working class can assure its final victory (MEW, vol. 16, p. 322, my translation—E.M.).

In an even more categorical way, Marx stated in his Instructions to the First International's General Council Delegates to the Geneva 1867 Congress of that Organisation:

> We declare the limitation of the working day to be a precondition, without which all other endeavours for amelioration and emancipation must fail (MEW, vol. 16, p. 192, my translation—E.M.)[8]

V

The struggle between the forces which push in the direction of long-term massive structural unemployment on the one hand, and of a new radical reduction of the working week on the other, are intimately related to the two basic motive forces of bourgeois society: Capital's drive to increase the production of relative surplus-value, i.e. the development of the 'objective' (objectivised, materialised) productive forces, machinery, machine systems, semi-automised systems, full-scale automisation, robots on the one hand; the counter-pressure of the class struggle between Capital and Wage-labour on the other. One of the main analytical achievements of Marx consisted precisely in indicating the *dialectical* (not mechanical, of the Malthus-Ricardo-Lassalle type) *inter-relation between the two.*

The increase in mechanisation has a *contradictory* effect on labour. It reduces skills, suppresses employment, bears down on wages through the rise of the industrial reserve-army of labour, effects which can be partially offset through the increase in the accumulation of capital ('economic growth'), international migration of labour, etc. But likewise, the increase in the mechanisation of production tends *to increase the intensity of the work effort* (physical and/or nervous), and therefore exercises objective pressure in the direction of a reduction of the working week. This second effect has often been overlooked by working class militants, including socialists and Marxists. It is strongly emphasised by Marx.[9]

But Capital will not grant this physically and economically indispensable reduction of the working week out of the kindness of its heart. It will only do so after a fierce struggle between Capital and Labour.

Workers' rebellion—as Marx called it—can however only be (temporarily) successful under relatively favourable relationships of forces. *These are created by the effects of employment and organisation of labour of the phase prior* to the long-term depression and surge of unemployment. And precisely in the late nineteen-seventies and nineteen-eighties, the international (especially the Western European) proletariat entered the growing confrontation with Capital around the issue 'austerity vs. shortening of the working week without a reduction in take-home pay or social security allowances', with a much increased numerical, organisational and militant strength accumulated during the nineteen-fifties, sixties and early-seventies, i.e. during the period of the long-term post-war 'boom'. *It is for that reason that resistance of the working class against the austerity offensive will increase, will spread, will become periodically explosive and will tend to be generalised* nationally and internationally. It is for the same reason that the capitalist class will not find it easy to implement its own historical 'solution' to the present depression.

Precisely because the *organic strength* of the working class (wage labour) is so large at the outset and in the first phase of this depression, the outcome of this intensified class offensive of Capital against Labour is far from certain. The likelihood that the proletariat will suffer a crushing defeat as in Germany in 1933, Spain in 1939 or France in 1940 in any of the larger capitalist key countries in the foreseeable future is limited.

This does not imply that a proletarian-socialist solution of the crisis is certain or already visible on the horizon. The main obstacle for such a crisis is *subjective* and not objective: the level of consciousness of wage labour and the capacity of its leadership are still absolutely inadequate. But this means that at least the *objective possibility* of a socialist working class solution of the crisis of mankind remains with us. The rest depends on the socialists themselves, their awareness of the gravity and the risks implied in the crisis (the very physical survival of mankind is now at stake), the impossibility of solving it within the framework of generalised market economy, i.e. 'exchange value production', i.e. capitalism, the necessity to develop an anti-capitalist programme of action starting from the real existing concerns and needs of the real existing wage labourers, in all their varieties, the necessity to unite this mighty force into a battering ram to shake the fortresses of capital, the necessity to organise for the overthrow of capitalism.

VI

Let us now make the hypothesis that all this will be disproved by experience during the coming decades; that both for economic reasons (robotisation) and political ones which we allegedly 'underestimate', wage-labour will decrease considerably between now and the end of the 20th century; that therefore the proletariat has already started to decline objectively (both in numbers and inner cohesion) and that for the same reason its *objective capacity* to transform society in a socialist sense will also decline more or less steadily. In that case, one should not only say 'goodbye' to the proletariat. One would also have to say:

- 'goodbye' to socialism and any realistic (materialistically based) project of human emancipation;
- 'goodbye' to the market economy and capitalism itself.

One of the basic theses of Marx, to which no evidence can be opposed on the basis of the last 100 years of experience, is that only the class of wage-labour acquires through its place in capitalist production and bourgeois society those 'positive qualities', i.e. the capacity for massive (self)-organisation, solidarity and co-operation, which are the *preconditions* for a socialist solution of the crisis of mankind. These qualities do not *automatically* create the emancipatory revolutionary role of the proletariat; they only lead to a *social potential* of that nature. But no other social class or layer has a similar potential, neither third-world peasants, nor revolutionary intellectuals, and certainly not technocrats and functionaries. Other social classes and layers have a huge revolutionary anti-capitalist (anti-imperialist) 'negative' potential, e.g. the peasantry in under-developed countries. But history has proved again and again that they don't have the 'positive' potential for conscious socialist organisation.

On the other hand, if a massive substitution of 'living' by 'dead' labour (robots) leads to a massive absolute decline of wage labour, it is not only the future of the proletariat and of socialism which is threatened. It is the very survival of capitalist market economy which becomes more and more impossible. This is expressed in a graphic, be it somewhat simplified way, by the already classical dialogue between the factory manager and the trade-union militant:

- 'What will become of your trade-union strength when all the workers

will be replaced by robots?'
— 'What will become of your profits in that case? Your profits are realised through the sale of your goods; robots unfortunately don't buy goods.'

Marx foresaw that development more than 125 years ago, in his *Grundrisse* (which, incidentally, confirms the point which I have made many times that, far from being an 'economist of the 19th century', he was a visionary who detected trends which would only come into their own in the late 20th century)' He wrote there:

> But to the degree that large industry develops, the creation of real wealth comes to depend less on labour time and on the amount of labour employed than on the power of the agencies set in motion during labour time, whose 'powerful effectiveness' is itself in turn out of all proportion to the direct labour time spent on their production, but depends rather on the general state of science and on the progress of technology, or the application of this science to production. . . Labour no longer appears so much to be included within the production process; rather, the human being comes to relate more as watchman and regulator to the production process itself.
>
> (*Grundrisse*, Pelican Marx Library, pp. 704–5.)

And again:

> *The theft of alien labour-time, on which the present wealth is based*, appears a miserable foundation in face of this new one, created by large-scale industry itself. As soon as labour in the direct form has ceased to be the great well-spring of wealth, labour time ceases and must cease to be its measure, and hence exchange-value [must cease to be the measure] of use value. *The surplus-labour of the mass* has ceased to be the condition for the development of general wealth, just as the *non-labour of the few*, for the development of the general powers of the human head. With that, production based on exchange value breaks down. . .'
>
> (*ibid.*, p. 705)

Obviously, this development cannot fully unfold under capitalism, because precisely under capitalism, economic growth, investment, the development of machinery (including robots), remain subordinated to the accumulation of capital, i.e. to the production and realisation of surplus-value, i.e. to profits for individual firms, both expected profits and realised profits. As I already indicated in *Late Capitalism* more than ten years ago,[10] under capitalism full automation, the development of robotism on a wide scale, is impossible, because it would imply the disappearance of commodity production, of market economy, of money, of capital and of profits (under a socialised economy robotism would be a wonderful instrument of human emancipation. It would make possible the reduction of the working week to a minimum of 10 hours.[11] It would grant men and women all the necessary leisure for self-management of the economy and society, the development of a rich social individuality for all, the disappearance of the social division of labour between the administrators and the administered, the withering away of the state and of the coercion between human beings).

So what is the most likely variant under capitalism is precisely the long duration of the present depression, with only the development of partial automation and marginal robotisation;[12] both accompanied by large-scale overcapacity (and over-production of commodities), by large-scale unemployment, and large-scale pressure to extract more and more surplus-value from a number of *productive* work-days and workers tending to stagnate and decline slowly, i.e. growing pressure to overexploitation of the working class (lowering of real wages and social security payments), to weaken or destroy the free organised labour movement and to undermine democratic freedoms and human rights.

VII

In his *Grundrisse*, Marx not only foresaw the basic trend of capitalist technology towards the progressive expulsion of human labour from the process of production. He also foresaw the basic contradictions this trend would lead to under *capitalism:*

- huge overproduction, or, what amounts to the same, under-capacity. During the last recession 1980–1982, over 35% of the capacity of output of USA industry remained unused. If one also deducts arms production—useless from a reproduction point of view—one arrives at the staggering amount of nearly 50% of America's productive capacity not being used for productive purposes;[13]

- high unemployment. Marx opposes the emancipatory *potential* of automation and robotism—its capacity to increase greatly the amount of human leisure time, time for full development of the all-round personality—to its oppressive tendency under *capitalism*. He synthesises this opposition precisely as being that between a class society and a classless society.

In a class society, appropriation of the social surplus by a minority means *capacity of extending leisure time for only a minority*, and therefore reproduction on a larger and larger scale of the division of society between those who administer and accumulate knowledge, and those who produce without or with only very limited knowledge.[14] In a classless society, appropriation and control of the social surplus product by all (by the associated producers) would mean a radical reduction of labour time (of necessary labour) *for all*, a radical extension of leisure *for all*, and thereby the disappearance of the division of society between administrators and producers, between those who have access to all knowledge and those who are cut off from most knowledge. In a striking passage of the

Grundrisse, linked to the above-quoted passage, Marx writes:

> *The creation of a large quantity of disposable time* apart from necessary labour time for society generally and each of its members (i.e. room for the development of the individuals' full productive forces, hence those of society also), this creation of not-labour-time, appears in the stage of capital, as all earlier ones, as not-labour-time, free time, for a few. . . But its tendency always, on the one side, *to create disposable time, on the other, to convert it into surplus labour.* If it succeeds too well at the first, then it suffers from surplus production, and then necessary labour is interrupted, because *no surplus labour can be realised by capital.* The more this contradiction develops, the more does it become evident that the growth of the forces of production can no longer be bound up with the appropriation of alien labour, but that the mass of workers must themselves appropriate their own surplus labour. Once they have done so—and *disposable time* thereby ceases to have an *antithetical* existence—then, on one side, necessary labour time will be measured by the needs of the social individual, and, on the other, the development of the power of social production will grow so rapidly that, even though production is now calculated for the wealth of all, *disposable time* will grow for all. For real wealth is the developed productive power of all individuals
>
> (*ibid.*, p. 708).

And Marx indicates how, *under capitalism*, science, the results of general social labour, i.e. general social knowledge, gets systematically divorced from labour, how—a striking anticipation of capitalist 'robotism'—science under capitalism becomes *opposed* to labour (MEGA, II, 3.6, p. 2164).

VIII

How does capitalism try to overcome this growing new contradiction, resulting from the reduction of the absolute amount of human labour necessary to produce even a growing mass of commodities saleable under the present (i.e. bourgeois) conditions of production and distribution? Its solution is that of the *dual society*, which divides the present proletariat into two antagonistic groups:

— those who continue to be included (or are newly incorporated, especially in the so-called 'third-world countries') into the process of production of surplus value, i.e. into the *capitalist process of production* (be it for tendentially declining wages);

— those who are expelled from that process and survive by all kinds of means other than the sale of their labour power to the capitalists (or the bourgeois state): welfare; increase of 'independent' activities; becoming small-scale peasants and handicraftsmen; returning to domestic labour (women); 'ludic' communities, etc.

A transitional form of 'dropping out' of the 'normal' capitalist production process is 'black' labour, 'precarious' labour, 'part-time jobs', etc., hitting especially women, youth, immigrant workers, etc.

	Part-time employment in 1979 as % of total employment	*of which female labour*
West Germany	11,4%	91,5%
Belgium	6.0%	89,3%
Denmark	22,7%	86,9%
USA	17,8%	66,0%
France	8,2%	82,0%
Italy	5,3%	61,4%
Holland	11,2%	82,5%
UK	16,4%	92,8%

(ILO: Le Travail dans le Monde, *op. cit.*)

What is the *capitalist rationale* of that dual society? It is a gigantic historical turning of the clock backward on one key issue: *indirect (socialised) wages.*

Through a long historical struggle, the working class of Western Europe, Australia and Canada (to a lesser degree that of the USA of Japan) had conquered from capital that *basic cement of class solidarity* that wages should not only cover the reproduction costs of *actually employed* living labour, but the reproduction costs of the proletariat *in its totality*, at least on a national scale: i.e. also the reproduction costs of the unemployed, sick, old, invalid male and female workers and their offspring. That is the historical meaning of social security, which is part and parcel of the wage bill (its socialised part, or at least that part of wages which 'transits' through the hands of social security institutions).

Through pressure in favour of a *dual society*, part-time labour, casual labour, 'dropping out of the rat-race', etc., capital now wants to reduce its wage-bill to directly paid-out wages only, which will then inevitably tend to decline as a result of a hugely inflated industrial reserve army of labour. It already succeeds with that goal with the mass of the 'casual' and 'precarious' labourers, who generally do not enjoy social security benefits. It wants to realise the same gains with regard to the unemployed as such.

In other words: the 'dual society' *under capitalism* is nothing but one of the key mechanisms to increase the rate of surplus-value, the rate of exploitation of the working class, and the mass and the rate of profit. Any excuse of a 'sophisticated' nature for supporting *this goal of capital* (be it 'third world-ism', ecologism, 'the immediate realisation of communism', the desire to 'break-up the capitalist consumers standard', etc.) is in the best of cases a mystified capitulation before bourgeois ideology and capital's economic purposes, in the worst of cases a direct help to the capitalist anti-working class offensive.

To advocate that unpaid labour should spread, even for 'socially useful purposes', when there is a huge number of unemployed, is not to build 'cells of communism' inside capitalism; it is to help the capitalists divide the working class through a new rise in unemployment, to help them increase profits.

But it is more than that. It puts new and formidable stumbling blocks on the *really emancipatory potential* of new technologies and 'robotism', in as much as it tends to perpetuate in an elitist way, the subdivision of society between those who receive the necessary leisure and potential to appropriate all the fruits of science and civilisation—which can only occur on the basis of the satisfaction of elementary fundamental material needs— and those who are condemned (including those who condemn themselves through self-chosen ascetism) to spend more and more of their time as 'beasts of burden', to quote again Marx's eloquent formula.

The real dilemma, which is the basic historical choice with which mankind is faced today, is the following one: *either a radical reduction of work-time for all*—to begin with the half-day of labour, or the half-week of labour—or the perpetuation of the division of society between those who produce and those who administer: the radical reduction of the work time *for all*—which was Marx's grandiose emancipatory vision—is indispensable both for the appropriation of knowledge and science by all, and for self-management by all (i.e. a regime of associated producers). Without such a reduction, both are a utopia. You cannot acquire scientific knowledge nor manage your own factory, neighbourhood or 'state' (collectivity), if you have to work at drudging mechanised labour in a factory or an office 8 hours a day, 5 or 6 days a week. To say otherwise is to lie to yourself or to lie to others.

The emancipatory potential of robotism is that it makes socialism, communism, much easier, by making a 20 hour, 15 hour, or 10 hour— working week possible *for all*. But any step in the direction of the *dual society*, even with the best of intentions, goes in the diametrically opposed direction.

We leave aside the question whether 'labour' reduced to 20 or 15 hours a week is still 'labour' in the classical sense of the word.[15] We also leave aside how far the development of the individual, to quote Marx again, is a development in which 'productive' activities remain separated from cultural, creative, scientific, artistic, sportive, purely recreative ones, in which, in other words, Lafargue's famous *droit à la paresse* becomes realised. Human happiness certainly does not depend on strenuous permanent activity, although a certain minimum amount of physical and mental activity and mobility seems to be an absolute precondition for a healthy growth including the growth of the mind.

But independently of any consideration of that nature—the future of labour in the secular sense of the word—one conclusion seems inescapable; what will happen to human labour and to humanity is not predetermined mechanically by technology or science, their present trends and the obvious dangers which they encompass. It is determined in the last analysis by the social framework in which they develop. And here the difference between a development in the framework of capitalism, competition, market economy on the one hand, and socialism, i.e. collective property and collective solidarity through the rule of the associated producers, through the mastery of all the producers over all their conditions of labour as a result of a radical reduction of the (productive) work-time, is absolutely basic.

The employers (and the bourgeois state) can likewise be helped in their strategic goal of introducing the *dual society* by the workers' obviously ambiguous attitude towards wage-labour, towards work under capitalism, and work in the modern factory in general.

It is true that workers are forced, *under capitalism*, to be attached to full-employment in order to receive a full (direct and indirect) wage. The alternative, again *under capitalism*, is a sharp decline in their standard of living, i.e. material and moral impoverishment and degradation.

But likewise, the workers are clearly aware of the increasingly degrading character of capitalist labour organisation and capitalist productive effort, especially under the conditions of extreme parcellisation of labour (Taylorism). Precisely when their standard of living is going up, as it did in the period 1950–1970, the needs of 'work satisfaction' and of increased leisure (increased health, increased culture, increased self-activity) take on a new dimension. This became strikingly evident through and after the May 1968 explosion.[16] This awareness still exists—and employers as well as the bourgeois state consciously try to capitalise upon it in order to make the appeal for the *dual society* appear as something else from what it really is: an attempt to have the working class itself pay the burden of unemployment, and thereby sharply increase the mass and rate of profit.

In the same way as the demagogic outcry that the workers (why not the capitalists?) should share their income with the unemployed, and as the myth that 'excessive wages and social security payments' are really responsible for the crisis, all the talk about 'meaningless labour which you had better do away with' is therefore today nothing less than an ideological weapon of the capitalists in their class struggle against wage labour for lowering the worker's shares in the national income.

IX

We have likewise to stress that any idea that present-day 'dirty', nature-destroying or directly life-threatening technology is an 'inevitable' outcome of the inner logic of natural science, has to be rejected as obscurantist, a-historical and in the last analysis an apologia for capitalism.

Under capitalism, technology develops in the framework of money-costs-accounting and money-profit-projection for the individual firm. Hence general social costs, human costs, ecological costs, are 'discounted', not only because they are 'externalised' (i.e. individual firms do not pay for them), but also because they appear often much later than the profits which the new technology permits on a short- or medium-term basis.

Examples of such technological choices which were profitable from the individual firm's point of view but irresponsible socially as a whole in the long run are the internal combustion-engine for vehicles and the detergent-vs-soap washing agents. In each of these cases choices were involved.

These were by no means the only technologies existing at these points of time.[17] On the contrary: many alternatives were present. The choices were not made for reasons of 'purely' scientific or 'technical' preferences. They were made for reasons of profit preferences by *specific* branches of industries, or better still leading firms in these branches, i.e. power relations inside the capitalist class. No 'technological determinism' was or is deciding humanity's fate. What is at stake is a socio-economic determinism, in which material interests of social classes or fractions of classes assert themselves, as long as these classes or fractions of classes have the actual power to impose their will (guided by these interests) upon the whole of society.

There is nothing new in understanding that technology developing under capitalism is not the only possible technology, but *specific* technology introduced for specific reasons closely linked to the specific nature of the capitalist economy and bourgeois society. Karl Marx was perfectly aware of this. He wrote in *Capital* vol. I:

> In modern agriculture, as in urban industry, the increase in the productivity and the mobility of labour is purchased at the cost of laying waste and debilitating labour-power itself. Moreover, all progress in capitalism is a progress in the art, not only of robbing the worker, but of robbing the soil; all progress in increasing the fertility of the soil for a given time is a progress towards ruining the more long-lasting sources of that fertility. The more a country proceeds from large-scale industry as the background of its development, as in the case of the United States, the more rapid is this process of destruction. Capitalist production, therefore, only develops the techniques and the degree of combination of the social process of production by simultaneously undermining the original sources of all wealth—the soil and the worker.
>
> (*Capital*, vol. I, Pelican Library edition, p. 638)

Marx also stressed that this tendency of applying specifically capitalistic technologies—i.e. only technologies which lead to an increase in the production of surplus value—implied that new techniques had to be not only means for reducing the value of labour power, for cheapening consumer goods, and for economising constant capital (cheaper machinery, raw materials and energy). They could also be means for breaking or reducing labour's power of resistance at factory, industrial branch or society's level:

> But machinery does not just act as a superior competitor to the worker, always on the point of making him superfluous. It is a power inimical to him, and capital

proclaims this fact loudly and deliberately, as well as making use of it. It is the most powerful weapon for suppressing strikes, those periodic revolts of the working class against the autocracy of capital. . . It would be possible to write a whole history of the inventions made since 1830 for the sole purpose of providing capital with weapons against working-class revolt.

(ibid., pp. 562–563)

The history of the introduction of numerically controlled machine-tools after the big 1946 strike wave in the USA is a striking confirmation of this rule.[18] Actually, when the balance-sheet is made 'after the facts', to-day less than 1% of the machine-tools used in US industry are numerically controlled ones. But the scare created by their initial introduction was sufficient to break union power at the machine tools producing plants.

A similar function is being played at present by the scare created in the trade union movement and the working class by the 'suppression of labour through robots'. Reality is still far removed from anything of the kind, as is indicated by the following table:

Robots per 10,000 wage-earners in manufacturing industry 1981

	1978	1980	1981
Sweden	13.2	18.7	29.9
Japan	4.2	8.3	13.0
W. Germany	0.9	2.3	4.6
USA	2.1	3.1	4.0
France	0.2	1.1	1.9
Britain	0.2	0.6	1.2

(L'Observateur de l'OECD no. 123, July 1983)

And to quote *Electronics Week*, January 1, 1985:

Even if the use of robots increases as predicted. . . by 1990, this would still affect only a few tenths of 1% of all employees in the industrialised countries, industry sources estimate.

It is necessary to answer this scare *by familiarising workers with computers*, by demanding that working class children's schools should put computers at their disposal without any costs. This year up to 5 million 'personal' home computers are supposed to be sold in the USA. Competition is ferocious. Prices will fall accordingly. Trade unions and other working class organisations should see to it, that workers and employees learn to master these mechanical slaves, whether or not endowed with 'artificial intelligence'. Then the scare will recede, and the working class will view new machines as it came to view old ones: as *instruments of labour* which can be transformed from instruments of despotism into instruments of emancipation, as soon as the workers become their collective masters.

Post-capitalist societies like that of the USSR generally borrow capitalist technology and suffer in addition from the consequences of bureaucratic management and bureaucratic power monopoly, i.e. the absence of free critical public opinion. But in a regime of associated self-managing producers under a socialist democracy with a plurality of political parties, no such constraints would operate. There is no reason to assume that such producers would be foolish enough to poison themselves and their environment, as soon as they knew the risks (when the risks are unknown, this is not due to too much but to too little scientific knowledge!). There is no reason to assume that they could not use machinery, including robots, as tools for the reduction or suppression of all mechanical, uncreative, burdensome, tedious, i.e. wasted human labour, as instruments for making possible the reunification of production, administration, knowledge, creative activity and full enjoyment of life, after having transformed them for that precise purpose.

X

There remains one unanswered question, a question which Marxists have not taken up till now because it was not posed before humanity. But after dwelling for decades in the realm of science fiction and futurology, this question has now been brought to the threshold of the materially conceivable, as a result of the huge leaps forward of applied science and technology in the last decade: could human labour construct machines which could escape the control of humanity, become completely autonomous of men and women, i.e. intelligent machines, and machines with a potential to rebel against their original creator? After a certain point, would robots start to build robots without human instructions (without programming), even robots inconceivable to humanity and largely superior to them from the point of view of intelligence?

In the abstract, such a possibility certainly is conceivable. But one should circumscribe more precisely the present and reasonably foreseeable material framework of the problem, before getting hysterical or feeling doomed concerning human mastery over machines.

To build a 'perfect' chess playing machine, which has an answer to *all* possible combinations (10^{120}) you would need *a number of combinations which far exceeds the number of atoms in the universe*. To have an existing computer calculate all numbers with 39,751 digits in order to discover a possible prime number among them, *it would take more time than the age of the universe up till now*. But with the help of the same existing computers, *human intelligence* in the month of September 1983, actually discovered such a prime number with 39,751 digits (which, if fully printed, would extend for sixty metres) at Chippewa Falls, Wisconsin, USA.[19]

Furthermore, there are 15 billion nerve cells and 15 trillion synapses in the human brain—in *one* human brain—a figure today's computers cannot compete with in any foreseeable future.

So the days in which we could become controlled, overwhelmed, mastered, by our chippy friends and slaves, are still far far off. They are all the more so as humanity, i.e. human labour, commands their product-ion and determines their calculating power. If necessary, humanity can decide to limit or stop the development of that power, or even to stop the production of robotised computers and computerised robots altogether. They are human tools, subordinated to specific human purposes. Humanity can avoid begetting sorcerers' apprentices, if it gains full control over its own tools and products.

But there we are at the heart of the matter: the structure and the laws of motion of *human society and economy*. That is what the problem is really all about, and not the undefined potential of mechanical calculating tools.

If humanity becomes master of its society, of the social organisation of labour, of the goals and purposes of labour, i.e. master of its own fate, then there is no danger of it becoming enslaved by thinking computers. But that presupposes abolition of private property, market economy, competition, and 'sacred egoism' as the main incentive for social labour. That presupposes a labour organisation based upon co-operation and solidarity for the common good, i.e. self-managing socialism. If we don't achieve that mastery, then the threats are innumerable: nuclear annihilation; suffocating in our own excrements, i.e. ecological destruction; massive poverty and decline of liberty; universal famine. Possible enslavement by machines would be only one of the threats, and probably not the worst.

What is therefore the rational kernel of that irrational scare is the fact that the changes in human consciousness necessary to bring about a socialist world might be rendered more difficult by the *short-term effects of new communication techniques on human thinking and sensibility*, in as much as these techniques are subordinated to particular goals of privileged social groups (ruling classes and *strata*). Substitution of video-cassettes for the written book; extreme narrowing of choices between conflicting sets of ideas; decline of critical thought and of research free from the tyranny of short-term 'profits'; decline of the theoretical, synthetical, imaginative thinking in favour of narrow pragmatism and short-sighted utilitarianism (generally combined with a generous zest of mysticism and irrationalism regarding 'broader' issues): there is the real danger that the robot and computer reshape our way of thinking,[20] but not through the fault of these poor mechanical slaves themselves but through the fault of those social forces who have an immediate social interest in achieving these disastrous effects.

Likewise, *human brains helped by computers* can more easily oppress, repress, exploit, enslave other human beings—the oppressed and exploited social classes in the first place!—than could human brains without computers. And this is so not because of the 'wickedness' of the computer or of applied science, but because of the wickedness of a given type of society, which creates the temptation and the incentives, for such types of behaviour and endeavour.[21]

Against these dangers we must mobilise, not under the slogan of 'Down with science and its dangerous potential', or 'destroy the computer' but under the slogan 'Let humanity become master of its social and technical fate, master of its economy and of all the products of its manual and intellectual labour'. That is still possible today. That is more necessary today than it ever was before.

NOTES

1. See, among others: André Gorz, *Adieux au prolétariat*, Paris, 1979; Daniel Bell, *The Post-Industrial Society; Ralf Dahrendorf, in *Geht uns die Arbeit aus?*, Bonn, 1983; Eric Hobsbawm, *Labour's Forward March Halted*, London, 1980.

2. Joseph Huber, *Die verlorene Unschuld der Oekologie*, Frankfurt, 1982; Ivan Ilich, *Le travail fantôme*, Paris, 1981; Club of Rome, *The Limits to Growth*, (1972); Rudolph Bahro, *From Red to Green*, London, 1981; André Gorz, *Adieux au prolétariat*, Paris.

3. OECD, *Robots industriels*, Paris, 1983.

4. Obviously, this does not imply that in given branches of industry (e.g. coal mining) there is no absolute decline in world employment, or in others (like textiles, shoe industry, ship-building, steel) a decline in employment in certain regions (USA, Western Europe) and a rise in others (Asia).

5. See the excellent study by Winfried Wolf, 'Volkswagen's Robots', in *Was Tun?*, December, 1983.

6. This phenomenon expresses itself among other things in the rise of drug addiction in the USA, hooliganism in Britain, etc.

7. Saga Ichiro, *The Development of New Technology in Japan*, Bulletin of the Socialist Research Centre, Hosei University, Tokyo, November 1983.

8. In his pamphlet *Lohn, Preis und Profit*, Marx stated equally:

   In their attempts at reducing the working day to its former rational dimensions, or, where they cannot enforce a legal fixation of a normal working day, at checking overwork by a rise of wages, a rise not only in proportion to the surplus time exacted, but in a greater proportion, workingmen fulfil only a duty to themselves and their race. They only set limits to the tyrannical usurpations of capital. Time is the room of human development. A man who has no free time to dispose of, whose whole lifetime, apart from the mere physical interruptions by sleep, meals, and so forth, is absorbed by his labour for the capitalist, is less than a beast of burden. He is a mere machine for producing foreign wealth, broken in body and brutalised in mind. (Marx: *Value, Price and Profit*, Selected Works, p. 329.)

9. It is especially developed in: Karl Marx, *Zur Kritik der Politischen Oekonomie* (Manuskript 1861–1863), in Karl Marx–Friedrich Engels Gesamtausgabe (MEGA), vol. 1–6, Part II, sub-part 3—quoted as Mega II/3/1–6, Berlin, Dietz-Verlag, 1976–1982). First comments on this hitherto unknown manuscript of Marx can be found in *Der Zweite Entwurf des 'Kapitals'*, Dietz-Verlag, Berlin, 1983.

10. Ernest Mandel, *Late Capitalism*, New Left Books, London, 1975, p. 2077.

11. A workers and trade-unionist group in France, writing under the pseudonym of Adret, published a book in 1977 under the title *Travailler deux heures par jour* (Le Seuil, Paris), which has had too little echo. It showed the material possibility of a radical reduction of the work day, even before the appearance of robotisation.

12. See in that respect the very subdued conclusion of a recent conference on robotics: P.H. Winston & K. Prendergast (eds.), *The A.I. Business—The Commercial Use of Artificial Intelligence*, MIT Press, Cambridge, Mass., London, 1984.

13. What most advocates of the capacity of capitalism to 'regulate' its present crisis forget, is the fact that *every* step forward in mechanisation, and certainly of automation, is accompanied by a *huge increase in the mass of goods produced* (see *Grundrisse, op. cit.*, p. 325 and *MEGA*, II, 3.6, *op. cit.*, p. 2164), *which have to be sold* before capital can realise and appropriate produced surplus-value.

14. Aristotle drew attention to the fact that those who deal with politics and science (i.e. those who 'administer', 'accumulate' in the Marxist sense of the word) can only do so because *others* produce for them their livelihood.

15. In his *Nicomachean Ethics*, Aristotle had already developed a view of the relationship between labour and leisure which comes near to that of Marx's *Grundrisse* and *Capital*. One should remember the etymology of 'leisure': the latin word licere, i.e. *to be free* to act as one likes.

16. See on this subject Danièle Linhart, *Crise et Travail, Temps Modernes*, January 1984.

17. Barry Commoner, *The Closing Circle*, 1972, London, Jonathan Cape.

18. See David F. Noble, *Forces of Production*, New York, 1984, Knopf.

19. See on this subject Reinhard Breuer, *Die Pfeile der Zeit*, München 1984, Meyster Verlag.

20. A.J. Ayer has dealt with the same question in a review of J. David Bolter's book, *Turing's Man: Western Culture in the Computer Age*, University of North Carolina Press, 1983, which appeared in the New York Review of Books, March 1, 1984.

21. 'Denning Mobile Robotics Inc., Woburn, Mass., said it had signed an agreement to provide Southern Steel Corp. with up to 680 robots for prison guard duty over the next three years. It said the contract was worth between $23 million and 30 million' (*The New York Times*, January 9, 1985).

WORK AND THE WORKING CLASS

Mateo Alaluf

Ever since Marx first systematised the theory that the proletariat is an agent of social change, there has been a great deal at stake in how the working class is conceptualised. Definitions of the working class always imply notions which allow us to understand social reality, the way that society is being transformed and the factors which determine whether or not the workers will support projects for social change. In their only exchange of letters, Proudhon justifies his reluctance to accept Marx's view of the working class by arguing that 'We should not view revolutionary action as a means of achieving social reforms. . . I must tell you in passing that the French working class appears to me to take the same view.'[1] If we assume that the working class bears within it an inherent political project, be it conservative, reformist or revolutionary, that project must be embodied in a party claiming to represent the working class.

The modern period is no exception to the rule. The period between the Second World War and the present crisis is frequently described as having been a period of social progress. According to this view, social progress was facilitated by increasing state intervention in economic life, by the routinisation of wage relations and by the regulation of capitalist development. This vision of the recent past also implies a particular vision of the working class.

The post-war period was dominated by a number of different conceptions of work. Initially, American sociologists developed the theory of the 'embourgeoisement' of the working class, whilst Serge Mallet developed his theory of the 'new working class' by stressing the fact that the workers had both technical skills and managerial aspirations.[2] Other writers concentrated upon the working conditions of unskilled workers and upon the effects of assembly-line work, and therefore developed a critique of Taylorist methods of work organisation.[3] The one thing that all these theories have in common is that they define the working class in terms of the tasks it has to perform. Mindless and exhausting work leads to apathy and resignation on the part of the workers. As a result, the working class is incapable of defining a radical project for the transformation of society. Such conceptions are then used to justify both the reformist aspirations which the labour organisations attribute to the workers and the legitimacy of those who negotiate on their behalf.

The current tendency to describe the period of post-war expansion as a specific form of regulation bound up with a social-democratic compromise also implies a specific vision of the working class. This vision itself is in part a product of social-democracy and it legitimises social democracy. It lends support to the tendency to explain the post-war mode of expansion in terms of regulation of wage relations. I will attempt here to explain the connection between a specific moment in the development of social-democracy (very schematically, the period between 1945 and 1975[4]) and the conception of the working class that went with it and which is, in many respects, still the dominant conception. I am not of course referring to the social-democratic theories and practices associated with Kautsky and Bernstein but to a more recent practice which accompanies the development of social-democracy and, more specifically, to the way in which the French 'regulationist' school interprets it.

Regulation Through Wage Relations
Does social-democracy imply a specific conception of the working class? In order to answer this question, we must first examine in detail the 'regulationist' interpretation of the regime of economic expansion which prevailed in Western Europe between the end of the Second World War and the mid-seventies and of the exhaustion of that mode of development's potential as its basis was destroyed. A number of economists[5] describe the post-war period of economic growth as 'Fordist' in that it was characterised by an intensive accumulation which allowed both mass production and mass consumption to rise. Their analysis is extremely interesting and it is pertinent to our argument in two senses. It represents an interpretation of the factors which produced both a period of expansion and the ensuing crisis, but it also implies that the working class is the key element in the Keynesian compromise.

According to this analysis, Taylorist work organisation was introduced between the wars. It required both mass production and rising sales, but it was introduced at a time when there was only a modest growth of consumption. The divorce between increased productive capacity and restricted consumption then led to the crisis of the thirties. In the post-war period, 'Fordism' was introduced in order to reduce the imbalance between intensive production and the absence of mass consumption. The coherent mechanism established after World War Two was based upon a combination of mass consumption and a rationalised use of labour-power in the factory (Taylorism).

Productivity gains led to an increase in the purchasing power of wage-earners, who thus became consumers. They also financed a generalised social security system which ensured regular consumption. The new 'Fordist' wage relations, which represented a specific mode of inserting wage-earners into society, were backed up by a whole system of consultation and negotiation which presupposed the existence of trade unions and employers' organisations working within the political framework of parliamentary democracy.[6]

Intensive accumulation was based upon both a rise in productivity and an increase in the volume of fixed capital. According to the 'regulationists', it was also based upon the incorporation of skills into the automated machine-system introduced both by Taylorist work organisation and by Henry Ford's use of the assembly line to speed up work. As a result, the labour process was constantly revolutionised during this period. Mass consumption guaranteed a market for the increasing number of commodities produced. The models of production were, then, closely bound up with the models of consumption.

Roger Boyer, for instance writes: 'The exceptional level of growth achieved in the fifties and sixties was due to the compromises reached by management and unions in the post-1945 period. Management was given a free hand to organise work and to take decisions concerning production, whilst the unions ensured that the subsequent rise in productivity was translated into an improved standard of living for wage-earners.'[7] For the productivist model which allowed this compromise, the application of science and technology was an imperative which transcended the class struggle.

This form of compromise, which some authors describe as 'social-democratic' because it is based upon structured and representative social organisations, implies the institutionalisation of collective bargaining and encourages social-democratic parties to participate in government. It is based upon a conception of the working class which is rarely made explicit but which legitimises its unions, parties, mutual benefit societies and co-operatives.

The 'Fordist' model makes three major assumptions about the working class. Because they have been deskilled by technological progress, the workers are to a certain extent passive; as a result, they have lost their identity as skilled workers, and their class consciousness has declined; at the same time, the working class has become more homogeneous and is therefore more willing to be represented by trade union officials and to accept forms of social and political democracy based upon delegation. Let us look at these assumptions in more detail.

Industrialisation and technological progress mean that dead labour (machines) becomes more important than living labour (workers). As a result, the worker is subordinated to the machines which dispossess him of his know-how and skills. Deskilled, devalued and dominated, he can no longer see any alternative to the capitalist organisation of labour and society. He therefore has no real identity as a skilled worker and his class consciousness declines. Even if workers do find ways to resist deskilling and do put forward economic demands, all their collective activities are characterised by a certain passivity. Machines and work organisation encourage or even produce this passivity by homogenising the labour-force. As early as 1870, a French industrialist and inventor could say that 'machines are civilisation's most powerful auxiliaries. . . You require intelligence and skill in a worker, and all men possess those qualities in varying degrees; look for machines which require so little intelligence and skill that anyone can operate them. If you do so, the worker who operates them will make a good living, realize that he can easily be replaced and will want to retain his lucrative position. If, on the other hand, he knows that you cannot do without him because he knows his trade—and this applies in many cases—he will ask of you what he likes and you will have to be grateful if he deigns to work for you.'[8] Here we have the two pre-conditions for a coherent social-democratic vision: workers are inter-changeable and they are sufficiently well paid to guarantee them a high regular purchasing power. The working class is represented as being relatively homogeneous and passive but as having enough room to negotiate for its representatives to be able to unite it in unions, parties, mutual benefit societies and cooperatives.

We have, then, the basis for a representation of the working class as having been dispossessed of its skills, as having no real ability to put forward proposals of its own and as being regimented by the social security system and by unions and parties which operate in a framework domina-ted by the state. The contractual and collective relations into which it enters imply a high degree of subordination. This form of division of labour and of collective contracts means that workers are increasingly interchangeable and that individual workers do not identify with specific tasks.

We can therefore agree with Pierre Rolle when he argues that 'capital-ism perpetuates itself, but it does so by becoming socialized in contra-dictory ways'.[9] To illustrate his point, Rolle cites the examples of social security contributions, which represent expenditure for all firms and a market for some firms, and domestic labour performed by women: it may well increase the family income, but it also reduces the potential labour force.

Whilst no social class is homogeneous and whilst competition between firms, and even between workers, has not disappeared, social conflicts are also a constant element in the 'Keynesian class compromise'. In a country like Belgium, the institutional framework for a very elaborate form of consultation was established long ago. Even before the Second World War had ended, representatives from the employers' associations, the unions and the administration were preparing for post-war reconstruction by drawing up an agreement for a social contract which defined the broad outlines of the institutionalised consensus implemented by the outline laws of 1948. By 1945, the government had already drafted an immigration policy designed to weaken the mineworkers' union and to reduce its wage militancy. Social peace implied the weakening of the labour movement.[10] Although there were periodic debates about various forms of worker participation, the question of democracy in the workplace was conspicuous by its absence. It was assumed that the worker could not participate fully because his position in the factory was ambiguous. The democratic compromise typical of political society always comes up against paralysing contradictions in the workplace. Thus, the 'planning' movement led by Henri de Man in the thirties tried to resolve the old 'revolution or reform' dilemma by using structural reforms (nationalising the banks and restricting credit) to implement economic democracy.[11] In many respects and despite its faults, de Man's view of planning prefigured the links that would later be established between social democracy and the state, but it never had the impact in the economic domain that universal suffrage had at the political level.[12]

The institutionalisation of tripartite labour relations involving the unions, employers' associations and the state can also lead to corporatism and to antagonisms. Although the state plays an increasingly important role in social and economic regulation, the class relations characteristic of capitalist societies do not disappear as a result. At best they are transformed and internationalised to produce a model which integrates a large number of markets and which uses a foreign labour force in the developed countries. The state which once dominated atomised workers gives way to the dominance of mass organisations. At the same time, both production and consumption are socialised to a certain extent. This form of social and state organisation does not, however, solve the problem. It reflects both the effects of working-class pressure and the Western bourgeoisie's fear of the Soviet Union at the end of the war. The labour movement finds that it is able to negotiate over issues relating to living standards, forms of guaranteed security and consumption. 'Even if class conflicts do not disappear, the interests which promote working-class reformism' thus find their institutional expression.[13]

Class Reformism?

The basic question raised by the development of social democracy is contained within Proudhon's answer to Marx. Christine Buci-Glucksmann and Göran Therborn put it this way: Is it possible to explain 'how and why a working class can be born reformist?'[14] If it is true that the working class is by definition reformist, what happens to it when the crisis in Europe dispossesses it of its project either by removing it from power or by allowing it to participate in government and subjecting it to such constraints that it is forced to adopt policies which will result in unemployment and reduced purchasing power and whose effects will be felt primarily by wage-earners? If that does happen, we might well have to 'bid farewell to the proletariat', as André Gorz puts it.[15]

The vision of the working class which dominated the period during which social democracy developed centred upon the conflict between workers and employers and upon how the employers succeeded in forcing the workers to accept specific forms of work organisation. Many authors, such as Touraine, Wieviorka and Dubet, argue that it is because they are conscious of their identity as skilled workers that the workers can challenge the dominance of their employers by putting forward a different schema for industrial production. It follows that 'class consciousness is at its highest when the work organisation involved in mass production comes into direct conflict with the autonomy of the skilled worker, particularly in the metal-working industry'.[16] The authors' central argument is as follows: 'The labour movement has a *centre* which can be defined as the point at which work organisation makes its most direct and most violent attack on the autonomy of skilled workers. Taylorism and Fordism are simply two of many forms of work organisation. Working-class consciousness is a response to this basic conflict. As we move away from the point at which that conflict is experienced as class struggle, the labour movement becomes weaker and trade unionism ceases to be a social movement.'[17] Just as working-class consciousness has a centre, it also has a central figure: the metal-worker of 1936.[18] As that figure disappears, the labour movement naturally becomes weaker and may even disappear too.

Touraine, Wieviorka and Dubet use this central figure to make a distinction between two types of class consciousness. The skilled worker's 'proud consciousness' means that his actions are determined by his skills and leads to political autonomy. It allows him to 'struggle against the power of his employer'.[19] The 'labourer's consciousness' or 'proletarian consciousness', on the other hand, is 'a poor man's consciousness'. It means that his actions are determined by economics and leads to political heteronomy. His demands are concerned primarily with wages and they are discontinuous; they do not pose any overall political or social challenge. 'Unskilled workers are at a disadvantage in that they cannot develop the "proud consciousness" of the worker who has mastered a skill, even if that skill is threatened.'[20] The unskilled worker, that is, has 'a negative class consciousness which is defined by a feeling of privation and by the absence of any project'.[21] 'It is by being deprived of skills and of any interesting or skilled activity that the unskilled worker is degraded.'[22]

Working class consciousness is weakened 'when workers are incorporated into a system of organisation and become operatives rather than workers'.[23] Mechanisation and rationalisation lead to deskilling. The 'proud consciousness' on which the workers relied to resist their employers is gradually whittled away and destroyed. The history of the labour process is in fact the history of the transition from a system centred upon skilled work to a technical system centred upon organisation. In a post-industrial or computerised society, the central conflict is that between 'the technocrats who create models of consumption and those who are reduced to being consumers or users, even though they would like to control their own lives'.[24] 'As we move away from the site of the conflict between managerial organisation of work and working class autonomy, the labour movement inevitably becomes weaker and more fragmented.'[25]

According to the authors of Le Mouvement ouvrier, working class consciousness is the product of a specific situation exemplified by the figure of the metal-worker of 1936. His situation is further identified with the mastery of certain well-determined skills. The worker is, then, shaped by his trade. His project for transforming society implies the application of his skills in such a way as to free him from the constraints imposed by the organisation which deprives him of the product of his labour.

Only those workers who have professional skills can become auto-nomous from the factory or resist the power of their employers. It is because they know they possess certain skills that they can put forward demands relating to the running of the factory itself. It is because they possess the requisite skills that they regard workers control as a real possibility. And it is because they wish to develop their skills without being constrained by their employers that they regard workers control as desirable.

The working class is, then, shaped by the worker's consciousness of his class. If work is transformed, the worker is deskilled and the working class becomes fragmented and may even disappear. As we move further away from the central moment of conflict between the workers and both work organisation and machines, the working class becomes weaker. Given the a priori identification of the working class with the 'metal-worker of 1936' this is of course inevitable. If the metal-working industries of 1936 disappear, the working class itself will inevitably wither away and disappear.

There is a close connection between this image of the worker and his class and the way in which many authors describe the changing structures of work. Contemporary accounts of work are in fact dominated by a theory which finds a link between technological progress, skills, job structures and the working class. This theory has been systematised by authors like Michel Freyssenet,[26] and it tends to dominate contemporary conceptions of the working class. The logic of the system is the logic of capital, which destroys the autonomy of work 'by materialising its order in the shape of machines and by moulding the labour force in accord-ance with that material order'.[27] Automation 'takes away what little intellectual activity was left to the worker and reduces his task to the reflex actions of machine-minding'.[28] It is, then, the quality of the labour performed which determines levels of skills, and machines are instruments for appropriating the workers' knowledge. Technological progress can be described as a process whereby men gradually come to be dominated by the machines which appropriate their knowledge. The future development of work will, then, be characterised by the deskilling of most workers and by the emergence of a highly skilled minority responsible for planning and supervision. It will thus lead to a polarisation of jobs.

Many conceptions of the working class are based upon the widely accepted view that working-class skills are being incorporated into machines and that a polarisation of skills is emerging. Some authors are, however, beginning to challenge this received opinion. Thus, a special issue of *Sociologie du travail* devoted to 'new technologies in industry and the question of skills' refers to 'changes, which are sometimes radical, but usually subtle, ignored or even unacknowledged' in these dominant conceptions. We will now look briefly at some of the contributions to this challenge to the dominant view.

Gilbert de Terssac and Benjamin Coriat base their conclusions on an analysis of 'the modes in which the functions required in concrete labour are realized'.[29] They base their work on job descriptions which are for the most part derived from research on ergonomics. They note that working procedures are complex and varied and that they involve elaborate operations and complex mental processes on the part of the workers. They note also that the workers' know-how is not being expropriated by machines and that workers are not being deskilled. The studies they quote to support their argument are not new and are in fact quite well known.

In an analysis of studies of German industry carried out some fifteen years ago, Horst Kern and Michaël Schumann previously claimed to detect a dynamic that was dispossessing workers of their skills and leading to a polarisation of job structures,[30] but the dynamic they now find in the same factories provides little support for their initial conclusions: the emphasis placed upon 'productive intelligence on the shop floor makes it more likely than ever before that industrial work will cease to be heteronomous'.

In their analysis of studies carried out in Great Britain, Bryn Jones and Stephen Wood[31] and, from a rather different perspective, Barry Wilkinson[32] criticise the deskilling thesis and then challenge Braverman's argument that technological progress results from a movement designed to deskill labour and that automation will lead to capital's complete domination of labour. Jones and Wood base their argument on the existence of 'tacit' skills which are not formally recognised by management. Even though new technologies have been introduced into production, it is still essential for the workers to possess certain skills. Thus, 'the irreducible dimension of skills based upon tacit knowledge' contradicts the hypothesis that technological changes are powerful instruments for deskilling. It should, however, be noted that 'workers' know-how', 'informal capacities' and 'tacit skills' are not really enough to overcome the tendency to marginalise labour; they merely restrict its marginalisation. Indeed, Terssac and Coriat claim that this analysis complements the deskilling argument rather than refuting it.[33]

The challenge to the theory that workers are being deskilled by machines and technological progress is in fact somewhat unconvincing in that it simply reinterprets existing data and presents the revised material as deriving from direct observation. The observation procedures involved in this sudden reassessment of developments in work are themselves based upon a theory of skills.

There is nothing new about this debate, which ultimately concerns different conceptions of the working class. In the sixties, the dominant view was that machines were instruments for expropriating workers, even though it was also hoped that automation would eventually lead to a recomposition of labour. Freyssenet's analysis belongs within this tradition, which is dominated by Georges Friedmann, in that he describes the history of work in terms of stages in the appropriation of workers' skills by machines. Skills are qualitative, and by transferring them to machines capitalism organises the deskilling of the majority of workers.

Pierre Naville, on the other hand, argues that skills are not 'things' which can gain or lose substance. He describes skills as a social appreciation of the value of labour. In the debate with Friedmann he therefore argues that skills cannot be reduced to immediately observable technical working conditions. If they are examined without reference to the educational system and to life styles, working conditions cannot in themselves explain skilling as a process of socialisation. This is why Naville attaches such importance to the view that skills must be measured in terms of the length of time it takes to acquire them: 'that is the only socially meaningful measure of skills. . . society demands variable and differential levels of skill and pays for them accordingly'.[34]

The distinction Naville makes between operations carried out by machines and operations carried out by workers leads him to conclude that whereas automatic machine systems simultaneously carry out operations which were formally separate, the same cannot be said of operations carried out by workers. Automation does not mean that the worker performs fewer or more tasks than before; he simply supervises their execution. Supervisory functions may well reflect a transformation of work in that they alienate the worker still further from the product of his labour, but they do not mean that work is being either fragmented or unified. From this point of view, the question of whether or not workers are being dispossessed of their skills loses much of its substance.

A Dominant Conception

Why should the idea that the worker is being deskilled by technological progress continue to dominate the sociology of work even though it has been under attack for a long time? Theories which see skill in terms of possession or dispossession of know-how are widespread because workers themselves discuss skill in those terms and because the related theorisations are both comprehensible and suitable for use in negotiations.

Class consciousness itself provides researchers with a further let out. Touraine, Wieviorka and Dubet's 'sociological intervention' leads them to the conclusion that skilled workers have 'lost their autonomy' and have been deskilled as a result of developments in technology: 'The role of the skilled worker, the central figure in the trade union movement, has been marginalised by changes in methods of production and work organisation. Ladle-men, smelters and crane-operators, many of whom have either undergone a long period of on-the-job training or have served an apprenticeship, constantly express their fears about mechanisation and rationalisation.'[35] A worker traces 'the history of how the methods of work organisation which destroyed skilled trades also destroyed the steel-makers' pride and autonomy: "Nowadays, workers are richer but less independent".'[36] Similarly, 'It is by being deprived of skills and of any interesting or skilled activity that the unskilled worker is degraded.'[37] and 'unskilled workers are at a disadvantage in that they cannot develop the "proud" consciousness' of the worker who has mastered a skill, even if that skill is threatened'.[38] All workers feel that they have lost their trade or are threatened with losing it,[39] and the labour movement remains such a central point of reference that the reader cannot fail to catch the nostalgic tone.

The authors of *Le Mouvement ouvrier* always interpret this nostalgia as a reflection of the disappearance of skilled trades and of the decline of the labour movement. Nostalgia for the days of the artisan is always present. But if we listen carefully to what the workers are saying, there is another possible interpretation. Whilst the artisan was trapped by his tools and by his working conditions and whilst the worker is trapped by being dispossessed of both his tools and the product of his labour, he can try to influence his living and working conditions by forming a coalition with other workers. A coalition of workers presupposes that the act of labour involves relationships which are strong enough to give birth to collective interests. If, on the other hand, we concentrate upon the identity of the skilled worker we tend to lapse into psychological interpretations ('skilled consciousness' and motivation to work) and to promote a nostalgic vision because any change is by definition perceived as leading to a loss of identity. The condition of the working class then has to be described in terms of deskilling, anomie and alienation. Work is assumed to have an atemporal value (know-how, solidarity and 'skilled consciousness') which is intrinsic to the worker and which is now being destroyed by changes in the technological environment. If we interpret working-class consciousness in terms of working-class trades, we simply describe the requirements of production and turn them into a source of professional pride. 'Proud consciousness' is also the complex psychological mechanism which enables a miner to accept the fact that his lungs are being turned into stone and to go on describing a period when working conditions led to frequent deaths as the age of gold.

The fact that the hypothesis formulated by the authors of *Le Mouvement ouvrier* finds favour with the workers does not mean that it has any real explanatory value. Just as workers speak in mythical terms of the heroic past of their unions and parties, Touraine, Wieviorka and Dubet mourn the disappearance of the identity of the skilled worker and the coalitions of the past. We then also see the worker as participating in his own alienation; the violence he experiences every day becomes insignificant and is transformed into positive images centring upon skilled consciousness and working class consciousness.

The notion of dispossession dominates the analysis of skills. It derives much of its strength from the discourse of the workers themselves. It gives rise to a theory of skills which encourages the worker to take a nostalgic view of his past conditions of exploitation and which at the same time promotes the notion that the working class is passive, that its aspirations have to be mediated by political or union affiliations and that it is dependent upon various branches of the social security system.

The Active Population and the Extension of the Wage System
The implications of the debate go far beyond differences of opinion as to the value of describing work situations in terms of the relative 'deskilling' or 'reskilling' of operatives. It is the notion of skill itself that is at stake, or in other words the theoretical conditions which allow us to understand how work valorises different generations of labour. Skill has to be understood in terms of socialisation, and not in terms of the gain or loss of substance, and the transformation of work has to be seen as an effect of the constant destructuring and restructuring of social relations.

No matter which part of the world we look at, changes in the active population show a sharp rise in the number of wage-earners and a considerable fall in the number of non-wage earners. OECD statistics for 1984 show that in the European countries surveyed, wage-earners represented between 70% (Spain) and 95% (Sweden) of the total active population.[40] The extension of wage-earning has, then, been the major tendency affecting the active population in recent years.

Whilst the fact that more people now work in offices than in factories and that there are considerable differences between the position of a teacher and that of a factory worker can be used to show that the working class is disappearing, the most striking trend is the increase in wage-earning as opposed to other forms of work. Despite their different status, non-wage-earners define themselves in relation to wage-earners and even model their economic demands on those made by wage-earners. In terms of pensions, unemployment benefit, the working week and holidays, and even use of the strike weapon, wage-earners always provide the model.

Although the extension of wage-earning is the dominant trend within the active population, wage-earners do not see themselves as equals or as having the same interests. They make distinctions between themselves and others in terms of their respective status (factory worker, office worker, manager, public sector, private sector, the unemployed. . .) and their position in the hierarchy. The mechanisms whereby skills are acquired are probably the key factor in the differentiation of workers.

Michel Aglietta and Anton Brender argue that the existence of a hierarchy is a component element of the wage-system.[41] Struggles over status are of central importance and effectively replace the class struggle. In the 'waged society' they describe, wage-earners have become so dominant, both in quantitative terms and in terms of forms of organisation and legitimation, that there is little room for other social groups. The unions and parties which represent wage-earners quite naturally come to see themselves as representing the general interest which, in waged societies, is synonymous with the national interest. In political terms, their ambition is to ensure that the state administers the solidarity systems of civil society and to develop new forms of consumption. It will then be possible to articulate a wage-system organised by the nation-state with multinational capital.

Taking into account the real differences that exist between wage-earners, describing divisions between them as a struggle for status, ensuring that they are controlled by the state and then adopting policies designed to promote equal opportunities and social justice results in a typically social-democratic contradiction. Pierre Rolle summarises the problem very accurately when he remarks that the wage-system embodies 'the contradiction which arises when wage-earners pay taxes and insurance contributions which are used to finance the system that creates differences between them and when they are forced to unite to defend the skills and hierarchies which divide them'.

The appearance of unemployment presupposes a division between time spent in paid work and time spent on domestic work and it means that, if they are to meet their needs, workers must sell their labour-power to an employer. In other words, labour becomes a commodity which can be exchanged. In that sense, the appearance of unemployment presupposes the existence of the wage-system.[42]

The fact that most industrialised countries in the West have experienced a considerable rise in unemployment since 1974 confirms that it is a collective phenomenon. The fact that unemployment is a selective process was recognised long ago.[43] It was for a long time assumed that workers with 'poorer skills', the uneducated, workers employed in sectors experiencing difficulties, and women were the most vulnerable. But the rise in unemployment tends now to blur such distinctions. In terms of education, it is no longer only those who have no qualifications who are affected. Unemployment is rising and it takes no account of the level of education or of the educational background of those who are seeking work. In fact those who have undergone vocational training in technical schools or institutes are often the most vulnerable. Unemployment is beginning to affect workers collectively; the selective processes simply affect the length of time they remain unemployed and the type of jobs that are available. In other words, finding work is a problem for more and more people: young school-leavers, women who have temporarily interrupted their professional activities, workers who have lost previous jobs. The whole process is becoming an area in which selectivity operates. The difficulties young people experience in finding work have less to do with inadequate preparation for the world of work while they were at school than with the fact that unemployment is becoming a process whereby certain skills are selected from amongst others. And, as so many studies have shown, that is also a process of social selection.

Insertion into social and professional life is not then a rapid or neutral moment which we can ignore in order to concentrate on what happens 'before' (being at school or losing one's job) and 'after' it (finding a job). The transition from unemployment to employment has become an important moment, and not only in terms of the development of the individual. It has become a major aspect of the conditions imposed upon all workers in a waged society. It is not, then, surprising to find that this phase is becoming institutionalised and organised, or to learn that it tends to be determined by changes in the productive system.

Although there are of course national variations, the crisis means that the pattern of unemployment in the developed capitalist countries is broadly similar.[44] The key dates are 1974–75 and 1979–80, when there was a sharp increase in unemployment and when governments had to alter their economic policies as a result of the oil crisis. The rise in unemployment began with the destruction of jobs, a process which affected all the developed countries, regardless of national variations.

After the Second World War, the labour market became institutionalised and the entire Mediterranean basin became a labour pool for Western Europe. But at the same time, the composition of the labour force in Western Europe itself was transformed. The arguments of many authors notwithstanding, the changes did not result in a polarisation of job structures and did not produce a pyramid with deskilled workers at the bottom and highly-skilled workers at the top.

The Challenge to the Division Between the Public and the Private Sector

As the working class asserts itself and as its organisations become vehicles for demands relating to working conditions, purchasing power and employment, the dividing line between the public and private sectors shifts to produce what Buci-Glucksmann and Therborn term 'the material basis for unprecedented demands upon the state'.[45] As a result, relations between the working class and the state are greatly modified. The outcome is the modern form of social-democracy exemplified by the Scandinavian countries, Great Britain and West Germany. This development is inseparable from the accumulation of capital on a large scale, the extension of the wage-system to new sections of the population, the development of mass consumption that results from increased working-class pressure, and from the expansion of the modern welfare state.

The argument that the deskilling and homogenisation of the working class by mechanisation and by the extension of the wage system has produced a mass of deskilled workers who are being both superexploited and internationalised by Fordism is closely connected with the view that representation inevitably takes the form of delegation, that bargaining has been institutionalised, that politics have become a mass phenomenon and that the masses can be organised from above. It follows that the labour movement has a corporatist economic basis but that its electoral strategy is designed to win a political majority. According to this view, the interests of the workers have a universal significance which transcends their specific interests: working-class organisations represent the interests of the collectivity as a whole, as opposed to sectional interests, and they become popular, inter-class parties, even if they are predominantly working-class based. They then become parties of government, though there may be national differences in terms of their form and content: socialist, social-democratic or labourist parties, or the Italian centre-left model.

The Keynesian state articulates the contradiction between the social nature of production and private ownership of the means of production by playing a central role in the regulation of wage relations and by attempting to implement a 'state socialisation' of production. Collective bargaining and participation in socialist, social-democratic or labourist governments subject working-class demands to increasing state mediation.

At the same time, the role of the state and the public sector is challenged more seriously than ever before. Although all demands are addressed to the state, there are constant complaints about state tyranny, the weight of state bureaucracy and about public servants. The present challenge to the state is far-reaching, and it represents neither a demand for the familiar strategy of socialising losses and privatising profits nor a response to the crisis in public finance. Still less is it simply an ideological phenomenon such as neo-liberalism. The challenge to the role of the state may take the form of deregulation (the abolition of rules governing the labour market and wages, or protecting certain economic agents from the effects of competition), decentralisation or privatisation. All these strategies reflect a desire to make various areas of economic and social life more responsive to market forces and competition.

The general tendency to increase profit rates means that the public sector is caught in a dilemma. On the one hand, the increasing inter-nationalisation of production undermines the old alliance between state and national industries, which was forged by the demands of a wartime economy and strengthened by the Cold War. On the other hand, what is usually termed the 'tertiary sector' (commerce, finance, education and services) becomes more important.

Table I below summarises changes in the active population in the USA and EEC member countries and shows the increasing importance of the service sector in both. It further shows that the structure of employ-ment in Europe in 1982 is very similar to that prevailing in the USA in 1960. The discrepancy relates both to differences in productivity levels and to differences in wage levels, collective relations and forms of accumulation.[46] Whilst the service sector as a whole is affected by rationalisation because of its low productivity, the public sector is even more severely affected because of the role it plays and because of the contradiction between its national structure and the multinational nature of production.

TABLE I

Percentage of Active Population Employed by Sector of Economic Activity

| | USA | | | EEC* | | |
	1960	1974	1982	1960	1974	1982
Agriculture	8.5	4.2	3.6	18.6	9.6	7.6
Industry	35.3	32.4	28.4	41.2	41.2	36.3
Services	56.2	63.4	68.0	40.2	49.2	56.1
	100	100	100	100	100	100

*Ten member countries.
Source: *Statistiques de population active*, Paris, OECD, 1984.

The public sector is the key element in the Keynesian state because of the high number of jobs it provides and because of its relations with the labour movement.

Management in public services departs from the usual commercial rules and has no direct contact with the public. It therefore becomes a target for neo-liberal ideology. The argument is that those public services which are seen to be inefficient must reduce their running costs, diversify their activities in response to demand and establish new relationships with their customers. In practice, however, the balance of power in a period of crisis and unemployment means that there is a tendency to dismantle certain public services, to pay more attention to big and profitable customers and to alter the very function of public services. Studies of the effects of computerisation show that in terms of occupational health, the management of funds is now regarded as more important than the prevention of illness.[47]

Unstable Employment and Changes in the Working Class

Unemployment is rising. Working conditions are becoming more precarious. Women make up a greater proportion of the active population than ever before. Public services and the status of public employees are coming under attack. Immigrant workers are joining trade unions. Standards of working-class education are rising, but young people find it increasingly difficult to obtain work. But can all these phenomena be regarded as resulting from the inescapable logic of technological progress? Attempts to explain them in such terms reduce socio-economic phenomena to expressions of technological change and make technology seem autonomous from the social system which produces it. Job losses, the relocation of industry and uneven regional development are seen as the 'natural' effects of a new 'technological' fate. These theories are often contradicted by empirical studies which show that, on the contrary, there is a close connection between the technical, organisational and social aspects of the application of new technologies. In her studies of employment prospects in the European chemicals industry, Marcelle Stroobants has shown that the new automated plants make it possible to adopt decentralised forms of work organisation which are quite in keeping with the existing division of labour.[48] They can also lead to a very supple combination of continuity and diversity in production and flexible use of the labour force. Even though these plants promote staff mobility and require workers who can carry out more than one task, they do not break down old divisions within the labour market. Automation means that, in many cases, office staff and middle management can take on the coordinating and supervisory tasks associated with Taylorist methods of work organisation. In the chemicals industry, for instance, the first phase of automation led to changes in work organisation and job structures. Those changes meant that the work force had to have multiple skills and led to the introduction of subcontracting, and it has been said that they are typical of processing industries.[49] But the same methods of labour-management immediately spread to other industries, regardless of technical considerations. Technological innovation thus seems to be an instrument of economic and management policies whose aims are social rather than technical.

'Modernisation' strategies designed to challenge the system of collective labour relations have to be seen as an effect of the way the system breaks down in periods of crisis. Measures which protect workers against the uncertainties of the market come to be seen as 'established rights' and as 'obstacles' to flexibility, which is defined as meaning that wage relations should be more responsive to market forces. The conditions under which new technologies are mastered and socialised becomes a major consideration in drawing up policies for labour-management and economic redeployment. In this context, what does it mean to say that jobs should respond to market forces?

It means, first of all, that collective bargaining should, as far as possible, be restricted to individual factories in order to make it responsive to the market and to competition. The workers, who have every reason to want the factory to survive, also find themselves competing. As unemployment rises and as both working conditions and wages deteriorate, the employers are in a position to make greater demands, and as collective bargaining breaks down, rivalry between the workers increases. It is not only 'secondary markets' that are vulnerable and it is not only jobs reserved for women and immigrants that are at risk. The same considerations apply in all areas, including basic industries and public services. Nor is the problem restricted to the workplace. The absence of jobs also has a profound effect on the school system: what is the point of staying on at school if education is useless in getting a job? As a result social, family, emotional and cultural life is seriously destabilised.

Productivity is still the main issue. Marx took the view that the war between capitalists would be won by sacking armies of workers and not by recruiting them.[50] He was right, but not completely right. Reducing the cost of labour is not enough. Wage-earners must also be involved in their work. They must agree to play the game and must further the factory's objectives by giving it not only their time, but also their know-know, their skills, their autonomy and their creativity. With automated factories, it is more important than ever before for information and know-how to circulate and to feed into the work of conceptualisation. Different forms of work organisation have been used to mobilise the work force, with varying degrees of success: 'Taylorism, human relations, semi-autonomous teams, autonomous groups. . . Improvements in productivity were paid for with wage increases, improvements in working conditions and by giving the unions more scope for action (better information, recognition of rights, consultation procedures).

The current change in collective labour relations stems from management's refusal to go on granting the traditional concessions over wages, working conditions and new rights. But management does demand loyalty. It demands that the workers accept the logic of the factory and identify with its interests, even when their jobs are at risk. They have to identify with the factory and its ethics, but in exchange they have to accept fewer concessions, especially over wages. This new ethics implies far-reaching changes in labour relations. It means that conflict inside the factory must give way to harmony and that there can be no solidarity with other workers. Once the trade unions have been confined inside individual factories, work organisation can be used to break them. Autonomous teams, for instance, are made up of volunteers and are designed to bypass union delegates.

How do changes in the labour market relate to the workers' ability to influence the balance of power and to changes in the labour movement? It is here that we can see the relevance of the distinction that Touraine, Wieviorka and Dubet make between the labour movement and working-class organisations. On the other hand, their views on the content of the labour movement are somewhat debatable. Given that they define workers as individuals who work with material things and who therefore have a political project, they are forced to conclude that workers are disappearing. They then argue that the labour movement is in decline, but that trade union organisations are not on the retreat.[51] They also claim that 'the very decline of the labour movement means that the unions take on a greater political role and become major participants in the formulation of economic and social policies'.[52] Finally, they predict that the labour movement will disappear in the near future, that the trade unions' political importance will grow accordingly,[53] and that the unions will be able to accommodate themselves to 'new social movements because they know that they alone have the capacity to convince and mobilise people on the same scale as the old labour movement'.[54]

According to Touraine, Wieviorka and Dubet, 'the social relations which the labour movement once supported are no longer central to society'.[55] But can operating machines and working with material things really be described as 'social relations'? Why should the working class be defined as a body of manual workers? Was there ever any clearcut definition of manual labour? Does it include the work performed by saleswomen in a department store, workers in a power station, airline pilots and maintenance staff? Production began to develop at a certain stage, and as it developed manual work on the shopfloor gradually gave way to collective administrative and supervisory work. The analysis should begin with labour relations and not with specific tasks.

In terms of the framework we have outlined, work in our societies can be defined primarily in terms of wage-earning, and it is constantly changing. In periods of crisis, both work and the working class are unstable. As unemployment rises, trade unions have less and less room to negotiate. They may even suffer a major decline in membership, even though wage-earners represent an increasing proportion of the active population. In other words, whilst the social relations which define work in our societies are expanding, and whilst the social base of the labour movement is growing, its ability to negotiate is declining. My conclusions are very different to those reached by Touraine, Wieviorka and Dubet. They claim that the crisis will lead to the disappearance of the labour movement, but that union organisations will survive. I would argue that, on the contrary, the social base of the labour movement is expanding considerably, even though the trade union movement's ability to negotiate is declining considerably.

The very idea of a social democratic compromise, which lies at the origins of the Keynesian state, presupposes the existence of a working class which is at once passive and homogeneous, but which can also use its own organisations—and only those organisations—to make the bourgeoisie agree to a different division of the product of increased productivity.

Earlier conceptions explained the reformism of working class consciousness in terms of the passivity induced by relations of production; the more recent theories attempt to justify the need for flexibility in labour management in terms of the need to introduce market forces into wage relations. They also try to make unemployment acceptable by claiming that there is a connection between the fact that young people are 'allergic to work' and the fact that jobs are precarious. Finally, they justify the alleged conservatism of trade unions which do not share these 'new values'.

In fact, there are no 'new' values as opposed to 'old values'; there is no 'new' working class, as distinct from the 'old'; work is constantly being transformed; and there is therefore no stable system of reference to judge it by. Work can only be understood in terms of the social relations which define it, and in our societies those relations are typified by the wage-system. The wage-earner differs from the artisan in that he is separated from both his tools and the product of his labour. Because its situation is by definition unstable, the working class is constantly and simultaneously broken up and recreated. The labour movement can control its destiny by returning to the practices which give it the strength to challenge the tendency to alienate the worker from the product of his labour. Its choice remains between constant pressure against exploitation and domination on the one hand and social democratic institutionalisation into the structures of capitalism on the other.

NOTES

1. Proudhon, letter of 17 May 1846 to Marx. For the full text see Pierre Haubt-mann, *Proudhon, Marx et la pensée allemande*, Grenoble Presses Universitaires de Grenoble, 1981.
2. Serge Mallet, *La Nouvelle Classe ouvrière*, Paris, Editions du Seuil, 1963.
3. Cf. Harry Braverman, *Labour and Monopoly Capital*, New York, Monthly Review Press, 1974; Claude Durand, *La Travail Enchainé*, Paris, Editions du

Seuil, 1978.

4. This periodisation is of course approximate in that in Scandinavia (and especially Sweden), this model appeared between the wars. It does however apply to most countries in Western Europe. .

5. Michel Aglietta, Robert Boyer, Alain Lipietz and Benjamin Coriat.

6. Cf. Robert Boyer, 'Les Transformations du rapport salarial dans la crise', *L'Emploi, Enjeux économiques et sociaux (Colloque de Dourdan)*, Paris, Maspero, 1982, pp. 50–102. Wage relations are defined as 'all those conditions which regulate the use and reproduction of labour power, including work organisation, hierarchies of skills, the mobility of the labour force, training and use of income from wages', *ibid.*, p. 80.

7. Robert Boyer, *L'Introduction du taylorisme en France à la lumière de recherches récentes*, Paris, CEPREMAP, 1983, p. 29. Cf. Michel Aglietta, *A Theory of Capitalist Regulation*, London, NLB, 1979; Benjamin Coriat, *L'Atelier et le chronomètre*, Paris Christian Bourgeois, 1979.

8. Denis Polot, (ed.), Alain Cottereau, *Le Sublime, ou le travailleur comme il est en 1870, et ce qu'il peut être*, Paris, Maspero, 1980, p. 406.

9. Pierre Rolle, 'Le Capitalisme perpétuel', *En Jeu*, no. 11, April 1984, p. 22.

10. Cf. Albert Martens, *Les Immigrés, flux et reflux d'une main-d-'oeuvre d'appoint*, Brussels, Editions Vie Ouvrière and Presses Universitaires de Louvain, 1976.

11. De Man's *planisme* has been described as 'a curious attempt to synthesise the aims of Lenin and those of Roosevelt', Christine Buci-Glucksmann and Göran Therborn, *Le Défi social-démocrate*, Paris, Maspero, 1981.

12. Although factory union branches were recognised after the war in some European countries, in others this is a recent phenomenon. In France, for instance, it took the events of May '68 for them to be recognised. Ever since the nineteenth century, the factory has been dominated by the authority of the employer and by work discipline. The political sphere is distinct from the 'social question' and the world of the factory.

13. Buci-Glucksmann and Therborn, *Le Défi*, p. 120.

14. *Ibid.*, p. 9.

15. André Gorz, *Farewell to the Working Class*, (Pluto, 1983).

16. Alain Touraine, Michel Wieviorka and François Dubet, *Le Mouvement ouvrier*, Paris, Fayard, 1984, p. 73.

17. *Ibid.*, p. 101.

18. *Ibid.*, p. 122.

19. *Ibid.*, p. 215.

20. *Ibid.*, p. 271.

21. *Ibid.*, pp. 273–274.

22. *Ibid.*, p. 119.

23. *Ibid.*, p. 73.

24. *Ibid.*, p. 55.

25. *Ibid.*, p. 321. It should, however, be noted that the authors make a constant distinction between the labour movement and the trade union movement. Thus, 'The decline of the labour movement does not mean that trade union struggles are on the decline. . . or that trade union organisations are on the retreat.' They then add (p. 327), that 'a distinction has to be made between unionism based upon class consciousness and forms of unionism which take their unifying principles from union policy alone.' However, 'the end of the labour movement inevitably leads to a decline in union activity; unionism cannot escape the effect of the social changes which are transforming industrial society into a post-industrial society', p. 386.

26. Michel Freyssenant, *La Division capitaliste du travail*, Paris, Savelli, 1977.

27. *Ibid.*, p. 31.
28. *Ibid.*, p. 53.
29. Gilbert de Terssac and Benjamin Coriat, 'Micro-électronique et travail ouvrier dans les industries de process', *Sociologie du travail*, 4, 1984, pp. 384–397.
30. Horst Kern and Michaël Schumann, 'Vers une professionalisation du travail industriel', *ibid.*, pp. 398–421.
31. Bryn Jones and Stephen Wood, 'Qualifications tacites, division du travail et nouvelles technologies', *ibid.*, pp. 407–421.
32. Barry Wilkinson, 'Technologie, qualifications et formation: une étude de cas sur les machines à commande numérique', *ibid.*, pp. 447–456.
33. Terssac and Coriat, 'Micro-électronique. . .'
34. Pierre Naville, 'Eclaircissements et discussions. Réflexions à propos de la division du travail', *Cahiers d'étude de l'automation et des sociétés industrielles'*, 3, 1962, p. 243.
35. Touraine *et al.*, *Le Mouvement ouvrier*, p. 162.
36. *Ibid.*, p. 163.
37. *Ibid.*, p. 118.
38. *Ibid.*, p. 271.
39. *Ibid.*, p. 270.
40. OECD, *Quarterly Labour Force Statistics*, 4, 1984. The percentage of wage-earners in countries like France, West Germany and the UK is between 85% and 90%.
41. Michel Aglietta and Anton Brender, *Les Métamorphoses de la société salariale*, Paris, Calmann-Lévy, 1984.
42. Unemployment is not to be confused with idleness. A survey I carried out on how ten-year-old children perceived unemployment showed that they had a very high opinion of unemployed women. They thought they were very active and busy with work in the home, whereas they regarded men as idle. This is an interesting inversion of the dominant perception of unemployment.
43. R. Ledrut, *Sociologie du chômage*, Paris, Presses Universitaires de France, 1966.
44. Robert Tollet, 'Emploi et chômage: des séquences différenciées dans la crise des économies industrialisées', *Critiques Régionales—Cahiers de sociologie et d'économie régionales*, 13, June 1985, pp. 5–15.
45. Buci-Glucksmann and Therborn, *Le Défi. . .*, p. 120.
46. Tollet, 'Emploi et chômage. . .'
47. Cf. The report on 'Technological Developments and Public Service' drawn up by M. Lacomblez, D. Lienard and A.S. Pollet for the Dublin Institute for the Improvement of Living and Working Conditions.
48. Marcelle Stroobants, 'Evolution de l'emploi et transformations des systèmes de travail dans les industries chimiques', *Critique régionale*, 7, September 1981, pp. 8–23. This article summarises the findings of studies carried out in connection with the EEC's FAST programme. Cf. *Les Perspectives d'emploi dans la chimie européenne*, Brussels, CEPEC, 1981.
49. Benjamin Coriat, 'Ouvriers et automates, procès du travail, économie du temps et théorie de la segmentation de la force de travail', in *Usines et ouvriers*, Paris, Maspero, 1980, pp. 40–76.
50. Cited, G. Labiche and G. Benussan, *Dictionnaire critique du marxisme*, Paris, Presses Universitaires de France, 1982, p. 150.
51. Touraine *et al.*, *Le Mouvement ouvrier*, p. 321.
52. *Ibid.*, p. 322.
53. *Ibid.*, p. 347.
54. *Ibid.*, pp. 384–385.
55. *Ibid.*, p. 388.

BEYOND SOCIAL DEMOCRACY*

Ralph Miliband and Marcel Liebman

In this essay, we seek to answer two closely related questions: first, why socialists in advanced capitalist countries should want to move beyond social democracy; and secondly, what are the requirements and implications of such a move. Until not so long ago, the first of these questions would have seemed rather indecent: *of course* all serious socialists wanted to move beyond social democracy. Today, no such intention or desire can be taken for granted. For even where there is sharp criticism of the limitations and derelictions of social democracy, there is also an implicit acceptance of it, based upon a despairing uncertainty about what *else* is possible. So both questions do need to be probed.

An answer to the first of them—why socialists should want to move beyond social democracy—requires a brief recapitulation of its nature and record. An initial distinction needs to be made for this purpose between social democracy before 1914, and social democracy after World War I and particularly since 1945. In its earlier formative phase, social democracy unambiguously stood for the wholesale transformation of the social order, from capitalism to socialism, on the basis of the social appropriation of the main means of production, distribution and exchange, a far reaching democratisation of the political system, and a drastic levelling out of social inequality. This was to be achieved by way of a long series of economic, social and political reforms, to be brought about by way of a parliamentary majority reflecting a preponderance of electoral and popular support. There were many differences between socialists as to the precise nature of the reforms to be realised, and the strategy to be employed in their advancement; and there were also revolutionary socialists in the ranks of social democracy, of whom Rosa Luxemburg was the most notable representative, who proposed a strategy of mass struggle far removed from the electoralism and parliamentarism of the predominant current. Still, 'reformists' could still very plausibly argue that they too were fully committed to the socialist project. As Jean Jaurès once said about the French Socialist Party, 'precisely because it is a party of revolution. . . the Socialist Party is the most actively reformist'.[1]

---

*We are very grateful to Leo Panitch and John Saville for their comments on an earlier version of this article.

What gave 'reformism' its pejorative connotations and made it all but synonymous with class collaboration and betrayal was not its reliance on gradual reforms as a path to socialist transformation, but the support for the war by the leaders of the Second International in August 1914 (and after) and their fierce opposition to left internationalists, of whom Lenin was of course the most conspicuous figure. With the triumph of the Bolsheviks in Russia in October 1917, Lenin's strictures against the 'reformist traitors' acquired a unique global authority and resonance. This has greatly affected the debate on the Left on the question of what strategy is most likely to advance matters, in socialist terms, in advanced capitalist countries with capitalist-democratic regimes. The debate has in fact often been conducted by the revolutionary Left in rather simplistic terms: on the one hand, reformism equals socialist betrayal; on the other, revolution equals socialist rectitude. But the questions that need to be raised in regard to the appropriate socialist strategy for these countries cannot be resolved in these terms.[2]

More will be said about this later, but the point that needs to be made here is that so far as social democracy after 1914 is concerned, the 'reformist' label has been of ever-decreasing relevance to its actual purposes, and is in fact quite misleading. For the purpose of social democracy, as expressed in practice by labour movements and parties everywhere since World War I has not been a 'reformist' socialist project in the classical sense at all. From that time onwards, and more and more definitely, it has in essence been a project of moderate reform within the framework of capitalism, a striving, at best, to achieve a better deal for organised labour and the 'lower income groups' inside capitalist society; and this has been linked to the wish to see the state make a more effective contribution to the management of capitalism. Social democracy became more and more attuned to the requirements of capitalism; and where these requirements clashed with reform, it was reform that was more often than not sacrificed on the altar of the 'national interest', 'pragmatism' and 'realism', or whatever else might serve to cover up compromise and retreat. The 'reformist', transformative project has remained part of the occasional rhetoric of social democratic leaders, to be brought out on suitable occasions such as party conferences; but the rhetoric has been consistently belied by the actual practice of social democracy. The most it has ever striven to achieve is capitalism with a more human face: the record is consistent across time and countries and continents– from Attlee to Wilson and Callaghan in Britain, from Léon Blum to Guy Mollet to Mitterrand in France, from Ebert to Brandt to Schmidt in Germany, etc.

Certainly, it would be quite wrong to ignore or undervalue the reforms which social democracy has helped to achieve in capitalist societies over the years, or the important role which its presence and pressure have played in forcing issues and policies on the political agenda which otherwise would have been ignored or differently handled. But acknowledging this and giving it its full weight should not obscure the deeply negative aspects of the record.

For one thing, social democracy has consistently sought to *limit* the scope and substance of the reforms which it has itself proposed and implemented, in an endeavour to pacify and accommodate capitalist forces, and to demonstrate how much these forces could count on the 'moderation' and 'reasonableness' of their social democratic opponents; and also because social democratic leaders in office have always readily endorsed conservative economic policies and submitted equally readily to the constraints this has imposed upon them. As a result, social democratic reforms, however useful, have tended to have a limited character and impact, and have been very vulnerable to conservative attack. Even when circumstances were most favourable, for instance in the years after World War II in such countries as Britain and France, when popular readiness and support for radical change was very high, it was timidity rather than boldness, submission to convention rather than innovative zeal which characterised social democratic reforming measures.

Secondly, social democracy has generally been deeply concerned to narrow the scope of political activity, to confine it as far as possible to carefully controlled party and parliamentary channels, to restrict and stifle grassroots activism except in the service of the party's electoral interests. Much of the energy of social democratic leaders has been devoted to the containment and channelling of the energies of their rank and file, and to the control of that rank and file by the party apparatus; and much the same concern has been evident among trade union leaders as well.

Thirdly and relatedly, social democratic leaders have always reserved their most energetic attacks for left activists in the labour movement. Social democratic hostility to the Left was already fierce and pervasive long before the Bolshevik Revolution and the coming into being of Communist parties. But the establishment of Soviet Russia and of Communist parties gave a new dynamic and legitimation to the struggle against anyone who demanded more radical policies and actions than social democratic leaders were themselves prepared to endorse, and provided these leaders with a convenient bogey to use against their opponents on the left, whatever their particular brand of socialism might be. Social democratic leaders, in parties and trade unions thus turned themselves into very effective watchdogs against the spread of socialist ideas and influence in the labour movement: no conservative politician could hope to have anything like the same impact in this respect. The effect of these endeavours has been of immense importance in the history of labour movements everywhere.

Fourthly, social democratic opposition to anything to the left of social democracy played a major role after 1945 in mobilising labour movements, or those parts of labour movements under their control, behind

the global counter-revolutionary crusade which capitalist governments
have been waging since World War II under the leadership of the United
States. Again and again, it is the social democratic leaders of Western
European labour movements who have proved the most faithful and
dedicated supporters and allies of the United States in this global enterprise, with the excuse that what was at stake was the defence of the West,
freedom, democracy and the rest, against the dire threat of Soviet
expansionism and aggression.

It would have been perfectly possible for social democratic leaders to
oppose the installation after World War II of Soviet-type regimes on
countries contiguous to the Soviet Union without lending their authority
to what has undoubtedly been one of the great myths of the second half
of the twentieth century, namely the myth of Soviet expansionism.[3]
Social democratic leaders did not choose that option, and thus made a
major contribution to the granting of respectability to that myth. In the
same context, these same leaders played a major part in supporting and
defending the defence policies of the United States, notwithstanding the
fact that these policies have been dominated by American determination
to maintain a preponderance in nuclear weaponry: at no point have social
democratic leaders made a serious contribution to the curbing of the
arms race.

Finally, social democracy played a notable—and utterly dishonourable—
role in the post-war decades in waging war, or in supporting the waging of
war, against independence movements in the colonial territories of their
countries. French social democracy was at the very centre of the murderous
struggle waged against the independence movements in Indochina and
Algeria, with names like Robert Lacoste and Guy Mollet forever inscribed
in annals of shame; and British social democracy was similarly involved in
the struggles of the 1940s and 1950s in British colonial territories—in
Malaya and Kenya, in Cyprus and Aden. Nowhere and at no time in those
years did social democratic leaders anywhere in imperialist countries show
any sign that they took the notion of socialist internationalism seriously.

In short, the record shows quite conclusively that social democracy has
never posed any real threat to the structure of domination and exploitation of capitalist societies. Throughout, its leaders have clearly demonstrated that they have been concerned with the management of capitalism,
not its supercession; and in the field of defence and foreign affairs, they
have always been much more the colleagues of conservative politicians
than their opponents. *In practice*, there has existed a very high degree of
consensus on the broad lines of policy, based upon the acceptance by
social democratic leaders of the policies of conservative governments:
occasional disagreements on specific issues, however sharp, have not
fundamentally disturbed this consensus. The point is particularly applicable
to defence and foreign policy; but it is hardly less relevant in other fields

as well.

There have always been many socialists in the ranks of social democratic parties who have opposed their leaders and sought to push them and their parties in more radical directions. They have on occasion had some successes, and their efforts have no doubt also prevented their leaders from moving even further in the direction of compromise and retreat. However, it must be noted that this socialist opposition inside social democratic parties has never managed to 'capture' these parties for the Left and given them a decisively different orientation and sets of programmes and policies. Social democratic leaders of the Centre and the Right have remained in command of their parties, and have continued to determine their policies and actions, notwithstanding the concessions they have occasionally had to make to their critics.

Nor does there seem to be any very good reason for thinking that matters are likely to be very different in the future. It is of course possible —indeed likely—that socialists will continue to extract occasional concessions from their leaders, in programmatic and even in practical terms; and it is equally possible that the pressure of events will compel these leaders to adopt different policies, even somewhat more radical ones—that they will, for instance be compelled to take a greater distance from American defence and foreign policies and seek to act as a more 'restraining' influence on the United States than has been the case in the past. To a limited extent, some such shift in these areas has already occurred in the years of the Reagan Presidency.

Anything of this sort must of course be welcome from a socialist point of view. But it should on no account obscure the fact that any such variation in programme or action occurs within a social democratic framework which is very set and solid. What socialists confront here—or ought to confront—is an ideological, political, even psychological, construct of great strength, which is open, flexible, loose on its right, but which is very unwilling, even unable, to yield much on its left. In other words, social democratic leaders find it much easier to compromise and consort with their conservative adversaries on the right than with their socialist critics on the left.

In seeking to explain the reasons for their opposition to the policies advocated by the Left, social democratic leaders themselves have often advanced the view that whatever the merits of these policies might be, extreme caution must be exercised in proposing anything which 'the electorate' could find 'extreme' and therefore unacceptable. On this view, the reluctance of social democratic leaders to endorse, let alone initiate, radical policies, is not due to their own predilections, but to their realism, and to their understanding of the fact that to move too far ahead of 'public opinion' and advocate policies for which 'the public' is not ready is to court electoral disaster and political paralysis.

This raises some very large and important points. It is undoubtedly true that 'the electorate' in the capitalist-democratic regimes of advanced capitalist countries does not support parties which advocate, or which appear to stand for, the revolutionary overthrow of the political system; and 'the electorate' here includes the overwhelming mass of the working class as well as other classes. This rejection by the working class and 'lower income groups' in general of parties committed or seemingly committed to the overthrow of the political and social order is a fact of major political importance, to say the least.

However, this does not at all mean that organised labour, the working class and the subordinate population of advanced capitalist countries (which constitutes the vast majority of their population) is also opposed to far-reaching changes and radical reforms. Social democratic parties have themselves been driven on many occasions to proclaim their trans-formative ambitions in their electoral manifestoes, and to speak of their firm determination to create 'a new social order'; and have nevertheless scored remarkable electoral victories with such programmes. Popular commitment to radical transformative purposes may not, generally speaking, be very deep; but there has at any rate been very little evidence of popular revulsion from such purposes.

The notion that very large parts of 'the electorate', and notably the working class, is bound to reject radical programmes is a convenient alibi, but little else. The real point, which is crucial, is that such programmes and policies need to be defended and propagated with the utmost determination and vigour by leaders totally convinced of the justice of their cause. It is *this* which is always lacking: infirmity of purpose and the fear of radical measures lies not with the working class but with the social democratic leaders themselves.

The same point must be made about social democratic governments. Such governments have never been disavowed by the working class because they were too 'extreme' or radical or over-zealous in pressing forward with reform: on the contrary, they have been disavowed precisely because they have regularly retreated from the promises enshrined in their mani-festoes, because they have adopted policies that ran counter to these promises, because they disillusioned and demoralised their supporters, and because they gave every indication that there was little to expect from their continuance in office. It is in this connection very odd that the lamentations which are so often heard on the Left about the decline of working class support for social democratic parties do not take greater account of the record of social democratic governments: the wonder is not the decline, but the resilience of support which, despite everything, endures for such parties in the working class and beyond.

It is also an important part of the picture that social democratic retreats and derelictions have disastrous repercussions on the labour movement. As social democratic governments retreat, so division and strife inside social democratic parties grow. The Left protests and attacks the leadership and seeks to deflect it from its courses; and the leadership turns on the Left and accuses it of disloyalty. Conservative forces rejoice; and the working class, or a large part of it, remains alienated or is further alienated from a divided and warring party.

We are therefore driven back to the leadership of social democratic parties. Again and again, social democratic governments have been elected with substantial, sometimes sweeping, parliamentary and popular majorities, on programmes of extensive reform and renewal, in a climate of genuine enthusiasm and support, and have very soon flagged and dissipated that enthusiasm and support, and retreated into the positions and policies just described.

It is of course true that even very 'moderate' and compromising social democratic governments confront very serious economic and financial constraints; that such governments operate in a generally unsympathetic or frankly hostile administrative context, in which other parts of the state tend to view social democratic ministers as interlopers; that they are subject to constant and often virulent attacks from an overwhelmingly conservative press; and that all conservative forces want to see the 'experiment' brought to an end as soon as possible, and do what they can to hasten the day.

All this must indeed be taken into account. It is perfectly reasonable—indeed essential—to appreciate the determination of this opposition even to social democracy. The point, however, is that most social democratic politicians are very ill-adapted to the politics of confrontation and struggle, at least with their conservative opponents—it is otherwise with their own activists on the Left.

This is not a matter of character but of ideological dispositions. Those who get to leadership positions in social democratic parties are generally 'safe' people, who can be relied on to pursue 'moderate', 'reasonable', 'sensible' courses. A process of co-optation, sifting and selection is at work on the way up, so that people who are deemed to be ideologically and politically 'unsound' can be kept at arm's length, and pushed back to the periphery of the party. The apparatus itself is under the control of 'moderate' men and women, and is used quite ruthlessly to ensure that the right people are brought in and the wrong people kept out. Where left socialists do nevertheless break through and cannot easily or safely be prevented from obtaining ministerial office, they are at least kept out of strategic offices such as finance, home affairs, foreign affairs and defence.

For most social democratic politicians, capitalist society (in so far as the existence of capitalism is acknowledged at all) is not a battlefield on which opposed classes are engaged in a permanent conflict, now more acute, now less, and in which they are firmly on one side, but a community, no doubt quarrelsome, but a community nonetheless, in which various groups—be they employers, workers, public employees, etc—make selfish and damaging demands, which it is the task of government to resist for the good of all; and it is a community in which help must naturally be extended to the weakest members. On this view, what is required of government, and what a social democratic government is peculiarly well able to provide, is good will, understanding, fairness, compassion, so that specific problems may be tackled and resolved; and it also follows that social democratic leaders, in practice as distinct from rhetoric or even sentiment, are by no means separated from their conservative opponents by an unbridgeable gulf. On the contrary, there are many channels of communication, understanding and even agreement between them. The business of social democratic leaders is conciliation and compromise. Their concern may be to advance reform, but also to contain the pressure for it. Gramsci spoke of intellectuals as 'managers of consent': the formulation is even more applicable to social democratic politicians. As such, they play a major role in the stabilisation of the politics of capitalist-democratic societies.

Given this, it is easy to understand why social democratic politicians, with the partial exception of Salvador Allende in Chile, have never sought to probe the limits of 'reformism', and have always retreated long before they faced a serious confrontation with conservative forces. To have done so would have required them to assume the leadership of a mass movement from which their whole view of the world led them to recoil. It is simply not realistic to expect such people to provide the inspiration and the leadership required to bring about a transformation of capitalist society in socialist directions: the task demands, at the very least, a set of ideological commitments which they do not possess.

What then, in socialist terms, is there beyond social democracy?

There have over the years been a good many different answers to this question. One of the main ones, of Leninist inspiration, proposes the building and nurturing of a 'vanguard' party, tightly organised on 'democratic centralist' lines, involved in a daily class struggle at the point of production and at all other points of tension in capitalist society, with the expectation that capitalist crisis must ultimately reach a point at which it will become unmanageable, as a result of which it will no longer be possible to contain popular anger within the confines of the political system. At that point, a revolutionary situation will have come to exist, which will make it possible for the 'vanguard' party to seize the moment and lead the working class towards a seizure of power. The bourgeois state will be smashed, and replaced by a dictatorship of the proletariat, on the basis of proletarian power, workers' councils and other authentically democratic forms.

Those who propose this strategy are well aware that in no advanced capitalist country has this 'scenario' come anywhere near to being realised. But they are of course able to argue that the realisation of the 'scenario' is only a matter of time, that the crisis is not yet far enough advanced but is developing, that the working class is still in the grip of social democratic 'reformist' illusions, but that it is bound to acquire greater class consciousness under the impact of events, and so forth. Some such beliefs have for many years—in fact since 1917—sustained a core of dedicated militants and revolutionaries in all advanced capitalist countries, and indeed in all other countries as well.

However, it needs to be said, that this revolutionary 'scenario' even with a marked aggravation of capitalist crisis, is very unlikely to be realised in advanced capitalist countries. If or when a revolutionary situation does arise in one or other such country, the chances are that it will play itself out very differently from what is envisaged in this 'scenario'.

This, however, is speculation of a fairly futile kind. For a very long time to come, what socialists will confront is crisis and conflict, but quite emphatically not a revolutionary situation; and all experience very strongly suggests that parties and groupings which base their intervention in political life on the lines just indicated, condemn themselves to marginality and ineffectiveness. Their problem is not that they are unable to attract any serious measure of popular support: the real problem is that they have generally proved unable to attract any serious measure of activist and socialist support.

There are a number of reasons for this. One of them is that the notion of a tightly-organised, democratic-centralist organisation has proved to be a very good recipe for top-down and manipulative leadership, for undemocratic centralism and the stifling of genuine debate, sharp divisions and resort to expulsions, and a turn-over of members so high as to make the organisation a transit camp from innocence and enthusiasm to disillusionment and bitterness. Only the leadership remains permanently entrenched, presiding year after year over a constantly renewed membership, and virtually irremovable save by internal upheavals, splits and excommunications. Parties and groupings such as this have shown very little capacity to think through the problems which the socialist project presents, and have tended instead to resort to incantation and sloganeering as a substitute. They have often included some very talented individuals, who have made important contributions to socialist thinking. But the groupings themselves have generated remarkably little that was fresh and innovative: the ardour and dedication of their members have more often than not been doomed to ineffectiveness because of the shortcomings of the organisations of which they were members and the distrust which these shortcomings engendered among socialist activists in the labour movement whom they needed to attract.

Secondly, the very notion of a 'vanguard' party has acquired an arrogant and 'imperialistic' ring, quite unacceptable in labour movements with a long history and with many different and contradictory or at least disparate tendencies. Vanguard parties are by definition unique and dominant: there cannot be two or more such parties. But it is only by compulsion and coercion that one party can impose itself as the 'vanguard' or 'leading' party. In the circumstances of advanced capitalist societies, with a high density of different organisations, interests, purposes, tendencies and aspirations, a socialist party can only expect to be one element in a comradely alliance between different formations. It may hope, by virtue of its conduct, clear sightedness and support, to become a major reference point in that alliance, even a senior partner in it, but without any pretension to an arbitrary and stifling predominance.

This is not only a matter of strategy in struggle. It raises larger issues concerning the political system appropriate to a socialist society. All the available evidence suggests that the concept of 'the leading party' (in effect the monopolistic party) tends to produce authoritarianism and the suppression of dissent—indeed the construal of all dissent as counter-revolutionary and therefore unacceptable. There are no doubt circum-stances of extreme peril where diversity, pluralism, and conflicting tenden-cies are very difficult to maintain: but failure to maintain them should be seen for what it is, namely a major retreat from socialist principles. What happened to the Bolshevik Party after the banning of 'factions' at the Xth Party Congress in 1921 offers an instructive lesson of what such banning entails for the life of a revolutionary party.

A further reason for the marginalisation and relative ineffectiveness of 'Marxist–Leninist' revolutionary groupings in advanced capitalist societies has to do with their failure to take seriously the context of capitalist democracy in which they operate. These groupings tend to treat capitalist democracy as a complete sham; and therefore to accord a wholly sub-ordinate place to electoral struggles, a form of activity for which they have great contempt. Whereas social democratic parties suffer from 'parlia-mentary cretinism', they tend to suffer from something akin to 'anti-parliamentary cretinism'. The fact is, that whatever the limitations of capitalist democracy may be—and they are drastic enough—no party or grouping operating within its context can afford not to seek some degree of electoral support, not least at local level. This requires a great deal more than a sudden irruption on the scene at election time.

What then, has been—and should be—the socialist alternative to these groupings? It has already been argued here that social democratic parties cannot realistically be taken to be such an alternative. That alternative entails a firm revolutionary commitment, namely the wholesale trans-formation of capitalist society in socialist directions. But it also involves a 'reformist' commitment, in so far as it also seeks all reforms which can be seen to form part of the larger revolutionary purpose.

Such 'revolutionary reformism' involves intervention in class struggle at all points of conflict in society, and pre-eminently at the site of work. It also involves electoral struggles at all levels and conceives these struggles as an intrinsic part of class struggle, without allowing itself to be absorbed into electoralism and parliamentarism; and it also means the permanent striving to strengthen the socialist presence on the political scene and in the political culture.

It should also be said that 'revolutionary reformism' does not postulate a smooth and uneventful transition to socialism by way of electoral support and parliamentary majorities. It acknowledges that, in the context of capitalist democracy, such a transition requires a massive degree of popular support and commitment, one of whose expressions (but by no means the only or even the most important one) is electoral strength and parliamentary representation. But 'revolutionary reformism' is also bound to be very conscious of the fact that any serious challenge to dominant classes must inevitably evoke resistance, and will be determined to meet that resistance with every weapon that this requires, including of course the mobilisation of mass support.

In historical terms, the parties which have embodied this 'revolutionary reformism' are the Communist Parties of the advanced capitalist countries (and others as well for that matter). To say this may seem paradoxical, since they themselves have always fiercely rejected the 'reformist' label, not surprisingly given the pejorative connotations it acquired after 1914. But the labelling is nevertheless wholly justified—it is in fact the 'revolutionary' part which may be the more problematic.

The reason for saying it is justified is that after the first years of *Sturm und Drang* following the Bolshevik Revolution and the foundation of these parties, it came to be understood that the overthrow of capitalism was not on the agenda; and Communist parties installed themselves as best they could (and in so far as bourgeois governments allowed them to do so) in the political life of their countries, and became in fact if not in name 'reformist' parties with an ultimately revolutionary vocation, a strong engagement in class struggle, taking part in electoral contests, and pressing for immediate as well as long term gains and reforms. There were periods when twists in Comintern policy (for instance the 'third period', 'class against class', social democrats are 'social fascists' phase between 1929 and 1934) or the twists in Soviet foreign policy (the 'imperialist war' phase between 1939 and 1941) forced the parties back into a more 'revolutionary' position. But this represented the exception rather than the rule, and that position has not on the whole been taken up since 1945.

What was fundamentally wrong with these Communist parties was two things: first, their total subservience to Stalin's policies and purposes; and secondly, closely related to this, their mode of organisation. Enough has been said and written about the Stalinism of Communist parties between the late twenties and the early fifties to take this as given here: for present purposes, it is enough to note the degree to which the combination of sectarianism and opportunism which characterised Stalinism, together with sudden changes of policy imposed from Moscow, blighted their politics and blunted their political effectiveness.

As for their mode of organisation, the 'democratic centralism' to which they subscribed, and which the nature of Stalinism made imperative (how else could total obedience be imposed?), helped to foster all the vices which have been discussed earlier, and which turned these parties into profoundly undemocratic institutions, in which 'deviation' was impermissible, and in which the word of the leadership was law, whatever that word might be, and however much the word of the moment contradicted the word that had gone before. Attempts might be made to provide the leaders with a simulacrum of democratic legitimation by the holding of Party Congresses. But these were manipulated and stunted affairs, which gave no real power or influence to 'ordinary' members.

Unquestioning subservience to the Soviet Union by Communist parties has generally speaking given way to a more flexible stance, though parties differ in the degree to which they allow themselves freedom to criticise Soviet policies and actions. On the other hand, 'democratic centralism' endures as a principle of organisation, and ensures the perpetuation of the stultifying practices of the past. Old habits die hard, particularly when they are so convenient to a leadership thus rendered irremovable by the party membership.

These are crippling weaknesses; and there is also much else in the mode of operation, the policies and positions of Communist parties which warrants severe criticism. But they are much less vulnerable to the charge which is usually levelled against them by their 'Marxist–Leninist' opponents on the Left, namely their 'reformism'. For there is a profound, fundamental sense in which revolutionary parties, in the context of capitalist democracy, do need to engage in a politics which it is very glib to denounce as 'reformist', and therefore as beyond the pale.

The real question is what kind of 'reformism' parties which affirm a revolutionary vocation actually do engage in. At one end, there is the 'revolutionary reformism' which was discussed earlier. At the other, there is a 'reformism' constituted by a practice which tends increasingly towards social democracy and is increasingly oblivious to the larger transformative purposes in which reforms are or ought to be inscribed, which comes to be dominated by electoral calculations to the detriment of principle, is more concerned with the control of class struggle than with its encouragement, and allows policy to be chopped and changed according to the opportunistic manoeuvres of party leaders. The French Communist Party provides a very good example of this kind of 'reformism'. The Italian

Communist Party, on the other hand, mirrors well the struggle between the two kinds of 'reformism'.

If it is the case, as has been argued here, that 'revolutionary reformism' (or whatever else the position encompassed by the formula may be called) does represent an alternative to social democracy, and points in realistic fashion beyond it, the very large question which this poses is what agencies are to push this forward. The argument so far developed is clearly intended to suggest that social democracy does not offer any reasonable hope of turning itself into such an agency; that Communist parties carry burdens from the past which make it very difficult for them to undergo the process of transformation which is required for the purpose; and that 'Marxist-Leninist' groupings to the left of Communist parties operate in far too narrow an ideological and political framework to make it possible for them to turn themselves from small sects into substantial parties.

How this situation will be resolved is not clear, and will in any case be resolved differently in different countries. In some, Communist parties may come to shed their negative features and form the basis for a socialist realignment on the Left; in others, that realignment will have to come from other left sources. However it comes to pass, the process is likely to be protracted: serious socialist parties cannot suddenly be conjured up out of nothing.

Be that as it may, the point is that the socialist cause *needs* political articulation, and that this political articulation, though not exclusively provided by parties, does nevertheless require the agency of party. However useful and effective other elements of pressure in the political system may be—trade unions, movements of women, blacks, ecologists, peace activists and many others—they cannot and do not for the most part wish to fulfil the main task of socialist parties, which is to inject a 'stream of socialist tendency', by word and action, into the political system and culture of their societies. Such parties are of course concerned with immediate issues, grievances and demands; but they are also, beyond this, concerned with the effective dissolution of the structures of power of capitalist society and their replacement by a fundamentally different social order, based upon the social ownership and control of the main means of economic activity, and governed by principles of co-operation, civic freedom, egalitarianism, and democratic arrangements far superior to the narrowly class-bound arrangements of capitalist democracy.

Many parties of the Left have advocated these principles over the years. For reasons given earlier, they have also suffered from great weaknesses, which reduced or nullified their effectiveness. The sooner these weaknesses are faced, and overcome, the better will become the prospects of socialist advance.

NOTES

1. Quoted in A. Przeworski, 'Social Democracy as a Historical Phenomenon', *New Left Review*, No. 122, July–August, 1980, p. 25.
2. For an earlier discussion of these and related issues, see R. Miliband, *Marxism and Politics* (1977), Ch. VI, 'Reform and Revolution'.
3. The 1984 *Socialist Register* was wholly devoted to 'The Uses of Anti-Communism' and discusses many facets of the issue.